7·50

Cotoneasters

Cotoneasters

A Comprehensive
Guide to Shrubs
for
Flowers, Fruit,
and Foliage

Jeanette Fryer
Bertil Hylmö

Foreword by
Roy Lancaster

Timber Press
Portland ◆ London

Page 2: *Cotoneaster salicifolius* 'Repens'. Drawing by Vojtěch Štolfa

Published in 2009 by
Timber Press, Inc.

The Haseltine Building
133 S.W. Second Avenue, Suite 450
Portland, Oregon 97204-3527
www.timberpress.com

2 The Quadrant
135 Salusbury Road
London NW6 6RJ
www.timberpress.co.uk

Printed in China

Library of Congress Cataloging-in-Publication Data
Fryer, Jeanette.
    Cotoneasters : a comprehensive guide to shrubs for flowers, fruit, and
foliage / Jeanette Fryer, Bertil Hylmö ; foreword by Roy Lancaster.
        p. cm.
    Includes bibliographical references and index.
    ISBN 978-0-88192-927-0 (alk. paper)
    1. Cotoneasters—Identification. I. Hylmö, Bertil. II. Title.
    QK495.R78F79 2009
    635.9'3373—dc22
                                                        2008034995
A catalog record for this book is also available from the British Library.

To my parents, Violet and Norman Giles,
my children, Glen, Conan, and Nicolette, and
especially to my husband, Dernford Woods,
all of whom have had to accept my passion
for cotoneasters.—JF

❧

To my wife, Ulla, and our family.—BH

Contents

Color photographs follow page 160

Foreword

Cotoneasters seem to have been in my life forever, most certainly before I ever knew their names or became aware of their significance. As a schoolboy with an interest in bird watching I had noticed their bright red fruits being eaten by birds but that was all I knew and it wasn't until I left school and began my career as a gardener with my local parks department that things changed. If memory serves me correctly, the sum total of cotoneasters, species and hybrids, grown in Bolton's parks amounted to just five—*Cotoneaster horizontalis*, *C. microphyllus*, *C. simonsii*, *C. franchetii*, and *C. salicifolius* with a possible sixth in the hybrid *C. ×watereri*. All were commonly used in a wide range of situations, *C. simonsii* mostly as a hedge. *Cotoneaster horizontalis* and *C. microphyllus* meanwhile were often employed as a low cover to hide unsightly objects like grids, sunken tanks, and the like. They were also used in a more ornamental role to cover rocks, low walls, and steep banks.

Cotoneaster salicifolius, or what was then sold by nurseries as such, was my favorite because of its graceful arching habit and its narrow willowlike shining green and wrinkled leaves, white hairy beneath. This was usually planted in groups in mixed shrub borders or occasionally as a single specimen in a lawn where its natural character could better be appreciated. Years later, I joined the Hillier Nurseries and was charged with checking out saleable stock in the nursery beds and writing up descriptions for their famous catalogues. Only then did I come to realize the great number of cotoneasters in cultivation and their remarkable variety of form and size as well as their ornamental merits of flower and fruit and, in some species, fall color.

When we came to prepare the *Hillier Manual of Trees and Shrubs*, published in 1971, the descriptions of cotoneasters grown by the nursery ran to 101 species, varieties, and cultivars large and small, evergreen and deciduous, with fruits ranging from red and orange to yellow, pink, purple, and black. It seemed an astonishing number and in garden terms it was, then. Thirty five years later it seems a paltry sum when compared with those cotoneasters now known to science. Over 400 species are described in the present work alone, a formidable number though comparatively few of these are as yet in general cultivation, a situation that should now improve dramatically as a result of this major reference and guide.

I met the late Bertil Hylmö only once but have known Jeanette Fryer for many years during which time through diligent work and research as well as gritty determination she has worked to make sense of what to a gardener represents a minefield of taxonomical complexity. From her days as a novice she has blossomed under the tutelage of her fellow author as well as other specialists in her field and is now an internationally recognized authority on the genus, checking specimens in the world's herbaria, describing new collections from the wild, as well as maintaining a national collection in her garden and her family nursery. All of this, aside from making her a respected taxonomist on the genus, has provided her with enough experience to advise on and recommend the wide range of cotoneasters available and suitable for today's gardens and parks.

I know from personal experience, having collected their seed and studied *Cotoneaster* species in the wild in China, the Himalaya, and Europe, just how hard Jeanette has worked to identify or describe those introduced into cultivation, and it is a tribute to her reputation that there are botanists exploring the wilds of Asia today who have been persuaded to keep a special eye open for cotoneasters. One result has been the describing and naming of many new species, some of which honor the collectors involved.

There have been times during the long gestation of this book when the authors must have wondered if it would ever reach fruition. The fact that it is now available speaks volumes for their strength of character and belief. It also says a great deal about their publishers that, despite the obstacles and pitfalls in editing an account that seeks to combine botanical accuracy and conformity with horticultural practicality, they have risen to the challenge and stayed the course. The result will be a relief to many, a source of argument to some, and to gardeners who want to use them, a key to a treasure chest of cotoneasters old and new for all situations and all seasons.

ROY LANCASTER

Preface

In preparation for this monograph the authors have both studied original material (unless stated, herbarium specimens quoted have been seen) and raised new introductions from wild sources, often studying them through three generations, to provide a thorough picture of the current scientific understanding of the genus and to obtain the most comprehensive descriptions of the species. In this survey of the genus *Cotoneaster* there are assessments of nearly all known species and cultivars (c. 460 taxa). It documents the popular and the well known, the new garden-worthy species and those purely of botanical interest, presenting both their botanical and horticultural aspects. New species are both named and validly published. Many of the cotoneasters described are in cultivation but are not yet freely available in the nursery trade, though they are deserving of recognition by gardeners.

This monograph unveils the genus with an introduction which includes the history and introduction of species by plant-hunters, garden value, cultivation, propagation, pests and diseases, garden escapes, taxonomy, genetics, and more. Keys are provided to subgenera, sections, series, and species in this complex genus, and enable the reader to research and identify cotoneasters.

Along with the descriptions of the species are also the distinguishing features of an extensive list of cultivars. Many of the species and some of the cultivars described are illustrated by color photographs as an additional aid to identification. Species descriptions include physical characteristics, seasons of flowering, fruiting and leaf-fall, genetics, hardiness, geographical range, primary garden attributes and any specific cultural requirements, history (including any awards), and if necessary relationships with closely related species.

The index includes every known name published for *Cotoneaster* from common names to synonyms and misnomers. It aims to be the most comprehensive listing yet published.

This monograph is a definitive treatment of the genus *Cotoneaster* and the culmination of at least 50 years' combined prodigious research by the two authors. It is a monumental work with the objective of being a comprehensive source of information on the classification, identification, cultivation, and nomenclature of the genus *Cotoneaster*. It is aimed at a broad audience of horticulturists, from the professional to the committed enthusiast, whether botanist, taxonomist, nursery owner, landscaper, or gardener. It aims to be scientifically accurate, practical, and readable.

We hope this book will provide authoritative information for people who grow and love cotoneasters, and for those about to grow them for the first time.

Acknowledgments

First, special thanks to Allen Coombes for his advice and support. We also thank (in alphabetical order) Poul Erik Brander, Rosalind Bucknall, Chris Chadwell, Raymond Cinovskis, Suzanne Cubey, Karl Evert Flinck, Brian Gale, Alberto Giussani, Anna Terentiyevna Grevtsova, Hillier Gardens and Arboretum, Peter Hylmö, the International Dendrology Society, Ewa Jerzak, Gerhard Klotz, Géza Kósa, Roy Lancaster, the Linnean Society of London, Hugh McAllister, the National Council for the Conservation of Plants and Gardens (NCCPG), Charles Nelson, Antonin Nohel, Hilde Nybom, Richard Pankhurst, Graham Pattison, the Oleg Polunin Trust, Chris Prior, the Royal Horticultural Society, Keith Rushforth, Tony Schilling, Clive Stace, William Stearn, Vojtěch Štolfa, Harry van de Laar, Roy Vickery, Linda Willms, Dernford Woods, Jacques Zeller, and Peter Zika.

Most of the photographs were taken in the living collections of Jeanette Fryer (JF) and Bertil Hylmö (BH).

Introduction to Cotoneasters

COTONEASTERS are among the most valuable and useful of hardy, ornamental shrubs due not only to their huge diversity in size and shape, but also for their potential for pruning or training to fit any size space. They also are easy to grow. Hardly a garden is without a relevant space for at least one of these very worthwhile shrubs.

For many years, only a small proportion of the vast range of species was utilized by the nursery trade in landscaping work and in sales to the public. Although thousands of cotoneasters were planted by parks departments in municipal settings, the range of plants used was so limited that this wide usage probably harmed, rather than helped, their reputation as a very diverse and most interesting genus of high horticultural value. Many beautiful, rare, and unusual cotoneasters were only to be seen in botanic gardens or specialist collections. However, recently enthusiasm has been kindled for cotoneasters with the publication and availability of many new and beautiful species.

Happily, the gardening public is becoming more adventurous in its taste for plants. Continental nurseries (and gardeners) have always tended to be more enterprising than those in the British Isles, and a wider selection of cotoneasters—especially cultivars, and shrubs trained as half standards (c. 1 m [3 ft.] high) and full standards (c. 2 m [6 ft.] high) on a single stem—is cultivated. In the United States, cotoneasters are used in horticulture on a large scale, but sadly, from only a relatively small number of taxa.

The wide range of fruit color and leaf size, color, and texture make cotoneasters popular with flower arrangers. Bonsai enthusiasts are fond of using some of the more diminutive, small-leaved species such as *Cotoneaster perpusillus* and *C. thymifolius* for their miniature specimens.

Cotoneasters can fill many penchants. They range in size from ground-hugging subshrubs of around 10 cm (4 in.) or less through to magnificent specimen trees of 15–18 m (50–60 ft.) in height. Many species are good for hedging. A good example is found in Dublin, Ireland, in the National Botanic Gardens at Glasnevin, where a truly majestic old hedge of *Cotoneaster lacteus* has grown to reach 6 m (20 ft.) high by 3 m (10 ft.) wide. Smaller species fruit abundantly when grown over walls or against them, also looking spectacular when grown to the top of a post, then left to hang down to the ground.

Sometimes grafting is used to create unusual, very small treelike shrubs (that is, *Cotoneaster adpressus* top-grafted onto *C. ×watereri*). Some shrubs are densely branched, others more open in habit. Branches can be stiffly erect, wide-spreading, arching, or gracefully pendulous; when bruised or broken, they emit a bitter cherrylike fragrance. Cotoneaster foliage can be evergreen, deciduous or, often depending on the climate, semi-evergreen. Many of the deciduous species are spectacular in autumn leaf color; in areas with warmer autumn temperatures, the colorful display will last further into the winter. Leaves range from minute to large, shiny or dull, while three or four species have very attractive variegated forms.

The main flowering season for cotoneasters is from midspring to late summer (April to August in the Northern Hemisphere). The flowers are produced from the axils of the leaves of the previous year, with the new shoot progressing beyond. Fruit, very often copiously produced, come in a range of colors—white or cream with a pink blush, shades of yellow, orange, red, and crimson, maroon and purple through to black—and are sometimes extremely shiny. The fruiting season is extended; in autumn, when other fruiting shrubs have lost their glory, cotoneasters still display for many more weeks. By careful selection of species, it is possible to have shrubs displaying their colorful fruit from as early as midsummer (July) in series *Cotoneaster* and *Melanocarpi*, throughout the year and into early to mid spring (March to April) of the following year with the evergreen, winter-fruiting species of series *Pannosi* and *Buxifolii*.

In addition to the ornamental purposes previously mentioned, cotoneasters are used by apiarists, as the flowers being plentiful in nectar are much loved by bees; the resulting honey is pale golden in color with a delicate flavor. In China, both the leaves and the fruit are used in tea, and the wood for making walking sticks, handles, and implements. In Iran and India cotoneasters are used as source of a sweet mannalike substance high in dextrose. In the past the fruit of *Cotoneaster integerrimus* has been used in the treatment of diarrhea.

Classification

Cotoneaster was long placed near *Crataegus* (hawthorn) in the family *Rosaceae*. Based on a reevaluation of flower and fruit characters, *Cotoneaster* is now believed to be more closely related to the genera *Pyracantha* (firethorn) and *Heteromeles* (Christmas berry) (Rohrer et al. 1992; Robertson et al. 1991), but lacks thorns and toothed leaf margins. Recent molecular studies also distance *Crataegus* from *Cotoneaster*; the latter has weak support for alliance with *Cydonia* and *Heteromeles*, and requires further study to resolve its placement (Campbell et al. 1995).

The genus *Cotoneaster* has long been separated into two distinct subgenera (sections according to Koehne 1893). The first subgenus, *Chaenopetalum*, has inflorescences in which the flowers open simultaneously, the corolla opens with petals spreading, rarely semispreading, and sometimes pink in bud, opening white. The second subgenus, *Cotoneaster*, has inflorescences in which the flowers open successively, frequently over a long period of time (often buds, open flowers, and fruit are present at the same time in the cluster); the corolla has only a small opening (or is closed), the petals are erect or suberect, off-white with red, pink, or green. These two subgenera are divided into sections using various botanical characters. Flinck and Hylmö (1966) further divided the sections into series, each series being based on botanical characters and the geographical origin of the species.

Subgenus *Chaenopetalum* comprises species with flowers that can be very showy and numerous, filling the air with the heady perfume peculiar to the family *Rosaceae*. The petals are spreading, white or sometimes pale-pink to mauve. Within this subgenus, series *Multiflori* includes species which are as free flowering as *Crataegus* but more graceful. Extremely hardy, they are sometimes used as street trees in municipal plantings in Central Europe, where they are often grafted onto *Crataegus* or *Sorbus* leaving a clear trunk of around 1.5–2 m (4-$\frac{1}{2}$ to 6 ft.) high. Excellent as small specimen trees for lawn or border, they can also be just as easily grown as a wall shrub. They are spectacular in spring and in autumn decorated with large globose fruit similar to small cherries. Inside the fruit are two firmly joined (fused) nutlets; these often need a knife to separate them.

Species in series *Hebephylli* have secondary branches growing at right angles to the main branches, and fruit with a single nutlet with a longitudinal groove, which resembles a grain of corn. The deciduous cotoneasters of this section, especially those of series *Racemiflori*, *Aitchisonioides*, and *Hissarici*, look good when grown in combination with the shorter, spring-flowering *Clematis*, which compliment their shape and open, often spreading, habit.

Species in series *Megalocarpi* have characteristics from both subgenera *Chaenopetalum* and *Cotoneaster*, and could be said to be the link between the two subgenera.

Subgenus *Cotoneaster* comprises species with flowers in which the petals are mostly erect. Though these flowers may be less showy than the flowers of subgenus *Chaenopetalum*, they are often unusual. Some flowers have pure-red, wide-erect petals (series *Sanguinei*); others are pink or white, or tricolored red, white, and green. Frequently flowers of this subgenus are plentiful in nectar.

The species in series *Horizontales* make excellent wall shrubs, fanning out their branches while climbing, and giving an excellent display of fruit and autumn color. Series *Verruculosi* has species that thrive in the moisture-laden air surrounding pools or streams. Series *Distichi* shrubs are shiny in all parts, and have flowers and fruit which hang attractively along the undersides of the branches. Series *Bullati* species are strong-growing large shrubs to small trees with attractive leaves. The fruit are much-loved by birds and quite a few species can be found bird-sown. Series *Cotoneaster* species are possibly the most widespread in geographical range of all the series, covering from Wales in the west, throughout Europe, western and central Asia to Kashmir and northwest to the area surrounding Lake Baikal. These species make attractive shrubs, many of which are diminutive in size, with a covering of soft pale grayish hairs which in early spring are a pleasing sight, especially as the leaves unfurl. Series *Cotoneaster* is probably the most problematic in Europe. Species in series *Melanocarpi* have small pinkish flowers which, combined with the softly hairy leaves, make an attractive display in early spring. Members of series *Melanocarpi* and series *Cotoneaster* are the earliest species to flower.

Habit

Gerhard Klotz (1982) has identified eight types of habit in *Cotoneaster*. The numbers in the list that follows correspond to the numbered habits in the drawing.

1. Large, erect and spreading shrubs to small to medium-sized trees of 3–15 m (10–50 ft.) high: series *Salicifolii, Pannosi, Frigidi, Aitchisonioides, Bacillares, Tomentelli*.
2. Medium or large, erect shrubs 2–5 m (6–16 ft.) high, branches stiffly erect: series *Racemiflori, Distichi, Kongboense, Sanguinei, Acuminati, Acutifolii, Bullati, Glomerulati, Melanocarpi, Ignavi, Megalocarpi*.
3. Medium, erect shrubs 2–3 m (6–10 ft.) high, branches arching or pendulous: series *Salicifolii, Pannosi, Racemiflori, Hissarici, Multiflori, Distichi, Nitentes, Kongboense, Mucronati, Bullati, Shannanense, Glomerulati, Franchetioides, Sterniani, Dielsiani, Zabelioides, Tomentosi, Cotoneaster, Melanocarpi, Ignavi*.
3a. Medium, erect shrubs 2–3 m (6–10 ft.) high, branches wide-spreading, often to 90 degrees: series *Tomentelli, Hebephylli, Conspicui*.

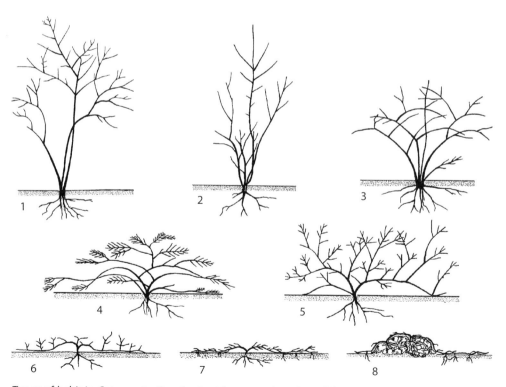

Types of habit in *Cotoneaster*. See the text for an explanation of the numbers. Drawings from G. Klotz (1982). Used by permission.

4. Small to medium, ascending shrubs 1–3 m (3–10 ft.) high, branches obliquely spreading, distichous: series *Rokujodaisanense, Distichi, Horizontales, Nitentes.*

5. Small to medium, erect or ascending shrubs 1–3 m (3–10 ft.) high, branches spreading, divaricate: series *Conspicui, Buxifolii, Microphylli, Sterniani, Tomentosi, Cotoneaster, Melanocarpi.*

5a. Dwarf to small, dense erect shrubs 0.5–1.5 m (1-$\frac{1}{2}$ to 4-$\frac{1}{2}$ ft.) high, branches divaricate: series *Verruculosi.*

6. Dwarf, prostrate or creeping shrubs 0.3–1 m (1–3 ft.) high, branches divaricate, not rooting: series *Buxifolii, Microphylli, Rokujodaisanense.*

7. Decumbent shrubs, mostly under 0.3 m (1 ft.) high, branches rooting: series *Microphylli, Radicantes, Adpressi.*

8. Creeping, carpeting shrubs under 0.3 m (1 ft.) high, branches rooting: series *Radicantes, Adpressi.*

Highly Recommended Cotoneasters

C. albokermesinus, C. amoenus, C. argenteus, C. atropurpureus 'Variegatus', *C. bradyi, C. brickellii, C. camilli-schneideri, C. chadwellii, C. cochleatus, C. conspicuus, C. cuspidatus, C. dammeri* 'Hybridus Pendulus', *C. dammeri* 'Major', *C. dielsianus, C. divaricatus, C. duthieanus, C. elatus, C. franchetii, C. frigidus, C. frigidus* 'Cornubia', *C. frigidus* 'Fructuluteo', *C. fulvidus, C. ganghobaensis, C. glabratus, C. glacialis, C. glaucophyllus, C. glomerulatus, C.* 'Gracia', *C. harrovianus, C. harrysmithii, C. hebephyllus, C. henryanus, C. henryanus* 'Corina', *C. hjelmqvistii, C. horizontalis, C. hualiensis, C. hummelii, C. hupehensis, C. hylmoei, C. ignescens, C. ignotus, C. incanus, C. induratus, C. insculptus, C. insolitus, C. integrifolius, C. konishii, C. kweitschoviensis, C. lacteus, C. lancasteri, C. laxiflorus, C. lidjiangensis, C. lucidus, C. marginatus, C. marquandii, C. meiophyllus, C. melanotrichus, C. meuselii, C. microphyllus, C. monopyrenus, C. morrisonensis, C. moupinensis, C. multiflorus, C. nanshan, C. naoujanensis, C. newryensis, C. ogisui, C. pannosus, C. parkeri, C. pluriflorus, C. polyanthemus, C. procumbens* 'Queen of Carpets', *C. prostratus* 'Arnold-Forster', *C. purpurascens, C. rehderi, C. rhytidophyllus, C. rokujodaisanensis, C. roseus, C. rotundifolius, C. salicifolius, C. salicifolius* 'Gnom', *C. salicifolius* 'Exburyensis', *C. salwinensis, C. shansiensis, C. serotinus, C. sherriffii, C. sikangensis, C. soczavianus, C. splendens, C. spongbergii, C. sternianus, C. ×suecicus* 'Juliette', *C. tengyuehensis, C. thimphuensis, C. tomentellus, C. transcaucasicus, C. turbinatus, C. uva-ursi, C. vandelaarii, C. vernae, C. vestitus, C. wilsonii, C. yalungensis, C. zabelii.*

Treatment of the Species

The number of *Cotoneaster* species described is steadily increasing. Rehder (1927) in the bibliography of his *Manual of Cultivated Trees and Shrubs* mentions about 80 species. Klotz (1957) has approximately the same number in his work. In the very first systematic division of described species into sections and series, 176 species are included (Flinck and Hylmö 1966). A similar compilation 25 years later (Phipps et al. 1990) shows 261 species. At present, as the Sino-Himalaya has become more accessible, new species of *Cotoneaster* are being discovered. Today, the total number known to science is around 400. Mostly the differences between the species are quite wide, but since the 1980s a number of species have been described with only minor differences, which have been brought to light by comparative cultivation.

Garden Escapes

Birds like to feed on the fruit of most species of *Cotoneaster*, but only when they are fully ripe, soft, and juicy. Some *Cotoneaster* species have late-ripening fruit which do not become soft until well after the winter frosts. In many areas, especially on chalky or sandy soil, cotoneasters are increasingly being found as bird-sown escapes from garden and roadside ornamentals. In Sweden, 11 species are mentioned in the *Lustgarden* (Flinck and Hylmö 1992) as escaped into the native flora. In the more temperate climate of the British Isles, around 70 *Cotoneaster* species have been found and included in the *New Flora of the British Isles* (Stace 1997). In the United States, the number found so far is around 36. Cotoneasters have also been recorded bird-sown among the native flora of both South Africa and Australia.

The History of Naming

At the time of the description of the genus *Cotoneaster*, the then-known species came from a tiny portion of the present-known distribution. The definition of species was usually quite vague, and at that time, the importance of apomixis was unknown. Several apomictic species were treated as varieties or forms, whereas others were treated as species. Our concept of the apomicts within the genus *Cotoneaster* is that they must be treated uniformly—all being given the rank of species. The only exceptions are the few ephemeral apomicts which do not show vitality, are incapable of natural regeneration, and therefore should be ignored.

Another difficulty in the history of naming plants is that sometimes several new species were described from a single collection. Moreover, species would sometimes be described and given a name from only a single piece on an herbarium sheet—no flowers, no fruit! Because such names are not connected with plants known in cultivation, it is impossible to place them with any specimens—living or herbarium. For some species no information of the geographical distribution was given. Several species were described in the past which were probably just synonyms of ones previously published.

Allowance has to be made when undertaking the identification of a *Cotoneaster* from a description made only from an herbarium specimen of wild-collected material. For example, when some leaves are dried, especially the more leathery ones, they can become slightly rugose with the leaf margins recurved. Also, in cultivation these specimens will more than likely be much larger in all parts, and sometimes with more flowers to the inflorescence. When growing a new or unknown cotoneaster it is preferable to wait until it is in its second season of flowering before making an exact identification, as immature shrubs can be atypical. When identifying, naming, and publishing a new species, it is preferable to compare it first in cultivation, preferably for several generations, making it possible to observe and research as to whether or not it is breeding true, and to make sure it deserves the rank of species.

Frequently, many taxa of differing horticultural value are sold in the nursery trade under the same species name. An example of this is *Cotoneaster horizontalis* hort. where about six apomictic species with constant characters have been found under the same name, despite the differences between them. Two of these species are *C. perpusillus*, a small-leaved dwarf shrub, and *C. hjelmqvistii*, a larger-leaved robust shrub which supported can reach a height of 7 m (21 ft.). When this *C. horizontalis* hort. mishmash is mistakenly planted as *C. horizontalis* Decaisne in large quantities in landscaping projects, the results can be disastrous.

A survey of Nepalese plants for sale to the general public undertaken by Chris Chadwell of the Sino-Himalayan Plant Society showed that around half of the species were wrongly named. Nursery owners and holders of large collections of *Cotoneaster* have, for many years, been aware of this problem of misidentified (or unidentified) and mixed species. Long they have waited for taxonomists to solve this awful, muddled situation.

One final note about naming is appropriate here. *Cotoneaster* as a genus name is properly treated as a masculine noun (T. T. Yu 1954), although horticultural works can still be found with feminine endings applied to species epithets.

History of the Genus

The name *cotoneaster* is derived from the Latin *cotoneum* for quince, with the suffix -*aster*, indicating an incomplete resemblance, and means "quincelike" or "mock quince" in reference to the similarity of the leaves in some species. The first mention of *Cotoneaster* is found in a book written by Casper Bauhin in Latin in 1623, where "*Cotonaster folio rotundo non serrato*"—the quincelike plant with round, not serrated, leaves—is mentioned. The spelling of the name was changed from *Cotonaster* to *Cotoneaster* by Conrad Gesner and Johannes Bauhin when they described what is now *C. integerrimus* from central Europe.

In 1737 in *Hortus Cliffortianus* and *Flora Suecica*, and later in 1753 in the first edition of *Species Plantarum*, Carl Linnaeus mentioned only one species, *Mespilus cotoneaster* (the red-fruited *Cotoneaster integerrimus* of Medikus). In *Hortus Kewensis*, a catalog of plants cultivated at the Royal Botanic Gardens Kew, William Aiton, in 1789, mentioned

Mespilus tomentosus (syn. *Cotoneaster tomentosus* (Aiton) Lindley). This was the second European species to be mentioned in literature. Some experts believed that Philip Miller described *C. tomentosus* earlier in 1768 as *Mespilus orientalis*, but today this name is accepted as a synonym for a species of *Amelanchier*.

The first publication of a *Cotoneaster* binominal was by Friedrich Kasimir Medikus in 1793. In *Geschichte der Botanik unserer Zeiten* he named two forms of *C. integerrimus* based on fruit color: *Fructu rubro* and *Fructu nigro*.

The very first survey of the genus was made by John Lindley in 1821 and included four species. Two of them were non-European, *Cotoneaster acuminatus* and *C. affinis*, both from the Himalaya. Botanical exploration of the Himalaya had begun around 1800 when Francis Buchanan-Hamilton, a Scottish medical man employed by the East India Company, collected in Nepal and the area east of it. In 1820, Nathaniel Wallich, often with the help of pilgrims, collected in Nepal, mostly in the area of Gossainkund.

Around this time, interest in the genus *Cotoneaster* arose in several other countries. In Sweden in 1820 Wahlgren described *Mespilus cotoneaster* b. *nigra* (syn. *Cotoneaster niger* Fries), and from Sicily in 1827 came *Pyrus nebrodensis* Gussone (syn. *C. nebrodensis* Koch). *Cotoneaster racemiflorus* Booth ex Bosse from the Caucasus was described from the botanic garden in Paris in 1829 as *Mespilus racemiflorus* Desfontaines. In addition, in 1829 *C. laxiflorus* Lindley from Central Asia, was described, although the origin of the species was unknown to the author at the time of publication. In 1830 from Kazakhstan and Altai came the Bunge species *C. multiflorus* and *C. uniflorus*. In addition, in 1830 the very first species from China, *C. acutifolius* Turczaninov, was described, a simple start to the naming (which took another five decades to emerge) of the Chinese cotoneasters from such an intensely species-rich country.

Before the explosion of the number of species discovered in China, single species were being found and described from various places throughout the area covered by the genus. *Cotoneaster nummularius* Fischer & C. A. Meyer came from Asia Minor in 1836, *C. ellipticus* (Lindley) Loudon from Kashmir in 1840; and in 1846 *C. roseus* Edgeworth from Kashmir and *C. granatensis* Boissier from the Granada area of Spain. The next decade produced *C. integrifolius* (Roxburgh) G. Klotz from Nepal in 1852; both *C. orbicularis* Schlechtendal from the Sinai peninsula of Egypt, and *C. lucidus* Schlechtendal from the area of Baikal Lake in Siberia in 1854; and later, in 1857 *C. nitidus* Jacques (now *C. rotundifolius* Wallich ex Lindley) from Nepal. In 1869, three new species were described by a Mr. Baker: *C. congestus* and *C. prostratus* from the Himalaya, and *C. simonsii* from northeastern India and Bhutan.

The descriptions of *Cotoneaster reflexus* Carrière in 1871 and *C. horizontalis* Decaisne in 1877, both from central China, signaled the beginning of that country's role as the epicenter of future *Cotoneaster* discoveries. Adrien René Franchet described in 1886 and 1890 seven new species, among them *C. salicifolius*, *C. pannosus*, and *C. cochleatus*. These seven species were collected in China by the French missionaries Armand David and Jean Delavay—two very skilled botanists and avid collectors.

David (1826–1900) made three journeys into China and worked for many years in various areas of the country. He was completely at home with almost every branch of natural history, and was one of the first to give an accurate account of China's natural history. Delavay (1834–1895) was a very systematic plant collector, who managed to send as many as 200,000 specimens to the National Museum of Natural History in Paris. Among them were more than 4000 plant species, of which 1500 were new to science. Delavay collected in a restricted area of Yunnan around Dali and Lijiang, an area today well combed by tourist plant collectors. We have to remember that for these two men, botanizing was only a sideline of secondary importance to their work as missionaries. Désiré Bois in 1902 described *C. franchetii*, which was collected by Delavay, and in 1904 *C. bullatus* from Sichuan, which was probably collected by M. E. Simon.

At the beginning of the 20th century, due to the immense interest in gardening and new species, the professional plant-hunter emerged. Ernest H. Wilson (1876–1930) born in Gloucester, England, was first sent to China by the nursery of James Veitch and Sons as a plant collector in 1899–1900, and for a second time in 1903–1905. Wilson's third expedition to China, from 1907 to 1909, was on the behalf of the Arnold Arboretum of Harvard University in Massachusetts. The collections made by Wilson were impressive, and many new species of *Cotoneaster* were described by him together with Alfred Rehder in 1912 and later. A number of our most frequently cultivated and valuable cotoneasters are Wilson collections: *C. apiculatus* Rehder & E. H. Wilson, *C. nanshan* Mottet, *C. divaricatus* Rehder & E. H. Wilson, and *C. rehderi* Pojarkova (syn. *C. bullatus* var. *macrophyllus* Rehder & E. H. Wilson). The Wilson collections were taken great care of and seed distributed to botanic gardens, where even now in some, such as the Royal Botanic Garden in Edinburgh, Scotland, and the National Botanic Gardens at Glasnevin, Ireland, shrubs can still be found which were raised from these seed.

Another professional plant collector was George Forrest (1873–1932) of Scotland, who made seven expeditions into China between 1904 and 1932, mostly to northwestern Yunnan. His travels were well-organized, costly plant collecting expeditions financed by garden syndicates. Forrest also trained a number of native collectors to collect independently. His *Cotoneaster* collection comprises at least 300 specimens and seed samples. The Forrest introductions were first described by Friedrich Diels in 1912 (*C. hebephyllus*, *C. insculptus*, and *C. verruculosus*). Later, ten more species were described by William W. Smith, of which *C. lacteus* is the most well known. Much later in 1963–1966 a further nine Forrest collections became holotypes due to Gerhard Klotz. Klotz described his species from mostly herbarium specimens only. Hence, as only a few of the original Forrest collection numbers are still in cultivation today, it is difficult to find the shrubs to fit all of the Klotz species descriptions. In 1998 another *Cotoneaster* from Forrest's collection was raised to the rank of species—*C. tardiflorus* J. Fryer & B. Hylmö. In some botanic gardens there are a few plant's with Forrest numbers still awaiting names.

The German botanist, dendrologist, and plant collector Camillo Schneider (1876–1951) gave his name to *Cotoneaster camilli-schneideri* Pojarkova in 1955. In his celebrated

Illustriertes Handbuch der Laubholzkunde (Illustrated handbook of woody plants culti-vated in central Europe) of 1906, he described six new cotoneasters. The most frequently cultivated of these are *C. aitchisonii*, *C. zabelii*, and *C. dammeri*. Schneider was in China in 1914, but his work was terminated by the First World War; he managed to get to Amer-ica where he worked at the Arnold Arboretum for four years. While there he named one of his own collections, *C. vernae*, for his daughter Verna.

An English plant collector and author born in Manchester, Frank Kingdon Ward (1885–1958), visited Yunnan (China) and southeast Tibet frequently from 1909 to 1956, taking in also Bhutan, Burma, and Assam (India). One of the first cotoneasters from his collections, *C. wardii*, was described in 1917 by W. W. Smith, along with *C. majusculus*. In 1954 T. T. Yu named *C. distichus* var. *parvifolius* (now *C. cordifolius* Klotz). Later in 1998 *C. cuspidatus* J. Fryer & B. Hylmö from the Burma-Tibet border was named.

Major George Sherriff from Scotland went on several plant hunting expeditions with various companions between 1933 and 1949: to Bhutan and Tibet in 1933–1934, with Frank Ludlow and F. Williamson, and again in 1936 when they were joined by K. Lums-den. In 1937 Sherriff went alone to central Bhutan. The following year found Sherriff and Ludlow, this time accompanied by George Taylor, again in Tibet. The years of 1942 to 1945 during the Second World War were spent by Sherriff and Ludlow stationed at Lhasa in Tibet. While there, they collected most of the plants within about a 97-kilometer (60-mile) radius of Lhasa. When the war was over, Sherriff and his wife Betty, along with Ludlow, went to southeastern Tibet, accompanied by Colonel H. Elliot. Sherriff's last expedition, again with his wife and Ludlow, but this time accompanied by J. H. Hicks, was to Tibet and Bhutan. On this expedition around 5000 collections were made. Sherriff also collected in India in Kashmir and the Punjab (Himachal Pradesh). These combined expeditions produced at least ten new species of *Cotoneaster*, among which are *C. gam-blei*, *C. kongboensis*, *C. sherriffii*, and *C. taylorii*.

Joseph F. Rock (1884–1962), an American explorer of Austrian birth, spent a great deal of time between 1922 and 1949 in China, mainly in Yunnan, Sichuan, and Gansu, and also in southeastern Tibet, financed by various American institutions. Rock collected a large number of cotoneasters, but to date only two of them—*C. taoensis* (commonly found in cultivation as *C. hessei*) and *C. notabilis* Klotz 1972—have been raised to new species. Several of the Rock collections are still awaiting names.

From Sweden came David Hummel (born in Smaland, the homeland of renown bot-anist Carl Linnaeus), the medical doctor with the Sino-Swedish expedition of 1927–1931 under the leadership of Sven Hedin, exploring the Gobi desert. Hummel collected seed in Gansu and compiled a large herbarium. Two of his cotoneasters in cultivation have been named by Jeanette Fryer and Bertil Hylmö—*C. hummelii* in 1997 and *C. flinckii* in 1998.

Another Swede, Harry (Karl August Harald) Smith (1889–1971), made three expedi-tions into China. He was not the usual plant hunter collecting only species deemed to be of garden value, but rather a skilled botanist looking for new taxa among the entire Chi-nese flora. On his first visit (1921) he went to northern Hebei (formerly Chili province) west of Beijing, and in 1922 to Sichuan. His second expedition in 1924 was to the northern province of Shanxi. In 1934 he made a return visit to Sichuan. He amassed at least 100 *Cotoneaster* specimens, both herbarium (which were beautifully mounted) and seed. Some of these were placed in the care of Karl Flinck and Bertil Hylmö, who, from 1962 to 1964, named three of his species *C. splendens*, *C. sikangensis*, and *C. harrysmithii*. Later, in 1995 E. C. Nelson and J. Fryer described *C. bradyi*, and in 1998, two species that had long been distributed under their names *C. albokermesinus* and *C. shansiensis* were published by J. Fryer and B. Hylmö. Because he was a professional botanist, Harry Smith often noticed minor differences between shrubs in the wild and saved material from these which would not have attracted the attention of previous collectors, so enhancing our scientific knowledge of the genus. We now understand, for example, that series *Nitentes* and *Adpressi* comprise a great variety of species, a common occurrence in an apomictic genus. Originating from northern China, several of Harry Smith's collections in cultivation can withstand the harsh winters of northern countries.

Tse-Tsun Yu (1908–1986), a distinguished Chinese botanist and plant collector, studied in England after the Second World War and compiled his doctoral thesis on Himalayan cotoneasters while working at the British Museum of Natural History in London. The outcome of his work was published in 1954. Yu described three new cotoneasters from eastern Tibet and Burma. Among them was the well-known *Cotoneaster sanguineus*. Yu became senior professor of the Institute of Botany, Chinese Academy of Sciences in Beijing. In 1937 he collected *Cotoneaster* seed and herbarium specimens in Yunnan and Sichuan for the Royal Botanic Garden Edinburgh. On 2 June 1949 he personally presented H. R. Fletcher, the principal scientific officer who later became Regius Keeper at the RBG Edinburgh, a list hand-written on rice paper of the proposed names for 93 *Cotoneaster* taxa of which he had collected seed and deposited material at the herbarium 12 years previous. The Yu collections were very well looked after at Edinburgh, and many of his introductions can still be seen in the gardens there. Again, some are still waiting to be scientifically named. Yu himself described three of his collections not on the Edinburgh list: *C. chengkangensis*, *C. rubens* var. *minimus*, and *C. salicifolius* var. *angustus*. Later (1968–1975) Gerhard Klotz raised five Yu collections to species rank, the most well known of these being *C. muliensis* and *C. langei*.

Since 1979 it has been possible again for foreigners to travel in previously closed areas of China. Botanists, both professional and amateur, gardeners, and tourists are today collecting seed of cotoneasters when seen in the autumn covered with colorful fruit. Yunnan and Sichuan are the most frequently visited provinces, closely followed by Tibet. The first of these interesting discoveries to be named was *Cotoneaster ganghobaensis* J. Fryer & B. Hylmö, collected by C. D. Brickell and A. C. Leslie in 1987. Other finds are confirming the origins of the old species.

In the 1930s, in another area of the range of *Cotoneaster* species, in what was previously part of the Soviet Union, several authors described new species. The most outstanding and skilled of these authors was Antonina Pojarkova, an expert on the genus *Coto-*

neaster. Pojarkova collected a number of species in different parts of the vast area of the former Soviet Union. She cultivated the seed she collected, and published perfect descriptions along with very good detailed drawings, making it relatively easy to identify the taxon belonging to the Pojarkova names. Pojarkova commands great respect as a botanical author. The most prominent species to be named by her from the Soviet area include *C. tauricus* from the Crimea, *C. soczavianus* from the Caucasus, *C. oliganthus* from Kazakhstan, and *C. zeravschanicus* from Tajikistan. Pojarkova also named a number of Chinese species—*C. tomentellus*, *C. przewalskii*, and *C. mongolicus*. Some of these were collected much earlier by Russian explorers of the natural history of northwestern China such as Nikolai M. Przewalski (1839–1888) and Grigorii N. Potanin (1835–1920).

Geographic Distribution of the Genus

The genus *Cotoneaster* is distributed widely throughout the Northern Hemisphere, including all of Europe, North Africa, and the temperate areas of Asia. The western limits are the Atlas mountains of Morocco, Granada and the Pyrenees in Spain, and northern Wales in Great Britain. In the east cotoneasters are found on the eastern coast of Russia opposite Sakhalin Island, in Taiwan, on the island of Ullüng between Korea and Japan, and in Korea (but not in Japan). The southern limits are the Sinai of Egypt, Jabalath Shan

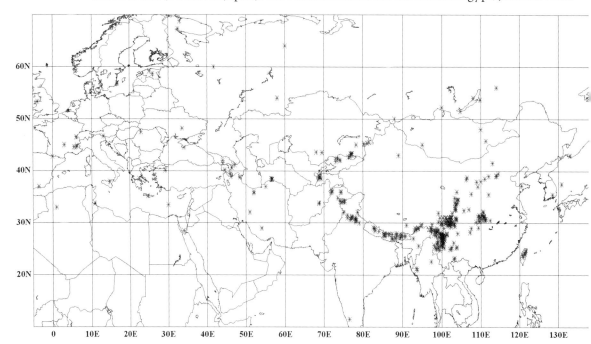

Distribution map for the type species of the genus *Cotoneaster.*

of Oman, the Nilgiri Hills of southern India, and Mount Victoria in Burma. In the north the genus occupies the Kola Peninsula and the area around Lake Baikal and Yatutsk in Siberia. The world center of distribution for the genus is the Himalaya and surrounding mountains of China in the provinces of Yunnan and Sichuan.

Apomixis

In the genus *Cotoneaster*, as with several other genera of the family *Rosaceae* (for example, *Crataegus*, *Rubus*, and *Sorbus*), species with apomictic breeding systems are very common. These mostly obligate apomicts produce seed which are formed without fertilization. This means that plants raised from these seed are usually genetically identical to the mother plant. A large number of groups of genetically similar individuals are produced. The morphological differences between species with such breeding systems can sometimes be small, making identification difficult. Apomixis facilitates the study of *Cotoneaster*, whereas sexual species in cultivation often hybridize, the majority of non-sexual apomictic species are constant generation after generation, despite the fact that they are surrounded by other species of the genus. Only rarely are any species of *Cotoneaster* facultative apomicts (some species in series *Bullati*, and maybe a few also in sections *Alpigeni* and *Franchetioides*).

Chromosome and DNA Research

As with several other genera of *Rosaceae*, the base chromosome number of *Cotoneaster* is $n = 17$. The majority of *Cotoneaster* taxa, about 70 percent, examined so far have proven to have a chromosome count of $2n = 68$ (tetraploids), while about 15 percent have $2n = 51$ (triploids), and another 10 percent have $2n = 34$ (diploids). The remaining few species have a count of $2n = 85$ (pentaploid), or an odd $2n = 102$ (polyploid), but these are extremely rare.

The outbreeding, variable species have proved to be diploids. Most of the in-breeding, apomictic species are tetraploids. The seed of the triploid species is a little less viable than the seed of the diploid and tetraploid species, very rarely producing a single, variable offspring among a batch of seedlings. Species with counts of $2n = 85$ and $2n = 102$ are extremely difficult to raise from seed, the seed frequently being malformed.

Recently, RAPD (random amplified polymorphic DNA) analysis showed that the European species differed strongly from the Chinese species. These in turn formed into related groups. Intra-specific variability was found to be very low; same species from different accessions were usually much more similar to each other than to accessions from any other species (Bartish et al. 2001; Bartish and Nybom 2005, 2007).

Hybrids

Although it is known that a high percentage (c. 85 percent) of cotoneasters will breed true from seed, the opposite is still believed by nurserymen. In countries with milder climates such as the British Isles, the most frequently grown cotoneasters are the hybrids between the diploid, outbreeding species—*C. salicifolius* and *C. frigidus*, and *C. dammeri* and *C. conspicuus*. Owing to their high ornamental value, these hybrids are common in cultivation.

Cotoneaster melanocarpus in its wider sense is known to spontaneously hybridize with *Sorbus aucuparia* subsp. *sibirica* (Hedlund) McAllister, forming ×*Sorbocotoneaster* Pojarkova. This natural hybrid was first discovered in Siberia in 1953.

Propagation

Seed propagation is the easiest method of propagation for the apomictic cotoneasters in which the seed is produced without fertilization and clonal reproduction takes place. These species will breed true from seed. Germination can sometimes be slow, one to eighteen months is normal, but infrequently seed will germinate after sitting in the pots for up to five years.

The seed are best removed from the fully ripened fruit as soon as possible, as chemicals present within the flesh can induce dormancy and thus delay germination. For best results a cold period of stratification is necessary for at least six weeks prior to sowing. This can be achieved by placing the cleaned, dry seed in a refrigerator with a temperature below 4°C (40°F). Sow in late winter to early spring into pots or trays made up with $^1/_3$ coarse grit, over which is placed $^1/_3$ loam-based compost onto which the seed are sown, and then covered with $^1/_3$ of vermiculite, or something similar. These should then be placed in a warm, sunny position. Move the pots to warm semishade as the seedlings germinate and pot on when large enough to safely handle without damaging.

If identical plants are required from the outbreeding, diploid cotoneasters or from cultivars, vegetative propagation should be used. Cuttings are best taken during July and early August when the current year's growth has sufficiently ripened and hardened. These can be taken with or without a heel, planted into a peat-and-sand mixture (about 50–50) and placed in a propagator or under polythene, preferably with bottom heat. Another method is to use Jiffy-7s (ready-prepared pressed peat blocks for cuttings), placing these into the plastic lids of clear glass (or plastic) jars, placing the jars over the top. These can then be stood on a warm windowsill.

Some of the low-growing, carpeting species are node rooting. New plants can be raised from these rooted branches. Also, cotoneasters can be layered to produce new plants.

Cotoneasters can be successfully grafted (best done in late winter under greenhouse conditions) onto other *Cotoneaster* species, or onto *Crataegus*, *Sorbus*, *Cydonia*, or *Malus*.

Diseases

Overall, *Cotoneaster* is a relatively trouble-free genus. Fireblight can sometimes be a problem, especially with some of the larger evergreen and later-flowering species.

I am indebted to Chris Prior, head of horticultural sciences at RHS Wisley for allowing the use of the following extracts from his *Plant Pathology Leaflet* (March 2005).

The causal agent [of fireblight] is a bacterium, *Erwinia amylovora*. It passes the winter in infected bark at the margins of the previous year's infections, but persists only very briefly on plant surfaces and does not survive in the soil. In the spring it multiplies in the infected back and oozes out on to the surface in mucilaginous drops, which may dry to a reddish deposit or form fine strands. Wind-blown rain or insects, including honey bees, spread the bacteria to healthy tissues where they infect via injuries or natural entry points such as lenticels, stigmas or leaf stomata. In susceptible hosts, the infection spreads down the inner bark into the main branches, causing bacterial slime to ooze out through lenticels. Slightly sunken cankers may appear on the bark and there is a reddish brown discoloration to the cambium, with a diffuse margin between healthy and diseased tissue while the disease is spreading, but becoming sharply demarcated as the canker stabilizes. The rate of spread may be as rapid as 50 mm (c. 2 in.) per day, and in severe cases the infection can spread to the main trunk and kill the tree. The name 'fireblight' describes a common symptom where all the leaves on one or more infected branches wilt and turn brown due to infection of the spur branches, giving the appearance of a fine scorch.

Fireblight originated in the United States, arriving in the United Kingdom in 1957 and is now present in parts of Europe, New Zealand and eastern Asia. It is still absent from some parts of Europe where it is regarded as an important quarantine organism. Certain areas where fireblight is not established are designated 'Protected Zones', and these include Northern Ireland, Channel Islands and the Isle of Man, the Republic of Ireland, Austria, Finland, Italy, Spain, Portugal, and parts of France.

In the United Kingdom, fireblight is usually of minor importance, but occasional epidemics occur at regular intervals, often of more than 10 years. These outbreaks are associated with the occurrence of favorable weather conditions for infection. These are warm (21°–30°C/70°–86°F), sunny days when insect activity is high, but when rain is also frequent, encouraging the production of the bacterial slime. Strong winds and hailstorms favor infection, both by dispersing the bacteria in wind-blown rain drops and by causing damage to leaves, blossoms and twigs which allows the bacteria to enter the plant. Trees are particularly susceptible at flowering, but in northern Europe most susceptible trees flower while temperatures are too low for a serious risk of infection. However, secondary summer blossoms (and late flowering species) are very important because they provide a warmer and much more favorable infection site. Insects are major vectors of the disease, feeding on the mucilaginous bacterial ooze and then carrying infective bacteria on their bodies to new hosts, which may become infected via feeding damage (e.g., by ants, beetles or leafhoppers) or by contamination of easily infected floral parts during pollination (e.g., by honey bees).

Fireblight cannot be cured, but several approaches can be adopted to control it. Cutting out and destroying infected branches can prevent the disease from spreading within the tree. It is important to act promptly because of the rapid rate of spread. Pruning tools should be sterilized after each cut to prevent the newly cut wood from becoming contaminated with infected bacteria. Biological control with harmless, antagonistic bacteria has also been investigated, using honey bees to carry them to flowers to protect against infection, but this technique is not yet in practice.

When cutting out affected branches, it is best to cut to around 30 cm (12 in.) down into the healthy, unaffected wood. It helps if the remainder of the shrub is then sprayed with a compound containing copper.

In the Netherlands, larger nurseries have had some success in raising fireblight-resistant cultivars such as *Cotoneaster salicifolius* 'October Glory' and 'Willeke' and *C. henryanus* 'Corina'.

Dieback, possibly caused or accentuated by coral-spot (*Nectria galligena*), can also occur, especially if for some reason the shrub is stressed. This is sometimes confused with fireblight. Treatment for dieback is much the same as for fireblight.

In the United States, leaf spots, canker, and fireblight are listed as the main problems of cotoneasters.

Pests

Pests are few, although some aphids seem to be attracted to the bullate-leaved species, which become covered in ants seeking out and destroying the aphids. In the United States, it seems pests are more of a problem, including hawthorn lace bug, scale and spider mites, cotoneaster webworm, sinuate pear tree borer, and pear leaf blister mite.

Birds (mainly thrushes and finches) will readily take the fruit of most cotoneasters when they are fully ripe. They prefer the red- and black-fruited taxa, orange next, and will only take yellow (or white) fruit if really hungry. The later-fruiting species mostly have fruit which take a long time to soften, hence are often left on the branches well into the winter.

Pruning

Prune in winter to encourage growth. Prune in summer to encourage flowers and hence fruit for the following season. Cotoneasters may be pruned at almost any time of the year and will tolerate regular pruning. Pruning of the most vigorous species can be undertaken in winter, and if necessary the young shoots can be shortened again in summer. If really overgrown or untidy, cotoneasters can be pruned severely, though the resulting vigorous regrowth will not produce flowers for several seasons. To keep hedges tidy and to display the fruit to its best advantage, prune out the current season's growth in September.

Soil and Situation

Cotoneasters thrive in most adequately drained soils. Although the plants seem to have a particular liking for chalk and limestone, they also do well on sandy or gravely soil. They are well adapted for poor or poorly structured soils if care is taken in establishing the plants initially, and their only dislikes are heavy, wet or waterlogged soils and excessive use of wood-chip or bark mulch. If wood-chip or bark mulch must be used, then feeding the plants with nitrogen and top-dressing with lime is essential; if this is not done the shrubs become stressed and susceptible to disease.

Sunny situations are ideal for most cotoneasters, but some species will tolerate semi-shade, especially the black-fruited species of series *Acutifolii*, *Nitentes*, and *Bullati*. Too much shade and the amount of flowers, and consequently the quantity of fruit, suffer. In addition, insufficient ripening of the wood makes the danger from winter damage substantially greater. Cotoneasters are useful in coastal areas, where many species will quite happily withstand the salt-laden winds. They are also tolerant of the atmospheric pollution of urban areas, and are hence invaluable for city plantings.

Cotoneasters include some of the most wind-hardy and valuable shrubs for exposed gardens.

Climate Tolerance

Winter hardiness is very complicated; low temperature is only one of several factors. After a warm autumn, or in areas where autumn is generally warm (for example, in North America), the new season's growth ripens and hardens, often making it possible for species to tolerate lower temperatures than in areas where autumn is cooler. The more northerly the species (native to areas with temperatures down to −25°C/−13°F), the more likely they are to be deciduous; the more southerly the species (native to areas with temperatures not falling below −15°C/5°F), the more likely they are to be evergreen. One species, *Cotoneaster lucidus*, which is native to the shores of Lake Baikal, Siberia, is one of the most hardy of all garden shrubs, and is frequently planted in Russia and Scandinavia, even north of the Arctic Circle. In areas with milder climates, evergreen species are more common in cultivation. Even in hot and dry countries, some species from series *Racemiflori*, *Hissarici*, and *Pannosi* can be successfully grown.

Identification

The most important and useful diagnostic characters for the determination of cotoneasters are the following: habit of growth; deciduous or evergreen; indumentum of new and one-year-old wood of sterile shoots; leaf sizes (taken from third leaf from apex to those at base of the sterile shoot), shape and indumentum; length of fertile shoots; number of flowers in the cyme; corolla with petals erect or spreading; petal color; stamen number and color; style number, plus whether free or joined along their entire length; anther color; fruit color and indumentum; nutlet number, and whether free or conjoined.

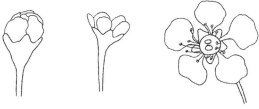

Petal orientation in *Cotoneaster* flowers: (from left to right) erect petals, semispreading petals, spreading petals. Drawings by Rosalind Bucknall.

Notes

In this publication, tree or shrub sizes quoted are ultimate heights, which are often reached only after an extended period of time.

Leaves of the sterile shoots only are used for all descriptions unless stated to the contrary. Hair type and covering should be taken from fully expanded leaves only. Hairs on the newly emerging leaves should mostly be ignored; only in series *Cotoneaster* is this feature used for identification purposes. Some species have glandular-based hairs, especially on the young bark of new branches; later, these hairs disappear leaving only the warty (verruculose) bases. This is most noticeable in series *Verruculosi*.

Flowers of subgenus *Cotoneaster* are measured by length, which includes the hypanthium (the structure on which the flower sits); in subgenus *Chaenopetalum* the width of the open flower is measured. The calyx lobes (sepals), at the top edge of the hypanthium, protect the unopened flowers. Petals sometimes have a tuft of hairs, or few or single hairs, at the base of the upper surface.

Stamen number in each flower varies from 6 to 22 throughout the species. The majority of species have 20 stamens in most flowers, although some may have a reduced number of 18, or even 16 stamens. Very seldom are more than 20 found. When the flower buds are opening these stamens can be seen arranged in two rings of 10, or occasionally, four rings of five; when fully open these stamens can be erect, erect-incurved, or erect to spreading (it is often possible to count the remains of the stamens in the fruit, making it feasible to separate species of the 10-stamen group from the 20-stamen group in the fruiting stage). The filaments of flowers with 20 stamens are narrowly subulate, whereas those of the 10 groups are mostly broadly subulate. Filament and anther color are best noted while in the bud or in the newly opened flower. Most species have white anthers, which age yellow when covered by pollen. However, there are large groups of species with anthers which are pale purple in the early stages of development, becoming purple ageing black. The effect of the black anthers in flowers with wide-open, white petals and spreading filaments is very dramatic.

Fruit sizes are given in length or length by width. Nutlet (seed) numbers per fruit are given. Each nutlet has a style attached from between halfway from the base to completely attached from the base to the apex (emerging at apex) in different species. This is a useful identification feature.

The following mathematical symbols have been used in the technical parts of the manuscript to save space and repetition:

≤ up to and including
< less than
> more than
± more or less

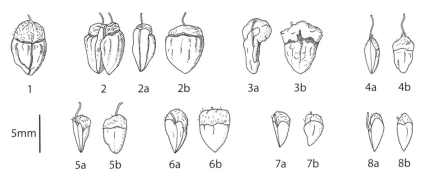

Types of nutlets in *Cotoneaster* fruit. View a shows the side of the nutlet. View b shows the back of the nutlet. 1: *C. monopyrenus*. 2: *C. przewalskii*. 3: *C. wallichianus*. 4: *C. lidjiangensis*. 5: *C. transcaucasicus*. 6: *C. schantungensis*. 7: *C. ogisui*. 8: *C. kuanensis*. Drawings by Rosalind Bucknall.

Plant Descriptions and Keys

Genus *Cotoneaster* Medikus, Philos. Bot. 1: 155 (1789). Synonyms: *Cotonea* Rafinesque; *Gymnopyrenium* Dulac; *Ostinia* Clairville.

Trees or shrubs varying in size from 15 to 18 m tall to prostrate subshrubs, no more than 2 cm tall. Branches alternate, erect, ascending, spreading or prostrate; branching varying from a central dominating trunk to multistemmed; branchlets irregular, distichous or spiraled. Leaves alternate, deciduous, semievergreen or evergreen; stipules linear or narrowly lanceolate, mostly inconspicuous and early deciduous; petioles cylindrical, 1–15 mm long, rarely with glands, frequently pubescent; blades simple and entire, flat, rugose or bullate, rarely with glands, frequently pubescent; venation pinnate, 2–14 pairs, secondary veins camptodromous, superficial or sunken adaxially. Inflorescences on lateral shoots, in thyrses or reduced thyrses of up to 200 flowers, to small clusters or solitary. Flowers epigynous; calyx without bractlets, 5-lobed, mostly persisting near fruit apex; sepals ± equal length, triangular, often fleshy; petals 5 free, white (sometimes pale pink) and spreading, or erect and pink to red, spathulate or ± orbicular and clawed; stamens 10–20; carpels and styles 1–5, 2 ovules per carpel, only one maturing, ovaries not connate, adnate to proximal half of hypanthium. Fruit a fleshy fruit 3–15 mm long, globose to obovoid or oblong; consisting of the swollen, succulent hypanthium surrounding the carpels, mostly orange to red or purple to black; flesh mostly yellow, soft-pulpy. Nutlets 1–5, not always covered by calyx lobes of the fruit; lacking in the intervening flesh between them, and shiny where interior faces are in contact, 1-seeded, brown, bony, planoconvex or trigonous, often pubescent distally, with the style remnants adnate, projecting from the apex or leaving a scar on the distal half.

Chromosomes: Basic chromosome number $\times = 17$. Majority (c. 90 percent) apomictic species.

Distribution: Throughout Eurasia and North Africa, with a marked concentration of species in the Himalaya and western China.

Key to the Subgenera, Sections, and Series of Genus *Cotoneaster*

1a. Flowering (fruiting) of inflorescence simultaneous; petals spreading at anthesis, sub-orbicular or broadly spathulate, white, rarely pale pink; filaments mostly white; anthers mostly violet or black; nutlets with conjoined style becoming free (leaving remains when dehisced) ± at apex. . . . . **Subgenus *Chaenopetalum* 2**

1b. Flowering (fruiting) of inflorescence extended; petals erect at anthesis, obovate or spathulate, pink, red, and off-white often with green, rarely white; filaments red or pink; anthers white, sometimes pink- or mauve-tinged; nutlets with conjoined style becoming free (leaving remains when dehisced) mostly $^2/_3$–$^3/_4$ from base . . . . **Subgenus *Cotoneaster* 5**

2a. Shrubs or small trees ≤ 18 m; branches erect, spreading or arched; leaves ≤ 177 mm, chartaceous or subcoriaceous, veins 3–14, petiole ≤ 18 mm; fertile shoots ≤ 100 mm; inflorescence ≤ 200 flowered; petals mostly with hair-tuft at base. **3**

2b. Dense shrubs mostly 0.2–3 m; branches prostrate, ascending or suberect, often mound-forming; leaves ≤ 45 mm, mostly coriaceous, veins 2–6(–8); petiole ≤ 9 mm; fertile shoots ≤ 50 mm; inflorescence ≤ 25-flowered; petals rarely with hair-tuft at base. . . . . **Section *Alpigeni* 11**

3a. Leaves deciduous, lower surface and petiole mostly initially pilose or villous; hypanthium mostly cupulate; fruit 6–15 mm; nutlets 1–3; very early to mid season **4**

3b. Leaves evergreen, lower surface and petiole mostly initially tomentose; hypanthium infundibulate; fruit 3–9 mm; nutlets (1–)2–4(–5); mid to very late season. . . . . **Section *Densiflori* 14**

4a. Height ≤ 18 m; fertile shoots ≤ 100 mm; inflorescence mostly compact, ≤ 200-flowered, pedicels ≤ 10 mm; anthers mostly white; nutlets (1–)2(–3). . . . . **Section *Chaenopetalum* 15**

4b. Height ≤ 8 m; fertile shoots ≤ 70 mm; inflorescence mostly lax, ≤ 30-flowered, pedicels ≤ 20 mm; anthers mostly purple-black; nutlets (1–)1 plus 1 coadunated (fused)(–2) . . . . **Section *Multiflori* 19**

5a. Branches procumbent or ascending; leaves evergreen or semi, subcoriaceous; fertile shoots ≤ 80 mm; anthers pink or purple. . . . . **Section (Series) *Rokujodaisanense***

5b. Branches erect, suberect or prostrate; leaves mostly deciduous and chartaceous; fertile shoots ≤ 170 mm; anthers white, rarely mauve **6**

6a. Leaf veins not impressed; petals semispreading, mostly white (1 sp. pink); filaments mostly white; nutlets (1–)2(–3), style remains $^4/_5$–$^9/_{10}$ from base . . . . **Section (Series) *Megalocarpi***

6b. Leaf veins mostly impressed; petals mostly erect, red or pink; nutlets 1–5, style remains $^1/_2$–$^4/_5$ from base. **7**

7a. Branchlets initially strigose or tomentose, rarely minutely verruculose; leaves elliptic or ovate, 6–85 mm, petiole 1–10 mm **8**

7b. Branchlets initially strigose, often verruculose; leaves mostly suborbicular, 4–38 mm, petiole 0.5–4 mm . . . . **Section *Adpressi* 21**

8a. Leaves 6–85 mm, veins 2–9; fertile shoots 5–100 mm; inflorescence < 60-flowered **9**

8b. Leaves 16–210 mm, veins 3–12; fertile shoots 15–170 mm; inflorescence < 150-flowered
. . . .**Section** *Acutifolii* **25**

9a. Branches loosely erect; branchlets distichous or divaricate; leaf apex acute or acuminate;
hypanthium strigose, pilose or villous; filaments red or pink **10**

9b. Branches narrowly erect; branchlets spiraled; leaf apex obtuse or acute; hypanthium
glabrous or few hairs at base; filaments white or pinkish . . . . **Section** *Cotoneaster* **28**

10a. Branchlets initially strigose; lower leaf surface mostly strigose or villous; inflorescences
mostly pendent, < 15-flowered; hypanthium campanulate; petals mostly red or pink . . . .
. . . .**Section** *Sanguinei* **32**

10b. Branchlets initially tomentose; lower leaf surface mostly tomentose; inflorescences mostly
erect, < 60-flowered; hypanthium cupulate or infundibulate; petals off-white with red or
pink. . . . .**Section** *Franchetioides* **35**

11a. Height 0.2–0.5 m; branches procumbent or prostrate, pliant; leaves distichous, very rarely
spiraled, veins impressed, petiole 2–9 mm; inflorescence 1- to 3(–4)-flowered, pedicels
3–15 mm; nutlets 2–5 . . . . **Series** *Radicantes*

11b. Height 0.5–5 m; branches ascending, prostrate or erect, stiff; leaves spiraled, rarely
distichous, veins not impressed or lightly impressed, petiole 1–6 mm; inflorescence ≤ 11-
flowered, pedicels ≤ 7 mm; nutlets (1–)2(–3) **12**

12a. Leaf apex acute, sometimes obtuse, veins lightly impressed, lower surface and petiole tomentose, sometimes villous-strigose; pedicels ≤ 3 mm; flower buds white; hypanthium in-
fundibulate; fruit villous-strigose. . . . . **Series** *Buxifolii*

12b. Leaf apex obtuse or rotund, veins not impressed, lower surface and petiole pilose-strigose;
pedicels 1–7 mm; flower buds pink; hypanthium cupulate; fruit glabrous or subglabrous .**13**

13a. Leaves mostly semievergreen, distichous or spiraled, subcoriaceous, ≤ 45 × 28 mm, upper
surface and petiole sparsely pilose-strigose; petals (3–)4–7 mm. . . . . **Series** *Conspicui*

13b. Leaves evergreen, spiraled, coriaceous, ≤ 24 × 11 mm, upper surface with single hairs, peti-
ole strigose, petals 2–5 mm . . . . **Series** *Microphylli*

14a. Branchlets mostly villous-strigose; leaves coriaceous, mostly lanceolate, veins impressed,
often deeply so; pedicels densely villous-strigose; nutlets 2–4(–5) . . . . **Series** *Salicifolii*

14b. Branchlets tomentose-strigose; leaves subcoriaceous, mostly elliptic, veins not impressed
or lightly impressed; pedicels tomentose; nutlets (1–)2 . . . . **Series** *Pannosi*

15a. Trees or large shrubs 6–18 m; leaves 30–177 mm, veins 6–12, petiole tomentose; fertile
shoots 25–100 mm; inflorescence 5- to 200-flowered; petals mostly without hair-tuft;
nutlets (1–)2(–3) . . . .**Series** *Frigidi*

15b. Shrubs sometimes small trees 5–8 m; leaves ≤ 100 mm, veins 3–10, petiole mostly strigose;
fertile shoots 8–70 mm; inflorescence 1- to 50-flowered; petals mostly with hair-tuft;
nutlets 1–2 . . . .**16**

16a. Lower leaf surface mostly sparsely villous or pilose; inflorescences mostly lax; fruit black;
nutlet with style remains 3/4–9/10 from base . . . . **Series** *Bacillares*

16b. Lower leaf surface densely pilose-villous or tomentose; inflorescences mostly compact, 2-
to 13-flowered; fruit red or black; nutlet with style remains ± apex **17**

17a. Leaves mostly subcoriaceous; inflorescence 2- to 13-flowered; petals with large hair-tuft; fruit mostly black . . . . **Series** *Hissarici*

17b. Leaves mostly chartaceous; inflorescence ≤ 50-flowered; petals mostly with hair-tuft; fruit red **18**

18a. Leaves spiraled, upper surface mostly pilose-strigose; pedicels 1–10 mm, flower buds pink; fruit with calyx lobes suberect or erect . . . . **Series** *Racemiflori*

18b. Leaves distichous or spiraled, upper surface mostly glabrous; pedicels 1–5(–8) mm, flower buds white; fruit with calyx lobes depressed or flat over apex . . . . **Series** *Aitchisonioides*

19a. Branches narrowly to loosely erect; branchlets spiraled or distichous, thin; petiole 4–18 mm; hypanthium and sepals mostly glabrous; petals white, rarely pale pink; anthers white, sometimes purple-margined; nutlets mostly 1 plus 1 coadunated (fused) . . . . **Series** *Multiflori*

19b. Branches mostly loosely erect; branchlets spiraled, moderately thick; petiole 2–12 mm; hypanthium and sepals pilose-strigose; anthers purple-black or mauve; nutlets 1–2 . . . . . **20**

20a. Branches erect to loosely erect; leaves distichous, upper surface mostly pilose; fertile shoots ≤ 50 mm; fruit mostly suborbicular; nutlets 1–2 . . . . **Series** *Tomentelli*

20b. Branches loosely erect; leaves distichous or spiraled, upper surface midrib few hairs or glabrous; nutlets 1(–2) . . . . **Series** *Hebephylli*

21a. Shrubs sometimes suckering; new growth strigose, verruculose, becoming glabrous and often densely verruculose; leaves spiraled or distichous, evergreen, subcoriaceous, veins impressed; inflorescence 1- to 2(–4)-flowered; petals caducous . . . . **Series** *Verruculosi*

21b. Shrub not suckering; new growth strigose becoming minutely verruculose and mostly subglabrous; leaves distichous, deciduous rarely semievergreen, mostly chartaceous, veins mostly not impressed; inflorescence 1- to 5(–8)-flowered; petals persistent **22**

22a. Leaves elliptic or ovate, 10–70 mm, upper surface pilose; sepal margin tomentose; petals red-brown, purple and off white; fruit black or maroon; autumn leaves yellows and golds . . . . **Series** *Nitentes*

22b. Leaves mostly suborbicular, 4–38 mm, upper surface glabrous or few strigose hairs; sepal margin villous; petals dark red or deep pink sometimes with off-white; fruit red or orange-red; autumn leaves purples and reds **23**

23a. Height ≤ 5 m; leaves dark green, lower surface strigose; flowers and fruit pendent; stamens 14–20(–26); nutlets 2–4(–5) . . . . **Series** *Distichi*

23b. Height ≤ 2.5 m; leaves mostly mid-green, lower surface glabrous or subglabrous; flowers erect; stamens (7–)10(–16); nutlets 1–3(–4) **24**

24a. Branches suberect or prostrate; branchlets mostly divaricate; leaf apex mostly acute or apiculate, margin often undulate; hypanthium cupulate; sepals mostly ligulate or obtuse; fruit globose or subglobose . . . . **Series** *Adpressi*

24b. Branches decumbent or ascending, rarely erect; branchlets mostly strongly distichous; leaf apex mostly obtuse or acute, margin flat, rarely slightly undulate; hypanthium infundibulate or narrowly cupulate; sepals mostly acute or acuminate; fruit cylindrical or obovoid . . . . **Series** *Horizontales*

25a. Leaves subcoriaceous, 20–210 mm, bullate, veins 3–11, very deeply impressed; fertile shoots 15–170 mm; inflorescence 3- to 150-flowered; corolla closed or only slightly open . . . . .Series *Bullati*

25b. Leaves chartaceous, 16–110 mm, flat or slightly bullate, veins 3–8, impressed; fertile shoots 14–70 mm; inflorescence 1- to 20-flowered; corolla mostly open 26

26a. Leaves 16–36 mm, dull, petiole 3–6 mm, pilose; fertile shoots 15–35 mm; inflorescence 3- to 9-flowered, pedicels 2–6 mm; sepals cuspidate or acuminate . . . . . . .Series *Shannanense*

26b. Leaves 25–90 mm, mostly shiny, petiole 1–10 mm, strigose; fertile shoots 15–70 mm; inflorescence 1- to 20-flowered, pedicels 1–12 mm; sepals acute or acuminate 27

27a. Branchlets mostly spiraled; leaves dark green; inflorescence lax; fruit cylindrical or obovoid, rarely subglobose, 7–15 mm; nutlets (1–)2–3 . . . . Series *Acutifolii*

27b. Branchlets distichous; leaves mostly mid or light green; inflorescence compact; fruit globose or depressed-globose, (5–)7–9 mm; nutlets (2–)3–5 . . . . Series *Glomerulati*

28a. Leaves spiraled or distichous, petiole villous; fertile shoots 15–100 mm; inflorescence lax, ≤ 50-flowered, pedicels 2–20 mm, mostly villous; hypanthium glabrous; fruit black, rarely maroon . . . . .Series *Melanocarpi*

28b. Leaves distichous, petiole tomentose or pilose; fertile shoots lax or compact, ≤ 20(–30)-flowered; pedicels ≤ 15 mm, tomentose or pilose; hypanthium pilose-villous or tomentose; fruit orange-red, red, ruby, or purple-black. 29

29a. Branchlets initially pilose; leaf veins mostly not impressed, lower surface and petiole pilose; inflorescences compact; stamens 10–20, filaments erect to semispreading; fruit with calyx lobes suberect . . . . .Series *Ignavi*

29b. Branchlets initially tomentose; leaf veins mostly impressed, lower surface and petiole tomentose; inflorescence compact or lax; stamens 20(–16), filaments erect-incurved; fruit with calyx lobes depressed or flat over apex. 30

30a. Branches narrowly erect; leaves mostly elliptic or obovate; inflorescence erect to spreading; pedicels 3–8 mm, tomentose; sepals mostly acute, tomentose, margin tomentose . . . . .Series *Tomentosi*

30b. Branches erect; leaves mostly ovate or elliptic; inflorescence spreading to pendent, pedicels ≤ 15 mm, pilose; sepals mostly obtuse or ligulate, glabrous or villous, margin villous 31

31a. Branchlets spiraled; inflorescence 1- to 10-flowered; hypanthium and sepals glabrous or subglabrous; petals erect-incurved; fruit globose, glabrous; nutlets 2–4(–5), style remains mostly $^2/_3$–$^4/_5$ from base. . . . . Series *Cotoneaster*

31b. Branchlets distichous; inflorescence 2- to 18(–30)-flowered; hypanthium and sepals villous; petals erect or semispreading; fruit obovoid, villous; nutlets 2(–3), style remains mostly $^1/_2$ from base . . . . .Series *Zabelioides*

32a. Branchlets mostly spiraled; leaves distichous or spiraled, chartaceous, ovate, elliptic or rarely lanceolate, 40–125 mm, veins not impressed; filaments white, greenish, or pale pink . . . . .Series *Acuminati*

32b. Branchlets mostly divaricate; leaves distichous, chartaceous or subcoriaceous, elliptic, ovate, sometimes suborbicular, 6–83 mm, veins impressed; filaments red or deep pink. . .33

33a. Branchlets minutely verruculose; leaves 6–88 mm; fertile shoots 10–35 mm; inflorescence 1- to 3(–4)-flowered; hypanthium broadly campanulate, sepals mostly obtuse; petals erect to semispreading, often caducous, rich red or deep pink sometimes with off-white margin . . . . **Series** *Sanguinei*

33b. Branchlets not verruculose; leaves 13–56 mm; fertile shoots 15–60 mm, inflorescence 1- to 15-flowered; hypanthium campanulate, sepals mostly acute or acuminate; petals erect or erect-incurved, red or brownish with pink, green, and/or off-white **34**

34a. Branchlets divaricate; leaves deciduous; hypanthium and sepals villous or villous-strigose; petals brownish red and off-white; fruit black or maroon . . . . **Series** *Kongboense*

34b. Branchlets divaricate, distichous or spiraled; leaves deciduous or semievergreen; hypanthium and sepals strigose; petals red, pink, and off-white; fruit red or orange-red . . . . **Series** *Mucronati*

35a. Leaves evergreen, lower surface sericeous-tomentose; inflorescence 1- to 60-flowered; pedicels sericeous-tomentose; sepals semispreading, sericeous-tomentose; petals semispreading or erect; anthers mostly mauve or pink; fruit with calyx lobes erect; nutlets mostly 2–3 . . . . **Series** *Franchetioides*

35b. Leaves mostly deciduous, lower surface tomentose; inflorescence ≤ 20-flowered; pedicels pilose-strigose; sepals erect, pilose-strigose; petals erect-incurved or erect; anthers mostly white; fruit with calyx lobes flat over navel; nutlets 2–5 . . . . **36**

36a. Leaves ≤ 60 mm, veins 2–5; fertile shoots ≤ 80 mm; inflorescence 1- to 20-flowered; hypanthium mostly cupulate; stamens 16(–20); fruit orange-red or orange . . . . **Series** *Sterniani*

36b. Leaves ≤ 26 mm; veins 2–3(–4); fertile shoots ≤ 40 mm; inflorescence 1- to 7(–10)-flowered; hypanthium mostly infundibulate; stamens 12–20; fruit mostly rich red (1 species orange-red) . . . . **Series** *Dielsiani*

1. Subgenus *Chaenopetalum* (Koehne) G. Klotz in *Beitr. Phytotax.* 10: 47 (1982).

Inflorescences mostly erect, flowers or fruit in inflorescence opening or ripening simultaneously. Corolla with petals spreading at anthesis, mostly suborbicular, white, rarely pale pink. Stamens erect to spreading, filaments narrowly subulate, mostly white; anthers violet to black, sometimes white. Nutlets with style/scar at or near apex.

4 sections: *Densiflori, Chaenopetalum, Multiflori, Alpigeni.*

1. Section *Densiflori* T. T. Yu in Acta Phytotax. Sin. 8: 217 (1963). As section *Densiflos.*

Mostly large shrubs or small trees. Branchlets initially densely villous-strigose. Leaves evergreen, mostly coriaceous, on sterile shoots distichous, lanceolate or elliptic, large (to 114–120 mm), apex mostly acute, veins impressed or deeply impressed. Inflorescences densely multiflowered. Hypanthium infundibulate, mostly villous-strigose. Fruit small (3–9 mm). Nutlets mostly 2–4, style/scar often on elongated apex.

2 series: *Salicifolii*, *Pannosi*.

1. Series *Salicifolii* T. T. Yu in Acta Phytotax. Sin. 8: 217 (1963).

Small shrubs to small trees. Branches ascending, erect (prostrate in some cultivars); branchlets mostly densely villous-strigose. Leaves mostly lanceolate, veins often deeply impressed, lower surface hairs sometimes dense. Inflorescences mostly lax. Hypanthium with sparse hairs; sepals mostly acute. Petals glabrous. Nutlets mostly 2–4.

Mid to late season.

China (Sichuan, Hubei).

8 species: *C. angustus*, *C. floccosus*, *C. glabratus*, *C. henryanus*, *C. hylmoei*, *C. rhytidophyllus*, *C. rugosus*, *C. salicifolius*.

Key to Series *Salicifolii*

1a. Leaf veins not impressed or rarely lightly impressed, lower surface mostly glabrous; inflorescence 5- to 200-flowered . . . .*C. glabratus*

1b. Leaf veins mostly deeply impressed, lower surface tomentose, floccose or villous; inflorescence 10- to 50-flowered 2

2a. Branchlets thin; leaves lanceolate, upper surface shiny; corolla 5–6 mm 3

2b. Branchlets mostly coarse; leaves lanceolate to elliptic, upper surface dullish; corolla 6–8 mm 4

3a. Lower leaf surface tomentose, mostly becoming subglabrous; inflorescence compact; sepals acute . . . .*C. salicifolius*

3b. Lower leaf surface floccose; inflorescence lax; sepals acuminate . . . . *C. floccosus*

4a. Inflorescence 15- to 30-flowered; nutlets 2–4 . . . .*C. rhytidophyllus*

4b. Inflorescence ≤ 40- to 50-flowered; nutlets 2–3 5

5a. Leaves 70–114 mm, lower surface villous; fruit blood-red with crimson . . . .*C. henryanus*

5b. Leaves 45–70 mm, lower surface tomentose; fruit orange-red 6

6a. Leaves extremely rugose, veins 8–11; inflorescence lax; nutlets mostly 2 . . . .*C. rugosus*

6b. Leaves rugose, veins 5–7; inflorescence compact; nutlets mostly 3 . . . . *C. hylmoei*

1. *Cotoneaster angustus* (T. T. Yu ex T. T. Yu & K. C. Kuan) G. Klotz in Mitt. Deutsch. Dendrol. Ges. 82: 71 (1996). Synonym: *C. salicifolius* Franchet var. *angustus* T. T. Yu ex T. T. Yu & K. C. Kuan (1963). Type: China, Sichuan, Emei Shan, 15 September 1935, *T. H. Tu 852* (holo PE).

Shrub large. Branches loosely erect. Leaves evergreen, coriaceous, on sterile shoots linear-lanceolate, 45–60 × 7–9 mm, apex subulate, base acuminate, veins 10–14 deeply impressed, lower surface yellowish tomentose. Fertile shoots 40–60 mm, including 4 leaves and an erect, lax, 10- to 20-flowered inflorescence. Carpels mostly 2.

Area: China (Sichuan).

Notes: *Cotoneaster angustus* is unknown in cultivation, but could easily be redis-covered as there are numerous botanical expeditions now visiting this area of China. Not in key.

2. *Cotoneaster floccosus* (Rehder & E. H. Wilson) Flinck & B. Hylmö in Bot. Not. (Lund) 119: 460 (1966). Synonyms: *C. salicifolius* Franchet var. *floccosus* Rehder & Wilson (1912); *C. sordidus* G. Klotz (1996). Type: China, W Sichuan, Wen-chuan Hsien, July 1908, *E. H. Wilson 1133a* (holo A, iso E, K). PLATE 1.

Shrub or tree to 8 m. Branches loosely erect, arched, pendulous, slender; branchlets spiraled or distichous, brown to purple-black, initially villous-strigose. Leaves evergreen, coriaceous, on sterile shoots distichous, lanceolate, 60–77 × 13–19 mm, apex acute or acuminate, base cuneate or acuminate, upper surface rugose, dark green, shiny, glabrous, margin slightly recurved, veins 9–14 deeply impressed, lower surface white tomentose-floccose, becoming villous to subglabrous and glaucous, sometimes a few remaining floccose tufts; petiole 3–5 mm, pilose-strigose. Fertile shoots 40–60 mm, including mostly 2–3 leaves and an erect, somewhat lax, 10- to 30-flowered inflorescence; pedicels densely strigose-villous. Hypanthium infundibulate, strigose-villous; sepals acuminate, densely strigose-villous, margin villous. Flower buds white. Corolla 5–6 mm, petals spreading, suborbicular, white, glabrous. Stamens 20; filaments white, anthers purple. Fruit globose, 5–7 mm, bright red with crimson, sparsely villous, calyx lobes depressed, navel slightly open with stamens and styles exserted. Nutlets (2–)3, rarely 4, style remains on elongated tip.

Seasons: Flowers June–July; fruit ripe November–December.

Chromosomes: Unknown. Reports of 2*n* = 34 counts probably belong to *C. salici-folius*.

Hardiness: −15°C (5°F).

Area: China (Sichuan).

Notes: *Cotoneaster floccosus* is an attractive shrub with a graceful, fanlike branching habit. It is highly recommended by its collector, Ernest Wilson, for the beauty of its fruit. This species is not common in cultivation; although the name *C. floccosus* is frequently used, it is usually in error for the related *C. salicifolius*. Recently reintroduced into culti-vation. Received RHS Award of Merit in 1920 and Award of Garden Merit in 1984.

3. *Cotoneaster glabratus* Rehder & E. H. Wilson in Sargent, Pl. Wilson. 1: 171 (1912). Type: China, W Sichuan, Wa-shan, 8 July 1906, *E. H. Wilson 2185* (holo A). PLATE 2.

Shrub or tree to 6 m. Branches somewhat loosely erect, ascending, spreading; branchlets spiraled, slender, maroon to purplish black, lenticellate, shiny, initially tomentose-pilose. Leaves evergreen, subcoriaceous, on sterile shoots lanceolate or elliptic, 60–90 × 18–39 mm, apex acuminate or acute, base cuneate, upper surface sometimes slightly rugose, dark green, dull or slightly shiny, initially pilose, margin slightly recurved, veins 7–10 sometimes lightly impressed, lower surface glaucous, initially sparsely pilose, midrib often red; petiole 5–10 mm, pilose. Fertile shoots 40–70 mm, including mostly 2 leaves and a somewhat lax, 50- to 200-flowered inflorescence; pedicels pilose. Hypanthium infundibulate, pilose; sepals obtuse or ligulate, glabrous, border broad, membranous, apex maroon, margin glabrescent. Flower buds white. Corolla 5–6 mm, petals spreading, white. Stamens 20, filaments white, anthers purple. Fruit globose, 3–5 mm, orange red to rich red, shiny, glabrescent, calyx lobes suberect or flat, navel open with stamens and styles exserted. Nutlets 2(–3), style remains on elongated tip.

Seasons: Flowers June–July; fruit ripe October–November.

Chromosomes: Tetraploid (McAllister, pers. comm.).

Hardiness: −15°C (5°F).

Area: China (Sichuan, possibly also Yunnan).

Notes: *Cotoneaster glabratus* is a magnificent species. With its shiny, purple-black branchlets, silvery-reversed leaves which are tinged with purple after frost, masses of large clusters of flowers and fruit, it is a very desirable shrub for growing instead of the ubiquitous *C.* ×*watereri*. Recently reintroduced into cultivation. Not to be confused with *C.* ×*watereri* 'Glabratus'.

4. *Cotoneaster henryanus* (C. K. Schneider) Rehder & E. H. Wilson in Sargent, Pl.
Wilson. 1: 174 (1912). Synonyms: *C. rugosus* E. Pritzel ex Diels var. *henryanus*
C. K. Schneider (1906); *C. pritzelii* (C. K. Schneider) G. Klotz (1996). Type: China,
W Hubei, received March 1889, *A. Henry 5752* (holo B, iso A, E). PLATE 3.

Shrub or tree to 5(–7) m. Branches erect and ascending, coarse, young lower growth horizontal; branchlets spiraled, greenish brown to purple-black, initially with tawny villous-strigose hairs. Leaves evergreen or semi, subcoriaceous, on sterile shoots lanceolate or elliptic, 70–114 × 22–44 mm, apex acute or acuminate, base cuneate, upper surface slightly rugose, dark green, dull, initially sparsely brownish pilose, margin slightly recurved, veins 7–10 impressed, lower surface initially densely brownish villous-strigose; petiole 5–10 mm, densely villous-strigose. Fertile shoots 40–80 mm, including 2–4 leaves and a lax, 10- to 40-flowered inflorescence; pedicels densely villous-strigose. Hypanthium infundibulate, densely villous-strigose; sepals acute, densely villous-strigose, margin villous. Flower buds white. Corolla 6–7 mm, petals spreading, white, glabrous. Stamens 20; filaments white, anthers purple. Fruit obovoid or subglobose, 5–6 mm, rich red with crimson, villous-strigose, calyx lobes depressed. Nutlets 2 rarely 1–3, style remains at slightly elongated and often densely villous apex.

Seasons: Flowers June–July; fruit ripe September–October.

Chromosomes: Diploid (Krügel 1992a; Bailey, pers. comm.; Jewsbury, pers. comm.). Sexual, outbreeding, variable from seed.

Hardiness: −15°C (5°F).

Area: China (Hubei, Sichuan).

Notes: *Cotoneaster henryanus*, due to its diploid nature, shows wide variation in width, thickness, and hair covering of leaves in its offspring. Klotz's (1996) *C. pritzelii* with its broader, less hairy leaves falls within the normal variation of *C. henryanus*. Sometimes found in cultivation as *C. rhytidophyllus* or *C. salicifolius*, *C. henryanus* itself is rather elusive in cultivation. It is a handsome and decorative shrub of spreading habit while young, with sturdy, erect or ascending branches later. The large leaves, which are sometimes bronzed in winter, can suffer wind damage. Received RHS Award of Merit in 1920. This being a variable species, some forms are forms are cultivated. Also a few hybrids are possibly produced with *C. frigidus*. Recently reintroduced into cultivation.

Cultivars: '**Anne Cornwallis**', height to 2.5 m, leaves semievergreen, ovate to lanceolate with margin slightly undulate, 60–100 × 25 mm, upper surface glabrous, lower surface glaucous and pubescent, fertile shoots short, pubescent, fruit obovoid, 7–8 mm, coral-red. Selected in England in 1967 by John Clarke of Frittenden, Cranbrook, Kent (WSY). '**Corina**' (PLATE 4), a handsome, sturdy, tall, and broad shrub with ascending branches, leaves large, coriaceous, with tawny tomentose hairs on lower surface, fruit abundant, light red to orange-red. Seemingly resistant to fireblight. '**Salmon Spray**', medium-sized, strongly erect shrub. Similar to *C. henryanus* but fruit salmon-red. Selected in England at the Hillier Nurseries before 1940.

5. ***Cotoneaster hylmoei*** Flinck & J. Fryer in The Plantsman 15: 26 (1993). Synonym:
   C. salicifolius Franchet var. *rugosus* Rehder & E. H. Wilson (1912), non *C. rugosus*
   E. Pritzel. Type: China, W Hubei, Ichang, October 1907, *E. H. Wilson 335* (holo A,
   iso BM). PLATE 5.

Shrub, 2–3 m. Branches erect, gracefully arched and pendulous; branchlets distichous, brownish purple, initially densely villous. Leaves evergreen, coriaceous, on sterile shoots elliptic or ovate-elliptic, 45–70 × 18–30 mm, apex acute or acuminate, mucronulate, base cuneate, upper surface rugose, dark green, dull, glabrescent, margin recurved, veins 5–7 deeply impressed, lower surface silvery-white tomentose; petiole 3–5 mm, tomentose. Fertile shoots 25–70 mm, including 2–3 leaves and an erect, compact, 15- to 50-flowered inflorescence; pedicels 0.5–2 mm, densely villous. Hypanthium infundibulate, densely villous; sepals often recurved, acute or obtuse, reddish purple, villous. Flower buds red. Corolla 7–9 mm, petals spreading, pale pink, glabrous. Stamens 20; filaments white or pale pink; anthers reddish black. Fruit globose, 5 mm, red, sparsely pilose, calyx lobes depressed, villous, navel slightly open. Nutlets 2–3, rarely 4, style remains at apex.

Seasons: Flowers July; fruit ripe November–December.

Chromosomes: Tetraploid (Bailey, pers. comm.). Apomictic, true from seed.

Hardiness: −15°C (5°F).

Area: China (Hubei, Sichuan).

Notes: *Cotoneaster hylmoei*, with its moderate height, elegant hanging branches, profusely borne pretty pink-tinged flowers, and long lasting bright, rusty red fruit, is especially suitable for today's modest-sized garden. The leaves turn reddish with age and are

most attractive when seen in winter sunshine. Received RHS Award of Merit in 1912 as
C. rugosus.

6. **Cotoneaster rhytidophyllus** Rehder & E. H. Wilson in Sargent, Pl. Wilson. 1: 175
(1912). Type: China, W Sichuan, Wa-Wu Shan, Hong-ya Xian, September 1908,
E. H. Wilson 2184 (holo A, iso BM, E). **PLATE 6**.

Shrub or small tree, 3–6(–7) m. Branches erect, ascending, spreading, coarse; branchlets
spiraled or distichous, purple-black, initially densely villous-strigose. Leaves evergreen,
coriaceous, on sterile shoots elliptic or ellipto-lanceolate, 45–88 × 15–40 mm, apex acute
or acuminate, base cuneate or narrowly cuneate, upper surface extremely rugose, reticulate, yellowish green to dark green, shiny, initially villous, margin recurved, veins 5–11
deeply impressed, lower surface pale yellowish green, tomentose-floccose; petiole coarse,
3–7 mm, densely villous-strigose. Fertile shoots 40–75 mm, including 3 leaves and a lax,
10- to 40(–50)-flowered inflorescence; pedicels 2–10 mm, strigose-villous. Hypanthium
infundibulate, densely villous-strigose; sepals acute, villous-strigose. Flower buds white.
Corolla 8–9 mm, petals spreading, white (sometimes fading pale pink), glabrous. Stamens 20; filaments white; anthers violet-purple. Fruit subglobose, 4–5 mm, orange-red,
slightly shiny, sparsely villous, calyx lobes densely villous. Nutlets (2–)3, rarely 4, style
remains at apex.

Seasons: Flowers July; fruit ripe October–November.

Chromosomes: Unknown. Apomictic, true from seed.

Hardiness: –15°C (5°F).

Area: China (Sichuan).

Notes: *Cotoneaster rhytidophyllus* is a handsome species which has been reintroduced into cultivation by Mikinori Ogisu. Shrubs in cultivation bearing the name *C.
rhytidophyllus* are mostly *C. henryanus*.

7. **Cotoneaster rugosus** E. Pritzel ex Diels in Bot. Jahrb. Syst. 29: 385 (1900). Type:
China, E Sichuan, Hoanch. Walv. Pensha Ai, Nanchuan, 30 August 1891, *C. Boch &
von A. Rosthorn 680* (holo B, iso O). **PLATE 7**.

Shrub or small tree, 4–5(–6) m. Branches loosely erect or ascending, coarse; branchlets
spiraled or distichous, light reddish brown, densely lenticellate, initially villous-strigose.
Leaves evergreen, coriaceous, on sterile shoots elliptic, lanceo-elliptic 70–90 × 25–30
mm, apex acute or acuminate, base cuneate, upper surface reticulate, extremely rugose,
dark green, shiny later dullish, initially villous-pilose, margin recurved, veins 7(–11)
deeply impressed, lower surface whitish villous-strigose; petiole 4–5 mm, densely villous-
strigose. Fertile shoots 30–50(–80) mm, including mostly 3 leaves and 10- to 40-flowered
inflorescence; pedicels densely villous-strigose. Hypanthium infundibulate; sepals acute,
rarely acuminate, densely villous-strigose; sepals acute, villous-strigose. Flower buds
white. Corolla 11–12 mm, petals spreading, white, glabrous. Stamens 20; filaments white;
anthers violet. Fruit obovoid or depressed-globose, 6–8 mm, orange-red, dullish, villous-

strigose, calyx lobes depressed, navel slightly open, stamens and styles exserted. Nutlets 2, very rarely 3, style remains at apex.

Seasons: Flowers June–July; fruit ripe October–November.

Chromosomes: Tetraploid (McAllister, pers. comm.). Apomictic, true from seed.

Hardiness: −15°C (5°F).

Area: China (Sichuan, Hubei).

Notes: *Cotoneaster rugosus* is a sturdy shrub with coral-red fruit. It is frequently confused with other species, especially *C. hylmoei*; many records of *C. rugosus* belong to other species in this series.

8. *Cotoneaster salicifolius* Franchet in Nouv. Arch. Mus. Hist. Nat., sér. 2, 8: 225 (1886). Synonym: *C. sargentii* G. Klotz (1996). Type: China, Sichuan, Moupine, in hills; leg. A. David, June 1869 (holo P). **PLATE 8.**

Shrub or small tree, 6–8 m. Branches loosely erect, arched; branchlets spiraled or distichous, slender, maroon, initially tomentose-strigose. Leaves evergreen, coriaceous, on sterile shoots lanceolate, 40–90 × 13–23 mm, apex acute or acuminate, base cuneate, upper surface rugose, dark green, shiny, initially sparsely pilose, margin recurved, veins 7–12 deeply impressed, lower surface grayish green, initially densely villous; petiole 4–8 mm, tomentose-strigose. Fertile shoots 30–60 mm, including 3–4 leaves and a compact, 10- to 50-flowered inflorescence; pedicels densely strigose-villous. Hypanthium pilose; sepals acute, sparsely pilose, border narrow, whitish and glabrous, margin very sparsely villous. Flower buds white. Corolla 5–6 mm, petals white, glabrous. Stamens 20; filaments white; anthers purple. Fruit globose, 5–7 mm, bright red with hint of crimson, sparsely pilose, calyx lobes depressed or flat, navel slightly open. Nutlets 2(–3), rarely 4–5, style remains at apex.

Seasons: Flowers June; fruit ripe October–November.

Chromosomes: Diploid (Broertjes 1956; Zeilinga 1964; Hensen 1966; Klotz 1968b; Jewsbury, pers. comm.). Sexual, outbreeding, variable from seed.

Hardiness: −15°C (5°F).

Area: China (Sichuan). Tibet.

Notes: *Cotoneaster salicifolius* is named for its willowlike (*Salix*) leaves. The fruit, of which there are also yellow and orange forms, are often abundant. This species has been reintroduced by Keith Rushforth (*KR 250*) and Roy Lancaster (*RL 606*) from the Emei Shan area of Sichuan. It is a very variable species of which many forms are cultivated. Also a few hybrids are produced (see *C. ×watereri*).

Cultivars: **'Aldenhamensis'**, fast-growing to around 3 m high, branches long, dark brown with many pale lenticels, leaves oblanceolate, 40–70 × 12–18 mm, apex and base acute, lower surface with long hairs, flowers in small, lax clusters, fruit long-lasting, rich red, nutlets 2. A handsome shrub selected by Vicary Gibbs of Aldenham House in England. Received RHS Award of Merit in 1927. **'Brno Orangeade'**, vigorous, low-growing, and wide-spreading with many light orange fruit. A good ground cover but sometimes sends up a few strong erect shoots which need to be removed to keep it low. Also excellent trained as a standard. '**Coral Bunch**', similar to *C. henryanus* 'Salmon Spray' with slightly lighter colored fruit. '**Decor**', widely erect with pendulous branches, leaves large and shiny, fruit bright red. From Germany. '**Emerald Carpet**', low-growing, compact shrub with small leaves and red fruit. Introduced by Monrovia nursery. '**Exburyensis**' (PLATE 9), erect, wide-spreading (especially when young), and strong-growing, with branches brownish, densely lenticellate, leaves darker green than 'Rothschildianus' with which it is often confused, fruit apricot-yellow becoming pink-tinged. Selected by Lionel Rothschild around 1930. Received RHS Award of Garden Merit in 1969. '**Fructuluteo**', a yellow-fruited form collected by Ernest Wilson (*Wilson 6909*) from Sichuan and raised by Rothschild at Exbury. The parent of various yellow-fruited cultivars. '**Gnom**', compact, height 20–30 cm, slow-growing, forming a low, wide mound, branches purplish black, internodes long, leaves lanceolate or oblong, c. 20 × 5 mm, base and apex obtuse, upper surface shiny bottle-green, veins 4–6, lower surface densely villous, inflorescence laxly 3- to 6-flowered, fruit 3–5 mm, light to bright red. Good ground cover, though more free-fruiting when trained against a wall or fence or trailed as curtain. Originated around 1938 from a prostrate seedling of *C. salicifolius* in the Juergl nursery, Cologne, Germany. Introduced in 1955. Received RHS Award of Garden Merit in 1984. '**Herbstfeuer**' (autumn fire), strong but fairly sparsely branched, height to 40 cm (often trained as a pendulous standard), long creeping and often rooting branches forming large carpet, leaves oval, 40–60 × 15–25 mm, upper surface slightly rugose, purple tinged in winter, veins 7–9, lower surface pale bluish green, subglabrous, base and apex acute, petiole 5 mm, inflorescence 5- to 12-flowered, fruit long-lasting, scarlet, 5 mm, nutlets usually 4. Discovered among seedlings purchased from Vilmorin of Paris by H. Bruns nursery, Westerstede, Germany, in 1930. '**Merriot Weeper**', wider than high (c. 150–200 cm) with weeping branches, flowers in small clusters, fruit red. '**October Glory**', wide-spreading, branches lax, remarkably rich red-brown, leaves broadly elliptic, 40 × 20 mm, upper surface slightly shiny. An excellent selection of outstanding hardiness discovered by Darthuizers in the Netherlands among *C. salicifolius*. Seemingly fireblight resistant. '**Parkteppich**' (park carpet), height 1–1.5 m, wide-spreading, long branches, leaves 20–30 × 6–12 mm, base and apex rounded, lower surface bluish white and pubescent, inflorescence 6- to 10-flowered, fruit not numerous, 4–6 mm, light red, nutlets 3–4. A good-looking ground-covering shrub, in cultivation since 1950. Introduced in 1957 by J. Hachmann, Barmstedt (Holstein), Germany. '**Pendulous**', branches prostrate and slowly spreading, pendulous when trained as a standard but then creeping again when touching the ground, leaves to 70 mm, upper surface slightly rugose, darkish green, fruit quite numerous, red. '**Perkeo**', dense, height to 1 m, branches pendulous, leaves 15–25 × 5–18 mm, lower surface white-tomentose, fruit few, very small, red. Resembles a dwarf *C. floccosus*. '**Pink Champagne**', large, dense, vigorous shrub, leaves narrow, fruit abundant, small, yellow becoming pink-tinged. Introduced by Hillier Nurseries in England in 1971. '**Red Flare**', vigorous, prostrate, and mound-forming, fruit bright red. '**Repens**' (syns. 'Avondrood', 'Sunset', 'Afterglow'), evergreen or semievergreen, low-growing, height to 80 cm, strongly branched, quickly forming a dense carpet, branches not rooting, green becoming dark brown with distinct lenticels, leaves ovate-lanceolate, 25–35 × 8–15 mm, upper surface slightly rugose, little autumn color but leaves reddening in cold winters, lower surface bluish green, glabrescent, petiole 4 mm, inflorescence 3- to 10-flowered, fruit not very numerous, bright red, nutlets 4–5. A good ground cover. Selected by W. Haalboom of Drierbergen, Netherlands. Introduced in 1948. **'Rothschildianus'**, branches distinctly spreading and green when young, leaves narrower than 'Exburyensis', yellowish green, fruit in large clusters, creamy-yellow. Due to a mix-up early in its distribution, 'Rothschildianus' is frequently grown as 'Exburyensis'. Less robust than 'Exburyensis'. Selected at Exbury Gardens in Hampshire, England. Received RHS Award of Garden Merit in 1984. **'Ruth'**, similar to 'Repens'. **'Saldam'**, habit similar to 'Herbstfeuer' but with leaves a slightly duller, paler green without much autumn color, producing only a few dark green or red variations. Selected as a seedling by J. Timm and Company, Elmshorn, Germany, before 1945 but not introduced until 1954. **'Scarlet Leader'**, low-growing, carpeting, height to around 1 m, spreading 2–3 m, leaves with red-purple autumn-winter color. An excellent ground cover; can form a dense mat in one year following planting. **'September Beauty'**, height at most 1 m, leaves similar to 'Herbstfeuer', fruit paler red. Selected by Darthuizers in Netherlands and introduced in 1990. Seemingly fireblight resistant. **'Stonefield Gnome'**, a dwarf, fastigiate shrub said to have originated from a witches' broom found growing in *C. salicifolius* at Scott's Nursery in Somerset, England, in the 1950s. **'Sympatie'**, a low-growing cultivar from the Czech Republic with salmon fruit finally turning red. **'Willeke'**, moderately high and wide in habit, leaves fairly large, narrow, fruit very numerous, orange-red. A cultivar of high ornamental value from Darthuizers in Netherlands. Has a good combination of attractive leaves and many bright-colored fruit. Also seemingly fireblight-free.

2. Series *Pannosi* Flinck & B. Hylmö in Bot. Not. (Lund) 119: 460 (1966).

Branches erect, arched; branchlets tomentose. Leaves mostly elliptic, veins lightly impressed, lower surface mostly tomentose. Inflorescences mostly compact. Hypanthium mostly tomentose; sepals cuspidate or acute. Petals often with tuft of hairs at base of upper surface. Nutlets (1–)2.

China (Yunnan, Sichuan, Guanxi). Tibet. Vietnam.

15 species: *C. brickellii, C. coriaceus, C. crispii, C. fulvidus, C. glaucophyllus, C. harrovianus, C. lacteus, C. meiophyllus, C. pannosus, C. poluninii, C. serotinus, C. tsarongensis, C. turbinatus, C. vernae, C. vestitus.*

Key to Series *Pannosi*

1a. Lower leaf surface soon glabrous; hypanthium glabrous except extreme base 2

1b. Lower leaf surface and hypanthium with hairs often dense 3

2a. Leaves ≤ 95 mm, apex mostly acute; inflorescence ≤ 60-flowered . . . . *C. glaucophyllus*

2b. Leaves ≤ 56 mm, apex obtuse or rotund, rarely acute; inflorescence ≤ 40-flowered . . . .
. . . . *C. meiophyllus*

3a. New growth tomentose, very soon glabrescent; leaves on sterile shoots often spiraled,
mostly obovate, 34–52 mm . . . .*C. coriaceous*

3b. New growth tomentose, villous or strigose, mostly remaining so, or only slowly glabrescent; leaves on sterile shoots distichous, mostly elliptic or lanceolate, if obovate
42–120 mm 4

4a. Leaves lanceolate, veins 6–12; corolla 5 mm 5

4b. Leaves elliptic or ellipto-lanceolate, veins 4–10; corolla 6–10 mm. 6

5a. Leaves ≤ 92 mm; inflorescence ≤ 70-flowered; hypanthium cupulate; petals glabrous
. . . . *C. tsarongensis*

5b. Leaves ≤ 52 mm; inflorescence ≤ 150-flowered; hypanthium infundibulate; petals with hair-
tuft . . . .*C. vernae*

6a. Leaf veins 4–6(–7); inflorescence 5- to 25-flowered 7

6b. Leaf veins 5–10; inflorescence 10- to 40(–150)-flowered 9

7a. Height 2–3 m; branches stiffly erect; leaves ≤ 29 mm, dark green. . . . .*C. poluninii*

7b. Height ≤ 5–6 m; branches arched, spreading; leaves ≤ 43 mm, mid-green. 8

8a. Fertile shoots ≤ 70 mm; inflorescence 7- to 25-flowered, fruit orient to blood-red; nutlets 2
. . . .*C. crispii*

8b. Fertile shoots ≤ 45 mm; inflorescence 5- to 15(–25)-flowered; fruit currant red; nutlets 1–2
. . . .*C. pannosus*

9a. Leaves ellipto-lanceolate; pedicels and sepals with silky hairs; anthers black or purple-
black. 10

9b. Leaves elliptic sometimes broadly so; pedicels and sepals hairs not silky; anthers red-
purple or purple. 12

10a. Leaves mostly < 47 mm; fertile shoots 30–50 mm. . . . . *C. harrovianus*

10b. Leaves ≤ 75 mm; fertile shoots 50–90 mm. 11

11a. Inflorescence lax, mostly 10- to 40-flowered; hypanthium base with dense silky hairs
. . . . *C. serotinus*

11b. Inflorescence compact; 20- to 100-flowered; hypanthium tomentose . . . .*C. turbinatus*

12a. Leaf apex obtuse or acute, veins not impressed or lightly impressed; inflorescence
10- to 40-flowered. 13

12b. Leaf apex mostly acute or acuminate, veins deeply impressed; inflorescence 20- to 150-
flowered 14

13a. Hypanthium densely strigose only at base; fruit light red; nutlet with style remains ¾ from base . . . .*C. fulvidus*

13b. Hypanthium tomentose; fruit cardinal-red; nutlet with style remains at apex . . . . .**C. vestitus**

14a. Leaves ≤ 70(–120) mm; fertile shoots 50–100 mm; inflorescence lax; fruit crimson . . . . *C. lacteus*

14b. Leaves ≤ 35 mm; fertile shoots 30–80 mm; inflorescence compact; fruit capsicum-red . . . .*C. brickellii*

1. *Cotoneaster brickellii* J. Fryer & B. Hylmö in New Plantsman 8: 236 (2001). Type: China, Yunnan, Lijiang to Dali roadside, 15 September 1987, *C. D. Brickell & A. C. Leslie 12415* [cult. England, Hampshire, Rumsey Gardens Nursery, J. Fryer (hort.) 1099, 16 January 1999] (holo WSY, iso E). **PLATE 10.**

Shrub, 1.5–2.5 m. Branches erect, arched, spreading; branchlets spiraled or distichous, purple-black, lenticellate, initially tomentose. Leaves evergreen, subcoriaceous or coriaceous, on sterile shoots elliptic, 19–35 × 10–19 mm, apex acute, base cuneate, upper surface slightly rugose, dark green, dull, glabrescent, veins 5–7 deeply impressed, lower surface white-tomentose; petiole 4–10 mm, tomentose. Fertile shoots 30–80 mm, including 4 leaves and a compact, 20- to 150-flowered inflorescence; pedicels 1–3 mm, tomentose-strigose. Hypanthium infundibulate, tomentose-strigose; sepals cuspidate or acuminate, tomentose, margin tomentose. Flower buds creamy-white. Corolla 6 mm, petals spreading, white, glabrous. Stamens 20, erect; filaments white; anthers red-purple. Fruit globose, 5–6 mm, orange-red, sparsely pilose, calyx lobes depressed. Nutlets 2, style remains at apex.

Seasons: Flowers July; fruit ripe October–December.

Chromosomes: Tetraploid (Bailey, pers. comm.; McAllister, pers. comm.). Apomictic, true from seed.

Hardiness: −12°C (10°F).

Area: China (Yunnan).

Notes: *Cotoneaster brickellii* is an excellent year-round shrub, wider than high with a fairly dense habit, attractive leaves, and masses of flowers covering the branches in mid-summer, followed by multitudes of fruit which last until the first hard frost.

2. *Cotoneaster coriaceus* Franchet in Pl. Delavay. 3: 222 (1890). Type: China, Yunnan, in thickets at Choui-tsin-yu, near Tapin-tze, 9 June 1889, *J. Delavay 3712* (holo P).

Shrub, 3–4 m. Branches erect, arched, spreading; branchlets light brown, initially tomentose. Leaves evergreen, coriaceous, on sterile shoots obovate or elliptic, 34–52 × 16–24 mm, apex rotund, obtuse or acute, base cuneate, upper surface rugose, dark green, shiny, glabrescent, veins 7–10 impressed, lower surface tomentose; petiole 7–8 mm, tomentose. Fertile shoots 30–50 mm, including 2–4 leaves and a compact, 10- to 50-flowered inflorescence; pedicels tomentose. Hypanthium infundibulate, silky tomentose; sepals cuspidate or acuminate, tomentose. Flower buds white. Corolla 7–10 mm, petals spreading, white, sometimes with hair-tuft. Stamens 20, filaments white, anthers red-purple. Fruit globose, 5–6 mm, red, sparsely pilose, calyx lobes suberect, tomentose. Nutlets 2, style remains at apex.

Seasons: Flowers July; fruit ripe November–December.

Chromosomes: Tetraploid (Jewsbury, pers. comm.).

Hardiness: −12°C (10°F).

Area: China (Yunnan).

Notes: *Cotoneaster coriaceus* has been reintroduced into cultivation by Keith Rushforth (*KR 2478*), collected in 1993 in Yunnan between Kunming and Xiaguan, and is proving to be a very garden-worthy shrub.

3. ***Cotoneaster crispii*** Exell (*pro. hybr.*) in Gard. Chron. 83: 44 (1928). Type: cult. *C. crispii*, as *C. frigida* × *C. pannosa*, Waterer & Sons, Bagshot, A. W. Exell, November 1927 (holo K).

Shrub or small tree, 4–6 m. Branches narrowly erect, arched; branchlets spiraled, purple-black, initially silky tomentose. Leaves evergreen or semi, subcoriaceous or coriaceous, on sterile shoots elliptic, sometimes ovate, 30–43 × 14–24 mm, apex acute, base cuneate, upper surface sometimes slightly rugose, mid to dark green, dull, pruinose, initially sparsely pilose, veins 4–7 sometimes lightly impressed, lower surface whitish tomentose; petiole 5–7 mm, tomentose. Fertile shoots 40–70 mm, including 4 leaves and a compact to somewhat lax, 7- to 25-flowered inflorescence; pedicels 1–7 mm, silky tomentose. Hypanthium infundibulate, silky tomentose; sepals cuspidate or acuminate, silky tomentose, border narrow, membranous, margin villous. Flower buds white. Corolla 7 mm, petals spreading, white, rarely with hair-tuft. Stamens 20; filaments white; anthers reddish purple. Fruit globose, 6–8 mm, red to rich red, glabrescent, calyx lobes depressed, densely villous. Nutlets (1–)2, style scar at apex.

Seasons: Flowers June–July; fruit ripe October–November.

Chromosomes: Triploid (Krügel 1992a; McAllister, pers. comm.; Bailey, pers. comm.).

Hardiness: −15°C (5°F).

Area: China (Yunnan).

Notes: Originally thought to be of hybrid origin, *Cotoneaster crispii* was found in the nursery of John Waterer, Sons & Crisp in England. It has proved (as with many other triploids) to breed around 99 percent true from seed, very rarely producing a rogue seedling. Repeat sowings of seed have been made, always giving the same results. *Cotoneaster crispii* has been collected in Yunnan in Cho Jiang He gorge in 1996 by Keith Rushforth (*KR 4072*) and Jeanette Fryer (*JFYU 081*).

4. ***Cotoneaster fulvidus*** (W. W. Smith) G. Klotz in Wiss. Z. Friedrich-Schiller-Univ. Jena, Math.-Naturwiss. 17: 335 (1968). Synonym: *C. hebephyllus* Diels var. *fulvidus* W. W. Smith (1917). Type: China, Yunnan, Yungchang-Mekong divide, May 1913, *G. Forrest 9888* (holo E, iso K). **PLATE 11.**

Shrub to small tree, 3–4 m. Branches erect, arched, spreading; branchlets spiraled, purple-black, initially yellowish tomentose-strigose. Leaves evergreen, coriaceous, on sterile shoots elliptic or obovate, 30–45 × 19–26 mm, apex obtuse or acute, base obtuse or cuneate, upper surface sometimes minutely rugose, dark green, shiny to dullish, glabrous, veins 6–7 lightly impressed, lower surface yellowish tomentose; petiole 6–9 mm, tomentose. Fertile shoots 30–80 mm, including 2–4 leaves and a compact, 10- to 40-flowered inflorescence; pedicels 2–5 mm, yellowish tomentose–strigose or tomentose-villous. Hypanthium infundibulate, base densely strigose, apex sparsely villous; sepals acute or cuspidate, glabrous or sparsely pilose, border broadly membranous, margin villous. Flower buds tinged pink. Corolla 6–7 mm, petals very pale pink, sometimes with hair-tuft. Stamens 20; filaments white; anthers purple. Fruit subglobose, 6–7 mm, light red, sparsely pilose, calyx lobes suberect, glabrous, navel open. Nutlets (1–)2, style remains ³/₄ from base.

Seasons: Flowers June–July; fruit ripe October–December.

Chromosomes: Tetraploid (Jewsbury, pers. comm.).

Hardiness: −12°C (10°F).

Area: China (Yunnan).

Notes: *Cotoneaster fulvidus* is in cultivation from a 1999 collection made by Keith Rushforth (*KR 2512*) in Yunnan between Bao Shan to Salween at Taiping Shan. It is a beautiful shrub and is an excellent addition to the available winter-fruiting species. This species is closely related to those in series *Hebephylli*.

5. ***Cotoneaster glaucophyllus*** Franchet in Pl. Delavay. 3: 222 (1890). Type: China, Yunnan, Kiao-che-tong, near Hee-chan-men, 6 December 1884, *J. Delavay 3747* (holo P). **PLATE 12**.

Shrub or small tree, to 4 m. Branches erect, arched, spreading; branchlets spiraled, greenish to purple-black, initially strigose. Leaves evergreen, subcoriaceous or chartaceous, on sterile shoots elliptic, 48–95 × 30–47 mm, apex acute, broadly acuminate or obtuse, base cuneate, upper surface mid-green, dull to slightly shiny, glabrescent, veins 6–9 lightly impressed, lower surface light-green, glaucous, reticulate, glabrescent; petiole 6–12 mm, villous. Fertile shoots 40–70 mm, including 2–4 leaves and a lax, 10- to 60-flowered inflorescence; pedicels 2–6 mm, strigose. Hypanthium infundibulate, sometimes sparsely strigose; sepals cuspidate or caudate, glabrous, margin sometimes with pilose or villous hairs. Flower buds white. Corolla 5–6 mm, petals spreading, white, with small hair-tuft. Stamens 20; filaments white; anthers black. Fruit globose, 6 mm, orange-red, shiny, glabrous, calyx lobes suberect, sometimes pilose. Nutlets 2, style remains at apex.

Seasons: Flowers August–September; fruit ripe December throughout winter.

Hardiness: −15°C (5°F).

Area: China (Yunnan). Possibly also in Tibet.

Notes: *Cotoneaster glaucophyllus* is a handsome year-round, wind-hardy shrub. The attractive leaves have a bluish white reverse and the many flowers are followed by long-lasting winter fruit. A fine specimen exists in Scotland at RBG Benmore. Collected by Keith Rushforth (*KR 4309*) in Yunnan, between Kaiyuan to Kunming at Mi Li in November 1996. Received RHS Award of Merit in 1924.

6. **Cotoneaster harrovianus** E. H. Wilson in Gard. Chron. 51: 3 (1912); Sargent, Pl. Wilson. 1: 173 (1912). Type: China, Yunnan, seed collected 10 miles southwest of Mengtze, November 1899, by Veitch expedition; specimens from Hort. Veitch 1315, June 1911 (lecto A).

Shrub or small tree, to 5 m. Branches erect, arched; branchlets spiraled or distichous, reddish purple, initially strigose. Leaves evergreen, coriaceous or subcoriaceous, on sterile shoots narrowly-elliptic, narrowly-obovate or lanceolate, 34–47 × 14–18 mm, apex acute or acuminate, base cuneate, upper surface becoming rugose, dark green, dull to shiny, initially sparsely pilose, veins 5–10 impressed, lower surface initially whitish pilose-villous; petiole 6–9 mm, tomentose. Fertile shoots 30–50 mm, including 4 leaves and a compact, 10- to 40-flowered inflorescence; pedicels 1–3 mm, silky tomentose. Hypanthium infundibulate, silky tomentose; sepals cuspidate or acuminate, silky tomentose, border narrow and membranous, margin villous. Flower buds white. Corolla 7–8 mm, petals spreading, white, sometimes with minute hair-tuft. Stamens 20; filaments white; anthers purple-black. Fruit depressed-globose, 4–6 mm, orange-red, shiny, very sparsely pilose, calyx lobes depressed, with silky hairs. Nutlets 2, style remains on elongated apex.

Seasons: Flowers July; fruit ripe November–January.

Chromosomes: Tetraploid (Zeilinga 1964; Klotz 1968b; Bailey, pers. comm.).

Hardiness: −12°C (10°F).

Area: China (Yunnan). Vietnam.

Notes: *Cotoneaster harrovianus* was discovered by Augustine Henry, introduced by Ernest Wilson, and found again in 2001 by Keith Rushforth (*KR 7332*) in Sapa, Lao Cai province, Vietnam. This is a very striking shrub, showy in flower, followed by large clusters of brilliant red fruit. It was named in honor of George Harrow, manager of the Coombe Wood Nurseries of Veitch in England. Received RHS Award of Merit in 1905.

7. **Cotoneaster lacteus** W. W. Smith in Not. Roy. Bot. Gard. Edinburgh 10: 23 (1917). Synonyms: *C. oligocarpus* C. K. Schneider (1917); *C. smithii* G. Klotz (1996). Type: China, Yunnan, descent to the Yangtze from the eastern boundary of Lijiang Valley, July 1913, *G. Forrest 10419* (holo E, iso BM, K). **PLATE 13**.

Shrub or small tree, 4–8 m. Branches erect, arched, spreading, slender; branchlets spiraled or distichous, purple-black, initially yellowish tomentose-villous. Leaves evergreen, coriaceous, on sterile shoots obovate or broadly elliptic, 42–120 × 20–60 mm, apex acute, acuminate or obtuse, base cuneate, upper surface slightly rugose, dark green, dull, initially sparsely pilose, veins 7–9 deeply impressed, lower surface yellowish tomentose-villous; petiole 5–8 mm, tomentose. Fertile shoots 50–100 mm, including 4 leaves and a lax, 20- to 150-flowered inflorescence; pedicels 1–5 mm, tomentose-strigose. Hypanthium infundibulate, tomentose-strigose; sepals cuspidate, tomentose, margin villous. Flower buds creamy-white, sometimes slightly pinkish. Corolla 6–8 mm, petals spreading, creamy-white, sometimes with hair-tuft. Stamens 20; filaments white; anthers purple. Fruit globose, 6–7 mm, crimson, sparsely villous, calyx lobes depressed, tomentose. Nutlets 2, style remains near apex.

Seasons: Flowers July; fruit ripe November.

Chromosomes: Tetraploid (Klotz 1968b; Bailey, pers. comm.). Apomictic, true from seed.

Hardiness: −15°C (5°F).

Area: China (Yunnan, Sichuan).

Notes: *Cotoneaster lacteus* is common in warm temperate zones of both the northern and southern hemispheres. It has naturalized in the United States on the Californian coastal hills, where it is often found in cultivation as *C. parneyi* hort. *Cotoneaster lacteus* is also cultivated in Mexico, Chile, Argentina, South Africa, and New Zealand. It is a very useful wind-hardy shrub. It can also be grown as a hedge where the summer growth is pruned to reveal the fruit. A magnificent hedge originating from George Forrest's collection (*Forrest 10419*) still stands in Ireland's National Botanic Gardens at Glasnevin, Dublin; planted in the late 1920s, it is now around 6 m high by 3 m thick. *Cotoneaster lacteus* has been collected by Jeanette Fryer (*JFYU 008*) and Keith Rushforth (*KR 3929*) in NW Yunnan in 1996. *Cotoneaster lacteus* in spring has striking, erect, tawny-haired new shoots, later covered with flowers which are followed by pretty red winter fruit. Received RHS Award of Merit in 1935 and Award of Garden Merit in 1984.

Cultivar: '**Milkmaid**' (PLATE 14), a variegated form, very arresting with fruit which ripens earlier and is shiny red, slower growing than the species. Nonvariegated growth needs to be pruned out.

8. ***Cotoneaster meiophyllus*** (W. W. Smith) G. Klotz in Wiss. Z. Friedrich-Schiller-Univ. Jena, Math.-Naturwiss. 17: 338 (1968). Synonym: *C. glaucophyllus* Franchet var. *meiophyllus* W. W. Smith (1917). Type: China, Yunnan, Mingkwong valley, June 1912, *G. Forrest 8325* (holo E, iso P). PLATE 15.

Evergreen shrub, to 5 m. Branches erect, arched; branchlets spiraled, greenish brown to reddish purple, initially tomentose-strigose. Leaves evergreen, subcoriaceous or coriaceous, on sterile shoots broadly elliptic, 37–56 × 27–31 mm, apex obtuse, rotund, rarely acute, base mostly obtuse, upper surface yellowish green becoming mid-green, shiny, glabrescent, veins 6–8 sometimes lightly impressed hairs, lower surface light green, glaucous, reticulate, tomentose only in bud; petiole 6–10 mm, sparsely pilose. Fertile shoots 50–80 mm, including mostly 3 leaves and a lax, 10- to 40-flowered inflorescence; pedicels 4–8 mm, tomentose-strigose. Hypanthium infundibulate, base densely strigose; sepals cuspidate, glabrous, border membranous, whitish, margin sometimes villous. Flower buds white. Corolla 6–7 mm, petals spreading, white, glabrous. Stamens 20; filaments white; anthers red-purple. Fruit globose or depressed-globose, 6 mm, orange-red, glabrous, calyx lobes suberect, navel wide open with nutlets exserted. Nutlets 2, style remains at apex.

Seasons: Flowers July–August; fruit ripe October–November.
Chromosomes: Tetraploid (Bailey, pers. comm.). Apomictic, true from seed.
Hardiness: −12°C (10°F).
Area: China (Yunnan, possibly also Sichuan and Guanxi).
Notes: *Cotoneaster meiophyllus* is a very beautiful shrub with year-round interest. It should be more frequently cultivated. The fruit persist long into winter. Closely related to *C. glaucophyllus*, *C. meiophyllus* is easily distinguished by its neater habit and smaller leaves which are rounded at the base and apex.

9. *Cotoneaster pannosus* Franchet in Pl. Delavay. 3: 223 (1890). Type: China, Yunnan, Tapin-tze, 1886, *J. Delavay 3743* (lecto designated P). PLATE 16.

Shrub, to 5 m. Branches erect, arched, pendulous, wide-spreading, slender; branchlets purple-black, tomentose-villous. Leaves evergreen, coriaceous, on sterile shoots elliptic, sometimes broadly elliptic, 20–37 × 10–26 mm, apex acute or obtuse, base cuneate, upper surface becoming slightly rugose, mid-green, dull, initially sparsely pilose, veins 4–6 lightly impressed, lower surface whitish tomentose; petiole 4–7 mm, tomentose. Fertile shoots 20–45 mm, including mostly 4 leaves and a compact, (3–)5- to 15(–25)-flowered inflorescence; pedicels 1–5 mm, tomentose. Hypanthium infundibulate or cupulate, silky-tomentose; sepals cuspidate, sometimes acute or obtuse, tomentose, border narrow, membranous, white with red apex, margin villous. Flower buds white. Corolla 7–10 mm, petals spreading, white, sometimes with hair-tuft. Stamens 20; filaments white; anthers purple. Fruit globose, 6–7 mm, red, shiny, villous, calyx lobes suberect, tomentose, navel open. Nutlets (1–)2, style remains at apex.

Seasons: Flowers June–July; fruit ripe November.
Chromosomes: Tetraploid (Krügel 1992a). Apomictic, true from seed. Some diploid counts reported but correct identification in doubt.
Hardiness: −15°C (5°F).
Area: China (Yunnan). Possibly in Tibet.
Notes: Seed of *Cotoneaster pannosus* was introduced into France and distributed from Paris to other botanic gardens, including the RBG Kew in England, in 1892. This species is common in cultivation in warm temperate zones of both the northern and southern hemispheres. In the United States, where it has escaped and naturalized, it can be found far from habitation in the Californian coastal area. It is cultivated in Mexico, Chile, Argentina, South Africa, and New Zealand. A remarkably wind-hardy shrub, it is excellent as a hedge or against a wall or fence (will tolerate even east-facing) where it hangs its long, silvery-hairy leaved branches gracefully, either full of flowers or weighed down with multitudes of small red fruit. Recently reintroduced into cultivation.

10. *Cotoneaster poluninii* G. Klotz in Wiss. Z. Friedrich-Schiller-Univ. Jena, Math.-
Naturwiss. 27: 21 (1978). Type: Nepal, Bheri River, Dunaihi, 2 June 1952, *O. Polunin,
W. R. Sykes & L. H. J. Williams 1037* (holo BM).

Shrub, 2–3 m. Branches narrowly erect; branchlets spiraled, purple-black, initially
tomentose-strigose. Leaves evergreen, coriaceous, on sterile shoots elliptic, 6–29 × 3–17
mm, apex acute or acuminate, base cuneate, upper surface slightly rugose, dark green,
dull, sparsely long-haired pilose, veins 4–6 lightly impressed, lower surface white-
tomentose; petiole 2–6 mm, tomentose-strigose. Fertile shoots 20–50 mm, including
mostly 4 leaves and a compact, 5- to 25-flowered inflorescence; pedicels 1–5 mm, silky
tomentose. Hypanthium infundibulate, silky tomentose; sepals cuspidate, long-haired
tomentose, border narrow, membranous, apex often dark red, margin tomentose. Flowers white in bud. Corolla 7–10 mm, petals spreading, white, hair-tuft at base of upper
surface. Stamens (16–)20; filaments white; anthers reddish purple. Fruit globose, obovoid,
7–8 mm, crimson to red, pilose, calyx lobes depressed, tomentose. Nutlets (1–)2, style
remains at apex.

Seasons: Flowers July; fruit ripe November.

Chromosomes: Tetraploid (Bailey, pers. comm.). Apomictic, true from seed.

Hardiness: −12°C (10°F).

Area: Nepal.

Notes: When *Cotoneaster poluninii* was described in 1978, it had long been in cultivation, although its origin was unknown. This is the largest species in this series. It is a
tall shrub with an unusual, somewhat fastigiate habit and numerous rich red fruit which
last well into the winter.

11. *Cotoneaster serotinus* Hutchinson in Bot. Mag. 146: t. 8854 (1920). Type: China,
Yunnan, open situations among shrubs at the north end of Hoching valley, November 1910, *G. Forrest 6756* (lecto designated E, iso K). Klotz neotype superseded.

PLATE 17.

Shrub or small tree, to 6 m. Branches erect, arched; branchlets spiraled, reddish purple,
initially tomentose-strigose. Leaves evergreen, subcoriaceous, on sterile shoots elliptic,
ellipto-lanceolate or obovate, 56–75 × 28–42 mm, apex acute or acuminate, base cuneate
or obtuse, upper surface sometimes slightly rugose, mid-green, dull, glabrescent, veins
7–10 sometimes lightly impressed, lower surface light green, reticulate, tomentose soon
villous; petiole 6–8 mm, tomentose-strigose. Fertile shoots 50–80 mm, including 2–5
leaves and a lax, 10- to 40(–100)-flowered inflorescence; pedicels 3–10 mm, with dense
silky hairs. Hypanthium infundibulate, with dense silky hairs, apex glabrescent; sepals
cuspidate or caudate, glabrescent, border broad, membranous, whitish, margin villous.
Flower buds white. Corolla 7–8 mm, petals spreading, white, sometimes with small hair-
tuft. Stamens 20; filaments white; anthers black. Fruit globose, 7 mm, rich red, sparsely
pilose or glabrous, calyx lobes depressed, sparsely pilose or glabrous, navel open. Nutlets
2, style remains at apex.

Seasons: Flowers August; fruit ripe November–December.

Hardiness: –12°C (10°F).

Area: China (Yunnan).

Notes: Klotz (1996) designated *Forrest 27770* as a neotype for *Cotoneaster serotinus* despite the fact that Hutchinson clearly indicated that this species was raised from *Forrest 6754*. *Cotoneaster serotinus* is not nowadays so common in cultivation (although many shrubs are mistakenly named as this species) as the closely related *C. turbinatus*, *C. glaucophyllus*, and *C. meiophyllus*. Previously *C. serotinus* was grown fairly extensively throughout warm temperate zones. It is one of the latest-fruiting species of *Cotoneaster*, holding its bright red fruit throughout winter. Awarded RHS First Class Certificate in 1919. Recently reintroduced into cultivation.

12. *Cotoneaster tsarongensis* J. Fryer & B. Hylmö, *sp. nov.* Type: SE Tibet, Tsarong, Salween-Kuichiang divide, October 1919, *G. Forrest 19116* (holo E). **PLATE 18.**

Shrub or small tree, densely branched, to 6 m. Branches erect, arched; branchlets spiraled or distichous, plum purple, initially tomentose-strigose. Leaves evergreen, chartaceous or subcoriaceous, on sterile shoots lanceolate, 48–92 × 17–24 mm, apex acuminate, sometimes acute, base cuneate or obtuse, upper surface sometimes minutely rugose, midgreen, shiny, glabrescent, veins 8–12 impressed, lower surface tomentose; petiole 7–12 mm, tomentose. Fertile shoots 30–60 mm, including up to 4 leaves and a lax, 20- to 70-flowered inflorescence; pedicels 3–10 mm, strigose-pilose. Hypanthium cupulate, strigose-pilose; sepals acute or acuminate, villous, border membranous, white, margin sparsely villous. Flowers buds white. Corolla 5 mm, petals spreading, white, glabrous. Stamens 20; filaments white; anthers purple-black. Fruit globose or obovoid, 4–5 mm, red with crimson, sparsely pilose, calyx lobes depressed. Nutlets 2, style remains 3/4 from base.

Seasons: Flowers June; fruit ripe November–December.

Chromosomes: Unknown. Possibly a diploid.

Hardiness: –12°C (10°F).

Area: Tibet. China (Yunnan).

Notes: *Cotoneaster tsarongensis* is unusual in having a very small hypanthium (2–3 mm including calyx), flowers, and fruit. It is extremely late fruiting, and unless the autumn is warm the fruit do not always fully ripen.

13. *Cotoneaster turbinatus* Craib in Curtis's Bot. Mag. 140: t. 8546 (1914). Type: cult. England, RBG Kew, from *Vilmorin 4484, 4547*, flowered 25 July 1913 (lecto designated K). **PLATE 19.**

Shrub or small tree, to 6 m. Branches erect, arched; branchlets spiraled, reddish purple, initially tomentose-strigose to villous. Leaves evergreen, subcoriaceous, on sterile shoots ellipto-lanceolate, elliptic or ovate, 55–70 × 23–31 mm, apex acute, acuminate or obtuse, base cuneate or obtuse, upper surface sometimes slightly rugose, mid to dark green, dull, initially sparsely pilose, veins 7–9 lightly impressed, lower surface grayish green, silky tomentose-villous; petiole 6–10 mm, tomentose-strigose. Fertile shoots 60–100 mm, including 3–5 leaves and a compact, 20- to 100-flowered inflorescence; pedicels 1–3 mm, silky tomentose. Hypanthium infundibulate, silky tomentose; sepals cuspidate or caudate, silky tomentose, border narrow, membranous, margin villous. Flower buds white. Corolla 6–8 mm, petals spreading, white, glabrous. Stamens (18–)20; filaments white; anthers black. Fruit obovoid, 6–7 mm, orange-red, sparsely silky pilose-villous, calyx lobes depressed, tomentose. Nutlets 2, style remains near apex.

Seasons: Flowers July–August; fruit ripe November–December.

Chromosomes: Tetraploid (Bailey, pers. comm.). Apomictic, true from seed.

Hardiness: –12°C (10°F).

Area: China (Yunnan, possibly also Sichuan).

Notes: *Cotoneaster turbinatus* is one of the most commonly grown species in series *Pannosi*. Apparently it was raised from seed from Vilmorin of France who believed it to have originated from collections made in China in eastern Sichuan or Hubei (Craib 1914). However, series *Pannosi* is not known from these provinces. This mix-up was probably made in the handling. It is quite likely that *C. turbinatus* originated from a collection made by Jean Delavay who collected extensively in Yunnan.

14. ***Cotoneaster vernae*** C. K. Schneider in Bot. Gaz. 64: 71 (1917). Synonyms: *C. pannosus* Franchet var. *robustior* W. W. Smith (1917); *C. robustior* (W. W. Smith) Flinck & B. Hylmö (1966). Type: China, Yunnan, Lijiang, Snow Mountain, October 1914, *C. K. Schneider 2676* (holo A). **PLATE 20.**

Tree or large shrub, to 9 m. Branches erect, arched; branchlets spiraled, purple-black, initially tomentose-villous. Leaves evergreen, subcoriaceous, on sterile shoots lanceolate or narrowly-elliptic, often conduplicate, 40–52 × 15–17 mm, apex acute or obtuse, base cuneate, upper surface sometimes slightly rugose, dark green, shiny, initially very sparsely pilose, veins 6–11, lower surface white-tomentose; petiole 5–8 mm, tomentose. Fertile shoots 30–70 mm, including 3–4 leaves and a compact, 20- to 150-flowered inflorescence; pedicels 1–3 mm, tomentose. Hypanthium infundibulate, silky tomentose, sepals cuspidate, silky tomentose. Flower buds creamy-white. Corolla 6 mm, petals semispreading to spreading, creamy-white, with hair-tuft. Stamens 20; filaments white; anthers reddish purple. Fruit globose or obovoid, 4–6 mm, red, pilose, calyx lobes erect, tomentose. Nutlets 2, style remains at apex.

Seasons: Flowers August; fruit ripe December–February.

Chromosomes: Tetraploid (Bailey, pers. comm.). Diploid (McAllister, pers. comm.). Sometimes variable from seed.

Hardiness: –12°C (10°F).

Area: China (Yunnan). Possibly also Tibet.

Notes: *Cotoneaster vernae* can form a trunk of up to around 0.3 m in diameter at the same distance from the ground. It has noticeable, brown-tomentose caduceus bracts and striking violet anthers. The late-forming fruit do not always fully ripen in colder temperate zones. Specimens of the original George Forrest collection (*Forrest 12869*) of *C. vernae* still exist in some botanic gardens as *C. pannosus* var. *robustior*. Recently reintroduced into cultivation.

15. *Cotoneaster vestitus* (W. W. Smith) Flinck & B. Hylmö in Bot. Not. (Lund) 119: 460 (1966). Synonym: *C. glaucophyllus* Franchet var. *vestitus* W. W. Smith (1917). Type: China, Yunnan, hills east of Tengchong, May 1912, *G. Forrest 7723* (holo E).
PLATE 21.

Shrub, 3.5–5 m. Branches erect, arched to pendulous; branchlets spiraled or distichous, slender, purple-black, initially tomentose-villous. Leaves evergreen, subcoriaceous or coriaceous, on sterile shoots elliptic, 35–54 × 18–25 mm, apex acute or obtuse, base cuneate or obtuse, upper surface mid-green, dull, initially sparsely pilose, veins 5–9, lower surface tomentose; petiole 3–7 mm, tomentose. Fertile shoots 30–60 mm, including mostly 3 leaves and a compact, 15- to 40-flowered inflorescence; pedicels 1–5 mm, tomentose. Hypanthium cupulate, tomentose; sepals cuspidate, acute or obtuse, tomentose, margin villous. Flower buds white. Corolla 7–9 mm, petals spreading, creamy-white, glabrous. Stamens 20; filaments white; anthers purple. Fruit globose, 6–7 mm, red to maroon, sparsely villous, calyx lobes suberect, navel open. Nutlets 1–2, style remains at apex.

Seasons: Flowers June–July; fruit ripe November.

Chromosomes: Tetraploid (McAllister, pers. comm.; Jewsbury, pers. comm.). Apomictic.

Hardiness: –15°C (5°F).

Area: China (Yunnan, Sichuan).

Notes: *Cotoneaster vestitus* is a beautiful shrub with hanging branches festooned with flowers and fruit. It is excellent as a specimen tree. It is also similar to *C. pannosus* but more pendulous with larger leaves and darker fruit.

2. Section *Chaenopetalum*

Variable-sized shrubs to large trees, sometimes multistemmed. Leaves deciduous, chartaceous or subcoriaceous, on sterile shoots mostly elliptic or suborbicular, sometimes large (4–177 mm). Inflorescences often compact, mostly multiflowered. Petals with tuft of hairs at base of upper surface. Anthers mostly white, sometimes purple or pink. Nutlets (1–) 2(–3).

5 series: *Frigidi, Aitchisonioides, Racemiflori, Bacillares, Hissarici.*

3. Series *Frigidi*. T. T. Yu in Bull. Brit. Mus. (Nat. Hist.), Bot. 1: 139 (1954).

Large shrubs to large trees up to 18 m. Branchlets tomentose or densely villous. Leaves deciduous or semievergreen, on sterile shoots elliptic, lanceolate or oblanceolate, 30–177 mm, veins 6–12 often slightly impressed. Inflorescences mostly lax, 5- to 100-flowered. Petals mostly glabrous. Anthers black or violet. Nutlets 2(–3).

Mid season.

India (Himachal Pradesh, Tamil Nadu, Sikkim, Bengal). Bhutan. Burma. Tibet.

3 species: *C. frigidus, C. gamblei, C. hedegaardii*. Also includes *C. ×watereri*.

Key to Series *Frigidi*

1a. Leaf veins 8–12; inflorescence 50- to 200-flowered; corolla 6–7 mm; fruit 4–7 mm . . . .
. . . . ***C. frigidus***

1b. Leaf veins 6–8; inflorescence 5- to 30-flowered; corolla 8–12 mm; fruit 10–12 mm **2**

2a. Upper leaf surface shiny; inflorescence lax; corolla 8–10 mm; fruit brownish red, dull
. . . . ***C. gamblei***

2b. Upper leaf surface dull; inflorescence compact; corolla 10–12 mm; fruit rich-red, shiny
. . . . ***C. hedegaardii***

1. ***Cotoneaster frigidus*** Wallich ex Lindley in Edward's Bot. Reg. 15: t. 1229 (1829).
Type: N Nepal in the alpine zone of Gossainkund, flowered August 1821, Herb. East
India Company, (Wallich's collectors) 657 (lecto K). **PLATE 22.**

Tree, 15–18 m. Branches somewhat narrowly erect, only slightly spreading; branchlets
spiraled, brown, initially tomentose to villous. Leaves deciduous, chartaceous or subcoriaceous, on sterile shoots elliptic, obovate or lanceolate, 105–177 × 37–56 mm, apex
acute, sometimes obtuse, base cuneate, upper surface dark green, slightly shiny, glabrescent, veins 8–12 lightly impressed, lower surface grayish green, tomentose-villous, petiole 8–12 mm, tomentose. Fertile shoots 40–100 mm, including 4 leaves and a lax, 50- to
200-flowered inflorescence; pedicels tomentose. Hypanthium cupulate, tomentose; sepals acuminate or acute, tomentose, margin villous. Flower buds white. Corolla 6–7 mm,
petals spreading, white, glabrous. Stamens 20; filaments white; anthers black. Fruit globose, 4–7 mm, red with crimson tint, shiny, sparsely villous, calyx lobes depressed,
densely villous, navel slightly open. Nutlets 2(–3), style remains at apex.

Seasons: Flowers June; fruit ripe October.

Chromosomes: Diploid (Zeilinga 1964; Hensen 1966; Mehra 1976 as quoted in Goldblatt 1981; Klotz and Krügel 1983a; Panigrahi and Kumar 1986; McAllister, pers. comm.).
Sexual, outbreeding; variable from seed.

Hardiness: −15°C (5°F).

Area: Nepal. India (Himachal Pradesh, Uttaranchal Pradesh, Tamil Nadu). Possibly
also in Tibet and Burma.

Notes: *Cotoneaster frigidus* was brought into cultivation in 1821 and is still one of the
finest cotoneasters. Highly ornamental and free growing, it often readily forms a trunk.
The Kennedy Park Research Centre in Ireland has an experimental plantation of *C. frigidus* for assessing the value of its wood. The species is extremely prolific in flower and
fruit. Because the fruit is not particularly liked by birds, it often remains on the totally
leafless branches all winter. The true species is seldom seen, hybrids with diploids of the

evergreen series *Salicifolii* (see *C.* ×*watereri*) being made to do duty for it. A magnificent specimen of *C. frigidus* can be seen at the Westonbirt Arboretum in Gloucestershire, England, which is at least 15–18 m high with a trunk girth of around 1.5 m. Received RHS Award of Garden Merit in 1925, Award of Merit in 1966, and again in 1986 as *C. gamblei*. In 1990 a collection of this species was made by Chris Chadwell and Alistair McKelvie in central Nepal, beyond Kalopani in Kali Gandaki. Forms of *C. frigidus* are found in the nursery trade.

Cultivars: '**Cornubia**' (PLATE 23), tree to 6 m or more, branches ascending diagonally, dark brown with many white lenticels, leaves semievergreen, 70–100 × 25–40 mm, dull green, slightly rugose, apex slightly acuminate, lower surface glabrescent, fruit copious, subglobose, 7–9 mm, bright red, nutlets 2–3. Diploid (Zeilinga 1964). Two forms of 'Cornubia' were originally distributed from L. Rothschild, Exbury, England in 1930: '**Exbury Variety**' and '**FCC Variety**', the former being maybe a little larger and more robust. Received RHS Award of Merit in 1933, First Class Certificate in 1936, and Award of Garden Merit in 1984. '**Fructuluteo**' (Bean) Rehder (syn. f. *fructuluteo*, 'Xanthocarpus') (PLATE 24), large clusters of creamy fruit slowly ripening to yellow. Introduced before 1914. Received RHS Award of Merit in 1932. '**Inchmery**', branches more arched and fruit larger than *C. frigidus*, fruit yellow becoming salmon-pink. '**Montana**', similar to 'Vicary'. '**Pendulous**', a shrub of weeping habit selected at the RBG Kew from seed obtained from Darjeeling, India, in 1924. Diploid (Zeilinga 1964). '**St. Monica**' (PLATE 25), branches strongly erect, leaves semievergreen, elliptic-oblong, 100–150 mm, some coloring in autumn, bears heavy crops of vivid scarlet fruit. Said to withstand windy situations. Selected at St. Monica Nursing Home, Bristol, England by Dr Bauer. Received RHS Award of Merit in 1933. '**Vicary**', robust growth, branches erect or ascending, shiny dark brown with many lenticels, leaves to 100 × 35 mm, apex acute, upper surface slightly rugose, pilose, lower surface with long hairs, midrib often red in winter, fruit ruby-red, not shiny. Originated at Aldenham House in England around 1920. '**Westonbirt Variety**', vivid red fruit. Selected by Vicary Gibbs at Aldenham House. Possibly the same as 'St. Monica'.

2. *Cotoneaster gamblei* G. Klotz in Wiss. Z. Martin-Luther-Univ. Halle-Wittenberg, Math.-Naturwiss. 15: 530 (1966). Type: Bhutan, Shabjetang, Bumthang Chu, 9 June 1949, *F. Ludlow, G. Sherriff & J. H. Hicks 19083* (holo BM, iso E, S, UPS). PLATE 26.

Tree, 6–10 m. Branches loosely erect and spreading; branchlets spiraled, brown or maroon-purple, initially tomentose-strigose. Leaves deciduous or semievergreen, chartaceous or subcoriaceous, on sterile shoots elliptic, 30–105 × 15–62 mm, apex acute or obtuse, base cuneate or obtuse, upper surface becoming rugose, dark green, shiny, subglabrous, veins 7–8, lower surface initially villous; petiole 4–10 mm, densely villous-strigose. Fertile shoots 40–70 mm, including 2–3 leaves and a lax, 5- to 30-flowered inflorescence; pedicels villous-strigose. Hypanthium cupulate, densely villous, sepals acute, densely villous, border maroon, margin tomentose. Flower buds white. Corolla 8–10 mm, petals white, sometimes with hair-tuft. Stamens 20; filaments white; anthers black. Fruit obovoid, 9–10 mm, brownish red to maroon tinted with green, dull, sparsely villous, calyx lobes depressed, villous, navel slightly open. Nutlets (1–)2, style remains near tomentose apex.

Seasons: Flowers June; fruit ripe October–November.

Chromosomes: Unknown. Apomictic, true from seed.

Hardiness: −15°C (5°F).

Area: Bhutan, India (Sikkim, Bengal).

Notes: Despite some previous reports of this species having red fruit, *Cotoneaster gamblei*, grown from the Rushforth collection (*KR 1576*), originating from the type area of the Bumthang region between Kunjey and Damphe in 1990, is most definitely much darker fruited. The original notes were probably taken from an unripe specimen. *Cotoneaster gamblei* is a very attractive wide-crowned small tree.

3. ***Cotoneaster hedegaardii*** J. Frycr & B. Hylmö, *sp. nov.* Type: cult. Sweden, Bjuv, raised from seed from Nepal, Phulchoki, 15 November 1974, Johannes Hedegaard 415, flowered 10 June 1990, *B. Hylmö 1446* (holo C); also fruited 45 September 1992.
    PLATE 27.

Tree or large shrub, to 6 m. Branches loosely erect, spreading; branchlets spiraled, greenish brown, minutely verruculose, initially tomentose-strigose. Leaves deciduous, chartaceous, on sterile shoots elliptic, 55–105 × 33–57 mm, apex acute or obtuse, base cuneate or obtuse, upper surface becoming slightly rugose, mid-green, dull to slightly shiny, subglabrous, veins 6–8 lightly impressed, lower surface grayish green, villous-pilose; petiole 4–8 mm, tomentose. Fertile shoots 25–45(–70) mm, including mostly 3 leaves, and a compact, 7- to 20-flowered inflorescence; pedicels 2–6 mm, tomentose. Hypanthium cupulate, tomentose-strigose, sepals acuminate or acute, tomentose-strigose, margin villous. Flower buds white. Corolla 10–12 mm, petals spreading, white, glabrous. Stamens 20; filaments white; anthers purple to reddish brown. Fruit globose, 12 mm, crimson to maroon, shiny, sparsely villous, calyx lobes depressed. Nutlets 2, very rarely 1 or 3; style/scar near apex.

Seasons: Flowers June; fruit ripe September–October.

Chromosomes: Unknown. Apomictic, true from seed.

Hardiness: −15°C (5°F).

Area: Nepal.

Notes: *Cotoneaster hedegaardii* commemorates Johannes Hedegaard, a Danish sculptor, *Rhododendron* expert, and writer, who was very knowledgeable on the Himalayan flora and collected *Cotoneaster* seed there for Bertil Hylmö. The Brian Halliwell collection (*Halliwell 148*) of *C. hedegaardii* from the south bank of the Langtang in Nepal is an interesting pale yellow-fruited form which seemingly keeps its yellow fruit color when raised from seed (*C. hedegaardii* Halliwell's Yellow). Recently reintroduced into cultivation.

4. *Cotoneaster* ×*watereri* Exell in Gard. Chron. 3: 83 (1928).

Variable hybrids (in cultivation) between *C. frigidus* and *C. salicifolius* and their forms. Semievergreen, medium to large shrubs or small trees of robust, erect growth with arched to pendent or ascending, dark brown shiny branches with few large lenticels. Leaves, mostly dull green and slightly rugose. Flowers abundant, followed by extremely heavy crops of usually red or orange-red fruit.

Originated from the nursery of John Waterer Sons & Crisp in England around 1920. Received RHS Award of Merit in 1951.

Cultivars: '**Brandekjaerhoej**', tall, branches ascending, fruit red. Possibly the hardiest clone of *C.* ×*watereri*. Originated in Denmark. '**Glabratus**', branches erect and arched, fruit smallish and dull-red. Introduced in England before 1951. '**Heaseland's Coral**', large, with more or less evergreen willowlike leaves which provide good background for the many heavy clusters of coral-red fruit. Received RHS Award of Merit in 1961. '**John Waterer**', a large erect shrub or small tree, branches long and spreading, becoming arched to pendent (displaying flowers and fruit to best advantage), leaves 70–100 × 25–50 mm, apex obtuse or acute, lower surface initially villous, flowers and fruit many in wide clusters, fruit 8–9 mm, bright shiny red and long lasting, nutlets usually 2. A chance seedling and its descendents by vegetative propagation from the nursery of John Waterer Sons and Crisp of Bagshot, England, around 1928. Type for group. Received RHS Award of Merit in 1951 and Award of Garden Merit in 1984. '**Notcutt's Variety**', an erect shrub, upper leaf surface bright green, lower surface often reddish in winter, fruit crimson. Very similar to *C. salicifolius* and probably a form of that species.

4. Series *Aitchisonioides* J. Fryer & B. Hylmö, *ser. nov.*

Small shrubs or small trees. Branchlets maroon or black-purple, tomentose or densely pilose-strigose. Inflorescences compact; pedicels tomentose. Hypanthium tomentose or densely villous. Petals often with hairs at base of upper surface. Stamens 10–20; anthers white, purple, or pink.

Mid season.

India (Himachal Pradesh). Kashmir. Afghanistan. Pakistan. Tajikistan. Kyrgyzstan. China (Xinjiang).

13 species: *C. afghanicus*, *C. aitchisonii*, *C. chadwellii*, *C. inexpectatus*, *C. lacei*, *C. lambertii*, *C. minutus*, *C. obovatus*, *C. pangiensis*, *C. royleanus*, *C. schubertii*, *C. suavis*, *C. verokotschyi*.

Key to Series *Aitchisonioides*

1a. Stamens mostly 20; anthers white; nutlets mostly 2 2
1b. Stamens 10–12(–16); anthers mostly pink; nutlets 1–2 7
2a. Height 0.5–1.2 m; leaves ≤ 15 mm; fruit orange-red . . . . *C. minutus*
2b. Height 1.5–5 m; leaves 15–70 mm; fruit rich-red 3

3a. Fertile shoots ≤ 25 mm; inflorescence 2- to 5-flowered ....*C. lacei*

3b. Fertile shoots 30–40 mm; inflorescence > 5-flowered.....................................**4**

4a. Leaf veins lightly impressed, petiole 5–10 mm; inflorescence 7- to 15-flowered **5**

4b. Leaf veins not impressed, petiole 8–12 mm; inflorescence mostly > 15-flowered...........**6**

5a. Leaves mostly suborbicular; sepals obtuse or acute; fruit red...................*C. schubertii*

5b. Leaves mostly elliptic; sepals acuminate or cuspidate; fruit maroon .... *C. suavis*

6a. Leaf veins 6–8; fertile shoots ≤ 30 mm; hypanthium mostly sparsely pilose-villous ....
....*C. aitchisonii*

6b. Leaf veins mostly 5; fertile shoots ≤ 40 mm; hypanthium tomentose .... *C. obovatus*

7a. Leaves 15–30 mm, petiole 3–9(–12) mm; anthers pale pink or white; fruit rich red with
crimson, or light ruby..**8**

7b. Leaves 44–70 mm, petiole 7–10 mm; anthers pink-red to violet; fruit light red ....
.... *C. chadwellii*

8a. Branches narrowly erect, petioles 5–7 mm; sepals mostly acuminate; corolla 9–11 mm, fruit
rich red with crimson ....*C. royleanus*

8b. Branches loosely erect, petioles 3–5 mm; sepals mostly obtuse; fruit pale ruby ....
....*C. verokotschyi*

1. *Cotoneaster afghanicus* G. Klotz in Wiss. Z. Martin-Luther-Univ. Halle-
Wittenberg, Math.-Naturwiss. 15: 532 (1966). Type: Afghanistan, Kuram Valley,
December 1879, *J. E. T. Aitchison 363* (holo DD, iso A, BM, CAL).
Shrub, densely branched, to 1 m. Branches erect, spreading; branchlets spiraled, purple-
black, shiny, initially grayish tomentose. Leaves deciduous, subcoriaceous, on sterile
shoots ovate or elliptic, 6–12 × 4–9 mm, apex rotund or obtuse, base obtuse or cuneate,
upper surface shiny, subglabrous, veins slightly impressed, lower surface tomentose; petiole 1–3 mm, pilose-strigose. Fertile shoots 10–25 mm, including a 1- to 4-flowered inflorescence; pedicels brief. Hypanthium cupulate, tomentose. Corolla 7–9 mm, petals spreading, white, with hair-tuft. Stamens 18–20. Fruit subglobose, 6–8 mm, orange or red, calyx
lobes with dense hairs. Nutlets 2.

Area: Afghanistan. Kashmir.

Notes: *Cotoneaster afghanicus* has not been discovered in cultivation. It is closely
related to *C. aitchisonii*. Not in key.

2. *Cotoneaster aitchisonii* C. K. Schneider in Illustr. Handb. Laubholzk. 1: 749 (1906);
cf. Feddes Repert. 3: 220 (1906). Type: Afghanistan, Kuram district, 5 July 1880,
J. E. T. Aitchison 277 (lecto designated K, iso A). **PLATE 28**.
Shrub or small tree, 3–5 m. Branches loosely erect, coarse; branchlets spiraled, greenish
brown, shiny, densely lenticellate, initially pilose-strigose. Leaves deciduous, chartaceous,
on sterile shoots broadly elliptic, broadly obovate or suborbicular, 44–59 × 24–50 mm,
apex acute, rotund or truncate, base cuneate or obtuse, upper surface grayish to dark
green, dull, glabrescent, veins 6–8, lower surface villous; petiole 8–12 mm, villous. Fertile

shoots 20–30 mm, including 2–3 leaves and a compact, (7–)11- to 25-flowered inflorescence; pedicels 3–8 mm, pilose-strigose. Hypanthium cupulate, sparsely pilose-villous; sepals obtuse, acute or acuminate, pilose-villous, border membranous, apex purple, glabrous, margin villous. Flower buds white. Corolla 8–12 mm, petals spreading, white, sometimes with hair-tuft. Stamens (16–)20; filaments white; anthers white. Fruit depressed-globose, 9–11 mm, red to cherry red, sparsely hairy, calyx lobes suberect, villous, navel open. Nutlets (1–)2, sometimes slightly conjoined, rarely 3, style remains at apex.

Seasons: Flowers June; fruit ripe September–October.

Chromosomes: Unknown. Apomictic, true from seed.

Hardiness: −21°C (−6°F).

Area: Pakistan. Afghanistan. Kashmir.

Notes: *Cotoneaster aitchisonii* has long been in cultivation, mostly as *C. montanus* hort. It is not common and is found mainly in specialist collections. Often abundantly fruitful, *C. aitchisonii* makes a pleasing sight in autumn.

3. *Cotoneaster chadwellii* J. Fryer & B. Hylmö, *sp. nov.* Type: India, Himachal Pradesh, Kinnaur, edge of a cultivated field near Chiktul in Baspa valley, September 1993, *C. Chadwell 1404* [cult. England, Froxfield, 19 September 2006, J. Fryer 1642] (holo WSY). PLATE 29.

Shrub, 1.5–3 m. Branches narrowly erect; branchlets spiraled and slender, maroon, minutely verruculose, initially sparsely pilose-strigose. Leaves deciduous, chartaceous, on sterile shoots elliptic or obovate, 44–70 × 27–40 mm, apex rotund or acute, base cuneate, upper surface mid to dark green, dull, subglabrous, veins 6–7, lower surface reticulate, sparsely villous; petiole 7–10 mm, densely villous-strigose. Fertile shoots 25–50 mm including 1–3 leaves and a dense, 10- to 50-flowered inflorescence; pedicels 2–5 mm, densely pilose-strigose. Hypanthium cupulate, densely pilose-strigose; sepals acute, obtuse or acuminate, densely pilose-strigose, border narrow, membranous, apex purple, margin villous. Flower buds white tipped red. Corolla 7–10 mm, petals spreading, white, sometimes with hair-tuft. Stamens 10–13; filaments white; anthers purple or rose-pink. Fruit depressed-globose, light red, 7–8 mm, subglabrous, calyx lobes flat, navel open. Nutlets 2, rarely 1, style remains at apex.

Seasons: Flowers May–June; fruit ripe October–November.

Chromosomes: Unknown. Apomictic, true from seed.

Hardiness: −18°C (−1°F).

Area: India (Himachal Pradesh). Kashmir.

Notes: *Cotoneaster chadwellii* is a most attractive species newly introduced into cultivation. Multistemmed, but fairly narrow in habit, it takes up little space in the smaller garden, but makes a fine display. Flowers and fruit are produced in profusion. The plant collector and botanist Chris Chadwell (pers. comm.) states that this *Cotoneaster* is the most ornamental found on his Himalayan travels.

4. *Cotoneaster inexpectatus* G. Klotz in Wiss. Z. Friedrich-Schiller-Univ. Jena,
   Math.-Naturwiss. 27: 23 (1978). Type: Nepal, Dunai, border of Bheri, 26 April 1974,
   J. F. Dobremez 2787 (holo BM iso E).

Shrub, to 2 m. Branches erect; branchlets maroon, initially strigose-tomentose. Leaves deciduous, chartaceous, on sterile shoots elliptic or broadly elliptic, 15–29 × 9–19 mm, apex obtuse, base cuneate or obtuse, upper surface dark grayish green, dull, glabrescent, veins impressed, lower surface reticulate, tomentose soon pilose; petiole 2–4 mm, strigose-tomentose. Fertile shoots 20–30 mm, including 2–3(–4) leaves and a compact, 3- to 6-flowered inflorescence; pedicels densely villous. Hypanthium infundibulate, densely villous; sepals acute, villous, margin villous. Corolla 8 mm, petals spreading, white, with large hair-tuft. Stamens 18–20; filaments white; anthers purple. Styles 2. Fruit probably red.

Area: Nepal. India (Himachal Pradesh).

Notes: *Cotoneaster inexpectatus* was originally wrongly assigned to series *Racemiflori*, which consists of species mainly from Caucasia, southern Europe, and southern Russia. *Cotoneaster inexpectatus* is not known in cultivation. Not in key.

5. *Cotoneaster lacei* G. Klotz in Wiss. Z. Martin-Luther-Univ. Halle-Wittenberg,
   Math.-Naturwiss. 15: 851 (1966). Type: NW India, Bashahr, Ralli forest, 29 May
   1890, *J. H. Lace 196* (holo E).

Shrub. Branches erect, slender; branchlets purple-black, shiny, initially tomentose. Leaves deciduous, chartaceous, on sterile shoots suborbicular or broadly elliptic, 18–50 × 13–39 mm, apex rotund or acute, base rotund or cuneate, upper surface dull, very sparsely villous, veins 6–8 lightly impressed, lower surface pilose-villous; petiole 3–7 mm, initially densely villous. Fertile shoots 15–25 mm, including a 2- to 5-flowered inflorescence; pedicels tomentose. Hypanthium tomentose; sepals acute, tomentose. Petals spreading or semispreading, 3 mm, white, with hair-tuft. Stamens 15–20. Fruit subglobose, crimson, glabrous, calyx lobes erect, pilose, navel open. Nutlets 2.

Area: India (Himachal Pradesh). Pakistan.

Notes: *Cotoneaster lacei* is possibly not in cultivation.

6. *Cotoneaster lambertii* G. Klotz in Wiss. Z. Friedrich-Schiller-Univ. Jena, Math.-
   Naturwiss. 19: 343 (1970). Type: Kashmir, in the Liddar mountains near Pahalgam,
   2 September 1927, *W. T. Lambert 200* (holo DD).

Shrub. Branches erect, arched; branchlets divaricate, purple-brown, shiny, initially subglabrous. Leaves deciduous, chartaceous, on sterile shoots broadly obovate, suborbicular or obcordate, 17–53 × 15–40 mm, apex emarginate or rotund, base obtuse or broadly cuneate, upper surface rich green, glabrous, veins impressed, lower surface sparsely villous, veins brown; petiole 4–11 mm, villous. Fertile shoots with a 15- to 30-flowered inflorescence; pedicels yellowish tomentose. Hypanthium glabrescent; sepals glabrous. Corolla 6–7 mm, petals spreading, possibly pink, glabrous. Stamens 15–20. Fruit subglobose, 7 mm, rich red, calyx open. Nutlets 1–2.

Area: Kashmir. Pakistan.

Notes: *Cotoneaster lambertii* is probably not in cultivation. Not in key.

7. *Cotoneaster minutus* G. Klotz in Wiss. Z. Martin-Luther-Univ. Halle-Wittenberg, Math.-Naturwiss. 12: 763 (1963). Type: Kashmir, near Chara-i-Sharif, Srinagar, 25 October 1962, H. Meusel (holo HAL).

Shrub dense, 0.5–1.2 m. Branches loosely erect and spreading; branchlets spiraled, brown, initially pilose-strigose. Leaves deciduous, subcoriaceous, on sterile shoots orbicular, suborbicular, cordate or broadly obovate, 3–7 × 3–6 mm, apex rotund or emarginate, base cuneate or obtuse, upper surface dull, initially densely pilose-strigose, veins 2–3, lower surface pilose-strigose, distinctly reticulate; petiole 1–3 mm, pilose-strigose. Fertile shoots 8–10 mm, including 1–2 leaves and a 1- to 5-flowered inflorescence; pedicels 1–3 mm, pilose-strigose. Hypanthium cupulate, base silky, apex pilose-strigose; sepals acuminate or acute, pilose-strigose, margin villous. Corolla 5–7 mm, petals spreading, with hair-tuft. Stamens 10–20; filaments white; anthers white. Fruit red. Nutlets 2.

Area: Afghanistan. Kashmir.

Notes: *Cotoneaster minutus* has not yet been found in cultivation.

8. *Cotoneaster obovatus* Wallich ex Dunn in Kew Bulletin p. 119 (1921). Type: India, NE Punjab, Kangra Chandaghery, 1829, *N. Wallich 655* (holo K).

Shrub, to 3 m. Branches somewhat narrowly erect; branchlets slender. Leaves deciduous, elliptic, c. 46 × 24 mm, apex acute, obtuse or rotund, base cuneate, veins 5 pairs. Fertile shoots 25–40 mm, including 2–3 leaves and a 15- to 50-flowered inflorescence. Hypanthium tomentose; sepals tomentose. Petals white (no pink).

Area: India (Himachal Pradesh). Pakistan. Kashmir.

Notes: Klotz (1966) preferred to exclude Wallich from the binomial and designated as the lectotype the later collection of *Ellis 1192* (K), in spite of the fact that Dunn had based *Cotoneaster obovatus* on the Wallich suggested name and used a Wallich collection as type. Klotz believed that Dunn's diagnosis better fitted *Ellis 1192* and stated that the Wallich specimens belonged to another taxon. *Cotoneaster obovatus* has yet to be discovered in cultivation. Dunn's description of *C. obovatus* was based on other collections and hence is not included in above description.

9. *Cotoneaster pangiensis* G. Klotz in Wiss. Z. Friedrich-Schiller-Univ. Jena, Math.-Naturwiss. 19: 342 (1970). Type: N India, Himachal Pradesh, Pangi, 7 June 1962, *N. C. Nair 22518* (holo BSD).

Shrub or small tree, 2–3 m. Branches erect, sometimes arched, spreading; branchlets spiraled, maroon, initially tomentose to densely pilose-strigose. Leaves deciduous, subcoriaceous or chartaceous, on sterile shoots suborbicular, broadly-elliptic or ovate, 21–70

× 21–50 mm, apex obtuse or rotund, base rotund or obtuse, upper surface dark green, dull, glabrous, sparsely villous, veins 7–9, lower surface reticulate, pilose-villous; petiole 8–12 mm, pilose-strigose. Fertile shoots 30–50 mm including 2–3 leaves and a 7- to 17-flowered inflorescence; pedicels 2–5 mm, villous-strigose. Hypanthium cupulate, densely villous-strigose; sepals acute or acuminate, densely villous-strigose, border membranous, purple, margin villous. Corolla 12–13 mm, petals spreading, white, with hair-tuft. Stamens 20; filaments white; anthers white. Fruit depressed-globose, 9–11 mm, maroon, slightly shiny, calyx lobes mostly flat, navel open. Nutlets 1–2, style remains near apex.

Seasons: Flowers June; fruit ripe October–November.

Hardiness: −21°C (−6°F).

Area: India (Himachal Pradesh).

Notes: *Cotoneaster pangiensis* has only fairly recently been discovered in cultivation at the botanic garden of the Institute of Botany in Strasbourg, France. Not in key.

10. *Cotoneaster royleanus* (Dippel) J. Fryer & B. Hylmö, stat. nov. *Basionym: C. racemiflorus* (Desfontaines) Booth ex Bosse var. *royleanus* Dippel in Handb. Laubholzk. 3: 415 (1893). Synonym: *C. royleanus* J. Booth ex Bosse (1849). Type: cult. Sweden, Bjuv from material received from Netherlands, Wageningen, 16 June 1973, B. Hylmö (hort.) 1813 (lecto designated GB).

Shrub, 1.5–2.5 m. Branches narrowly erect; branchlets spiraled, coarse, purple-black, lenticellate, minutely verruculose, initially pilose-strigose. Leaves deciduous, chartaceous, on sterile shoots suborbicular, broadly obovate or broadly elliptic, 18–30 × 14–27 mm, apex rotund, truncate or apiculate, base cuneate, upper surface dark-green, dull, initially sparsely pilose-villous, veins 4–5 lightly impressed, lower surface grayish green, reticulate, pilose-villous; petiole 5–7 mm, pilose-villous. Fertile shoots 15–25 mm, including 1–3 leaves and a compact, 5- to 9(–12)-flowered inflorescence; pedicels 1–4 mm, pilose-villous. Hypanthium cupulate, pilose-villous; sepals acuminate or acute, pilose-villous, margin villous. Flower buds white. Corolla 9–11 mm, petals spreading, white, sometimes very small hair-tuft. Stamens 10–12(–14); filaments white; anthers white or very pale pink. Fruit globose, 9–10 mm, rich red to red with crimson, calyx lobes suberect, navel open. Nutlets 1(–2), style remains near or at apex.

Seasons: Flowers June; fruit ripe September–October.

Chromosomes: Tetraploid (Broertjes 1956; Zeilinga 1964).

Hardiness: −18°C (−1°F).

Area: N India.

Notes: *Cotoneaster royleanus* has been in cultivation since the early 1800s, often as either *C. orbicularis* or *C. nummularius*. When describing *C. kotschyi* in his new species of Iran, Klotz (1963) mistakenly included *C. royleanus* as a synonym without taking into consideration that the latter species is only found in N India. Recently reintroduced into cultivation.

11. ***Cotoneaster schubertii*** G. Klotz in Wiss. Z. Martin-Luther-Univ. Halle-
      Wittenberg, Math.-Naturwiss. 12: 759 (1963). Type: Kashmir, Chara-i-Sharif,
      Srinagar, 25 October 1962, H. Meusel & R. Schubert (holo HAL).

Shrub, 2–3 m. Branches loosely erect, spreading; branchlets spiraled, grayish brown, lenticellate, initially densely pilose-strigose. Leaves deciduous, subcoriaceous, on sterile
shoots suborbicular, broadly elliptic or broadly obovate, 29–48 × 27–39 mm, apex rotund,
acute, truncate or emarginate, base cuneate or obtuse, upper surface sometimes slightly
rugose, grayish to mid-green, slightly shiny, glabrescent, veins 4–7, lightly impressed,
lower surface grayish green, densely pilose-villous; petiole 5–10 mm, densely pilose-
villous. Fertile shoots 25–35 mm, including 2–3 leaves and a compact, 7- to 15-flowered
inflorescence; pedicels 1–7 mm, densely pilose-villous. Hypanthium cupulate, tomentose
to silky; sepals obtuse, acute, some long acute, densely pilose-villous, border membranous, margin villous. Flower buds white. Corolla 10–12 mm, petals spreading, white,
with large hair-tuft. Stamens 20; filaments white; anthers white. Fruit depressed-globose
or obovoid, 8–9 mm, rich red, to pale ruby with cherry, villous, calyx lobes depressed,
tomentose. Nutlets 2, style remains at apex.
      Seasons: Flowers June; fruit ripe October.
      Chromosomes: Triploid (Klotz 1968b; Krügel 1992a).
      Hardiness: −18°C (−1°F).
      Area: Kashmir. Pakistan.
      Notes: The type for *Cotoneaster schubertii*, collected in the autumn of 1962, had al-
ready been described by spring 1963. Klotz based his description on this Meusel &
Schubert herbarium specimen, but in cultivation in the botanic garden of the Martin
Luther University in Halle (from where it was spread to other gardens), the nurtured
shrub grew more robust (as is often the case) than was depicted by the specimen collected
in the wild. The description made from the herbarium sheet was of fertile shoot leaves,
which differ widely from sterile shoot leaves which are more normally used when making
a diagnosis. Also, the dried fruit were seen to be purple but when fresh they are rich red.
Therefore, the above description differs somewhat from that of the original diagnosis.
Indeed, *C. schubertii* is closely related to *C. suavis* and species of series *Aitchisonioides*,
rather than those of series *Racemiflori* as was originally believed.

12. ***Cotoneaster suavis*** Pojarkova in Not. Syst. Inst. Bot. Acad. Sci. USSR 16: 118 (1954).
      Type: Tajikistan, Hissar Mountains, Kondara river (a tributary of the Varzob river),
      30 August 1944, *A. Pojarkova 1909/948* (holo LE). PLATE 30.

Shrub, 2–3 m. Branches erect and spreading; branchlets maroon, lenticellate, minutely
verruculose, initially densely pilose-strigose. Leaves deciduous, chartaceous to subcoriaceous, on sterile shoots elliptic, broadly elliptic, broadly ovate or broadly obovate, 35–50
× 27–29 mm, apex acute, obtuse or rotund, base cuneate, upper surface sometimes slightly rugose, light green, slightly shiny, glabrescent, veins 5–7 lightly impressed, lower surface densely pilose-villous; petiole 6–10 mm, pilose-strigose. Fertile shoots 30–40 mm,

including 2–3 leaves and a dense, 7- to 15-flowered inflorescence; pedicels 2–8 mm, pilose-strigose. Hypanthium cupulate, densely pilose-strigose; sepals acuminate, cuspidate or acute, densely pilose-strigose, border narrow, membranous, often reddish purple, margin villous. Flower buds white. Corolla 8–12 mm, petals spreading, white, with large hair-tuft. Stamens 20; filaments white; anthers white. Fruit globose, 9–10 mm, ruby to maroon, villous, calyx lobes depressed, navel slightly open. Nutlets 2, style remains $^9/_{10}$ from base.

Seasons: Flowers June; fruit ripe October.

Chromosomes: Tetraploid (Gladkova 1968). Triploid (Bailey, pers. comm.; Jewsbury, pers. comm.). Pentaploid (Jewsbury, pers. comm.).

Hardiness: −21°C (−6°F).

Area: Tajikistan. Kyrgyzstan. China (Xinjiang).

Notes: *Cotoneaster suavis* is an extremely handsome shrub which should be more frequently grown. Its open white flowers and unusual rich maroon fruit are abundantly produced. Recently reintroduced into cultivation.

13. *Cotoneaster verokotschyi* J. Fryer & B. Hylmö, *sp. nov.*, non *C. kotschyi* (C. K. Schneider) G. Klotz (1963). Type: cult. Sweden, Bjuv, *B. Hylmö 1499*, 20 September 1992, from the botanic garden in Halle, Germany, as *C. bornmulleri* (holo GB).

PLATE 31.

Shrub, 2–3 m. Branches narrowly erect; branchlets spiraled, reddish to purple-black, initially pilose-strigose. Leaves deciduous, chartaceous, on sterile shoots orbicular, suborbicular or broadly elliptic, 15–26 × 13–20 mm, apex rotund, obtuse or apiculate, base cuneate or rotund, upper surface slightly rugose, dark green, dull, initially pilose, veins 3–4, lower surface grayish, densely pilose-villous; petiole 3–5 mm, pilose-strigose. Fertile shoots 10–25 mm, including 2–3 leaves and a compact, 3- to 5-flowered inflorescence; pedicels 1–3 mm, tomentose. Hypanthium cupulate, silky-tomentose; sepals obtuse or acute, tomentose, margin villous. Flower buds white. Corolla 7–8 mm, petals spreading, white, with hair-tuft. Stamens 10–16; filaments white, anthers white. Fruit depressed-globose or obovoid, 8–9 mm, pale ruby to ruby, pruinose, dull, villous, calyx lobes villous, navel open. Nutlets 1(–2), style remains at or near apex.

Seasons: Flowers June; fruit ripe September.

Chromosomes: Tetraploid (Zeilinga 1964; Hensen 1966; Klotz and Krügel 1983a). Apomictic, true from seed.

Hardiness: −21°C (−1°F).

Area: Caucasus, probably Iran.

Notes: *Cotoneaster verokotschyi* has long been in cultivation, possibly since around at least 1850, but mostly confused with *C. royleanus*.

5. Series *Racemiflori* (Pojarkova) G. Klotz in Wiss. Z. Martin-Luther-Univ. Halle-Wittenberg, Math.-Naturwiss. 12: 759 (1963).

Dwarf to large shrubs. Branchlets red-brown. Leaves with upper surface olive green to mid-green, mostly dull, veins 3–7 mostly not impressed, lower surface tomentose or pilose-strigose. Inflorescences mostly compact. Flower buds mostly pink. Sepals obtuse or acute. Anthers white. Fruit with calyx suberect to erect, navel open. Early to mid season.

Iran. Greece. Turkey. Azerbaijan. Turkmenistan. Armenia. Georgia. Morocco. Algeria. Tajikistan. France. Spain. Ukraine. Pakistan. Uzbekistan. Macedonia. Egypt. Oman. Cyprus. Syria. Lebanon. Italy. Tunisia.

17 species: *C. assadii, C. atlanticus, C. creticus, C. delphinensis, C. discolor, C. esfandiarii, C. granatensis, C. nebrodensis, C. nummularius, C. orbicularis, C. ovatus, C. parnassicus, C. persicus, C. racemiflorus, C. tauricus, C. transcaucasicus, C. uzbezicus.*

Key to Series *Racemiflori*

1a. Leaves elliptic or ovate, rarely suborbicular, apex mostly acute 2

1b. Leaves orbicular, suborbicular, broadly elliptic, broadly ovate or broadly obovate, apex mostly rotund 5

2a. Inflorescence (1–)2- to 5-flowered . . . .*C. parnassicus*

2b. Inflorescence 5- to 9(–13)-flowered 3

3a. Branches stiffly erect; upper leaf surface mid-green, dull . . . . **C. tauricus**

3b. Branches erect, ascending, spreading or arched; leaves upper surface dark green, shiny . . . 4

4a. Height 3–4 m; upper leaf surface very sparsely pilose-strigose, veins and petiole also margin of sepals green . . . . **C. persicus**

4b. Height 1–2 m; upper leaf surface glabrous or initially few hairs on midrib, veins, petiole and margin of sepals reddish purple . . . .*C. discolor*

5a. Upper leaf surface glabrous or subglabrous; stamens 12–20; fruit depressed-globose or subglobose 6

5b. Upper leaf surface pilose-strigose, sometimes only on midrib; stamens mostly 20; fruit obovoid or ellipsoid 9

6a. Branches loosely erect; leaves subcoriaceous; fruit orange-red . . . .*C. assadii*

6b. Branchlets erect; leaves mostly chartaceous; fruit red or maroon 7

7a. Leaf apex mostly apiculate or acuminate; pedicels 1–4 mm; hypanthium densely villous-strigose . . . .*C. racemiflorus*

7b. Leaf apex mostly rotund or obtuse; pedicels 3–10 mm; hypanthium sparsely pilosestrigose 8

8a. Height 3–5 m; fertile shoots 20–50 mm; calyx persistent . . . .*C. granatensis*

8b. Height ≤ 1.5 m; fertile shoots 15–25 mm; calyx dehiscing early from fruit exposing apex of nutlets . . . .*C. creticus*

9a. Inflorescence 1- to 7-flowered; petals with large hair-tuft 10

9b. Inflorescence 3- to 13(–20)-flowered; petals with small hair-tuft 12

10a. Leaves mostly chartaceous, broadly ovate or broadly elliptic, rarely suborbicular, apex
mostly obtuse or acute, upper surface dull . . . .*C. atlanticus*

10b. Leaves subcoriaceous, orbicular or suborbicular, apex mostly rotund or truncate, upper
surface somewhat shiny 11

11a. Inflorescence 3- to 7-flowered; hypanthium tomentose; sepals acute or acuminate . . . .
. . . . *C. nummularius*

11b. Inflorescence 1- to 4-flowered; hypanthium sparsely pilose-strigose; sepals mostly obtuse
or acute . . . . *C. orbicularis*

12a. Leaves dark green, shiny; fertile shoots 10–25 mm. 13

12b. Leaves light to mid-green, dull; fertile shoots 15–40 mm 14

13a. Branches mostly ascending, spreading; leaves mostly ovate or broadly elliptic, upper
surface pilose-strigose. . . . . *C. ovatus*

13b. Branches erect, arched; leaves orbicular to broadly obovate, upper surface sparsely pilose-
strigose . . . . *C. uzbezicus*

14a. Leaves base mostly cuneate; hypanthium densely pilose-strigose or tomentose; fruit light
red. . . . .*C. transcaucasicus*

14b. Leaves base rotund; hypanthium sparsely pilose-strigose; fruit dark red. 15

15a. Height 2–3 m; leaves ≤ 50 mm; sepals acute or obtuse . . . . *C. delphinensis*

15b. Height 1–1.5 m; leaves ≤ 26 mm; sepals acute, acuminate or ligulate . . . . *C. nebrodensis*

1. ***Cotoneaster assadii*** Khatamsaz in Iran. Journ. Bot. 4: 116 (1988). Type: Iran,
Mazanderan, Siahbisheh, *Khatamsaz & Assadi 43257* (holo TARI).
Shrub, 2–3 m. Branches loosely erect and spreading; branchlets spiraled, maroon, initially pilose-strigose. Leaves deciduous, subcoriaceous, on sterile shoots broadly obovate,
16–31 × 13–22 mm, apex rotund, base cuneate, upper surface light green, dull, glabrescent, veins 3–5, lower surface grayish green, pilose-strigose; petiole 3–7 mm, pilose-
strigose. Fertile shoots 15–35 mm, including 2–3 leaves and a compact, 3- to 10-flowered
inflorescence; pedicels 1–3 mm, pilose-strigose. Hypanthium cupulate, mostly sparsely
pilose-strigose; sepals acute or acuminate, sparsely pilose-strigose, margin villous. Flower
buds pinkish. Corolla 7–9 mm, petals spreading, white, with small hair-tuft. Stamens
16–20; filaments white; anthers white. Fruit globose or obovoid, 7–9 mm, orange, sparsely
pilose, calyx lobes suberect, navel open. Nutlets (1–)2, style remains at apex.
Seasons: Flowers June; fruit ripe September–October.
Chromosomes: Tetraploid (Bailey, pers. comm.). Apomictic, true from seed.
Hardiness: –18°C (–1°F).
Area: Iran.
Notes: *Cotoneaster assadii*, from the Elburz mountains, is very similar to *C. trans-
caucasicus*. It is an attractive, tough shrub for dry and sunny situations.

2. *Cotoneaster atlanticus* G. Klotz in Wiss. Z. Martin-Luther-Univ. Halle-Wittenberg, Math.-Naturwiss. 12: 759 (1963). Synonym: *C. fontanesii* Spach var. *tomentella*
  Maire (1923). Type: Algeria, Grand Atlas Mountains, Ourika, 9 July 1921, C. Monts
  de Batna, Djebel Chlala, A. Joly (holo AL) as *C. fontanesii* Spach var. *tomentella*.
Shrub, 1–2 m. Branches erect, irregularly spreading; branchlets spiraled, maroon, initially pilose-strigose. Leaves deciduous, chartaceous or subcoriaceous, on sterile shoots
broadly ovate, elliptic or suborbicular, 19–27 × 15–18 mm, apex obtuse, acute or rotund,
base obtuse or cuneate, upper surface mid-green, dull, pilose-strigose, veins 4–6, lower
surface tomentose; petiole 5–7 mm, pilose-strigose. Fertile shoots 15–25 mm, including
2–4 leaves and a compact, 3- to 6-flowered inflorescence; pedicels 2–5 mm, pilose-
strigose. Hypanthium cupulate, base densely pilose-strigose, apex subglabrous; sepals
obtuse or acute, villous-strigose or subglabrous, margin villous. Corolla 7–9(–10) mm;
petals spreading, white, with large hair-tuft. Stamens 20; filaments white; anthers white.
Fruit subglobose or obovoid, 6–8 mm, dark red, pilose, calyx lobes erect, tomentose.
Nutlets 2.
  Seasons: Flowers June.
  Hardiness: −18°C (−1°F).
  Area: Algeria. Morocco.
  Notes: *Cotoneaster atlanticus* differs from *C. granatensis* in its more open habit, lower
stature, less rounded leaves with upper surface persistently pilose-strigose, and shorter
fertile shoots, with fewer-flowered inflorescences. This same phenomenon of two closely
related species with much the same degree of difference between them can be found in
the Western Alps (*C. delphinensis*) and in the Pyrenees (*Cotoneaster sp. nov.*). Further
observation in cultivation is necessary for the complete understanding of this situation.
Recently reintroduced into cultivation.

3. *Cotoneaster creticus* J. Fryer & B. Hylmö, *sp. nov.* Type: Crete, Drakona mountains, rare, 7 July 1883, *E. Reverchon 7548* (holo LD). **PLATE 32.**
Shrub, 1.5–2 m. Branches erect, spreading; branchlets spiraled, purple-black, lenticellate,
minutely verruculose, initially pilose-strigose. Leaves deciduous, chartaceous, on sterile
shoots suborbicular, 20–37 × 15–29 mm, apex rotund or obtuse, base obtuse or cuneate,
upper surface mid-green, dull, glabrescent, veins 5–6, lower surface grayish green, reticulate, sparsely pilose. Fertile shoots 15–25 mm, including 2–4 leaves and a dense, 5- to
11-flowered inflorescence; pedicels 4–9 mm, sparsely pilose-strigose. Hypanthium cupulate, sparsely pilose-strigose; sepals acute or obtuse, sparsely pilose-strigose, margin
sparsely villous. Flower buds pinkish. Corolla 8–10 mm, petals spreading, white, with
large hair-tuft. Stamens 16–20; filaments white; anthers white. Fruit shortly obovoid, 6–9
mm, ruby to maroon, slightly shiny, glabrous, calyx often dehiscing early as coronet exposing nutlets. Nutlets (1–)2, style remains at or near apex.
  Seasons: Flowers June; fruit ripe September.
  Hardiness: −15°C (5°F).

Area: Greece (Crete).

Notes: *Cotoneaster creticus* has been introduced into cultivation by Italian geologist and *Cotoneaster* enthusiast Alberto Giussani, who created a collection near Lake Como in Italy for the production of *Cotoneaster* honey.

4. *Cotoneaster delphinensis* Chatenier in Bull. Soc. Bot. France 69 (9–10): 712 (1923).
   Type: France, Drôme, Berignan à Montland de Saules-Laminière, 24 June 1898,
   Chatenier (holo GRM).

Shrub, 2–3 m. Branches erect and spreading; branchlets spiraled, slender, reddish brown, minutely verruculose, initially pilose-strigose. Leaves deciduous, chartaceous, on sterile shoots broadly elliptic or suborbicular, 25–50 × 18–40 mm, apex rotund and mucronate, base rotund, upper surface light to mid-green, dull, sparsely pilose-strigose, veins 4–5, lower surface densely villous; petiole 5–11 mm, pilose-strigose. Fertile shoots 30–50 mm, including 2–3 leaves and a lax, 7- to 13(–20)-flowered inflorescence; pedicels 3–18 mm, pilose-strigose. Hypanthium cupulate, sparsely pilose-strigose; sepals acute or obtuse, sometimes ligulate, very sparsely pilose-strigose, border broad, reddish purple, glabrous, margin villous. Flower buds white or pinkish. Corolla 6–8 mm, petals semispreading, white, with hair-tuft. Stamens 20; filaments white; anthers white. Fruit obovoid, 7–8 mm, rich red to ruby, sparsely pilose-strigose, calyx lobes suberect, navel open. Nutlets (1–)2, style remains at apex.

   Seasons: Flowers June; fruit ripe August–September.

   Chromosomes: Tetraploid (Jewsbury, pers. comm.).

   Hardiness: –21°C (–6°F).

   Area: France.

Notes: It was quite unexpected that a species of *Cotoneaster* with spreading, white-petaled flowers belonging to series *Racemiflori* of section *Chaenopetalum* would be discovered growing in the Western Alps. More specimens of series *Racemiflori* have been discovered recently in this same area and are still under observation. *Cotoneaster delphinensis* has been introduced into cultivation (Garraud 1994).

5. *Cotoneaster discolor* Pojarkova in Not. Syst. Inst. Bot. Acad. Sci. USSR 16: 116
   (1954). Type: Turkmenistan, Kopet-Dag mountains, 30 July 1912, *Androssov &*
   Bubyrj 2546 (holo LE).

Shrub, 1–2 m. Branches erect or ascending, spreading; branchlets spiraled or distichous, light brown, initially pilose-strigose. Leaves deciduous, chartaceous, on sterile shoots elliptic, ovate or ellipto-lanceolate, 22–35 × 12–18 mm, apex acute or obtuse, base cuneate, upper surface slightly rugose, reticulate, dark green, shiny, glabrescent, veins 4–7 impressed, often reddish purple, lower surface densely pilose-strigose; petiole 5–10 mm, often reddish purple, pilose-strigose. Fertile shoots 15–25 mm, including 2–3 leaves and a compact, 5- to 9(–13)-flowered inflorescence; pedicels 1–3 mm, pilose-strigose. Hypanthium cupulate, tomentose; sepals acute, densely pilose-strigose, apex reddish purple, margin tomentose. Flower buds pinkish. Corolla 8–10 mm, petals spreading, white, with large hair-tuft. Stamens (14–)20; filaments white; anthers white. Fruit globose or obovoid, 8–9 mm, red to brownish red, sparsely pilose, calyx lobes suberect, villous, navel open. Nutlets 1–2, style remains $^9/_{10}$ from base.

Seasons: Flowers May–June; fruit ripe September–October.

Chromosomes: Triploid (Klotz 1968b; Klotz and Krügel 1983a; Krügel 1992b). Tetraploid (Jewsbury, pers. comm.). Apomictic, true from seed.

Hardiness: –18°C (–1°F).

Area: Iran. Turkmenistan.

Notes: Open in habit with quite distinct colored margins to the sepals, *Cotoneaster discolor* is not common in cultivation, mainly being found in botanic gardens and larger private collections. Recently reintroduced into cultivation.

6. Cotoneaster esfandiarii Khatamsaz in Iran. Journ. Bot. 5: 1 (1991). Type: Iran, Tehran, Firuzkuh, Lazour Kuh-e Mishin-e Marg, *Khatamsaz, Akari & Abouhamzeh 64756* (TSARI).

Shrub, 0.3–0.4 m. Branchlets dark purple, initially with short adpressed hairs. Leaves deciduous, lanceolate or elliptic, 10–16 × 4–8 mm, apex acute, base cuneate, upper surface with scattered hairs, lower surface tomentose, petiole 2–3 mm, pilose. Fertile shoots with a spreading to slightly pendent 3- to 7-flowered inflorescence. Hypanthium and sepals tomentose. Flower buds reddish. Corolla 4 mm, petals erect to semispreading, white. Stamens 16–20. Fruit subglobose, 6 mm, red, villous. Nutlets 3–4.

Area: Iran.

Notes: *Cotoneaster esfandiarii* is not known in cultivation. The above is compiled from the Khatamsaz type description. Said to be related to *C. integerrimus*, but due to the area from which *C. esfandiarii* originates, and to the illustration which accompanies the type description, this species possibly belongs here in series *Racemiflori*. This species definitely needs further investigation. Not in key.

7. Cotoneaster granatensis Boissier in Elench. Pl. Nov. Hisp. (January 1836); cf. in Elench. Pl. Hisp. Austr. 71 (1838). Type: *Cotoneaster granatensis* Boissier, El. 71 (Spain) in valleys of the Sierra Nevada, July 1837, Herb. E. Boissier (lecto designated B).

Shrub, 3–5 m. Branches somewhat loosely erect, irregularly spreading; branchlets spiraled, brown, initially pilose-strigose. Leaves deciduous, chartaceous to subcoriaceous, on sterile shoots orbicular, suborbicular or broadly ovate, 26–34 × 19–32 mm, apex rotund, obtuse, apiculate or acute, base obtuse or cuneate, upper surface mid-green, dull, glabrescent, veins 4–6, lower surface pilose-strigose; petiole 6–9 mm, sparsely pilose-strigose. Fertile shoots 20–50 mm, including 2–3 leaves and a lax, 5- to 15-flowered inflorescence; pedicels 3–10 mm, sparsely pilose-strigose. Hypanthium cupulate, sparsely pilose-strigose; sepals obtuse or acute, glabrescent, margin villous. Flower buds pink-tinged. Corolla 8–11 mm, petals spreading, white, with small hair-tuft. Stamens 12–20; filaments white; anthers white. Fruit depressed globose, 8–9 mm, dark red to maroon, subglabrous, calyx lobes suberect, navel wide open. Nutlets 2, rarely 1, style remains $^9/_{10}$ from base.

Seasons: Flowers May–June; fruit ripe October.
Chromosomes: Tetraploid (McAllister, pers. comm.). Apomictic, true from seed.
Hardiness: –18°C (–1°F).
Area: Spain. Morocco. Algeria. Tunisia.
Notes: *Cotoneaster granatensis* is a well-known species. Described in 1836, it was later reduced to a variety of *C. multiflorus*. Klotz (1957) intended to demote *C. granatensis* further to a form but declined owing to the distance between the two areas of origin—Spain and Kazakhstan, the latter being the natural area for *C. multiflorus*. Although originally believed to belong to series *Multiflori*, *C. granatensis* is typical of a number of related species originating from the Mediterranean area with fruit containing 2 free nutlets, which, along with other characters, classifies them to series *Racemiflori*. Recently reintroduced into cultivation.

8. *Cotoneaster nebrodensis* (Gussone) K. Koch in Hort. Dendrol. 179: 6 (1853).
Synonym: *Pyrus nebrodensis* Gussone (1827). Type: *Pyrus nebrodensis* (lecto designated LD).

Shrub, 1–1.5 m. Branches erect and spreading; branchlets spiraled or distichous, brown, initially densely pilose-strigose. Leaves deciduous, chartaceous to subcoriaceous, on sterile shoots ovate, broadly elliptic or suborbicular, 20–26 × 16–19 mm, apex rotund or obtuse, base rotund, upper surface light green, dull, sparsely strigose-pilose, veins in 6, lower surface tomentose-pilose; petiole 4–7 mm, pilose-strigose. Fertile shoots 15–35 mm, including a 5- to 9-flowered inflorescence. Hypanthium cupulate, sparsely pilose-strigose; sepals acute or acuminate, sparsely villous. Flower buds pinkish. Petals spreading, white. Filaments white; anthers white. Fruit ellipsoid, red, calyx lobes sparsely villous, navel slightly open. Nutlets 2, style remains $^4/_5$ from base.

Seasons: Flowers June; fruit ripe September.
Hardiness: –15°C (5°F).
Area: Italy (Sicily, Calabria).
Notes: *Cotoneaster nebrodensis* is rare in the wild and is very seldom found in cultivation. Its identification has caused great confusion. Indeed, in the past the question was raised as to whether it was actually *Cotoneaster* or *Amelanchier*. When in 1853 K. Koch designated this species to *Cotoneaster*, he believed it to be synonymous with *C. tomentosus*. The same mistake was repeated in *Flora Europaea* (Tutin et al. 1968) and unfortunately accepted by several modern floras. In *Flora Sicula* (Lojocano 1891) it was treated as a *Cotoneaster*, but it was named as the related *C. nummularius*. Klotz (1982), having seen no reference material, was not sure if it was a *Cotoneaster*; however, he recognized that *C. nebrodensis* was described by Koch as having fruit containing 2 nutlets, while Aiton

(1789) described his *C. tomentosus* as having fruit with 5 nutlets. Recently reintroduced into cultivation.

9. *Cotoneaster nummularius* Fischer & C. A. Meyer in Ind. Semin. Hort. Bot. Petrop. 2: 34 (1835). Type: as *Cotoneaster tomentosus*, pl. Cauc. Casp. (1831), *C. A. Meyer 1527* (holo LE).

Shrub, 0.5–1.5 m. Branches ascending, spreading; branchlets spiraled, maroon, lenticellate, initially pilose-strigose. Leaves deciduous, subcoriaceous, on sterile shoots orbicular or suborbicular, 10–24 × 8–20 mm, apex rotund, base rotund, obtuse or cuneate, upper surface mid-green, slightly shiny, sparsely pilose-strigose, veins 3–5 lightly impressed, lower surface tomentose becoming densely villous-pilose; petiole 3–6 mm, pilose-strigose. Fertile shoots 10–25 mm, including mostly 3 leaves and a compact, 3- to 7-flowered inflorescence; pedicels 1–4 mm, tomentose. Hypanthium cupulate, tomentose or densely pilose-strigose; sepals acute or acuminate, densely pilose-strigose, margin villous. Flower buds pinkish or white. Corolla 7–9 mm, petals spreading, white, with large hair-tuft. Stamens 20; filaments white; anthers white. Fruit obovoid to subglobose, 7–8 mm, red to cherry-red, pilose, calyx lobes erect, villous, navel open. Nutlets (1–)2, style remains at apex.

Seasons: Flowers June; fruit ripe September–October.

Chromosomes: Tetraploid (Gladkova 1968; Krügel 1992a). Apomictic, true from seed.

Hardiness: −18°C (−1°F).

Area: Georgia (republic). Azerbaijan. Armenia. Turkey. Greece (Chios). Cyprus. Syria. Lebanon.

Notes: *Cotoneaster nummularius* was described from a cultivated shrub grown in the garden of the V. K. Komarov Botanical Institute in St. Petersburg, Russia, raised from seed which originated from the area of the Caucasus between the Talish mountains on the border between Iran and Azerbaijan and Mount Samamis in Georgia. In this same region the related species *C. transcaucasicus* is also found. The latter differs (among other features) in its leaves being larger and mostly elliptic and in the inflorescences up to 12-flowered. *Cotoneaster nummularius* is a shrub of open habit which is able to withstand quite a wide range of variation in temperature. Recently reintroduced into cultivation.

10. *Cotoneaster orbicularis* Schlechtendal in Linnaea 27: 544 (1854). Type: Egypt, Sinai peninsula, Mount St. Catherine, 19 May 1835, *W. Schimper 270-445* (holo HAL, iso K, M).

Shrub, 1–2 m. Branches erect and spreading; branchlets spiraled, initially pilose-strigose. Leaves deciduous or semievergreen, on sterile shoots subcoriaceous, orbicular or suborbicular, 4–15 × 3–11 mm, apex rotund or truncate, base obtuse, upper surface dark green, shiny, sparsely pilose-strigose, veins 3–4, lower surface tomentose to pilose-strigose; petiole 2–5 mm, pilose-strigose. Fertile shoots 10–15 mm, including mostly 2–3 leaves and a compact, 1- to 4-flowered inflorescence; pedicels 1–3 mm, pilose-strigose.

Hypanthium cupulate, sparsely pilose-strigose; sepals obtuse, acute or acuminate, sparsely pilose-strigose, margin villous. Corolla 7–8 mm, petals spreading, white. Stamens 20; filaments white; anthers white. Fruit red to dark red, calyx lobes erect, navel open. Nutlets 2.

Area: Egypt (Sinai). Oman.

Notes: *Cotoneaster orbicularis* is not known in cultivation. Shrubs grown under this name usually belong to other species, most commonly *C. sherriffii*. Cotoneasters have been discovered in several areas of the Arabian peninsula which could prove to be *C. orbicularis*. It is imperative to study these recent collections in cultivation. Klotz (1963) made *C. orbicularis* the type for his new series *Orbiculares*. It is preferable though to include this species in series *Racemiflori*.

11. *Cotoneaster ovatus* Pojarkova in Not. Syst. Inst. Bot. Acad. Sci. USSR 16: 111 (1954). Type: Turkmenistan, in the eastern Kopet-Dag mountains near Gaudan, 29 May 1898, *D. Litwinov 929* (holo LE, iso E).

Shrub, 1–2 m. Branches ascending spreading, sometimes erect; branchlets spiraled, maroon, lenticellate, initially pilose-strigose. Leaves deciduous, subcoriaceous, on sterile shoots ovate, broadly elliptic, broadly ovate or suborbicular, 12–35 × 10–25 mm, apex rotund, base cuneate or obtuse, upper surface dark green, shiny, sparsely pilose-strigose, veins 3–5 lightly impressed, lower surface tomentose; petiole 4–5 mm, pilose-strigose. Fertile shoots 10–20 mm, including 2–3 leaves and a compact, 3- to 9-flowered inflorescence; pedicels 1–3 mm, pilose-strigose. Hypanthium cupulate, tomentose or densely pilose-strigose; sepals acute or acuminate, densely pilose-strigose, margin villous. Flower buds pink. Corolla 10–12 mm, petals, white, with small hair-tuft. Stamens 20; filaments white; anthers white. Fruit rich red, villous, calyx lobes erect, tomentose, navel open. Nutlets 2, style remains $^3/_4$ from base.

Seasons: Flowers May–June; fruit ripe September.

Chromosomes: Tetraploid (Krügel 1992a; Jewsbury, pers. comm.). Apomictic, true from seed.

Hardiness: –18°C (–1°F).

Area: Iran. Turkmenistan.

Notes: Antonina Pojarkova described the filaments of *Cotoneaster ovatus* as "atropurpureus" (black-purple), but we have always found them to be white. Maybe Pojarkova's specimen was not fresh when examined. Details such as this do tend to become distorted if studied a few hours after the specimen is gathered. *Cotoneaster ovatus* is seldom in cultivation but was recently reintroduced.

12. *Cotoneaster parnassicus* Boissier & Heldreich in Diagn. Pl. Orient. 2: 48 (1856). Type: Greece, on Mount Parnassus, near Cararia (rarely), 4 July 1854, leg. Theodorus G. Orphanides 420, Herb. Th. v. Heldreich (lecto designated B, iso K, LD, UPS, WAG).

Shrub, 1.5–2(–4) m. Branches erect and spreading; branchlets spiraled, purple-black, minutely verruculose, initially pilose-strigose. Leaves deciduous, chartaceous, on sterile shoots ovate or elliptic, 18–36 × 13–29 mm, apex acute or obtuse, base obtuse or cuneate, upper surface mid-green, dull to slightly shiny, sparsely strigose, veins 3–4, lower surface tomentose; petiole 4–7 mm, tomentose. Fertile shoots 15–30 mm, including mostly 2 leaves and a compact, (1–)2- to 5-flowered inflorescence; pedicels 3–10 mm, tomentose. Hypanthium cupulate, tomentose to pilose-strigose; sepals obtuse or acute, pilose-strigose, border reddish purple, glabrous, margin villous. Flower buds pink. Corolla 7–9 mm, petals spreading, white, with hair-tuft. Stamens 20; filaments white; anthers white. Fruit red, pilose, remains of styles projecting through navel. Nutlets 2.

    Area: Greece. Macedonia.

    Notes: *Cotoneaster parnassicus* has yet to be discovered in cultivation. This seemingly lost species was included in *C. tomentosus* in *Flora Europaea* (Tutin et al. 1968). In *The Mountain Flora of Greece* (Strid 1986) it was included in *C. ×intermedius*. It is understood to be rare in its native habitat; nevertheless, when field studies were undertaken for the latter publication, this cotoneaster was reportedly seen growing in a number of locations.

13. ***Cotoneaster persicus*** Pojarkova in Not. Syst. Inst. Bot. Acad. Sci. USSR 16: 118
    (1954). Synonym: *C. rechingeri* G. Klotz (1967). Type: S Iran, Kuh-Delu, 13 June
    1842, *Th. Kotschy 504* (holo LE, iso BM, H, HAL, K, S, STR).
Shrub, 3–4 m. Branches erect and spreading; branchlets spiraled, initially pilose-strigose. Leaves deciduous, chartaceous, on sterile shoots elliptic or ellipto-lanceolate, 20–25 ×10–14 mm, apex acute or obtuse, base cuneate, upper surface slightly rugose, dark green, shiny, very sparsely pilose-strigose, veins 5–7, lower surface tomentose; petiole 4–8 mm, pilose-strigose. Fertile shoots 15–25 mm, including 2–3 leaves and a compact, 5- to 9-flowered inflorescence; pedicels 1–3 mm, pilose-strigose. Hypanthium cupulate, pilose-strigose; sepals obtuse or acute, pilose-strigose, margin tomentose. Corolla 7–9 mm, petals spreading, white, with large hair-tuft. Stamens 20; filaments white; anthers white. Styles 2. Fruit not seen, probably red.

    Area: Iran. Pakistan.

    Notes: *Cotoneaster persicus* is closely related to *C. discolor* differing only in its slightly narrower leaves with fewer hairs on the upper surface. The unpublished name *C. bornmulleri* G. Klotz is so very similar to *C. persicus* that we believe it to be a synonym.

14. ***Cotoneaster racemiflorus*** (Desfontaines) Booth ex Bosse in Vollstandiges
    Handbuch der Blumengartneri 4: 177 (1849). Synonym: *C. fontanesii* Spach (1834).
    Type: cult. France, Paris, botanic garden, 8 September 1936, as *C. fontanesii* Spach
    (syn. *Mespilus racemiflorus* Desfontaines) (lecto designated K).
Shrub, 1.5–2 m. Branches narrowly erect, arched; branchlets spiraled, slender, reddish brown, initially densely pilose-strigose. Leaves deciduous, chartaceous, on sterile shoots

suborbicular, broadly elliptic or broadly ovate, 25–39 ×16–28 mm, apex apiculate, acuminate or acute, base obtuse or cuneate, upper surface olive green, dull, initially sparsely pilose-strigose, veins 4–5, lower surface tomentose; petiole 6–10 mm, villous-strigose or villous. Fertile shoots 20–30 mm, including 2–4 leaves and a compact, 7-to 15-flowered inflorescence; pedicels 1–4 mm, densely villous-strigose. Hypanthium cupulate, densely villous-strigose; sepals acute, tomentose, margin villous. Flower buds pinkish. Corolla 8–10 mm, petals spreading, white, with large hair-tuft. Stamens (16–)20; filaments white; anthers white. Fruit depressed-globose, 8–9 mm, succulent, red, pilose, calyx lobes suberect, navel open. Nutlets (1–)2, rarely connate, style remains $^9/_{10}$ from base.

Seasons: Flowers May–June; fruit ripe September–October; autumn leaves intense yellow.

Chromosomes: Tetraploid (Hensen 1966; Kroon 1975; Klotz and Krügel 1983a). Apomictic, true from seed.

Hardiness: –21°C (–6°F).

Area: Georgia. Azerbaijan. Armenia.

Notes: Initially, *Cotoneaster racemiflorus* was thought to have originated from Lebanon. However, no trace has been found of this species in herbaria among specimens from this area. Pojarkova (1939) included Caucasus as one of several areas of origin, but she also included under *C. racemiflorus* several taxa which today are separated as new species. *Cotoneaster racemiflorus* is probably endemic to the Caucasus. From the St. Petersburg botanic garden in Russia it reached Réné Desfontaines in France at the Jardin des Plantes in Paris around 1829 and was introduced into England shortly thereafter. *Cotoneaster racemiflorus* was common in cultivation during the late 1800s, often as *C. fontanesii* or *C. desfontainii*. Shrubs in cultivation today bearing the name *C. racemiflorus* frequently belong to other species. *Cotoneaster racemiflorus* produces a combination of butter-yellow leaves and rich red fruit which look most striking in autumn sunshine.

15. *Cotoneaster tauricus* Pojarkova in Not. Syst. Inst. Bot. Acad. Sci. USSR 8: 138 (1940); cf in Fl. USSR 9: 333 (1939). Type: Ukraine, Crimea, Yalta, Koschka mountain, 7 May 1916, Petunnikov (holo LE). PLATE 33.

Shrub, to 1.5 m. Branches narrowly erect; branchlets spiraled, brown and shiny, lenticellate, initially pilose-strigose. Leaves deciduous, chartaceous, on sterile shoots ovate or elliptic, 22–40 × 13–21 mm, apex acute or obtuse, base cuneate or obtuse, upper surface mid-green, dull, glabrescent, veins 3–5 lightly impressed, lower surface grayish green, densely pilose; petiole 4–8 mm, villous. Fertile shoots 15–30 mm, including 2–4 leaves and a compact, 5- to 9-flowered inflorescence; pedicels 2–4 mm, villous. Hypanthium cupulate, sparsely villous; sepals obtuse or ligulate, sparsely villous or subglabrous, margin villous. Flower buds red or pink. Corolla 7–9 mm, petals spreading, white, sometimes hair-tuft. Stamens (11–)16–20 in two rings; filaments white; anthers white. Fruit obovoid, succulent, 8–9 mm, red, glabrescent, calyx lobes erect or suberect, navel open. Nutlets (1–)2, style remains $^4/_5$ from base.

Seasons: Flowers May–June; fruit ripe September.

Chromosomes: Tetraploid (Gladkova 1968; Klotz 1968b; Krügel 1992a). Apomictic, true from seed.

Hardiness: −21°C (−6°F).

Area: Ukraine.

Notes: *Cotoneaster tauricus*, endemic to the thin woodlands of the stony mountain slopes of the Crimea peninsula, is a delightful, scantily branched shrub which is pretty in flower and ornamental during fruiting. It has been in cultivation since around 1938.

16. ***Cotoneaster transcaucasicus*** Pojarkova in Not. Syst. (Leningrad) 21: 117 (1961).

Synonym: *C. obovatus* Pojarkova (1954), non Wallich ex Dunn. Type: SE Armenia, Megri district, descending from Primazra village to Lischk village in *Quercus macranthera* forest, 30 September 1936, *A. Pojarkova 733* (holo LE). PLATE 34.

Shrub, 1.5–3 m. Branches erect and spreading; branchlets spiraled, maroon, lenticellate, initially pilose-strigose. Leaves deciduous, chartaceous to subcoriaceous, on sterile shoots elliptic to suborbicular, 19–28 × 16–21 mm, apex rotund or obtuse, base cuneate or obtuse, upper surface mid-green, dull, pilose, veins 3–5, lower surface tomentose-pilose; petiole 4–7 mm, tomentose. Fertile shoots 15–35 mm, including 2–3 leaves and a compact, 3- to 12-flowered inflorescence; pedicels 1–5 mm, pilose-strigose. Hypanthium cupulate, densely pilose-strigose or tomentose; sepals obtuse, acute or acuminate, densely pilose-strigose, margin villous. Flower buds pinkish. Corolla 8–10 mm, petals spreading, white, with hair-tuft. Stamens 20; filaments white; anthers white. Fruit obovoid, 8–9 mm, light red, sparsely villous, calyx lobes suberect, villous, navel wide open. Nutlets (1–)2, style remains at apex.

Seasons: Flowers June; fruit ripe September–October.

Chromosomes: Unknown. Apomictic, true from seed.

Hardiness: −18°C (−1°F).

Area: Armenia. Iran. Turkey. Azerbaijan.

Notes: *Cotoneaster transcaucasicus* is a tough shrub of open habit for dry exposed situations. It is spectacular both in flower and in fruit. Recently reintroduced into cultivation.

17. ***Cotoneaster uzbezicus*** Grevtsova ex J. Fryer & B. Hylmö. Synonym: *C. uzbezicus* Grevtsova in Atlas Cotoneasters, p. 307 (1999), without holotype dedicated. Type: Tajikistan, Hissar Mountains, valley of Siome, October 1978, *A. Nohel 1035* [cult. Sweden, Bjuv, (hort.) 2523, B. Hylmö, 28 September 2000, from Czech Republic, Mendel University, Brno] (lecto designated GB). PLATE 35.

Shrub, slow growing to 0.5–1.5 m. Branches erect, arched, horizontally spreading; branchlets spiraled or distichous, slender, maroon, lenticellate, pilose-strigose, glabrescent. Leaves deciduous, subcoriaceous, on sterile shoots distichous or spiraled, orbicular, suborbicular, broadly obovate or broadly elliptic, 16–24 × 14–21 mm, apex rotund or truncate, base rotund or cuneate, upper surface slightly rugose, dark green, mostly shiny, sparsely pilose-strigose, veins 4–5 lightly impressed, lower surface grayish green, densely pilose-strigose; petiole 2–5 mm, densely pilose-strigose. Fertile shoots 10–25 mm, including 2–4 leaves and a dense, 5- to 9(–12)-flowered inflorescence; pedicels 2–5 mm, pilose-strigose. Hypanthium cupulate, densely pilose-strigose; sepals acute, acuminate or obtuse, densely pilose-strigose, margin tomentose. Flower buds pinkish. Corolla 8–11 mm, petals spreading, white, with hair-tuft. Stamens 18–20; filaments white; anthers white. Fruit obovoid or globose, 7–9 mm, rich red with crimson, villous, calyx lobes depressed, tomentose, navel open. Nutlets (1–)2, style remains $4/5$ from base.

Seasons: Flowers May–June; fruit ripe September–October.

Chromosomes: Tetraploid (Kroon 1975) as *C. karatavicus*. Apomictic, true from seed.

Hardiness: −18°C (−1°F).

Area: Tajikistan (Hissar Mountains). Uzbekistan. (Parnia).

Notes: *Cotoneaster uzbezicus* is an attractive species introduced into cultivation from the collection made in Tajikistan by Antonin Nohel, emeritus director of the botanic garden at Mendel University in Brno, Czech Republic. A correction has to be made to the illustration on page 248 in Grevtsova's (1999) work, where the name is wrongly given as *C. uzbetzicus*.

6. Series *Bacillares* G. Klotz in Wiss. Z. Friedrich-Schiller-Univ. Jena, Math.-Naturwiss. 19: 336 (1970).

Large shrubs to small trees. Branchlets greenish brown to purple-brown. Leaves on sterile shoots obovate, elliptic, or suborbicular, 22–100 mm, veins 4–10, petiole 5–15 mm. Inflorescences mostly lax, 5- to 30-flowered. Fruit 6–14 mm, plum-purple or black, often pruinose, calyx often wide open with nutlets protruding.

Mid season.

India (Himachal Pradesh, Uttaranchal Pradesh). Nepal. Kashmir. Pakistan.

7 species: *C. affinis*, *C. bacillaris*, *C. confusus*, *C. ignotus*, *C. insignis*, *C. obtusus*, *C. wattii*.

Key to Series *Bacillares*

1a. Height 4–8 m; leaves elliptic or obovate; nutlets 2 2

1b. Height 3–5 m; leaves orbicular, suborbicular, broadly obovate or broadly elliptic; nutlets 1–2 . . . . **4**

2a. Leaves obovate, apex mostly rotund; inflorescence ≤ 30-flowered; sepals obtuse or acute . . . . *C. bacillaris*

2b. Leaves elliptic, apex mostly acute; inflorescence ≤ 20-flowered; sepals cuspidate or acuminate. **3**

3a. Hypanthium densely pilose-strigose; fruit obovoid, 12–14 mm................... *C. affinis*

3b. Hypanthium very sparsely pilose-strigose; fruit globose, 8–9 mm...............*C. obtusus*

4a. Lower leaf surface and hypanthium with sparse hairs; sepals mostly cuspidate; fruit glabrous ....*C. ignotus*

4b. Lower leaf surface and hypanthium with dense hairs; sepals mostly acute; fruit sparsely villous..*C. insignis*

1. ***Cotoneaster affinis*** Lindley in Trans. Linn. Soc. London 13: 101 (1822); illustr. Loddiges' Bot. Cab. 1522 (1830). Synonym: *C. virgatus* G. Klotz (1978). Type: Kashmir, 1876, *C. B. Clarke 29166* (holo BM). PLATE 36.

Shrub or small tree, 4–6 m. Branches erect, spreading; branchlets greenish brown, minutely verruculose, initially densely pilose-strigose. Leaves deciduous, chartaceous, on sterile shoots elliptic, 47–100 × 37–50 mm, apex acute or obtuse, base rotund, obtuse or cuneate, upper surface ageing slightly rugose, dark green, dull to slightly shiny, subglabrous, veins 5–6, lower surface grayish green, sparsely long-haired pilose-villous, midrib often red; petiole 6–10 mm, pilose-strigose. Fertile shoots 30–70 mm, including 2–4 leaves and a compact, 7- to 20-flowered inflorescence; pedicels 1–4 mm, pilose-strigose. Hypanthium cupulate, densely pilose-strigose; sepals acuminate or cuspidate, densely pilose-strigose, margin villous. Flower buds white and pale pink. Corolla 10–12 mm, petals spreading, white, with hair-tuft. Stamens 20; filaments white; anthers white ageing purple. Fruit obovoid, 10–14 mm, purple-black, pruinose, sparsely villous, calyx lobes depressed, navel closed. Nutlets (1–)2, obovate, 7 × 5 mm, style remains ¾ from base.

Seasons: Flowers June; fruit ripe October–November.

Chromosomes: Tetraploid (Kroon 1975). Apomictic, true from seed.

Hardiness: −18°C (−1°F).

Area: Kashmir. Nepal. India (Himachal Pradesh).

Notes: *Cotoneaster affinis* has been known in cultivation for many years. It is quite vigorous and very showy in flower and fruit. The species was already introduced by 1822 and, although not common, has been constantly in cultivation ever since. It has been much confused; many shrubs known as *C. affinis* belong to other species.

2. ***Cotoneaster bacillaris*** Wallich ex Lindley in Edward's Bot. Reg. 15: t. 1229 (1829). Synonym: *C. obtusus* Klotz (1970), non Wallich ex Lindley. Type: N India, Kumaon, Herb. East India Company, *Wallich 660* (lecto K, iso BM, E, LD).

Shrub to small tree, 4–8 m. Branches erect, wide-spreading; branchlets spiraled, slender, greenish yellow to light brown, lenticellate, minutely verruculose, initially pilose-strigose. Leaves deciduous, chartaceous, on sterile shoots obovate, 63–90 × 32–63 mm, apex rotund or apiculate, base cuneate, upper surface ageing slightly rugose, light green, dull to slightly shiny, subglabrous, veins 5–9, lower surface grayish green, subglabrous; petiole 7–12 mm, pilose-strigose. Fertile shoots 30–50 mm, including 2–3 leaves and a compact, 7- to 30-flowered inflorescence; pedicels 2–6 mm, sparsely pilose-strigose. Hypanthium cupulate, sparsely pilose-strigose; sepals obtuse or acute, rarely acuminate, sparsely pilose-strigose, margin villous. Flower buds white. Corolla 9–11 mm, petals spreading, white, with long hair-tuft. Stamens 20; filaments white; anthers pale purple. Fruit depressed-globose, 8 mm, purple-black, pruinose, glabrous, calyx lobes erect, navel wide open with nutlets exserted. Nutlets 2, orbicular or broadly obovate, 5–6 mm, style remains at apex.

Seasons: Flowers June; fruit ripe October–November.

Chromosomes: Counts differ greatly (diploid, triploid, and tetraploid), probably due to misidentifications. Further counts are needed on verified specimens.

Hardiness: −18°C (−1°F).

Area: India (Uttaranchal Pradesh). Nepal.

Notes: *Cotoneaster bacillaris* is often greater in width than height. Its wood is hard and durable and is said to have long been used in its countries of origin for walking sticks and implement handles. It is handsome in autumn when bearing an abundance of black fruit which, being produced in long sprays, are apparently useful in flower arrangements. *Cotoneaster bacillaris* was collected in the Langtang area of Nepal in 1997 by Alistair McKelvie, Fred Carrie, and Ian Christie.

3. *Cotoneaster confusus* G. Klotz in Wiss. Z. Friedrich-Schiller-Univ. Jena, Math.-
   Naturwiss. 19: 340 (1970). Type: India, Himachal Pradesh, Simla, 24 June 1903,
   Kalha Perchad 19008 (holo CAL).

Shrub or small tree, to 5 m. Branches erect and slightly spreading; branchlets purple-black and shiny, initially strigose-pilose. Leaves deciduous, chartaceous, on sterile shoots elliptic or obovate-elliptic, 22–74 × 12–39 mm, apex obtuse or emarginate, base cuneate, upper surface subglabrous, lower surface sparsely pilose to subglabrous; petiole 3–11 mm, pilose or subglabrous. Fertile shoots with a narrow (to 40 mm in diameter), 10- to 30-flowered inflorescence; pedicels initially pilose. Hypanthium sparsely initially pilose. Corolla 8–9 mm, petals spreading, white, with hair-tuft. Stamens 18–20; anthers purple. Fruit globose, 6–8 mm, purple-black, pruinose, navel open. Nutlets 2.

Area: India (Himachal Pradesh, Uttaranchal Pradesh).

Notes: Type for *Cotoneaster confusus* not seen. Refound by Chris Chadwell (*CC 5107*) in Himachal Pradesh near Manali in the Upper Kulu valley in 2005. Not in key.

4. *Cotoneaster ignotus* G. Klotz in Wiss. Z. Friedrich-Schiller-Univ. Jena, Math.-
   Naturwiss. 19: 339 (1970). Type: E Nepal, Kali valley near Kawa, 28 July 1883,
   J. F. Duthie 5528 (holo BM, iso K, DD). **PLATE 37**.

Shrub or small tree, 3–5 m. Branches erect, spreading; branchlets spiraled, green to light brown and minutely verruculose, initially pilose-strigose. Leaves deciduous, chartaceous, on sterile shoots broadly obovate, broadly elliptic or suborbicular, 34–82 × 26–79 mm, apex rotund, truncate or acute, base cuneate or rotund, upper surface ageing slightly rugose, light becoming dark green, dull to slightly shiny, subglabrous, veins 5–7 pairs lightly impressed, lower surface light yellowish green, reticulate, sparsely pilose-villous; petiole 5–13 mm, pilose-strigose. Fertile shoots 30–50 mm, including 2–3 leaves and a lax, 5- to 19-flowered inflorescence; pedicels 2–6 mm, sparsely pilose-strigose. Hypanthium cupulate, sparsely pilose-strigose; sepals cuspidate or acuminate, sparsely pilose-strigose, border narrow, membranous, white, apex reddish purple, margin villous. Flower buds white. Corolla 9–12 mm, petals spreading, white, with large hair-tuft. Stamens 20; filaments white; anthers white ageing purple. Fruit subglobose, 8 mm, purple-black, pruinose, glabrous, calyx lobes erect, navel wide open with nutlets exserted. Nutlets (1–)2, obovate, 7 × 5 mm, style remains $^9/_{10}$ from base.

Seasons: Flowers June; fruit ripe October–November.
Chromosomes: Tetraploid (McAllister, pers. comm.). Apomictic, true from seed.
Hardiness: –18°C (–1°F).
Area: India (Himachal Pradesh, Uttaranchal Pradesh). Kashmir. Nepal.
Notes: *Cotoneaster ignotus* has long been in cultivation but often as *C. affinis* or *C. bacillaris*. It is very striking in flower and later when laden with clusters of sooty black fruit. It retains its large round leaves and fruit well into winter. A spectacular and unusual shrub.

5. *Cotoneaster insignis* (Pojarkova) Fl. USSR 9: 330 (1939). Synonym: *C. insignoides* hort. Type: Tajikistan, Kuljab province, Dashtidshum district, Obiniou river, at Czernov, 10 October 1943, *A. Pojarkova 6512* (lecto designated H).

Shrub or small tree, 4–5 m. Branches loosely erect, spreading, slender; branchlets maroon to dark brown, lenticellate, initially pilose-strigose. Leaves deciduous, chartaceous, on sterile shoots broadly obovate, broadly elliptic or suborbicular, 33–70 × 27–48 mm, apex rotund, truncate or apiculate, base rotund or cuneate, upper surface ageing slightly rugose, mid-green, dull to slightly shiny, glabrescent, veins 4–7 lightly impressed, lower surface light green, initially densely villous; petiole 7–11 mm, pilose-strigose. Fertile shoots 25–50 mm, including 2–3 leaves and a lax, 7- to 25-flowered inflorescence; pedicels 2–4 mm, pilose-strigose. Hypanthium cupulate, densely pilose-strigose; sepals acuminate or acute, pilose, border membranous, whitish, apex purple, margin villous. Flower buds white. Corolla 8–10 mm, petals spreading, white, with hair-tuft. Stamens 20; filaments white; anthers white ageing purple. Fruit depressed-globose, 7–9 mm, purple-black, pruinose, sparsely villous, calyx lobes depressed, villous, navel open with styles projecting 1–2 mm. Nutlets (1–)2, broadly ovate with apex slightly recurved, style remains $^9/_{10}$ from base.

Seasons: Flowers May–June; fruit ripe October–November.
Chromosomes: Unknown. Apomictic, true from seed.
Hardiness: –21°C (–6°F).
Area: Tajikistan. Kyrgyzstan. Azerbaijan.
Notes: Much confusion has occurred in cultivation between *Cotoneaster insignis* from the Caucasus and *C. ellipticus* from Kashmir and Pakistan. *Cotoneaster insignis* has

thinner, larger leaves and a lax rather than compact inflorescence with twice as many flowers than *C. ellipticus*. Distributed as *C. insignis* from Tashkent and Dushambe botanic gardens after 1946.

6. *Cotoneaster obtusus* Wallich ex Lindley in Edward's Bot. Reg. 15: t. 1229 (1829).
Type: N India, E Kumaon, Herb. East India Company, *Wallich 659.1* (holo LD, iso E, K). PLATE 38.

Shrub or small tree, 4–8 m. Branches spiraled, greenish yellow to light brown, lenticellate, minutely verruculose, initially pilose-strigose. Leaves deciduous, chartaceous, on sterile shoots elliptic, 50–60 × 28–37 mm, apex acute rarely obtuse, base cuneate or obtuse, upper surface slightly rugose, dark green, dull soon shiny, subglabrous, veins 5–10, whitish, lower surface reticulate, grayish green, subglabrous, midrib red; petiole 5–15 mm, often red, pilose-strigose. Fertile shoots 30–50 mm, including 3–4 leaves and a somewhat lax, 7- to 20-flowered inflorescence, pedicels 2–5 mm, very sparsely villous. Hypanthium cupulate, very sparsely pilose-strigose; sepals acuminate or cuspidate, very sparsely villous, margin villous. Flower buds white. Corolla 9–10 mm, petals spreading, white, sometimes with small hair-tuft. Stamens 20; filaments white; anthers white, often with purple margin. Fruit globose or depressed-globose, 8–9 mm, purple-black, bluish pruinose, glabrous, calyx lobes depressed. navel wide open with nutlets slightly exserted. Nutlets 2, orbicular or broadly obovate, 5 mm, style remains at apex.

Seasons: Flowers June; fruit ripe October–November.
Chromosomes: Tetraploid (Jewsbury, pers. comm.).
Hardiness: –18°C (–1°F).
Area: India (Himachal Pradesh, Uttaranchal Pradesh).
Notes: *Cotoneaster obtusus* is common in cultivation but mostly misnamed. It is a very showy shrub both in flower and in fruit. It should not be confused with *C. obtusus* Klotz (1970), which is a synonym of *C. bacillaris*.

7. *Cotoneaster wattii* G. Klotz in Wiss. Z. Friedrich-Schiller-Univ. Jena, Math.-Naturwiss. 19: 342 (1970). Type: India, Himachal Pradesh, Simla, near Nag Kanda in Baggi forest, May 1884, *G. Watt 8073* (holo DD).

Large shrub or small tree. Branches erect, spreading or arched; branchlets purple-brown and shiny, initially subglabrous. Leaves deciduous, chartaceous, on sterile shoots elliptic or lanceolate, 25–68 × 13–34 mm, apex acute or obtuse, base cuneate, upper and lower surface with midrib sparsely pilose; petiole 8 mm, glabrous. Fertile shoots with a narrow (30–45 mm in diameter) 6- to 25-flowered inflorescence; pedicels glabrescent. Hypanthium and sepals glabrous or sparsely pilose. Corolla 8–10 mm, petals spreading, white, with hair-tuft. Stamens 15–20. Fruit globose, 6–8 mm, black or purple-black, apex open. Nutlets 2.

Area: India (Himachal Pradesh).

Notes: Type specimen not seen. A recent collection made in Uttaranchal Pradesh by Chris Chadwell (*CC 5114*) may prove to be this species. Not in key.

7. **Series *Hissarici*** G. Klotz in Wiss. Z. Martin-Luther-Univ. Halle-Wittenberg, Math.-Naturwiss. 15: 535 (1966a). Synonym: series *Insignes* (Pojarkova) G. Klotz (1966a).

Dwarf to large shrubs. Branchlets spiraled or divaricate, slender. Leaves on sterile shoots suborbicular, orbicular, obovate, or elliptic, 5–45 mm, veins 3–7, lower surface tomentose or with dense hairs; petiole 1–8 mm. Fertile shoots 8–40 mm, inflorescence mostly compact, 1- to 13-flowered. Fruit plum-purple or ruby, mostly pruinose. Nutlets 1–2.

Mid season.

Tajikistan. Turkmenistan. Kashmir. Pakistan. Afghanistan. Iran. Georgia. Kyrgyzstan. Armenia. Turkey.

12 species: *C. ellipticus*, *C. falconeri*, *C. hissaricus*, *C. luristanicus*, *C. morulus*, *C. nummularioides*, *C. pruinosus*, *C. saxatilis*, *C. subacutus*, *C. subuniflorus*, *C. turcomanicus*, *C. tytthocarpus*.

Key to Series *Hissarici*

1a. Pedicels ≤ 10 mm; small tuft of hairs at petal base; fruit ruby or maroon 8

1b. Pedicels ≤ 5(–6) mm; large tuft of hairs at petal base; fruit black. 2

2a. Leaves elliptic or ovate; pedicels 1–2 mm; corolla c. 7 mm; fruit 6–7 mm, glabrous . . . .
. . . . **C. tytthocarpus**

2b. Leaves orbicular, suborbicular or obovate; pedicels ≤ 6 mm; corolla ≤ 11 mm; fruit 7–10 mm, sparsely villous 3

3a. Leaves mostly obovate, apex apiculate, acute or acuminate; fruit obovate or cylindrical, calyx closed . . . .**C. turcomanicus**

3b. Leaves orbicular or suborbicular; apex rotund, obtuse or truncate; fruit mostly globose, calyx open 4

4a. Leaves ≤ 17 mm, upper surface with long pilose hairs, veins not impressed; fertile shoots 8–15 mm, inflorescence 2- to 4(–5)-flowered; hypanthium villous-tomentose. . . . .
. . . .**C. nummularioides**

4b. Leaves ≤ 43 mm, upper surface glabrous or few hairs at midrib, veins impressed; fertile shoots 10–40 mm, inflorescence ≤ 13-flowered 5

5a. Leaf apex obtuse; fertile shoots 20–40 mm; pedicels tomentose-villous; sepals long-acuminate. . . . . **C. morulus**

5b. Leaf apex rotund or truncate; fertile shoots 10–30 mm; pedicels pilose-strigose; sepals acute or acuminate 6

6a. Height 0.5–1 m; branches ascending; leaves 10–20 mm; inflorescence 3- to 8-flowered; anthers white; fruit obovoid to depressed globose . . . .*C. falconeri*

6b. Height 1.5–4 m; branches erect; leaves ≤ 40 mm; inflorescence 5- to 13-flowered; fruit globose 7

7a. Height 1.5–2 m; leaves ≤ 30 mm, lower surface pilose; inflorescences lax; pedicels 2–6 mm; nutlets (1–)2 . . . .*C. hissaricus*

7b. Height 3–4 m; leaves 20–40 mm, lower surface tomentose to densely villous; inflorescences compact; pedicels 1–3 mm; nutlets 1(–2) . . . .*C. ellipticus*

8a. Leaves suborbicular or broadly elliptic; sepals acute or acuminate; nutlets 1(–2) . . . .
. . . . *C. saxatilis*

8b. Leaves elliptic, broadly elliptic or suborbicular; sepals cuspidate or acuminate; nutlets 2. . . .
. . . . *C. subacutus*

1. *Cotoneaster ellipticus* (Lindley) Loudon in Trans. Linn. Soc. London 13: 102 (1822), as *Eriobotria elliptica*. Synonyms: *C. lindleyi* Steudel (1840); *C. arborescens* Zabel (1897). Type: Kashmir, Waziristan, *J. L. Stewart 274b* (lecto designated K).

Shrub or small tree, 3–4 m. Branches loosely erect, wide-spreading, slender; branchlets spiraled, maroon, initially pilose-strigose. Leaves deciduous, subcoriaceous, on sterile shoots orbicular, suborbicular, broadly obovate or broadly elliptic, 21–40 × 19–33 mm, apex rotund or truncate, base rotund or cuneate, upper surface ageing slightly rugose, dark bluish green, slightly shiny, glabrescent, veins 4–6 lightly impressed, lower surface pale bluish green with midrib often red, initially densely villous; petiole 4–8 mm, pilose-villous. Fertile shoots 15–25 mm, including 2–3 leaves and a compact, 5- to 13-flowered inflorescence; pedicels 1–3 mm, pilose-strigose. Hypanthium cupulate, densely pilose-strigose; sepals acute or acuminate, pilose-strigose, border narrow, whitish, apex purple, glabrous, margin villous. Flower buds pale pink. Corolla 8–10 mm, petals spreading, white, with large hair-tuft. Stamens 20; filaments white, anthers white ageing purple. Fruit globose, 7–8 mm, purple-black, pruinose, sparsely villous, calyx lobes depressed, villous, navel slightly open. Nutlets 1(–2), style remains at apex.

Seasons: Flowers June; fruit ripe October–November.

Chromosomes: Tetraploid (Gladkova 1967, 1968; Kroon 1975)—although these counts could possibly relate to other species.

Hardiness: −18°C (−1°F).

Area: Kashmir. Pakistan.

Notes: *Cotoneaster ellipticus* was introduced in 1824 and has been fairly common in cultivation since around 1830. It is a good-sized shrub with long, sweeping branches. It can be found in cultivation as *C. nummularius* or *C. lindleyi*.

2. *Cotoneaster falconeri* G. Klotz in Wiss. Z. Martin-Luther-Univ. Halle-Wittenberg, Math.-Naturwiss. 15: 535 (1966). Type: N Pakistan, Chitral, Jambatai, 5 May 1895, *S. A. Harris 16109* (holo CAL, iso BM, DD).

Shrub, 0.5–1 m. Branches loosely ascending, spreading; branchlets spiraled, light brown, lenticellate, pilose-strigose. Leaves deciduous, chartaceous, on sterile shoots suborbicular or broadly obovate, 9–20 × 9–19 mm, apex rotund or truncate, base rotund or cuneate, upper surface ageing slightly rugose, dark grayish green, dull to slightly shiny, glabrescent, veins 3–5 lightly impressed, lower surface densely pilose; petiole 2–4 mm, pilose-strigose. Fertile shoots 10–20 mm, including mostly 2 leaves and a compact, 3- to 8-flowered inflorescence; pedicels 2–4 mm, pilose-strigose. Hypanthium cupulate, densely pilose-strigose; sepals acuminate, pilose-strigose, border membranous, whitish, apex purple, margin villous. Flower buds white. Corolla 8–11 mm, petals spreading, white, with hair-tuft. Stamens 20 (2 rings of 10); filaments white; anthers white or initially slightly brownish. Fruit obovoid or depressed-globose, 7–8 mm, maroon to purple-black, pruinose, subglabrous, calyx lobes depressed, pilose, navel slightly open. Nutlets (1–)2, style remains near apex.

Seasons: Flowers May–June; fruit ripe September–October.

Chromosomes: Tetraploid (Klotz 1968b). Apomictic, true from seed.

Hardiness: –18°C (–1°F).

Area: Pakistan. Kashmir.

Notes: *Cotoneaster falconeri* is the earliest species to flower in series *Hissarici*. Recently reintroduced into cultivation.

3. *Cotoneaster hissaricus* Pojarkova in Not. Syst. Inst. Bot. Acad. Sci. USSR 16: 124
    (1954). Type: Tajikistan, Hissar Mountains, Kondara river, 30 September 1944,
    A. Pojarkova 1117 (holo LE).

Shrub, 1.5–2 m. Branches erect, arched; branchlets spiraled, slender, maroon, densely lenticellate and minutely verruculose, densely pilose-strigose. Leaves deciduous, chartaceous or subcoriaceous, on sterile shoots orbicular, suborbicular or broadly obovate, 23–30 × 21–24 mm, apex rotund or truncate, base rotund or cuneate, upper surface ageing slightly rugose, dark green, slightly shiny, glabrescent, veins 4–6 lightly impressed, lower surface initially densely pilose; petiole 4–6 mm, pilose-strigose. Fertile shoots 15–30 mm, including 2–4 leaves and a somewhat lax, 4- to 10(–13)-flowered inflorescence; pedicels 2–6 mm, pilose-strigose. Hypanthium cupulate, densely pilose-strigose; sepals acuminate or acute, pilose-strigose, border broad, membranous, whitish, apex purple, margin villous. Flower buds white tinged-pink. Corolla 7–9 mm, petals spreading, white, with large hair-tuft. Stamens 14–20; filaments white; anthers white ageing slightly purple. Fruit globose, 7–9 mm, maroon, purple-black to black, pruinose, sparsely villous, calyx lobes depressed, villous, navel open. Nutlets (1–)2, style remains near apex.

Seasons: Flowers June; fruit ripe October–November.

Chromosomes: Triploid (Klotz 1968b; Krügel 1992a; Bailey, pers. comm.). Tetraploid (Gladkova 1968; Krügel 1992a). Pentaploid (Krügel 1992a).

Hardiness: –18°C (–1°F).

Area: Tajikistan. Afghanistan.

Notes: *Cotoneaster hissaricus*, with its variable chromosome counts, is possibly not always breeding completely true from seed. Included in this species are the recently (invalidly) named *C. bilokonii*, *C. fominii*, and *C. zaprjagaevae* Grevtsova. *Cotoneaster hissaricus*, originating from the Hissar Mountains, is not common in the nursery trade but can be seen in most botanic gardens and large collections. Recently reintroduced into cultivation.

4. *Cotoneaster luristanicus* G. Klotz in Feddes Repert. 76: 201 (1967). Type: W Iran, Bakhtiari, Gahar, 27 May 1941, *W. N. Koelz 17846* (holo W).

Shrub, to 2 m. Branches loosely erect; branchlets red-brown or gray-brown, initially tomentose. Leaves deciduous, chartaceous or subcoriaceous, on sterile shoots suborbicular or obcordate, 5–25 × 5–24 mm, apex rotund or emarginate, base cuneate or rotund, upper surface initially densely villous, dull, lower surface villous; petiole (1–)2–4 mm, tomentose. Inflorescence (1–)3- to 7(–9)-flowered; pedicels initially densely villous. Hypanthium initially pilose; sepals acute, initially densely villous. Corolla 7–8 mm, petals spreading, white, with hair-tuft. Stamens 18–20; filaments white; anthers pink. Mature fruit not seen. Nutlets 2.

Notes: Type specimen not seen. Living shrubs have not been found in cultivation. It is unclear whether the fruit are red or black. Klotz's statement that the anthers are pink was possibly taken from anthers that were ageing. Not in key.

5. *Cotoneaster morulus* Pojarkova in Not. Syst. Inst. Bot. Acad. Sci. USSR 21: 177 (1961). Type: Transcaucasia, NE Azerbaijan, Nucha, 12 September 1949, *A. Pojarkova 1156* (holo LE).

Shrub, 1.5–2 m. Branches erect, spreading; branchlets spiraled or divaricate, grayish brown to purple-black, minutely verruculose, initially tomentose. Leaves deciduous, chartaceous or subcoriaceous, on sterile shoots suborbicular or broadly elliptic, 26–43 × 21–34 mm, apex obtuse, base obtuse or cuneate, upper surface mid-green, dull to shiny, subglabrous, veins 5–7 lightly impressed, lower surface grayish green, tomentose-villous to pilose; petiole 3–8 mm, villous. Fertile shoots 20–40 mm, including 3 leaves and a lax, 6- to 11-flowered inflorescence; pedicels 2–4 mm, tomentose-villous. Hypanthium cupulate, pilose; sepals long acuminate, villous, border membranous, often reddish purple, glabrous, margin villous. Flower buds greenish white. Corolla 6–9 mm, petals spreading, white, with large hair-tuft. Stamens 20; filaments white; anthers white. Fruit depressed-globose or obovoid, 7–9 mm, maroon to purple-black, sparsely villous, calyx lobes depressed, sparsely villous, navel slightly open. Nutlets (1–)2, style remains near apex.

Seasons: Flowers May–June; fruit ripe October.

Chromosomes: Triploid (Krügel 1992a).

Hardiness: −21°C (−6°F).

Area: Azerbaijan. Turkey, Georgia. Armenia. Iran.

Notes: *Cotoneaster morulus* is newly introduced into cultivation from a collection by

Flanagan and Pitman (#38) in Turkey. It is proving to be very garden-worthy, pretty in flower, and with numerous fruit.

6. *Cotoneaster nummularioides* Pojarkova in Not. Syst. Inst. Bot. Acad. Sci. USSR 16: 128 (1954). Type: Tajikistan, Hissar Mountains, Varzob river, Bigar, Kondara river, 1 November 1944, *A. Pojarkova 1120* (holo LE).

Shrub, 1.5–2.5 m. Branches erect, spreading, rigid and slender; branchlets spiraled, reddish brown to purple-black, minutely verruculose, initially tomentose-villous. Leaves deciduous, subcoriaceous, on sterile shoots orbicular, broadly obovate or broadly elliptic, 13–17 × 10–15 mm, apex obtuse or truncate, base obtuse or cuneate, upper surface ageing slightly rugose, mid-green or grayish, dull to slightly shiny, adpressed pilose, veins mostly 4, lower surface densely villous-pilose; petiole 2–4 mm, villous. Fertile shoots 8–15 mm, including 1–3 leaves and a compact, 2- to 4(–5)-flowered inflorescence; pedicels 1–3 mm, villous-tomentose. Hypanthium cupulate, villous-tomentose; sepals acuminate or acute, villous, border membranous, apex reddish purple, margin villous. Flower buds white tinged pink. Corolla 7–8 mm, petals spreading, white, with large hair-tuft. Stamens (16–) 20; filaments white; anthers white. Fruit globose, 6–8 mm, purple-black, pruinose, villous, calyx lobes depressed, villous, navel open. Nutlets 1–2, style remains $^9/_{10}$ from base.

Seasons: Flowers June; fruit ripe October.

Chromosomes: Triploid (Gladkova 1967, 1968; Klotz 1968b; Krügel 1992a). Tetraploid (Klotz and Krügel 1968).

Hardiness: –21°C (–6°F).

Area: Tajikistan. Turkmenistan.

Notes: Although V. N. Gladkova, Tamara Krügel, and indeed Gerhard Klotz himself found *Cotoneaster nummularioides* to be triploid, a further count by Klotz on a shrub originating from the Kopet-Dag mountains in the area near Ashgabat, Turkmenistan, revealed a tetraploid. This is an exquisite and unusual little shrub, suitable for growing in a container. Recently reintroduced into cultivation.

7. *Cotoneaster pruinosus* G. Klotz in Wiss. Z. Martin-Luther-Univ. Halle-Wittenberg, Math.-Naturwiss. 15: 533 (1966). Type: N Pakistan, south of Chitral village, 16 April 1958, *J. D. A. Stainton 2212* (holo BM).

Shrub, 1.5–2 m. Branches erect, slender; branchlets spiraled or divaricate, slender, purple-black, initially villous. Leaves deciduous, chartaceous or subcoriaceous, on sterile shoots broadly obovate or suborbicular, 5–24 × 3.5–17 mm, apex rotund, emarginate, sometimes obtuse, mucronulate, base cuneate or obtuse, upper surface grayish green, glabrescent, veins 4(–5), lower surface glaucous, reticulate, sparsely pilose or glabrous, midrib pilose; petiole 1.5–3(–4) mm. Fertile shoots 10–12 mm, including 1–3 leaves and a compact, 1- to 5(–9)-flowered inflorescence, pedicels 1–3 mm, initially villous. Hypanthium cupulate, sometimes sparsely villous; sepals acute, acuminate or cuspidate, sometimes sparsely villous, apex red, margin villous. Flower buds greenish white. Corolla 6–9 mm, petals spreading, white, with hair-tuft. Stamens 10–12; filaments white; anthers creamy-white. Fruit subglobose, 5–8 mm, purple-black, pruinose, very sparsely villous, calyx lobes depressed or flat. Nutlets (1–)2, style remains at or near apex.

Seasons: Flowers May–June; fruit ripe October.

Hardiness: –18°C (–1°F).

Area: Pakistan. Kashmir.

Notes: *Cotoneaster pruinosus* is very uncommon in cultivation. Not in the key.

8. *Cotoneaster saxatilis* Pojarkova in Not. Syst. Inst. Bot. Acad. Sci. USSR 8: 7 (1938); cf. Fl. USSR 9: 333 (1939). Type: Azerbaijan, Kirovabad, Aksu river, Czajkend, 21 September 1937, *A. Pojarkova 243* (holo LE).

Shrub, 2–3 m. Branches erect, spreading; branchlets dark brown and shiny, lenticellate, initially pilose-strigose. Leaves deciduous, on sterile shoots suborbicular or broadly elliptic, 24–35 × 17–28 mm, apex rotund, truncate or acute, base rotund or cuneate, upper surface grayish to mid-green, dull, subglabrous, veins 3–5, lower surface long-haired pilose; petiole 5–8 mm, pilose-strigose. Fertile shoots 20–40 mm, including mostly 3 leaves and a lax, 5- to 13-flowered inflorescence; pedicels 2–7 mm, pilose-strigose. Hypanthium cupulate, pilose-strigose; sepals acute or acuminate, pilose-strigose, border narrow, membranous, apex purple, margin villous. Flower buds white. Corolla 8–10 mm, petals spreading, white, with small hair-tuft. Stamens 18–20; filaments white; anthers white. Fruit globose, 8–9 mm, ruby to dark maroon, pruinose, villous, calyx lobes villous, navel open with nutlets exserted. Nutlets 1–2, style remains at apex.

Seasons: Flowers June; fruit ripe October-November.

Chromosomes: Tetraploid (Klotz 1968b). Apomictic, true from seed.

Hardiness: –21°C (–6°F).

Area: Azerbaijan. Tajikistan. Armenia.

Notes: *Cotoneaster saxatilis* is frequently confused with *C. subacutus* in botanic gardens and collections (see notes for *C. subacutus*). Recently reintroduced into cultivation.

9. *Cotoneaster subacutus* Pojarkova in Not. Syst. Inst. Bot. Acad. Sci. USSR 21: 165 (1961). Type: W Tian Shan, Tschatkalense, Sary-Tschilek, 24 August 1950, *A. Pojarkova 668* (holo LE).

Shrub, 1.5–2.5 m. Branches erect, spreading; branchlets spiraled, slender, maroon, lenticellate, minutely verruculose, initially pilose-strigose. Leaves deciduous, chartaceous, on sterile shoots broadly elliptic, elliptic or suborbicular, 25–28 × 17–21 mm, apex rotund, obtuse or acute, base broadly cuneate, upper surface dark green, dull, subglabrous, veins 5–7, lower surface densely pilose; petiole 5–8 mm, pilose-strigose. Fertile shoots 15–30 mm, including 3–4 leaves and a compact, 7- to 13-flowered inflorescence; pedicels 3–10 mm, pilose-strigose. Hypanthium cupulate, initially pilose-strigose; sepals cuspidate, acuminate or acute, pilose-strigose, margin villous. Flower buds white. Corolla 9–10 mm, petals spreading, white, with small hair-tuft. Stamens 20 in 2 rings; filaments white;

anthers white. Fruit globose or obovoid, 8–9 mm, ruby, pruinose, villous, calyx lobes sub-erect, subglabrous, navel open with nutlets exserted. Nutlets 2, sometimes joined, style remains $^9/_{10}$ from base.

Seasons: Flowers May-June; fruit ripe September-October.

Chromosomes: Tetraploid (Gladkova 1968; Klotz 1968b; Krügel 1992a). Apomictic, true from seed.

Hardiness: –21°C (–6°F).

Area: Kazakhstan. Kyrgyzstan. Tajikistan.

Notes: *Cotoneaster subacutus* is similar to *C. saxatilis* but differs in its more elliptic leaves, the lighter shade of its fruit, and in having 2 nutlets.

10. *Cotoneaster subuniflorus* (Kitamura) Klotz in Wiss. Z. Martin-Luther-Univ.
    Halle-Wittenberg, Math.-Naturwiss. 12: 765 (1963). Type: Afghanistan, Nuristan,
    between Kandai and Seprigal, 28 July 1955, S. Kitamura (KYOTO).
Shrub. Branchlets purple, initially densely tomentose. Leaves deciduous, on sterile shoots broadly obovate, 6–10 × 7–11 mm, apex emarginate, mucronate, base rotund, truncate, upper surface dark green, lower surface glaucous, adpressed-pilose; petiole 1.5–2 mm. Flowers 1(–2); pedicels 2–3 mm, pilose. Fruit oblong, 3–5 mm, black. Nutlets 2.

Area: Afghanistan.

Notes: *Cotoneaster subuniflorus* is not known in cultivation. The above description is compiled only from the original description. Not in key.

11. *Cotoneaster turcomanicus* Pojarkova in Not. Syst. Inst. Bot. Acad. Sci. USSR 21:
    162 (1961). Type: Turkmenistan, Kopet-Dag mountains, Ai-Dere, 23 September
    1953, T. Egorova (holo LE).
Shrub, 2–3 m. Branches loosely erect, spreading; branchlets spiraled purple-black, minutely verruculose, initially tomentose. Leaves deciduous, subcoriaceous, on sterile shoots obovate, elliptic or suborbicular, 28–45 × 29–33 mm, apex apiculate, acute or acuminate, mucronate, base cuneate or obtuse, upper surface ageing slightly rugose, mid to dark green, dull to slightly shiny, subglabrous, veins 5–7 lightly impressed, lower surface grayish green, tomentose to pilose-villous; petiole 6–8 mm, villous. Fertile shoots 15–20 mm, including 2–3 leaves and a compact, 7- to 13-flowered inflorescence; pedicels 1–5 mm, tomentose. Hypanthium cupulate, tomentose-villous; sepals acuminate, villous, border membranous, white, apex reddish purple, margin villous. Flower buds white. Corolla 8–10 mm, petals spreading, with large hair-tuft. Stamens 20; filaments white; anthers white. Fruit obovoid or cylindrical, 7–11 mm, purple-black, pruinose, villous, calyx lobes depressed, villous, navel closed. Nutlets (1–)2 (when unripe slightly joined), style remains near to apex.

Seasons: Flowers May–June; fruit ripe October.

Chromosomes: Unknown. Apomictic, true from seed.

Hardiness: –21°C (–6°F).

Area: Turkmenistan. Tajikistan.

Notes: *Cotoneaster turcomanicus* is native to the Kopet-Dag and Hissar mountains. Recently reintroduced into cultivation. This species has vigorous basal shoots which can reach a length of 2 m in one growing season. It is similar to *C. tytthocarpus* (see notes for this species).

12. *Cotoneaster tytthocarpus* Pojarkova in Not. Syst. Inst. Bot. Acad. Sci. USSR 21: 181 (1961). Type: Turkmenistan, Kopet-Dag mountains, Ai-Dere, 11 October 1940, *K. Blinovsky 58* (holo LE, iso E).

Shrub, 2–3(–4) m. Branches erect, arched, slender; branchlets spiraled, reddish brown to purple-black, initially villous. Leaves deciduous, chartaceous, on sterile shoots elliptic or ovate, 18–32 × 16–23 mm, apex obtuse or acute, base cuneate or obtuse, upper surface ageing slightly rugose, dark green, dull to slightly shiny, subglabrous, veins 4–6, lower surface tomentose-villous; petiole 3–7 mm, villous. Fertile shoots 15–20 mm, including 2(–3) leaves and a compact, 3- to 4(–6)-flowered inflorescence; pedicels 1–2 mm, tomentose-villous. Hypanthium cupulate, tomentose-villous; sepals acute or acuminate, tomentose-villous, border membranous, margin villous. Flower buds white tinged pink. Corolla 7 mm, petals spreading, white, with hair-tuft. Stamens 16–20; filaments white; anthers white. Fruit obovoid, 6–7 mm, purple-black, glabrous, calyx lobes villous, navel open. Nutlets 1–2, sometimes joined, style remains near apex.

Seasons: Flowers June; fruit ripe September–October.

Chromosomes: Tetraploid (Jewsbury, pers. comm.). Apomictic, true from seed.

Hardiness: −21°C (−6°F).

Area: Georgia. Turkmenistan. Tajikistan. Iran.

Notes: *Cotoneaster tytthocarpus* is native to the Elburz Mountains of Georgia, the Kopet-Dag mountains of Turkmenistan, and the Hissar Mountains of Tajikistan. It is similar to *C. turcomanicus* but differs in its smaller leaves, shorter fertile shoots, and mostly 3- to 4-flowered inflorescences. Recently reintroduced into cultivation.

3. Section *Multiflori*, stat. nov. Basionym: series *Multiflori* (Pojarkova) T. T. Yu in Bull. Brit. Mus. (Nat. Hist.), Bot. 1 (5): 137 (1954).

Large shrubs or small trees. Branches often wide-spreading. Leaves deciduous, mostly chartaceous. Inflorescences lax, multiflowered. Hypanthium cupulate or campanulate. Corolla often wide, up to 15 mm, petals often with hairs at base of upper surface. Fruit often large (to 15 mm). Nutlets 1, or 2 conjoined.

3 series: *Multiflori, Tomentelli, Hebephylli*.

8. Series *Multiflori* including series *Hupehenses* Hurusawa (1973).

Large shrubs to small trees of 8 m. Branchlets slender. Corolla widely campanulate, petals sometimes reflexing, white or pale purple. Filaments white or pale purple; anthers white, rarely with pale purple margin. Fruit often large (6–15 mm). Nutlets 2 connate (fused tightly together).

Mostly early, rarely mid season.

China (Sichuan, Hubei, Gansu, Shanxi, Hebei, Henan, Nei Monggol, Ningxia). Kazakhstan. Mongolia. Armenia. Georgia. Azerbaijan. Iran. Turkey.

16 species: *C. borealichinensis*, *C. calocarpus*, *C. hupehensis*, *C. kaschkarovii*, *C. latifolius*, *C. magnificus*, *C. meyeri*, *C. multiflorus*, *C. przewalskii*, *C. purpurascens*, *C. reflexus*, *C. silvestrii*, *C. submultiflorus*, *C. tanpaensis*, *C. tumeticus*, *C. veitchii*.

Key to Series *Multiflori*

1a. Lower leaf surface, hypanthium and sepals tomentose or densely villous; late flowering and fruiting **2**

1b. Lower leaf surface, hypanthium and sepals glabrous or few hairs; early flowering and fruiting. **3**

2a. Leaves ovate or ovate-lanceolate, upper surface soon glabrous; fruit subglobose . . . . **C. silvestrii**

2b. Leaves broadly elliptic or broadly ovate, upper surface densely villous becoming sparsely so; fruit globose . . . . **C. veitchii**

3a. Fertile shoots ≤ 60–70 mm; sepals sometimes ligulate; fruit with sparse hairs **4**

3b. Fertile shoots 35–45(–60) mm; sepals not ligulate; fruit glabrous. **6**

4a. Leaves suborbicular or broadly ovate, apex obtuse or acute; sepals mostly obtuse; stamens 20–24 . . . .*C. reflexus*

4b. Leaves broadly elliptic or broadly ovate, apex acuminate; sepals mostly acute; sepals 18–20 . . . .**5**

5a. Upper leaf surface dark green, petiole ≤ 12 mm; pedicels ≤ 8 mm; fruit maroon-purple to black . . . .*C. meyeri*

5b. Upper leaf surface light green, petiole ≤ 7 mm; pedicels ≤ 15 mm; fruit crimson . . . . **C. przewalskii**

6a. Leaf apex mostly acute or obtuse or apiculate; corolla with petals spreading; stamens (13–)20 . . . .**7**

6b. Leaf apex mostly acuminate or acute; corolla mostly widely campanulate; stamens 12–20 . . . .**11**

7a. Branchlets maroon; leaves elliptic or ovate, veins 6–9. . . . .**8**

7b. Branchlets light brown; leaves suborbicular or broadly ovate, veins 4–7 . . . .**10**

8a. Leaves mostly 35–50 mm; fertile shoots ≤ 60 mm; corolla 12–15 mm in diameter fruit ruby . . . .*C. calocarpus*

8b. Leaves mostly 20–40 mm; fertile shoots ≤ 35 mm; corolla 10–12 mm diameter; fruit crimson or cherry **9**

9a. Upper leaf surface brownish green becoming dark green, pilose; hypanthium campanulate .... *C. borealichinensis*

9b. Upper leaf surface mid-green, glabrous; hypanthium cupulate .... *C. hupehensis*

10a. Leaves light green initially reddish, inflorescence 10- to 20-flowered; corolla 9 mm; fruit crimson .... *C. multiflorus*

10b. Leaves dark green initially blackish brown, inflorescence 5- to 10-flowered; corolla 13 mm; fruit becoming maroon.. *C. tumeticus*

11a. Upper leaf surface light green; flower buds white; corolla with petals spreading, white; fruit crimson 12

11b. Upper leaf surface dark green; flower buds with pink, red or purple; corolla campanulate, petals pale purple or white; fruit ruby to maroon 13

12a. Branches stiffly erect; corolla 7–9 mm; fruit 6–8 mm .... *C. submultiflorus*

12b. Branches erect, arched and spreading; corolla 12–14 mm; fruit 10–12 mm .... *C. magnificus*

13a. Leaves elliptic, ≤ 45 mm; petals pure white..... ....*C. tanpaensis*

13b. Leaves mostly broadly ovate or broadly elliptic, ≤ 50–66 mm petals pale purple or white with pale purple dots.. 14

14a. Leaves 50–66 mm, lower surface sparsely pilose soon glabrous; inflorescence 7- to 20-flowered; petals white with purple dots ....*C. latifolius*

14b. Leaves 31–50 mm; lower surface strigose-pilose; inflorescence 5- to 11-flowered; petals mauve .... *C. purpurascens*

1. *Cotoneaster borealichinensis* (Hurusawa) Hurusawa in Inf. Ann. Hort. Bot. Fac. Sci. Univ. Tokyo. p. 14 (1967). Synonym: *C. multiflorus* Bunge var. *borealichinensis* Hurusawa (1943). Type: China, Hebei, Mount Wutai, 21 August 1913, *F. N. Meyer 1259* (lecto designated TI). **PLATE 39.**

Shrub, 2–3 m. Branches narrowly erect, arched, slender; branchlets distichous, red-brown, densely lenticellate, minutely verruculose, initially densely pilose-strigose. Leaves deciduous, chartaceous, on sterile shoots ovate, 20–35 × 11–17 mm, apex acute, base cuneate or obtuse, upper surface brownish green soon dark green, dull, pilose, veins 6–9, lower surface reticulate, initially pilose-villous; petiole 6–10 mm, pilose-strigose. Fertile shoots 25–35 mm, including 2–3 leaves and a lax, 5- to 15-flowered inflorescence; pedicels 3–6 mm, sparsely pilose or glabrous. Hypanthium campanulate, glabrescent; sepals obtuse or acute, glabrescent, margin villous. Flower buds white. Corolla 10–12 mm, sometimes 6- to 8-petaled; petals spreading, wide-spaced, white, with short hair-tuft. Stamens 13–20; filaments white; anthers white. Fruit globose or depressed globose, 11–13 mm, rich red to cherry red (drying purple-black), glabrous, calyx lobes suberect, navel open with stamens and styles exserted. Nutlets 2 connate, rarely 1, style remains at elongated apex.

Seasons: Flowers May–June; fruit ripe August–September.
Chromosomes: Unknown. Apomictic, true from seed.
Hardiness: −18°C (−1°F).

Area: China (Hebei, Shaanxi, Henan, Gansu, Shanxi).

Notes: *Cotoneaster borealichinensis* is seldom seen in cultivation, although seed was distributed in 1960 (as *C. multiflorus*) from the Chinese National Herbarium in Beijing. Recently reintroduced into cultivation. This species is later flowering than the closely related *C. multiflorus*.

2. **Cotoneaster calocarpus** (Rehder & E. H. Wilson) Flinck & B. Hylmö in Bot. Not. (Lund) 119: 457 (1966). Synonym: *C. multiflorus* Bunge var. *calocarpus* Rehder & E. H. Wilson (1912). Type: China, W Sichuan, Min river near Sung-pan Ting, September 1910, *E. H. Wilson 4015* (holo A). PLATE 40.

Shrub, 2–3 m. Branches erect and arched; branchlets maroon, lenticellate, initially pilose-strigose. Leaves deciduous, chartaceous, on sterile shoots ovate or broadly ovate, 40–52 × 23–31 mm, apex acute or acuminate, base obtuse or cuneate, upper surface reddish brown soon dark green, dull, initially sparsely villous, veins 6–8, lower surface initially densely villous; petiole 5–7 mm, villous. Fertile shoots 25–60 mm, including 3–5 leaves and a lax, 5- to 15-flowered inflorescence; pedicels 5–10 mm, sparsely villous. Hypanthium cupulate, sparsely villous; sepals acute or obtuse, glabrous. Flower buds white with pink dots. Corolla 12–15 mm, petals spreading, white, with hair-tuft. Stamens 18–20; filaments white; anthers white, margin with some pale purple. Fruit globose, succulent, 10–11 mm, red maturing ruby, glabrous, calyx lobes flat. Nutlets 2 connate, style remains at apex.

Seasons: Flowers May–June; fruit ripe August; autumn leaves shades of yellow.

Chromosomes: Tetraploid (Krügel 1992a). Apomictic, true from seed.

Hardiness: –18°C (–1°F).

Area: China (Sichuan).

Notes: *Cotoneaster calocarpus* is the earliest species to flower in series *Multiflori*. It makes a beautiful shrub with flowers and fruit very freely produced. Fairly common in cultivation, especially in Central Europe, the plant is often found in cultivation as *C. racemiflorus* var. *soongoricus*. Shrubs still exist in some collections under the *Wilson 4015* type.

3. **Cotoneaster hupehensis** Rehder & E. H. Wilson in Sargent, Pl. Wilson. 1: 169 (1912). Type: China, W Hubei (formerly Hupeh), Xingshan Xian, October 1907, *E. H. Wilson 334* (holo A). PLATE 41.

Shrub, 2–4 m. Branches loosely erect, arched, pendulous, slender; branchlets spiraled, maroon, lenticellate, initially pilose-strigose. Leaves deciduous, chartaceous, on sterile shoots elliptic or ovate, 24–40 × 15–23 mm, apex acute, base cuneate or obtuse, upper surface mid-green, dull, glabrous, veins 6–9, lower surface initially sparsely pilose; petiole 5–7 mm, pilose-strigose. Fertile shoots 23–35 mm, including 2–4 leaves and a lax, 5- to 11-flowered inflorescence; pedicels 3–6 mm, pilose-strigose. Hypanthium cupulate, pilose-strigose; sepals acute or obtuse, glabrescent, margin villous. Flower buds white. Corolla 12 mm, petals spreading, white, with short hair-tuft. Stamens 20; filaments white;

anthers white. Fruit globose or depressed-globose, succulent, 11–14 mm, cherry red, dull, glabrescent, calyx lobes depressed, navel open. Nutlets 2 connate, style remains at apex.

Seasons: Flowers June; fruit ripe September.

Chromosomes: Tetraploid (Kroon 1975). Apomictic, true from seed.

Hardiness: −15°C (5°F).

Area: China (Hubei).

Notes: All specimens of *Cotoneaster hupehensis* in cultivation probably originate from the *Wilson 334* type collection. The shrub is very graceful in habit, with whiplike maroon, pendulous branches covered with cascading masses of open white flowers and in turn strewn with cherry-red fruit. This species is very closely related to those in series *Tomentelli*.

4. *Cotoneaster kaschkarovii* Pojarkova in Not. Syst. Inst. Bot. Acad. Sci. USSR 21: 194 (1961). Type: China, Sichuan, Kangding (Ta-tsien-lu) and Batang, Olunschi and Natschuka, 18 May 1893, V. Kaschkarov (holo LE).

Shrub, 2–4 m. Branches erect, long and slender; branchlets divaricate, purple-black, shiny, initially pilose. Leaves deciduous, chartaceous, on sterile shoots elliptic, oblong-rhomboid-elliptic, 12–30 × 7–15 mm, apex acuminate, acute or obtuse, base narrowly cuneate, upper surface light green, dull, sparsely pilose, lower surface pale green, glaucous, reticulate; petiole 3–7 mm, pilose. Fertile shoots 10–25 mm, including 2–3 leaves and an erect, lax, 2- to 12-flowered inflorescence; pedicels 2–3 mm, pilose. Hypanthium initially pilose; sepals triangular, subobtuse, margin membranous, shortly pilose. Corolla 8–10 mm, petals spreading to recurved, white. Stamens 16–20; filaments white. Fruit subglobose, crimson to dark red. Nutlets 2 connate or 2 free.

Seasons: Flowers May; fruit ripe August–September.

Chromosomes: Unknown.

Hardiness: −18°C (−1°F).

Area: China (Sichuan). Tibet.

Notes: *Cotoneaster kaschkarovii* is rare in cultivation. Not in key.

5. *Cotoneaster latifolius* J. Fryer & B. Hylmö in New Plantsman 8: 228, 237 (2001). Type: China, NW Shanxi, Pa-Shui-Kou Shan, C. Blom, *Harry Smith 77* (seed) (holo GB).

Shrub, 3–6 m. Branches 4–5 m. erect, arched and wide-spreading; branchlets spiraled or distichous, maroon with large white lenticels, initially pilose-strigose. Leaves deciduous, chartaceous or subcoriaceous, on sterile shoots broadly elliptic or broadly ovate, 50–66 × 29–49 mm, apex acuminate or acute, base cuneate or obtuse, upper surface brownish to reddish green, soon dark green, dull, veins 4–6, lower surface grayish green, initially pilose, petiole 6–9 mm, pilose. Fertile shoots 30–50 mm, including 3–4 leaves and a lax, 7- to 20-flowered inflorescence; pedicels 3–10 mm, sparsely pilose or glabrous. Hypanthium campanulate, glabrescent; sepals obtuse or acute, party-coloured red-purple, glabrous, margin villous. Flower buds pink and red. Corolla widely campanulate, 12–13 mm, petals concave, white with few pale purple dots and sometimes small hair-tuft. Stamens 18–20; filaments white; anthers white. Fruit obovoid or globose, 11–14(–17) mm, crimson to ruby red, skin splitting at maturity, glabrous, calyx lobes flat. Nutlets 2 connate, style remains at apex.

> Seasons: Flowers May-June; often reflowers August; fruit ripe August-September.
> Chromosomes: Unknown. Apomictic, true from seed.
> Hardiness: –25°C (–13°F). Very hardy.
> Area: China (Shanxi, Gansu, Hebei).
> Notes: *Cotoneaster latifolius* was collected by Harry Smith on his second expedition to China. It is probably the largest fruited of all cotoneasters. It is also extremely heavily fruiting. In autumn the ground beneath the shrubs becomes carpeted with the large, cherrylike fruit.

6. *Cotoneaster magnificus* J. Fryer & B. Hylmö in New Plantsman 5: 138 (1998). Type: China, W Sichuan, north of Kangding, September 1910, *E. H. Wilson 4131* (holo A, iso BM, K).

Shrub, 3–5 m. Branches erect, arched and spreading; branchlets spiraled and distichous, maroon, initially tomentose-pilose. Leaves deciduous, subcoriaceous, on sterile shoots suborbicular, broadly elliptic, ovate or rhomboid, 34–40 × 20–32 mm, apex acute, acuminate or apiculate, base obtuse or cuneate, upper surface brownish green soon light green, glabrescent, veins 5–6, lower surface initially densely pilose; petiole 5–8 mm, pilose-villous. Fertile shoots 25–40 mm, including 3–4 leaves and a lax, 5- to 12-flowered inflorescence; pedicels 3–12 mm, subglabrous. Hypanthium cupulate, glabrous; sepals acute or obtuse, glabrous, margin sparsely villous. Flower buds white. Corolla 12–14 mm, petals spreading, white, with hair-tuft. Stamens (16–)20; filaments white; anthers white. Styles often unequal in length. Fruit depressed-globose, 10–13 mm, crimson to rich red with cherry, glabrous, calyx lobes suberect, stamens and style exserted. Nutlets 2 connate, rarely 1, style remains at or near apex.

> Seasons: Flowers May; fruit ripe September–October.
> Chromosomes: Tetraploid (Sax 1954, as *C. multiflorus*). Apomictic, true from seed.
> Hardiness: –18°C (–1°F).
> Area: China (Sichuan).
> Notes: *Cotoneaster magnificus* is a very decorative shrub with a multitude of large, wide-open flowers in spring, followed by an abundance of huge fruit which weigh down the branches in the autumn. This species is commonly cultivated in the United States and Canada. It was distributed by the Arnold Arboretum as *C. multiflorus* #1334-1910.

7. *Cotoneaster meyeri* Pojarkova in Not. Syst. Inst. Bot. Acad. Sci. USSR 17: 185 (1955). Type: Azerbaijan, Ganja, Kjurai-Czai river, 27 September 1937, *A. Pojarkova 289* (holo LE).

Shrub, 2–3 m. Branches erect, arched and spreading; branchlets spiraled or distichous, khaki to maroon, slightly verruculose, initially pilose-strigose. Leaves deciduous, chartaceous, on sterile shoots broadly elliptic, broadly ovate or ovate, 35–60 × 21–38 mm, apex acute or acuminate, base obtuse or cuneate, upper surface reddish or brownish green, shiny, soon dark green and dull, initially sparsely long-haired pilose, veins 5–7, lower surface light green, dull, sparsely pilose; petiole 5–12 mm, pilose. Fertile shoots 40–60 mm, including 4–5 leaves and a lax, 7- to 12-flowered inflorescence; pedicels 3–8 mm, minutely verruculose, pilose. Hypanthium cupulate, minutely verruculose, sparsely villous-strigose; sepals acute, apiculate, ligulate or obtuse, sparsely villous, border broad, membranous, apex purple, glabrous, margin tomentose. Flower buds white with faint brown stripes. Corolla campanulate, 12 mm, petals slightly concave, white, sometimes with small hair-tuft. Stamens 20; filaments white; anthers white. Fruit globose or ellipsoid, 8–11 mm, maroon-purple drying black, pruinose, glabrescent, calyx lobes flat, navel open. Nutlets 2 connate, style remains $^4/_5$ from base.

Seasons: Flowers May; fruit ripe August.

Chromosomes: Tetraploid (Krügel 1992a). Apomictic, true from seed.

Hardiness: −18°C (−1°F).

Area: Turkey. Armenia. Georgia. Azerbaijan. Iran.

Notes: *Cotoneaster meyeri* is native to an isolated outpost to the west of the range of other species in series *Multiflori*. Its nearest relative is *C. submultiflorus* in the Tian Shan range of Kyrgyzstan. This shrub is especially handsome when covered with its richly colored fruit. Recently reintroduced into cultivation.

8. **Cotoneaster multiflorus** Bunge in Ledebour, Fl. Altaica 2: 220 (1830); illustr. Ic.
   Plant. Fl. Rossicae t. 274 (1831). Type: Kazakhstan, Chingiz-tau mountains, *Meyer 1528* (holo LE). **PLATE 42**.

Shrub or small tree, 3–6 m. Branches erect, arched, spreading, sometimes pendulous, slender; branchlets spiraled and distichous, light brown, slightly verruculose, initially sparsely pilose-strigose. Leaves deciduous, chartaceous, on sterile shoots broadly ovate or suborbicular, 30–46 × 21–40 mm, apex acute seldom obtuse, base obtuse, upper surface reddish brown, soon light green, dull, initially pilose, veins 4–7, lower surface initially densely pilose; petiole 6–10 mm, pilose. Fertile shoots 25–40 mm, including 3–4 leaves and a lax, 10- to 20-flowered inflorescence; pedicels 3–7 mm, subglabrous. Hypanthium cupulate, glabrous; sepals obtuse or acute, glabrous. Flower buds white. Corolla 9–10 mm, petals spreading, wide-spaced, white, with hair-tuft. Stamens 20; filaments white; anthers white. Fruit globose or depressed-globose, succulent, 10–11 mm, red, glabrous, calyx lobes flat. Nutlets 2 connate, style remains at apex.

Seasons: Flowers May; fruit ripe September.

Chromosomes: Tetraploid (Hensen 1966; Gladkova 1968; Kroon 1975; Krügel 1992a). Apomictic, true from seed.

Hardiness: −21°C (−6°F).

Area: Kazakhstan.

Notes: The above description for *Cotoneaster multiflorus* is based on the type held in the herbarium of the V. L. Komarov Botanical Institute in St. Petersburg; the illustration made by Bunge in 1831 (branch showing unripe fruit); and the taxon known as *C. multiflorus* which has long been common in cultivation in Central Europe and Scandinavia. *Cotoneaster multiflorus* is similar to *C. reflexus* which came into cultivation around 1870, but in an 1892 publication, an illustration of *C. reflexus* shows a long fertile shoot of around 60 cm and a corolla which is mostly widely campanulate, contrary to *C. multiflorus*. In spring *C. multiflorus* is smothered with streamers of flowers along its slender hanging branches and in autumn is dotted with bright fruit. It was first introduced to the RBG Kew in England in 1837. It is commonly cultivated in Europe and sometimes used in amenity plantings.

9. *Cotoneaster przewalskii* Pojarkova in Not. Syst. Inst. Bot. Acad. Sci. USSR 21: 196 (1961). Type: China, SE Gansu, Choni monastery at T'ao-ho river, 7 June 1885, G. N. Potanin (holo LE).

Shrub or small tree, 3–5 m. Branches erect, arched and wide-spreading; branchlets spiraled and distichous, purple-brown with large lenticels, initially pilose. Leaves deciduous, chartaceous, on sterile shoots elliptic or broadly elliptic, 45–50 × 30–27 mm, apex acuminate or acute, base obtuse or cuneate, upper surface with brownish flush, soon light green, glabrescent, veins 5–6, lower surface slightly reticulate, glabrescent; petiole 5–7 mm, pilose. Fertile shoots 30–70 mm, including 4 leaves and a lax, 5- to 15-flowered inflorescence; pedicels 4–15 mm, pilose. Hypanthium campanulate, very sparsely pilose; sepals acute or obtuse, glabrescent, border membranous, red-purple, margin villous. Flower buds white with brownish pink dots. Corolla mostly widely campanulate, 11–13 mm, petals spreading, concave, white tinged pale purple, sometimes with hair-tuft. Stamens (18–)20; filaments white with pale purple base; anthers white. Fruit globose, 12–13 mm, succulent, crimson with cherry, skin splitting at maturity, glabrous, calyx lobes flat. Nutlets 2 connate, style remains at apex.

Seasons: Flowers May–June; fruit ripe August.

Chromosomes: Unknown. Apomictic, true from seed.

Hardiness: –21°C (–6°F).

Area: China (Gansu, Sichuan, Qinghai, Ningxia).

Notes: *Cotoneaster przewalskii* is fairly common in cultivation, often as *C. multiflorus*, and is a very pretty and elegant shrub with an open habit. It looks good with a low-growing *Clematis* draped through it. Recently reintroduced into cultivation.

10. *Cotoneaster purpurascens* J. Fryer & B. Hylmö in New Plantsman 8: 228, 237 (2001). Type: cult. England, Sussex, Highdown (garden of Sir Frederick Stern), 28 June 1988, as *C. multiflorus* var. *calocarpus* #821, raised from seed collected in S Gansu, *R. Farrer 403* (holo WSY). PLATE 43.

Shrub or small tree, 4–8 m. Branches erect and wide-spreading; branchlets spiraled or distichous, slender, maroon, minutely verruculose, initially strigose-tomentose. Leaves deciduous, chartaceous, on sterile shoots broadly ovate or ovate, 31–50 × 21–28 mm, apex acute or acuminate, base obtuse or cuneate, upper surface brownish red to purple soon dark green, dull, sparsely pilose, veins 5–8, lower surface initially densely strigose-pilose; petiole 5–8 mm, strigose. Fertile shoots 25–35 mm, including 2–4 leaves and a 5- to 11-flowered inflorescence; pedicels 3–6 mm, sparsely pilose. Hypanthium campanulate, glabrescent; sepals acute, apiculate or obtuse, glabrescent, margin villous. Flower buds pale purple and red. Corolla mostly widely campanulate, 10–12 mm, petals slightly concave, mauve with purple base, sometimes with small hair-tuft. Stamens 12–18(–20); filaments pale pink or pale purple; anthers white. Styles often unequal in length. Fruit globose or subglobose, succulent, 11–12 mm, crimson to maroon, glabrous, calyx lobes flat. Nutlets 2 connate, rarely 1, style remains at apex.

   Seasons: Flowers May–June; fruit ripe October–November.
   Chromosomes: Unknown. Apomictic, true from seed.
   Hardiness: −21°C (−6°F).
   Area: China (Gansu, Sichuan).
   Notes: With its myriad of pale purplish pink flowers and rich purple leaves which age dark purplish green, *Cotoneaster purpurascens* is a striking and unusual shrub. In Sir Frederick Stern's garden at Highdown in Sussex, England, there is a fine display of this species grown from seed collected by Reginald Farrer, cascading from top to bottom of the old chalk-pit garden. Although the exact origin of this species is slightly obscure, Farrer's notes indicate that it was collected in 1914–1915 in China in the hills of Gansu province, where it was found growing on one roadside only; he notes that it was a small, lax tree-shrub with long sprays and big bunches of small cherrylike fruit.

11. *Cotoneaster reflexus* Carrière in Rev. Hort. 342: 520 (1871); illustr. Rev. Hort. p. 327 (1892). Type: cult. Sweden, Malmö Kungsparken, planted c. 1890, 20 May 1934, Bertil Hylmö (lecto designated GB).

Shrub or small tree, 3–4 m. Branches erect, arched and spreading; branchlets spiraled or distichous, reddish brown, initially sparsely pilose-strigose. Leaves deciduous, chartaceous, on sterile shoots suborbicular or broadly ovate, 36–54 × 25–36 mm, apex obtuse or acute, base obtuse, upper surface reddish, soon light green, dull, glabrescent, veins 6–8, lower surface reticulate, midrib often reddish, glabrescent; petiole 6–12 mm, pilose. Fertile shoots 40–70 mm, including 3–4 leaves and lax, 8- to 18-flowered inflorescence; pedicels 3–12 mm, glabrescent. Hypanthium campanulate, glabrescent; sepals obtuse or ligulate, erose, glabrous. Corolla widely campanulate, 10–12 mm, petals spreading, slightly concave, white, with hair-tuft. Stamens 20–24; filaments white; anthers white. Fruit globose, crimson, glabrous, calyx lobes flat. Nutlets 2 connate, style remains at apex.

   Seasons: Flowers May; fruit ripe September.
   Chromosomes: Unknown. Apomictic, true from seed.

Hardiness: −18°C (−1°F).

Area: China (exact origin unknown).

Notes: *Cotoneaster reflexus* was introduced by M. E. Simons from his 1863 travels in China in the provinces of Hubei, Hunan, and Sichuan. The herbarium labels for his collections were sadly destroyed, so the exact origin was lost.

12. *Cotoneaster silvestrii* Pampanini in Nuov. Giorn. Bot. Italy 17: 288 (1910). Type: China, Hubei, Mount Niang Niang, July 1907, *C. Silvestri 900* (holo FI).

Shrub, 2–3 m. Branchlets maroon, initially densely pilose. Leaves deciduous, subcoriaceous, on sterile shoots ovate or ovate-lanceolate, 30–45 × 14–23 mm, apex acute, base obtuse, upper surface dark green, dull, glabrous, veins 6–8 lightly impressed, lower surface tomentose or densely pilose; petiole 5–8 mm, tomentose. Fertile shoots 25–40 mm, including 3–4 leaves and a lax, 5- to 10-flowered inflorescence; pedicels 3–7 mm, densely pilose. Hypanthium densely pilose; sepals acute, tomentose, margin tomentose. Stamens 20. Fruit subglobose, calyx lobes flat, navel open. Nutlets 2 connate, style remains at apex.

Area: China (Hubei).

Notes: *Cotoneaster silvestrii* is not known in cultivation. This species is closely related to *C. veitchii* but differs, among other details, in its narrower leaves.

13. *Cotoneaster submultiflorus* Popov in Bull. Soc. Imp. Nat. Mosc. 44: 126 (1935). Synonym: *C. pseudomultiflorus* Popov (1935). Type: Kazakhstan, Alma Ata, Almatinka Minor river, 18 June 1933, M. Popov (holo LE).

Shrub, 2–3 m. Branches narrowly erect; branchlets spiraled, light brown, densely lenticellate, initially pilose-strigose. Leaves deciduous, chartaceous, on sterile shoots often spiraled, suborbicular or broadly ovate, 33–60 × 25–49 mm, apex apiculate or acuminate, base cuneate or obtuse, upper surface light green (without initial color flush), dull, glabrescent, veins 5–8, lower surface initially sparsely pilose; petiole 10–18 mm, villous. Fertile shoots 20–45 mm, with up to 4 leaves and a lax, 5- to 17-flowered inflorescence; pedicels 2–6 mm, sparsely pilose. Hypanthium narrowly cupulate, sparsely pilose; sepals acute or obtuse, glabrous, apex often purple, margin villous. Flower buds white. Corolla 7–9 mm, petals spreading, white, sometimes with hair-tuft. Stamens 18–20, equaling petals in length; filaments white; anthers white. Fruit globose or depressed-globose, succulent, skin often splitting at maturity, 6–8 mm, crimson to cherry, glabrous, calyx lobes suberect, navel open with stamens and style exserted. Nutlets (1–)2 connate, style remains near apex.

Seasons: Flowers June; fruit ripe August–September.

Chromosomes: Unknown. Apomictic, true from seed.

Hardiness: −21°C (−6°F).

Area: Kazakhstan (Tian Shan and Pamirs). Kyrgyzstan.

Notes: *Cotoneaster submultiflorus* is unusual among species in series *Multiflori* in being quite erect in habit. It has prettily shaped, delicate leaves, little flowers, and many fruit. This species shows some similarity to those in series *Megalocarpi*.

14. *Cotoneaster tanpaensis* J. Fryer & B. Hylmö, *sp. nov.* Type: China, Sichuan, Tanpa district, Maoniu, 1 October 1934, *Harry Smith 12646* (holo UPS). **PLATE 44**.
Shrub, 2–3 m. Branches erect, spreading; branchlets spiraled, maroon, minutely verruculose, initially pilose-strigose. Leaves deciduous, chartaceous, on sterile shoots elliptic or broadly elliptic, 32–45 × 21–25 mm, apex acute or acuminate, base cuneate or obtuse, upper surface becoming dark green, sparsely pilose-strigose, veins 5–6, lower surface initially pilose; petiole 5–10 mm, pilose. Fertile shoots 30–45 mm, including 3–4 leaves and a lax, 5- to 10-flowered inflorescence; pedicels 3–10 mm, glabrous. Hypanthium widely campanulate, glabrous; sepals obtuse or acute, glabrous, apex reddish, margin sparsely villous. Flower buds pinkish or white. Corolla 11–12 mm, petals semispreading, deeply concave, white, sometimes with small hair tuft. Stamens 14–20; filaments white, ageing slightly purple; anthers white or with margin somewhat purple. Fruit globose, succulent, 10–11 mm, crimson to pale ruby, glabrous, calyx lobes flat, navel open. Nutlets 1(–2) connate, style remains at apex.
   Seasons: Flowers May; fruit ripe September.
   Chromosomes: Tetraploid (Bailey, pers. comm.). Apomictic, true from seed.
   Hardiness: –18°C (–1°F).
   Area: China (Sichuan).
   Notes: *Cotoneaster tanpaensis* is one of the many collections of *Cotoneaster* made by Harry Smith. It has distinct, wide bell-shaped flowers with petals which are very noticeably concave. The species is often found in botanic gardens in Scandinavia where it is sometimes frozen back to the ground by the extreme cold, but frequently regrows to its former beauty.

15. *Cotoneaster tumeticus* Pojarkova in Not. Syst. Inst. Bot. Acad. Sci. USSR 21: 204 (1961). Type: China, Ningxia, Toumet, May 1855, A. David (holo LE).
Shrub, 2–3 m. Branches loosely erect, arched and spreading; branchlets spiraled, maroon, densely lenticellate, initially pilose-strigose. Leaves deciduous, chartaceous, on sterile shoots suborbicular, broadly ovate or broadly elliptic, 36–60 × 37–47 mm, apex obtuse, acute or apiculate, base widely cuneate or obtuse, upper surface brownish to blackish green, soon dark green, shiny, sparsely pilose, veins 4–7, lower surface light green, initially densely villous; petiole 5–13 mm, tomentose. Fertile shoots 30–40 mm, including 3–4 leaves and a lax, 5- to 10-flowered inflorescence; pedicels 3–12 mm, sparsely pilose. Hypanthium cupulate, glabrescent; sepals acute or obtuse, red to maroon, glabrous, margin pilose. Flower buds pale purple. Corolla 13 mm, petals spreading, white, with hairtuft. Stamens erect, 20; filaments white or with pale purple base; anthers white. Fruit globose or depressed-globose, succulent, 11–12 mm, crimson to maroon, glabrous, calyx lobes suberect, stamens and style exserted. Nutlets 2 connate, style remains at apex.

Seasons: Flowers May; fruit ripe August–September.

Chromosomes: Tetraploid (Jewsbury, pers. comm.). Apomictic, true from seed.

Hardiness: –21°C (–6°F).

Area: China (Ningxia, Heilongjiang). Mongolia and adjacent areas.

Notes: *Cotoneaster tumeticus* is an outstanding species. In spring multitudes of showy flowers contrast well with the bronzed new leaves; later the branches are laden with huge fruit. A lovely shrub. Recently reintroduced into cultivation.

16. ***Cotoneaster veitchii*** (Rehder & E. H. Wilson) G. Klotz in Wiss. Z. Martin-Luther-Univ. Halle-Wittenberg, Math.-Naturwiss. 6: 974 (1957). Synonym: *C. racemiflorus* (Desfontaines) Booth ex Bosse var. *veitchii* Rehder & E. H. Wilson (1917). Type: cult. United States, Arnold Arboretum, Veitch-Wilson II 1079 as *C. acutifolius*, June 1916, *1316 A. R.* (holo A); raised from seed collected in China, W Hubei, Xingshan Xian. PLATE 45.

Shrub or small tree, 3–5 m. Branches erect, arched and wide-spreading; branchlets distichous, reddish brown, initially tomentose-strigose. Leaves deciduous, coriaceous or subcoriaceous, on sterile shoots broadly elliptic, ovate or suborbicular, 28–41 × 22–31 mm, apex acute or acuminate, base obtuse, upper surface mid-green to dark brownish green, shiny, initially villous, veins 4–5 lightly impressed, lower surface grayish green, densely villous; petiole 4–6 mm, tomentose. Fertile shoots 25–45 mm, including 3–4 leaves and a lax, 4- to 15-flowered inflorescence; pedicels 3–8 mm, densely villous–strigose. Hypanthium campanulate, villous-tomentose; sepals acute or apiculate, tomentose, border mostly reddish, glabrous, margin tomentose. Flower buds white tinged pink. Corolla 12–15 mm, petals spreading, slightly concave, white, with small hair-tuft. Stamens 20; filaments white; anthers white. Fruit globose, succulent, 13 mm, crimson ageing maroon, skin often splitting at maturity, sparsely villous, calyx lobes flat, navel slightly open. Nutlets (1–)2(–3) connate, style remains at constricted apex.

Seasons: Flowers June; fruit ripe October; autumn leaves yellow and gold.

Chromosomes: Tetraploid (Krügel 1992a). Apomictic, true from seed.

Hardiness: –21°C (–6°F).

Area: China (Hubei, Shaanxi).

Notes: *Cotoneaster veitchii* is the last species to flower and fruit in series *Multiflori*. It is the odd species within the series inasmuch that it has coriaceous leaves, a tomentose hypanthium, and some of the fruit containing three nutlets. Despite these differences, C. veitchii is placed in this series because of the firmly fused nutlets. It makes a very attractive shrub which is extremely floriferous and heavily fruited. It is especially popular in cultivation in Central Europe, where it is sometimes used as a street tree grafted onto *Crataegus*.

9. Series *Tomentelli* G. Klotz in Wiss. Z. Martin-Luther-Univ. Halle-Wittenberg, Math.-Naturwiss. 12: 760 (1963).

Small shrubs to small trees. Branchlets growing at 45- to 90-degree angle to branch, initially shortly pilose-strigose. Leaves with lower surface mostly shortly pilose, often densely so. Hypanthium pilose. Anthers mostly purple-black or pale pink. Fruit red or crimson, sometimes initially white or pale yellow. Nutlets 1, or 2 connate (fused).

Very early to mid season.

China (Sichuan, Gansu, Qinghai).

6 species: *C. albokermesinus*, *C. gonggashanensis*, *C. hersianus*, *C. microcarpus*, *C. potaninii*, *C. tomentellus*.

Key to Series *Tomentelli*

1a. Upper leaf surface pilose-villous; hypanthium villous or densely pilose-villous; fruit obovoid or subglobose 2

1b. Upper leaf surface glabrous or subglabrous; hypanthium sometimes pilose-strigose; fruit mostly globose 3

2a. Leaves ≤ 44 × 30 mm, petiole 5–9 mm; pedicels 1–7 mm, fruit milky red, nutlets 1 sometimes 2 . . . .*C. tomentellus*

2b. Leaves ≤ 26 × 15 mm, petiole 3–5 mm; pedicels 1–15 mm, fruit purple-red, nutlets mostly 2 . . . . *C. potaninii*

3a. Leaves 12–27 mm; fertile shoots 15–20 mm; corolla 6–7 mm; fruit 7–8 mm . . . .*C. microcarpus*

3b. Leaves 30–44 mm; fertile shoots 20–50 mm; corolla 7–10(–12) mm; fruit 9–11 mm 4

4a. Leaves subcoriaceous, veins 3–4; fertile shoots 40–50 mm; anthers purple-black; fruit white-pink . . . .*C. albokermesinus*

4b. Leaves chartaceous, veins 5–7; fertile shoots 20–30 mm; anthers mauve; fruit pink-red . . . .*C. gonggashanensis*

1. *Cotoneaster albokermesinus* J. Fryer & B. Hylmö in New Plantsman 5:132 (1998). Type: China, Sichuan, Taofu district, 14 September 1934, *Harry Smith 12226* (holo UPS). PLATE 46.

Shrub or small tree, 3–5 m. Branches loosely erect and wide-spreading, long and slender; branchlets spiraled, dark purple, initially pilose-strigose. Leaves deciduous, subcoriaceous, on sterile shoots broadly elliptic, broadly ovate or suborbicular, 30–44 × 25–32 mm, apex obtuse or acute, base obtuse or cuneate, upper surface dark bluish green, dull, glabrescent, veins 3–5, lower surface pale grayish green, reticulate, initially pilose; petiole 5–10 mm, densely pilose. Fertile shoots 40–50 mm, including (1–)2–3 leaves and a lax, 7- to 15-flowered inflorescence; pedicels 4–8 mm, sparsely pilose-strigose. Hypanthium cupulate, initially sparsely pilose; sepals acute or obtuse, subglabrous, apex red-purple, margin tomentose. Flower buds white. Corolla 8–10(–12) mm, petals spreading, white, with long hair-tuft. Stamens (10–)12(–20); filaments white; anthers purple-black. Fruit depressed-globose, 9–11 mm, white with yellowish pale crimson, glabrous, calyx lobes glabrous. Nutlets mostly 1, sometimes 2 connate, style remains at or near apex.

Seasons: Flowers May; fruit ripe August–September.

Chromosomes: Unknown. Apomictic, true from seed.

Hardiness: –21°C (–6°F).

Area: China (Sichuan).

Notes: In spring *Cotoneaster albokermesinus* is covered with masses of snowy white flowers. Its fruit, also produced in great profusion, are an unusual creamy white with a deep pink blush on the side which faces the sun. These fruit are disliked by birds. A magnificent species, *C. albokermesinus* is well worthy of cultivation. It is seemingly resistant to fireblight.

2. *Cotoneaster gonggashanensis* J. Fryer & B. Hylmö, *sp. nov.* Type: China, Sichuan, Liuba, 13 September 1981, *Kim Sorvig 104* (holo K); cult. England, RBG Kew, J. Fryer, 22 May 1991 (holo GB). **PLATE 47.**

Shrub or small tree, 3–6 m. Branches erect, arched, wide-spreading; branchlets spiraled, maroon, minutely verruculose, initially pilose-strigose. Leaves deciduous, chartaceous, on sterile shoots broadly elliptic to suborbicular, 30–42 × 20–33 mm, apex acute or obtuse, base obtuse, upper surface mid-green, dull, subglabrous, veins 5–7, lower surface densely pilose, glabrescent; petiole 5–11 mm, initially pilose-strigose. Fertile shoots 20–35 mm, including 2–4 leaves and a lax, 5- to 15-flowered inflorescence; pedicels 2–10 mm, minutely verruculose, pilose-strigose. Hypanthium campanulate, minutely verruculose, strigose with a pilose base; sepals acute or obtuse, minutely verruculose, glabrous, margin sparsely villous. Flower buds white. Corolla 7–9 mm, petals spreading, white, with long hair-tuft. Stamens 15–20; filaments white; anthers purple. Fruit globose, succulent, 8–10 mm, pale crimson to red, dull, calyx lobes flat, navel wide open with nutlets exserted. Nutlets 1, sometimes 2 connate, style remains at apex.

Seasons: Flowers April–May; fruit ripe August.

Hardiness: probably around –18°C (–1°F).

Area: China (Sichuan).

Notes: With its verruculose pedicels, hypanthium, and sepals, *Cotoneaster gonggashanensis* is a unique species. It is rare in cultivation.

3. *Cotoneaster hersianus* J. Fryer & B. Hylmö, *sp. nov.* Type: China, Shaanxi, 1923, *J. Hers 2825* [cult. England, Froxfield, J. Fryer 1021, 11 September 2001] (holo GB). **PLATE 48.**

Shrub, 1.5–2 m. Branches loosely erect, arched, pendulous, very slender. Branchlets spiraled, brown-violet, initially pilose. Leaves deciduous, chartaceous, on sterile shoots broadly obovate or broadly elliptic, 53–60 × 35–40 mm, apex acute or obtuse, base cuneate, upper surface dark green, dull or slightly shiny, glabrescent, veins 4–6, lower surface grayish green, pilose; petiole 5–9 mm, initially pilose. Fertile shoots 25–60 mm, including 2–3 leaves and a lax, 4- to 7-flowered inflorescence; pedicels 5–12 mm, sparsely pilose. Hypanthium campanulate, shiny, glabrescent; sepals obtuse, apiculate or acute, glabrous, margin villous. Flower buds rose-pink. Corolla 9–11 mm, petals spreading or semi-spreading, emarginate, white with rose-pink, sometimes with hair-tuft. Stamens (14–)20; filaments white; anthers white. Fruit succulent, subglobose or turbinate, 14–17 mm, crimson to rich ruby, glabrous, calyx lobes flat. Nutlets 1–2 connate, style remains at apex.

Seasons: Flowers May, reflowers October; fruit ripe September.

Chromosomes: Unknown. Apomictic, true from seed.

Hardiness: –18°C (–1°F).

Area: China (Shaanxi).

Notes: *Cotoneaster hersianus* is a little-known species originally collected by the Belgian diplomat and plant collector J. Hers. This unusual *Cotoneaster* is often 4-petaled. It has the largest fruit of any species, often splitting when fully ripe. Well worth growing. Not in key.

4. *Cotoneaster microcarpus* (Rehder & E. H. Wilson) Flinck & B. Hylmö in Bot. Not. (Lund) 119: 459 (1966). Synonym: *C. racemiflorus* (Desfontaines) Booth ex Bosse var. *microcarpus* Rehder & E. H. Wilson (1912). Type: China, W Sichuan, Min valley, near Sung-pan Ting, September 1910, *E. H. Wilson 4014* (holo A).

Shrub, 1.5–2 m. Branches loosely erect, arched, pendulous, slender; branchlets spiraled, maroon, shiny, lenticellate, initially short-haired strigose-villous. Leaves deciduous, chartaceous or subcoriaceous, on sterile shoots ovate, elliptic or suborbicular, 12–27 × 10–22 mm, apex obtuse or acute, base cuneate or obtuse, upper surface mid-green, dull, glabrescent, veins 5–7 lightly impressed, lower surface initially densely pilose-villous; petiole 4–7 mm, initially strigose-villous. Fertile shoots 15–20 mm, including 3–4 leaves and a 5- to 18-flowered inflorescence; pedicels 1–3, thin, initially strigose-villous. Hypanthium widely cupulate, pilose-strigose; sepals acute or acuminate, pilose-strigose, apex red, margin villous. Flower buds white. Corolla 6–7 mm, petals spreading, white, with small hair-tuft. Stamens 20; filaments white; anthers white to pale pink. Fruit subglobose, 7–8 mm, rich red, shiny, glabrous, calyx lobes suberect, navel open. Nutlets 1(–2 connate), style remains at apex.

Seasons: Flowers May–June, reflowers August–September; fruit ripe September; autumn leaves gold-dappled.

Chromosomes: Unknown. Apomictic, true from seed.

Hardiness: –15°C (5°F).

Area: China (Sichuan and bordering Yunnan).

Notes: *Cotoneaster microcarpus* is an extremely elegant and pretty species, resembling a *Spiraea* in habit and in its numerous white flowers, with small beadlike red fruit. Recently reintroduced into cultivation.

5. *Cotoneaster potaninii* Pojarkova in Not. Syst. Inst. Bot. Acad. Sci. USSR 21: 202 (1961). Type: China, Sichuan, Kam in Fu-piang-ho river valley, between Sching-tien-tze village and the lamasery, 2 August 1893, G. Potanin (holo LE).

Shrub, 1.5–2 m. Branches erect, arched and pendulous, slender; branchlets spiraled, brown and shiny, initially villous. Leaves deciduous, chartaceous, on sterile shoots ovate, 9–26 × 5–15 mm, apex and base rotund, upper surface dark green, dull, densely pilose, veins 4–5, lower surface densely pilose-villous; petiole 3–5 mm, thin, villous. Fertile shoots 15–35 mm, including 2–3 leaves and a lax, 2- to 10-flowered inflorescence; pedicels 1–15 mm, thin, villous or subglabrous. Hypanthium cupulate, densely pilose-villous; sepals acute, densely pilose-villous. Corolla 9–11 mm, petals spreading, white, frequently with hair-tuft. Stamens with filaments white; anthers purple. Fruit obovoid, 6–8 mm, red to purple-red, pilose, calyx lobes densely pilose, navel open. Nutlets (1–)2 connate, style remains $^9/_{10}$ from base.

Area: China (Sichuan, Yunnan).

Notes: *Cotoneaster potaninii* is not yet known in cultivation. The ovate leaves with rounded ends are very typical and are good identification features for this species.

6. *Cotoneaster tomentellus* Pojarkova in Not. Syst. Inst. Bot. Acad. Sci. USSR 21: 200 (1961). Synonym: *C. racemiflorus* (Desfontaines) Booth ex Bosse var. *soongoricus* Rehder & E. H. Wilson (1912), non *C. soongoricus* (Regel) Popov (1935). Type: China, W Sichuan, Kangding, October 1908, *E. H. Wilson 1317* (holo A, iso LE).

Shrub, 3–5 m. Branches loosely erect and spreading; branchlets spiraled, light to reddish brown, and lenticellate, initially pilose-villous. Leaves deciduous, chartaceous to subcoriaceous, on sterile shoots broadly elliptic, broadly obovate or suborbicular, 29–44 × 19–30 mm, apex obtuse, base obtuse or cuneate, upper surface dark grayish green, dull, pilose-villous, veins 4–5, lower surface grayish green, villous; petiole 5–9 mm, villous. Fertile shoots 25–40 mm, including 4 leaves and a lax, 5- to 20-flowered inflorescence; pedicels 1–7 mm, villous. Hypanthium cupulate, villous; sepals acute or obtuse, villous, margin densely villous. Flower buds white. Corolla 12 mm, petals spreading, white, with long hair-tuft. Stamens (16–)20; filaments white; anthers purple to black. Fruit globose to obovoid, 10–13 mm, cherry-red with pale yellow on shaded side, villous or glabrous, calyx lobes flat, navel open. Nutlets 1(–2 connate), rarely 2–3 free, style remains at or near apex.

Seasons: Flowers May–June; fruit ripe September.

Chromosomes: Tetraploid (Hensen 1966). Apomictic, true from seed.

Hardiness: −18°C (−1°F).

Area: China (Sichuan).

Notes: *Cotoneaster tomentellus* is common in cultivation, most, if not all, shrubs originating from the *Wilson 1317* type collection. It is often grown as *C. racemiflorus* var. *songoricus*. This shrub is a beautiful sight, even from afar, with its soft gray leaves contrasting well with the abundant coral- to crimson-colored fruit. Received RHS Award of Merit in 1960.

10. Series *Hebephylli* G. Klotz in Wiss. Z. Martin-Luther-Univ. Halle-Wittenberg,
     Math.-Naturwiss. 12: 766 (1963). Including series *Tibetici* G. Klotz (1968).

Medium shrubs to small trees. Branchlets growing at (60–)90-degree angle to branch.
Leaves deciduous or semievergreen, on sterile shoots distichous or spiraled. Hypanthium
campanulate or cupulate. Anthers purple-black. Nutlets mostly 1, sometimes 2 connate
or 2 free.

    Early to mid season.

    China (Yunnan). Tibet. Bhutan. India (Arunachal Pradesh).

    12 species: *C. arbusculus*, *C. chungtiensis*, *C. cooperi*, *C. hebephyllus*, *C. incanus*, *C. majusculus*, *C. monopyrenus*, *C. muliensis*, *C. omissus*, *C. tibeticus*, *C. transens*, *C. zayulensis*.

Key to Series *Hebephylli*

1a. Leaves lanceolate or lanceo-elliptic; flower buds sometimes with pink dots; corolla
    5–7 mm . . . . ***C. cooperi***

1b. Leaves elliptic, obovate or suborbicular; flower buds white; corolla 7–12 mm 2

2a. Branchlets tomentose-pilose; leaves ≤ 103 mm, apex acute; fruit often with villose hairs
    . . . . ***C. transens***

2b. Branchlets pilose-strigose; leaves ≤ 25–60 mm, apex mostly obtuse; fruit glabrous 3

3a. Leaves 25–30 mm, petiole 2–8 mm; sepals mostly cuspidate 4

3b. Leaves 38–60 mm, petiole 4–12 mm; sepals mostly obtuse 5

4a. Inflorescence 5- to 20-flowered; stamens 12–16; fruit ruby . . . . ***C. incanus***

4b. Inflorescence 3- to 9-flowered; stamens 20; fruit purple-black . . . . ***C. muliensis***

5a. Leaf veins lightly impressed, base mostly obtuse; fruit mostly obovoid, ruby becoming
    purple-black . . . . ***C. monopyrenus***

5b. Leaf veins not impressed, base mostly cuneate; fruit mostly globose, crimson, cherry or
    ruby. 6

6a. Leaves coriaceous, dark green; fertile shoots 40–70 mm; inflorescence ≤ 25-flowered
    . . . . ***C. omissus***

6b. Leaves chartaceous, mid-green; fertile shoots 15–40 mm; inflorescence ≤ 16-flowered 7

7a. Leaves mostly suborbicular; hypanthium cupulate; corolla 10–12 mm; fruit crimson with
    yellow. . . . . ***C. chungtiensis***

7b. Leaves mostly broadly elliptic; hypanthium mostly campanulate; corolla 7–11 mm; fruit red
    to ruby. 8

8a. Leaves ≤ 40 mm, petiole 4–7 mm; fertile shoots 25–40 mm; nutlet 1 . . . . ***C. hebephyllus***

8b. Leaves ≤ 50 mm; petiole 5–12 mm; fertile shoots 15–30 mm; nutlets (1–)2 . . . . . ***C. zayulensis***

1. ***Cotoneaster arbusculus*** G. Klotz in Wiss. Z. Friedrich-Schiller-Univ. Jena, Math.-
   Naturwiss. 17: 337 (1968). Type: China, Yunnan, Shunning, Wumulung, 8 July
   1938, *T. T. Yu 16603* (holo E).

Shrub or small tree, 5–6 m. Branches erect and spreading; branchlets spiraled, pilose-strigose. Leaves deciduous, chartaceous, on sterile shoots elliptic, 17–52 × 9–24 mm, apex acute or obtuse, base cuneate or obtuse, upper surface mid-green, dull, sparsely strigose midrib, veins impressed, lower surface sparsely villous-strigose; petiole 2–7 mm, densely villous-strigose. Fertile shoots with a 9- to 15-flowered inflorescence; pedicels 10–20 mm, strigose-villous. Hypanthium sparsely pilose-strigose; sepals glabrous. Corolla 8–9 mm, petals spreading, white, glabrous. Stamens 18–20. Styles 2. Fruit not seen.

    Area: China (Yunnan).

    Notes: *Cotoneaster arbusculus* is not known in cultivation. This species is very closely related to *C. transens*. Not in key.

2. ***Cotoneaster chungtiensis*** (T. T. Yu) J. Fryer & B. Hylmö stat. et nom. nov. Synonym: *C. multiflorus* Bunge var. *atropurpureus* T. T. Yu in Acta Phytotax. Sin. 8: 219
   (1963). Type: China, Yunnan, Atuntze, September 1935, *C. W. Wang 70235* (holo PE).
   PLATE 49.

Shrub, 2–3 m. Branches loosely erect, irregularly wide-spreading; branchlets spiraled, maroon, shiny, lenticellate, initially pilose-strigose. Leaves deciduous, chartaceous, on sterile shoots suborbicular, broadly elliptic or broadly obovate, 26–38 × 20–25 mm, apex obtuse or acute, base cuneate, upper surface mid-green, dull, glabrous, veins 5–7, lower surface pilose-villous; petiole 4–8 mm, pilose-strigose. Fertile shoots 20–35 mm, including 3–4 leaves and a lax, 9- to 16-flowered inflorescence; pedicels 1–4 mm, pilose-strigose. Hypanthium cupulate, glabrescent; sepals acute or obtuse, subglabrous, often with broad, membranous whitish green border, apex red, margin villous. Flower buds white. Corolla 10–12 mm, petals spreading, white, with hair-tuft. Stamens 20; filaments white; anthers mauve to purple. Fruit depressed-globose, 7–8 × 8–10 mm, crimson with yellow, glabrous, calyx lobes depressed. Nutlets 1(–2), sometimes 2 connate, style remains $^9/_{10}$ from base.

    Seasons: Flowers May–June; fruit ripe August–September.

    Chromosomes: Tetraploid (Bailey, pers. comm.). Apomictic, true from seed.

    Hardiness: −15°C (5°F).

    Area: China (Yunnan).

    Notes: A beautiful shrub of *Cotoneaster chungtiensis*, originally collected by T. T. Yu in 1937, was discovered growing in the nursery of the Royal Botanic Garden Edinburgh in Scotland in 1993. Excelling in both flower and in its luminous pink fruit, this species should be more widely grown. *Cotoneaster chungtiensis* is very similar to (if not the same) as *C. takpoensis* G. Klotz, an unpublished name.

3. ***Cotoneaster cooperi*** C. Marquand in Hooker's Ic. Plantarum, t. 3146 (1930). Synonyms: *C. cooperi* C. Marquand var. *microcarpus* C. Marquand (1937); *C. griffithii*

G. Klotz (1970). Type: cult. England, RBG Kew, May 1924, origin as *R. E. Cooper 3311* (holo K). **PLATE 50.**

Shrub or small tree, 4–6 m. Branches loosely erect, arched and pendulous, slender; branchlets spiraled, maroon, minutely verruculose, initially pilose-strigose. Leaves deciduous, chartaceous, on sterile shoots lanceolate, lanceo-elliptic or elliptic, 24–90 × 7–39 mm, apex acute or acuminate, base cuneate, upper surface mid-green, dull, few hairs on midrib, veins 6–9, lower surface grayish green, pilose-villous; petiole 4–8 mm, pilose-strigose. Fertile shoots 25–70 mm, including 4 leaves and a lax, 8- to 30-flowered inflorescence; pedicels 1–5 mm, pilose-strigose. Hypanthium campanulate, sparsely pilose-strigose; sepals obtuse, acute or apiculate, glabrescent, margin villous. Flower buds white sometimes few pink dots. Corolla 5–7 mm, petals spreading, white, large hair-tuft. Stamens 16–20; filaments white; anthers purple. Fruit obovoid or globose, 6–9 × 6–8 mm, red to purple-black, sparsely pilose, calyx lobes suberect, navel open. Nutlets 2, rarely 1, style remains at often elongated apex.

Seasons: Flowers May–June; fruit ripe August–September.

Chromosomes: Diploid (McAllister, pers. comm.; Bailey, pers. comm.). Sexual, outbreeding, variable from seed.

Hardiness: −12°C (10°F).

Area: Bhutan. Tibet. India (Arunachal Pradesh).

Notes: When first introduced, *Cotoneaster cooperi* was cultivated under the wrong collection number, *Cooper 3311*. In herbaria this Cooper number is a *Viburnum*. Cecil Marquand used *Cooper 3315* as a paratype for *C. cooperi*. Originally described as having purple-black fruit, living shrubs of *Cooper 3315* in the Royal Botanic Garden Edinburgh produced red fruit. These red fruit impelled Marquand to describe *Cooper 3315* as *C. cooperi* var. *microcarpus*, which Klotz later raised to a species—*C. griffithii*. Both *C. cooperi* and *C. griffithii* have been propagated many times from seed and the resulting offspring have always been very variable, including the fruit color. At RBG Edinburgh, under a small tree of *C. cooperi* with purple-black fruit, seedlings germinated giving offspring with red fruit. *Cotoneaster cooperi* is a sexual species and *C. griffithii* fits into its range of variability. After delving into the history of the introduction of this species which was so intensely discussed by Marquand, it is most plausible that both *C. cooperi* and *C. griffithii* were raised from the same seed lot, namely, *Cooper 3315*. *Cotoneaster cooperi*, being extremely variable from seed, causes great confusion in identification in large *Cotoneaster* collections where the shrubs are allowed to freely seed themselves. Some forms with long narrow leaves can be easily mistaken for *C. salicifolius* when without flower or fruit. Recently reintroduced into cultivation.

Cultivars: '**Nicolette**' (syn. 'Jeanette'), beautiful in flower with numerous, long-lasting, bright red fruit. '**Rumsey Gardens**', a small dense shrub resembling *Lonicera nitida* with few shiny red fruit. '**Taranto**', bottle-green, shiny leaves and maroon fruit.

4. *Cotoneaster hebephyllus* Diels in Not. Roy. Bot. Gard. Edinburgh 5: 273 (1912).
   Type: China, Yunnan, north end of Zhongdian plateau on pass leading to Yangtze
   valley, September 1904, *G. Forrest 283* (holo E). **PLATE 51.**

Shrub, 2–3 m. Branches loosely erect, irregularly spreading; branchlets spiraled, slender, maroon, lenticellate, initially pilose-strigose. Leaves deciduous, chartaceous, on sterile shoots broadly elliptic or broadly obovate, 18–40 × 15–22 mm, apex obtuse or truncate, base cuneate or obtuse, upper surface mid-green, dull, sometimes single hairs on midrib, veins 3–6, lower surface reticulate, sparsely pilose-villous; petiole 4–7 mm, pilose-strigose. Fertile shoots 25–40 mm, including 2–4 leaves and a lax, 5- to 16-flowered inflorescence; pedicels 3–6 mm, sparsely pilose-strigose. Hypanthium campanulate to cupulate, sparsely pilose-villous; sepals acute or obtuse, glabrescent, border narrow, membranous, yellowish white, maroon-tipped, margin villous. Flower buds white. Corolla 8–10 mm, petals spreading, white, with hair-tuft. Stamens (16–)20; filaments white; anthers purple to black. Fruit pendent on thin pedicels, globose or depressed-globose, 7–8 mm, red ripening pale ruby, glabrous, calyx lobes flat. Nutlet 1.

   Seasons: Flowers May–June; fruit ripe September.
   Chromosomes: Unknown. Apomictic, true from seed.
   Hardiness: –15°C (5°F).
   Area: China (Yunnan). Tibet.
   Notes: The type herbarium specimen of *Cotoneaster hebephyllus* is in full bloom and incorrectly said to have been collected in September. Klotz (1963) made *C. monopyrenus* a synonym of *C. hebephyllus* and based his description of series *Hebephylli* on *C. monopyrenus*. He incorrectly proclaimed that *C. hebephyllus* fruit contained 2 nutlets, later creating a further series, *Tibetici*, for species with fruit containing only one nutlet. All *C. hebephyllus* in cultivation probably originated from the Kingdon Ward collection of 1931 from the Burma-Tibet border. *Cotoneaster hebephyllus*, wreathed with flowers and later laden with pendulous fruit, has fruit which always contain only one nutlet, resembling a grain of corn.

5. *Cotoneaster incanus* (W. W. Smith) G. Klotz in Wiss. Z. Martin-Luther-Univ.
   Halle-Wittenberg, Math.-Naturwiss. 12: 766 (1963). Synonym: *C. hebephyllus* Diels
   var. *incanus* W. W. Smith (1917). Type: China, Yunnan, Tong Shan, in the Yangtze
   bend, August 1913, *G. Forrest 10837* (holo E, iso BM, K). **PLATE 52.**

Shrub, to 3 m. Branches erect, spreading, arched and pendulous, thin; branchlets spiraled, light brown, lenticellate and minutely verruculose, initially pilose-strigose. Leaves deciduous, subcoriaceous, on sterile shoots broadly elliptic or suborbicular, 16–30 × 10–22 mm, apex obtuse or rotund, base obtuse or cuneate, upper surface mid-green, dull, glabrous or subglabrous, veins 4–6, lower surface grayish green, densely pilose-strigose; petiole 2–8 mm, pilose-strigose. Fertile shoots 20–40 mm, including 4 leaves and a compact, 5- to 20-flowered inflorescence; pedicels 2–5 mm, densely pilose-strigose. Hypanthium campanulate, initially villous; sepals cuspidate, acuminate or acute, initially villous, apex red, margin densely long-haired villous. Flower buds white. Corolla 8–10 mm, petals spreading, white, with hair-tuft. Stamens 12–16; filaments white; anthers purple. Fruit pendent on long pedicels, obovoid, 7–12 mm, rich red maturing ruby and slightly purplish pruinose, calyx lobes suberect, greenish. Nutlets 1(–2), style remains at elongated apex.

Seasons: Flowers May–June; fruit ripe September–October.

Chromosomes: Unknown. Apomictic, true from seed.

Hardiness: −12°C (10°F).

Area: China (Yunnan).

Notes: *Cotoneaster incanus* is an elegant and graceful shrub with long hanging branches which are crowded with flowers and long-lasting fruit. It is beautiful as a specimen shrub. Recently reintroduced into cultivation.

6. ***Cotoneaster majusculus*** (W. W. Smith) G. Klotz in Wiss. Z. Martin-Luther-Univ. Halle-Wittenberg, Math.-Naturwiss. 12: 766 (1963). Synonym: *C. hebephyllus* Diels var. *majusculus* W. W. Smith (1917). Type: China, NW Yunnan near Tibetan frontier, 1913, *F. Kingdon Ward 492* (sometimes quoted as 482) (holo E).

Shrub, 3–4 m. Branches loosely erect; branchlets spiraled, maroon, initially pilosestrigose. Leaves deciduous, chartaceous, on sterile shoots elliptic, 20–36 × 12–19 mm, apex acute or obtuse, base cuneate or obtuse, upper surface green, dull, glabrous, veins 5–9, lower surface pilose-strigose; petiole 4–6 mm, pilose-strigose. Fertile shoots 30–50 mm, including a 12- to 20-flowered inflorescence; pedicels 2–7 mm, pilose-strigose. Hypanthium campanulate, pilose-strigose; sepals acute, acuminate or cuspidate, sparsely pilose-strigose, margin villous. Corolla 10–12 mm, petals spreading, white, with hair-tuft. Stamens 18–20; anthers purple to black. Fruit subglobose, 8–9 mm, red to crimson. Nutlets 1–2.

Area: China (Yunnan).

Notes: *Cotoneaster majusculus* is a recent introduction into cultivation through the Alpine Garden Society expedition. Although previously collected by Frank Kingdon Ward, it is not known in cultivation from this collection. Not in key.

7. ***Cotoneaster monopyrenus*** (W. W. Smith) Flinck & B. Hylmö in Bot. Not. (Lund) 119: 459 (1966). Synonym: *C. hebephyllus* Diels var. *monopyrenus* W. W. Smith (1917). Type: China, Yunnan, Lijiang range, September 1913, *G. Forrest 11422* (holo E). PLATE 53.

Shrub or small tree, 3–5 m. Branches loosely erect and arched, spreading; branchlets spiraled, maroon, lenticellate, initially pilose-strigose. Leaves deciduous, subcoriaceous, on sterile shoots suborbicular, broadly elliptic or broadly obovate, 25–45 × 15–40 mm, apex obtuse or truncate, seldom acute, base obtuse or cuneate, upper surface dark green, dull, glabrescent, veins 4–5 lightly impressed, lower surface tomentose-pilose, reticulate; petiole 5–9 mm, pilose-strigose. Fertile shoots 30–50 mm, including 3–4 leaves and a lax,

7- to 20-flowered inflorescence; pedicels 2–5 mm, pilose-strigose. Hypanthium campanulate to cupulate, sparsely pilose-strigose; sepals acute, acuminate or obtuse, sparsely pilose-strigose, border membranous, reddish, maroon-tipped, margin villous. Flower buds white. Corolla 10–12 mm, petals spreading, wide-spaced, white, sometimes with hair-tuft. Stamens (16–)20; filaments white; anthers purple to black. Fruit obovoid or globose, 10–11 mm, ruby to maroon maturing purple-black, pruinose, glabrous, calyx lobes flat, navel open. Nutlets 1(–2 free or connate), style remains at apex.

Seasons: Flowers June; fruit ripe October–November.

Chromosomes: Unknown. Apomictic, true from seed.

Hardiness: −15°C (5°F).

Area: China (Yunnan).

Notes: Marquand (1935) reported that the fruit of *Cotoneaster monopyrenus* contained 2 nutlets united into one. Consequently Klotz (1963), when mistakenly using *C. monopyrenus* (instead of *C. hebephyllus*) as the base for his description of series *Hebephylli*, denoted 2 nutlets per fruit—but species belonging to this series mostly have only one nutlet, similar to a grain of corn, per fruit. This species is often grown as *C. hebephyllus*.

8. *Cotoneaster muliensis* G. Klotz in Wiss. Z. Friedrich-Schiller-Univ. Jena, Math.-Naturwiss. 17: 336 (1968). Type: China, Yunnan, Muli, Tou-li-gou, 7 September 1937, *T. T. Yu 14196* (holo E, iso A). **PLATE 54.**

Shrub, 2–3 m. Branches loosely erect, arched, irregularly spreading; branchlets spiraled, slender, maroon and minutely verruculose, initially strigose. Leaves semievergreen, subcoriaceous, on sterile shoots broadly elliptic or suborbicular, 16–25 × 14–20 mm, apex obtuse, base obtuse or cuneate, upper surface dark green, dull, glabrescent, veins 5–7, lower surface grayish green, tomentose-pilose; petiole 3–7 mm, pilose-strigose. Fertile shoots 20–30 mm, including 3–4 leaves and a lax, 3- to 9-flowered inflorescence; pedicels 1–4 mm, densely strigose. Hypanthium campanulate, glabrous; sepals cuspidate or acuminate, glabrous, border broad, membranous, maroon, margin villous. Flower buds white. Corolla 8 mm, petals spreading, wide-spaced, white, with hair-tuft. Stamens 20; filaments white; anthers purple. Fruit obovoid or globose, 7–10 mm, maroon maturing purple-black, glabrous, calyx lobes flat. Nutlets 1(–2 free), style remains at apex.

Seasons: Flowers June; fruit ripe September–October.

Chromosomes: Tetraploid (Bailey, pers. comm.; Jewsbury, pers. comm.). Apomictic, true from seed.

Hardiness: −15°C (5°F).

Area: China (Yunnan, Sichuan).

Notes: *Cotoneaster muliensis* is not common in cultivation. All shrubs in cultivation are probably descended from the *Yu 14196* collection. This sparsely branched, graceful, and pretty shrub throws only dappled shade, and hence can be easily grown above low-growing species.

9. *Cotoneaster omissus* J. Fryer & B. Hylmö, *sp. nov.* Type: China, Yunnan, mountains northeast of the Yangtze bend, October 1913, *G. Forrest 11463* (holo E, iso BM). **PLATE 55.**

Shrub or small tree, 4–8 m. Branches loosely erect, spreading horizontally; branchlets spiraled, maroon, lenticellate and lightly verruculose, initially pilose-strigose. Leaves evergreen, coriaceous, on sterile shoots obovate or broadly elliptic, 35–60 × 23–34 mm, apex obtuse, acute or broadly acuminate, base cuneate or obtuse, upper surface dark green, glaucous, dull, glabrescent, veins 6–8, lower surface pale grayish green, reticulate, sparsely pilose-villous; petiole 6–10 mm, pilose-strigose. Fertile shoots 40–70 mm, including 3(–4) leaves and a lax, 7- to 25-flowered inflorescence; pedicels 3–7 mm, pilose-strigose. Hypanthium campanulate, pilose-strigose; sepals acute or obtuse, glabrescent, border broad, membranous, reddish purple, margin villous. Flower buds white. Corolla 9–10 mm, petals spreading, white, with large hair-tuft. Stamens 20; filaments white; anthers purple to black. Fruit globose, 10 mm, rich red with cherry, glabrescent, calyx lobes flat, navel open. Nutlets (1–)2, style remains $^4/_5$ from base.

Seasons: Flowers May–June; fruit ripe October.

Chromosomes: Tetraploid (Bailey, pers. comm.; Jewsbury, pers. comm.). Apomictic, true from seed.

Hardiness: −12°C (10°F).

Area: China (Yunnan).

Notes: William W. Smith treated *Forrest 11463*, the type for *Cotoneaster omissus*, as a paratype of *C. hebephyllus* var. *majusculus* (syn. *C. majusculus* (W. W. Smith) G. Klotz). *Cotoneaster omissus*, although for many years overlooked as a species in its own right, can sometimes be found in cultivation as *C. glaucophyllus*. *Cotoneaster omissus* flowers and sets fruit at least one month earlier than species belonging to series *Pannosi* to which *C. glaucophyllus* belongs.

10. *Cotoneaster tibeticus* G. Klotz in Wiss. Z. Friedrich-Schiller-Univ. Jena, Math.-Naturwiss. 17: 334 (1968). Type: S Tibet, Lhasa, 1 June 1942, *F. Ludlow & G. Sherriff 8626* (holo BM, iso E).

Shrub, 3–4 m. Branches loosely erect, spreading, slender; branchlets spiraled. Branchlets maroon and shiny, initially pilose-strigose. Leaves deciduous, chartaceous, on sterile shoots broadly obovate, 11–22 × 8–16 mm, apex obtuse or apiculate, base cuneate, upper surface dark green, dull, glabrescent, lower surface grayish green, pilose-strigose; petiole 3–5 mm, pilose-strigose. Fertile shoots 20–30 mm, including a 6- to 12-flowered inflorescence; pedicels pilose-strigose. Hypanthium pilose-strigose; sepals acute, glabrescent, margin villous. Corolla 8 mm, petals spreading, with hair-tuft. Stamens 15–20; anthers purple. Fruit red. Nutlet 1.

Area: Tibet.

Notes: The Ludlow and Sherriff collections of *Cotoneaster tibeticus* are not known in cultivation. Until the 1995 Keith Rushforth collections (*KR 2546, KR 354*) from Pe, Tibet, were introduced into cultivation, this species was thought to be a synonym of the closely related *C. hebephyllus*. Not in key.

11. **Cotoneaster transens** G. Klotz in Wiss. Z. Friedrich-Schiller-Univ. Jena, Math.-
    Naturwiss. 17: 337 (1968). Type: China, Yunnan, Chi-tsu mountains, 1933,
    McLaren's collector *C 157* (holo E, iso A). PLATE 56.
Shrub or small tree, 4–6 m. Branches loosely erect, spreading, stiff; branchlets spiraled, maroon and minutely verruculose, initially pilose-strigose. Leaves deciduous, chartaceous, on sterile shoots elliptic, 47–103 × 24–42 mm, apex acute or obtuse, base cuneate, upper surface brownish green soon mid-green, dull, subglabrous, veins 6–10 lightly impressed, lower surface villous-strigose; petiole 4–6 mm, densely pilose-strigose. Fertile shoots 40–50 mm, including 2–4 leaves and a lax, 10- to 25-flowered inflorescence; pedicels 3–5 mm, densely pilose-strigose. Hypanthium cupulate, villous-strigose; sepals acute, sparsely villous, margin villous. Flower buds white. Corolla 10–12 mm, petals spreading, white, with large hair-tuft. Stamens (16–)20; filaments white; anthers black. Fruit obovoid, 10 × 9 mm, maroon to purple-black, sometimes with few villous hairs, calyx lobes flat, navel slightly open. Nutlets 1(–2), style remains $^9/_{10}$ from base.
    Seasons: Flowers June; fruit ripe October–November.
    Chromosomes: Unknown. Apomictic, true from seed.
    Hardiness: −18°C (−1°F).
    Area: China (Yunnan).
    Notes: *Cotoneaster transens* can be found in many botanic gardens and large collections, frequently as *C. affinis*. This species may possibly cover a wider geographical range than previously thought. Records from Bhutan and Nepal need to be checked.

12. **Cotoneaster zayulensis** G. Klotz in Wiss. Z. Friedrich-Schiller-Univ. Jena, Math.-
    Naturwiss. 17: 334 (1968). Type: SE Tibet, Zayul, Ata in valley Rong To, 29 May
    1933, *F. Kingdon Ward 10439* (holo BM, iso UPS).
Shrub, 3–5 m. Branches loosely erect, irregularly spreading; branchlets spiraled, slender, light brown, lenticellate, initially pilose-strigose. Leaves deciduous or semievergreen, chartaceous, on sterile shoots broadly elliptic, broadly obovate or suborbicular, 30–50 × 18–30 mm, apex obtuse, acute or apiculate, base cuneate or obtuse, upper surface mid-green, dull, subglabrous, veins 4–7, lower surface reticulate, sparsely pilose; petiole 5–12 mm, pilose-strigose. Fertile shoots 15–30 mm, including 2–4 leaves and a 5- to 15-flowered inflorescence; pedicels 2–5 mm, pilose-strigose. Hypanthium campanulate, sparsely pilose-strigose; sepals acute, obtuse or ligulate, subglabrous, margin villous. Corolla 7–11 mm, petals spreading, white, with hair-tuft. Stamens 18–20; filaments white; anthers purple. Fruit depressed-globose, 7–8 mm, red to ruby, glabrous, calyx lobes flat. Nutlets (1–)2, style remains $^9/_{10}$ from base.
    Seasons: Flowers May–June; fruit ripe September.
    Chromosomes: Unknown. Apomictic, true from seed.

Hardiness: −15°C (5°F).

Area: China (Yunnan). Tibet.

Notes: Although *Cotoneaster zayulensis* is rarely found in cultivation, it is reported to be common in the vicinity of Zhongdian in Yunnan. The problem with refinding *C. zayulensis* is that this is an early fruiting species and the fruit are usually gone when the Western hunting troops arrive for seed collecting in September to November.

4. Section *Alpigeni* (Koch) Hurusawa in Acta Phytotax. Geobot. 13: 231 (1943).

Mostly low-growing or carpeting, often densely branched shrubs. Branchlets mostly spiraled. Leaves mostly evergreen, coriaceous, on sterile shoots mostly spiraled, small (4–45 mm). Fertile shoots short (5–50 mm), including a mostly 1- to 9(–12)-flowered inflorescence. Petals mostly glabrous. Stamens often 2-ranked; anthers violet. Nutlets (1–)2(–5).

4 series: *Conspicui, Buxifolii, Microphylli, Radicantes.*

11. Series *Conspicui* G. Klotz in Wiss. Z. Martin-Luther-Univ. Halle-Wittenberg, Math.-Naturwiss. 12: 781 (1963).

Creeping to medium shrubs. Branches erect or prostrate, often wide-spreading; branchlets maroon. Leaves mostly semievergreen, subcoriaceous, upper surface mostly grayish green or mid-green, mostly dull, veins not impressed. Hypanthium cupulate. Corolla 8–17 mm, petals sometimes with hairs at base of upper surface. Fruit coral, orange, red, ruby or crimson. Nutlets (1–)2(–3).

Early to mid season.

China (Yunnan). Tibet. Nepal. Bhutan.

5 species: *C. conspicuus, C. ludlowii, C. pluriflorus, C. schlechtendalii, C. sherriffii.*

Key to Series *Conspicui*

1a. Flower buds white; petals with hair-tuft; nutlets 1, rarely 2 connate or 2 free .... ***C. ludlowii***

1b. Flower buds pink; petals mostly glabrous; nutlets 1–3 2

2a. Leaves broadly elliptic or suborbicular; pedicels, hypanthium and sepals villous-strigose
.... ***C. sherriffii***

2b. Leaves elliptic or lanceolate; pedicels, hypanthium and sepals pilose-strigose............. 3

3a. Leaves elliptic or obovate; inflorescence 3- to 10-flowered.............. ***C. schlechtendalii***

3b. Leaves lanceo-elliptic or lanceolate; inflorescence 1- to 4-flowered 4

4a. Fertile shoots 8–12 mm; inflorescence 1(–3)-flowered; corolla 9–13 mm ...... ***C. conspicuus***

4b. Fertile shoots 15–25 mm; inflorescence 2- to 4-flowered; corolla 12–17 mm.... ***C. pluriflorus***

1. *Cotoneaster conspicuus* J. B. Comber ex C. Marquand in Kew Bulletin p. 119 (1937). Synonyms: *C. conspicuus* Messel (1934) nom. nud.; *C. conspicuus* Comber ex C. Marquand (1939); *C. permutatus* G. Klotz (1963); *C. nanus* G. Klotz (1963). Type:

cult. England, Sussex, Nymans Handcross, 4 October 1933, Comber, raised from seed Kingdon Ward 6400, SE Tibet, Kongbo province, Tsangpo river area, Gyala, seed only, 18 November 1924, *F. Kingdon Ward 6400* (lecto designated K). **PLATE 57.** Shrub dense, 0.5–2.5 m. Branches to 2.5 m, prostrate, mound-forming or erect; branchlets spiraled or distichous, maroon, initially strigose. Leaves evergreen, subcoriaceous or coriaceous, on sterile shoots distichous or spiraled, ellipto-lanceolate or lanceolate, 6–20 × 2–8 mm, apex obtuse or acute, base cuneate, upper surface mid or grayish green, slightly shiny, sparsely pilose or glabrous, veins 3–5, lower surface grayish green, initially pilose-strigose, reticulate; petiole 1–3 mm, pilose-strigose. Fertile shoots many, 8–12 mm, including 3–4 leaves and 1(–3) flower(s); pedicel 1–3 mm, pilose-strigose. Hypanthium cupulate, pilose-strigose; sepals acute or obtuse, pilose-strigose, border membranous, mostly reddish, margin villous. Flower buds pink. Corolla 9–13 mm, petals spreading, white. Stamens 20; filaments white; anthers purple-black. Fruit erect, depressed-globose, 8–10 × 9–11 mm, orange-red to red, shiny, glabrous, calyx lobes suberect, pilose. Nutlets 2(–3), style remains at elongated apex.

Seasons: Flowers May–June; fruit ripe October–December.

Chromosomes: Diploid (Zeilinga 1964; Klotz 1968b; Kroon 1975; Krügel 1992a; McAllister, pers. comm.; Jewsbury, pers. comm.). Sexual, outbreeding, variable from seed. Hybridizes with other outbreeding cotoneasters.

Hardiness: –15°C (5°F).

Area: Tibet.

Notes: In 1924 Frank Kingdon Ward collected seed (only) of his collection *6400*. Later he recalled the vivid memory of the impression of this as "a bubbling red cauldron of berries produced by this collection as seen from the top of the cliff." Seed of *Kingdon Ward 6400* was widely distributed to botanic gardens and private collections; the variation in the resulting offspring was large. The U.S. Department of Agriculture in Washington, D.C., selected a prostrate form for vegetative propagation and gave it the name *Cotoneaster conspicuus* var. *decorus* Russell (1938). In the United Kingdom, more erect forms were most frequently cultivated. Flinck and Hylmö (1966) reported *C. conspicuus* to be diploid (Zeilinga 1964) and outbreeding. Klotz (1963b) was not aware of this variability and selected as type for *C. conspicuus* the variety *decorus*. The original *C. conspicuus* holotype of Comber in 1933 was given another name. This same sheet is now by us converted to the lectotype of *C. conspicuus* Comber ex C. Marquand. This type sheet was made by the author Comber and is the earliest sheet to be found in herbaria named *C. conspicuus*.

Cotoneaster conspicuus received the RHS Award of Merit in 1933, RHS Award of Garden Merit in 1947, and First Class Certificate (as *C. conspicuus* 'Decorus') in 1953. Good as a specimen shrub or for massed plantings. Top grafted onto *C.* ×*watereri* it makes a lovely and unusual standard. The conspicuus profusion of flowers and shiny, orange-red fruit make this a very ornamental, strikingly beautiful shrub. As with many of the species in section *Alpigeni*, in flower alone *C. conspicuus* rivals a multitude of other spring-flowering shrubs. Frank Kingdon Ward stated that the fruit were not attractive to birds and usually persisted throughout the winter. *Cotoneaster conspicuus* has been collected in Tibet by Keith Rushforth (*KR 3626*) between Gyala and Tripe in 1995, and by Hugh McAllister and Rushforth (*KR 5763*) from Showa La, Pome, in 1997.

Cultivars: '**Decorus**' Russell (1938), a prostrate clone. '**Flameburst**', a handsome, low-growing, spreading and mat-forming shrub with numerous, brilliant orange-red fruit. '**Leicester Gem**', leaves lanceolate, masses of flowers and fruit, unusually the calyx falling as a coronet leaving nutlets exposed. This lovely cultivar originated from the botanic garden of the University of Leicester, England, in 1987. '**Red Glory**', tall and elegant, in time, trained, can form a small tree to 3 m, fruit red. '**Red Pearl**', a low to medium-sized shrub with spreading branches and large, bright orange-red fruit. '**String of Pearls**', a shrub to c. 1.75 m high, branches somewhat lax and pendulous, large fruit very numerous, wreathing the branches. Very striking. Found as seedling at Darthuizers in the Netherlands. '**Tiny Tim**', a dwarf (to 0.8 m) mat-forming shrub with fruit orange washed red.

2. ***Cotoneaster ludlowii*** G. Klotz in Wiss. Z. Martin-Luther-Univ. Halle-Wittenberg, Math.-Naturwiss. 12: 775 (1963). Type: *Cotoneaster* sp.,*F. Ludlow & G. Sherriff 19632B*, Bhutan [cultivated at the botanic garden of Martin-Luther-Univ. in Halle, Germany] (holo HAL).

Shrub, 1–2 m. Branches loosely erect, irregularly spreading; branchlets spiraled, maroon to grayish brown, lenticellate, initially yellowish strigose. Leaves deciduous or semi-evergreen, subcoriaceous, on sterile shoots distichous or spiraled, elliptic or obovate, 20–32 × 11–18 mm, apex acute rarely obtuse, base cuneate rarely obtuse, upper surface dull green, glabrescent, veins 4–5, lower surface gray initially pilose-villous; petiole 2–3 mm, pilose-strigose. Fertile shoots 15–25 mm, including 2–4 leaves and an erect, 5- to 12-flowered inflorescence; pedicels 2–4 mm, pilose-strigose. Hypanthium campanulate, sparsely pilose-strigose; sepals acuminate or acute, subglabrous, border broad, membranous, greenish white, red-tipped, margin villous. Flower buds white sometimes with pink dots. Corolla 8–10 mm, petals spreading, white, with hair-tuft. Stamens 20; filaments white; anthers purple to black. Fruit globose or depressed-globose, 8–10 mm, pale crimson with yellow (coral-red), finally cherry-red, glabrous, calyx lobes flat. Nutlets 1, rarely 2 connate or 2 free, style remains $^9/_{10}$ from base.

Seasons: Flowers June; fruit ripe September–October.

Chromosomes: Tetraploid (Klotz 1968b). Apomictic, true from seed.

Hardiness: −15°C (5°F).

Area: Bhutan, also borders of Nepal and Tibet.

Notes: *Cotoneaster ludlowii* is a fast-growing shrub which is outstanding both in flower and in fruit. The type shrub of the species originated from seed distributed by the University of Washington Botanic Gardens, Seattle, where it was first raised in 1950.

3. Cotoneaster pluriflorus G. Klotz in Wiss. Z. Martin-Luther-Univ. Halle-Wittenberg, Math.-Naturwiss. 12: 781 (1963). Type: SE Tibet, Kongbo province, Lusha, Tsangpo valley, 17 June 1938, *F. Ludlow, G. Sherriff & G. Taylor 4855* (holo BM, iso A, E). **PLATE 58.**

Shrub, 0.5–1.5 m. Branches prostrate or erect; branchlets spiraled, maroon, initially strigose. Leaves semievergreen, subcoriaceous, on sterile shoots spiraled, narrowly elliptic or lanceo-elliptic, 14–20 × 8–9 mm, apex obtuse, base cuneate or obtuse, upper surface mid to dark green, dull or slightly shiny, sparsely pilose-strigose or glabrous, veins 4–6 lightly impressed, lower surface grayish green, pilose-strigose; petiole 1–4 mm, pilose-strigose. Fertile shoots 15–25 mm, including mostly 4 leaves and an erect (1–)2- to 4-flowered inflorescence; pedicels 2–6 mm, strigose. Hypanthium cupulate, sparsely pilose-strigose; sepals acute or acuminate, sparsely pilose-strigose, border broad, membranous, often red, margin sparsely villous. Flower buds pink. Corolla 12–17 mm, petals spreading, white, sometimes with few hairs. Stamens 15–20, arranged in four rings of differing lengths; filaments white; anthers purple-black. Fruit erect, obovoid or globose, 10–11 mm, pale pinkish orange to coral, shiny, glabrous, calyx lobes suberect, pilose, navel open. Nutlets (1–)2, style remains at apex.

    Seasons: Flowers June; fruit ripe October–November.

    Chromosomes: Tetraploid (McAllister, pers. comm.). Apomictic, true from seed.

    Hardiness: −15°C (5°F).

    Area: Tibet.

    Notes: *Cotoneaster pluriflorus* was introduced in 1948 and has sometimes been cultivated both as *C. permutatus* hort., non G. Klotz, and as *C.* 'Highlight'. Closely related to *C. conspicuus*, it differs in its broader and darker leaves, longer fertile shoots, larger flowers and fruit, and in the fruit being coral-red. This spectacular shrub forms a mound of arching shoots, with masses of white flowers followed by closely packed, large and unusually colored, almost luminous fruit. *Cotoneaster pluriflorus* has also been collected by Keith Rushforth in 1995 (*KR 3573*) in Tibet between Tripe and Gyala.

4. Cotoneaster schlechtendalii G. Klotz in Wiss. Z. Martin-Luther-Univ. Halle-Wittenberg, Math.-Naturwiss. 12: 776 (1963). Type: SE Tibet, Sanga Choling, Chan Chu, 27 September 1936, *F. Ludlow & G. Sherriff 2709* (holo BM, iso E).

Shrub, to 1.5 m. Branches erect, stiff; branchlets gray-brown, initially grayish villous. Leaves spiraled, evergreen, coriaceous, on sterile shoots elliptic rarely obovate-elliptic, 7–25 × 5–14 mm, apex rotund sometimes emarginate, mucronate, base obtuse, upper surface becoming slightly shiny, sparsely strigose-villous to pilose, lower surface initially densely strigose-villous; petiole 1–3 mm. Fertile shoots with an erect, 1- to 5-flowered inflorescence. Fruit globose, 7–8 mm, crimson. Nutlets 2.

    Hardiness: −15°C (5°F).

    Area: Tibet.

Notes: *Cotoneaster schlechtendalii* has been discovered among the cotoneasters collected by Hugh McAllister and Keith Rushforth in the Tsangpo area of SE Tibet.

5. *Cotoneaster sherriffii* G. Klotz in Wiss. Z. Martin-Luther-Univ. Halle-Wittenberg, Math.-Naturwiss. 12: 776 (1963). Type: SE Tibet, Kongbo province, Molo, Lilung Chu, 26 June 1938, *F. Ludlow, G. Sherriff & G. Taylor 5677* (holo BM, iso E). **PLATE 59**.
Shrub dense, 0.5–2.5 m. Branches erect, ascending, rarely prostrate, wide-spreading; branchlets spiraled, maroon, lenticellate, initially strigose. Leaves semievergreen, subcoriaceous, on sterile shoots spiraled or distichous, broadly elliptic or suborbicular, 6–14 × 4–12 mm, apex rotund or obtuse, base rotund or obtuse, upper mid-green, dull, glabrescent, veins 3–4, lower surface grayish green, villous; petiole 1–3 mm, pilose-strigose. Fertile shoots 15–35 mm, including 4–6 (often obovate) leaves and an erect, 3- to 9(–11)-flowered inflorescence; pedicels 3–7 mm, villous-strigose. Hypanthium cupulate or infundibulate, villous-strigose; sepals acute or apiculate, villous, border broad, membranous, mostly red, margin erose and villous. Flower buds pink. Corolla 9–10 mm, petals spreading, white. Stamens (16–)20, in 2 rows; filaments white; anthers purple-black. Fruit obovoid, 9–11 × 8–10 mm, pale orange to pale orange-red, glabrescent, calyx lobes suberect, villous. Nutlets (1–)2, style remains at apex.
  Seasons: Flowers May–June; fruit ripe September–October.
  Chromosomes: Triploid (McAllister, pers. comm., Jewsbury, pers. comm.).
  Hardiness: –15°C (5°F).
  Area: Tibet.
  Notes: *Cotoneaster sherriffii* is a dense and spreading shrub with pretty dutch-vermilion (orange-red; RHS 40a) fruit, and leaves which turn purple in late autumn. Sometimes grown as *C. conspicuus* or *C. orbicularis*, it is frequently found in cultivation as *C.* 'Highlight'. *Cotoneaster sherriffii* has been collected by Keith Rushforth (*KR 3596*) in Tibet near Gyala in the Nancha Barwa valley, in 1996.

12. Series *Buxifolii* G. Klotz in Wiss. Z. Martin-Luther-Univ. Halle-Wittenberg, Math.-Naturwiss. 12: 773 (1963).
Dwarf to small shrubs. Branches erect, ascending or prostrate; branchlets dark purple, initially densely pilose-strigose or tomentose. Leaves elliptic or lanceolate, veins 2–5, impressed, lower surface tomentose. Inflorescences 1- to 25-flowered. Flower buds mostly white. Hypanthium infundibulate, villous, pilose or tomentose; sepals mostly cuspidate or acuminate. Corolla 7–10 mm, petals sometimes with hairs at base of upper surface. Fruit 5–8 mm. Nutlets (1–)2(–3).
  Mid to late season.
  China (Yunnan, Sichuan). Tibet. Nepal. India (Tamil Nadu).
  9 species: *C. argenteus, C. astrophoros, C. brevirameus, C. buxifolius, C. delavayanus, C. hodjingensis, C. insolitus, C. lidjiangensis, C. rockii.*

Key to Series *Buxifolii*

1a. Inflorescence 3- to 9-flowered (S. India) . . . . *C. buxifolius*
1b. Inflorescence 1- to 4-flowered (N.W. China) 2
2a. Leaves elliptic; hypanthium and sepals mostly pilose-strigose, sometimes villous-strigose
. 3
2b. Leaves lanceolate or lanceo-elliptic; hypanthium and sepals tomentose 5
3a. Fertile shoots ≤ 30 mm; hypanthium becoming glabrous . . . . *C. rockii*
3b. Fertile shoots ≤ 15–20 mm; hypanthium with persistent hairs 4
4a. Leaves ≤ 9 mm, apex acute, veins 2–3 . . . . *C. astrophoros*
4b. Leaves ≤ 13 mm, apex mostly obtuse, veins 3–5 . . . . *C. lidjiangensis*
5a. Branches erect; leaf apex rostrate . . . . *C. hodjingensis*
5b. Branches ascending or decumbent; leaf apex rotund, obtuse or acute 6
6a. Leaf base cuneate or obtuse, upper surface with sparse hairs becoming glabrous . . . .
. . . . *C. delavayanus*
6b. Leaf base acute or cuneate, upper surface densely villous-strigose . . . . *C. brevirameus*

1. ***Cotoneaster argenteus*** G. Klotz in Wiss. Z. Martin-Luther-Univ. Halle-Wittenberg, Math.-Naturwiss. 12: 775 (1963). Type: China, Yunnan, northeast of the Yangtze bend, August 1913, *G. Forrest 10780* (holo BM, iso A, E, K). **PLATE 60**.
Shrub dense, to 1 m. Branches erect; branchlets spiraled, gray-brown, initially silvery tomentose. Leaves evergreen, coriaceous or subcoriaceous, on sterile shoots spiraled, elliptic or narrowly elliptic, rarely oblong or oblong-obovate, 5–12 × 3–5 mm, apex obtuse, rarely rotund, mucronate, base cuneate, upper surface dull or slightly shiny, initially densely villous, lower surface gray-tomentose; petiole 1–3 mm, tomentose. Inflorescence erect, (1–)2- to 3-flowered. Hypanthium and sepals initially villous-tomentose. Corolla 7–9 mm. Fruit not seen.
Hardiness: −15°C (5°F).
Area: China: Yunnan.
Notes: *Cotoneaster argenteus* is similar to *C. brevirameus* but more erect in habit, with narrower leaves and flowers mostly 2–3 together. It has not yet been positively found in cultivation. Not in key.

2. ***Cotoneaster astrophoros*** J. Fryer & E. C. Nelson in Glasra 2: 128 (1995); illustr. Walsh and Nelson (1990). Type: cult. Ireland, National Botanic Gardens, Glasnevin, Rock Garden (accession XX006849), E. C. Nelson, 14 June 1991 (holo DBN, iso E, K).
Shrub dense, 0.5–1 m. Branches to 2 m, prostrate, decumbent or ascending, stiff; branchlets spiraled, purple-black, initially tomentose-strigose. Leaves evergreen, coriaceous, on sterile shoots spiraled or distichous, elliptic, 5–9 × 3–4 mm, apex acute or obtuse, base cuneate or obtuse, margin recurved, upper surface sometimes slightly rugose, dark green, slightly shiny, initially sparsely long-haired pilose-strigose, veins 2–3 impressed, lower

surface reticulate, tomentose; petiole 1–2 mm, tomentose. Fertile shoots 10–15 mm, including 2–4 leaves and an erect, 1(–3) flower(s); pedicel 1–3 mm, strigose-villous. Hypanthium infundibulate, villous-strigose; sepals cuspidate, acuminate or acute, strigose-villous, border membranous, often red, margin villous. Flower buds white. Corolla 8–10 mm, petals spreading, white. Stamens (17–)20; filaments white; anthers violet-black. Fruit depressed-globose, 6–8 mm, orient-red, glabrescent, calyx lobes suberect. Nutlets 2(–3), style remains at apex.

Seasons: Flowers June; fruit ripe October–March.

Chromosomes: Tetraploid (Bailey, pers. comm.; Jewsbury, pers. comm.). Triploid and pentaploid counts have also been recorded.

Hardiness: −15°C (5°F).

Area: China (Yunnan, Sichuan).

Notes: *Cotoneaster astrophoros* is sometimes confused with the closely related *C. hodjingensis*, which was also collected by Tse Tsun Yü, but has leaves with apex more acute and lower surface with strigose hairs. These two species are often found growing mixed together in collections. *Cotoneaster astrophoros* is a splendid shrub, especially in June when the arching branches sparkle with masses of white, starry flowers which overlay the softly hairy gray-tinted new leaves. Each leaf has a silvery margin due to the felting of hairs of the lower surface extending beyond the margin. The fruit are produced very freely on this lovely dwarf evergreen shrub. The species has also been collected between Lijiang and Dali, at Yua Hau south of Jianchuan on 11 November 1996, by Jeanette Fryer (*JFYU 141*).

3. ***Cotoneaster brevirameus*** Rehder & E. H. Wilson in Sargent, Pl. Wilson. 1: 177 (1912). Type: China, W Sichuan, without locality but believed to be Wa Shan, south of Emei Shan, July 1903, Veitch expedition, *E. H. Wilson 3513* (holo A).

Shrub dense, 0.5–0.8(–1) m. Branches short, often bent in different directions; branchlets many, spiraled, grayish brown and slightly verruculose, initially densely villous-strigose. Internodes short, leaves evergreen or semi, subcoriaceous, on sterile shoots spiraled or distichous, elliptic, elliptic-oblong or oblong, 8–15 × 4–6 mm, apex acute or obtuse, mucronate, base cuneate, upper surface minutely reticulate, becoming slightly shiny, initially densely villous, veins 4 lightly impressed, lower surface white tomentose-villous; petiole 1–2 mm, tomentose, base minutely verruculose. Fertile shoots with a subsessile, 1(–3) flower(s). Hypanthium ovoid-turbinate, adpressed-villous; sepals broadly-triangular, acute, villous-strigose, margin villous. Corolla 7–9 mm, petals spreading, white. Stamens 20; filaments white; anthers violet-black. Fruit subglobose, 5–6 mm, red. Nutlets 2, apex densely villous, style remains at elongated apex.

Seasons: Flowers June; fruit ripe October–November.

Hardiness: −12°C (10°F).

Area: China (Sichuan, Yunnan).

Notes: *Cotoneaster brevirameus* is similar to *C. argenteus* but differs in its more compact habit and mostly single flowers. It is a miniature, slow-growing species useful for rockery or containers. Recently reintroduced into cultivation.

4. *Cotoneaster buxifolius* Wallich ex Lindley in Edward's Bot. Reg. 15: t. 1229 (1829).
Type: (India) Nilgiri, E. Nolan, Herb. East India Company, *Wallich 661* (holo K).
Shrub dense, 0.5–2 m. Branches erect and spreading; branchlets spiraled, divaricate, dark brown, initially densely gray pilose-strigose. Leaves evergreen, subcoriaceous, on sterile shoots spiraled, elliptic or ovate, 5–17 × 3–13 mm, apex obtuse, acute, rarely rotund or shortly-acuminate, mucronate, upper surface minutely rugose, becoming slightly shiny, initially villous, veins 2–4 lightly impressed, lower surface grayish to yellowish tomentose-villous; petiole 1–4 mm, tomentose-strigose. Fertile shoots 10–30 mm, including 4 leaves and an erect 1- to 9(–20)-flowered inflorescence; pedicels 1–3 mm, tomentose-strigose. Hypanthium infundibulate, tomentose-strigose; sepals cuspidate or acuminate, mucronate, initially tomentose-strigose, margin long-haired tomentose. Flower buds white. Corolla 7–9 mm, petals spreading, white, sometimes few hairs at base of upper surface. Stamens 20; filaments white; anthers black. Fruit crimson, villous, calyx lobes erect, strigose. Nutlets 2, style remains near apex.
Hardiness: −12°C (10°F).
Area: S India.
Notes: *Cotoneaster buxifolius* is an intricately branched woody shrub which is very rare in cultivation. It is native to the Madras or Nilgiri hills of southern India. It is hoped that this species will be refound in its native habitat in the not-too-distant future. This would be invaluable to further the understanding of this species and its relationship to other species in this series. Records of *C. buxifolius* from N India and the Himalaya are due to misidentifications. The true species was introduced into the RGB Kew in England in 1919 and may still be in cultivation in old private collections somewhere yet to be found. There are further species of *Cotoneaster* growing in the Nilgiri Hills area, one of which, at present under observation, has leaves with lower surface strigose and is more closely related to *C. integrifolius* and *C. prostratus*.

5. *Cotoneaster delavayanus* G. Klotz in Wiss. Z. Martin-Luther-Univ. Halle-Wittenberg, Math.-Naturwiss. 12: 774 (1963). Type: China, W Yunnan, Schweli-Salween divide, November 1924, *G. Forrest 26055* (holo K, iso E).
Shrub. Branches rooting; branchlets black-purple to gray-brown, initially strigose-villous. Leaves evergreen, coriaceous, on sterile shoots spiraled, lanceolate, oblanceolate or narrowly-elliptic oblong or oblong-oblanceolate, 3–12 × 2–5 mm, apex acute and mucronate or rotund with thick mucro, upper surface initially sparsely villous, lower surface strigose-tomentose; petiole 1–3 mm. Fertile shoots with an erect, solitary flower. Sepals triangular, mucronate. Fruit globose, 6–8 mm, crimson. Nutlets 2.
Area: China (Yunnan). Tibet.
Notes: *Cotoneaster delavayanus* has been discovered among the Hugh McAllister

and Keith Rushforth 1997 collections from Tibet. It is more prostrate than other species in this series, with branches rooting and leaves less hairy, and could belong to another series.

6. *Cotoneaster hodjingensis* G. Klotz in Wiss. Z. Martin-Luther-Univ. Halle-Wittenberg, Math.-Naturwiss. 12: 774 (1963). Synonym: *C. exellens* C. Marquand hort. Type: China, Yunnan, Heqing (formerly Hodjing), 20 May 1916, *Handel-Mazzetti 8748* (holo W).

Shrub dense, 0.5–1.5 m. Branches erect becoming suberect, ascending, wide-spreading; branchlets spiraled, stiff, maroon and minutely verruculose, initially densely pilose or villous-strigose. Leaves evergreen, coriaceous, on sterile shoots spiraled, lanceolate or lanceo-elliptic, 5–11 × 2–5 mm, apex rostrate, acute or obtuse with a long mucro, base narrowly cuneate, upper surface minutely rugose and verruculose, dark green, shiny, initially pilose-strigose, veins 2–4 impressed, lower surface grayish white tomentose; petiole 1–2 mm, tomentose. Fertile shoots 10–20 mm, including 4 leaves and an erect 1(–3)-flowered inflorescence; pedicel 1–3 mm, tomentose. Hypanthium densely villous; sepals cuspidate or acuminate, tomentose, margin villous. Flower buds white. Corolla 7–8 mm, petals spreading, white. Stamens 20; filaments white, anthers violet. Fruit globose or depressed-globose, 6–7 mm, crimson-cherry, villous, calyx lobes suberect or erect as coronet, navel open with nutlets exserted. Nutlets 2, style remains near apex.

Seasons: Flowers June; fruit ripe October–November.

Chromosomes: Tetraploid (Krügel 1992a; Bailey, pers. comm.; McAllister, pers. comm.); diploid (Jewsbury, pers. comm.). Apomictic, true from seed.

Hardiness: –12°C (10°F).

Area: China (Yunnan).

Notes: *Cotoneaster hodjingensis* has been in cultivation since around 1920–1930 (about the same time as *C. buxifolius* with which it is possibly easily confused), probably introduced from a George Forrest collection. This species is reported as being frequent on roadsides in Yunnan along which many plant collectors pass. It can be found in some collections as *C. exellens* (an unpublished name). *Cotoneaster hodjingensis* was found in Yunnan near Chiuxiong in 1996 by Jeanette Fryer (*JFYU 001*). In western California this species is used as hedging where it looks beautiful, not least in winter.

7. *Cotoneaster insolitus* G. Klotz in Wiss. Z. Martin-Luther-Univ. Halle-Wittenberg, Math.-Naturwiss. 15: 536 (1966). Type: China, Yunnan, Kiao-che-tong, on the eastern slope of Hee-chan-men, 15 May 1884, *J. Delavay 1079* (holo P). **PLATE 61.**

Shrub dense, 0.5–1 m. Branches erect, spreading, stiff; branchlets spiraled or distichous, maroon, initially densely pilose or pilose strigose. Leaves evergreen, coriaceous, on sterile shoots spiraled or distichous, elliptic or obovate, 6–15 × 5–9 mm, apex acute or obtuse, mucronate, base obtuse or cuneate, margin long-ciliate, upper surface dark green, dull to slightly shiny, initially pilose-strigose, veins 2–4 lightly impressed, lower surface tomentose-pilose; petiole 1–3 mm, pilose-strigose. Fertile shoots 20–30 mm, including 4 leaves and an erect, (1–)2- to 8-flowered inflorescence. Hypanthium infundibulate, initially pilose-strigose; sepals acute, cuspidate or acuminate, subglabrous, margin densely villous. Flower buds pinkish. Corolla 7–9 mm, petals spreading, white, sometimes with hairs. Stamens 20; filaments white; anthers purple-black. Fruit globose or obovoid. 5–6 mm, red to rich red, pilose, calyx lobes suberect. Nutlets (1–)2(–3), style remains at apex.

Seasons: Flowers June; fruit ripe October–December.

Chromosomes: Unknown. Apomictic, true from seed.

Hardiness: –12°C (10°F).

Area: China (Yunnan).

Notes: *Cotoneaster insolitus* is a neat, well-shaped shrub which looks good at all times of the year. Unusually, the flowers and fruit often appear on the shrub together. Roy Lancaster's collection (*RL 680*) from Hu Hong Dong, west of Kunming, in 1980 is also *C. insolitus*. Not in key.

8. *Cotoneaster lidjiangensis* G. Klotz in Wiss. Z. Martin-Luther-Univ. Halle-Wittenberg, Math.-Naturwiss. 12: 773 (1963). Type: China, Yunnan, Lijiang range, 8 July 1914, *C. Schneider 1781* (holo A). **PLATE 62**.

Shrub dense, 0.5–1.5 m. Branches erect or ascending, wide-spreading; branchlets spiraled or distichous, maroon, initially densely pilose-strigose. Leaves evergreen, coriaceous, on sterile shoots spiraled or distichous, elliptic, obovate-elliptic, rarely oblong-obovate, 10–18 × 5–8 mm, apex obtuse, rotund or acute, base cuneate, upper surface dark green, dull or slightly shiny, initially pilose-villous, veins 3–5 very slightly impressed, lower surface white tomentose-villous; petiole 2–3 mm, tomentose. Fertile shoots 10–30 mm, including 4–5 leaves and an erect, compact 1- to 8-flowered inflorescence, pedicels densely pilose-villous. Hypanthium infundibulate, densely pilose or villous-strigose; sepals cuspidate or acuminate, densely pilose or villous-strigose, border membranous, red with white, glabrous, margin villous. Flower buds white with pink. Corolla 8–9 mm, petals semispreading to spreading, white. Stamens 17–20; filaments pale-purple or white; anthers mauve. Fruit globose or obovate, 5–6 mm, red to crimson, base pilose, calyx lobes erect. Nutlets 2, rarely 1, style remains at apex.

Seasons: Flowers June, fruit ripe October–November.

Hardiness: –12°C (10°F).

Area: China (Yunnan).

Notes: This is a very pretty shrub with its pale mauve anthers, bottle-green leaves, and late-ripening fruit, making it useful for many sunny situations. It was collected in 1996 in Yunnan between Lijiang and Dali, Tei-jia Shan, by Jeanette Fryer (*JFYU 137*).

Cultivar: **'Erin Faye'** (**PLATE 63**), very similar to *C. lidjiangensis* but denser in habit with slightly smaller leaves and many orange-red fruit.

9. *Cotoneaster rockii* G. Klotz in Wiss. Z. Martin-Luther-Univ. Halle-Wittenberg, Math.-Naturwiss. 12: 775 (1963). Type: SE Tibet, Mount Kenichunpo, Salween-Irrawaddy divide, May to July 1932, *J. F. Rock 22077* (holo A, iso BM, K, E).

Shrub, 0.5–1 m. Branches suberect or prostrate; branchlets black-purple to gray-brown, initially densely strigose-villous. Leaves evergreen, subcoriaceous, on sterile shoots spiraled, elliptic, broadly-elliptic, rarely obovate-elliptic or oblong-oblanceolate, 6–12 × 5–8 mm, apex obtuse, rarely rotund or acute, mucronate, base cuneate or obtuse, upper surface slightly rugose, slightly shiny, initially sparsely pilose, lower surface villous; petiole 1–3 mm. Fertile shoots with a 1- to 2-flowered inflorescence; pedicels initially villous. Hypanthium initially villous; sepals triangular acute often mucronate, initially villous. Petals spreading, white. Stamens 20; filaments white; anthers violet. Styles 2–3. Fruit subglobose, 6–7 mm, crimson. Nutlets 2–3.

Seasons: Flowers June; fruit ripe October–November.

Hardiness: −12°C (10°F).

Area: Tibet. China (Yunnan, Sichuan).

Notes: *Cotoneaster rockii* is not common in cultivation, although it will quite probably be discovered in the Hugh McAllister and Keith Rushforth 1994 collections from Tibet.

13. Series *Microphylli* T. T. Yu in Bull. Brit. Mus. (Nat. Hist.), Bot. 1 (5): 134 (1954). Prostrate to medium shrubs, densely branched. Branches suberect or prostrate; branchlets dark purple, sometimes striate. Leaves on sterile shoots 4–45 mm. Inflorescences mostly erect. Hypanthium narrowly cupulate. Fruit crimson, cherry, or ruby, rarely pure red.

Early to mid season.

Nepal. India (Uttaranchal Pradesh, Himachal Pradesh, Sikkim, Tamil Nadu). Bhutan. China (Sichuan, Yunnan). Tibet.

9 species: *C. brandisii, C. congestus, C. glacialis, C. integrifolius, C. marginatus, C. meuselii, C. microphyllus, C. thymifolius, C. uva-ursi.*

Key to Series *Microphylli*

1a. Leaves mostly chartaceous, obovate, pale to mid-green, dull; pedicels and hypanthium sparsely pilose . . . . **C. congestus**

1b. Leaves mostly coriaceous, dark green, shiny; pedicels and hypanthium mostly strigose . . .2

2a. Leaves linear or narrowly obovate, 5–12 × 2–3 mm; fertile shoot leaves 3–6; fruit 3–6 mm . . . . **C. thymifolius**

2b. Leaves mostly elliptic or oblanceolate, ≤ 45 × 28 mm; fertile shoot leaves 2–4; fruit 6–10(–12) mm 3

3a. Leaves 7–45 mm, veins 4–6, petiole 3–6 mm; fertile shoots 15–35 mm, inflorescence 2- to 10-flowered; fruit 8–12 mm . . . . *C. marginatus*

3b. Leaves 5–20 mm, veins 2–5, petiole 1–5 mm; fertile shoots 5–20 mm; inflorescence 1- to 3(–4)-flowered; fruit 6–9(–10) mm **4**

4a. Leaves mostly narrowly elliptic, upper surface midrib sparsely pilose; inflorescence (1–)2- to 3(–4)- flowered . . . . *C. meuselii*

4b. Leaves mostly broadly elliptic, upper surface midrib strigose; inflorescence 1- to 2(–3)-flowered. **5**

5a. Fertile shoots 10–20 mm; buds greenish white with red stripes; hypanthium and calyx pale green; fruit red with some crimson, glabrous . . . . *C. uva-ursi*

5b. Fertile shoots 8–15 mm; buds white tinged pink; hypanthium and calyx mid dark green; fruit crimson, sparse hairs. **6**

6a. Branches often procumbent; leaves 5–10 mm; sepals sometimes ligulate, pilose . . . . *C. glacialis*

6b. Branches mostly prostrate; leaves ≤ 17 mm, sepals not ligulate, strigose-villous **7**

7a. Leaves mid-green, petiole 1–3 mm; fertile shoots 8–15 mm; corolla 7–12 mm. . . . .*C. microphyllus*

7b. Leaves dark, often blackish green, petiole ≤ 5 mm; fertile shoots 5–12 mm; corolla ≤ 15 mm **8**

8a. Leaves oblanceolate, oblong, rarely lanceolate, 8–17 mm; hypanthium narrowly cupulate; fruit dark red-crimson, dull or slightly shiny . . . . *C. integrifolius*

8b. Leaves elliptic, oblong or lanceolate, 5–15 mm; hypanthium widely cupulate; fruit crimson, dull . . . .*C. brandisii*

1. ***Cotoneaster brandisii*** G. Klotz in Wiss. Z. Martin-Luther-Univ. Halle-Wittenberg, Math.-Naturwiss. 15: 537 (1966). Type: India, Garhwal-Himalaya, Chakarta, 17 August 1946, *M. B. Raizada 98015* (holo DD).

Shrub, 0.5–1.5 m. Branches prostrate or ascending, spreading and rooting; branchlets spiraled, black-purple to gray-brown and green striate, initially strigose-villous. Leaves evergreen, coriaceous, on sterile shoots spiraled, elliptic, oblong, or lanceolate, 5–15 × 3–8 mm, apex obtuse or acute, mucronate, base cuneate or obtuse, margin slightly undulate and recurved, villous, upper surface dark green, dull becoming shiny, initially with sparse strigose-villous hairs mostly on midrib, veins mostly 4, lower surface gray-green, initially strigose-villous; petiole 2–5 mm, densely strigose-pilose. Fertile shoots 10–12 mm, including mostly 2 leaves and 1(–2) flower(s); pedicel densely strigose-villous. Hypanthium widely-cupulate, densely villous-strigose; sepals acute or obtuse, often recurved, villous-strigose, border membranous. Flower buds white with a pink spot. Corolla 12–15 mm, petals spreading, white. Stamens 18–20; filaments white, anthers red-purple. Fruit depressed-globose or subglobose, 6–9 mm, crimson, dull, few sparse hairs, calyx lobes erect, green, villous, naval with small opening. Nutlets 2, style remains at apex.

Seasons: Flowers May–June; fruit ripe October–November.

Chromosomes: Triploid (Bailey, pers. comm.).

Hardiness: −15°C (5°F).

Area: India (Uttaranchal Pradesh, Himachal Pradesh, Tamil Nadu). Kashmir.

Notes: *Cotoneaster brandisii* is not common, although it sometimes is seen in cultivation as *C. marginatus* or *C. integrifolius*. *Cotoneaster brandisii* has also been collected in the Nilgiri hills of Tamil Nadu in 1970 by collectors for Flinck and Hylmö (hort. 1681), and it is grown in the Czech Republic at the botanic garden of Mendel University in Brno (#29-00).

2. ***Cotoneaster congestus*** Baker in Saunder's Ref. Bot. 1: pl. 51 (1869). Type: cult. *C. congesta*, original of Saunder's *Refugium* plate 51, from W. W. Saunder's garden (1868) (lecto designated K).

Shrub variable, mostly dense and congested, sometimes mound-forming or carpeting, 0.2–1 m. Branches suberect, prostrate or decumbent, often rooting; branchlets spiraled, purple, initially sparsely pilose-strigose. Leaves evergreen or semi, chartaceous or sub coriaceous, on sterile shoots spiraled, obovate, obovate-elliptic, obovate-oblong, 4–13 × 3–8 mm, apex rotund, obtuse or emarginate, base cuneate or obtuse, upper surface smooth, pale to mid-green, dull or rarely slightly shiny, glabrous or initially with single hairs on midrib, veins 2–3, lower surface light grayish green, initially sparsely pilose; petiole 3–5 mm, thin, often reddish, initially sparsely pilose. Fertile shoots 10–25 mm, including mostly 4 leaves and 1(–2) flower(s); pedicel 3–7 mm, initially sparsely pilose. Hypanthium cupulate, initially sparsely pilose; sepals acute or apiculate, rarely obtuse, sparsely pilose or glabrous, margin villous. Flower buds pink and white. Corolla 7–9 mm, petals spreading, white. Stamens 20, white; anthers violet. Fruit depressed-globose or globose, 8–10 mm, crimson to cherry, dull, glabrous, calyx lobes subglabrous. Nutlets 2, rarely 1 or 3, obovoid, style remains at apex.

Seasons: Flowers May–June; fruit ripe October.

Chromosomes: Diploid (Klotz and Krügel 1983a; McAllister, pers. comm.; Jewsbury, pers. comm.). Sexual, outbreeding, very variable from seed.

Hardiness: −10°C (14°F).

Area: Nepal. India (Sikkim, Himachal Pradesh). Kashmir. Bhutan.

Notes: The herbarium sheet of *Cotoneaster congestus* at the RGB Kew is of a specimen cultivated by William Saunders from seed given to him by Dr. Royle from the western Himalaya in northern India, and it was this plant on which John Baker based his original description. The species was introduced before 1868. *Cotoneaster congestus* and its forms are very useful slow-growing little shrubs for the smaller garden. They need shelter from cold north winds. This outbreeding diploid needs more research. Recently reintroduced into cultivation.

Cultivars: '**Nanus**', a dwarf form suitable for pots and rock garden pockets. '**Nymans**' (syn. 'Pyramidalis'), dense and bushy, height to 1 m, leaves large (13 × 8 mm), pale green with red petiole and some autumn color. '**Seattle**', branches 1.5 m, prostrate; leaves dark green; pedicels, hypanthium, and sepals with strigose-pilose hairs; stamens 16–18, fruit red. Tetraploid (Bailey, pers. comm.). Probably a new species.

3. *Cotoneaster glacialis* (J. D. Hooker ex Wenzig) Panigrahi & Kumar in Bull. Surv. India 28: 75 (1986). Synonyms: *C. microphyllus* f. *glacialis* J. D. Hooker ex Wenzig (1874); *C. nivalis* (G. Klotz) Panigrahi & Kumar (1986). Type: India, Sikkim, Lachen, 15 July 1845, J. D. Hooker (lecto B, iso CAL, K, LD). **PLATE 64.**

Shrub often dense, sometimes mound-forming, 0.2–1 m. Branches prostrate, suberect or procumbent; branchlets spiraled, purple-black, initially strigose. Leaves evergreen, coriaceous or subcoriaceous, on sterile shoots broadly elliptic or broadly obovate, 5–10 × 4–7 mm, apex rotund, obtuse or emarginate, base obtuse or broadly cuneate, margin strigose, upper surface dark green, shiny, ageing slightly rugose, initially strigose, veins 2–4, lower surface light to whitish green with veins darker, pilose-strigose; petiole 2–3 mm, strigose. Fertile shoots 8–15 mm, including 4 leaves, and a single (–3) flower; pedicel strigose. Hypanthium cupulate, strigose; sepals acute, obtuse or ligulate, pilose, margin tomentose. Flower buds pinkish. Corolla 8–11 mm, petals spreading, white, glabrous. Stamens 20; filaments white; anthers violet. Fruit depressed-globose, 7 mm, crimson to cherry, sparsely pilose, calyx lobes erect, pilose. Nutlets (1–)2(–3), style/scar at elongated apex.

Seasons: Flowers May–June; fruit ripe September–November.

Chromosomes: Tetraploid (McAllister, pers. comm.).

Hardiness: –15°C (5°F).

Area: Nepal. India (Sikkim).

Notes: *Cotoneaster glacialis* is a smart little year-round shrub with lovely shiny leaves which in spring are covered with a multitude of flowers and then followed by many bright fruit. Recently reintroduced into cultivation. This species is closely related to both *C. microphyllus* and *C. congestus*, and more research is needed into the complexities of these three species.

4. *Cotoneaster integrifolius* (Roxburgh) G. Klotz in Wiss. Z. Martin-Luther-Univ. Halle-Wittenberg, Math.-Naturwiss. 12: 779 (1963). Synonym: *Crataegus integrifolius* Roxburgh (1832). Type: *Crataegus integrifolia* Roxburgh, (Nepal) from the alpine zone of Gossainkund, August 1821, herb. *Wallich 662* (b=662.B) (lecto designated K).

Shrub, 0.5–1.5 m. Branches 1–1.5 m, suberect, decumbent, wide-spreading; branchlets spiraled, purple-black, sometimes green and brown striate, initially strigose. Leaves evergreen, coriaceous, on sterile shoots spiraled, oblanceolate, oblong, rarely lanceolate, 8–17 × 3–8 mm, apex rotund or obtuse, rarely emarginate or acute, base cuneate, upper surface dark green sometimes blue-green, shiny, initially strigose, veins 2–4, lower surface grayish white and faintly reticulate, densely strigose or strigose-pilose; petiole 1–5 mm, strigose. Fertile shoots 5–12 mm, including 2–3 leaves and 1 (rarely 2) subsessile flower(s); pedicel densely strigose. Hypanthium narrowly cupulate, strigose hairs often dense;

sepals acute or obtuse, sometimes shortly mucronate, strigose-villous hairs often dense, border membranous, apex often red, margin densely villous-strigose. Flower buds pink. Corolla 7–15 mm, petals spreading, white, glabrous. Stamens 20, erect; filaments narrowly subulate, white; anthers red-purple. Styles 2(–3). Fruit erect, depressed-globose, 7–9 mm, dark rich red with crimson, dull or slightly shiny, sparsely villous, calyx lobes suberect or erect, villous. Nutlets 2, rarely 3, obovate 3–4 mm, style remains at apex.

Seasons: Flowers May–June; fruit ripe October–November.

Chromosomes: Tetraploid (Zeilinga 1964; McAllister, pers. comm., Krügel 1992a; Bailey, pers. comm.; Jewsbury, pers. comm.). Apomictic, true from seed.

Hardiness: −15°C (5°F).

Area: Nepal. India (Himachal Pradesh, Sikkim), Bhutan.

Notes: *Cotoneaster integrifolius* is very common in cultivation under various names, often as *C. microphyllus*. This species is frequently found as a garden escape, naturalizing on coastal cliffs. It is a tough little shrub which is extremely wind-hardy. Recently reintroduced into cultivation.

Cultivar: '**Silver Shadow**, a particularly dark, shiny blue-green leaved form.

5. ***Cotoneaster marginatus*** Lindley ex Loudon in Encycl. Trees & Shrubs, p. 411 (1842). Synonyms: *C. marginatus* Lindley ex Schlechtendal (1854); *C. lanatus* Jacques (1859). Type: as *Cotoneaster microphyllus*, Hort. Berlin, herb. Schlechtendal (lecto designated by G. Klotz [1963] HAL). **PLATE 65**.

Shrubs variable, 1–5 m. Branches erect, ascending, sometimes prostrate, wide-spreading, often 3 m or more; branchlets spiraled, red-purple, initially yellowish pilose-strigose. Leaves evergreen or semi, coriaceous or subcoriaceous, on sterile shoots spiraled or distichous, elliptic, obovate or lanceolate-elliptic, 7–45 × 3–28 mm, apex obtuse or acute, rarely emarginate, base cuneate or obtuse, margin villous-strigose, upper surface sometimes minutely rugose, dark green, slightly shiny, initially sparsely strigose, veins 4–6 lightly impressed, lower surface light green and reticulate, initially strigose-pilose or strigose-villous; petiole (1–)3–6 mm, strigose-pilose. Fertile shoots 15–35 mm, including mostly 4 leaves and an erect, 2- to 10-flowered inflorescence; pedicels 3–7 mm, strigose-pilose. Hypanthium widely-cupulate, strigose-pilose; sepals acute, sometimes apiculate, pilose-strigose, membranous border sometimes red, margin villous. Flower buds white with pink tinge. Corolla 8–12 mm, petals spreading, white. Stamens (18–)20; filaments white; anthers violet-black. Fruit depressed-globose, often succulent, 8–10 mm, crimson, ruby to dark ruby, dull, sparsely villous, calyx lobes erect or suberect, villous. Nutlets 2(–3), style remains at or near apex.

Seasons: Flowers May–June; fruit ripe October–November.

Chromosomes: Diploid (Jewsbury, pers. comm.). Sexual, outbreeding, variable from seed. Outbreeding shrubs with triploid counts (McAllister 1989; Bailey, pers. comm.) need further investigation as several taxa may be involved. It is possible that this species is producing offspring with varying counts.

Hardiness: −15°C (5°F).

Area: India (Himachal Pradesh, Uttaranchal Pradesh). Nepal.

Notes: *Cotoneaster marginatus* was introduced into cultivation in 1838. Often hybridizing with other diploid species, it can produce very variable offspring, some of which have previously been accredited to other species. It caused much confusion before its diploid nature was realized. The Chadwell and McKelvie collection of *C. marginatus* made at Langtang, in Sing Gompa, Gossainkund, Nepal, in 1990, from the original seed produced shrubs which varied between lower growing, small leaved specimens and erect, larger-leaved specimens. *Cotoneaster marginatus* is vigorous growing, often forming a dense mass of branches which project from the shrub in all directions. The abundant fruit are slow-ripening and hence are not taken by birds until well into winter. *Cotoneaster marginatus* and *C. cooperi* are two of the most promiscuous species in the genus.

Cultivars: '**Antonin Nohel**', large and wide-spreading, height to 3 m, extremely heavily fruiting, fruit light crimson to light red, persisting throughout winter and into spring. A very valuable shrub for winter fruit color. '**Blazovice**', similar to 'Antonin Nohel' and 'Brno' but slightly taller and more narrowly erect, leaves larger and darker green, fruit becoming rich red. '**Brno**', very similar to 'Antonin Nohel' but more dense in habit. Due to the fruit remaining hard for a long period, these three cultivars are untouched by birds until the depths of winter when the fruit begin to soften and, due to the vast quantity of fruit produced, provide welcome food until spring. '**Eastleigh**', vigorous and much-branched, leaves blackish green, fruit huge, succulent, deep crimson to rich dark red, dull, skin splitting at maturity, produced in profusion. Selected around 1960 by Hillier Nurseries in Hampshire, England.

6. *Cotoneaster meuselii* G. Klotz in Wiss. Z. Martin-Luther-Univ. Halle-Wittenberg, Math.-Naturwiss. 12: 777 (1963). Type: W Himalaya, in well-drained cedar-oak forest, near the town of Mussoori, 13 October 1962, Meusel & Schubert (holo HAL).
   PLATE 66.

Shrub dense, 0.5–1.5 m. Branches suberect or prostrate; branchlets spiraled, red-brown to grayish, initially strigose-pilose. Leaves evergreen, subcoriaceous or coriaceous, on sterile shoots spiraled, narrowly-elliptic, oblong-oblanceolate or narrowly-obovate, 8–16 × 4–9 mm, apex obtuse, base cuneate or obtuse, upper surface mid to dark green, shiny, midrib initially sparsely pilose, veins 2–4, lower surface gray-green, initially pilose-strigose; petiole 2–4 mm, initially pilose-strigose. Fertile shoots 10–20 mm, including 3–4 leaves and an erect, mostly 1(–4) flower(s); pedicels 2–5 mm, pilose-strigose. Hypanthium cupulate, shiny, strigose; sepals acute, acuminate or obtuse, pilose-strigose, margin villous-tomentose. Flower buds white with red stripes. Corolla 12–14 mm, sometimes 6-petaled; petals spreading becoming recurved, white. Stamens 20; filaments white; anthers violet. Fruit globose or subglobose, 6–8 mm, crimson, dull, glabrous, calyx lobes erect, green, navel open. Nutlets 2(–3), style remains at apex.

Seasons: Flowers May–June; fruit ripe October–November.

Chromosomes: Triploid (Bailey, pers. comm.; Jewsbury, pers. comm.).

Hardiness: −15°C (5°F).

Area: Nepal. India (Uttaranchal Pradesh, Himachal Pradesh)

Notes: *Cotoneaster meuselii* is fairly common in botanic gardens and large collections, primarily from the Major Tom Spring-Smythe collection (*138-64*) from Dhorpatan, Nepal, in 1964. It is exceedingly floriferous but rarely sets many fruit.

7. *Cotoneaster microphyllus* Wallich ex Lindley in Edward's Bot. Reg. 13: t. 1114 (1827). Type: (Nepal) from the alpine zone of Gossainkund, August 1821, *Wallich 662* (a = 662.1) (holo K). **PLATE 67**.

Shrub dense, often mound-forming, 0.6–1 m. Branches suberect, prostrate, decumbent, spreading; branchlets spiraled, maroon to purple-black, initially strigose. Leaves evergreen, coriaceous, on sterile shoots spiraled, rarely distichous, elliptic, obovate, broadly-elliptic or broadly-obovate, 7–13 × 4–9 mm, apex rotund, obtuse, sometimes acute or emarginate, base obtuse or cuneate, margin strigose, upper surface mid to dark green, shiny, sparsely strigose, veins 2–4, lower surface gray-green, initially strigose; petiole 1–3 mm, strigose. Fertile shoots 8–15 mm, including 4 leaves and an erect, mostly 1(–3) flower(s); pedicels strigose. Hypanthium cupulate, base strigose-villous; sepals acute, obtuse or acuminate, sparsely strigose-villous, margin villous. Flower buds pink. Corolla 7–11 mm, petals spreading, white. Stamens 20; filaments white; anthers violet-black. Fruit depressed-globose, 6–8 mm, crimson, subglabrous, calyx lobes erect or suberect, pilose. Nutlets 2(–3), style remains at apex.

Seasons: Flowers May–June; fruit ripe October–November.

Chromosomes: Tetraploid (McAllister, pers. comm.; Krügel 1992a).

Hardiness: −18°C (−1°F).

Area: Nepal.

Notes: Klotz (1963b) included within *Cotoneaster microphyllus* a number of taxa from a wide area ranging from the Western Himalaya, India, Uttaranchal Pradesh (Kumaon division), through to eastern Tibet and the provinces of Yunnan and Sichuan in China, but *C. microphyllus* in its strictest sense has only been recorded from Nepal. Many chromosome counts have been published for this species, but it is uncertain if *C. microphyllus* in its strictest sense was always involved. A number of taxa are incorrectly cultivated as this species. It is possible though that this species is producing offspring with variable counts. More research is desperately needed. *Cotoneaster microphyllus*, according to John Lindley (1827) is "a beautiful little evergreen shrub, clothed with deep-green shiny foliage, which no winter will impair and when in blossom strewed with snow-white flowers, which, reposing on a rich couch of green, have so brilliant an appearance, that a poet would compare them to diamonds lying on a bed of emeralds." *Cotoneaster microphyllus* is not so commonly cultivated as in the past, many shrubs grown under this name are the closely related *C. integrifolius*. Recently reintroduced into cultivation.

Cultivar: '**Emerald Spray**', branches dense, spreading, and arching, leaves shiny and emerald green, flowers white, fruit red, 8–9 mm. Probably *C. microphyllus*.

8. *Cotoneaster thymifolius* Baker in Saunder's Ref. Bot. 1:50 (1869). Synonyms: *C. linearifolius* (G. Klotz) G. Klotz (1978); *C. microphyllus* Wallich ex Lindley f. *linearifolius* G. Klotz (1957). Type: India (Himachal Pradesh) Simla, 11 June 1848, T. Thomson (holo K, iso BM, LD).

Shrubs variable, dense, slow-growing, 0.3–1 m. Branches stiff, congested, ascending, suberect or decumbent; branchlets spiraled, red-brown, initially yellowish strigose. Leaves evergreen, coriaceous, on sterile shoots spiraled, linear or narrowly obovate, 5–12 × 2–3 mm, apex rotund, obtuse or emarginate, base cuneate, rarely obtuse, margin recurved, upper surface dark green (blackish green), shiny, sparsely strigose-pilose, veins 2–4, lower surface grayish, strigose; petiole 0.5–3.5 mm, strigose. Fertile shoots 5–12 mm, including 4–6 leaves and topped by 1(–2) subsessile flower(s). Hypanthium narrowly cupulate, strigose; sepals acute or obtuse, pilose-strigose, margin tomentose-strigose. Flower bud pink, red and white. Corolla 6–9 mm, petals spreading, white with a little pink from reverse often showing. Stamens 15–20, white; anthers violet-black. Fruit globose or depressed-globose, 3–6 mm, crimson, dull, glabrescent, calyx lobes erect, villous, navel open. Nutlets (2–)3, style remains at apex.

Seasons: Flowers May–June; fruit October–December.

Chromosomes: Diploid (Krügel 1992a; McAllister, pers. comm.). Sexual, outbreeding, variable from seed.

Hardiness: −15°C (5°F).

Area: India (Himachal Pradesh). Nepal.

Notes: *Cotoneaster thymifolius* is a bit of puzzle. Previously thought to possibly be a form of *C. integrifolius*, *C. thymifolius* seems to be much more closely related to *C. congestus*. More study is needed into the relationship between these two diploid species. This lovely miniature cotoneaster is a real little treasure. It is very pretty at all times—in leaf, covered with its pinkish white flowers, or when its little beadlike fruit are sprinkled over its branches. Recently reintroduced into cultivation.

9. *Cotoneaster uva-ursi* (Lindley) G. Don in Loudon Hort. Brit. (1830). Synonyms: *C. microphyllus* Wallich ex Lindley var. *uva-ursi* Lindley in Bot. Reg. 14: 1187 (1828); *C. rotundifolius* hort. non Wallich ex Lindley. Type: Nepal, herb. Lambert, *Mespilus rotundifolia* Ehrhart (lecto designated UPS). PLATE 68.

Shrub, 0.5–1.5 m. Branches to 2 m, ascending, arched or prostrate, robust; branchlets spiraled, purple-black to brown, initially yellow-green strigose. Leaves evergreen, coriaceous, on sterile shoots spiraled, broadly elliptic or broadly obovate, rarely suborbicular or oblong, 7–21 × 5–15 mm, apex obtuse or acute, mucronate, base obtuse or cuneate, margin strigose, upper surface dark green, shiny, initially sparsely strigose midrib, veins

3–5, lower surface yellowish green, pilose-strigose; petiole 2–3 mm, strigose. Fertile shoots 10–20 mm, including 2–3 leaves and 1(–3) flower(s); pedicel strigose. Hypanthium cupulate, pale green, sparsely strigose, sepals mostly acute, villous-strigose with a broad membranous border, margin tomentose. Flower buds white with greenish stripes. Corolla 10–14 mm, petals slowly becoming spreading, white. Stamens 20; white; anthers purple. Fruit depressed-globose or globose, 7–10 mm, currant to cherry-red, dull, glabrous, calyx lobes suberect, pilose. Nutlets 2, style remains at elongated apex.

Seasons: Flowers May–June; fruit ripe October–November.

Chromosomes: Tetraploid (Moffett 1931; Broertjes 1956; Zeilinga 1964; Hensen 1966; Klotz 1968b; Jewsbury, pers. comm.). Apomictic, true from seed.

Hardiness: –15°C (5°F).

Area: Nepal. Bhutan.

Notes: *Cotoneaster uva-ursi* is fairly frequently found in cultivation mistakenly named *C. rotundifolius*, which is correctly the name of a species belonging to series *Distichi* in subgenus *Cotoneaster* (see notes for *C. rotundifolius*). Introduced in 1825, *C. uva ursi* has, according to the type description and figure, 2–3 flowers per inflorescence, although in cultivation it is known to produce mostly single flowers, rarely 2–3 together. In common with many species in series *Microphylli*, *C. uva-ursi* can be grafted to form a standard. It is vigorous growing and can also be used to make a low and wide hedge which needs little maintenance. Recently reintroduced into cultivation.

14. Series *Radicantes* G. Klotz in Wiss. Z. Martin-Luther-Univ. Halle-Wittenberg, Math.-Naturwiss. 12: 785 (1963). Including series *Procumbentes* G. Klotz (1968).
Type: *C. radicans* Dammer ex C. K. Schneider (1906), lecto designated here. Klotz (1963) named his new series *Radicantes* but mistakenly used *C. dammeri* C. K. Schneider as the type. Hereby corrected.

Carpeting to prostrate shrubs. Branches 1–3 m, procumbent, easily rooting, slender; branchlets distichous or spiraled. Leaves on sterile shoots distichous, rarely spiraled. Inflorescences sometimes becoming pendent, 1- to 3(–4)-flowered; pedicels 2–15 mm. Hypanthium widely cupulate. Nutlets 2–5, sometimes reddish, style remains at or near apex.

Early to mid season.

China (Yunnan, Sichuan, Hubei, Gansu). Tibet. India (Himachal Pradesh, Uttaranchal Pradesh, Ladakh). Kashmir. Taiwan.

9 species: *C. cashmiriensis*, *C. cochleatus*, *C. dammeri*, *C. elatus*, *C. melanotrichus*, *C. morrisonensis*, *C. procumbens*, *C. prostratus*, *C. radicans*. Also including *C.* ×*suecicus*.

Key to Series *Radicantes*

1a. Leaves 15–40 mm, light to mid-green, very shiny, veins 5–6, deeply impressed; fertile shoots 20–40 mm; pedicels 4–15 mm; nutlets 4–5 . . . . *C. dammeri*

1b. Leaves mostly dark green, shiny, veins 2–4(–5), level or lightly impressed; fertile shoots 8–30 mm; pedicels 2–8 mm; nutlets 2–3(–4) 2

2a. Leaves sometimes lanceolate; flower buds white; anthers deep pink; fruit pendent, ellipsoid or subglobose. . . . . *C. melanotrichus*

2b. Leaves not lanceolate; flower buds mostly pink; anthers purple-black; fruit ± erect, globose or depressed-globose 3

3a. Branches coarse; inflorescence 1- to 4-flowered; hypanthium mostly infundibulate; corolla 7–8 mm . . . . *C. elatus*

3b. Branches slender; inflorescence 1(–3)-flowered; hypanthium cupulate or campanulate; corolla 8–12 mm. 4

4a. Branches plaint; pedicels 3–8 mm, thin; sepals apiculate or acute; fruit orange-red to red with crimson . . . . *C. radicans*

4b. Branches rigid; pedicels 2–6 mm, coarse; sepals mostly acute or obtuse; fruit crimson or ruby. 5

5a. Upper leaf surface mostly dull; flowers solitary; fruit 5–6 mm, pale red with crimson . . . . *C. procumbens*

5b. Upper leaf surface shiny; inflorescences 1(–3)-flowered; fruit 6–11, rich red or ruby and crimson 6

6a. Leaves 12–22 mm, upper surface glabrous, veins 3–5 impressed, petiole 3–8 mm; fruit mostly obovate. . . . . *C. morrisonensis*

6b. Leaves 4–14 mm, upper surface sparse hairs especially at midrib, veins 2–4 not impressed, petiole 1–5 mm; fruit mostly subglobose. 7

7a. Leaves mostly broadly obovate or suborbicular; fertile shoots 8–15 mm; fruit 7–9 mm; nutlets 2–3 . . . . *C. cochleatus*

7b. Leaves mostly elliptic or obovate-elliptic; fertile shoots 15–25 mm; fruit 8–11 mm; nutlets 2 8

8a. Leaves coriaceous, elliptic or obovate elliptic, 4–11; corolla 8–10 mm; fruit subglobose, crimson . . . . *C. cashmiriensis*

8b. Leaves subcoriaceous, broadly obovate-elliptic or oblong, 6–13 mm; corolla 10–12 mm; fruit crimson to ruby. . . . . *C. prostratus*

1. *Cotoneaster cashmiriensis* G. Klotz in Wiss. Z. Martin-Luther-Univ. Halle-Wittenberg, Math.-Naturwiss. 12: 778 (1963). Type: Kashmir, near Sinthan Pass, 4 July 1939, *F. Ludlow 179* (holo BM).

Shrub dense and carpeting, 0.2–0.5 m. Branches prostrate, often rooting; branchlets distichous or spiraled, black-purple to gray-brown, initially yellow-strigose. Leaves evergreen, coriaceous, on sterile shoots distichous or spiraled, elliptic or obovate-elliptic, 4–

11 × 3–7 mm, apex obtuse or acute, mucronate, base obtuse or cuneate, upper surface mid to dark green, shiny, initially sparsely long-haired pilose-strigose, veins 2–3, lower surface grayish green, reticulate, pilose-strigose; petiole 1–4 mm, pilose-strigose. Fertile shoots 15–25 mm, including 3–4 leaves, and 1(–2) flower(s); pedicel 2–5 mm, pilose-strigose. Hypanthium campanulate, pilose-strigose; sepals acute or acuminate, pilose-strigose, margin densely villous. Flower buds white or very pale pink. Corolla 8–10 mm, petals spreading, white. Stamens 18–20; filaments white; anthers purple. Fruit subglobose, 8–10 mm, crimson, dull, few pilose hairs, calyx lobes erect, pilose. Nutlets 2, style remains at apex.

Seasons: Flowers June; fruit ripe October–November.

Chromosomes: Tetraploid (Klotz and Krügel 1983a; McAllister, pers. comm.). Apomictic, true from seed.

Hardiness: −15°C (5°F).

Area: India (Himachal Pradesh, Uttaranchal Pradesh, Ladakh). Kashmir.

Notes: Discovered in September 1993 by Chris Chadwell (*CC 1359*) in the Ladakh region of India, *Cotoneaster cashmiriensis* is a useful little evergreen which is frequently confused with the very similar *C. prostratus*.

2. *Cotoneaster cochleatus* (Franchet) G. Klotz in Wiss. Z. Martin-Luther-Univ. Halle-Wittenberg, Math.-Naturwiss. 6: 952 (1957). Synonym: *C. buxifolius* Lindley f. *cochleatus* Franchet (1890). Type: China, Yunnan, in Mount Koua-la-po, near Hokin, 27 May 1884, *J. Delavay 784* (lecto P). **PLATE 69.**

Shrub dense and carpeting, 0.2–0.4 m. Branches prostrate, rooting; branchlets spiraled and distichous, red to purple-black, initially yellow-green strigose. Leaves evergreen, coriaceous, on sterile shoots spiraled, obovate, broadly-obovate or suborbicular, 5–14 × 3–9 mm, apex rotund or obtuse, sometimes emarginate, base obtuse or broadly cuneate, margin slightly recurved, upper surface sometimes lightly rugose, dark green, shiny, glabrescent, veins 2–3, lower surface grayish, reticulate, initially densely strigose-villous; petiole 1–4 mm, strigose. Fertile shoots 8–15 mm, including mostly 4 leaves and 1(–3) flower(s); pedicels 3–5 mm, strigose. Hypanthium cupulate, strigose or pilose-strigose; sepals obtuse or acute, initially sparsely pilose-strigose, border broad, membranous, margin villous. Flower buds pinkish. Corolla 8–10 mm, petals spreading, white. Stamens (15–)20; filaments white; anthers purple. Styles 2(–3). Fruit subglobose, 7–9 mm, crimson, sparsely pilose, calyx lobes suberect, sparsely strigose. Nutlets 2(–3), style remains at apex on small projection.

Seasons: Flowers May–June; fruit ripe September–November.

Chromosomes: Tetraploid (Zeilinga 1964; Krügel 1992a; Bailey, pers. comm.). Apomictic, true from seed.

Hardiness: −15°C (5°F).

Area: China (Yunnan, Sichuan). Tibet.

Notes: *Cotoneaster cochleatus* is a charming little shrub. Low and neat, it is effective as ground cover tumbling over any obstacles in its path. It often bears numerous fruit. This species was collected in Cangshan, Dali, Yunnan, in 1996, by Jeanette Fryer (*JFYU 017*). Received RHS Award of Merit in 1930, and Award of Garden Merit in 1984.

3. ***Cotoneaster dammeri*** C. K. Schneider, Ill. Handb. Laubholzk. 1: 761 (1906); cf. Feddes Repert. 3: 222 (1906). Synonym: *C. humifusus* Duthie ex Veitch (1906). Type: China, W Hubei, without locality, June 1900, Veitch expedition, *E. H. Wilson 1966* (holo W, iso A, B).

Shrub carpeting, to 0.2 m. Branches to 1.5 m, procumbent, pliant, rooting; branchlets distichous or spiraled, greenish to light brown, densely lenticellate, initially pilose-strigose. Leaves evergreen, coriaceous, on sterile shoots distichous, elliptic, obovate, rarely suborbicular, 15–40 × 7–21 mm, apex obtuse, rotund, or acute, base cuneate or obtuse, upper surface rugose, light to mid-green, intensely shiny, often single hairs on midrib, veins 5–8 deeply impressed, lower surface grayish green, reticulate, initially villous; petiole 2–9 mm, villous-strigose. Fertile shoots 20–40 mm, including mostly 4 leaves and a (1–)2- to 3(–4)-flowered, slightly pendent inflorescence; pedicels 4–15 mm, thin, villous-strigose. Hypanthium cupulate, pale green, sparsely pilose-strigose; sepals obtuse or acute, sparsely pilose-strigose, border narrow, membranous, often red-tipped, margin sparsely villous. Flower buds white. Corolla 10–12 mm, petals spreading, white. Stamens 20, erect, filaments white; anthers purple-black. Fruit globose, 6–7 mm, red, shiny, glabrous, calyx lobes suberect, glabrous, navel open. Nutlets (4–)5, style remains c. apex.

Seasons: Flowers May–June; fruit ripe October–November.

Chromosomes: Diploid (Zeilinga 1964; Hensen 1966; Klotz 1968b; Klotz and Krügel 1983a; Bailey, pers. comm.). Sexual, outbreeding, variable from seed.

Hardiness: –18°C (–1°F).

Area: China (Hubei).

Notes: *Cotoneaster dammeri* is common in cultivation, frequently as *C. dammeri* var. *radicans* or *C. dammeri* 'Major', causing confusion. This species can fairly quickly cover large areas, adapting to all levels and angles over which it spreads. Once established it makes an effective ground cover. It is excellent for walls, down or trained up, and is good as a carpet over bulbs. The leaves are sometimes bronzed by frost during winter. This useful and pleasant species was discovered in 1886 by Augustine Henry and introduced in 1900 by Ernest Wilson. It occurs at around 1500–2000 m in the Hubei province of China.

Cotoneaster dammeri subsp. ***songmingensis*** C. Y. Wu & L.-H. Zhou in Acta Bot. Yunnan. 22: 380 (2000), from Yunnan, Songmin, Liangwang Shan, Li-Hua Zhou (KUN), is said to differ from *C. dammeri* only in its 2–3 mm petioles and pedicels, and 3 nutlets.

Cultivars: 'Cardinal', height 30–50 cm, wider than high, leaves to 30 mm, somewhat oblong, fruit red, quite large. This cultivar from Germany is said to have arisen as a seedling from *C. dammeri* 'Hybridus Pendulus'. 'Gelre', a robust, ground-hugging form, leaves quite large, fruit few. '**Holstein Resi**', very low growing, leaves fresh green, fruit sparse, red. Of German origin. '**Hybridus Pendulus**' (PLATE 70), prostrate, leaves 40–70

× 15–25 mm, upper surface dark green and slightly shiny, autumn color yellow, flowers in small clusters, fruit rich red, produced in abundance. Attractive as a specimen shrub. Valuable as a ground-cover but more often trained as a standard by tying main branch in for the first years to achieve an erect shrub with side branches which hang in a narrowly pendulous fashion until they reach the ground where they run along. Can also be grafted onto *C. ×watereri* to form wider head. Received RHS Award of Merit in 1953. Possibly a hybrid between *C. dammeri* and *C. salicifolius*. 'Klampen', fast growing with a partly procumbent, partly ascending habit, leaves to 30 mm, dark green with striking red petiole, fruit numerous, bright red. Said to perhaps be of hybrid origin. 'Lofast', height c. 30 cm, densely branched, rapidly forming a ground-cover, leaves attractive dark green, fruit abundant, shiny red. Said to be extremely hardy. Raised in the United States at Hopkins Nursery in Bothell, Washington, by Harold T. Hopkins, pre 1960. 'Major' (PLATE 71), robust form, leaves mostly suborbicular, occasional ones yellow-orange in autumn, fruit sparse. Hardy and commonly grown. Often found in cultivation as *C. dammeri* var. *radicans*. 'Mooncreeper', prostrate and carpeting, leaves fresh green and lustrous, flowers quite large, fruit small and numerous, red. A hardy, valuable ground-cover. 'Schoon', creeping, leaves dark green, fruit red. Originating in Germany. 'Thiensen', creeping, low and dense, leaves 40–50 mm, fruit sparse, red. Similar to 'Major'. 'Typ Reisert', small and compact, branches short, stiff, and numerous. Possibly of hybrid origin. In the Italian nursery trade.

4. *Cotoneaster elatus* G. Klotz in Wiss. Z. Martin-Luther-Univ. Halle-Wittenberg, Math.-Naturwiss. 12: 781 (1963). Type: China, Yunnan, Lan-ping Hsien, 26 September 1933, *H. T. Tsai 56142* (A). PLATE 72.

Shrub, 0.5 (–1) m high (3–4 m supported). Branches wide-spreading, prostrate or decumbent, coarse, rooting; branchlets spiraled, maroon, minutely verruculose, initially pilose-strigose. Leaves evergreen, coriaceous or subcoriaceous, on sterile shoots spiraled or distichous, elliptic or narrowly-elliptic, 7–17 × 5–10 mm, apex acute or obtuse, base cuneate or obtuse, upper surface dark green, shiny, initially very sparsely strigose-pilose, veins 3, lower surface light green, reticulate, sparsely pilose or pilose-strigose; petiole 3–5 mm, strigose. Fertile shoots 10–30 mm, including 4 leaves and an erect 1- to 4-flowered inflorescence; pedicels 2–5 mm, pilose-strigose. Hypanthium narrowly-cupulate, pilose-strigose; sepals acute sometimes obtuse, sparsely pilose-strigose, margin villous. Flower buds pink. Corolla 7–9 mm, petals spreading, white. Stamens 20; filaments white; anthers purple-black. Fruit depressed-globose, obovoid, rarely ellipsoid, 5–6 mm, dark ruby with crimson, dull, glabrous, calyx lobes erect. Nutlets 2, style remains at apex.

Seasons: Flowers May; fruit ripe October–November.

Chromosomes: Triploid (Klotz and Krügel 1983a; Bailey, pers. comm.; Jewsbury, pers. comm.). Apomictic, true from seed.

Hardiness: −15°C (5°F).

Area: China (Yunnan).

Notes: *Cotoneaster elatus* has been around for many years, probably originating from a George Forrest collection, but grown under an assortment of names. Klotz stated (his notes were made from an herbarium sheet) that the height was around 1.5 m, but this assumption of height was probably based on the coarse branch on the herbarium sheet. The species has been collected by Jeanette Fryer (*JFYU 087*) in Napa Hai, Zhongdian, Yunnan, in 1996.

Cultivar: '**Ruby**' (*C. sikkimensis* hort.), similar if not the same as *C. elatus* except the lower surface of the leaves is more bluish green with the midrib frequently ageing red. Tetraploid (Hensen 1966; Klotz and Krügel 1983a).

5. ***Cotoneaster melanotrichus*** (Franchet) G. Klotz in Mitt. Deutsch. Dendrol. Ges. 82: 65 (1996). Synonym: *C. buxifolius* Lindley f. *melanotrichus* Franchet (1890). Type: China, Yunnan, Hee-chan-men (Longkong), 6 December 1884, *J. Delavay 3742* (holo P, iso A, K). **PLATE 73**.

Shrub dense and carpeting, to 0.4 m. Branches prostrate, decumbent, rooting; branchlets distichous or spiraled, purple-black to gray-brown, initially strigose-villous. Leaves evergreen, coriaceous, on sterile shoots distichous or spiraled, elliptic, obovate or lanceolate, 6–14 × 4–8 mm, apex acute or obtuse, base cuneate or obtuse, upper surface dark green, shiny, initially sparsely villous, lower surface reticulate, long-haired pilose-strigose; petiole 1–3 mm, strigose. Fertile shoots 18–20 mm, including 2–4 leaves and a pendent, 1(–3) flower(s); pedicel 2–7 mm, strigose. Hypanthium cupulate, long-haired pilose-strigose; sepals acute, sometimes obtuse, mucronate, sparsely long-haired pilose-strigose; margin villous. Flower buds white. Corolla 10–12 mm, petals spreading, white. Stamens 20, white; anthers deep pink. Fruit ellipsoid to subglobose, 7–9 mm, scarlet-red, glabrous, calyx lobes suberect, succulent, red, glabrous. Nutlets (1–)2, style at apex.

Seasons: May–June; Fruit ripe October–November.

Chromosomes: Tetraploid (Bailey, pers. comm.).

Hardiness: −15°C (5°F).

Area: China (Yunnan, Sichuan).

Notes: There are no black hairs on *Cotoneaster melanotrichus*—this was a mistake made by Franchet when looking at a specimen on an herbarium sheet on which the hairs appeared to be black, probably the result of a fungal attack. For a long time this specimen was thought to be *C. cochleatus*, but Klotz (1996) quite rightly corrected this mistake. *Cotoneaster melanotrichus* is very similar in habit to *C. cochleatus* but has more acute leaves and fruit which are somewhat pendent, ellipsoid, and more red than crimson. The species has been found below Yulong Shan in Gan Hai Zi, Yunnan, in 1996, by Jeanette Fryer (*JFYU 122*).

6. ***Cotoneaster morrisonensis*** Hayata in Ic. Pl. Formosa 5: 62 (1915); illustr. Fl. Taiwan 62: pl. 478 (1977). Type: Taiwan, Mount Morrison, 3000 m, October 1906, U. Mori (holo TI).

Shrub mound-forming and carpeting, to 0.4 m. Branches 0.5–1 m, prostrate, rooting; branchlets spiraled or distichous, maroon with abundant lenticels, initially strigose. Leaves evergreen, coriaceous, on sterile shoots distichous, elliptic or obovate, 12–21 × 8–14 mm, apex obtuse or acute, base obtuse or cuneate, upper surface rugose, dark green, shiny, glabrous, veins 3–5 impressed, lower surface grayish green, reticulate, pilose-strigose; petiole 3–8 mm, pilose-strigose. Fertile shoots 15–20 mm, including 4 leaves and 1(–2) flower(s); pedicel 3–6 mm, strigose. Hypanthium cupulate, densely pilose-strigose; sepals obtuse or acute, villous-strigose, border broad, membranous, margin villous. Flower buds pinkish. Corolla 10–12 mm, petals spreading, white. Stamens 16–20 in 4 rings; filaments white; anthers purple-black. Fruit obovoid or globose, 6–7 mm, red, shiny, glabrous, calyx lobes suberect, often green, navel open. Nutlets 2(–3), pale reddish, style remains at apex.

Seasons: Flowers June; fruit ripe October–November.

Chromosomes: Tetraploid (Bailey, pers. comm.; Jewsbury, pers. comm.). Apomictic, true from seed.

Hardiness: −15°C (5°F).

Area: Taiwan.

Notes: *Cotoneaster morrisonensis* has long been in cultivation in Japan where it is frequently grown in containers and can be seen hanging in cascades from balconies in urban areas.

7. *Cotoneaster procumbens* G. Klotz in Wiss. Z. Martin-Luther-Univ. Halle-Wittenberg, Math.-Naturwiss. 6: 982 (1957); cf Wiss. Z. Martin-Luther-Univ. Halle-Wittenberg, Math.-Naturwiss. 12: 784 (1963). Type: cult. Germany BG, hort. Halle, as *C. prostratus* (lecto HAL).

Shrub dense and carpeting, to 0.2 m. Branches 1–1.5 m, procumbent, rooting; branchlets spiraled or distichous, brown, lenticellate, initially sparsely strigose. Leaves evergreen, subcoriaceous, on sterile shoots distichous or spiraled, obovate, 9–13 × 5–9 mm, apex rotund, often emarginate, sometimes obtuse, base cuneate, upper surface rugose, initially flushed purple, soon dark green, dull or slightly shiny, glabrous, veins 2–4 lightly impressed, lower surface whitish green, reticulate, pilose or pilose-strigose; petiole 2–5 mm, sparsely pilose-strigose. Fertile shoots 8–20 mm, including 3–4 leaves and 1 somewhat pendent flower; pedicel 3–5 mm, villous-strigose. Hypanthium cupulate, long-haired pilose-strigose; sepals acute, obtuse, or ligulate, sparsely pilose-strigose, margin densely villous. Flower buds white or pinkish. Corolla 8–10 mm, petals spreading, white. Stamens 20; filaments white; anthers purple to black. Fruit globose or depressed-globose, 5–6 mm, pale-red to crimson, sparsely pilose, calyx lobes erect, pilose. Nutlets 2(–3), style remains at apex.

Seasons: Flowers May–June; fruit ripe October–November.

Chromosomes: Tetraploid (Krügel 1992a; Bailey, pers. comm.; Jewsbury, pers. comm.). Apomictic, true from seed.

Hardiness: −15°C (5°F).

Area: China (Yunnan and bordering Sichuan).

Notes: The origin of *Cotoneaster procumbens* was for a long time unknown as it was described from a cultivated shrub of a taxon commonly grown in Central Europe. However, on several occasions this species has been discovered in Yunnan, China. The type at the botanic garden in Halle, Germany, probably originated from a Schneider collection from this region. This species has been collected by Jeanette Fryer (*JFYU 030*) in Yunnan near Dali in 1996. It is a very useful and attractive, compact, ground-hugging shrub.

Cultivars: **'Queen of Carpets'** (PLATE 74), closely follows every contour over whatever it grows, leaves thicker (coriaceous), larger, more orbicular, and of a paler green than *C. procumbens*, few fruit produced. Pentaploid (McAllister, pers. comm.). Extremely difficult to raise from seed. Although collections of this taxon from Yunnan, China, have produced good sturdy plants, more research is needed on this *Cotoneaster*. **'Streibs's Findling'**, a dense, congested shrub, height 10–15 cm, branches low, arching, prostrate, leaves 8–9 mm, dark blue-green and rather dull. Introduced from Germany around 1960. Very similar to if not the same as *C. procumbens*.

8. *Cotoneaster prostratus* Baker in Saunder's Ref. Bot. 1:53 (1869), non Bean (1950).
> Type: cult. original of Saunder's *Refugium* plate 53, from W. W. Saunder's garden, 1868 (lecto designated K).

Shrub, 0.5–1 m. Branches prostrate, wide-spreading and rooting; branchlets distichous or spiraled, maroon to gray-brown, initially sparsely strigose-pilose. Internodes long, leaves evergreen, subcoriaceous, on sterile shoots spiraled or distichous, broadly obovate-elliptic, elliptic, or oblong, rarely suborbicular, 6–13 × 4–8 mm, apex obtuse, acute or rotund, rarely emarginate, base obtuse or cuneate, upper dark green, slightly shiny, initially sparsely pilose-strigose, veins 2–4, lower surface gray-green and slightly glaucous, initially pilose or villous strigose; petiole 2–5 mm, pilose or villous strigose. Fertile shoots 15–25 mm, including 3–6 leaves and 1(–3) erect flower(s); pedicels 2–5 mm, pilose-strigose. Hypanthium widely cupulate, villous-strigose or pilose-strigose; sepals acute or obtuse, rarely acuminate, pilose-strigose or villous-strigose, margin densely villous. Flower buds pale pink or white. Corolla 10–12 mm, petals spreading, white, glabrous. Stamens 20, erect-spreading; filaments narrowly subulate, white; anthers purple. Styles 2. Fruit depressed-globose or slightly turbinate, 9–11 mm, crimson to ruby, dull, hairs sparse, calyx lobes flat, green, subglabrous, navel slightly open. Nutlets (1–)2.

Seasons: Flowers June; fruit ripe October–November.

Chromosomes: Tetraploid (Broertjes 1956; Bailey, pers. comm.). Triploid (Jewsbury, pers. comm.).

Hardiness: −15°C (5°F).

Area: N India. Bhutan. Nepal.

Notes: *Cotoneaster prostratus* has proved to be a somewhat elusive species. Baker states that it is intermediate in leaf and fruit between *C. uva-ursi* and *C. marginatus*.

Originating from seed sent by Dr. Royle from the Western Himalaya to William Saunders, who said (1869) that "planted on a south-facing bank, *C. prostratus* grows freely with a prostrate straggling habit, has large leaves and fruit, although both sparingly produced, and that it tends to drop many of its leaves in autumn." *Cotoneaster prostratus* has been collected by Keith Rushforth in 1990 in Bhutan, in the Bumthang region, between Damphe and Phephet. With its varying chromosome counts and possibly a tendency to not always breed 100 percent true from seed, *C. prostratus* needs more research.

Cultivar: '**Arnold-Forster**' (PLATE 75), leaves 12–21 × 5–14 mm, margins revolute and slightly undulated, blackish green, inflorescence 1- to 2(–9)-flowered, corolla 12–14 mm in diameter, fruit numerous. This attractive cultivar has long been in cultivation.

9. *Cotoneaster radicans* Dammer ex C. K. Schneider in Illustr. Handb. Laubholzk. 1: 761 (1906). Synonyms: *C. dammeri* C. K. Schneider var. *radicans* Dammer ex C. K. Schneider (1906); *C. radicans* (C. K. Schneider) G. Klotz (1963). Type: China, W Sichuan and Tibetan frontier, chiefly near Kangding, December 1890, *Pratt 2* (holo B, iso A, CAL, E).

Shrub carpeting, to 0.2 m. Branches 0.5–1 m, procumbent, pliant, rooting; branchlets spiraled or distichous, maroon, densely lenticellate, initially pilose-strigose. Leaves evergreen, coriaceous, on sterile shoots distichous, elliptic or obovate, 12–20 × 7–10 mm, apex acute or obtuse, base cuneate or obtuse, upper surface rugose, dark green, shiny, initially sparsely pilose, veins 3–4 impressed, lower surface whitish green, reticulate, pilose-strigose; petiole 4–8 mm, strigose. Fertile shoots 15–25 mm, including 4–5 leaves and an erect, 1(–3) flower(s); pedicel 3–8 mm, pilose-strigose. Hypanthium cupulate, pilose-strigose; sepals apiculate, acute or acuminate, pilose-strigose, border broad, membranous, margin villous. Flower buds pinkish. Corolla 8–10 mm, petals spreading, white. Stamens 20; filaments white; anthers purple to black. Fruit globose or obovoid, 7–8 mm, scarlet to rich red with crimson, shiny, glabrous, calyx lobes erect, pilose. Nutlets 3(–4), rarely 2, style remains near apex.

Seasons: Flowers May–June; fruit ripe November.

Chromosomes: Tetraploid (Bailey, pers. comm.). Apomictic, true from seed. Zeilinga (1964) produced a diploid count from a misnamed *C. dammeri*. Other diploid counts of Broertjes (1956) and Klotz and Krügel (1983a) were mistakenly based on clones of *C. dammeri*.

Hardiness: –15°C (5°F).

Area: China (Sichuan and borders with Yunnan and Tibet).

Notes: *Cotoneaster radicans* has long been in cultivation, especially in Central Europe. In Denmark it is grown under the name *C. dammeri* 'Rami' Dafo. Brander (1990). Most plants bearing the name *C. dammeri* var. *radicans* are not *C. radicans* but the sexual and variable *C. dammeri*. *Cotoneaster radicans* gained a RHS Award of Garden Merit in 1973, but from its description this may have been awarded mistakenly to *C. dammeri* 'Major'. Recently reintroduced into cultivation.

10. *Cotoneaster* ×*suecicus* G. Klotz in *Beitr. Phytotax.* 10: 47 (1982). Type: [cult.
Germany, Jena BG], leg. G. Klotz, 10 June 1980, flowers and fruits, 25 October 1980
fruits (holo JE).

Shrub, 0.4–0.6 m. Branches semiprocumbent, arched, ends rooting; branchlets purple-
black above, green beneath, initially densely strigose. Leaves semievergreen, subcoriaceous, on sterile shoots spiraled, elliptic, 10–23 × 4–10 mm, apex rotund or emarginate,
base cuneate, upper surface dark green, shiny, initially sparsely long-haired pilose, lower
surface gray-green, initially strigose-villous, midrib often red; petiole 1–3 mm, often red,
strigose. Fertile shoots 8–40 mm long, including 3–4 leaves and a 2- to 6-flowered inflorescence; pedicels initially sparsely pilose. Hypanthium initially sparsely pilose. Corolla
with petals spreading, white. Stamens 15–20; anthers purple-black. Styles 2–4. Fruit subglobose, 4–7 mm, scarlet. Nutlets 2–4.

Seasons: Flowers May–June; fruit ripen October–November.

Chromosomes: Diploid (Zeilinga 1964; Krügel 1992a).

Hardiness: −18°C (−1°F).

Notes: *Cotoneaster* ×*suecicus*, the Swedish cotoneaster, is known only in cultivation.
It is reported to be a hybrid between *C. conspicuus* and *C. dammeri* (Flinck & B. Hylmö
1967), of which many forms are cultivated.

Cultivars: '**Coral Beauty**' (Hoogendoorn 1967), somewhat dense and low-growing,
0.3–0.8 × 1–2 m, resembling 'Skogholm' but remaining lower, branches arching and
wide-spreading, leaves evergreen, ovate-elliptic, 18–20 mm, rich, shiny green, fruit abundant, bright orange-red. Hardy. Good for ground cover. One of the most frequently
planted low-growing cotoneasters. '**Erlinda**', branches pendulous (trained) or carpeting,
leaves variegated with creamy-white border, pink-tinged in autumn, shy flowering and
fruiting. An elegant, highly ornamental cultivar from Belgium. Originated as a variegated sport from 'Skogholm'. Selected by André van Beek and named after his wife
Erlinda. Received a gold medal at the Plantarium Show in the Netherlands (1992). With
its small red fruit 'Erlinda' shows more of its *C. dammeri* parent than does the other variegated *C.* ×*suecicus* cultivar, 'Juliette'. '**Ifor**', vigorous, extremely free fruiting, fruit bright
orange, raised in the RBG Edinburgh nursery. '**Juergl**', broad, evergreen shrub, height to
50 cm, branches long and arched, branchlets light green to red-brown, leaves 10–15 × 19
mm, ovate, apex obtuse, upper surface slightly rugose, fruit single or paired, 9 mm, light
orange-red, nutlets 2–3. Similar to 'Skogholm' but lower growing, leaves with shorter
petioles, and heavier fruiting. A good ground-cover. '**Juliette**' (PLATE 76), more vigorous
than 'Erlinda', displaying the more numerous, larger, and more orange fruit of its *C. conspicuus* parent. A beautiful cultivar giving year-round pleasure. '**Little Beauty**', compact
habit, height c. 40 cm, leaves small and narrow. A sport of 'Coral Beauty'. '**Minipolster**',
slower growing than other cultivars, developing into a dense, rounded cushion similar to
an evergreen *C. adpressus*. Introduced in 1967. '**Royal Beauty**' (1968), very similar to if
not the same as 'Coral Beauty'. '**Royal Carpet**' (1970), very similar to if not the same as
'Coral Beauty'. '**Skogholm**' (syn. *C. dammeri* 'Mrs. Kennedy'), spreading and strongly

branched, to 0.6 m high by 2–3 m wide, branches prostrate and arching, lightly rooting where touching ground, leaves evergreen, slightly shiny, not rugose, 10–30 mm, elliptic, both ends rounded, few turning yellow-orange in late autumn, flowers 2–6 together, corolla 8 mm, fruit not numerous, 4–6 mm, dull red, nutlets 3–4. Very hardy. Due to its strong growth which rapidly covers the ground allowing few weeds to grow, it is used in large quantities for amenity plantings (very popular in Europe). Any vertical shoots should be pruned to maintain ground-cover effect. Selected as a seedling of *C. dammeri* in 1941 by O. Goeransson of Hindby, near Malmö in Sweden. Introduced into commerce around 1950 by Skogsholmens Planteskolor, Sweden. '**Skogholm White Form**', white variegated form exhibited by Boot and Company, Boskoop, Netherlands, at the 1965 Flora Nova Show in that country. '**Smaragdpolster**', similar in habit to 'Coral Beauty' but slightly more compact and densely branched, semievergreen, leaves dark green, fruit more abundantly produced. From Johannes Hachmann of Barmstedt, Germany. '**Sukinek**', similar to 'Skogholm', raised in the Czech Republic. '**Surth**', lowish growing, height 30–50 cm, leaves small, broadly elliptic, shining dark green, fruit orange-red. An excellent, hardy German selection. '**Ursinov**', similar to 'Ifor' but more wide-spreading, originating from Poland. '**Winter Jewel**', prostrate and mat-forming, height to 40 cm, leaves very dark green, fruit numerous, orange-red. A good ground-cover.

2. Subgenus *Cotoneaster*

Inflorescences spreading or pendent, flowers or fruit in inflorescence opening or ripening over a period of time (not simultaneously). Corolla with petals mostly erect at anthesis, obovate or spathulate, frequently with apex incurved, pink, red and off-white, often with green, rarely completely white. Stamens incurved to erect; filaments subulate, often broadly so, red or pink; anthers white, rarely pale pink or mauve. Nutlets with conjoined style becoming free (leaving remains when dehisced) $1/2$–$3/4$ from the base.

    7 sections: *Rokujodaisanense, Adpressi, Sanguinei, Acutifolii, Franchetioides, Cotoneaster, Megalocarpi.*

5. Section *Rokujodaisanense*, stat. nov. Basionym: series *Rokujodaisanense*
    J. Fryer & B. Hylmö in New Plantsman 8: 238 (2001).

Leaves evergreen or semievergreen, rarely deciduous, subcoriaceous or coriaceous, extremely shiny, veins often deeply impressed. Petals semispreading or erect. Anthers pink or purplish red.

    1 series: *Rokujodaisanense.*

15. Series *Rokujodaisanense*
Shrubs prostrate to small. Branches not rooting (at least not readily). Fertile shoots with

an erect, 1- to 7(–60)-flowered inflorescence. Flowers red and pink in bud. Petals wide-spaced, spathulate.

Early to late season.

China (Sichuan, Yunnan, Guizhou). Taiwan.

4 species: *C. chuanus, C. kweitschoviensis, C. rokujodaisanensis, C. vandelaarii*. Also including *C.* 'Gracia' and *C.* 'Valkenburg'.

Key to Series *Rokujodaisanense*

1a. Leaves 32–55 mm; inflorescence (10–)30- to 70-flowered . . . . *C. vandelaarii*
1b. Leaves 15–24 mm; inflorescence 1- to 4(–7)-flowered 2
2a. Branches ascending; petioles 2–4 mm; fertile shoots 10–25 mm; stamens 10(–14) . . . .
. . . . *C. chuanus*
2b. Branches procumbent; petioles 4–8 mm; fertile shoots 15–40 mm; stamens 16–20 3
3a. Leaves broadly elliptic or broadly ovate; inflorescence 1- to 3-flowered; fruit 7–10 mm. . . . . .
. . . . *C. rokujodaisanensis*
3b. Leaves ellipto-lanceolate or elliptic; inflorescence (1–)2- to 4(–7)-flowered; fruit 5–7 mm. . . .
. . . .*C. kweitschoviensis*

1. ***Cotoneaster chuanus*** J. Fryer & B. Hylmö, *sp. nov.* Type: China, Sichuan, Tian-chuan Hsien, 26 October 1936, *K. L. Chu 4125* (holo E, iso BM). **PLATE 77.**
Shrub, 1–1.5 m. Branches 1.5–2 m, ascending horizontally; branchlets distichous, maroon to brown, slightly verruculose, strigose, glabrescent. Leaves deciduous or semi-evergreen, subcoriaceous, on sterile shoots orbicular, suborbicular, broadly elliptic or broadly obovate, 15–20 × 11–16 mm, apex obtuse, rotund, apiculate or acute, base obtuse, upper surface rugose, mid to dark green, extremely shiny, glabrescent, veins 3–4 deeply impressed, lower surface reticulate, sparsely strigose; petiole 2–4 mm, strigose. Fertile shoots 10–25 mm, including 3–4 leaves and a (1–)3(–5)-flowered inflorescence; pedicels 1–3 mm, strigose; flowers (including hypanthium) 5–6 mm, pink in bud. Hypanthium cupulate, pilose-strigose, sepals acute, obtuse or acuminate, sparsely pilose-strigose, border membranous, glabrous, margin densely yellow-villous. Corolla with large opening; petals erect, pink with red base and pale pinkish to off-white border. Stamens 10(–14) dark red; anthers pink to purple. Fruit obovoid, 8–10 mm, rich red, subglabrous, calyx lobes flat with tips erect. Nutlets 3(–4), rarely 2, style remains ²/₃–³/₄ from base.

Seasons: Flowers June; fruit ripe November; autumn leaves orange-red.

Chromosomes: Tetraploid (Bailey, pers. comm.; Jewsbury, pers. comm.). Apomictic, true from seed.

Hardiness: –18°C (–1°F).

Area: China (Sichuan).

Notes: *Cotoneaster chuanus* is a vigorous shrub which is very attractive both in flower and in fruit. Unfortunately, it is not common in cultivation. It is sometimes found as *C.*

taoensis or *C. trinervis* hort. *Cotoneaster chuanus* was also found by Roy Lancaster (*RL 624*) in Sichuan in the Temple Garden at Leshen on Emei Shan.

2. *Cotoneaster* 'Gracia' in Ir. F. Schneider in Dendroflora 1: 35 (1964). PLATE 78.
Shrub, to 1 m. Branches prostrate or ascending horizontally 1.5–2 m; branchlets distichous, maroon, minutely verruculose, initially strigose. Leaves semievergreen, subcoriaceous, on sterile shots elliptic, 16–20 mm, apex obtuse or apiculate, base cuneate or obtuse, upper surface rugose, light green, extremely shiny, glabrous, veins 5–6 deeply impressed, lower surface yellowish green, initially strigose-villous; petiole 3–5 mm, strigose. Fertile shoots 15–25 mm, including 3–4 leaves and a 1- to 5-flowered inflorescence; pedicels 1–5 mm, strigose; flowers (including hypanthium) 5–7 mm long. Hypanthium widely cupulate, strigose; sepals apiculate, acute, obtuse, mucronate, red, sparsely long-haired villous, border broad, membranous, red, margin tomentose-villous. Corolla 6 mm with large opening; petals erect, red with rich pink border. Stamens 12–15; filaments red; anthers pink. Fruit subglobose, bright red, shiny, glabrous, calyx lobes depressed with tips erect. Nutlets (2–)3, style remains $^2/_3$ from base.

Seasons: Flowers May–June; fruit ripe October; autumn leaves red, purple, and bottle green.

Chromosomes: Triploid (Bailey, pers. comm.; Boskoop Experimental Station 1961 as quoted in Ir. F. Schneider 1964).

Hardiness: –15°C (5°F).

Notes: *Cotoneaster* 'Gracia' was introduced by C. Broertjes in the Netherlands in 1961 and was said to have arisen from a cross between *C. salicifolius* and *C. hjelmqvistii* made in 1951 at the Boskoop Experimental Station. The possibility of a hybrid between two such unrelated species from two different subgenera of *Cotoneaster* was questioned by Klotz (1970, p. 331) and others. *Cotoneaster* 'Gracia' is possibly a species. This attractive, broad shrub has branches that are ornamentally arching. It is free-flowering with large showy pink flowers which smother the branches in spring but produce few fruit. The shiny, crinkly leaves color beautifully in autumn and are retained into late December. Not in key.

3. *Cotoneaster kweitschoviensis* G. Klotz in Wiss. Z. Martin-Luther-Univ. Halle-Wittenberg, Math.-Naturwiss. 12: 785 (1963). Type: China, Guizhou, Fanjing Shan, 7 September 1931, *Steward, Chiao & Cheo* 408 (holo LE, iso A, BM, E, K, S).
PLATE 79.
Shrub, to 0.2 m. Branches 1.5–2 m, procumbent, creeping, pliant, non-rooting; branchlets somewhat distichous, reddish purple with numerous large lenticels, initially strigose. Leaves evergreen or semievergreen, coriaceous, on sterile shoots elliptic or ellipto-lanceolate, 15–20 × 9–11 mm, apex acute or obtuse, base cuneate or obtuse, upper surface rugose, dark green, slightly shiny, sometimes single hairs on midrib, veins 3–5 deeply impressed, lower surface grayish green, strigose-pilose; petiole 4–6 mm, strigose. Fertile

shoots 15–40 mm, including mostly 4 leaves and a (1–)2- to 4(–7)-flowered inflorescence; pedicels 3–6 mm, slender, strigose. Hypanthium cupulate, strigose, apex pilose-strigose; sepals acute, acuminate or obtuse, villous-strigose, border broad, membranous, margin short-haired villous. Corolla 6–9 mm, sometimes with 3–4 petals instead of usual 5; petals semispreading, off-white with pinkish border. Stamens 16–20 in two rings; filaments white with pink base becoming red; anthers purple, ripening in 2 stages. Fruit obovoid or subglobose, 5–7 mm, bright red, sparsely pilose, calyx lobes erect, sparsely pilose, caudate as coronet. Nutlets 2–4, apex sometimes red, style remains $^3/_4$–$^4/_5$ from base.

Seasons: Flowers May–June; fruit ripe November.

Chromosomes: Tetraploid (McAllister, pers. comm.). Apomictic, true from seed.

Hardiness: –15°C (5°F).

Area: China (Guizhou).

Notes: *Cotoneaster kweitschoviensis* is extremely garden-worthy and is pretty both in flower and in fruit. It is excellent for trailing over walls and banks, where the lovely fan-shaped branching habit is shown to its best advantage. Recently reintroduced into cultivation.

4. *Cotoneaster rokujodaisanensis* Hayata in Icon. Plant. Formosa (Taiwan) 5: 63 (1915). Type: Taiwan, Byōritsu, Mount Rokujōdaisan, 3000 m, October 1908, U. Mori (holo TI). **PLATE 80.**

Shrub, to 0.5 m. Branches 2–3 m, procumbent or decumbent, pliant, non-rooting; branchlets somewhat distichous, reddish purple, initially yellowish strigose. Leaves evergreen or semi, subcoriaceous, on sterile shoots broadly elliptic or broadly ovate, 20–24 × 12–16 mm, apex acute or obtuse, base cuneate or obtuse, upper surface rugose, dark green, intensely shiny, glabrous, veins 3–5 impressed, lower surface grayish green, reticulate, pilose-strigose; petiole 4–8 mm, strigose. Fertile shoots 15–30 mm, including mostly 4 leaves and a 1- to 3-flowered inflorescence; pedicels 3–5 mm, strigose. Hypanthium cupulate, pilose-strigose; sepals long acute, acuminate or obtuse, pilose-strigose, border broad, membranous, margin villous. Corolla 9–10 mm, petals semispreading, widely spaced, pink. Stamens 16–20; filaments red and pink; anthers pink soon dark purple. Fruit obovoid or subglobose, 7–10 mm, light yellowish orange to light red, shiny, glabrescent, calyx lobes suberect. Nutlets 3–4(–5), style remains $^3/_4$ from base.

Seasons: Flowers June; fruit ripe November.

Chromosomes: Triploid (Bailey, pers. comm.).

Hardiness: –15°C (5°F).

Area: Taiwan.

Notes: *Cotoneaster rokujodaisanensis* is another good species of *Cotoneaster* recently introduced into cultivation. It is said to be found in windy, rocky grassland in northern and central Taiwan at altitudes above 2500 m. This good all-rounder shrub has a creeping and climbing habit, attractive leaves, very pretty flowers, and large-sized shiny late-ripening fruit.

5. *Cotoneaster* **'Valkenburg'** in Ir. F. Schneider in Dendroflora 1: 35 (1964). **PLATE 81.**
Shrub, 1–2 m. Branches ascending, spreading; branchlets distichous, maroon, initially strigose-villous. Leaves evergreen, subcoriaceous, on sterile shoots ovate or elliptic, 32–55 × 17–29 mm, upper surface slightly rugose, extremely shiny, initially strigose-villous, veins 4 lightly impressed, lower surface sparsely strigose-villous. Fertile shoots with a 1- to 5-flowered inflorescence. Hypanthium widely cupulate, strigose-villous. Corolla with large opening; petals erect, pink, with red base and white border. Stamens with filaments red; anthers pink. Fruit subglobose, often misshapen, light red. Nutlets (2–)3, often deformed.

Seasons: Flowers May–June; fruit ripe October.

Chromosomes: Triploid (Boskoop Experimental Station 1961 as quoted in Ir. F. Schneider 1964).

Hardiness: −15°C (5°F).

Notes: *Cotoneaster* 'Valkenburg' was introduced by C. Broertjes in the Netherlands in 1961. It was said to have arisen at the Boskoop Experimental Station from a crossing in 1951 between *C. floccosus* and *C. hjelmqvistii*, but this is extremely unlikely between two such unrelated species (see *C.* 'Gracia'). *Cotoneaster* 'Valkenburg' is possibly a species. It is a handsome, dense, and broadly growing shrub of medium height (to 1.7 m) with branches bowed. It is free-flowering but produces few fruit. The leaves are much the same as *C.* 'Gracia' but not as crinkly and remaining green over winter, abscising in spring. Not in key.

6. *Cotoneaster vandelaarii* J. Fryer & B. Hylmö in New Plantsman 8:229,238 (2001).
Type: China, Yunnan, Kunming Western Hills, Hua Hong Dong, October 1980, *H. van de Laar 80671* (holo WAG). **PLATE 82.**
Shrub, to 1.5 m. Branches erect and ascending, horizontally spreading; branchlets distichous, reddish brown, lenticellate, initially strigose. Leaves evergreen, subcoriaceous, on sterile shoots ovate or elliptic, 30–55 × 17–29 mm, apex acute or acuminate, base obtuse or truncate, upper surface bullate, mid-green, extremely shiny, strigose, veins 4–5 deeply impressed, lower surface villous-strigose; petiole 5 mm, strigose. Fertile shoots 30–70 mm, including 4 leaves and a compact, (10–)30- to 70-flowered inflorescence; pedicels 3–9 mm, strigose. Hypanthium cupulate, villous or villous-strigose; sepals acuminate, acute or sometimes obtuse, villous or glabrous, margin villous. Corolla 9 mm, petals semispreading, deep pink with white or pale pink border. Stamens 20; filaments pink or white with a red base; anthers deep red or purple. Fruit obovoid or subglobose, 7–8 mm, orange to light red, shiny, sparsely strigose, calyx lobes flat, green, navel open with remains of stamens and styles exserted. Nutlets 3(–4), rarely 2, style remains ¾ from base.

Seasons: Flowers June–July; fruit ripe October–December.

Chromosomes: Unknown. Apomictic, true from seed.

Hardiness: −10°C (14°F).

Area: China (Yunnan).

Notes: *Cotoneaster vandelaarii* is named in honor of the late Harry van de Laar, professional plantsman of the Dutch Boskoop Research Station for Nursery Stock. This species gives year-round pleasure. Many clusters of open pink flowers are followed by lovely shiny, late, and long-persisting fruit which complement the extremely shiny, corrugated leaves. In mild winters the fruit can remain until spring.

6. Section *Adpressi* Hurusawa in Acta Phytotax. Geobot. 13: 237 (1943).

Low-growing shrubs. Branchlets sometimes verruculose. Leaves on sterile shoots suborbicular or elliptic, small (4–40 mm), lower surface mostly strigose or glabrous, petiole short (0.5–5 mm). Inflorescence 1- to 5(–8)-flowered. Petals red, base frequently purple. Stamens mostly 10–16.

5 series: *Verruculosi, Distichi, Adpressi, Horizontales, Nitentes.*

16. Series *Verruculosi* G. Klotz in Wiss. Z. Friedrich-Schiller-Univ. Jena, Math.-Naturwiss. 21: 1004 (1972).

Dwarf or small shrubs. Branchlets mostly irregular, strigose and verruculose, often densely so. Leaves evergreen or semievergreen, subcoriaceous or coriaceous, on sterile shoots distichous or spiraled, 4–24 mm, upper surface extremely shiny. Stipules red, often very noticeable, especially in winter. Fertile shoots with flowers mostly pendent. Hypanthium campanulate. Corolla with large opening; petals mostly erect or semispreading, often caducous.

Early to mid season.

China (Yunnan, Sichuan). Nepal. India (Sikkim). Taiwan. Burma.

12 species: *C. chulingensis, C. encavei, C. farreri, C. ganghobaensis, C. konishii, C. langei, C. milkedandaensis, C. nantouensis, C. sandakphuensis, C. subadpressus, C. verruculosus, C. yalungensis.*

Key to Series *Verruculosi*

1a. Leaves mostly > 15 mm 2

1b. Leaves mostly < 15 mm. 4

2a. Height ≤ 0.8 m; branches decumbent or procumbent; upper leaf surface glabrous; sepals obtuse . . . . *C. chulingensis*

2b. Height ≤ 1.5 m; branches erect; upper leaf surface with hairs; sepals acute and acuminate 3

3a. Leaves mostly suborbicular, apex mostly obtuse, veins 2–3; fertile shoots 30–50 mm; stamens 16–18 . . . . *C. ganghobaensis*

3b. Leaves mostly elliptic, apex mostly acute, veins 3–5; fertile shoots 10–25 mm; stamens 10(–15) . . . .*C. konishii*

4a. Upper leaf surface glabrous or nearly so, veins not impressed; nutlet with style remains
near apex **5**

4b. Upper leaf surface persistently strigose, veins mostly impressed; nutlet with style remains
3/4 from base **7**

5a. Branchlets divaricate; leaves < 10 mm, apex mostly emarginate; petals semispreading . . . . .
. . . . *C. sandakphuensis*

5b. Branchlets spiraled; leaves > 15 mm, apex mostly obtuse or truncate; petals mostly erect . .
. . . .**6**

6a. Branches erect; leaves strongly undulate, broadly elliptic or suborbicular; stamens 15–16 . .
. . . . *C. milkedandaensis*

6b. Branches prostrate or ascending; leaves flat, suborbicular to subquadrate; stamens 10 . . . . .
. . . . *C. nantouensis*

7a. Upper leaf surface persistently strigose; hypanthlum densely strigose, sepals acute or
acuminate. . . . . *C. langei*

7b. Upper leaf surface strigose soon sparsely so; hypanthium glabrous or sparsely strigose,
sepals obtuse or broadly acute. **8**

8a. Height 0.2–1 m; branches procumbent or ascending; hypanthium sparsely strigose; nutlets
2–3. . . . . *C. subadpressus*

8b. Height 0.8–1.5 m; branches mostly erect; hypanthium glabrous; nutlets mostly 2. . . . .**9**

9a. Upper leaf surface slightly rugose, veins 2–3; filaments pinkish; nutlets mostly 2 . . . .
. . . . *C. verruculosus*

9b. Upper leaf surface not impressed, veins mostly 3–4; filaments red; nutlets 2–3 . . . .**10**

10a. Branchlets distichous; leaf veins mostly 3; pedicels 1–2 mm; stamens 20 . . . . . *C. yalungensis*

10b. Branchlets divaricate; leaf veins mostly 4; pedicels 2–4 mm; stamens 10–15 . . . . . . *C. encavei*

1. *Cotoneaster chulingensis* J. Fryer & B. Hylmö, *sp. nov.* Synonym: *C. pseudorubens*
'Coru' hort. Type: China, Yunnan, Weixi, north of Tung Chuling, 9 November 1937,
T. T. Yu 10662 (holo E, iso BM). **PLATE 83.**
Shrub, 0.8 m. Branches decumbent or procumbent; branchlets divaricate, maroon, verruculose, strigose, glabrescent. Leaves evergreen or semi, coriaceous, on sterile shoots
orbicular, broadly elliptic or broadly obovate, 13–20 × 11–18 mm, apex obtuse, base
obtuse, upper surface dark green, shiny, glabrous, veins 3–5 impressed, lower surface
initially densely strigose; petiole 3 mm, strigose, glabrescent. Fertile shoots 10–20 mm,
including 2–3 leaves and 1(–2) pendent flower(s); pedicel absent to 2 mm, glabrous; flowers (including hypanthium) 5–6 mm long. Hypanthium campanulate, initially sparsely
strigose, shiny; sepals obtuse, dark red, glabrescent, margin erose and villous. Petals semispreading to spreading, caducous, dark red. Stamens 10–14; filaments dark red; anthers
white. Fruit globose or depressed-globose, succulent, 10–13, orange-red to rich red, shiny,
glabrous, calyx lobes depressed, navel wide open. Nutlets 2(–3), apex swollen and recurved, style remains 3/4 from base.
Seasons: Flowers May–June; fruit ripe September–October.

Chromosomes: Unknown. Apomictic, true from seed.

Hardiness: −15°C (5°F).

Area: China (Yunnan).

Notes: Dietrich Hobbie, a *Rhododendron* breeder in Oldenburg, Germany, purchased seed of *Rhododendron* in 1937–1938 from Professor Hu in China. As a gift Hu included a few samples of *Cotoneaster* collected in the mountains of NW Yunnan by his assistant T. T. Yu. In 1959 Karl Evert Flinck and Bertil Hylmö visited Hobbie's gardens and noticed this rather unusual *Cotoneaster* from which seed was collected and raised in Sweden. In 1966 Poul Erik Brander of the Danish State Research Gardens gathered seed in Sweden from the offspring and gave it the name *C. pseudorubens* 'Coru'.

2. ***Cotoneaster encavei*** J. Fryer & B. Hylmö, *sp. nov.* Synonym: *C. cavei* hort., non
   G. Klotz (1963). Type: Nepal, Mount Kanchenjunga, Guphar, Pokhari, 5 October
   1989, Kew/Edinburgh Kanchenjunga Expedition, *KEKE 1239* (holo E). **PLATE 84.**
Shrub, dense, 0.8–1.2 m. Branches erect, stiff; branchlets divaricate or distichous, maroon, verruculose, initially densely strigose. Leaves evergreen or semi, subcoriaceous, on sterile shoots orbicular, suborbicular or broadly elliptic, 10–14 × 10–11 mm, apex obtuse, truncate or emarginate and mucronate, base obtuse, margin slightly undulate, upper surface dark green, intensely shiny, initially strigose, veins 3–4, very lightly impressed, lower surface glabrous, midrib and margin strigose; petiole 3–4 mm, sparsely strigose; stipules red, margin long-haired villous-strigose. Fertile shoots 8–12 mm, including 2–4 leaves and 1(–2) pendent flower(s); pedicel 2–4 mm, glabrous; flowers (including hypanthium) 5–6 mm long. Hypanthium campanulate, shiny, glabrous; sepals broadly obtuse or broadly acute, border membranous, margin erose and sparsely villous. Petals erect to semispreading, red with pink border. Stamens 10–15; filaments red-pink; anthers white. Fruit globose or obovoid, 8–9 mm, orange-red, shiny, glabrous, calyx lobes suberect, navel open. Nutlets 2(–3) apex swollen and recurved, style remains $^3/_4$ from base.

Seasons: Flowers May–June; fruit ripe September–October.

Chromosomes: Tetraploid (McAllister, pers. comm.). Apomictic, true from seed.

Hardiness: −15°C (5°F).

Area: Nepal. India (Sikkim).

Notes: Klotz (1963a) described a new species, *Cotoneaster cavei*, as a synonym of *C. distichus* var. *parvifolius* T. T. Yu, in part. In the same publication Klotz elevated *C. cordifolius* to species level and described it, using the same synonym, *C. distichus* var. *parvifolius* T. T. Yu, in large part. The holotype for both new taxa thus has to be the type of *C. distichus* var. *parvifolius* T. T. Yu, namely, *Kingdon Ward 6788*. How to divide an herbarium specimen having only one piece of branch on the sheet between two holotypes is not easy to understand. *Cotoneaster cavei* G. Klotz has to be treated as a synonym of *C. cordifolius* G. Klotz. Klotz made another holotype for his *C. cavei*, but this is not legitimate. *Cotoneaster encavei* is a very useful shrub for the smaller garden. It is neat in habit, the young growth is densely covered with small red warts and noticeable red stipules, the shiny bottle-green leaves are attractive at all times of the year, and the fruit are long persistent. Recently reintroduced into cultivation.

3. **Cotoneaster farreri** G. Klotz in Wiss. Z. Friedrich-Schiller-Univ. Jena, Math.-Naturwiss. 21: 1006 (1972). Type: NE Burma, Mokuji Pass, 8 August 1920, *R. Farrer 1830* (holo E).

According to the type description, *Cotoneaster farreri* differs from *C. langei* only in leaves with upper surface being sparsely hairy, and the hypanthium and calyx glabrous.

Notes: Not known in cultivation. Not in key.

4. **Cotoneaster ganghobaensis** J. Fryer & B. Hylmö in New Plantsman 5: 136 (1998). Type: cult. England, Hampshire, Clanfield, Rumsey Gardens Nursery, N. R. Giles, Jeanette Fryer 118 from seed collected in China, Yunnan, N Lijiang, at base of Gang Ho Ba valley, on the eastern side of Yulong Shan, October 1987, *C. D. Brickell & A. C. Leslie 12234*, Jeanette Fryer (holo WSY). **PLATE 85.**

Shrub, 1–1.5 m. Branches erect, spreading and arched, often suckering at base; branchlets divaricate, maroon, minutely verruculose, initially tomentose-strigose. Leaves evergreen, subcoriaceous, on sterile shoots suborbicular or broadly elliptic, 21–24 × 15–23 mm, apex obtuse or apiculate, base truncate or obtuse, upper surface rugose, dark green, intensely shiny, pilose-strigose, veins 2–3 deeply impressed, lower surface reticulate, densely villous-strigose; petiole 2–3 mm, villous-strigose. Fertile shoots 30–50 mm, including 4 leaves and an erect, compact (1–)3(–4)-flowered inflorescence; pedicels 1–3 mm, strigose; flowers (including hypanthium) 5–6 mm long. Hypanthium campanulate, greenish brown, densely villous-strigose; sepals acute or acuminate, villous-strigose, border red, glabrous, margin long-haired villous. Corolla with small opening; petals erect-incurved, red with dark red base and pink and off-white border. Stamens (14–)16–18(–20); filaments red with pink; anthers white. Fruit subglobose or obovoid, succulent, 10–12 mm, orange-red, base villous, calyx lobes flat, villous. Nutlets 2(–3), style remains ¾ from base.

Seasons: Flowers June–July; fruit ripe October–November.

Chromosomes: Triploid (Bailey, pers. comm.).

Hardiness: −18° C (−1°F).

Area: China (Yunnan).

Notes: *Cotoneaster ganghobaensis* is a compact, densely branched shrub which seems to be more winter hardy than most evergreen cotoneasters. Its rounded leaves are attractively deep-veined and shiny. Bees love its abundant flowers and the fruit are large, colorful, and showy. The plant can be grown successfully in a large pot for the patio. It is another excellent year-round shrub.

5. **Cotoneaster konishii** Hayata in Icon. Plant. Formosa (Taiwan) 3: 100 (1913). Type: Taiwan, Bataiankei, at 2690 m, June 1902, leg. N. Konishi (holo TI). **PLATE 86.**

Shrub, 1–1.5 m. Branches erect, slightly arched; branchlets divaricate, red-brown, minutely verruculose, initially strigose. Leaves semievergreen, chartaceous or subcoriaceous, on sterile shoots elliptic, ovate or suborbicular, 15–23 × 11–15 mm, apex acute, obtuse or acuminate, base obtuse or cuneate, upper surface slightly rugose, dark green, shiny, sparsely strigose, margin strigose, veins 3–5 deeply impressed, lower surface sparsely strigose, midrib more dense; petiole 2–3 mm, strigose. Fertile shoots 10–25 mm, including 3–4 leaves and an erect 1- to 4-flowered inflorescence; pedicels 1–3 mm, strigose; flowers (including hypanthium) 5–6 mm long. Hypanthium campanulate, strigose-villous; sepals acute or acuminate, strigose, margin villous. Corolla open; petals, erect-incurved, red and pink with white border. Stamens 10(–15); filaments dark red; anthers white. Fruit orange-red, glabrous, shiny. Nutlets 2(–3), rarely 4, apex slightly swollen and recurved, style remains $^2/_3$–$^3/_4$ from base.

    Seasons: Flowers May–June; fruit ripe October.

    Chromosomes: Tetraploid (McAllister, pers. comm.). Apomictic, true from seed.

    Hardiness: −15°C (5°F).

    Area: Taiwan.

    Notes: The above description is compiled from Hayata's type diagnosis, added to and corrected with the aid of minute pieces and a photograph of the type donated by the University of Tokyo. Also included are details from the Wynn-Jones collection (#*394*) from NE Taiwan, Nakuta Shan, near Yukon tunnel in 1993, which is in cultivation. This description of *C. konishii* diverges considerably from those of *C. konishii* in later floras of Taiwan, which were probably including the new species *C. hualiensis* belonging to series *Bullati*. This problem was initiated by Hayata stating in his description of *C. konishii* that the fruit contained 3–5 nutlets instead of only 2–3. *Cotoneaster konishii* is a pretty little shrub with good autumn color.

    6. Cotoneaster langei G. Klotz in Wiss. Z. Friedrich-Schiller-Univ. Jena, Math.-
        Naturwiss. 21: 1000 (1972). Type: China, Yunnan, Tschungtien, Shiarentung, 18
        October 1937, *T. T. Yu 13743* (holo E, iso A).

Shrub, 0.5–1.5 m. Branches erect and spreading, sometimes rooting where touching the ground; branchlets divaricate, maroon, slightly verruculose, initially densely yellow-strigose. Leaves evergreen or semi, subcoriaceous, on sterile shoots broadly ovate or suborbicular, 7–13 × 6–13 mm, apex obtuse and mucronate, base obtuse, upper surface slightly rugose, dark green, shiny, strigose, veins 2–3 impressed, lower surface strigose; petiole 2–3 mm, strigose. Fertile shoots 10–20 mm, including 2–4 leaves, and 1(–2) flower(s); pedicel 3–10 mm, strigose; flowers (including hypanthium) 6–7 mm long. Hypanthium campanulate, densely strigose; sepals attenuated-acute, acute or acuminate, strigose, margin long-haired villous. Corolla open; petals erect-incurved, red with dark red base and broad pale crimson or off-white border. Stamens 10(–12); filaments pink; anthers white. Fruit succulent, broadly obovoid or globose, 10–12 mm, yellow, ripening orange-red with yellow cheek, shiny, sparsely strigose, calyx lobes suberect, glabrous, navel open. Nutlets 2(–3), apex slightly swollen and recurved, style remains ³/₄ from base.

Seasons: Flowers May–June; fruit ripe September–November.

Chromosomes: Tetraploid (Bailey, pers. comm.; Jewsbury, pers. comm.). Apomictic, true from seed.

Hardiness: –15°C (5°F).

Area: China (Yunnan, Sichuan).

Notes: *Cotoneaster langei* was refound in Yunnan in 1996 at Xiao Zhongdian by Jeanette Fryer (*JFYU 097*), and near Zhongdian at Shu Du Hu by Keith Rushforth (*KR 4094*). This is a beautiful shrub with unusually large and shiny fruit which remain yellow until the end of the season when one cheek finally becomes flushed with orange-red. As with other yellow fruited cotoneasters, the fruit are not readily eaten by birds.

7. *Cotoneaster milkedandaensis* J. Fryer & B. Hylmö, *sp. nov.* Type: Nepal, Milke Danda, 23 October 1974, *J. Hedegaard 304* (holo C). **PLATE 87.**

Shrub, dense and often somewhat fastigiate, 0.5–1 m. Branches narrowly erect; branchlets spiraled, red-maroon, densely verruculose, initially densely strigose. Leaves evergreen, chartaceous, on sterile shoots broadly elliptic or suborbicular, 7–15 × 5–10 mm, apex obtuse, acute or emarginate and mucronate, base obtuse or cuneate, margin extremely undulate, often reddish, upper surface mid-green, shiny, initially sparsely strigose, veins 3–4, lower surface midrib sparsely strigose; petiole 3–5 mm, often red, sparsely strigose; stipules conspicuous, rich red, strigose. Fertile shoots 10–12 mm, including 3–4 leaves, and 1 pendent, subsessile flower; flower (including hypanthium) 7 mm long. Hypanthium campanulate, glabrous; sepals obtuse or ligulate, glabrous, border membranous, margin sparsely villous. Petals erect to semispreading, dark red. Stamens 15–16; filaments red and pink; anthers white. Fruit globose or subglobose, 7–8 mm, orange-red to red, shiny, glabrous, calyx lobes erect or suberect, navel open. Nutlets (1–)2(–3), apex swollen and recurved, style remains near apex.

Seasons: Flowers May–June; fruit ripe September–October.

Chromosomes: Diploid (Jewsbury, pers. comm.). Sexual, outbreeding, variable from seed.

Hardiness: –15°C (5°F)

Area: Nepal.

Notes: *Cotoneaster milkedandaensis* is an unusual dwarf evergreen with pretty little red flowers. Recently reintroduced into cultivation. The collection (*#3494*) of J. D. Adam Stainton, William Sykes, and John Williams at the Natural History Museum in London, made from above Dhorpatan in Nepal in 1954, is very closely related to *C. milkedandaensis* if not the same.

8. *Cotoneaster nantouensis* J. Fryer & B. Hylmö *sp. nov.* Synonym: *C. horizontalis*, non Decaisne in Hsieh & Huang, Taiwania, 42 (1): 48, Figs. 1, 21, 22 (1997). Type: Taiwan, Noho, Nanto, 6 August 1918, *E. H. Wilson 10072* (holo A, iso K).

Shrub, 0.3–0.8 m. Branches prostrate or ascending; branchlets spiraled or distichous, brown, verruculose, initially densely strigose-verruculose. Leaves evergreen or semi, chartaceous or subcoriaceous, on sterile shoots suborbicular, subquadrate or orbicular, 5–10 × 5–12 mm, apex truncate or obtuse, base obtuse, upper surface dark green, shiny, glabrous, veins 2–3, lower surface glabrous or few strigose hairs; petiole 2–4 mm, strigose. Fertile shoots 8–12 mm, including 2 leaves and 1 flower; pedicel 1–2 mm. Hypanthium campanulate, sparsely strigose; sepals obtuse or acute, sparsely strigose. Petals erect to semispreading, 4–5 mm (Hsieh & Huang 1997}, reddish purple. Stamens 10; filaments dark red; anthers white. Fruit broadly obovoid, 6 mm, red. Nutlets 2.

Area: Taiwan.

Notes: Subsequent to studying both the herbarium specimen *Wilson 10072* and the excellent color photo by T.-H. Hsieh and T.-C. Huang (1997), which is incorrectly named *Cotoneaster horizontalis*, it was possible to identify this as a new species. *Cotoneaster nantouensis* is not yet known in cultivation.

9. *Cotoneaster sandakphuensis* G. Klotz in Bull. Bot. Surv. India 5:213 (1963). Type: Sikkim-Himalaya, Sandakphu, Rimbick, 9 October 1941, *K. Biswas 5721* (holo CAL, iso A).

Shrub, dense, 0.2–0.8 m. Branches suberect; branchlets divaricate, rich red to maroon, densely verruculose-strigose. Leaves evergreen coriaceous, on sterile shoots suborbicular, broadly elliptic or elliptic, 4–9 × 3–7 mm, apex emarginate, mucronate, base obtuse or cuneate, upper surface dark green, shiny, initially sparsely strigose, veins 2–3, lower surface glabrous or few hairs on midrib; petiole 1–3 mm, red, subglabrous; stipules red. Fertile shoots 6–10 mm, including 2 leaves and 1 pendent flower; pedicel 1–3 mm, glabrous; flower (including hypanthium) 5 mm long. Hypanthium campanulate, pale yellowish green, shiny, glabrous; sepals obtuse sometimes acute, border membranous, margin erose and villous. Petals semispreading, wide-spaced, caducous, dark red. Stamens 10–16, filaments greenish white tinged pink; anthers off-white. Fruit subglobose or shortly obovoid, 6–7 mm, bright red, shiny, glabrous. Nutlets 2(–3), style remains near apex.

Seasons: Flowers June; fruit ripe September–October.

Chromosomes: Diploid (Krügel 1992a; McAllister, pers. comm.; Jewsbury, pers. comm.). Sexual, outbreeding, variable from seed. However, the Woodland collection when propagated from seed gives offspring in which no variation has been observed. Further investigation on this species, including new chromosome counts, is needed.

Hardiness: −15°C (5°F).

Area: Nepal. India (Sikkim).

Notes: Klotz (1970) stated that he had been unsuccessful in germinating seed of *Cotoneaster sandakphuensis* and was of the opinion that vegetative propagation was the only method of reproduction. He (Klotz 1970, 334) assumed that this must therefore be a hybrid, guessing at the parentage as being possibly *C. microphyllus* and *C. verruculosus*, two species which are very far apart in relationship, coming one from each of the two subgenera of *Cotoneaster*. But, due to its characteristics, *C. sandakphuensis* undoubtedly belongs in series *Verruculosi*. There is no evidence of any relationship whatsoever with series *Microphylli*. In England, a number of new collections of *C. sandakphuensis* have been successfully propagated from seed. *Cotoneaster sandakphuensis* is a slow-growing little beauty resembling what could be a natural bonsai of a *Cotoneaster*. In winter its red shoots are shown to their best advantage. It is best grown where it will not be smothered by other plants. A rockery situation is ideal, but preferably where it is not too dry.

10. *Cotoneaster subadpressus* T. T. Yu in Acta Phytotax. Sin. 8: 219 (1963). Synonym:
   C. subalpinus G. Klotz (1972). Type: China, Yunnan, Chungtien, Haba, 2 June 1937,
   T. T. Yu 11552 (holo PE).
Shrub, 0.2–1 m. Branches procumbent, ascending or prostrate, occasionally suckering; branchlets gray-brown, verruculose, initially densely strigose. Leaves evergreen or semi, subcoriaceous, on sterile shoots suborbicular or broadly ovate, 5–15 × 4–12 mm, apex obtuse or acute, base obtuse or cuneate, upper surface dark green, shiny, initially strigose, veins 2–3 impressed, lower surface sparsely strigose; petiole 1–2 mm, sparsely strigose. Fertile shoots 6–12 mm, including 2 leaves, and 1(–2) subsessile flower(s); pedicel absent to 1 mm, strigose; flowers (including hypanthium) 5–9 mm long. Hypanthium campanulate, sparsely strigose; sepals obtuse or acute, sparsely strigose, margin villous. Petals erect, 3–4 mm, red, pink and off-white. Stamens 10–15; filaments pale pink; anthers white. Fruit subglobose or broadly-obovoid, 5–8 mm, yellow-orange to orange-red, shiny, glabrescent, calyx lobes erect, pilose, margin densely villous, navel open. Nutlets 2(–3), apex swollen and slightly recurved, style remains $^3/_4$ from base.
   Seasons: Flowers May–June; fruit ripe September–October; autumn leaves red and yellow.
   Chromosomes: Tetraploid (Klotz and Krügel 1983a). More counts are needed for a clearer understanding of the behavior of this species.
   Hardiness: −15°C (5°F).
   Area: China (Yunnan and bordering Sichuan).
   Notes: In the past *Cotoneaster subadpressus* was only occasionally found in cultivation, but now, thanks to recent collections from Yunnan, this species is becoming more widely grown. It was collected in Yunnan by the Alpine Garden Society China expedition (#*1666*) in 1999 and by Jeanette Fryer (*JFYU 101*) at Thong Giang gorge, Yunnan, in 1996. This attractive, spreading subshrub is suitable for rockery or container growing.

11. *Cotoneaster verruculosus* Diels in Not. Roy. Bot. Gard. Edinburgh 5: 272 (1912).
   Synonym: *C. distichus* Lange var. *verruculosus* (Diels) T. T. Yu (1954). Type: China,

NW Yunnan, eastern flank of the Dali range, June–July 1906, *G. Forrest 4427* (holo E).

Shrub, 1–1.5 m. Branches erect or ascending; branchlets spiraled or distichous, brown, densely verruculose, initially densely strigose. Leaves evergreen or semi, subcoriaceous, on sterile shoots orbicular, suborbicular or broadly obovate, 6–14 × 5–14 mm; apex obtuse, acute or emarginate and mucronate, base obtuse, upper surface dark green, very shiny, sparsely strigose, veins 2–3 slightly impressed, lower surface sometimes few strigose hairs on midrib; petiole 2–4 mm, strigose; stipules red, long-haired strigose. Fertile shoots 8–12 mm, including 3–4 leaves and 1(–2) pendent flower(s); pedicel 1–2 mm; flowers (including hypanthium) 5–6 mm long. Hypanthium campanulate, shiny, glabrescent; sepals obtuse or broadly acute, shiny, glabrescent, margin erose. Petals semispreading, rich red. Stamens 12–16; filaments pink and white; anthers white. Fruit pendent, subglobose or broadly obovoid, 8–10 mm, rich red, glabrous, shiny, calyx lobes suberect. Nutlets 2, rarely 3–4, style remains ³/₄ from base.

Seasons: Flowers May–June; fruit ripe October.

Chromosomes: Tetraploid (Jewsbury, pers. comm.). Apomictic, true from seed.

Hardiness: −15°C (5°F).

Area: China (Yunnan).

Notes: The notes accompanying the holotype of *Cotoneaster verruculosus* disagree with the five small specimens on the herbarium sheet. The branches have lost most of their leaves and there is an absence of new spring growth; therefore, it is more probable that it was collected in winter and not during June-July as stated. Also the notes state that the flowers are white, but flowers are absent. In all probability the label was confused with that of another specimen during handling. It is feasible that this label belongs to C. *cochleatus* or related species. Recently reintroduced into cultivation.

12. ***Cotoneaster yalungensis*** J. Fryer & B. Hylmö, *sp. nov.* Type: E Nepal, Kanchenjunga, S of Yalung Ridge, 9 November 1981, *A. D. Schilling 2568* (holo K). **PLATE 88.**

Shrub, to 1 m. Branches erect, ascending, spreading, stiff, apex of flowering branches often forked; branchlets distichous or spiraled, maroon, verruculose, initially strigose. Leaves evergreen, subcoriaceous, on sterile shoots suborbicular or orbicular, 10–15 × 10–13 mm, apex obtuse, sometimes emarginate and mucronate, base obtuse or cuneate, margin mostly flat, upper surface dark green, intensely shiny, initially strigose, veins 3(–4) sometimes lightly impressed, lower surface glabrous except sparsely strigose midrib and margin; petiole 3–5 mm, maroon-green, strigose; stipules maroon, strigose. Fertile shoots 8–12 mm, including 2–4 leaves and 1 pendent flower; pedicel 1–2 mm; flowers (including hypanthium) 5–6 mm long. Hypanthium campanulate, red, shiny, glabrous; sepals obtuse, border membranous, margin erose, sometimes with single villous hairs. Corolla 5–6 mm, petals erect to semispreading, dark-red with pink border. Stamens 20; filaments red; anthers white. Fruit globose or subglobose, 7–8 mm, orange-red, shiny, glabrous, calyx lobes erect, navel open. Nutlets 2(–3), apex slightly swollen and recurved, style remains $^3/_4$ from base.

   Seasons: Flowers May–June; fruit ripe October.

   Chromosomes: Tetraploid (Bailey, pers. comm.). Apomictic, true from seed.

   Hardiness: –15°C (5°F).

   Area: Nepal.

   Notes: *Cotoneaster yalungensis* is a striking species with rich red flowers and bright shiny fruit which hang attractively along the undersides of the branches.

17. Series *Distichi* T. T. Yu in Bull. Brit. Mus. (Nat. Hist.), Bot. 1 (5): 127. (1954).

   Including series *Simonsioides* J. Fryer & B. Hylmö (2001).

Dwarf to large shrubs. Branches stiffly erect or ascending; branchlets distichous, spiraled or divaricate. Leaves deciduous, semievergreen, rarely evergreen. Flowers pendent. Corolla often globose, mostly open. Stamens (14–)18–20. Fruit pendent. Nutlets often moderately swollen and slightly recurved at apex.

   Mostly mid to late season, rarely early.

   Bhutan. Burma. China (Yunnan). Tibet. India (Arunachal Pradesh, Sikkim). Nepal.

   14 species: *C. assamensis, C. bumthangensis, C. capsicinus, C. cordifolius, C. cuspidatus, C. forrestii, C. hicksii, C. marquandii, C. nagaensis, C. natmataungensis, C. rotundifolius, C. salwinensis, C. simonsii, C. taylorii.*

Key to Series *Distichi*

1a. Leaves 9–15 mm; pedicels ≤ 4 mm 2

1b. Leaves 13–38 mm; pedicels ≤ 10 mm 5

2a. Fertile shoots 5–10 mm; flowers single, subsessile . . . .***C. natmataungensis***

2b. Fertile shoots 10–20 mm; flowers 1–2(–3), pedicels 1–4 mm 3

3a. Leaves often cordate or obcordate, veins 2–3, petiole 0.5–2 mm; corolla closed, petals pink and white . . . . ***C. cordifolius***

3b. Leaves not cordate or obcordate, veins 3–4, petiole 2–4 mm; corolla open, petals red and pink. 4

4a. Leaves broadly elliptic or suborbicular, 13–14 mm; fertile shoots to 15 mm; fruit 7–8 mm . . . . ***C. nagaensis***

4b. Leaves orbicular or broadly obovate, 9–12 mm; fertile shoots ≤ 20 mm; fruit 10–11 mm. . . . . ***C. rotundifolius***

5a. Flowers 1(–3) 6

5b. Flowers (1–)2–4(–8) 8

6a. Leaves elliptic, 17–30 mm, apex mostly acuminate; hypanthium campanulate. . . . . ***C. hicksii***

6b. Leaves broadly obovate or suborbicular, 15–22 mm, apex mostly obtuse; hypanthium cupulate 7

7a. Branches ascending horizontally; leaf veins 3–4, petiole 3–5 mm; flower (including hypanthium) 5 mm . . . . *C. capsicinus*

7b. Branches erect; leaf veins 2–3, petiole 2–3 mm; flowers (including hypanthium) 6–7 mm
. . . . *C. forrestii*

8a. Branchlets spiraled or distichous; leaf upper surface strigose, veins mostly not impressed
. . . . **9**

8b. Branchlets mostly divaricate; leaf upper surface villous or pilose-strigose, veins lightly impressed **12**

9a. Branches ascending; leaves mostly orbicular, apex obtuse or truncate; nutlets (3–)4–5 . . . . .
. . . . *C. salwinensis*

9b. Branches erect; leaves mostly elliptic, apex acuminate or acute; carpels (1–)2–3(–5). **10**

10a. Leaves ≤ 22 mm; fertile shoots 10–20 mm; fruit depressed-globose or obovoid . . . .
. . . .*C. marquandii*

10b. Leaves 33–36 mm; fertile shoots 15–30 mm; fruit obovoid or cylindrical. **11**

11a. Leaves somewhat dull, veins 3–4 lightly impressed; sepals erect; fruit rich-red, nutlets 2–3
. . . . *C. assamensis*

11b. Leaves shiny, veins 4–5 not impressed; sepals recurved; fruit orange-red, nutlets 3–4(–5)
. . . . *C. simonsii*

12a. Leaf veins 2–3; fertile shoots to 30 mm; pedicels ≤ 5 mm; fruit orange-red; nutlets 2–3 . . . . .
. . . . *C. bumthangensis*

12b. Leaf veins 3–4; fertile shoots ≤ 20 mm; pedicels ≤ 10 mm; fruit rich-red; nutlets (2–)3, rarely 4. . . . .*C. cuspidatus*

1. *Cotoneaster assamensis* G. Klotz in Wiss. Z. Friedrich-Schiller-Univ. Jena, Math.-Naturwiss. 21: 996 (1972). Type: NE India, Assam, Balipara frontier, Manda La, 6 July 1938, *F. Kingdon Ward 13858* (holo BM).

Shrub, 3–5 m. Branches erect, stiff; branchlets distichous, often ending in forked fertile shoots, maroon, initially strigose. Leaves deciduous, chartaceous, on sterile shoots elliptic or ovate, 22–36 × 14–19 mm, apex acuminate, base cuneate or obtuse, upper surface mid-green, dull, strigose, veins 3–4 lightly impressed, lower surface yellowish strigose; petioles 3–5 mm, strigose. Fertile shoots 20–30 mm, including 4(–5) leaves and a pendent, compact 2- to 5-flowered inflorescence; pedicels 2–5 mm, strigose; flowers (including hypanthium) 6–7 mm long. Hypanthium campanulate, sparsely strigose; sepals acuminate, cuspidate or acute, sparsely strigose, border broad, reddish green, glabrous, margin pilose. Corolla globose, finally with wide opening; petals erect-incurved, off-white with pink, base greenish. Stamens (18–)20; filaments base pink, apex white; anthers white. Fruit obovoid, 11–13 mm, rich red, shiny, glabrous, calyx lobes flat to suberect, navel open, glabrous. Nutlets (2–)3, rarely 4, apex swollen and recurved, style remains ³/₄ from base.

Seasons: Flowers June–July; fruit ripe October–November; autumn leaves deep gold.
Chromosomes: Triploid (Bailey, pers. comm.; Jewsbury, pers. comm.).

Hardiness: −18°C (−1°F).

Area: India (Arunachal Pradesh).

Notes: *Cotoneaster assamensis*, a striking shrub with many large shiny red fruit and good autumn color, can sometimes be found in cultivation as *C. distachyus* hort. (Hillier).

2. Cotoneaster bumthangensis J. Fryer & B. Hylmö, *sp. nov.* Type: East central Bhutan, Tang valley, Bumthang district, 7 May 1988, *A. D. Schilling 2991* [cult. Sweden, Bjuv, B. Hylmö 2411, 6 July 1996] (holo GB). **PLATE 89.**

Shrub, 1–2 m. Branches narrowly erect and ascending, coarse; branchlets distichous and divaricate, red-brown, initially strigose-tomentose. Leaves deciduous or semievergreen, chartaceous, on sterile shoots suborbicular or broadly elliptic, 13–24 × 11–17 mm, apex obtuse or apiculate, base obtuse, margin slightly undulate, upper surface slightly concave, mid to dark green, dull becoming shiny, sparsely villous-strigose, veins 2–3 lightly impressed, lower surface mid-green, sparsely strigose, midrib densely yellow-strigose; petiole 2–5 mm, strigose. Fertile shoots 15–30 mm, including 4–5 leaves and a pendent, 1- to 4-flowered inflorescence; pedicels 2–5 mm, sparsely strigose; flowers (including hypanthium) 7–8 mm long. Hypanthium widely cupulate, sparsely strigose; sepals obtuse, apiculate or acute, green, sparsely strigose, border broad, membranous, white, margin erose, sparsely long-haired villous. Corolla globose, open; petals erect-incurved, pale pink with red base and broad white border. Stamens 14–20; filaments pink and white; anthers white. Fruit obovoid, 10–11 mm, orange-red, shiny, glabrous, calyx lobes flat, navel open. Nutlets (2–)3, rarely 4, style remains $^{2}/_{3}$ from base.

Seasons: Flowers June–July; fruit ripe October–November; autumn leaves rich red.

Chromosomes: Tetraploid (Jewsbury, pers. comm.). Pentaploid (Jewsbury, pers. comm.). Apomictic.

Hardiness: −15°C (5°F).

Area: Bhutan.

Notes: *Cotoneaster bumthangensis* is an attractive shrub, excellent for its striking combination of autumn fruit and leaf color. The species has also been collected by Keith Rushforth (*KR 1474*) in Bhutan on the Mongar road, 8 km east of Sengor, in 1988.

3. Cotoneaster capsicinus J. Fryer & B. Hylmö, *sp. nov.* Type: SE Tibet, Tsarong Salween-Kuichiang divide, 3700 m, July 1921, *G. Forrest 19875* (holo E, iso A, UPS). **PLATE 90.**

Shrub, 0.5–1 m. Branches ascending horizontally, slightly arched; branchlets distichous, maroon, verruculose, initially densely strigose. Leaves deciduous, chartaceous or subcoriaceous, on sterile shoots broadly obovate or subcordate, 15–22 × 12–16 mm, apex obtuse, cuneate, apiculate or emarginate, base cuneate, upper surface dark green, shiny, strigose, veins 3–4, lower surface light green, sparsely strigose, glabrescent; petiole 3–5 mm, mostly sparsely strigose. Fertile shoots 10–20 mm, including 2–4 leaves and pendent, 1(–3) flower; pedicel 1–5 mm, sparsely strigose; flowers (including hypanthium) 5 mm long. Hypanthium cupulate, shiny, glabrescent; sepals obtuse or acute, glabrescent, border membranous, margin erose, sparsely villous. Corolla with small opening; petals erect-incurved, reddish with white border. Stamens 20; filaments pink; anthers white. Fruit shortly obovoid, 9–10 mm, orange, glabrous, calyx lobes flat, glabrous, navel open. Nutlets 3(–4), style remains $2/3$ from base.

> Seasons: Flowers July; fruit ripe October–November; autumn leaves red.
> Chromosomes: Tetraploid (Jewsbury, pers. comm.).
> Hardiness: –15°C (5°F).
> Area: Tibet.
> Notes: *Cotoneaster capsicinus* has long been in cultivation, usually as *C. apiculatus.*

4. *Cotoneaster cordifolius* G. Klotz in Bull. Bot. Surv. India 5: 212 (1963). Synonyms: *C. distichus* Lange var. *parvifolius* T. T. Yu (1954); *C. cavei* hort., non G. Klotz (1963). Type: N Burma, Seinghku Wang, 29 May 1926, *F. Kingdon Ward 6788* (holo K).

Shrub, 1–2 m. Branches erect and spreading, stiff; branchlets distichous or divaricate, reddish brown, minutely verruculose, initially densely strigose. Leaves deciduous or semi-evergreen, chartaceous to subcoriaceous, on sterile shoots orbicular, cordate, obcordate or broadly obovate, 9–11 × 7–10 mm, apex obtuse, truncate or emarginate and mucronate, base obtuse or broadly cuneate, margin often undulate, upper surface mid to dark green, shiny, initially strigose, veins 2–3, lower surface light green, sparsely strigose, more dense on midrib; petiole 0.5–2 mm. Fertile shoots 10–20 mm, including 4 leaves and 1–2(–3) pendent flowers; pedicels 1–4 mm, strigose; flowers (including hypanthium) 5–6 mm long. Hypanthium campanulate, glabrescent; sepals truncate, obtuse or acute, border broad, membranous, white or red, glabrous, tip recurved, margin erose and sparsely villous. Corolla globose, closed; petals erect-incurved, red and pink with greenish base and white apex. Stamens 18–20; filaments off-white, apex pinkish; anthers white. Fruit obovoid, succulent, 10–11 mm, orange-red, shiny, glabrous, calyx lobes flat, glabrous, navel with small opening. Nutlets (2–)3, rarely 4, apex with long hairs, style remains $2/3$ from base.

> Seasons: Flowers May–June; fruit ripe October–November; autumn leaves brilliant orange-red and purple.
> Hardiness: –15°C (5°F).
> Area: Burma. Tibet. Bhutan.
> Notes: *Cotoneaster cordifolius* is a beautiful shrub and should be more widely grown. It is very effective in its habit, its multitude of tiny closely spaced leaves which have good autumn color, and its vivid pendent fruit. This species was reintroduced when it was collected in 1990 by Keith Rushforth (*KR 1677*) in Bhutan, Sengor, beside Sengor Chu.

5. *Cotoneaster cuspidatus* C. Marquand ex J. Fryer & B. Hylmö in New Plantsman 5: 138 (1998). Type: Burma-Tibet frontier, Ata, Zayul, 21 October 1933, *F. Kingdon Ward 10907* (holo B, iso E). PLATE 91.

PLATE 1. *Cotoneaster floccosus*

PLATE 2. *Cotoneaster glabratus*

PLATE 3. *Cotoneaster henryanus*

PLATE 4. *Cotoneaster henryanus* 'Corina'

PLATE 5. *Cotoneaster hylmoei*

PLATE 6. *Cotoneaster rhytidophyllus*

PLATE 7. *Cotoneaster rugosus*

PLATE 8. *Cotoneaster salicifolius*

PLATE 9. *Cotoneaster salicifolius* 'Exburyensis'

PLATE 10. *Cotoneaster brickellii*

PLATE 11. *Cotoneaster fulvidus*

PLATE 12. *Cotoneaster glaucophyllus*

PLATE 13. *Cotoneaster lacteus*

PLATE 14. *Cotoneaster lacteus* 'Milkmaid'

PLATE 15. *Cotoneaster meiophyllus*

PLATE 16. *Cotoneaster pannosus*

PLATE 17. *Cotoneaster serotinus*

PLATE 18. *Cotoneaster tsarongensis*

PLATE 19. *Cotoneaster turbinatus*

PLATE 20. *Cotoneaster vernae*

PLATE 21. *Cotoneaster vestitus*

PLATE 22. *Cotoneaster frigidus*

PLATE 23. *Cotoneaster frigidus* 'Cornubia'

PLATE 24. *Cotoneaster frigidus* 'Fructuluteo'

PLATE 25. *Cotoneaster frigidus* 'St. Monica'

PLATE 26. *Cotoneaster gamblei*

PLATE 27. *Cotoneaster hedegaardii*

PLATE 28. *Cotoneaster aitchisonii*

PLATE 29. *Cotoneaster chadwellii*

PLATE 30. *Cotoneaster suavis*

PLATE 31. *Cotoneaster verokotschyi*

PLATE 32. *Cotoneaster creticus*

PLATE 33. *Cotoneaster tauricus*

PLATE 34. *Cotoneaster transcaucasicus*

PLATE 35. *Cotoneaster uzbezicus*

PLATE 36. *Cotoneaster affinis*

PLATE 37. *Cotoneaster ignotus*

PLATE 38. *Cotoneaster obtusus*

PLATE 39. *Cotoneaster borealichinensis*

PLATE 40. *Cotoneaster calocarpus*

PLATE 41. *Cotoneaster hupehensis*

PLATE 42. *Cotoneaster multiflorus*

PLATE **43**. *Cotoneaster purpurascens*

PLATE **44**. *Cotoneaster tanpaensis*

PLATE **45**. *Cotoneaster veitchii*

PLATE **46**. *Cotoneaster albokermesinus*

PLATE **47**. *Cotoneaster gonggashanensis*

PLATE **48**. *Cotoneaster hersianus*

PLATE 49. *Cotoneaster chungtiensis*

PLATE 50. *Cotoneaster cooperi*

PLATE 51. *Cotoneaster hebephyllus*

PLATE 52. *Cotoneaster incanus*

PLATE 53. *Cotoneaster monopyrenus*

PLATE 54. *Cotoneaster muliensis*

PLATE 55. *Cotoneaster omissus*

PLATE 56. *Cotoneaster transens*

PLATE **57.** *Cotoneaster conspicuus*

PLATE **58.** *Cotoneaster pluriflorus*

PLATE **59.** *Cotoneaster sherriffii*

PLATE **60.** *Cotoneaster argenteus*

PLATE 61. *Cotoneaster insolitus*

PLATE 62. *Cotoneaster lidjiangensis*

PLATE 63. *Cotoneaster lidjiangensis* 'Erin Faye'

PLATE 64. *Cotoneaster glacialis*

PLATE 65. *Cotoneaster marginatus*

PLATE 66. *Cotoneaster meuselii*

PLATE **67**. *Cotoneaster microphyllus*

PLATE **68**. *Cotoneaster uva-ursi*

PLATE **69**. *Cotoneaster cochleatus*

PLATE **70**. *Cotoneaster dammeri* 'Hybridus Pendulus'

PLATE **71**. *Cotoneaster dammeri* 'Major'

PLATE **72**. *Cotoneaster elatus*

PLATE **75**. *Cotoneaster prostratus* 'Arnold-Forster'

PLATE **73**. *Cotoneaster melanotrichus*

PLATE **74**. *Cotoneaster procumbens* 'Queen of Carpets'

PLATE **76**. *Cotoneaster* ×*suecicus* 'Juliette'

PLATE 77. *Cotoneaster chuanus*

PLATE 78. *Cotoneaster 'Gracia'*

PLATE 79. *Cotoneaster kweitschoviensis*

PLATE 80. *Cotoneaster rokujodaisanensis*

PLATE 81. *Cotoneaster 'Valkenburg'*

PLATE 82. *Cotoneaster vandelaarii*

PLATE 83. *Cotoneaster chulingensis*

PLATE 84. *Cotoneaster encavei*

PLATE 85. *Cotoneaster ganghobaensis*

PLATE **86**. *Cotoneaster konishii*

PLATE **87**. *Cotoneaster milkedandaensis*

PLATE **88**. *Cotoneaster yalungensis*

PLATE **89**. *Cotoneaster bumthangensis*

PLATE 90. *Cotoneaster capsicinus*

PLATE 91. *Cotoneaster cuspidatus*

PLATE 92. *Cotoneaster hicksii*

PLATE 93. *Cotoneaster marquandii*

PLATE 94. *Cotoneaster natmataungensis*

PLATE 95. *Cotoneaster rotundifolius*

PLATE 97. *Cotoneaster beimashanensis*

PLATE 96. *Cotoneaster salwinensis*

PLATE 98. *Cotoneaster cardinalis*

PLATE 99. *Cotoneaster duthieanus*

PLATE 100. *Cotoneaster nanshan*

PLATE 101.*Cotoneaster atropurpureus* 'Variegatus'

PLATE 102. *Cotoneaster atrovirens*

PLATE 103. *Cotoneaster divaricatus*

PLATE 104. *Cotoneaster hjelmqvistii*

PLATE 105. *Cotoneaster horizontalis*

PLATE 106. *Cotoneaster spongbergii*

PLATE 107. *Cotoneaster yinchangensis*

PLATE 108. *Cotoneaster atrovinaceus*

PLATE 109. *Cotoneaster drogochius*

PLATE 110. *Cotoneaster harrysmithii*

PLATE 111. *Cotoneaster kangdingensis*

PLATE 112. *Cotoneaster marroninus*

PLATE 113. *Cotoneaster naninitens*

PLATE 114. *Cotoneaster tripyrenus*

PLATE 115. *Cotoneaster convexus*

PLATE 116. *Cotoneaster decandrus*

PLATE 117. *Cotoneaster* 'Marketa'

PLATE 118. *Cotoneaster campanulatus*

PLATE 119. *Cotoneaster mirabilis*

PLATE 120. *Cotoneaster mucronatus*

PLATE 121. *Cotoneaster newryensis*

PLATE 122. *Cotoneaster nepalensis*

PLATE 123. *Cotoneaster parkeri*

PLATE 124. *Cotoneaster thimphuensis*

PLATE 125. *Cotoneaster coadunatus*

PLATE 126. *Cotoneaster hummelii*

PLATE 127. *Cotoneaster lucidus*

PLATE 128. *Cotoneaster washanensis*

PLATE **129**. *Cotoneaster yulingkongensis*

PLATE **130**. *Cotoneaster ataensis*

PLATE **131**. *Cotoneaster atuntzensis*

PLATE **132**. *Cotoneaster bullatus* 'Samantha Jane'

PLATE **133**. *Cotoneaster cornifolius*

PLATE 134. *Cotoneaster emeiensis*

PLATE 135. *Cotoneaster hillieri*

PLATE 136. *Cotoneaster hualiensis*

PLATE 137. *Cotoneaster ignescens*

PLATE 138. *Cotoneaster lancasteri*

PLATE **139**. *Cotoneaster moupinensis*

PLATE **140**. *Cotoneaster ogisui*

PLATE **141**. *Cotoneaster pseudoobscurus*

PLATE **142**. *Cotoneaster rehderi*

PLATE **143**. *Cotoneaster sikangensis*

PLATE 144. *Cotoneaster wanbooyensis*

PLATE 145. *Cotoneaster kingdonii*

PLATE 146. *Cotoneaster shansiensis*

PLATE 147. *Cotoneaster camilli-schneideri*

PLATE 148. *Cotoneaster daliensis*

PLATE 149. *Cotoneaster glomerulatus*

PLATE 150. *Cotoneaster kuanensis*

PLATE 151. *Cotoneaster tengyuehensis*

PLATE 152. *Cotoneaster amoenus*

PLATE 153. *Cotoneaster franchetii*

PLATE 154. *Cotoneaster nohelii*

PLATE 155. *Cotoneaster tardiflorus*

PLATE 156. *Cotoneaster teijiashanensis*

PLATE 157. *Cotoneaster vilmorinianus*

PLATE 158. *Cotoneaster wardii*

PLATE 159. *Cotoneaster aurantiacus*

PLATE 160. *Cotoneaster fastigiatus*

PLATE 163. *Cotoneaster induratus*

PLATE 161. *Cotoneaster huahongdongensis*

PLATE 164. *Cotoneaster insculptus*

PLATE 162. *Cotoneaster hypocarpus*

PLATE 165. *Cotoneaster leveillei*

PLATE **166.** *Cotoneaster naoujanensis*

PLATE **167.** *Cotoneaster qungbixiensis*

PLATE **168.** *Cotoneaster sternianus*

PLATE **169.** *Cotoneaster taofuensis*

PLATE **170.** *Cotoneaster bradyi*

PLATE **171.** *Cotoneaster declinatus*

PLATE 172. *Cotoneaster dielsianus*

PLATE 173. *Cotoneaster floridus*

PLATE 174. *Cotoneaster froebelii*

PLATE 175. *Cotoneaster fruticosus*

PLATE 176. *Cotoneaster splendens*

PLATE 177. *Cotoneaster kitaibelii*

PLATE 179. *Cotoneaster zabelii*

PLATE 178. *Cotoneaster svenhedinii*

PLATE 180. *Cotoneaster soczavianus*

PLATE 181. *Cotoneaster estiensis*

PLATE 182. *Cotoneaster favargeri*

PLATE 183. *Cotoneaster integerrimus*

PLATE 185. *Cotoneaster scandinavicus*

PLATE 184. *Cotoneaster kullensis*

PLATE 186. *Cotoneaster altaicus*

PLATE **187**. *Cotoneaster hylanderi*

PLATE **188**. *Cotoneaster laxiflorus*

PLATE **189**. *Cotoneaster melanocarpus*

PLATE **190**. *Cotoneaster narynensis*

PLATE **191.** *Cotoneaster polyanthemus*

PLATE **193.** *Cotoneaster yakuticus*

PLATE **194.** *Cotoneaster browiczii*

PLATE **192.** *Cotoneaster rannensis*

PLATE **195.** *Cotoneaster erratus*

PLATE **196**. *Cotoneaster ignavus*

PLATE **198**. *Cotoneaster osmastonii*

PLATE **197**. *Cotoneaster cinovskisii*

PLATE **199**. *Cotoneaster roseus*

PLATE **200**. *Cotoneaster wilsonii*

Shrub, 2.5–3 m. Branches ascending and erect, stiff, bowed in fruit; branchlets divaricate, red-brown, minutely verruculose, initially yellowish strigose-villous. Leaves deciduous or semievergreen, subcoriaceous, on sterile shoots broadly obovate, broadly elliptic or suborbicular, 21–26 × 17–24 mm, apex obtuse or truncate and mucronulate or cuspidate, base cuneate, upper surface slightly rugose, dark green, shiny, yellowish strigose-pilose, veins mostly 3–4 lightly impressed, lower surface mid-green, shiny, strigose; petiole 3–4 mm, strigose. Fertile shoots 15–20 mm, including 2–4 leaves and a pendent, (1–)3(–8)-flowered inflorescence, branch apex inflorescences to 8-flowered; pedicels 2–10 mm, strigose; flowers (including hypanthium) 6–8 mm long. Hypanthium widely cupulate, few long strigose hairs; sepals obtuse or acute, glabrescent, border membranous, tip recurved, margin erose and sparsely villous. Corolla open; petals erect-incurved, dark red, border pink. Stamens (16–)20; filaments pale pink, apex off-white; anthers white to yellowish. Fruit globose or ellipsoid, 8–10 mm, rich red, shiny, glabrous, calyx lobes depressed, margin villous. Nutlets (2–)3, rarely 4, apex villous, style remains ²/₃ from base.

Seasons: Flowers May–June; fruit ripe October; autumn leaves fiery orange-red.
Chromosomes: Tetraploid (Klotz 1968b as *C. strigosus;* Bailey, pers. comm.).
Hardiness: −18°C (−1°F).
Area: Burma. Tibet.
Notes: Cecil Marquand studied this *Cotoneaster* in cultivation at the RBG Kew and in 1939 noted his conclusion on the herbarium sheet that this was a new species. He gave it the name *C. cuspidatus*, but neither his observations nor his name for this species were published. *Cotoneaster cuspidatus* is a very handsome shrub with polished, bottle-green leaves showing brilliant autumn color, and striking pendent fruit which hang in profusion on short pedicels along the undersides of the branches. This plant is frequently found in cultivation as *C. khasiensis, C. strigosus,* or *C. distichus* var. *tongolensis.*

6. **Cotoneaster forrestii** G. Klotz in Bull. Bot. Surv. India 5: 209 (1963). Type: China, central W Yunnan, September 1924, *G. Forrest 25215* (holo K, iso E).
Shrub, 2–3 m. Branches narrowly erect, stiff; branchlets distichous, maroon, minutely verruculose, initially densely strigose. Leaves deciduous or semievergreen, chartaceous or subcoriaceous, on sterile shoots broadly obovate, broadly elliptic or suborbicular, 15–21 × 11–17 mm, apex obtuse or truncate, base cuneate or obtuse, upper surface dark green, shiny, strigose, veins 2–3 lightly impressed, lower surface light green, shiny, sparsely strigose; petiole 2–3 mm, strigose. Fertile shoots 10–20 mm, including 2–4 leaves and pendent, 1(–3) flowers; pedicel 3–4 mm, sparsely strigose; flowers (including hypanthium) 6–7 mm long. Hypanthium cupulate, shiny, glabrescent; sepals obtuse or apiculate, shiny, glabrous, border narrow, membranous, margin slightly erose, villous. Corolla with small opening; petals erect-incurved, greenish and red with off-white border. Stamens (14–)18–20; filaments pink, apex white; anthers white. Fruit shortly obovoid, 8 mm, orange-red shiny, glabrous, calyx lobes depressed, glabrous, navel opening small with stamens and style exserted. Nutlets 3(–4), rarely 2, style remains ²/₃ from base.

Seasons: Flowers June–July; fruit ripe November; autumn leaves purple-red.
Chromosomes: Unknown. Apomictic, true from seed.
Hardiness: –18°C (–1°F).
Area: China (Yunnan). Possibly in Tibet.
Notes: *Cotoneaster forrestii*, with its erect habit and lovely autumn display of fruit and leaf color, makes a beautiful specimen shrub. It was rediscovered in Yunnan in 1996 by Maurice Foster (*MF 96102*).

7. *Cotoneaster hicksii* J. Fryer & B. Hylmö, *sp. nov.* Type: Bhutan, Gyaza Dzong, Mo Chu, 3 October 1949, *F. Ludlow, G. Sherriff & J. H. Hicks 17405* (holo E, iso BM). **PLATE 92.**

Shrub, 2–3 m. Branches stiffly erect becoming arched; branchlets spiraled or distichous, maroon, minutely verruculose, densely strigose. Leaves deciduous, chartaceous, on sterile shoots mostly elliptic, 17–30 × 10–18 mm, apex acuminate or acute, base cuneate, upper surface mid-green, shiny, initially densely strigose, veins 3–6, lower surface light green, sparsely strigose; petiole 4–5 mm, strigose. Fertile shoots 15–25 mm, including 4 leaves and pendent, 1(–2) flower; pedicel 3–8 mm, strigose; flower (including hypanthium) 7 mm long. Hypanthium campanulate, maroon, mostly sparsely strigose; sepals obtuse, sparsely strigose, border broad, membranous, brown and whitish, margin erose and villous. Corolla open; petals erect-incurved, red with white border. Stamens (16–)20; filaments pink; anthers white. Fruit obovoid, 7–9 mm, orange-red, shiny, glabrous, calyx lobes suberect, green, glabrous. Nutlets (2–)4, apex somewhat swollen and recurved, style remains ²⁄₃ from base.

Seasons: Flowers May–June; fruit ripe November.
Chromosomes: Unknown. Apomictic, true from seed.
Hardiness: –15°C (5°F).
Area: Bhutan.
Notes: *Cotoneaster hicksii* is very pretty with the autumn sun highlighting the shiny orange droplet-shaped pendent fruit. Known only from the type collection.

8. *Cotoneaster marquandii* G. Klotz in Bull. Bot. Surv. India 5: 209 (1963). Type: cult. Wales, Tal-y-cafn, Bodnant, in garden of Lord Aberconway (mistakenly as Kingdon Ward 6788) (holo K). **PLATE 93.**

Shrub, 2–3 m. Branches narrowly erect, stiff; branchlets distichous or spiraled, maroon, minutely verruculose, initially densely strigose. Leaves deciduous or semievergreen, chartaceous, on sterile shoots elliptic, 13–22 × 9–15 mm, apex acuminate or acute, base cuneate, upper surface dark green, shiny, initially sparsely strigose, veins 3–4, lower surface mid-green, glabrescent, midrib more densely so; petiole 2–3 mm, strigose. Fertile shoots 10–20 mm, including 4 leaves and a pendent, 1- to 3(–4)-flowered inflorescence; pedicels 1–4 mm, sparsely strigose; flowers (including hypanthium) 5–6 mm long. Hypanthium cupulate, subglabrous; sepals broadly obtuse or ligulate, subglabrous, border broad, membranous, white, margin erose, sparsely villous. Corolla with large opening; petals erect-incurved, dark red with white border. Stamens (14–)20; filaments red and pink; anthers white. Fruit depressed globose or obovoid, 7–8 mm, orange-red, shiny, glabrous, calyx lobes suberect, navel wide open. Nutlets (2–)3(–4), style remains $^2/_3$ from base.

Seasons: Flowers June–July; fruit ripe November–December; autumn leaves red.

Chromosomes: Tetraploid (Krügel 1992a; McAllister, pers. comm.; Jewsbury, pers. comm.). Apomictic, true from seed.

Hardiness: –15°C (5°F).

Area: China (Yunnan).

Notes: *Cotoneaster marquandii* has as its type a cultivated specimen said to have been raised from the Kingdon Ward collection *6788*. However, this number is the type for *C. cordifolius*, and the herbarium specimen of *Kingdon Ward 6788* verifies this as correct. *Cotoneaster marquandii* has been rediscovered in the Yunnan province of China, in the area surrounding Dali, through which a number of plant collectors traversed throughout the years. It was collected by Jeanette Fryer (*JFYU 056*) in Yunnan in 1996. Its often fan-shaped branching habit, scarlet autumn leaves, and conspicuous, pendent fruit (both colorful leaves and fruit long persisting) make *C. marquandii* a very garden-worthy shrub.

9. *Cotoneaster nagaensis* G. Klotz in Bull. Bot. Surv. India 5: 212 (1963). Synonym: *C. khasiensis* G. Klotz (1963). Type: India, Assam, Naga Hills, Kohima, 1 September 1939, *C. K. Deka 15452* (holo ASSAM).

Shrub, 1–3 m. Branches erect; branchlets spiraled or distichous, brown, minutely verruculose, initially strigose. Leaves deciduous or semievergreen, subcoriaceous, on sterile shoots broadly elliptic or suborbicular, 13–14 × 8–13 mm, apex obtuse or acute, base obtuse or cuneate, upper surface dark green, shiny, strigose, veins 3–4, lower surface sparsely strigose on veins and midrib; petiole 2–4 mm, strigose. Fertile shoots 10–15 mm, including 4 elliptic leaves and 1–2 pendent flowers; pedicels 1–3 mm, glabrous. Hypanthium glabrous; sepals obtuse or acute, glabrous, margin sparsely villous. Petals erect-incurved, 3 mm, probably red. Stamens 20. Fruit obovoid, 7–8 mm, orange-red to crimson, calyx lobes suberect. Nutlets 2–3, apex slightly swollen and recurved, style remains $^2/_3$ from base.

Seasons: Fruit ripe October–November.

Hardiness: –12°C (10°F).

Area: India (Arunachal Pradesh).

Notes: Rarely found in cultivation, *Cotoneaster nagaensis* was in cultivation in the United States at the University of Washington Botanic Gardens in Seattle in 1966.

10. *Cotoneaster natmataungensis* J. Fryer, B. Hylmö & E. C. Nelson, *sp. nov.* Type: central W Burma, S Chin Hills, Mount Victoria region, top section, 9 April 1956 (Kingdon Ward expedition), *Ingrid Alsterlund 230* (holo GB). **PLATE 94.**

Shrub, 1–2 m. Branches erect and spreading, stiff; branchlets distichous or spiraled, brown with raised lenticels, minutely verruculose, initially densely strigose. Leaves evergreen, subcoriaceous, on sterile shoots orbicular, obcordate, broadly obovate or broadly elliptic, 8–16 × 8–14 mm, apex obtuse or truncate, base obtuse or cuneate, upper surface light to mid-green, slightly shiny, sparsely strigose, margin densely strigose, veins in 2–5 sometimes lightly impressed, lower surface sparsely strigose or glabrous; petiole 3–5 mm, strigose. Fertile shoots 5–10 mm, including 2–4 leaves and 1 pendent flower; pedicels absent to 2 mm, glabrous or with few strigose hairs; flowers (including hypanthium) 4–8 mm long. Hypanthium widely cupulate, glabrous; sepals obtuse or apiculate, glabrous, border narrow, membranous, brown, margin sparsely villous. Corolla with small opening; petals erect-incurved, greenish, red, pink and off-white. Stamens 20; filaments pink; anthers white. Fruit obovoid, 8–11 mm, orange-red, shiny, glabrous, calyx lobes suberect, navel open. Nutlets 2–4, style remains $^2/_3$–$^3/_4$ from base.

Seasons: Flowers June–July; fruit ripe November.

Chromosomes: Unknown. Possibly not breeding true from seed.

Hardiness: −15°C (5°F).

Area: Burma.

Notes: *Cotoneaster natmataungensis* has been rediscovered in the same location as the collection made by the Kingdon Ward expedition in 1956—Victoria Mountain National Park summit in Chin state. In 1998, C. Nelson and D. Sayers collected it twice (*CNDS 22, CNDS 27*), the latter at 3000 m. Open in habit with bright shiny fruit, this *Cotoneaster* is an attractive species for the smaller garden.

11. *Cotoneaster rotundifolius* Wallich ex Lindley in Edward's Bot. Reg. 15: t. 1229 (1829); illustr. Saunder's Refug. Bot., t. 54 (1869); Curtis's Bot. Mag. 131: t. 8010 (1905) (petals incorrectly illustrated as spreading). Synonyms: *C. nitidus* Jacques (1859); *C. distichus* Lange (1882). Type: Nepal, from the alpine zone of Gossainkund, October 1821, *Wallich 663* (holo K). **PLATE 95.**

Shrub, 2–3 m. Branches erect or suberect, stiff; branchlets distichous or spiraled, brown, verruculose initially densely strigose. Leaves evergreen or semi, subcoriaceous, on sterile shoots orbicular or broadly obovate, 9–12 × 8–11 mm, apex obtuse or truncate, base obtuse, upper surface dark green, shiny, sparsely strigose, veins 3–4, lower surface mid-green, sparsely strigose; petiole 2–4 mm, strigose. Fertile shoots 10–20 mm, including 4 leaves and 1(–2) pendent flower(s); pedicel 3–4 mm, sparsely strigose; flowers (including hypanthium) 6–7 mm long. Hypanthium campanulate, red, shiny, subglabrous; sepals obtuse, glabrous, border broad, membranous, whitish, margin erose, sparsely villous. Corolla with large opening; petals erect-incurved, dark red with pink border. Stamens (12–)18–20; filaments dark red; anthers white. Fruit obovoid, 10–11 mm, orange-red to red, shiny, glabrous, calyx lobes suberect, navel open. Nutlets (2–)3, rarely 4, apex slightly swollen and recurved, style remains $^2/_3$ from base.

Seasons: Flowers June–July; fruit ripe November–December; autumn leaves (some) shades of red.

Chromosomes: Tetraploid (Klotz and Krügel 1983a; McAllister, pers. comm.; Bailey, pers. comm.). Apomictic, true from seed.

Hardiness: –15°C (5°F).

Area: Nepal.

Notes: *Cotoneaster rotundifolius* Wallich ex Lindley has been blighted by a predicament caused by the illustration attached to the type description of *C. microphyllus* var. *uva-ursi* Lindley (1828), which later Lindley (1829) included in *C. rotundifolius*. The illustration, with its white, spreading petals, clearly shows a very different taxon from *C. rotundifolius*. Unfortunately, being more common in cultivation than *C. rotundifolius*, this misnamed taxon, which rightly belonged in series *Microphylli* in subgenus *Chaenopetalum*, took over the name completely. Baker (1869) tried to correct this problem of two species under one name with an excellent illustration of *C. rotundifolius* showing erect red-pink petals. Lange (1882) mistakenly bequeathed this taxon with another name, *C. distichus*, by which it was known until Exell (1930) found the overlooked name *C. nitidus* Jacques. From then, *C. nitidus* was commonly used for *C. rotundifolius* and has been to the present day. A letter exists in the herbarium of the RBG Kew, England, written to the Arnold Arboretum in the United States, dated 18 September 1918, in which Hutchinson remonstrates with Rehder for using the names incorrectly. Hutchinson concluded that Lange's *C. distichus* was the same as *C. rotundifolius*. Rehder (1930) accepted this and changed *C. distichus* var. *tongolensis* to *C. rotundifolius* var. *tongolensis*—a species now known as *C. soulieanus* G. Klotz. *Cotoneaster rotundifolius* is a dense shrub with small, polished leaves which color brilliantly in autumn, and large pendent, bright scarlet fruit, which, not being particularly relished by birds, persist until spring. Excellent for amenity plantings. Received RHS Award of Garden Merit in 1927.

12. *Cotoneaster salwinensis* G. Klotz in Wiss. Z. Friedrich-Schiller-Univ. Jena, Math.-Naturwiss. 21: 1003 (1972). Type: China, Yunnan, Mekong-Salween divide, July 1919, *G. Forrest 18188* (holo E, iso A, K). **PLATE 96.**

Shrub, 1–1.5 m. Branches ascending, stiff; branchlets distichous, curved, often fertile shoots at apex, maroon, minutely verruculose, initially densely strigose. Leaves deciduous, chartaceous, on sterile shoots orbicular, subcordate or broadly obovate, 14–22 × 10–17 mm, apex obtuse or truncate, base cuneate or obtuse, upper surface dark green, shiny, strigose, veins 3–4, lower surface mid-green, strigose; petiole 2–4 mm, long-haired strigose. Fertile shoots 15–25 mm, including 4–5 leaves and an outspread, (1–)3(–4)-flowered (end shoots 5- to 8-flowered) inflorescence; pedicels 2–5 mm, densely strigose; flowers (including hypanthium) 5–6 mm long. Hypanthium cupulate, strigose or sparsely long-haired strigose; sepals obtuse or acute, subglabrous, border membranous, whitish, glabrous, margin erose, sparsely villous. Corolla closed; petals erect-incurved, green and red with off-white border. Stamens 18–20, rarely to 26; filaments pale pink; anthers white. Fruit obovoid, 8–9 mm, orange-red, shiny, glabrous, calyx lobes erect. Nutlets (3–)4–5, style remains ²/₃ from base.

Seasons: Flowers June; fruit ripe October–November; autumn leaves red.

Chromosomes: Triploid (Bailey, pers. comm.; Jewsbury, pers. comm.).

Hardiness: −18°C (−1°F).

Area: China (Yunnan).

Notes: *Cotoneaster salwinensis* is a good shrub for the smaller garden, dense and tidy in habit and with excellent autumn leaf and fruit color. Recently reintroduced into cultivation.

13. *Cotoneaster simonsii* Baker in Saunder's Ref. Bot. 1: t. 55 (1869). Type: India, Himachal Pradesh, Lailankote, Khasia, 26 September 1886, *C. B. Clarke 45543* (K).

Shrub, 3–4 m. Branches erect, stiff; branchlets divaricate, spiraled, grayish brown, initially densely strigose. Leaves deciduous, rarely semievergreen, chartaceous or subcoriaceous, on sterile shoots broadly elliptic or suborbicular, 19–33 × 13–24 mm, apex acuminate or acute, base obtuse or cuneate, upper surface mid to dark green, shiny, sparsely strigose, veins 4–5, lower surface light green, initially strigose; petiole 3–5 mm, strigose. Fertile shoots 15–30 mm, including 4 leaves and a pendent, 2- to 6-flowered inflorescence; pedicels 2–5 mm, strigose; flowers (including hypanthium) 5–7 mm long. Hypanthium campanulate, strigose, sepals long acuminate or cuspidate, strigose, border narrow, glabrous, apex recurved, margin villous. Corolla open; petals erect-incurved, dark red with white border. Stamens 20; filaments pink; anthers white. Fruit mostly cylindrical or obovoid, 10–12 mm, bright orange to orange-red, shiny, glabrous, calyx lobes erect. Nutlets 3(–4), rarely 2, rarely 5 in apex fruit, style remains ²/₃ from base.

Seasons: Flowers June; fruit ripe October–November; autumn leaves yellow to fiery red.

Chromosomes: Tetraploid (Zeilinga 1964; Hensen 1966; McAllister, pers. comm.). Apomictic, true from seed.

Hardiness: −18°C (−1°F).

Area: India (Sikkim). Bhutan.

Notes: *Cotoneaster simonsii* is frequently found as an escape from cultivation in areas with only moderately cold winters. The fruit are often produced in copious quantities, frequently remaining on the leafless branches well into the following season. When closely clipped, this shrub makes an excellent, dense hedge which is full of fruit. This species was also collected by Keith Rushforth (*KR 721*) in Bhutan on a hillside above Olathang Hotel at Paro in 1985. Received RHS Award of Garden Merit in 1984.

14. *Cotoneaster taylorii* T. T. Yu in Bull. Brit. Mus. (Nat. Hist.), Bot. 1 (5): 129 (1954).
   Type: SE Tibet, below Kongbo Nga La, Takpo, 13 May 1938, *F. Ludlow, G. Sherriff & G. Taylor 4246* (holo BM).

Shrub, sometimes multistemmed, 2–3 m. Branches narrowly erect, becoming arched, stiff; branchlets spiraled, reddish brown, minutely verruculose, initially densely strigose. Leaves deciduous, chartaceous, on sterile shoots elliptic or obovate, often broadly so, 17–38 × 12–24 mm, apex acuminate or acute, base cuneate, upper surface dark to mid-green, shiny, strigose, veins 3–5 slightly impressed, lower surface strigose-villous, midrib more dense; petiole 3–5 mm, strigose. Fertile shoots 15–25 mm, including 2–4 often orbicular leaves and a lax 1- to 3(–4)-flowered inflorescence; pedicels 5–10 mm, strigose; flowers (including hypanthium) 6 mm long. Hypanthium campanulate, sparsely strigose or subglabrous; sepals obtuse or acute, subglabrous, border broad, membranous, white to brownish, margin villous. Corolla globose with large opening; petals erect, red or deep pink with darker red base and off-white border. Stamens (14–)20; filaments broadly lanceolate, pink and white; anthers white. Fruit obovoid, 8–9 mm, bright red, calyx lobes depressed. Nutlets (2–)3(–4), apex pilose, style remains $^3/_4$ from base.
   Seasons: Flowers May–June; fruit ripe September–October.
   Chromosomes: Unknown. Apomictic, true from seed.
   Hardiness: −18°C (−1°F).
   Area: Tibet.
   Notes: *Cotoneaster taylorii* is rare in cultivation, but can be found in some U.S. botanic gardens and parks. Not in key.

18. Series *Adpressi*

Dwarf shrubs. Branches decumbent or procumbent, easily rooting; branchlets irregular or spiraled. Leaves deciduous, thinly chartaceous, margin undulate. Flowers erect, subsessile. Sepals mostly ligulate or obtuse, sometimes acute. Petals with margin often very erose. Anthers white, often with pinkish dots. Fruit succulent. Nutlets 1–3.
   Early season.
   China (Yunnan, Sichuan, Gansu). Tibet. India (Uttaranchal Pradesh, Himachal Pradesh, Sikkim). Nepal. Pakistan (Hindukush).
   9 species: *C. adpressus, C. apiculatus, C. beimashanensis, C. cardinalis, C. duthieanus, C. garhwalensis, C. kerstanii, C. nanshan, C. taoensis.*

Key to Series *Adpressi*

1a. Branches decumbent or prostrate; flowers 1(–2); nutlets (1–)2(–3) 2
1b. Branches erect or suberect, spreading; flowers 1–4; nutlets 1–2(–3) 7
2a. Leaves ≤ 25 × 15 mm; stamens 10–12(–18) . . . . *C. garhwalensis*
2b. Leaves ≤ 20 × 17 mm; stamens 8–12(–15) 3

3a. Leaves mostly elliptic; sepals mostly ligulate; fruit 6–8 mm, red or rich–red; nutlets mostly 2. . . . .**4**

3b. Leaves mostly suborbicular; sepals not ligulate; fruit 8–12 mm, orange-red; nutlets 1–3. . . .**5**

4a. Branches compact, rigid; upper leaf surface glabrous, veins 2–3; hypanthium infundibulate . . . . *C. adpressus*

4b. Branches somewhat lax, pliant; upper leaf surface sparsely strigose, veins 3–4(–5); hypanthium cupulate. . . . . *C. taoensis*

5a. Fertile shoots 10–20 mm; sepals obtuse or acute; fruit depressed-globose . . . . *C. beimashanensis*

5b. Fertile shoots 8–12 mm; sepals mostly acuminate; fruit globose. **6**

6a. Height ≤ 1 m; leaf apex mostly obtuse; flowers deep rich-pink; nutlets mostly 2. . . . . *C. cardinalis*

6b. Height ≤ 0.7 m; leaf apex mostly apiculate; flowers dark red; nutlets mostly 3 . . . . *C. apiculatus*

7a. Leaves broadly obovate-elliptic or obcordate, ≤ 15 mm, apex mostly obtuse; filaments red and pink . . . . *C. kerstanii*

7b. Leaves suborbicular or broadly elliptic, ≤ 25 mm, apex mostly apiculate; filaments dark red **8**

8a. Leaves strongly undulate; flowers 7–10 mm; hypanthium sparsely strigose; anthers white with pink stripes. . . . .*C. nanshan*

8b. Leaves slightly undulate; flowers 5–6 mm; hypanthium sparsely pilose; anthers pink becoming red . . . . *C. duthieanus*

1. ***Cotoneaster adpressus*** Bois in Bull. Soc. Bot. France 51: 149 (1904). Type: France, Les Barres garden (M. Vilmorin), from type plant collected by W. J. Bean, 14 July 1904, cult. (lecto K).

Shrub, mound-forming, to 0.3 m. Branches to 0.8 m, stiff, divaricate, rooting; branchlets distichous, maroon, initially strigose-villous. Internodes short, leaves deciduous, charta-ceous, on sterile shoots elliptic, ovate or suborbicular, 8–15 × 5–12 mm, apex acute or obtuse, base obtuse, margin slightly undulate, upper surface dull green, glabrous, veins 2–3, lower surface subglabrous, midrib strigose; petiole 1–2 mm, glabrescent. Fertile shoots 6–10 mm, including 2–3 leaves and 1(–2) subsessile flower(s); flower (including hypanthium) 4–7 mm long. Hypanthium infundibulate, maroon, subglabrous; sepals ligulate or acute, sometimes recurved, glabrous, margin villous. Corolla open; petals erect, dark red. Stamens 10(–13); red and pink; anthers white. Fruit globose, succulent, 6–7 mm, bright red. Nutlets 2, style remains ⁴/₅ from base.

Seasons: Flowers April–May; fruit ripe September; autumn leaves yellow-red.

Chromosomes: Diploid (Zeilinga 1964; Hensen 1966). Sexual, outbreeding, variable from seed.

Hardiness: –15°C (5°F).

Area: China (Sichuan, Yunnan).

Notes: *Cotoneaster adpressus* is a shrub well suited for rockeries, growing against a wall or fence. The branches layer themselves where they touch the ground, are slow growing, with an attractive tufted growth habit, and in time can cover a considerable area. Flowers and hence fruit are not numerous. Probably introduced by Armand David, who in 1869–1870 was collecting in the same area of Sichuan in which K. L. Chu discovered *C. adpressus* in 1936. First grown and distributed in 1895 by Vilmorin of Les Barres garden in France. Recently reintroduced into cultivation.

Cultivars: '**Canu**', more diminutive than *C. adpressus*, fairly dense and regular in habit, at 10 years a maximum 50 cm high × 150 cm wide, fruit red. A Danish cultivar. '**Conglomeratus**', very densely branched, slightly larger than 'Canu'. '**Kovalosky**', selected in the Czech Republic at the botanic garden of Mendel University, Brno. '**Little Gem**', miniature, slow-growing, forming a small, compact cushion to 10 × 25 cm. A little gem for the rockery, trough, or even a hanging basket. Introduced before 1946 by Verboom of Boskoop, Netherlands, from a chance seedling. Triploid (Zeilinga 1964) and thus not a clone of the diploid *C. adpressus*. '**Tangstedt**', procumbent, dense habit with good ground-cover qualities, leaves becoming dark-red in autumn. Very hardy. A German selection. '**Tom Thumb**', similar to 'Little Gem'.

2. *Cotoneaster apiculatus* Rehder & E. H. Wilson in Sargent, Pl. Wilson. 1: 156
   (1912). Type: China, W Sichuan, Pan-lan Shan, west of Guan Xian, October 1910,
   E. H. Wilson 4311 (holo A).
Shrub, to 0.7 m. Branches 1–1.5 m, spreading, tips ascending; branchlets spiraled and divaricate, maroon, minutely verruculose, initially strigose. Leaves deciduous, chartaceous, on sterile shoots orbicular or suborbicular, 10–20 × 8–16 mm, apex apiculate or acute, base broadly cuneate or obtuse, margin flat or slightly undulate, strigose, upper surface dark green, shiny, glabrous, veins 2–3 lightly impressed, lower surface sparsely strigose; petiole 1–2 mm, becoming purple, strigose. Fertile shoots 10 mm, including 2–4 leaves and 1(–2) subsessile flower(s); flower (including hypanthium) 5–8 mm long. Hypanthium cupulate, often dark red, very sparsely strigose; sepals acuminate, acute or obtuse, hairs few, margin villous. Corolla closed or small opening; petals erect-incurved, erose, blackish purple-red and red. Stamens 10(–12); filaments dark red; anthers white with mauve dots. Fruit globose, 10–11 mm, succulent, orange-red to red, shiny. Nutlets (2–)3, style remains ²⁄₃ from base.

Seasons: Flowers April–May; fruit ripe September; autumn leaves coppery to purple-red.

Chromosomes: Tetraploid (Zeilinga 1964; Kroon 1975; Klotz and Krügel 1983a; Bailey, pers. comm.). Apomictic, true from seed.

Hardiness: −18°C (−1°F).

Area: China (Sichuan).

Notes: *Cotoneaster apiculatus* is a charming shrub, denser in habit than *C. nanshan*, forming hummocklike mounds with closely overlapping branches. Striking fruit and long-lasting autumn leaf color follow the pretty little red flowers. This cotoneaster is useful for coastal areas as once established it is considerably drought and salt tolerant. It is commonly cultivated in the United States, where it was ranked the most popular cotoneaster in 1989 by *American Nurseryman*. It is less frequently grown in Europe, where it can be found as *C. nanshan* 'Boer' or *C.* 'Hessei'. Recently reintroduced into cultivation.

Cultivar: '**Copra**', said to have robust growth, reaching c. 1 m high × 3 m wide in 10 years, leaves dark green and very abundant, fruit large, red. From Denmark. Probably same as *C. apiculatus*.

3. ***Cotoneaster beimashanensis*** J. Fryer & B. Hylmö, *sp. nov.* Type: China, NW Yunnan, Atuntze, Bei-ma Shan, November 1937, *T. T. Yu 10844* (holo E, iso BM). PLATE 97.

Shrub, 0.5–1 m high. Branches 1–1.5 m, stiff, prostrate, spreading, mound-forming; branchlets divaricate, maroon, initially strigose. Leaves deciduous, chartaceous, on sterile shoots suborbicular or broadly elliptic, 13–20 × 8–15 mm, apex acute or apiculate, base obtuse or cuneate, margin undulate, strigose, upper surface mid-green, shiny, initially sparsely strigose, veins 3–4, lower surface sparsely strigose; petiole 3–4 mm. Fertile shoots 10–25 mm, including 2–3 leaves and 1(–2) flower(s); flower (including hypanthium) 6–7 mm long. Hypanthium cupulate, strigose; sepals obtuse or acute, sparsely strigose, margin villous. Corolla with large opening; petals erect, pink with red base and pale-pink border. Stamens 10; filaments dark-red; anthers pink to purple. Fruit depressed-globose, 10–13 mm, orange-red to red, often with yellow cheek, navel open. Nutlets (1–)2, rarely 3, style remains 4/5 from base.

Seasons: Flowers May–June; fruit ripe September; autumn leaves red and purplish brown.

Chromosomes: Tetraploid (Jewsbury, pers. comm.). Apomictic, true from seed.

Hardiness: –18°C (–1°F).

Area: China (Yunnan, Tibet).

Notes: *Cotoneaster beimashanensis* is fairly common in botanic gardens and collections from the *Yu 10844* collection. It has been reintroduced from the many recent expeditions to the same mountainous area in Yunnan. It was collected by Jeanette Fryer (*JFYU 089*) in Yunnan, Zhongdian, on the Napa Hai logging route.

4. ***Cotoneaster cardinalis*** J. Fryer & B. Hylmö *sp. nov.* Type: China, Sichuan, Kangding, on the western side on sunny slopes, 4 November 1934, *Harry Smith 13038* (holo UPS). PLATE 98.

Shrub, 0.5–1 m. Branches 1–1.5 m, stiff, prostrate to suberect, creeping and rooting; branchlets divaricate, red-brown, initially densely yellowish strigose. Leaves deciduous, chartaceous, on sterile shoots suborbicular, broadly elliptic or broadly obovate, 12–20 × 8–17 mm, apex obtuse and apiculate, base obtuse or broadly cuneate, margin slightly undulate, strigose, upper surface light to mid-green, shiny, glabrous or subglabrous, lower surface sparsely strigose-pilose, midrib more dense; petiole 2 mm, strigose. Fertile shoots 8–12 mm, including 2–3 leaves and a single (–2) subsessile flower; flowers (including hypanthium) 5–8 mm long. Hypanthium cupulate, maroon, shiny, sparsely pilose-strigose; sepals acute or acuminate, sparsely pilose, margin villous. Corolla closed or small opening; petals erect-incurved, deep rich pink to crimson with purple base. Stamens 10, sometimes to 15; filaments purple-red; anthers white tinted pink or purple. Fruit globose, 8–10 mm, orange-red, shiny, glabrous, calyx lobes erect, navel open. Nutlets (1–)2(–3), style remains ³/₄ from base.

Seasons: Flowers May–June; fruit ripe September–October; autumn leaves reddish brown.

Chromosomes: Unknown. Apomictic, true from seed.

Hardiness: –15°C (5°F).

Area: China (Sichuan).

Notes: *Cotoneaster cardinalis* is a lovely little shrub which is neat in habit with shiny, fresh green leaves and unusual, attractive cardinal pink flowers. It should be more frequently grown.

5. *Cotoneaster duthieanus* (C. K. Schneider) G. Klotz in Bull. Bot. Surv. India 5: 211 (1963). Synonym: *C. distichus* Lange var. *duthieanus* C. K. Schneider (1907). Type: N India, Kumaon, in birch forest near Naffi in the Kutti valley, 11 September 1884, *J. F. Duthie 2874* (holo K, iso CAL, E). **PLATE 99**.

Shrub, to 1 m. Branches erect and spreading; branchlets divaricate and spiraled, maroon, initially strigose. Leaves deciduous, chartaceous, on sterile shoots suborbicular or broadly elliptic, 10–24 × 7–21 mm, apex apiculate or obtuse, base obtuse, margin undulate, upper surface shiny, glabrous, veins 3–4(–5), lower surface initially sparsely strigose-pilose, midrib remaining dense; petiole 1.5–4 mm, strigose. Fertile shoots 10–25 mm, including 4 leaves and a subsessile 1- to 4-flowered inflorescence; pedicels initially strigose; flowers (including hypanthium) 5–6 mm long. Hypanthium cupulate, sparsely pilose; sepals obtuse or acute, sometimes acuminate, sparsely pilose. Corolla closed or small opening; petals erect-incurved, red, with blackish purple base and pinkish white border. Stamens 10–11, filaments dark red; anthers pinkish red to red. Fruit globose, 8–10 mm, succulent, rich red, glabrous, calyx lobes erect, navel open. Nutlets (1–)2, style remains ³/₄ from base.

Seasons: Flowers May–June; fruit ripe September–October; autumn leaves shades of purple and red.

Chromosomes: Tetraploid (McAllister, pers. comm.). Apomictic, true from seed.

Hardiness: –18°C (–1°F).

Area: India (Uttaranchal Pradesh, Himachal Pradesh, Sikkim). Nepal. Tibet.

Notes: Originating from the Himalaya, *Cotoneaster duthieanus* is a good dwarf shrub for flower, fruit, and autumn color. Recently reintroduced into cultivation.

6. **Cotoneaster garhwalensis** G. Klotz in Wiss. Z. Martin-Luther-Univ. Halle-
   Wittenberg, Math.-Naturwiss. 15: 543 (1966). Type: India, Garhwal, Nila Valley,
   Phuladaru, 20 June 1883, *J. F. Duthie 1061* (holo K, iso DD).

Shrub, 0.3–0.5 m. Branches 0.5–1 m, decumbent, prostrate, suberect or creeping, becoming rigid with age; branchlets divaricate, reddish brown and slightly verruculose, initially strigose. Leaves deciduous, chartaceous, on sterile shoots broadly elliptic, broadly obovate or suborbicular, 5–25 × 5–15 mm, apex obtuse, mucronate, base obtuse, margin slightly undulate, strigose, upper surface mid-green, slightly shiny, glabrous, veins 3–4, lower surface initially sparsely pilose-strigose, petiole 1–2.5 mm, sparsely strigose. Fertile shoots 10–20 mm, including 3–4 leaves and 1(–2) subsessile flower(s); pedicel sparsely strigose; flower (including hypanthium) 7–9 mm long. Hypanthium cupulate, purplish or brownish red, shiny, sparsely pilose-strigose; sepals obtuse, ligulate or acute, sparsely pilose or glabrous, color as hypanthium, margin villous. Corolla wide open; petals erect to semispreading, rich pink with dark red base and pink border. Stamens 10–12(–18); filaments dark red; anthers white tinged pink. Fruit subglobose, 8–10 mm, orange to orange-red. Nutlets 2(–3).

Seasons: Flowers April–May; fruit ripe September; autumn leaves scarlet to purple-brown.

Chromosomes: Unknown. Apomictic, true from seed.

Hardiness: –18°C (–1°F).

Area: India (Uttaranchal Pradesh, Himachal Pradesh). Nepal.

Notes: *Cotoneaster garhwalensis* is a useful little scrambling, ground-covering shrub with large, attractive flowers and fruit and excellent autumn color. Recently reintroduced into cultivation.

7. **Cotoneaster kerstanii** G. Klotz in Wiss. Z. Friedrich-Schiller-Univ. Jena, Math.-
   Naturwiss. 21: 1010 (1972). Type: cultivated at the botanic garden in Halle, Germany,
   from seed collected in the Hindukush mountains, leg. G. Kerstan 1936, leg. G. Klotz,
   14 May 1969 (holo JE).

Deciduous shrub, c. 0.6 m. Branches suberect; branchlets divaricate, purple-black and shiny, initially strigose-villous. Leaves chartaceous, broadly obovate-elliptic or obcordate, 8–15 × 5–10 mm, apex obtuse or emarginate, base obtuse or broadly cuneate, margin flat, upper surface initially sparsely pilose, shiny, lower surface initially pilose; petiole 0.5–3 mm, strigose. Fertile shoots with a (1–)3-flowered inflorescence; pedicels initially pilose. Hypanthium narrowly campanulate; sepals ligulate, acute or acuminate, initially pilose. Petals erect, 3–4 mm, red with pale crimson border. Stamens 10–13; filaments with base red. Fruit globose, 8–10 mm, deep red, glabrous. Nutlets 1–2, style remains ⁴/₅ from base.

Area: Pakistan.

Notes: *Cotoneaster kerstanii* is known in cultivation only from the type shrub growing in the botanic garden in Halle, Germany. Its frequently obovate leaves make it easily recognizable.

8. *Cotoneaster nanshan* M. Vilmorin ex Mottet in Arbres Arbustes d'ornament p. 207 (1925). Synonym: *C. adpressus* Bois var. *praecox* Bois & Berthault (1918). Type: Arnold Arboretum, Harvard University, *C. adpressus* var. *praecox* 7519B. Plant from M. Chenault & Son, Orléans, 1915, cult. Arnold Arboretum, 1 June 1936 (lecto designated A). **PLATE 100.**

Shrub, 0.5–1 m. Branches 1.5–2 m, erect, suberect or prostrate, rising and falling then running along ground; branchlets spiraled, red-maroon, initially strigose. Leaves deciduous, chartaceous, on sterile shoots suborbicular or broadly elliptic, 12–25 × 9–24 mm, apex apiculate or acute, base obtuse, margin extremely undulate, strigose, upper surface dull green, initially few strigose hairs, veins 3–4, lower surface sparsely strigose, midrib densely so; petiole 2–3 mm, strigose. Fertile shoots 10–20 mm, including 4–5 leaves and a 2- to 4-flowered inflorescence; pedicels absent to 1 mm, strigose; flowers (including hypanthium) 7–10 mm long. Hypanthium widely cupulate, reddish, sparsely strigose; sepals ligulate, obtuse or acute, sparsely strigose, margin villous. Corolla with large opening; petals erect-incurved, margins undulate an extremely erose, red and pink with off-white border. Stamens 10–12(–14); filaments dark red; anthers white with pinkish stripe. Fruit subglobose, very succulent, 10–12 mm, bright red, glabrous, calyx lobes suberect, navel open. Nutlets (1–)2, rarely 3, style remains $^9/_{10}$ from base.

Seasons: Flowers May; fruit ripe September; autumn leaves brilliant red.

Chromosomes: Tetraploid (Broertjes 1954; Zeilinga 1964; Hensen 1966; Klotz and Krügel 1983). Apomictic, true from seed.

Hardiness: –18°C (–1°F).

Area: China (Sichuan, Yunnan).

Notes: *Cotoneaster adpressus* var. *praecox* Bois & Berthault was described from shrubs growing in the garden of M. Chenault of Orléans, France. It was first grown and distributed in 1895 by Vilmorin of Les Barres garden in France. These shrubs originated from Vilmorin, who exchanged an immense amount of plants and seed with the Arnold Arboretum in the United States. When Séraphin Joseph Mottet raised this taxon to species *C. nanshan*, he mentioned that it originated from China around 1910. Ernest Wilson, in fact, collected it (*Wilson 2187*), with accompanying notes "China, western Sichuan, Tachien-lu [Kangding], rocky places in alpine regions, 2800–3230 m, September 1908, fruit bright red." *Wilson 2187* was still present in the living collection of the Arnold Arboretum in 1970, identified as *C. nanshan*. Vilmorin used the name *C. spec. de Nan Shan* as early as 1902 but for another taxon, *C. adpressus*, which was collected by a Russian expedition. *Cotoneaster nanshan* was brought into cultivation on a large scale by the German and Scandinavian nurseries around 1930. It became popular in landscaping for low plantings, being hardier than *C. horizontalis*. In the United States, *C. apiculatus* is more popular than *C. nanshan* for low plantings, but *C. nanshan* can also be found. The effect of the abundant, conspicuus rose-pink flowers covering *C. nanshan* is very striking, as are its large squashy fruit. Recently reintroduced into cultivation.

9. *Cotoneaster taoensis* G. Klotz in Wiss. Z. Friedrich-Schiller-Univ. Jena, Math.-Naturwiss. 21: 1010 (1972). Synonym: *C. ×hessei* (Hesse) G. Klotz (1957). Type: China, SW Gansu, Tao River Basin, beyond Taochow, September 1925, *J. F. Rock 13203* (holo K).

Shrub, compact, to 0.5 m. Branches 0.5–1 m, mostly procumbent, weak and slender; branchlets divaricate, red-brown, initially strigose-pilose. Leaves deciduous, chartaceous, on sterile shoots elliptic or suborbicular, 12–18 × 8–11 mm, apex acute or acuminate, base cuneate or obtuse, margin undulate, strigose, upper surface initially sparsely strigose hairs mostly at midrib, veins 3–4(–5), lower surface initially sparsely strigose; petiole 3–4 mm, glabrescent. Fertile shoots 8–10 mm, including mostly 2 leaves and 1(–2) flower(s); pedicel c. 1 mm, very sparsely pilose; flowers (including hypanthium) 5–7 mm long. Hypanthium cupulate, dark red, sparsely short-haired strigose; sepals ligulate or acute, without membranous border, dark red, sparsely short haired strigose, margin short haired villous-strigose. Petals erect, dark red with pink border. Stamens 8–12; filaments dark red; anthers white, tinted pink. Fruit globose, 7–8 mm, deep red, hairs few, calyx lobes suberect. Nutlets (1–)2(–3), style remains ³/₄ from base.

Seasons: Flowers May; fruit ripe September–October; autumn leaves orange and red.

Chromosomes: Tetraploid (Krügel 1992a) as *C. adpressus* 'Hessei'. Apomictic, true from seed.

Hardiness: −18°C (−1°F).

Area: China (Gansu, Sichuan).

Notes: *Cotoneaster taoensis* used to be frequently found in cultivation in botanic gardens and private collections as *C.* 'Hessei', sometimes labeled *Rock 13535*. This is a good, garden-worthy dwarf shrub. Recently reintroduced into cultivation.

19. Series *Horizontales* Hurusawa in Inf. Ann. Hort. Bot. Fac. Sci. Univ. Tokyo. 11 (5–7): 216 (1967), as subsection. Synonym: series *Horizontales* (Hurusawa) G. Klotz (1972).

Dwarf to medium shrubs. Branches mostly horizontally spreading and distichous, not rooting; branchlets strongly distichous (very noticeably herringbone in habit). Leaves mostly deciduous, margins flat or only slightly undulate. Flowers erect. Hypanthium mostly infundibulate; sepals mostly acute or cuspidate, sometimes obtuse.

Early to mid season.

China (Hubei, Sichuan, Gansu, Hunan).

11 species: *C. ascendens, C. atropurpureus, C. atrovirens, C. divaricatus, C. flinckii, C. hjelmqvistii, C. horizontalis, C. kansuensis, C. perpusillus, C. spongbergii, C. yinchangensis.*

Key to Series *Horizontales*

1a. Upper leaf surface initially sparsely strigose; fruit cylindrical, rarely subglobose, 8–11 mm, rich-red **2**

1b. Upper leaf surface glabrous or single hairs from bud; fruit obovoid, rarely globose, 4–9 mm, orange-red. **4**

2a. Branches erect and spreading; leaves ≤ 30 mm, petiole 3–4 mm; fruit ruby; nutlets mostly 2 . . . .*C. divaricatus*

2b. Branches ascending; leaves ≤ 10–23 mm, petiole 1–2 mm; fruit red; nutlets mostly 2–3 . . . .**3**

3a. Branchlets distichous; leaves elliptic, 14–23 mm, veins 4(–5); petals border white. . . . .*C. ascendens*

3b. Branchlets mostly divaricate; leaves suborbicular, 7–10 mm, veins 2–3; petals border pink . . . .*C. atrovirens*

4a. Leaves 13–25 mm, veins 3–5, petiole 3–5 mm; hypanthium cupulate. **5**

4b. Leaves 5–15 mm, veins 2–4, petiole 1–3 mm; hypanthium infundibulate **6**

5a. Branches arched, slender; branchlets mostly divaricate; leaves dark green, ≤ 18 mm, apex apiculate. . . . .*C. flinckii*

5b. Branches ascending, coarse; branchlets mostly distichous; leaves light green, ≤ 25 mm, apex obtuse. . . . .*C. hjelmqvistii*

6a. Branchlets verruculose; leaves base obtuse; sepals cuspidate or caudate. . . . *C. spongbergii*

6b. Branchlets not or slightly verruculose; leaves base cuneate; sepals acute or acuminate **7**

7a. Leaves chartaceous, apex obtuse or truncate, margin slightly undulate; fruit 8 mm. . . . .*C. atropurpureus*

7b. Leaves subcoriaceous, apex mostly apiculate or obtuse, margin flat; fruit 4–6 mm. **8**

8a. Leaves ≤ 12 mm; fertile shoots 8–20 mm; stamens 10(–13) . . . .*C. horizontalis*

8b. Leaves ≤ 8(–10) mm; fertile shoots 5–8 mm; stamens 7–10 . . . .*C. perpusillus*

1. ***Cotoneaster ascendens*** Flinck & B. Hylmö in Bot. Not. (Lund) 119: 453 (1966). Synonyms: *C. horizontalis* Decaisne var. *wilsonii* Havemeyer ex E. H. Wilson (1927); *C. horizontalis* Decaisne var. *ascendens* Krüssmann (1951). Type: cult. United States, Arnold Arboretum, C.C.P. 330, 2 June 1919, A.R. (holo A).

Shrub, 1–2 m. Branches ascending; branchlets strongly distichous, maroon, verruculose, initially densely yellowish strigose. Leaves deciduous, chartaceous, on sterile shoots elliptic, 14–23 × 8–14 mm, apex acute or acuminate, base obtuse, margin undulate, upper surface light green, shiny, subglabrous, veins 4(–5) impressed, lower surface sparsely strigose, midrib more dense; petiole 1–2 mm. Fertile shoots 15–20 mm, including 4–5 leaves and a subsessile, (1–)2- to 3-flowered inflorescence; flowers (including hypanthium) 6–7 mm long. Hypanthium infundibulate, strigose; sepals acute or acuminate, strigose, margin yellowish villous. Corolla closed or with small opening; petals erect-incurved, red and pink with white border. Stamens 10–15; filaments pink with red base and white apex;

anthers white. Fruit cylindrical, often maturing subglobose, 7–8 mm, rich red, shiny, calyx lobes depressed, tips erect. Nutlets 2(–3), style remains $^3/_5$ from base.

Seasons: Flowers May; fruit ripe September–October.

Chromosomes: Tetraploid (Zeilinga 1964). Apomictic, true from seed.

Hardiness: –18°C (–1°F).

Area: China (Hubei).

Notes: The name *Cotoneaster horizontalis* var. *wilsonii* was given to a shrub of unknown origin cultivated in the Arnold Arboretum. At the RBG Edinburgh, this same species has long been cultivated under *Wilson 227* (Hylmö 1993). When the Edinburgh shrub was compared with the Arnold Arboretum specimen, both were found to be *C. ascendens Wilson 227*, a collection from Fang Hsien in western Hubei, China, at 2300 m, dated November 1907. *Cotoneaster ascendens* has long been common in cultivation in the United States as well as throughout Europe, often as *C. horizontalis* or *C. horizontalis* f. *fructu-sanguinea*. Large amenity plantings of *C. horizontalis* are sometimes grown from seed mistakenly containing both *C. horizontalis* and *C. ascendens* with disastrous results in the intended uniform effect of the planting. *Cotoneaster ascendens* is a more vigorous shrub than *C. horizontalis* with ascending branches, narrower leaves, and longer, darker red fruit. *Cotoneaster ascendens* has also been confused with *C. wilsonii* Nakai which is a very different species with open, pink flowers and maroon to purple-black fruit. *Cotoneaster apiculatus* 'Cotali', originating from Denmark is said to be extremely hardy, low-growing, and spreading, with small acute leaves and numerous red fruit; it is probably *C. ascendens*.

2. *Cotoneaster atropurpureus* Flinck & B. Hylmö in Watsonia 18: 311 (1991). Synonyms: *C. horizontalis* Decaisne var. *prostratus* hort; *C. horizontalis* Decaisne 'Prostratus' Vilmorin (non Baker) Grootendorst (1946); *C. apiculatus* 'Blackburn' Morton Arboretum. Type: China, W Hubei, Ichang, October 1907, *E. H. Wilson 496* (holo A).

Shrub, 0.5–1 m (supported 3–4 m). Branches decumbent or ascending, arched; branchlets divaricate, few distichous, red-purple, initially densely yellowish strigose-villous. Leaves deciduous, chartaceous, on sterile shoots obovate-orbicular, 9–14 × 8–12 mm, apex obtuse or truncate, mucronulate, base obtuse or acute, margin slightly undulate, upper surface mid to dark green, shiny, glabrous, veins 2–3, lower surface very sparse shiny golden-yellow pilose; petiole 1–2 mm, yellow-villous. Fertile shoots 9–11 mm, including 3 leaves and a (1–)3(–2)-flowered inflorescence; pedicels 0.2–1 mm, pilose; flowers (including hypanthium) 6 mm long. Hypanthium infundibulate, sparsely yellow pilose-strigose; sepals acuminate or acute, green and red-purple, sparsely pilose, margin yellow-villous. Corolla closed or small opening; petals erect-incurved, dark red with purple-black base and narrow white border. Stamens 10; filaments dark purple-red with white apex; anthers white, tinged pink. Fruit obovoid, 7–8 mm, orange-red, subglabrous, calyx lobes suberect. Nutlets 2(–3), style remains $^3/_4$ from base.

Seasons: Flowers May; fruit ripe September–October; autumn leaves rich ruby-red.

Chromosomes: Tetraploid (Zeilinga 1964; Hensen 1966). Apomictic, true from seed.

Hardiness: −18°C (−1°F).

Area: China (Hubei).

Notes: The holotype for *Cotoneaster atropurpureus* was identified by Rehder and Wilson (1912) as *C. horizontalis* Decaisne var. *perpusillus* C. K. Schneider. The Arnold Arboretum has several sheets of *C. atropurpureus* material from plants which were cultivated in the arboretum as *Cotoneaster* sp. *Wilson 496*, the earliest dated 1911.

Cultivar: '**Variegatus**' (Osborn R.H. 1916) (**PLATE 101**), height to 50 cm, leaves edged white, pink-tinged in autumn, margin sometimes wavy, flowers white, fruit red. The most commonly cultivated variegated form of *Cotoneaster*. Often grown as *C. horizontalis* 'Variegatus', but when sometimes reverting occurs in the odd branch, then the orbicular, truncate leaves and darker flowers of *C. atropurpureus* can clearly be seen. Received RHS Award of Garden Merit in 1993.

3. ***Cotoneaster atrovirens*** J. Fryer & B. Hylmö, *sp. nov.* Type: China, Sichuan, Kangding toward Cheto, on sunny slopes, 22 October 1934, *Harry Smith 12918* (holo UPS, iso A, LD, S). **PLATE 102**.

Shrub, dense, 0.5–1 m (supported 2 m). Branches ascending and decumbent; branchlets divaricate sometimes distichous, purple-brown, initially densely yellowish strigose. Leaves deciduous, subcoriaceous, on sterile shoots suborbicular, broadly obovate or broadly elliptic, 7–10 × 5–9 mm, apex obtuse, mucronulate, base obtuse or cuneate, margin undulate, upper surface blackish green, shiny, initially sparsely pilose-strigose, veins 2–3 lightly impressed, lower surface grayish green, sparsely pilose-strigose; petiole 1–3 mm, purple-green, strigose. Fertile shoots 7–10 mm, including 2–4 leaves and a 1- to 2(–3)-flowered inflorescence; pedicels 0.5–3 mm, strigose; flowers (including hypanthium) 5–6 mm long. Hypanthium infundibulate, purple, sparsely strigose; sepals acute or acuminate, sparsely strigose, border purple, margin villous. Corolla closed or small opening; petals erect-incurved, blackish purple with pale-crimson border. Stamens 10(–12); filaments purple-red; anthers white with pink dots. Fruit globose or depressed-globose, succulent, 9–11 mm, rich red with hint of orange, apex sparsely pilose, calyx lobes erect. Nutlets 3(–4), rarely 2, style remains 2/3 from base.

Seasons: Flowers May-June; fruit ripe October-November; autumn leaves reddish maroon.

Chromosomes: Unknown. Apomictic, true from seed.

Hardiness: −18°C (−1°F).

Area: China (Sichuan).

Notes: *Cotoneaster atrovirens* was collected by Harry Smith on his third (1934) expedition to the area of western China in which many interesting species, previously found by earlier explorers such as George Forrest and Ernest Wilson, were rediscovered. This neat little spreading shrub has an unusual (for series *Horizontales*) divaricate branching habit and attractive, dark blackish green leaves. Its fruit are often very abundant.

4. *Cotoneaster divaricatus* Rehder & E. H. Wilson in Sargent, Pl. Wilson. 1: 157 (1912). Type: China, W Hubei, Xingshan Xian, September 1907, *E. H. Wilson 232* (holo A, iso K). PLATE 103.

Shrub, 1.5–2 m. Branches erect and spreading; branchlets divaricate or spiraled, brownish violet, initially strigose. Leaves deciduous, chartaceous, on sterile shoots broadly elliptic or suborbicular, 10–30 × 7–19 mm, apex acuminate or acute, base obtuse, margin undulate; upper surface dark green, shiny, initially sparsely strigose, veins 3–4 lightly impressed, lower surface initially strigose; petiole 3–4 mm, strigose. Fertile shoots 10–20 mm, including 4 leaves and a (1–)2(–4)-flowered inflorescence; pedicels 1–3 mm, strigose; flowers (including hypanthium) 6–8 mm long. Hypanthium cupulate, strigose; sepals acute or acuminate, strigose, margin villous. Corolla with small opening; petals erect-incurved, pale-crimson with dark red base and white border. Stamens 10–15; filaments pale rose-pink or white; anthers white. Fruit cylindrical, 10–11 mm, dark red to ruby, shiny, sparsely pilose, calyx lobes suberect. Nutlets (1–)2(–3) rarely 4, style remains $^{2}/_{3}$ from base.

Seasons: Flowers May; fruit ripe October; autumn leaves orange to reddish purple.
Chromosomes: Tetraploid (Zeilinga 1964; Hensen 1966). Apomictic, true from seed.
Hardiness: –15° to –18°C (5° to –1°F).
Area: China: (Hubei).
Notes: In autumn *Cotoneaster divaricatus* becomes profusely laden with shiny rich red fruit and leaves varying from lustrous bottle green to brilliant orange-red and rich purple. This most desirable, ornamental, hardy, and trouble-free species is excellent as a specimen shrub or for hedging. Received RHS First Class Certificate in 1912 and Award of Garden Merit in 1969.

5. *Cotoneaster flinckii* J. Fryer & B. Hylmö in New Plantsman 5: 140 (1998). Type: China, Gansu, Gahoba, Sven Hedin expedition, 23 October 1930, *D. Hummel 5331 (2331)* (holo S).

Shrub, 1–1.5 m (supported 5 m). Branches spreading, ascending, arched; branchlets mostly divaricate, purple, initially densely strigose-pilose. Leaves deciduous, chartaceous, on sterile shoots orbicular or suborbicular, 13–18 × 11–16 mm, apex apiculate, mucronulate, base rotund or obtuse, margin flat, upper surface dark green, shiny, glabrous, veins 3–5, lower surface sparsely pilose-strigose; petiole 3–5 mm, strigose. Fertile shoots 12–20 mm, including 4 leaves and a (1–)3-flowered inflorescence; pedicels 2–4 mm, strigose; flowers (including hypanthium) 6–7 mm long. Hypanthium cupulate, sparsely pilose-strigose, sepals cuspidate, acute or obtuse, sparsely pilose-strigose, margin villous. Corolla with large opening; petals erect-incurved, red with dark red base and pink and off-white border. Stamens 10; filaments red; anthers white. Fruit obovoid, 8–9 mm, orange-red, shiny, glabrous or sparsely pilose, calyx lobes erect, pilose. Nutlets 2(–3), style remains ³/₅ from base.

Seasons: Flowers May; fruit ripe September–October; autumn leaves purple-red.

Chromosomes: Tetraploid (Bailey, pers. comm.; McAllister, pers. comm.). Apomictic, true from seed.

Hardiness: –15°C (5°F).

Area: China (Gansu).

Notes: The pretty little flowers of *Cotoneaster flinckii* are abundant in nectar and hence much loved by bees. These shrubs produce numerous fruit and show good autumn leaf color. The species was collected by David Hummel, a physician with the 1931 Sven Hedin expedition to China. It was named in honor of Karl Evert Flinck in recognition of his work on the genus *Cotoneaster*.

6. *Cotoneaster hjelmqvistii* Flinck & B. Hylmö in Watsonia 18: 312 (1991). Synonym: *C. horizontalis* Decaisne 'Coralle', 'Robusta', and 'Dart's Splendid'. Type: cult. Sweden, Alnarp BG, 4 June 1959, *B. Hylmö 9300* (holo LD). **PLATE 104.**

Shrub, 0.5–1 m (supported 7 m). Branches decumbent, ascending, arched; branchlets mostly distichous, brownish red, initially densely strigose. Leaves deciduous, chartaceous, on sterile shoots orbicular or broadly obovate, concave, 13–25 × 10–25 mm, apex obtuse, mucronulate, base obtuse, margin flat, upper surface vivid light green, shiny, glabrous, veins 3–4(–5) lightly impressed, lower surface yellowish pilose-strigose; petiole 2–4 mm, pilose. Fertile shoots 10–25 mm, including 3–4 leaves and a (1–)3(–4)-flowered inflorescence; pedicels 0.5–2(–3) mm, glabrescent; flowers (including hypanthium) 5 mm long. Hypanthium cupulate, glabrescent; sepals acuminate or acute, green and reddish purple, glabrous, margin villous. Corolla open; petals erect-incurved, dark pink with red base and pink border. Stamens 10–16; filaments red and pale-crimson; anthers white. Fruit globose to obovoid, 8 mm, orange-red, glabrous, calyx lobes obliquely erect. Nutlets 2(–3), style ¹/₂–²/₃ from base.

Seasons: Flowers May; fruit ripe October–November; autumn leaves intense red-purple.

Chromosomes: Tetraploid (Bailey, pers. comm.). Apomictic, true from seed.

Hardiness: –15°C (5°F).

Area: China (Gansu).

Notes: *Cotoneaster hjelmqvistii* is vigorous and free-fruiting with brilliant autumn leaf color. Arriving at the botanic garden in Lund, Sweden, from Hungary in 1943, it was introduced to the nursery trade by the Belgian nursery Vuyk Van Nes in 1954, from where it was spread to the large Dutch nurseries.

7. *Cotoneaster horizontalis* Decaisne in Fl. Ser. Jard. l'Europe 22: 168 (1877). Synonym: *C. acuminata* Lindley var. *prostrata* J. D. Hooker ex Wenzig (1874). Type: W China, Sichuan, A. David (holo P). **PLATE 105.**

Shrub, 0.5–1 m (supported 3.5 m). Branches decumbent, ascending, spreading horizontally; branchlets distichous, maroon, initially densely yellow-strigose. Leaves mostly deciduous, subcoriaceous, on sterile shoots suborbicular, orbicular or broadly obovate, 5–12 × 5–9 mm, apex apiculate or obtuse, mucronulate, base obtuse or cuneate, margin flat, upper surface dark green, shiny, glabrescent, veins 2–4, lower surface sparsely long-haired strigose; petiole 2–3 mm, strigose. Fertile shoots 8–20 mm, including 3–4 leaves, and a 1- to 3-flowered inflorescence; pedicels 1–2 mm, strigose; flowers (including hypanthium) 5–7 mm long. Hypanthium infundibulate, sparsely pilose-strigose; sepals acute or acuminate, sparsely strigose, margin villous. Corolla closed; petals erect-incurved, dark-red with blackish red base and pale crimson border. Stamens 10(–13); filaments dark red; anthers white. Fruit subglobose, 5–6 mm, orange-red, shiny, subglabrous. Nutlets (2–)3, style remains ³/₄ from base.

    Seasons: Flowers May; fruit ripe October–November; autumn leaves rich red.

    Chromosomes: Tetraploid (Zeilinga 1964; Hensen 1966). Apomictic, true from seed.

    Hardiness: −15° to −18°C (5° to −1°F).

    Area: China (Sichuan, Gansu).

    Notes: *Cotoneaster horizontalis* was originally described from shrubs growing in the garden of the National Museum of Natural History in Paris, raised from seed received from the missionary Armand David around 1870. It was first sold commercially in France in 1885. *Cotoneaster horizontalis* is an old favorite The plant is incredibly tough, invaluable for north- or east-facing situations, and much used for covering walls, but when grown freestanding produces mounded irregular masses. The leafless branches in winter are attractive with their curious herringbone habit. In spring these branches are covered with multitudes of flowers. W. Arnold-Forster (1948) stated that "bees love its flowers, so that when summer is coming in, *C. horizontalis* makes more welcoming noise than any other plant." In autumn the lower leaves are ablaze with color while at branch ends green leaves remain—often enduring throughout winter. The innumerable fruit add to the display. Recently reintroduced into cultivation. Received RHS First Class Certificate in 1897, Award of Merit in 1925, and Award of Garden Merit in 1984.

    Cultivar: '**Variegatus**', most (if not all) forms seen as *C. horizontalis* 'Variegatus' belong to the closely related *C. atropurpureus.*

    8. *Cotoneaster kansuensis* G. Klotz in Wiss. Z. Friedrich-Schiller-Univ. Jena, Math.-Naturwiss. 21: 1001 (1972). Type: Central China, Gansu, 2 May 1919, *E. Licent 5181* (holo K, iso BM).

Shrub. Branches erect, robust; branchlets divaricate, initially strigose-tomentose. Leaves deciduous or semievergreen, chartaceous to subcoriaceous, on sterile shoots suborbicular or orbicular, 7–13 × 6–12 mm, apex rounded, rarely emarginate, base obtuse, upper surface initially subglabrous, veins 3–4 impressed, lower surface sparsely strigose-villous, midrib more dense; petiole 1.5–2 mm, strigose-villous. Fertile shoots with a (1–)2- to 3-

flowered inflorescence; pedicels short. Hypanthium glabrous or subglabrous; sepals acute, margin villous. Petals 3 mm. Stamens 12–15. Carpels 3.

Area: China (Gansu).

Notes: *Cotoneaster kansuensis* is rarely found in cultivation. A vigorous-growing shrub at the botanic garden of Mendel University, Brno (#71-00), named *C. trinervis* 'Brno', has masses of pink-red flowers and bright red fruit and is most likely this species. Not in key.

9. *Cotoneaster perpusillus* (C. K. Schneider) Flinck & B. Hylmö in Bot. Not. (Lund) 119: 453 (1966). Synonyms: *C. horizontalis* Decaisne var. *saxatilis* (Hesse) Boom (1959); *C. perpusillus* G. Klotz (1966). Type: China, W Hubei, Chang-yang, May 1900, Veitch expedition, *E. H. Wilson 564* (lecto designated W, iso A, DBN).

Shrub, slowly reaching 0.5–0.8 m. Branches horizontal, decumbent or ascending, or arched to ground then horizontal; branchlets strongly distichous, maroon-purple, initially strigose. Leaves deciduous, subcoriaceous, on sterile shoots suborbicular or broadly ovate, 6–10 × 5–8 mm, apex acute, apiculate or obtuse, mucronate, base obtuse, margin flat, upper surface mid-green, shiny, glabrous, veins 3–4, lower surface sparsely strigose; petiole 1–2 mm, strigose. Fertile shoots 5–8 mm, including 4–5 leaves and 1(–2) subsessile flower(s); flower (including hypanthium) 4–5 mm long. Hypanthium infundibulate, green and red, sparsely strigose; sepals ligulate or acute, sparsely strigose, margin villous. Corolla closed; petals erect-incurved, red with blackish red base and pale crimson border. Stamens 7–10; filaments red; anthers white. Fruit oblong to subglobose, 4–5 mm, orange-red. Nutlets (2–)3, rarely 1 or 4, style remains $^2/_3$ from base.

Seasons: Flowers May; fruit ripe October–November; autumn leaves good color.

Chromosomes: Tetraploid (Zeilinga 1964; Krügel 1992a). Apomictic, true from seed.

Hardiness: −15°C (5°F).

Area: China (Hubei, Sichuan, possibly also Shaanxi).

Notes: A lovely little shrub, *Cotoneaster perpusillus* is more diminutive in all parts than the related *C. horizontalis*. *Cotoneaster perpusillus* is well-suited to growing in tubs and containers, especially as a bonsai specimen. Ernest Wilson said that this was the common *Cotoneaster* of the moorlands of the Hubei province in China, being abundant in open rocky areas. Received RHS Award of Merit in 1916.

10. *Cotoneaster spongbergii* J. Fryer & B. Hylmö, *sp. nov.* Type: 1980 Sino-American Botanical Expedition (SABE) to China, W Hubei, Metasequoia region of Lichuan Xian, vicinity of Lojiaba on west side of the valley, SABE 1933, 6 October 1980, (holo A, iso E). **PLATE 106.**

Shrub, 0.5–1 m. Branches 1–1.5 m, decumbent, spreading, rarely ascending; branchlets distichous, brown, verruculose, initially densely yellowish strigose. Leaves deciduous, chartaceous, on sterile shoots obovate or elliptic, 10–16 × 6–11 mm, apex obtuse, broadly acute or acuminate, mucronulate, base cuneate, margin slightly undulate, upper surface dark green, shiny, glabrous, veins 3–4, lower surface initially strigose; petiole 2–3 mm, strigose. Fertile shoots 8–20 mm, including 1–4 (5) leaves and a 1- to 3-flowered inflorescence; pedicels 0.5–2 mm, strigose; flowers (including hypanthium) 5–7 mm long. Hypanthium infundibulate, often brownish red, shiny, sparsely pilose-strigose; sepals long-cuspidate or caudate, reddish, pilose-strigose, margin densely yellowish villous. Corolla closed or small opening; petals erect-incurved, light ruby with red base and pink border. Stamens 10; filaments dark red and pink; anthers white. Fruit obovoid, 7–8 mm, orange-red, glabrescent, calyx lobes depressed or suberect, strigose. Nutlets 2(–3), style remains $^2/_3$ from base.

Seasons: Flowers May; fruit ripe October; autumn leaves ruby-red.

Chromosomes: Unknown. Apomictic, true from seed.

Hardiness: −15°C (5°F).

Area: China (Hubei).

Notes: *Cotoneaster spongbergii*, named in honor of Stephen Spongberg, a participant in the 1980 SABE expedition, is a neat little shrub which covers the ground closely, layering its branches so that little else can grow beneath it. For this reason it is very effective as ground-cover, allowing few weeds to grow. It flowers and fruits extremely well and has good autumn color. Frequently grown in Europe. Distributed by the Dutch nursery trade.

11. *Cotoneaster yinchangensis* J. Fryer & B. Hylmö, *sp. nov.* Type: China, Sichuan,
Emei Shan, 8 August 1938, *C. Y. Chiao & C. S. Fan 624* (holo E). **PLATE 107.**

Shrub, 1–1.5 m. Branches 2–3 m, ascending, horizontally wide-spreading, straight; branchlets distichous, purple-brown, shiny, minutely verruculose, initially densely strigose-villous. Leaves deciduous or semi, chartaceous, on sterile shoots broadly elliptic, 10–12 × 8–11 mm, apex acute or acuminate, base cuneate, margin flat, upper surface mid-green, slightly shiny, pilose, veins 2–3, lower surface pilose; petiole 1–2 mm, strigose. Fertile shoots 10–13 mm, including 2–4 leaves and a 1- to 3-flowered inflorescence; pedicels 3–4 mm, strigose-pilose; flowers (including hypanthium) 6–7 mm long. Hypanthium infundibulate, pilose; acute, sparsely pilose, margin villous. Corolla with small opening; petals erect-incurved, dark red and pink with black-red base and white border. Stamens 10–12; filaments dark red; anthers white. Fruit subglobose, 5–6 mm, orange-red to rich red, calyx lobes erect, navel open. Nutlets 2(–3), style remains $^2/_3$ from base.

Seasons: Flowers May; fruit ripe October–November; autumn leaves fiery red to bronze.

Chromosomes: Tetraploid (Bailey, pers. comm.). Apomictic, true from seed.

Hardiness: −18°C (−1°F).

Area: China (Sichuan).

Notes: *Cotoneaster yinchangensis* is a magnificent species, robust, with long straight branches which shoot out in all directions. This cotoneaster has also been collected by Roy Lancaster (*RL 1505*) in NW Sichuan, Wolong valley, in the Yin Chang gorge in 1986. Not in key.

20. Series *Nitentes* Flinck & B. Hylmö in Bot. Not. (Lund) 119: 453 (1966).

Dwarf to large shrubs. Branches erect or ascending; branchlets mostly distichous. Leaves deciduous, on sterile shoots elliptic, broadly elliptic, or ovate, mostly mid-green. Lower surface pilose-strigose. Inflorescences erect. Hypanthium widely cupulate. Petals red with a purple-black base and white border. Fruit mostly cylindrical or ellipsoid, purple-black or sometimes maroon.

　　Early season.

　　China (Sichuan, Gansu). Tibet.

　　10 species: *C. atrovinaceus, C. drogochius, C. harrysmithii, C. kangdingensis, C. marroninus, C. naninitens, C. nitens, C. tenuipes, C. tripyrenus, C. undulatus.*

Key to Series *Nitentes*

1a. Leaves ≤ 35–40 mm, mostly broadly ovate, veins 4–5 mostly lightly impressed 2

1b. Leaves 13–27 mm, mostly elliptic, veins 2–4 not impressed 4

2a. Leaves broadly ovate to suborbicular, margin undulate, upper surface soon glabrous, petiole 1–3 mm. . . . . *C. undulatus*

2b. Leaves ovate or elliptic, mostly flat, upper surface pilose, petiole 2–6 mm 3

3a. Fertile shoots 30–40 mm; stamens 10(–12), filaments pale pink; nutlets 2 . . . . *C. tenuipes*

3b. Fertile shoots 10–20 mm; stamens (10–)12(–16), filaments dark red; nutlets (2–)3(–4) . . . . *C. drogochius*

4a. Leaves broadly elliptic to suborbicular, base obtuse, upper surface glabrous; fruit glabrous or single hairs 5

4b. Leaves elliptic or ellipto-ovate, base mostly cuneate, upper surface with hairs; fruit sparsely pilose 7

5a. Leaves ≤ 27 mm; fertile shoots 15–30 mm; stamens 10–12(–15); nutlets mostly 2 . . . *C. nitens*

5b. Leaves ≤ 16 mm; fertile shoots 10–20 mm; stamens 10; nutlets mostly 3 6

6a. Leaf apex apiculate or acute; pedicels 2–3 mm; sepals acute or acuminate; fruit ellipsoid . . . . *C. tripyrenus*

6b. Leaf apex obtuse or broadly acute; pedicels 3–5 mm; sepals obtuse or broadly acute; fruit globose . . . .*C. naninitens*

7a. Leaves dark green; fertile shoots 15–30 mm; fruit obovoid, maturing maroon, intensely shiny . . . .*C. marroninus*

7b. Leaves mid or light green; fertile shoots 10–20 mm; fruit ellipsoid or cylindrical, maturing black, somewhat dull 8

8a. Leaf veins 4, lower surface pilose; pedicels 1–3 mm; hypanthium pilose soon glabrous . . . . *C. harrysmithii*

8b. Leaf veins 2–3, lower surface strigose; pedicels 2–5 mm; hypanthium strigose. . . . .*C. kangdingensis*

1. ***Cotoneaster atrovinaceus*** J. Fryer & B. Hylmö, *sp. nov.* Type: cult. Czech Republic, Mendel University botanic garden, Brno (#53), as *C. 'hnedoplody'*, September 1990, from Slovakia, Mlynany BG (holo BRN). **PLATE 108.**

Shrub dense, c. 0.5–1 m. Branches erect then arching to ground, thin; branchlets mostly divaricate, maroon, minutely verruculose, initially strigose. Leaves deciduous, chartaceous, on sterile shoots broadly ovate or suborbicular, 15–27 × 11–20 mm, apex acuminate or acute, base obtuse or cuneate, upper surface mid to dark green, shiny, strigose-villous, veins 3–4 impressed, lower surface sparsely strigose-villous; petiole 3–4 mm, strigose-villous. Fertile shoots 10–30 mm, including mostly 2 leaves and a 2- to 3-flowered inflorescence; pedicels 3–8 mm, strigose-villous; flowers (including hypanthium) 4–6 mm long. Hypanthium widely cupulate, strigose-villous; sepals obtuse or acute, margin villous. Corolla with small opening, petals erect-incurved, dark red with a white border. Stamens 10–12, filaments pink-red; anthers white. Fruit cylindrical, ellipsoid to obovate, 9 × 7–8 mm, ruby, maroon to purple-black, dull, pilose, calyx lobes erect, margins densely pilose-villous. Nutlets 2, style remains $^9/_{10}$ from base.

Seasons: Flowers April–May, often reflowers in autumn; fruit ripe September–October; autumn leaves orange-gold.

Chromosomes: Pentaploid (Bailey, pers. comm.; Jewsbury, pers. comm.). Apomictic, true from seed.

Hardiness: −18°C (−1°F).

Area: Unknown.

Notes: *Cotoneaster atrovinaceus* is a slow-growing cotoneaster which is similar size in height and width. It has attractive port-wine-colored fruit which finally turn nearly black. Despite its unusual chromosome number this species breeds true from seed. Uncommon. Not in key.

2. ***Cotoneaster drogochius*** J. Fryer & B. Hylmö, *sp. nov.* Type: China, Sichuan, northwestern Drogochi in meadows and shrubby grassland, 26 September 1922, *Harry Smith 4543* (holo UPS, iso A, S). **PLATE 109.**

Shrub, 3–4 m. Branches erect and gracefully arched, slender; branchlets distichous, reddish brown, verruculose, initially densely strigose. Leaves deciduous, chartaceous, on sterile shoots ovate or elliptic, 25–40 × 11–23 mm, apex acute or acuminate, base obtuse, margin slightly undulate, upper surface mid-green, initially densely pilose-strigose, veins 4, lower surface pilose-strigose; petiole 2–4 mm, densely pilose-strigose. Fertile shoots 10–20 mm, including 2–3 leaves and a (2–)3(–4)-flowered inflorescence; pedicels densely pilose-strigose; flowers (including hypanthium) 6–7 mm long. Hypanthium widely cupulate, densely pilose-strigose; sepals acuminate or acute, densely pilose-strigose, margin tomentose. Corolla with large opening; petals erect, red with dark-purple, border off-white. Stamens (10–)12(–16), filaments dark red; anthers white. Fruit ellipsoid, obovoid or globose, 7–9 mm, maroon to purple-black, white papillose, villous, calyx lobes depressed, pilose, margin tomentose. Nutlets 3, rarely 2 or 4, style remains $^2/_3$ from base.

Seasons: Flowers May, often reflowers August–September; fruit ripe September; autumn leaves lime green to gold.

Chromosomes: Tetraploid (Bailey, pers. comm.; Jewsbury, pers. comm.). Apomictic, true from seed.

Hardiness: –15°C (5°F).

Area: China (Sichuan).

Notes: The Harry Smith collection of *Cotoneaster drogochius* is in cultivation. Also, there is a specimen of *C. drogochius* growing in RBG Edinburgh (*#19932756*) from Shanghai BG, wild collected in Sichuan in 1992.

3. *Cotoneaster harrysmithii* Flinck & B. Hylmö in Bot. Not. (Lund) 115: 29 (1962).
   Type: China, Sichuan, Tanpa district, Maoniu, 10 October 1934, *Harry Smith 12647* (holo UPS, iso BM). **PLATE 110.**

Shrub, 1–2 m. Branches erect and ascending; branchlets distichous, reddish brown, initially strigose-pilose. Leaves deciduous, chartaceous, on sterile shoots elliptic or elliptic-ovate, 13–17 × 8–9 mm, apex acute or acuminate, mucronulate, base cuneate or obtuse; upper surface mid-green, initially papillose, dull, sparsely pilose-villous, veins 4, lower surface pilose; petiole 2–3 mm, pilose-strigose. Fertile shoots 10–20 mm, including 2–4 leaves and a (1–)2- to 3(–4)-flowered inflorescence; pedicels 1–3 mm, pilose; flowers (including hypanthium) 4–6 mm long. Hypanthium widely cupulate, initially pilose; sepals acute or acuminate, initially pilose, margin tomentose. Corolla open; petals erect-incurved, pink with maroon base and white border. Stamens (10–)12(–14); filaments red; anthers white. Fruit ellipsoid, 6–7 mm, maroon to black, calyx lobes erect. Nutlets 2–3, rarely 4, apex pilose, style remains 3/4 from base.

Seasons: Flowers May, often reflowers August; fruit ripe September–October; autumn leaves intense yellow.

Chromosomes: Tetraploid (Klotz 1968b). Apomictic, true from seed.

Hardiness: –15°C (5°F).

Area: China (Sichuan).

Notes: *Cotoneaster harrysmithii* is less vigorous than the related *C. nitens*. An unusual shrub bearing some resemblance to *C. horizontalis* but with black fruit.

4. *Cotoneaster kangdingensis* J. Fryer & B. Hylmö, *sp. nov.* Type: China, Sichuan,
   Kangding toward Cheto, in sunny meadows, 22 October 1934, *Harry Smith 12919* (holo UPS, iso A, S). **PLATE 111.**

Shrub, 1–1.5 m. Branches ascending, spreading; branchlets distichous, brown, verruculose, initially densely strigose-pilose. Leaves deciduous, chartaceous, on sterile shoots elliptic or elliptic-ovate, 18–21 × 9–13 mm, apex acuminate or acute and mucronate, base cuneate or obtuse; upper surface light green. Initially long-haired pilose-strigose, veins 2–3, lower surface initially strigose; petiole 2–4 mm, strigose. Fertile shoots 10–15 mm, including 3–4 leaves and a (1–)2(–3)-flowered inflorescence; pedicels 2–5 mm, strigose;

flowers (including hypanthium) 4–5 mm long. Hypanthium widely cupulate, strigose; sepals obtuse, acute or apiculate, strigose, border broad, membranous, purple-red, glabrous, margin villous. Corolla closed; petals erect-incurved, red with purple-black, border white. Stamens 10–12; filaments purple-red or crimson; anthers white. Fruit cylindrical, 7–8 mm, purple-black, shiny, sparsely pilose, calyx lobes erect, pilose, margin villous. Nutlets (1–)2(–3), style remains $^2/_3$ from base.

    Seasons: Flowers May; fruit ripe September–October; autumn leaves greenish gold.

    Chromosomes: Unknown. Apomictic, true from seed.

    Hardiness: −15°C (5°F).

    Area: China (Sichuan).

    Notes: *Cotoneaster kangdingensis* is mostly in cultivation from the Harry Smith collection, but this species has also been collected by Mikinori Ogisu (*MO 05200*) in Sichuan, Kangding, Zhedo Shan, in 2005.

    5. *Cotoneaster marroninus* J. Fryer & B. Hylmö *sp. nov.* Type: China, Sichuan, Paoma Shan, a hill beyond Kangding, 2 November 1988, Erskine, Fliegner, Howick & McNamara, *SICH 335* (holo K). **PLATE 112.**

Shrub, 1–2 m. Branches erect, spreading, lateral ones sometimes horizontal; branchlets distichous, maroon, initially densely strigose. Leaves deciduous, chartaceous, on sterile shoots elliptic, 15–22 × 10–14 mm; apex acute or acuminate, base cuneate or obtuse; margin slightly undulate, upper surface dark green, sparsely long-haired pilose-strigose, initially shiny, veins 3–4, lower surface pilose-villous; petiole 2–3 mm, villous-strigose. Fertile shoots 15–30 mm, including 2–3 leaves and a (1–)2- to 3(–4)-flowered inflorescence; pedicels strigose; flowers (including hypanthium) 5–6 mm long. Hypanthium widely cupulate, densely strigose; sepals long-acuminate, densely strigose, margin tomentose. Corolla closed or with small opening; petals erect-incurved, red with dark purple-red base and broad, white border. Stamens 10(–14); filaments dark red, apex white; anthers white. Fruit obovoid, 8–9 mm, maroon, intensely shiny, subglabrous, calyx lobes depressed. Nutlets 2–3, style remains $^2/_3$ from base.

    Seasons: Flowers May–June; fruit ripe September.

    Chromosomes: Tetraploid (Klotz and Krügel 1983a) as *C. tripyrenus*. Apomictic, true from seed.

    Hardiness: −15°C (5°F).

    Area: China (Sichuan).

    Notes: Between 1957 and 1960 at the RBG Kew, prior to so many of the beautiful specimens there sadly being ravaged by fireblight, seed was fortunately saved of the cotoneasters. One of these specimens was unlabelled. This seed was raised in Bjuv, Sweden, and distributed from there to other European *Cotoneaster* collections. The unlabelled specimen with the lovely, shiny maroon fruit is hereby named *C. marroninus*.

6. *Cotoneaster naninitens* J. Fryer & B. Hylmö, *sp. nov.* Type: China, Sichuan, Chosodja, in sunny meadows and rocky terrain, 18 October 1922, *Harry Smith 4648* (holo UPS, iso A, S). **PLATE 113.**

Shrub, 1–1.5 m. Branches ascending, spreading, slender; branchlets distichous or divaricate, grayish brown, verruculose, initially densely strigose. Leaves deciduous, chartaceous, on sterile shoots broadly elliptic or suborbicular, 10–13 × 7–10 mm, apex obtuse or broadly acute, mucronulate, base obtuse, upper surface mid-green, subglabrous, veins 4, lower surface sparsely strigose, midrib densely so; petiole 1–3 mm, densely strigose. Fertile shoots 10–20 mm, including 3–4 leaves and a 1- to 3-flowered inflorescence; pedicels 3–5 mm, sparsely pilose-strigose; flowers (including hypanthium) 5 mm long. Hypanthium widely cupulate, sparsely pilose-strigose; sepals obtuse or broadly acute, sparsely pilose-strigose, border purple, glabrous, margin tomentose. Corolla opening small; petals erect-incurved, red with purple-black, border white. Stamens mostly 10; filaments dark red; anthers white. Fruit depressed-globose or globose, 5–7 mm, maroon to purple-black, glabrescent, calyx lobes erect (as coronet), glabrous, margin tomentose. Nutlets 3, rarely 2 or 4, style remains ³/₄ from base.

Seasons: Flowers May; fruit ripe September; autumn leaves apricot to gold.

Chromosomes: Unknown. Apomictic, true from seed.

Hardiness: –15°C (5°F).

Area: China (Sichuan).

Notes: *Cotoneaster naninitens*, so named due to its similarity to *C. nitens* but smaller in all parts, is cultivated in European gardens, all shrubs probably descending from *Harry Smith 97* (seed) (corresponding with herb. sheet 4648).

7. *Cotoneaster nitens* Rehder & E. H. Wilson in Sargent, Pl. Wilson. 1: 156 (1912).

Type: China, W Sichuan, Min valley, near Sung-pan Ting, September 1910, *E. H. Wilson 4021* (holo A, iso BM, DBN, K).

Shrub, 1.5–3 m. Branches erect becoming pendulous; branchlets divaricate, red-brown, initially strigose. Leaves deciduous, chartaceous, on sterile shoots broadly elliptic, broadly ovate or suborbicular, 10–27 × 9–19 mm, apex obtuse or acute and mucronulate, base obtuse; upper surface initially reddish soon bright green, glabrous, veins 3, lower surface initially densely pilose-strigose; petiole 2–3(–4) mm, pilose-strigose. Fertile shoots 15–30 mm, including 3–4(–5) leaves and a 1- to 3(–4)-flowered inflorescence; pedicels 2–4 mm, glabrescent; flowers (including hypanthium) 6–7 mm long. Hypanthium widely cupulate, sparsely pilose; sepals obtuse, acute or apiculate, sparsely pilose, margin tomentose. Corolla open; petals erect, pink with purple-maroon base and white border. Stamens 10–12(–15); filaments red-purple with dark pink apex; anthers white with pale crimson border. Fruit ellipsoid, 7–10 mm, purple-black, shiny, subglabrous, calyx lobes erect. Nutlets 2(–3), style remains ³/₄ from base.

Seasons: Flowers May; fruit ripe September; autumn leaves shades of gold and red.

Chromosomes: Tetraploid (Kroon 1975; McAllister, pers. comm.; Krügel 1992a). Apomictic, true from seed.

Hardiness: −15°C (5°F).

Area: China (Sichuan, Gansu).

Notes: *Cotoneaster nitens* has polished leaves which give dazzling autumn color, but the fruit are not usually numerous. Fairly common in cultivation.

8. Cotoneaster tenuipes Rehder & E. H. Wilson in Sargent, Pl. Wilson. 1: 171 (1912).

   Type: China, W Sichuan, Min valley, Sung-pan Ting, August 1910, *E. H. Wilson 4544* (holo A).

Shrub, 3(–4) m. Branches erect, ascending, spreading, becoming pendulous, slender and graceful; branchlets distichous, yellowish red, initially villous-strigose. Leaves deciduous, chartaceous, on sterile shoots elliptic-ovate, 12–35 × 10–12 mm, apex acute or acuminate, base broadly cuneate or obtuse, upper surface dark green, shiny, pilose, veins 4–5 lightly impressed, lower surface pilose; petiole 3–6 mm. Fertile shoots 30–40 mm, including 4 leaves and a lax, (1–)3(–5)-flowered inflorescence; pedicels 4–8 mm, sparsely villous; flowers (including hypanthium) 6–8 mm long. Hypanthium cupulate, tomentose; sepals acute or apiculate, pilose-tomentose, margin tomentose. Corolla open; petals erect-incurved, off-white with reddish brown or pale pink base and off-white border, or entirely off-white. Stamens 10(–12); filaments pale pink, apex sometimes white; anthers white. Fruit cylindrical or ellipsoid, 10–11 mm, purple-black, pilose, calyx lobes flat, densely pilose. Nutlets 2, style remains $^9/_{10}$ from base.

Seasons: Flowers April–May, often reflowers August; fruit ripe August–September.

Chromosomes: Tetraploid (Klotz and Krügel 1983a). Apomictic, true from seed.

Hardiness: −15°C (5°F).

Area: China (Sichuan, Gansu). Tibet.

Notes: *Cotoneaster tenuipes* is an elegant shrub with an open habit, the branches cascading with coppery colored frondlike endings. Very floriferous but the fruit quickly taken by birds. Recently reintroduced into cultivation.

9. Cotoneaster tripyrenus J. Fryer & B. Hylmö, *sp. nov.* Type: China, Sven Hedin expedition, S Gansu, Min Shan, Gahoba, 20 October 1930, *D. Hummel 5332 (2332)* (holo S). **PLATE 114.**

Shrub, to 2 m. Branches erect, arched; branchlets distichous, reddish brown, verruculose, initially densely strigose. Leaves deciduous, chartaceous, on sterile shoots broadly elliptic or suborbicular, 12–16 × 9–14 mm, apex apiculate or acute with mucro, base obtuse, margin sometimes slightly undulate, upper surface mid-green, dull, glabrescent, veins mostly 3, lower surface initially strigose; petiole 2–3 mm, strigose. Fertile shoots 10–15 mm, including (2–)3(–4) leaves and a 1- to 3-flowered inflorescence; pedicels 2–3 mm, sparsely strigose; flowers (including hypanthium) 3–5 mm long. Hypanthium widely cupulate, shiny, sparsely strigose; sepals acute or acuminate, glabrescent, margin long-haired villous. Corolla open; petals erect-incurved, red with purple-black, border narrow, white. Stamens mostly 10; filaments dark red; anthers white. Fruit ellipsoid, 7–8 mm, maroon to purple-black, glabrescent, calyx lobes erect, subglabrous, margin villous. Nutlets (2–)3, style remains ³/₄ from base.

Seasons: Flowers May–June; fruit ripe September–October.

Chromosomes: Tetraploid (Bailey, pers. comm.; Jewsbury, pers. comm.). Apomictic, true from seed.

Hardiness: −15°C (5°F).

Area: China (Gansu).

Notes: *Cotoneaster tripyrenus* J. Fryer & B. Hylmö has been in cultivation since 1939. *Cotoneaster tripyrenus* Flinck & B. Hylmö, a name published without description (Klotz 1972, 1983), was raised from seed collected by Klotz when visiting Bertil Hylmö's garden in Sweden in 1967 but the seed became mixed with another and the resulting offspring were not *C. tripyrenus* but *C. marroninus*.

10. *Cotoneaster undulatus* J. Fryer & B. Hylmö, *sp. nov.* Type: China, Gansu, Min Shan, 1914–1915, *R. Farrer 404* (holo WSY).

Shrub, 1.5–2 m. Branches erect, arched, spreading; branchlets reddish brown, initially densely pilose-strigose. Leaves deciduous, chartaceous, on sterile shoots broadly ovate, broadly elliptic or suborbicular, 29–40 × 20–35 mm, apex shortly acuminate or acute and mucronulate, base obtuse, margin extremely undulate, upper surface light green, shiny, initially sparsely pilose, veins 4 slightly impressed, lower surface initially strigose-villous; petiole 1–3 mm, strigose. Fertile shoots 15–35 mm, including 3–4 leaves and a 3- to 4(–5)-flowered inflorescence; pedicels 2–4 mm, sparsely pilose-strigose; flowers (including hypanthium) 7–8 mm long. Hypanthium conoid to campanulate, shiny, sparsely strigose; sepals obtuse, acute or emarginate, purple, often verruculose, subglabrous, margin villous-strigose. Corolla closed; petals erect-incurved, red and purple-black, border white. Stamens 10(–12); filaments dark red; anthers white. Fruit cylindrical or ellipsoid, 7–8 mm, purple-black, subglabrous, calyx lobes erect. Nutlets 2–3, style remains ³/₄ from base.

Seasons: Flowers June, often reflowers September–November; fruit ripe September–November; autumn leaves dark red.

Hardiness: −15°C (5°F).

Area: China (Gansu).

Notes: *Cotoneaster undulatus* is cultivated in central and northern Europe. *Farrer 405* is probably this species.

7. Section *Sanguinei*, stat. nov. Basionym: series *Sanguinei* G. Klotz in Wiss. Z. Friedrich-Schiller-Univ. Jena, Math.-Naturwiss. 21: 969 (1972).

Branchlets irregularly spiraled. Leaves mostly chartaceous. Hypanthium mostly campanulate, often red and shiny; sepals mostly low. Corolla with large opening at apex, petals mostly dark red, deep pink, or brownish, sometimes with sparse hairs at base of upper surface. Stamens mostly 10–16. Nutlets often with apex swollen and recurved.

4 series: *Kongboense, Sanguinei, Mucronati, Acuminati.*

21. Series *Kongboense* J. Fryer & B. Hylmö nom. nud. Synonym: series *Orientales* G. Klotz (1972). Type: *C. kongboensis* G. Klotz. In 1868 the name *C. orientalis* Kerner was used for a species belonging to the now series *Melanocarpi.* Hence Klotz's series name *Orientales* has become a permanent source of confusion and error and must be rejected.

Small to large shrubs. Branchlets irregular, spiraled or divaricate. Petals brownish, red and off-white, rarely with small hair-tuft at base of upper surface. Fruit pendent, large (11–15 mm), purple-black, rarely maroon, pilose or villous.

Early to mid season.

China (Yunnan, Sichuan). Tibet.

6 species: *C. burmanicus, C. convexus, C. decandrus, C. dokerensis, C. kongboensis, C. notabilis.*

Key to Series *Kongboense*

1a. Leaves ≤ 18 mm, veins 3, petiole ≤ 3 mm; stamens 10 . . . .*C. dokerensis*

1b. Leaves ≤ 53 mm, veins 4–6, petiole ≤ 7 mm; stamens 10–20 2

2a. Fertile shoots 20–60 mm; inflorescence 2- to 10-flowered; pedicels 6–8 mm; anthers pinkish; nutlets 2 . . . . **C. decandrus**

2b. Fertile shoots 15–30 mm; inflorescence 1- to 4(–5)-flowered; pedicels 2–5 mm; anthers white; nutlets 2–3(–4). 3

3a. Leaves elliptic, apex acuminate, petiole 4–6 mm, villous; stamens 10–14(–18); fruit cylindrical. . . . .*C. kongboensis*

3b. Leaves broadly elliptic to suborbicular, apex mostly obtuse or acute, petiole 2–4 mm, strigose, stamens 15–20; fruit obovoid . . . .**C. notabilis**

1. *Cotoneaster burmanicus* G. Klotz in Wiss. Z. Friedrich-Schiller-Univ. Jena, Math.-Naturwiss. 21: 1004 (1972). Type: W central Burma, Mount Victoria, 6 June 1956, *F. Kingdon Ward 22135* (holo BM).

Shrub. Branches erect; branchlets spiraled, strigose-villous, becoming maroon, verruculose and glabrous. Leaves deciduous, chartaceous, on sterile shoots ovate or elliptic, 16–35 × 12–21 mm, apex acuminate, base cuneate, upper surface initially sparsely pilose, lower surface veins strigose-pilose, margin strigose-villous; petiole 2–5 mm, strigose-villous. Flowers not seen. Fruit not seen.

Area: Burma.

Notes: This species is not known other than by the type herbarium specimen which possesses neither flowers nor fruit—just a sterile branch. It is probably not possible to discover *Cotoneaster burmanicus* in cultivation from such an inadequate description. Not in key.

2. *Cotoneaster convexus* J. Fryer & B. Hylmö, *sp. nov.* Type: cult. from seed from Arnold Arboretum, October 1958 as *C. acutifolia* var. *villosa* SD, Rock, China 1926. Cult. Sweden, Bjuv, 30 May 1994, *B. Hylmö 9289* (holo E). **PLATE 115**.

Shrub, 2–4 m. Branches erect, arched, ascending; branchlets divaricate, reddish brown, initially villous-tomentose. Leaves deciduous, chartaceous and flaccid, on sterile shoots ovate or elliptic, 52–70 × 25–34 mm, apex acuminate or acute, base obtuse or cuneate; margin strigose, upper surface convex, mid to dark green, shiny, pilose-villous, veins 4–5 lightly impressed, lower surface villous; petiole 2–3 mm, tomentose. Fertile shoots 25–45 mm, including 4 leaves and a lax, 3- to 4-flowered inflorescence; pedicels 2–8 mm, pilose-villous; flowers (including hypanthium) 7 9 mm long. Hypanthium cupulate, tomentose; sepals acute or acuminate, base tomentose, border broad and glabrous, margin tomentose. Corolla open; petals erect-incurved, pink-red with reddish brown base and greenish white border, subglabrous. Stamens (10–)12–14(–18); filaments pale pink or off-white; anthers white. Fruit cylindrical or obovoid, 12–13 mm, purple-black, villous, apex tomentose, calyx lobes suberect, tomentose. Nutlets 2(–3), style remains $^3/_4$ from base.

Seasons: Flowers June, often reflowers September; fruit ripe September.

Chromosomes: Tetraploid (Bailey, pers. comm.; Jewsbury, pers. comm.). Apomictic, true from seed.

Hardiness: −15°C (5°F).

Area: China (Gansu).

Notes: *Cotoneaster convexus*, with its unusual, convex leaves, is not common. All plants in cultivation probably descend from the Joseph Rock collections. Not in key.

3. *Cotoneaster decandrus* J. Fryer & B. Hylmö, *sp. nov.* Type: China, Sichuan, southwest of Kangding by Pala river near Liuba, autumn 1980, *R. Lancaster 1001* (holo BM). **PLATE 116**.

Shrub, 1.5–2 m. Branches ascending or erect, arched; branchlets purple-brown, initially densely pilose. Leaves deciduous, chartaceous, on sterile shoots ovate or elliptic, 28–36 × 17–18 mm, apex acute or acuminate, base obtuse or cuneate, upper surface slightly rugose, dark green, intensely shiny, initially sparsely pilose, veins 4–6 impressed, lower surface villous-tomentose; petiole 5–7 mm, densely pilose-villous. Fertile shoots 20–60 mm, including 4 leaves and a distichous, 2- to 10-flowered inflorescence; pedicels 6–8 mm, densely pilose; flowers (including hypanthium) 5–6 mm long. Hypanthium campanulate, densely villous-strigose; sepals acute or acuminate, densely villous, margin tomentose. Petals erect, not overlapping, caducous, red with brownish red base and off-white border, glabrous or subglabrous. Stamens 10(–12); filaments red with pink apex; anthers pinkish. Fruit cylindrical, 12–15 mm, purple-black, shiny, sparsely pilose, calyx lobes flat, pilose. Nutlets 2, apex swollen and recurved, style remains $^2/_3$ from base.

Seasons: Flowers May–June, often reflowers August; fruit ripe August.

Chromosomes: Unknown. Apomictic, true from seed.

Hardiness: –18°C (–1°F).

Area: China (Sichuan).

Notes: Shrubs of *Cotoneaster decandrus* (so named for its 10 stamens per flower) in cultivation have probably all been raised from the Roy Lancaster collection.

4. *Cotoneaster dokerensis* G. Klotz in Wiss. Z. Friedrich-Schiller-Univ. Jena, Math.-Naturwiss. 21: 974 (1972). Type: China, NW Yunnan and E Tibet, Doker La, 8 July 1913, *F. Kingdon Ward 699* (holo E).

Shrub, to 2 m. Branches erect; branchlets divaricate, villous-strigose. Leaves deciduous, chartaceous or subcoriaceous, on sterile shoots broadly elliptic, 14–18 × 8–10 mm, apex obtuse or acute, rarely acuminate, base cuneate or obtuse, upper surface shiny, strigose, veins 3, lower surface villous-strigose; petiole 2–3 mm, villous-strigose. Fertile shoots 15–25 mm, including 3–4 leaves and a 3- to 6-flowered inflorescence; pedicels strigose; flowers (including hypanthium) 6–8 mm long. Hypanthium campanulate, villous-strigose; sepals obtuse, acute or acuminate, villous-strigose, margin densely villous. Corolla with petals semispreading, red with pink or off-white border, few single hairs at base of upper surface. Stamens 10. Carpels 2.

Area: China (Yunnan). Tibet.

Notes: *Cotoneaster dokerensis* has yet to be discovered in cultivation. The above description is compiled from the original diagnosis plus the type herbarium specimen. This species is probably going to be discovered in recent collections made in the area of the original collection.

5. *Cotoneaster kongboensis* G. Klotz in Wiss. Z. Friedrich-Schiller-Univ. Jena, Math.-Naturwiss. 21: 997 (1972). Type: SE Tibet, valley of Lilung Chu (west bank of river), 29 May 1938, *F. Ludlow, G. Sherriff & G. Taylor 4423* (holo BM, iso A, E, K).

Shrub, 1.5–2.5 m. Branches erect and arched; branchlets divaricate, red to grayish brown, shiny, initially villous. Leaves deciduous, chartaceous, on sterile shoots elliptic, 40–53 × 19–23 mm, apex acuminate, base cuneate or obtuse, upper surface mid-green, shiny, initially densely long-haired pilose, veins 4–5 slightly impressed, lower surface villous; petiole 4–6 mm, villous. Fertile shoots 15–30 mm, including 3–4 leaves and a 3- to 4(–5)-flowered inflorescence; pedicels 3–5 mm, villous; flowers (including hypanthium) 8 mm long. Hypanthium campanulate, densely villous-strigose; sepals obtuse, acute or apiculate, villous, margin villous. Petals semispreading, red with brownish red base and off-white border. Stamens 10–14(–18); filaments red; anthers white. Fruit cylindrical, 10–11 mm, purple-black, shiny, pilose, calyx lobes erect, pilose. Nutlets 2–3, apex swollen and recurved.

Seasons: Flowers May, frequently reflowers July at ends of long shoots; fruit ripe July–August.

Chromosomes: Unknown. Apomictic, true from seed.

Hardiness: −18°C (−1°F).

Area: Tibet.

Notes: The fruit of *Cotoneaster kongboensis* were originally described as red; however, the type collection is from a flowering branch, and the syntypes have no fruit color mentioned. In cultivation *C. kongboensis* has purple-black fruit. The species is frequently cultivated in central and northern Europe. It tolerates semishade. Reintroduced by Keith Rushforth (*KR 3648*) from Tibet above Timpe on the way to Nyima La in 1995.

6. *Cotoneaster* 'Marketa'. Synonym: *C. klotzii* hort. Type: cult. Czech Republic, Mendel University botanic garden, Brno (#186), May 1992, as *C.* 'Cerrenoplody', from Slovakia, Mlynany Arboretum (WSY). PLATE 117.

Shrub, 2.5–4 m. Branches erect, arched, thin. Leaves deciduous, chartaceous, or subcoriaceous, on sterile shoots broadly ovate, 26–42 × 15–28 mm, apex acute or acuminate, base obtuse, upper surface shiny, light green, sparsely strigose-villous, veins 3–4 impressed, lower surface strigose-villous; petiole 3–4 mm, strigose-villous. Fertile shoots 15–25 mm, including 2–4 leaves and a compact, 3- to 11-flowered inflorescence; pedicels 1–5 mm, strigose; flowers (including hypanthium) 7 mm long. Hypanthium widely cupulate, strigose-villous; sepals obtuse, acute or acuminate with a red, glabrous border, margin villous. Corolla closed; petals erect-incurved, purple with off-white border. Stamens 16–20; filaments red; anthers white. Fruit obovoid, 8 × 6 mm, ruby, maroon to purple-black, pilose, calyx open, lobes depressed. Nutlets 2–3(–4), style remains 2/3 from base.

Seasons: Flowers May–June, reflowers autumn; fruit ripe September–October.

Hardiness: −18°C (−1°F).

Notes: The wild origin of *Cotoneaster* 'Marketa ' is unknown. Originating from the Mlynany Arboretum in Slovakia, it likely is a Schneider collection. Not common. Not in key.

7. *Cotoneaster notabilis* G. Klotz in Wiss. Z. Friedrich-Schiller-Univ. Jena, Math.-Naturwiss. 21: 972 (1972). Type: China, Yunnan, Lao Chun Shan, SW Shiku and the Yangtze, May 1932, *J. F. Rock 25093* (holo E).

Shrub, 3–4 m. Branches erect, arched; branchlets maroon, initially densely strigose. Leaves deciduous, chartaceous, on sterile shoots broadly elliptic or suborbicular, 13–44 × 9–24 mm, apex obtuse, acute or acuminate, base obtuse or cuneate, upper surface dark green, strigose, veins 4–6 slightly impressed, lower surface strigose-villous; petiole 2–4 mm, strigose. Fertile shoots 15–30 mm, including 4 leaves and a 1- to 4-flowered inflorescence; pedicels 2–4 mm, strigose; flowers (including hypanthium) 6–8 mm long. Hypanthium campanulate, strigose-villous; sepals acute, acuminate or cuspidate, maroon, strigose-villous, margin villous. Corolla with large opening; petals erect or semispreading, dark red with off-white border. Stamens 15–20; filaments pink and white; anthers white. Fruit obovoid, 9 mm, maroon to black, shiny, pilose, calyx lobes flat, pilose. Nutlets 2–3, apex slightly swollen and recurved, densely villous, style remains ¾ from base.

Seasons: Flowers May–June; fruit ripe September–October; autumn leaves intense coppery orange, red, and purple.

Chromosomes: Probably diploid, but more research is needed. Variable from seed.

Hardiness: –18°C (–1°F).

Area: China (Yunnan, Sichuan).

Notes: *Cotoneaster notabilis* is beautiful in autumn color. Recently reintroduced into cultivation.

22. Series *Sanguinei*. Synonym: series *Strigosi* G. Klotz (1972).

Dwarf to large, sparsely branched shrubs, branches frequently terminating in fertile shoots. Flowers pendent. Hypanthium often widely campanulate; sepals short, mostly obtuse. Petals often caducous, mostly rich red. Anthers white, often becoming purple. Fruit often succulent, glabrous. Nutlets with apex very swollen and recurved.

Very early to mid season.

Nepal. China (Sichuan, Yunnan). Tibet. Bhutan. India (Sikkim).

10 species: *C. bis-ramianus, C. campanulatus, C. chengkangensis, C. minimus, C. paradoxus, C. rubens, C. sanguineus, C. sichuanensis, C. staintonii, C. wallichianus.*

Key to Series *Sanguinei*

1a. Lower leaf surface and petiole mostly tomentose; petals spreading, caducous, dark red; stamens 10–12(–13); anthers mostly with pink or purple dots 2

1b. Lower leaf surface and petiole strigose or strigose-villous; petals erect to semispreading, persistent, red and off-white; stamens (7–)10–16 (–20); anthers white. 5

2a. Leaves broadly elliptic or suborbicular, ≤ 28 mm, petiole 2–4 mm, strigose; fertile shoots 10–15 mm; fruit mostly globose. . . . .*C. rubens*

2b. Leaves ovate or elliptic, ≤ 36–83 mm, petiole 3–9 mm, villous-strigose; fertile shoots 15–25 mm; fruit cylindrical or obovoid. 3

3a. Leaves 48–83 mm; pedicels 5–12 mm; fruit purple-black; nutlets 2 . . . . *C. campanulatus*

3b. Leaves 17–40 mm; pedicels 1–2 mm; fruit orange or red; nutlets 2–3 4

4a. Leaves elliptic, apex mostly obtuse; flowers single; hypanthium glabrous except strigose base; sepals glabrous; fruit obovoid. . . . .*C. wallichianus*

4b. Leaves ovate, apex mostly acute; flowers 1–3; hypanthium and sepals strigose; fruit cylindrical. . . . .*C. sanguineus*

5a. Leaves 5–20 mm, veins not impressed, petiole 1–3 mm; fertile shoots 10–20 mm 6

5b. Leaves 20–50 mm, veins impressed, petiole 3–5 mm; fertile shoots 25–35 mm 7

6a. Branches erect to loosely erect; leaves elliptic, 6–10 mm; inflorescence erect; 5–10 mm . . . . .
. . . .*C. sichuanensis*
6b. Branches narrowly erect; leaves ovate or broadly elliptic, 11–18 mm; inflorescence pendent;
pedicels 2–4 mm . . . . *C. chengkangensis*
7a. Petiole 3–5 mm; fertile shoots 10–25 mm; stamens (14–)16–20 . . . . *C. bis-ramianus*
7b. Petiole 5–8 mm; fertile shoots 20–35 mm; stamens 7–16(–18) **8**
8a. Leaves elliptic or ovate; hypanthium glabrous except extreme base, sepals glabrous;
stamens 7–13; fruit ruby . . . .*C. paradoxus*
8b. Leaves ovate or lanceolate; hypanthium and sepals strigose; stamens 13–18; fruit
orange-red . . . . *C. staintonii*

1. ***Cotoneaster bis-ramianus*** G. Klotz in Wiss. Z. Friedrich-Schiller-Univ. Jena,
Math.-Naturwiss. 21: 994 (1972). Type: Nepal, W Gadhibasa, Khaptar, 29 May 1929,
Bis Ram 563 (holo DD, iso BM).

Shrub, 2–3 m. Branches narrowly erect, robust, frequently terminating in fertile shoots;
branchlets divaricate, brown, initially densely strigose. Leaves deciduous, chartaceous,
on sterile shoots elliptic or ovate, 19–50 × 11–23 mm, apex acute or acuminate, base cuneate, upper surface slightly rugose, dark green, shiny, strigose, veins 4–5 impressed, lower
surface strigose-villous; petiole 3–5 mm, strigose. Fertile shoots 10–25 mm, including 4
leaves and single (–2) pendent flower; pedicels 1–5 mm, glabrous; flowers (including hypanthium) 9–10 mm long. Hypanthium campanulate, light green flushed red, shiny, glabrous; sepals broadly obtuse, shiny, glabrous, margin villous. Corolla wide open; petals
erect, greenish white flushed red with brownish red base and off-white border, glabrous
or subglabrous. Stamens (14–)16–20; filaments white, base sometimes pinkish; anthers
white. Fruit obovoid, 11–12 × 10–11 mm, succulent, orange-red, shiny, glabrous, calyx
lobes flat, subglabrous, navel open. Nutlets 2, apex very swollen and recurved, villous,
style remains 2/3 from base.

Seasons: Flowers May–June; fruit ripe September–October.
Chromosomes: Unknown. Apomictic, true from seed.
Hardiness: –15°C (5°F).
Area: Nepal.
Notes: *Cotoneaster bis-ramianus* came into cultivation when it was collected by Len
Beer, Roy Lancaster, and David Morris (*BLM 163*) in Topkegola, Nepal, in 1971. It is an
unusual shrub, sparsely branched, with huge orange, shiny, succulent fruit that the birds
do not seem to like and so remain on the branches longer than fruit of some other
species.

2. ***Cotoneaster campanulatus*** J. Fryer & B. Hylmö, *sp. nov.* Type: China, NW Yunnan,
Atuntze, Dokerla, 4 November 1937, *T. T. Yu 7866* (holo E, iso BM). **PLATE 118**.

Shrub, 2–3 m. Branches erect and arched, long young branches often terminating in fertile shoots; branchlets spiraled or divaricate, maroon, minutely verruculose, initially densely strigose. Leaves deciduous, chartaceous, on sterile shoots ovate or elliptic, 48–83 × 19–46 mm, apex acuminate or acute, base obtuse or cuneate, upper surface mid-green, densely villous-strigose, veins 5–6 lightly impressed, lower surface yellowish villous-tomentose; petiole 7–9 mm, strigose-villous. Fertile shoots 20–25 mm, including 2–5 leaves and a (1–)2- to 3-flowered inflorescence; pedicels 5–12 mm, strigose; flowers (including hypanthium) 7–8 mm long. Hypanthium campanulate, green or maroon, densely villous-strigose; sepals acute, obtuse or apiculate, base villous, margin densely so. Corolla wide open, semispreading, caducous, red with dark ruby, border pink, glabrous. Stamens 10; filaments ruby; anthers white, sometimes with pink dots. Fruit cylindrical or obovoid, 10–12 mm, purple-black. Nutlets (1–)2, rarely 3, apex very swollen and recurved, densely villous, style remains $^3/_4$ from base.

Seasons: Flowers May; fruit ripe August–October; autumn leaves fiery orange-red.
Chromosomes: Tetraploid (Jewsbury, pers. comm.). Apomictic, true from seed.
Hardiness: −15°C (5°F).
Area: China (Sichuan, Yunnan). Tibet.
Notes: *Cotoneaster campanulatus*, with its distinctly bell-shaped hypanthium, was first noticed by Karl Flinck and Bertil Hylmö in the nursery of *Rhododendron* breeder Dietrich Hobbie at Linswege, Oldenburg, Germany, in 1959. Hobbie had obtained an assortment of seed in 1937–1938 from Professor Hu of China; this seed had been collected by Hu's assistant, T. T. Yu, in the mountains of NW Yunnan. Recently reintroduced into cultivation.

3. *Cotoneaster chengkangensis* T. T. Yu in Acta Phytotax. Sin. 8: 220 (1963). Synonyms: *C. improvisus* G. Klotz (1972); *C. strigosus* G. Klotz (1972). Type: China, Yunnan, Cheng-kang, 27 July 1938, *T. T. Yu 16959* (holo PE, iso A).

Shrub dense, 1–2 m. Branchlets divaricate, becoming gray-brown to black, initially densely yellow strigose. Leaves deciduous, on sterile shoots ovate or broadly elliptic or suborbicular, 10–18 ×7–15 mm, apex acute, base broadly cuneate or rotund, upper surface dark-green, veins 3–5 deeply impressed, lower surface sparsely strigose-pilose; petiole 1–3 mm, yellow pilose. Fertile shoots with a pendent, 2- to 3-flowered inflorescence; pedicels 2–4 mm, sparsely yellow pilose. Hypanthium campanulate, sparsely pilose; sepals triangular, acute or obtuse, pilose, margin villous. Corolla with petals erect 3–4 mm, white. Stamens 20. Fruit ellipsoid, 8–9 mm, scarlet. Nutlets 3(–5).

Area: China (Yunnan).
Notes: *Cotoneaster chengkangensis* has yet to be studied in cultivation. It does not sit easily here in series *Sanguinei*, but most of T. T. Yu's description leads to this series. It is hoped that this species will be among the recent collections made on the Zhongdian plateau in the Yunnan province of China. Yu reported *C. chengkangensis* to be common in this area. Klotz (1972b) described *C. improvisus* from a specimen collected by Yu at the same locality on the Snow Range the day before the type collection of *C. chengkangensis*. These two collections are very similar. *Cotoneaster strigosus* G. Klotz (1972) is also prob-

ably *C. chengkangensis*. Klotz (1972) identified his *C. strigosus* with a taxon distributed in cultivation as *C. distichus* var. *tongolensis*; however, this is *C. cuspidatus*, a species first recognized by Cecil Marquand as belonging to series *Distichi*. More confusing, *C. splendens* can also be found as *C. distichus* var. *tongolensis* in some botanic gardens.

4. *Cotoneaster minimus* (T. T. Yu) J. Fryer, stat. nov. Basionym: *C. rubens* W. W. Smith var. *minimus* T. T. Yu in Acta Phytotax. Sin. 8: 220 (1963). Type: China, Sichuan, Wa-se-kou, 5 September 1940, *K. L. Chu 7919* (holo PE).

Shrub, 0.2–0.5 m. Branches horizontally spreading; branchlets distichous and divaricate, purple-red to brown, shiny, minutely verruculose, initially strigose-villous. Leaves deciduous, distichous, subcoriaceous, on sterile shoots broadly elliptic or suborbicular, 10–20 × 8–18 mm, apex obtuse or acute, sometimes mucronate, base obtuse, upper surface slightly bullate, dark green, shiny, glabrescent, veins 4(–5) lightly impressed, lower surface strigose-pilose, petiole 3–5 mm, initially strigose. Fertile shoots 6–10 mm, including 3–4 leaves and a single, subsessile, pendent flower. Hypanthium widely campanulate, maroon, sparsely strigose or glabrous; sepals truncate or broadly obtuse, green with a red border, sparsely strigose-villous, margin villous. Corolla 10–12 mm, petals erect to semi-spreading, purple-red to crimson with pink margin. Stamens 12–13; filaments purple-red; anthers white, dotted red in bud. Fruit cylindrical, 12–14 mm, yellow-orange to bright rich red, shiny, glabrous. Nutlets 2(–3), large, style remains $^4/_5$ from base.

Seasons: Flowers April–May; fruit ripe September–October; autumn leaves red-maroon.

Hardiness: –15°C (5°F).

Area: China (Sichuan, Yunnan).

Notes: T. T. Yu's description of this species as a miniature version of *Cotoneaster rubens* is very appropriate. *Cotoneaster minimus* differs also in its distinct, horizontal branching habit. Rare in cultivation. Not in key. Recently reintroduced into cultivation.

5. *Cotoneaster paradoxus* G. Klotz in Wiss. Z. Friedrich-Schiller-Univ. Jena, Math.-Naturwiss. 27: 24 (1978). Type: C Nepal, Kolagaon, Barbung Khola, 3 June 1952, *O. Polunin, W. R. Sykes & L. H. J. Williams 1051* (holo BM).

Shrub, to 2.5 m. Branches erect, arched, often terminating in fertile shoots; branchlets divaricate, maroon and minutely verruculose, initially densely strigose. Leaves deciduous, chartaceous, on sterile shoots elliptic or ovate, 22–44 × 10–19 mm, apex acute, acuminate or obtuse, base cuneate or obtuse, upper surface dark-green, shiny, sparsely villous-strigose, veins 4–5 slightly impressed, lower surface sparsely pilose-strigose; petiole 5–8 mm, strigose. Fertile shoots 20–35 mm, including 4 leaves and 1–2 flowers; pedicels strigose; flowers (including hypanthium) 5–7 mm long. Hypanthium widely campanulate, red, base sparsely long-haired strigose; sepals sometimes 6–8 in number instead of normal 5, broadly ligulate, obtuse or acute, reddish brown, glabrous, margin villous. Corolla wide open, petals erect to semispreading, dark red with black-red base and pink or off-white border. Stamens 7–13, erect; filaments dark-red and pink; anthers white. Fruit cylindrical or obovoid, 10–11 mm, red to ruby, shiny, sparsely villous-strigose. Nutlets (1–)2(–3), apex very swollen and recurved, densely strigose, style remains ²/₃ from base.

Seasons: Flowers April–June; fruit ripe August–October; autumn leaves maroon and purple.

Hardiness: –15°C (5°F).

Area: Nepal. India (Sikkim). Bhutan.

Notes: *Cotoneaster paradoxus* is a very unusual shrub with deep red flowers continually produced for up to three months, and rich ruby fruit, which are slow to ripen, also on the branches for a long time. Recently reintroduced into cultivation.

6. *Cotoneaster rubens* W. W. Smith in Not. Roy. Bot. Gard. Edinburgh 10: 24 (1917).

Type: China, NW Yunnan, Zhongdian plateau, July 1914, *G. Forrest 12663* (holo E). Shrub, 1–2 m. Branches erect, often terminating in fertile shoots; branchlets divaricate, maroon and verruculose, initially densely strigose. Leaves deciduous or semievergreen chartaceous or subcoriaceous, on sterile shoots broadly elliptic or suborbicular, 18–28 × 16–21 mm, apex obtuse or acute, base obtuse, upper surface slightly rugose, dark-green, sparsely strigose-villous, veins 4–5 impressed, lower surface densely strigose-villous; petiole 2–4 mm, strigose. Fertile shoots 10–15 mm, including 2–4 leaves and a single (on branch ends sometimes 2–3), pendent flower; pedicels 1–2 mm, strigose; flowers (including hypanthium) 5–6 mm long. Hypanthium campanulate, reddish brown, densely strigose, sepals obtuse or acute, sparsely strigose, margin tomentose. Corolla wide open, petals semispreading, dark-red and deep-pink. Stamens 10; filaments red; anthers white. Fruit globose or obovoid, 10–11 mm, succulent, bright-red, shiny, glabrous. Nutlets (1–)2(–3), apex very swollen and recurved, tomentose, style remains ²/₃ from base.

Seasons: Flowers May; fruit ripe September–October; autumn leaves gold and rich orange.

Chromosomes: Unknown. Apomictic, true from seed.

Hardiness: –15°C (5°F).

Area: China (Yunnan). Records of *C. rubens* from India (Sikkim) and Bhutan (Klotz 1972) belong to other species.

Notes: *Cotoneaster rubens* was very rarely in cultivation, but now, with recent collections from Yunnan, it is possible to see this lovely species more often.

7. *Cotoneaster sanguineus* T. T. Yu in Bull. Brit. Mus. (Nat. Hist.), Bot. 1 (5): 130 (1954). Synonym: *C. bakeri* G. Klotz (1972). Type: SE Tibet, Chickchar, Tsari, 13 June 1936, *F. Ludlow & G. Sherriff 2157* (holo BM, iso A, E).

Shrub, 2–3 m. Branches narrowly erect, arched; branchlets spiraled, maroon, initially sparsely villous. Leaves deciduous, chartaceous, on sterile shoots ovate, 19–40 × 9–19 mm, apex acute or acuminate, base cuneate, upper surface dark green, sparsely strigose-villous, veins 4–5 impressed, lower surface strigose-villous; petiole 5–7 mm, strigose-villous. Fertile shoots 15–25 mm, including 4 leaves and a pendent, 1- to 3-flowered inflorescence; pedicels 1–2 mm, strigose; flowers (including hypanthium) 8–9 mm long. Hypanthium campanulate, red, strigose; sepals obtuse or acute, sparsely strigose, margin villous. Corolla wide open, petals erect to semispreading, caducous, pale ruby. Stamens 10–13; filaments red, apex pink; anthers white becoming purple. Fruit cylindrical, 10–12 mm, succulent, orange-red, scattered lenticels, sparsely pilose. Nutlets 2(–3), apex very swollen and recurved.

Seasons: Flowers May–June; fruit ripe September–October.

Hardiness: −15°C (5°F).

Area: Tibet. Bhutan.

Notes: *Cotoneaster sanguineus*, with its wide-open, red flowers and large, fleshy, orange-red fruit, should be more frequently cultivated. Ludlow, Sherriff, and Taylor stated that this shrub was not common where they found it growing among *Abies-Rhododendron* forest in SE Tibet. Reintroduced by Keith Rushforth (*KR 1492*), who collected it in Bhutan, N Ura below Gompa at Samsong in 1988.

8. ***Cotoneaster sichuanensis*** G. Klotz in Wiss. Z. Friedrich-Schiller-Univ. Jena,
   Math.-Naturwiss. 21: 1013 (1972). Type: China, Sichuan, Tongolo, June 1908,
   E. H. Wilson 2186 (holo A, iso BM, E, K).

Shrub, 0.5–1 m. Branches ascending, often terminating in fertile shoots; branchlets divaricate or distichous, brown, initially strigose. Leaves deciduous, chartaceous, on sterile shoots elliptic, 6–10 × 4–7 mm, apex obtuse or acute, base obtuse or cuneate, upper surface initially long-haired strigose, veins 3–4, lower surface initially densely strigose; petiole 1–2 mm, strigose. Fertile shoots 10–20 mm, including 4 leaves and an erect, 1- to 4-flowered inflorescence; pedicels 5–10 mm, strigose. Hypanthium campanulate, strigose; sepals low, acute or obtuse, villous, border membranous, glabrous, margin villous. Corolla wide open, petals erect to semispreading, pink with dark red base and off-white or pale pink border. Stamens 10(–15); filaments pink. Carpels 2–3.

Area: China (Sichuan).

Notes: Owing to its distichous and divaricate branching habit, *Cotoneaster sichuanensis* was placed by Klotz (1972b) in series *Horizontales*, but the characteristics of both the leaves and the flowers give no doubt that this species belongs here in series *Sanguinei*. This species has been found among the recent collections from Sichuan still under observation. Not in key.

9. ***Cotoneaster staintonii*** G. Klotz in Wiss. Z. Friedrich-Schiller-Univ. Jena, Math.-
   Naturwiss. 21: 971 (1972). Type: E Nepal, Tamur Valley, Kamsachen, east of
   Walungchung Gola, 27 July 1956, *J. D. A. Stainton 1146* (holo BM, iso A, E).

Shrub, 2–3(–4) m. Branches narrowly erect, slightly arched, longer ones often terminating in fertile shoots; branchlets divaricate, maroon, initially strigose-villous. Leaves deciduous, chartaceous, on sterile shoots ovate or lanceolate, 30–40 × 12–22 mm, apex acute or acuminate, base cuneate or obtuse, margin slightly undulate, upper surface dark green, intensely shiny, strigose, veins 3–5 impressed, lower surface shiny, strigose-villous hairs more dense on midrib; petiole 5–8 mm, strigose. Fertile shoots 20–30 mm, including 4 leaves and a 1- to 3-flowered inflorescence; pedicels 1–4 mm, strigose; flowers (including hypanthium) 8–10 mm long. Hypanthium campanulate, brownish, strigose; sepals semispreading, broadly obtuse, often brown, sparsely strigose-villous, border narrow, membranous, white, margin villous. Corolla wide open, petals erect to semispreading, caducous, off-white tinged greenish and pink with purple-red base, sometimes small hair-tuft at base of upper surface. Stamens 10–13; filaments white or pink; anthers white. Fruit obovoid, 12–13 mm, orange red, shaded side yellow, shiny, glabrous, calyx lobes suberect, glabrescent, margin tomentose, navel slightly open. Nutlets 2, apex very swollen and recurved, villous, style remains ²/₃ from base.

Seasons: Flowers May–June; fruit ripe September–October; autumn leaves red and gold.

Chromosomes: Unknown. Apomictic, true from seed.

Hardiness: –15°C (5°F).

Area: Nepal.

Notes: Although said to grow to a height of 4 m in the wild, *Cotoneaster staintonii* in cultivation is slow growing and would take some years to attain such a height. The large orange pendent fruit are relatively untouched by birds. Recently reintroduced into cultivation.

10. *Cotoneaster wallichianus* G. Klotz in Wiss. Z. Martin-Luther-Univ. Halle-Wittenberg, Math.-Naturwiss. 15: 541 (1966). Type: (India), Sikkim-Himalaya, Tankra Mountains, 5 August 1892, *G. A. Gammie 634* (holo CAL, iso BM).

Shrub, sparsely branched, 3–4 m. Branches narrowly erect, slightly arched, often terminating in fertile shoots; branchlets divaricate or distichous, maroon, initially strigose-villous. Leaves deciduous, rarely semievergreen chartaceous or subcoriaceous, on sterile shoots elliptic, 20–36 × 12–17 mm, apex obtuse or acute, base cuneate or obtuse, upper surface dark green, shiny, sparsely villous, veins 4 deeply impressed, lower surface villous-strigose; petiole 3–5 mm, villous-strigose. Fertile shoots 15–25 mm, including 2 leaves and a mostly single (in apex shoots ends paired), pendent flower; pedicel 1–2 mm, strigose; flowers (including hypanthium) 4–5 mm long. Hypanthium campanulate, maroon, base strigose; sepals obtuse, ligulate or acute, glabrous, margin sparsely villous. Corolla wide open, petals spreading, maroon and dark red. Stamens 10–12; filaments dark red; anthers white to purple. Fruit obovoid, 10–12 mm, orange-red, shiny, glabrous, calyx lobes suberect, navel wide open, nutlets exserted. Nutlets 2(–3), apex red, strigose, very swollen and recurved, style remains ²/₃ from base.

Seasons: Flowers May–June; fruit ripe September; autumn leaves good color.

Chromosomes: Triploid (Bailey, pers. comm.).

Hardiness: –15°C (5°F).

Area: Nepal. India (Sikkim). Bhutan.

Notes: *Cotoneaster wallichianus* is a slow-growing species which takes a long time to reach its ultimate height. The large, shiny orange fruit with exposed nutlets are an unusual sight. Recently reintroduced into cultivation.

23. Series *Mucronati* J. Fryer & B. Hylmö, *ser. nov.*

Medium to large shrubs, rarely small trees. Leaves often semievergreen, apex mostly acute. Fertile shoots with a spreading or semierect 1- to 15-flowered inflorescence. Sepals acute, acuminate or cuspidate. Petals often tuft of hairs at base of upper surface. Anthers red, pink, or white. Nutlets apex slightly swollen and recurved.

Early to mid season.

China (Yunnan).

3 species: *C. mirabilis, C. mucronatus, C. newryensis.*

Key to Series *Mucronati*

1a. Upper leaf surface strigose-pilose, petiole ≤ 5 mm, strigose; inflorescence 1- to 3(–6)-flowered; petals erect and incurved; anthers white . . . . *C. mucronatus*

1b. Upper leaf surface glabrous or midrib sparse hairs, petiole ≤ 7 mm, mostly villous; inflorescence 3- to 15-flowered; petals semispreading; anthers red or pink 2

2a. Branches wide-spreading; leaves mostly suborbicular, apex obtuse; stamens (10–)12(–14); nutlets mostly 2 . . . .*C. mirabilis*

2b. Branches erect; leaves mostly elliptic, apex acute; stamens 18–20; nutlets 2–3 . . . . *C. newryensis*

1. *Cotoneaster mirabilis* G. Klotz & Krügel (*pro. hybr.*) in Wiss. Z. Friedrich-Schiller-Univ. Jena, Math.-Naturwiss. 32: 909 (1983). Synonym: *C. ×mirabilis* G. Klotz & Krügel (1893). Type: cult. Jena BG, 19 May 1980 and 23 September 1981. Leg. T. Krügel (holo JE). **PLATE 119.**

Shrub, 1.5–2.5 m. Branches erect, ascending and wide-spreading; branchlets distichous, reddish brown, initially strigose. Leaves deciduous or semievergreen, chartaceous or subcoriaceous, on sterile shoots broadly ovate or suborbicular, 22–39 × 19–33 mm, apex obtuse or cuneate, upper surface dark green, slightly shiny, glabrous or few strigose hairs on midrib, veins 3–5 lightly impressed, lower surface villous, veins densely so; petiole 3–7 mm, villous. Fertile shoots 20–40 mm, including 3–4 leaves and a 3- to 12-flowered inflorescence; pedicels 2–8 mm, strigose-villous; flowers (including hypanthium) 8 mm long. Hypanthium campanulate, green, sparsely strigose; sepals acute, acuminate or obtuse, sparsely strigose, margin villous. Corolla 8–10 mm, petals semispreading to spreading, pink, with hair-tuft at base of upper surface. Stamens (10–)12(–14); filaments deeppink; anthers white tinted red. Fruit obovoid to subglobose, 7–9 mm, crimson to purple. Nutlets 2(–3), apex slightly swollen and recurved.

Seasons: Flowers May–June; fruit ripe September–October.

Chromosomes: Pentaploid (Klotz and Krügel 1983b). Variable from seed.

Hardiness: probably –15°C (5°F).

Area: China (Yunnan, Sichuan).

Notes: Originally published by Klotz and Krügel as *Cotoneaster ×mirabilis*, a sensational hybrid between *C. hissaricus* and a species belonging to section *Adpressi*. *Cotoneaster mirabilis* has been discovered growing wild in China by not only the CLD (Chungtien Lijiang Dali) and SICH (Erskine, Fliegner, Howick, and McNamara) expeditions, but also by Maurice Foster (*MF 96044*), near the monastery of Qi-fu-ping Shan, Zhongdian, Yunnan, in 1996.

2. *Cotoneaster mucronatus* Franchet in Pl. Delavay. 3: 223 (1890). Type: China, Yunnan, Ouchay, flowered 18 May 1882, *J. Delavay 3738* (holo P). **PLATE 120.**

Shrub, to 2 m. Branches erect and ascending, sometimes terminating in fertile shoots; branchlets distichous, brown, initially densely strigose. Leaves evergreen or semi, chartaceous, on sterile shoots elliptic, ovate or suborbicular, 20–50 × 10–30 mm, apex acuminate or acute, base obtuse or cuneate, upper surface dark-green, shiny, strigose-pilose, veins 3–4 impressed, lower surface strigose-villous hairs initially dense; petiole 3–4 mm, strigose. Fertile shoots 15–40 mm, including 2–5 leaves and a 1- to 3(–6)-flowered inflorescence; pedicels 5–8 mm, strigose; flowers (including hypanthium) 6–8 mm long. Hypanthium campanulate, red-maroon, strigose; sepals acuminate, cuspidate or acute, tips often recurving, pilose-strigose, border membranous, glabrous, margin villous. Corolla with large opening; petals erect-incurved, red, pink and green, narrow white border, glabrous. Stamens 18–20; filaments red and pink or off-white; anthers white. Fruit obovoid, 10–12 mm, succulent, orange-red to red, shiny, subglabrous, calyx lobes flat, tips erect. Nutlets 2–3, rarely 4, apex slightly swollen and recurved, style remains ³/₄ from base.

Seasons: Flowers May; fruit ripe September–October; autumn leaves yellow to deep gold.

Chromosomes: Tetraploid (McAllister, pers. comm.; Panigrahi and Kumar 1986). Apomictic, true from seed.

Hardiness: –16°C (3°F).

Area: China (Yunnan).

Notes: *Cotoneaster mucronatus* was introduced to the RBG Kew in 1907. It has been reintroduced from collections made in Yunnan by Keith Rushforth (*KR 2722*) and Maurice Foster (*MF 93096*) in 1993. A good sturdy and fairly dense shrub which is useful for hedging. Fruits well.

3. *Cotoneaster newryensis* Barbier in Barbier & Son nursery trade list, Orléans, France, p.121 (autumn 1908–spring 1909). Type: cult. Ireland, County Down, Newry, Daisy Hill Nurseries, June 1949 (lecto designated E). **PLATE 121.**

Shrub or small tree, 3–5 m. Branches erect, arched, spreading, coarse, often terminating in fertile shoots; branchlets spiraled, divaricate or distichous, maroon, initially densely yellowish strigose-villous. Leaves deciduous, chartaceous or subcoriaceous, on sterile shoots broadly elliptic, 31–43 × 18–28 mm, apex acute, base obtuse or cuneate, upper surface dark green, initially sparsely strigose, veins 4–5 impressed, lower surface sparsely yellowish villous, denser on midrib; petiole 5–7 mm, strigose-villous. Fertile shoots 30–50 mm, including 3–5 leaves and a 5- to 15-flowered inflorescence; pedicels 3–7 mm, strigose; flowers (including hypanthium) 7–8 mm long. Hypanthium widely cupulate, strigose; sepals acute, acuminate or cuspidate, maroon, sparsely strigose, border glabrous, margin villous. Petals semispreading, red and pink, sometimes with hair-tuft at base of upper surface. Stamens 18–20; filaments pink and white; anthers pale crimson. Fruit obovoid or globose, 7– 8 mm, red, shiny, calyx lobes flat, green. Nutlets (2–)3, style remains ²/₃ from base.

Seasons: Flowers June; fruit ripe September–October.

Chromosomes: Although a tetraploid count has been reported, this could have been the result of a labeling error. *Cotoneaster newryensis* is not easy to raise from seed, and when successful the offspring are variable, also sometimes deformed and short-lived.

Hardiness: –15°C (5°F).

Area: China, probably Yunnan or Sichuan.

Notes: *Cotoneaster newryensis* was probably brought into cultivation around 1900 by the industrious plant collectors working in China in Yunnan and Sichuan. It was first raised at Thomas Smith's Daisy Hill Nursery in Ireland and distributed by the French nursery of Barbier. In 1911 it appeared in the catalogue of Lemoine nursery of Nancy, France. *Cotoneaster newryensis* is a vigorous shrub which is fairly rare in cultivation, beautiful in flower, with good autumn color. It was originally thought to be a hybrid between *C. franchetii* and *C. simonsii*. There is a beautiful drawing of *C. newryensis* in Walsh and Nelson's *A Prospect of Irish Flowers* (1990, plate 7).

24. Series *Acuminati* T. T. Yu in Bull. Brit. Mus. (Nat. Hist.), Bot. 1 (5): 132 (1954).

Medium shrubs to small trees. Branches often narrowly erect; branchlets distichous or spiraled. Leaves on sterile shoots 40–125 mm, apex mostly acuminate, margin often undulate, upper surface frequently extremely shiny, good autumn color. Hypanthium mostly campanulate. Petals greenish white, pinkish, and red, sometimes with hair-tuft at base of upper surface; nectar often abundant. Fruit pendent.

Early to mid season.

Nepal. Pakistan. India (Himachal Pradesh, Sikkim). Kashmir. Bhutan.

6 species: *C. acuminatus, C. humilis, C. kaganensis, C. nepalensis, C. parkeri, C. thimphuensis.*

Key to Series *Acuminati*

1a. Branches ascending; leaves 10–30 mm; flowers 4–5 mm; fruit 5–7 mm...........**C. humilis**

1b. Branches erect; leaves 40–125 mm; flowers 7–10 mm; fruit 11–14 mm **2**

2a. Leaf veins deeply impressed; pedicels 5–10 mm; fruit yellow finally orange; nutlets 2–4 ....
....*C. thimphuensis*

2b. Leaf veins not impressed; pedicels 1–5 mm; fruit red or ruby; nutlets (1–)2(–3).............**3**

3a. Petioles 4–6 mm; fertile shoots 10–20 mm; sepals mostly obtuse or acute, inflorescence
1(–2)-flowered; nutlet with style remains $^9/_{10}$ from base......................*C. acuminatus*

3b. Petioles 5–10 mm; fertile shoots 15–70 mm; sepals acute or acuminate; inflorescence 2- to
13-flowered; nutlet with style remains $^2/_3$ from base **4**

4a. Leaves 40–70 mm; fertile shoots 15–35 mm; inflorescence 2- to 8-flowered; hypanthium
campanulate, villous; anthers white...*C. nepalensis*

4b. Leaves 60–125 mm; fertile shoots 25–70 mm; inflorescence 3- to 13-flowered; hypanthium
cupulate, strigose; anthers white or pale mauve................................. *C. parkeri*

1. *Cotoneaster acuminatus* Lindley in Trans. Linn. Soc. London 13: 101 (1822);
illustr. Loddiges' Bot. Cab. 919 (1824) as *Mespilus acuminatus*. Type: Nepal, 1821,
Herb. East India Company, *Wallich 664* (holo K, iso BM, LD).
Shrub, vigorous, 2–3 m. Branches narrowly erect; branchlets spiraled, light brown to maroon, verruculose, lenticellate, initially densely strigose. Leaves deciduous, chartaceous,
on sterile shoots ovate or lanceolate, 41–57 × 15–29 mm, apex acuminate, base cuneate,
margin undulate, upper surface light green, intensely shiny, sparsely pilose-strigose,
veins 4–5, lower surface shiny, villous; petiole 4–6 mm, villous-strigose. Fertile shoots
10–20(–35) mm, including 2–4 leaves and 1–2 flowers; pedicels 2–5 mm, pilose-strigose;
flowers (including hypanthium) 7–8 mm long, reddish brown in bud. Hypanthium campanulate, shiny, sparsely strigose; sepals obtuse, acute or apiculate, sparsely pilose-
strigose, border membranous, margin villous. Corolla with large opening, petals erect,
greenish white ageing pinkish. Stamens (18–)20; filaments greenish white or white; anthers white; nectar abundant. Fruit obovoid or cylindrical, succulent, 11–13 mm, red,
shiny, subglabrous, calyx lobes erect to semispreading, sparsely villous, navel open. Nutlets 2(–3), apex slightly swollen, villous, style remains $^4/_5$ from base.
Seasons: Flowers May–June; fruit ripe September–October; autumn leaves vivid
orange-red to purple.
Chromosomes: Diploid (Hensen 1966). Sexual, outbreeding, variable from seed.
Hardiness: −18°C (−1°F).
Area: Nepal. India (Sikkim, Ladakh). Possibly also Pakistan.
Notes: *Cotoneaster acuminatus* has been brought into cultivation through a number
of collections. However, some of the earlier collections thought to be this species were the
closely related *C. nepalensis*. Several descriptions of *C. acuminatus* are unfortunately
based on *C. nepalensis*. The two species are fairly easy to separate: *C. nepalensis* has fertile

shoots 15–35 mm, with 2–8 flowers, whereas those of *C. acuminatus* are mostly 10–20 mm long with single or paired flowers. According to Brandis (1974), *C. acuminatus* often occurs as understory in oak forests of the western Himalaya. It was first raised in England in 1802 by Loddiges of Hackney. Recently reintroduced into cultivation.

2. ***Cotoneaster humilis*** Dunn in Kew Bulletin p. 384 (1924). Synonym: *C. gilgitensis* G. Klotz (1966). Type: NW Himalaya, Kashmir, Sonamarg, 9 August 1921, *R. R. Stewart 6619* (holo K, iso DD).

Shrub, to 1 m. Branches ascending, spreading; branchlets divaricate, brown, initially pilose-strigose. Leaves deciduous, chartaceous, on sterile shoots broadly elliptic, 10–30 × 6–22 mm, apex acute or acuminate, base cuneate or obtuse, upper surface initially sparsely pilose, veins 4–5, lower surface densely villous; petiole 2–5 mm, villous. Fertile shoots 15–30 mm, including 2–4 leaves and a 1- to 7-flowered inflorescence; pedicels pilose; flowers (including hypanthium) 4 mm long. Hypanthium cupulate, sparsely villous; sepals acute or apiculate, glabrous, margin villous. Petals spreading to semispreading, probably off-white tinged pink. Stamens (18–)20; filaments white; anthers white. Fruit obovoid, 5–7 mm, red, glabrous. Nutlets 2–3(–4), style remains ²/₃ from base.

Area: Pakistan. Kashmir. India (Himachal, Uttaranchal Pradesh).

Notes: *Cotoneaster humilis* is probably not in cultivation. It is closely related to *C. parkeri*, differing only in its shorter growth, smaller, more rounded leaves, shorter fertile shoots with fewer-flowered inflorescences, and fruit containing mostly 3 nutlets.

3. ***Cotoneaster kaganensis*** G. Klotz in Wiss. Z. Martin-Luther-Univ. Halle-Wittenberg, Math.-Naturwiss. 15: 541 (1966). Type: N Pakistan, Hazara, Kagan valley, Bhorj, 12 July 1897, *J. F. Duthie 21276* (holo DD, iso CAL).

Shrub, to 0.4 m high. Flowers and fruit single.

Notes: This species is described as a dwarf shrub similar to *Cotoneaster acuminatus* but with much smaller leaves and fruit, and with single flowers and fruit. The two species have been confused in the past. The only difference between them is the smaller growth habit of *C. kaganensis*. It is quite probable this is just a diminutive form of the diploid and variable *C. acuminatus*. *Cotoneaster kaganensis* has not been discovered in cultivation. Not in key.

4. ***Cotoneaster nepalensis*** André in L'illustr. Hort. 22: 95 (1875); illustr. Rev. Hort. 61: 349 (1889). Synonym: *C. stracheyi* G. Klotz (1966). Type: Nepal, Bhoté Khasi river, 14 October 1954, A. Zimmermann 1676, cult. Sweden, Bjuv, 28 June 1974, *B. Hylmö 1213* (lecto designated GB). **PLATE 122.**

Shrub, multistemmed, 2–3 m. Branches narrowly erect; branchlets spiraled, brown to maroon with few large lenticels, initially densely pilose-strigose. Leaves deciduous, chartaceous, on sterile shoots ovate or elliptic, 40–70 × 21–30 mm, apex acute or acuminate, base cuneate or obtuse, margin undulate, upper surface mid-green, shiny, sparsely strigose, veins 4–5, lower surface grayish green, reticulate, pilose-villous, midrib dense; petiole 5–10 mm, densely villous. Fertile shoots 15–35 mm, including 3–4 leaves and a compact, 2- to 8-flowered inflorescence; pedicels 2–5 mm, pilose-strigose; flowers (including hypanthium) 8–9 mm long, red in bud. Hypanthium campanulate, villous; sepals acuminate or acute, villous, margin long-haired villous. Petals semispreading to erect, greenish white ageing pinkish, sometimes with hair-tuft at base of upper surface. Stamens 18–20; filaments white or pale pink; anthers white; nectar plentiful. Fruit obovoid or cylindrical, 12–13 mm, red to ruby, intensely shiny, sparsely villous, calyx lobes semispreading, densely villous. Nutlets (1–)2(–3), apex slightly swollen and recurved, densely villous, style remains $^2/_3$ from base.

Seasons: Flowers May–June; fruit ripe October.

Chromosomes: Tetraploid (Zeilinga 1964; Krügel 1992a), both as *C. acuminatus*. Apomictic, true from seed.

Hardiness: −18°C (−1°F).

Area: Nepal. India (Himachal Pradesh, Uttaranchal Pradesh).

Notes: *Cotoneaster nepalensis*, described in France in 1875, was for over one hundred years an overlooked species (Flinck and Hylmö 1992). It has been in cultivation since at least 1830 (RBG Kew and the Arnold Arboretum), commonly as *C. acuminatus*. In *Flora Europaea* (Tutin et al. 1968) *C. nepalensis* is treated as *C. acuminatus* and reported to be commonly naturalized in central Europe. From the description there is no doubt that this is *C. nepalensis*. *Cotoneaster stracheyi* Klotz (1966) was described as a hybrid between *C. acuminatus* and *C. obtusus* Lindley or *C. confusus* G. Klotz. A mistake was made in this description, incorrectly stating the inflorescences as 10- to 25-flowered. *Cotoneaster nepalensis* is a beautiful sight with its large, shiny, drop-shaped fruit and yellow-gold leaves in the autumn sunshine.

5. *Cotoneaster parkeri* G. Klotz (*pro. hybr.*) in Wiss. Z. Friedrich-Schiller-Univ. Jena, Math.-Naturwiss. 15: 850 (1966). Synonym: *C.* ×*parkeri* G. Klotz (1970). Type: India, Punjab, Bashahr state, Simla, Khadrala, 18 June 1928, *R. N. Parker 3053* (holo DD, iso A, K). **PLATE 123**.

Shrub or small tree, 3–4 m. Branches narrowly erect; branchlets spiraled, yellowish brown becoming maroon with large lenticels, initially pilose-strigose. Leaves deciduous, chartaceous, on sterile shoots ovate or elliptic, 60–125 × 30–55 mm, apex acuminate or acute, base cuneate; margin often undulate, upper surface mid-green, slightly shiny, sparsely long-haired pilose, veins 4–5, lower surface sparsely long-haired pilose-strigose, midrib densely so; petiole 5–10 mm, villous-strigose. Fertile shoots 25–70 mm, including 1–3 leaves and a 3- to 13-flowered inflorescence; pedicels 1–5 mm, villous-strigose; flowers (including hypanthium) 7–9 mm long, white in bud. Hypanthium cupulate, strigose; sepals acute or acuminate, strigose, margin villous. Petals spreading to semispreading, transparent off-white or pale pink, with hair-tuft at base of upper surface. Stamens (15–)20; filaments white; anthers white or pale mauve; copious nectar. Fruit obovoid, 10–12 mm, ruby to maroon, dull, sparsely villous, calyx lobes semispreading, villous-strigose. Nutlets (1–)2, apex densely villous, style remains ⅔ from base.

Seasons: Flowers May–June; fruit ripe September–October.

Chromosomes: Tetraploid (Bailey, pers. comm.). Apomictic, true from seed.

Hardiness: –18°C (–1°F).

Area: Pakistan. India (Himachal Pradesh). Kashmir.

Notes: *Cotoneaster parkeri* was originally considered a hybrid with *C. roseus* as one of the parents, but there is no evidence to indicate any relationship whatever with *C. roseus*. The suggestion probably arose from the collection notes stating that both *C. acuminatus* and *C. roseus* were growing in the locality. *Cotoneaster parkeri* is, however, closely related to *C. acuminatus*. Klotz (1970, 1972b) uses this hybrid assumption in complicated discussions about the origin of *Cotoneaster* species, using *C.* ×*parkeri* as an example of hybrids between species of different sections. As yet there have been no intersubgenera hybrids discovered in *Cotoneaster*. *Cotoneaster parkeri* has been in cultivation for many years and its behavior is the same as that of other apomictic species. A highly attractive shrub, it has many, wide-open flowers that are much loved by bees for their abundant nectar which often overspills the corolla. The shrub also fruits heavily, the branches often bowing under the weight of the numerous fruit.

6. *Cotoneaster thimphuensis* J. Fryer & B. Hylmö in New Plantsman 8: 230, 237 (2001). Type: Bhutan, Thimphu district between Paro and Chelai La, 14 October 1984, *I. Sinclair & D. Long 5726* (holo E). **PLATE 124.**

Shrub, 3–5 m. Branches erect and arched; branchlets distichous, maroon, initially strigose. Leaves deciduous, chartaceous, on sterile shoots ovate or elliptic, 65–85 × 27–35 mm, apex acuminate, base cuneate, margin slightly undulate, upper surface bullate, dark green, intensely shiny, initially strigose, veins 3–5 deeply impressed, lower surface yellowish strigose-villous; petiole 6–7 mm, strigose. Fertile shoots 25–50 mm, including 4 leaves and a 3- to 10-flowered inflorescence; pedicels 5–10 mm, strigose; flowers (including hypanthium) 7–10 mm long. Hypanthium campanulate, strigose; sepals acute and mucronate or acuminate, subglabrous, border broad, membranous, glabrous, margin erose, long-haired tomentose-villous. Corolla with large opening; petals erect-incurved, red and maroon with off-white border, sometimes with hair-tuft at base of upper surface. Stamens 20; filaments white or pale pink; anthers white. Fruit obovoid, succulent, 11–14 mm, yellow to orange-yellow, shiny, glabrous, calyx lobes depressed. Nutlets (2–)3(–4), apex somewhat swollen and recurved, styles remains ⅔ from base.

Seasons: Flowers June; fruit ripe September–November.

Chromosomes: Tetraploid (Jewsbury, pers. comm.). Apomictic, true from seed.

Hardiness: –15°C (5°F).

Area: Bhutan.

Notes: *Cotoneaster thimphuensis* is a beautiful newcomer to our gardens. Vigorous in growth with large, showy, shiny yellow fruit which finally turn orange, often persisting well into the winter, it also has excellent autumn leaf color. This strange and unusual cotoneaster is difficult to classify. It was originally classified to series *Simonsioides*, which has now been included in series *Distichi*. The species has been found to be closely related to series *Acuminati* and *Bullati*.

8. Section *Acutifolii* Hurusawa in Acta Phytotax. Geobot. 13: 234 (1943). As *Acutifoliae*.

Leaves with good autumn color, 16–210 mm, veins 3–11, sometimes deeply impressed. Fertile shoots 15–170 mm; inflorescence 2- to 50(–70)-flowered. Fruit black or red.

4 series: *Acutifolii, Bullati, Shannanense, Glomerulati.*

25. Series *Acutifolii*. Synonym: series *Lucidi* Pojarkova (1939).

Small shrubs to small trees, often multistemmed. Leaves acute or acuminate; upper surface flat or sometimes bullate; petiole 2–10 mm. Fertile shoots 15–70 mm. Pedicels 2–12 mm. Fruit 7–13 mm, mostly purple-black. Nutlets mostly 2–3.

Early season.

Extremely hardy.

China (Sichuan, Gansu, Shanxi, Hebei, Yunnan). Mongolia. Russia (Siberia).

15 species: *C. acutifolius, C. ambiguus, C. coadunatus, C. dissimilis, C. hsingshangensis, C. hummelii, C. hurusawanus, C. laetevirens, C. lucidus, C. otto-schwarzii, C. pekinensis, C. pseudoambiguus, C. villosulus, C. washanensis, C. yulingkongensis.*

Key to Series *Acutifolii*

1a. Sterile shoot leaves ≤ 42 mm; fruit red slowly becoming black . . . . *C. acutifolius*

1b. Sterile shoot leaves mostly > 42 mm; fruit purple-black to black 2

2a. Sterile shoots leaves elliptic to ellipto-lanceolate, oblong, lanceolate or ovate; fertile shoot leaves lanceolate 3

2b. Sterile shoot leaves elliptic or ovate, often broadly so; fertile shoots leaves not lanceolate 5

3a. Leaf apex long-apiculate, veins 6–8; inflorescence 5- to 11-flowered; fruit mostly globose, c. 8 mm . . . . *C. ambiguus*

3b. Leaf apex acuminate, veins 4–6; inflorescence 1- to 8-flowered; fruit mostly cylindrical or elliptic, ≤ 11–15 mm 4

4a. Leaves elliptic or lanceolate, veins 5–6, petiole 5–10; inflorescence 3- to 8-flowered; stamens 12–20; nutlets sometimes fused . . . . *C. coadunatus*

4b. Leaves oblong-ovate or lanceolate, veins 4–5, petiole 2–3 mm; inflorescence (1–)3(–4)-flowered; stamens (10–)11–13(–18); nutlets free . . . . *C. otto-schwarzii*

5a. Leaves ≤ 105–110 mm; petals base maroon; fruit mostly globose, calyx margin with dense
hairs, forming fringed star **6**

5b. Leaves ≤ 50–75 mm; petals base mostly red; fruit mostly cylindrical, calyx margin hairs not
dense **8**

6a. Upper leaf surface sparsely pilose, very shiny, petiole 2–3 mm; fertile shoots 25–40 mm,
inflorescence (3–)4- to 7(–9)-flowered . . . .***C. hsingshangensis***

6b. Upper leaf surface densely pilose or strigose soon becoming glabrous, fertile shoots 40–70
mm, inflorescence 4- to 15-flowered **7**

7a. Leaves chartaceous, veins 5–6, petiole 4–6 mm, villous; nutlets (2–)3; fruit obovoid,
11–13 mm . . . .***C. hummelii***

7b. Leaves subcoriaceous, veins 6–8, petiole 6–10 mm, strigose-pilose; nutlets (3–)4; fruit
globose, 7–9 mm . . . .***C. washanensis***

8a. Leaves broadly elliptic or broadly ovate; sepals glabrous or few villous hairs; fruit mostly
ellipsoid or globose **9**

8b. Leaves elliptic or ovate; sepals strigose; fruit cylindrical or obovoid **10**

9a. Leaves intensely shiny; inflorescence 5- to 15-flowered; corolla open. . . . . ***C. lucidus***

9b. Leaves dull; inflorescence 4- to 7-flowered; corolla closed. . . . . ***C. pseudoambiguus***

10a. Leaf veins 3–5; fertile shoots 15–40 mm; inflorescence 2- to 4(–5)-flowered. **11**

10b. Leaf veins 5–8; fertile shoots 25–70 mm; inflorescence 3- to 9(–12)-flowered. **12**

11a. Leaves 30–50 mm, base cuneate or obtuse; fertile shoots 20–40 mm; stamens 14–20;
nutlets 2(–3). . . . .***C. hurusawanus***

11b. Leaves 36–62 mm, base truncate; fertile shoots 15–20 mm; stamens 15–20; nutlets 2–3. . . . .
. . . .***C. pekinensis***

12a. Leaves mostly subcoriaceous; inflorescence 3- to 5(–7)-flowered; hypanthium tomentose-
strigose; nutlet style remains ⁴/₅ from base . . . . ***C. villosulus***

12b. Leaves chartaceous; fertile shoots 30–70 mm; hypanthium mostly strigose; nutlet style ³/₄
from base **13**

13a. Leaves 30–90 mm, dark green, dull; hypanthium 6–9 mm. ***C. dissimilis***

13b. Leaves 20–75 mm, mid-green, shiny; hypanthium 5–6 mm **14**

14a. Leaves 43–66 mm; fertile shoots ≤ 50 mm; sepals acute or apiculate; stamens (15–)20;
nutlets 2 . . . . ***C. laetevirens***

14b. Leaves 55–75 mm; fertile shoots ≤ 70 mm; sepals obtuse or shortly acute; stamens 10–16;
nutlets 2–3 . . . . ***C. yulingkongensis***

1. *Cotoneaster acutifolius* Turczaninov in Bull. Soc. Imp. Nat. Mosc. 4: 190 (1832).
Type: Mongolia, Hongor Obo, 27 August 1920, *J. Eriksson 918* (lecto designated GB).
Shrub or small tree, 2–4 m. Branches erect, arched; branchlets spiraled or distichous,
reddish brown, initially strigose-pilose. Leaves deciduous, chartaceous, on sterile shoots
elliptic or ovate, 15–34 × 21–42 mm, apex acuminate or acute, base obtuse or cuneate,
upper surface mid-green, dull, initially pilose-villous, veins 3–5 lightly impressed, lower
surface villous hairs decreasing; petiole 3–5 mm, pilose. Fertile shoots 20–25 mm, in-

cluding 3–4 leaves and 2–3(–5) flowers; pedicels 4–7 mm, densely pilose. Hypanthium cupulate, densely villous; sepals acute or apiculate, villous, margin tomentose. Corolla erect, open, petals white with red base. Stamens 20. Fruit obovoid or subglobose, 7–10 × 4–7 mm, ruby-red, finally black, slightly shiny, subglabrous, calyx lobes flat forming star over open navel. Nutlets 2(–3), style remains ³/₄–⁴/₅ from base.

Seasons: Flowers May–June, sometimes reflowering later in season; fruit ripe September–October.

Chromosomes: Unknown. Apomictic, true from seed.

Hardiness: –25°C (–13°F).

Area: Mongolia. N China.

Notes: In his diagnosis, Nicolai Turczaninov gives the fruit of *Cotoneaster acutifolius* as red. This was queried by Schneider (1906), Klotz (1972b), and others, as related species all have black fruit. The lectotype, which was collected in August, also has red fruit. But the fruit of this species are not fully ripened until well into September. Confusion with this species and the widely cultivated *C. lucidus* has been caused by *C. lucidus* long being misnamed as *C. acutifolius*, especially by the nursery trade. True *C. acutifolius* is rarely in cultivation, but can be found in Ukraine in the University of Kiev botanical garden.

2. *Cotoneaster ambiguus* Rehder & E. H. Wilson in Sargent, Pl. Wilson. 1: 159 (1912). Type: China, W Sichuan, Pan-lan Shan, west of Kuan-hsien, June 1908, *E. H. Wilson 2179* (holo A, iso E).

Shrub, 2–3 m. Branches narrowly erect; branchlets spiraled or distichous, light brown to maroon with large lenticels, initially strigose. Leaves deciduous, chartaceous, on sterile shoots elliptic or lanceolate, 53–73 × 26–30 mm, apex acuminate, base cuneate, upper surface slightly rugose, reddish green, soon dark green, slightly shiny, sparsely pilose-strigose, veins 6–8 impressed, lower surface mid-green, initially sparsely pilose-strigose; petiole 3–5 mm, pilose-strigose. Fertile shoots 20–45 mm, including 4 lanceolate leaves and a lax, 5- to 11-flowered inflorescence; pedicels 3–10 mm, sparsely strigose; flowers (including hypanthium) 6–7 mm long. Hypanthium cupulate, sparsely long-haired pilose-strigose; sepals acute or apiculate, subglabrous, margin long-haired villous. Corolla closed or small opening; petals erect-incurved, greenish white tinged red, base dark red, border greenish white, glabrous. Stamens 16–20; filaments pale-pink; anthers white. Fruit globose or obovoid, 7–9 mm, purple-black, shiny, sparsely villous, calyx lobes flat forming star over open navel. Nutlets 2(–3), style remains ³/₄ from base.

Seasons: Flowers May–June; fruit ripe September; autumn leaves golden yellow.

Chromosomes: Unknown. Apomictic, true from seed.

Hardiness: –21°C (–6°F).

Area: China (Sichuan).

Notes: The holotype for *Cotoneaster ambiguus* was taken from a flowering specimen. Seed distributed under this name came from the paratype *Wilson 1270*, which later became the type for *C. pseudoambiguus*. Most plants of *C. ambiguus* in cultivation are known to have originated from the *Harry Smith 766* collection.

3. **Cotoneaster coadunatus** J. Fryer & B. Hylmö, *sp. nov.* Type: cult. Sweden, Göteborg University botanic garden, raised from seed from China, Sichuan, Matang, 1922, *Harry Smith 1047* (seed only), 8 July 1960, Bertil Hylmö (holo GB).
   PLATE 125.

Shrub or small tree, 3–5 m. Branches erect, spreading and arched; branchlets spiraled or distichous, brown, initially strigose. Leaves deciduous, chartaceous, on sterile shoots elliptic or lanceolate, 48–80 × 20–30 mm, apex acuminate, base cuneate, upper surface slightly rugose, dark green, shiny, sparsely pilose-strigose, glabrescent, veins 5–6 lightly impressed, lower surface sparsely villous, glabrescent; petiole 5–10 mm, strigose. Fertile shoots 20–50 mm, including 4–5 large lanceolate leaves and a lax 3- to 8-flowered inflorescence; pedicels 3–10 mm, mostly sparsely pilose-strigose; flowers (including hypanthium) 6–7 mm long. Hypanthium cupulate, sparsely pilose-strigose; sepals acute, apiculate or acuminate, glabrescent, margin villous. Corolla with small opening; petals erect-incurved, white with ruby and greenish white base, sometimes with sparse hairs. Stamens 12–20; filaments pale pink and white; anthers white. Fruit cylindrical or obovoid, 10–15 mm, purple-black, subglabrous, calyx lobes suberect. Nutlets (1–)2, often partly or wholly coadunated, apex swollen and recurved, style remains 3/4 from base.

Seasons: Flowers May–June, seldom reflowers; fruit ripe August–September; autumn leaves coloring.

Chromosomes: Unknown. Apomictic, true from seed.

Hardiness: −21°C (−6°F).

Area: China (Sichuan).

Notes: *Cotoneaster coadunatus* is an exceptional species in this series. The leaves are lanceolate, the petals have hairs at the base, and the large fruit have nutlets which are (not normal for this subgenus) often joined together.

4. **Cotoneaster dissimilis** G. Klotz in Wiss. Z. Friedrich-Schiller-Univ. Jena, Math.-Naturwiss. 21: 984 (1972). Type: N China, Shanxi, Sikoumen, 5 July 1884, G. N. Potanin (holo LE, iso CAL).

Shrub, 1.5–3 m. Branches erect, arched; branchlets divaricate or distichous, maroon, initially strigose. Leaves deciduous, chartaceous, on sterile shoots elliptic or ovate, 30–90 × 15–45 mm, apex acuminate, apiculate, rarely acute, base obtuse or cuneate, upper surface dark green, dull, sparsely strigose-villous, veins 5–8 impressed, lower surface sparsely pilose-strigose; petiole 3–8 mm, villous. Fertile shoots 20–60 mm, including 4 leaves and a lax, 3- to 8(–12)-flowered inflorescence; pedicels 3–12 mm, strigose-villous; flowers (including hypanthium) 6–9 mm long. Hypanthium cupulate, strigose-villous; sepals acuminate, acute, apiculate, glabrescent, margin tomentose. Petals erect-incurved, open, red and brownish red with off white border, glabrous. Stamens 15–20; filaments pink; anthers white. Fruit cylindrical or obovoid, 9–14 mm, plum-purple to black, shiny, strigose-pilose, calyx lobes flat to suberect, margin tomentose forming star over open navel. Nutlets 2(–3), style remains ³/₄ from base.

Area: China (Shanxi, Shaanxi).

Notes: *Cotoneaster dissimilis* has only recently come into cultivation with a collection made in Shaanxi by the University of Alnarp in Sweden. Prior to this discovery this species was known only from the type herbarium specimen, plus an herbarium collection made by Lao Chin for Harry Smith.

5. *Cotoneaster hsingshangensis* J. Fryer & B. Hylmö in Watsonia 21: 335 (1997). Type: cult. Sweden, Bjuv, garden of K. E. Flinck. Plant 1027 from Arnold Arboretum as "*C. foveolatus* 13431-D SD China, Wilson 1907," 5 July 1964, B. Hylmö (holo E).

Shrub, multistemmed, 2–3 m. Branches erect, arched and spreading; branchlets spiraled or distichous, blackish maroon, initially pilose-strigose. Leaves deciduous, chartaceous or subcoriaceous, on sterile shoots elliptic-ovate, 75–105 × 40–50 mm, apex acuminate or acute, base obtuse, upper surface bullate, maroon-purple, soon dark green, extremely shiny, sparsely pilose, veins 5–6 deeply impressed, lower surface light green, initially sparsely pilose; petiole 2–3 mm, pilose. Fertile shoots 25–40 mm, including 3–4 leaves and a (3–)4- to 7(–9)-flowered inflorescence; pedicels 2–10 mm, pilose; flowers (including hypanthium) 6–8 mm long. Hypanthium infundibulate, pilose-strigose; sepals obtuse, acute or cuspidate, subglabrous, margin tomentose. Corolla closed; petals erect-incurved, white with maroon central stripe and few red dots, red base and white border, glabrous. Stamens 16–20; filaments pink and white; anthers white. Fruit globose, 10–11 mm, purple-black, shiny, pilose, calyx lobes depressed, glabrous, margin tomentose forming star over open navel. Nutlets 2(–3), style remains ³/₄ from base.

Seasons: Flowers May, often reflowers September–October; fruit ripe September–October; autumn leaves greenish yellow to intense red.

Chromosomes: Tetraploid (Zeilinga 1964). Apomictic, true from seed.

Hardiness: –21°C (–6°F).

Area: China (Hubei, Sichuan).

Notes: *Cotoneaster hsingshangensis*, found in the Arnold Arboretum labelled as a Wilson collection from China in 1907, was discovered to have been grown from *Wilson 187* (seed only) from Xingshan Xian (formerly Hsing-shan Hsien) in western Hubei (notes: in thickets, altitude 1300–2000 m, 1907, bush 2–3 m). From this source, *C. hsingshangensis* (distributed as *C. foveolatus*) has been widely cultivated in central and northern Europe. This shrub has an unusual tendency to prematurely burst into life during mild spells in January or February; it causes leaf damage appearing as whitish areas which remain throughout the season.

6. *Cotoneaster hummelii* J. Fryer & B. Hylmö in Watsonia 21: 336 (1997). Type: cult. Sweden, Göteborg University botanic garden (#9182), D. Hummel, 1931 II, 461, 8 June 1960, B. Hylmö (holo E). **PLATE 126.**

Shrub, multistemmed, 3–4 m. Branches narrowly erect and arched; branchlets spiraled, light brown to maroon, initially pilose-strigose. Leaves deciduous, chartaceous, on sterile shoots obovate, elliptic or ovate, 80–110 × 30–45 mm, apex acuminate, base cuneate, margin slightly undulate, upper surface bullate, reddish brown and shiny, soon dark green, dull or slightly shiny, initially densely pilose, veins 5–6 impressed, lower surface grayish to gold-green, initially villous-pilose; petiole 4–6 mm, villous. Fertile shoots 40–60 mm, including 4 leaves and a 7- to 15-flowered inflorescence; pedicels 3–10 mm, sparsely pilose; flowers (including hypanthium) 4–5 mm long. Hypanthium cupulate, with sparse long, yellow villous hairs; sepals acute, sparsely villous, margin densely villous. Corolla with small opening; petals erect-incurved, reddish brown, border white. Stamens 16–20; filaments white with pink base, ageing red; anthers white. Fruit obovoid, 11–13 mm, purple-black, shiny, glabrous with villous apex, calyx lobes depressed, sparsely villous, margin densely villous forming star over open navel. Nutlets (2–)3, style remains 2/3 from base.

Seasons: Flowers May, reflowers August; fruit ripe September–October; autumn leaves intense maroon-purple.

Chromosomes: Tetraploid (Jewsbury, pers. comm.). Apomictic, true from seed.

Hardiness: −21°C (−6°F).

Area: China (Gansu).

Notes: Seed of *Cotoneaster hummelii* was collected in the Gansu province of China, in the Min Shan range at Ngan-Dre-Liang, on 31 October 1930, by the Swedish traveler David Hummel, a medical doctor with the Sven Hedin expedition to central China in 1927–1931. A magnificent 4-m-high specimen of this *Cotoneaster* was growing in the botanic garden at Göteborg University in 1958, laden with great hanging clusters of shiny black fruit and leaves of most beautiful autumn tints. It was distributed throughout Europe from this botanic garden. Some shrubs named as *C. moupinensis* belong here.

7. *Cotoneaster hurusawanus* G. Klotz in Wiss. Z. Friedrich-Schiller-Univ. Jena, Math.-Naturwiss. 21: 984 (1972). Synonym: *C. acutifolius* Turczaninov f. *glabriusculus* Hurusawa (1943). Type: China, Hebei province, Mount Wutai, 21 August 1913, *F. N. Meyer 1263* (holo TI, iso LD, K).

Shrub, 1.5–2 m. Branches erect, arched; branchlets spiraled or distichous, slender, light brown, initially strigose. Leaves deciduous, chartaceous, on sterile shoots elliptic or ovate, 30–49 × 12–26 mm, apex acuminate or acute, base cuneate or obtuse, upper surface convex, light green, slightly shiny, villous-strigose, veins 3–5 lightly impressed, lower surface initially villous; petiole 3–5 mm, villous. Fertile shoots 20–40 mm, including 4 leaves and a 2- to 4-flowered inflorescence; pedicels 3–5 mm, strigose; flowers (including hypanthium) 6–7 mm long. Hypanthium cupulate, strigose; sepals acute or acuminate, strigose, border broad, brown, glabrous, margin villous. Corolla closed; petals erect-incurved, pink with maroon base and white border, upper surface glabrous, lower surface sub-glabrous. Stamens 14–20; filaments red and pink; anthers white. Fruit obovoid or cylindrical, 11–12 mm, black, sparsely pilose, calyx lobes flat. Nutlets 2(–3), style remains $^4/_5$ from base.

Seasons: Flowers May; fruit ripe August; autumn leaves intense red-purple.
Chromosomes: Unknown. Apomictic, true from seed.
Hardiness: −25°C (−13°F). Very hardy.
Area: China (Hebei).
Notes: *Cotoneaster hurusawanus* is a beautiful shrub for autumn color. It is similar to *C. pekinensis* but, among other separating characters, has fertile shoots which are twice the length of those of *C. pekinensis* and the leaf upper surface has more hairs.

8. *Cotoneaster laetevirens* (Rehder & E. H. Wilson) G. Klotz in Wiss. Z. Friedrich-Schiller-Univ. Jena, Math.-Naturwiss. 21: 985 (1972). Synonym: *C. acutifolius* Turczaninov var. *laetevirens* Rehder & E. H. Wilson (1912). Type: China, W Sichuan, Tapao Shan, NE of Kangding, 4 July 1908, *E. H. Wilson 2177* (holo A, iso E, K).

Deciduous shrub, 2–4 m. Branches narrowly erect and gracefully arched; branchlets distichous, slender, brown, initially pilose-strigose. Leaves deciduous, chartaceous, on sterile shoots elliptic or ovate, 20–66 × 10–37 mm, apex acuminate or acute, base obtuse or cuneate, upper surface slightly rugose, reddish brown soon light green, slightly shiny, initially pilose-strigose, veins 5–7 impressed, lower surface villous-strigose; petiole 3–8 mm, pilose-strigose. Fertile shoots 15–50 mm, including 3–4 leaves and a 2- to 7-flowered inflorescence; pedicels 3–8 mm, strigose or sparsely so; flowers (including hypanthium) 5–7 mm long. Hypanthium cupulate, strigose; sepals acute, acuminate or apiculate, sparsely strigose, border broad, brown, glabrous, margin villous. Corolla with small opening; petals erect-incurved, off-white with ruby and green base. Stamens (15–)20; filaments pink; anthers white. Fruit cylindrical or obovoid, 10–11 mm, purple-black, villous, calyx lobes flat, villous margins forming star over open navel. Nutlets 2, very rarely 3, style remains $^3/_4$ from base.

Seasons: Flowers June; fruit ripe September; autumn leaves good color.
Chromosomes: Unknown. Apomictic, true from seed.
Hardiness: −21°C (−6°F).
Area: China (Gansu, Sichuan).
Notes: Due to the fact that fruit were not present on the type herbarium specimen, the identification of *Cotoneaster laetevirens* in cultivation has not been an easy task. At one time it was thought that maybe the Rock collections from Gansu were a separate species (temporarily named *C. tebbutus* but never published), but after further investigation they proved more likely to be *C. laetevirens*. This is a good shrub for autumn color, and useful as it will withstand partial shade.

9. *Cotoneaster lucidus* Schlechtendal in Linnaea 27: 541 (1854); illustr. Svensk.
   Tidskr. 87: 313 (1993). Synonym: *C. acutifolius* (Lindley ex Bunge) Ledebour, non
   Turczaninov (1844). Type: Mongolia, Anerk Bogda, 8 July 1920, J. G. Andersson
   (lecto designated LD). **PLATE 127.**

Shrub, densely branched, 1.5–2.5 m. Branches narrowly erect, spreading; branchlets spiraled or distichous, greenish gray to maroon, initially strigose. Leaves deciduous, chartaceous, on sterile shoots elliptic or ovate, 30–60 × 17–39 mm, apex acuminate or acute,
base cuneate or obtuse, upper surface slightly rugose, dark green, intensely shiny, initially sparsely strigose, veins 3–5 impressed, lower surface mid-green, sparsely pilose-
strigose; petiole 4–8 mm, strigose. Fertile shoots 25–50 mm, including 4–5 leaves and a
lax, 5- to 15-flowered inflorescence; pedicels 5–12 mm, sparsely pilose; flowers (including
hypanthium) 6–7 mm long. Hypanthium cupulate, glabrescent, extreme base sparsely
pilose; sepals acute or acuminate, glabrous, margin villous. Corolla with large opening;
petals erect, off-white with pink and green tints. Stamens 20; filaments pink; anthers
white. Fruit ellipsoid or globose, 8–10 mm, black with blue tint, shiny, glabrous, calyx
lobes flat. Nutlets 2–3, style remains ²/₃ from base.

Seasons: Flowers April–May; fruit ripe August; autumn leaves intense dark red.

Chromosomes: Tetraploid (Zeilinga 1964; Hensen 1966; Gladkova 1968; Krügel
1992a). Apomictic, true from seed.

Hardiness: −25°C (−13°F). Very hardy.

Area: Russia (Siberia). Mongolia.

Notes: *Cotoneaster lucidus*, from the area south of Lake Baikal, has long been in cultivation. Because it withstands clipping well and has an iron constitution, it is excellent
for hedges, especially in exposed areas. The species is grown extensively in Scandinavian
countries. It is a handsome shrub with leaves emerging in early spring, and in early autumn giving an outstanding display of brilliant color. The species was also found in Mongolia in the subalpine pastures of the Chinghiltey Mountains, NE of Ulaan Baátar, by
Géza Kósa, #1129-87, of the Institute of Ecology and Botany of the Hungarian Academy
of Sciences at Vácrátót.

10. *Cotoneaster otto-schwarzii* G. Klotz in Wiss. Z. Friedrich-Schiller-Univ. Jena,
   Math.-Naturwiss. 24: 402 (1975). Type: cult. Jena BG from seed collected in the
   mountains of S China (Yunnan), T. T. Yu 13592. Exsicc. G. Klotz, 8 June 1974
   (holo JE).

Shrub, 2–3 m. Branches narrowly erect, slender; branchlets divaricate, brown, initially
strigose-villous. Leaves deciduous, chartaceous, on sterile shoots oblong-ovate or lanceolate, 42–62 × 18–26 mm, apex acuminate, base obtuse or cuneate, upper surface brownish
green, soon light green, shiny, initially pilose, veins 4–5 impressed, lower surface initially villous; petiole 2–3 mm, pilose. Fertile shoots 20–35 mm, including 2–4 leaves and
a lax (1–)3(–4)-flowered inflorescence; pedicels 3–8 mm, villous. Flowers (including hy-

panthium) 6–8 mm long. Hypanthium cupulate, densely villous; sepals acute, apiculate or cuspidate, often reddish, sparsely villous or glabrous, border broad, membranous, glabrous, margin yellowish tomentose. Corolla closed or with small opening; petals erect-incurved, pink with brownish red, border off-white, glabrous. Stamens (10–)11–13; filaments red or pale pink, apex white; anthers white. Fruit ellipsoid, 8–11 mm, purplish black, calyx lobes erect. Nutlets 2(–3), apex sometimes slightly swollen and recurved, style remains ³/₄ from base.

Seasons: Flowers May-June, often reflowers September; fruit ripe September; autumn leaves rich red to purple.

Chromosomes: Tetraploid (Klotz and Krügel 1983a; Jewsbury, pers. comm.). Apomictic, true from seed.

Hardiness: –21°C (–6°F).

Area: China (Yunnan).

Notes: *Cotoneaster otto-schwarzii* is an attractive shrub with bronzed green leaves emerging early in spring, later giving a blaze of autumn color contrasting with the shiny black fruit. Also collected by Keith Rushforth (*KR 4079*) in Yunnan near Zhongdian on track leading to Bita Hai in 1996.

11. *Cotoneaster pekinensis* (Koehne) Zabel in Mitt. Deutsch. Dendrol. Ges. 7: 384
   (1898). Synonym: *C. acutifolius* Turczaninov f. *pekinensis* Koehne (1893). Type: cult.
   Munich BG, 22 May 1918 (lecto designated M).

Shrub, 1.5–2 m. Branches erect, arched and spreading; branchlets spiraled, divaricate, clustered, yellowish to light brown, initially strigose. Leaves deciduous, chartaceous to subcoriaceous, on sterile shoots elliptic or ovate, 36–62 × 19–30 mm, apex acuminate or acute, base truncate, upper surface dark green, dull, very sparsely long-haired strigose or subglabrous, veins 4–5 lightly impressed, lower surface initially sparsely pilose-strigose; petiole 3–7 mm, strigose. Fertile shoots 15–20 mm, including 4 leaves and a 2- to 4(–5)-flowered inflorescence; pedicels 3–7 mm, strigose; flowers (including hypanthium) 6–7 mm long. Hypanthium strigose, base densely so; sepals acute, apiculate or obtuse, strigose, margin villous. Petals erect-incurved, brownish and red with purple base, border white or greenish. Stamens 11–16; filaments pink, apex white; anthers white. Fruit cylindrical or obovoid, 8–10 mm, black, calyx lobes flat. Nutlets 2–3, sometimes joined.

Seasons: Flowers May; fruit ripe July–August; autumn leaves outstanding color.

Chromosomes: Unknown. Apomictic, true from seed.

Hardiness: –21°C (–6°F).

Area: China (Hebei, Shanxi).

Notes: Zabel (1898) noted that the offspring of *Cotoneaster pekinensis* were true from seed—an early observation of apomixis. Rehder and Wilson (Sargent 1912, 158) reported this species was introduced into the Arnold Arboretum in 1883 by Emil Bretschneider from the mountains near Beijing. *Cotoneaster pekinensis* is unusual in that the sterile shoots often end with an inflorescence.

12. *Cotoneaster pseudoambiguus* J. Fryer & B. Hylmö in Watsonia 21: 337 (1997).
Type: China, W Sichuan, west of Kangding, October 1908, during the 1907–1909
China expedition, *E. H. Wilson 1270* (holo A).

Shrub, multistemmed, 3–4 m. Branches erect, arched and spreading; branchlets spiraled
or distichous, light reddish brown, initially pilose-strigose. Leaves deciduous, chartaceous, on sterile shoots broadly elliptic, broadly ovate or rhomboid, 34–55 × 24–34 mm,
apex acuminate, base cuneate, upper surface rugose, reddish green, pilose-strigose, soon
dark green, dull, subglabrous, veins 4–5 impressed, lower surface initially villous-strigose;
petiole 3–5 mm, villous-strigose. Sterile shoots 25–35 mm, including 4 leaves and a 4- to
7-flowered inflorescence; pedicels 2–12 mm, yellowish villous; flowers (including hypanthium 5 mm. Hypanthium cupulate, yellowish villous-strigose; sepals obtuse or acute,
sparsely villous, margin yellowish tomentose. Corolla closed; petals erect-incurved, pink
with red base and off white border. Stamens 15–20, filaments white and pale pink;
anthers white. Fruit globose or obovoid, 8–9 mm, purple-black, shiny, sparsely villous,
calyx lobes depressed, glabrous, navel wide open, glabrous. Nutlets (2–)3, style remains
$^4/_5$ from base.

Seasons: Flowers May–June, sometimes reflowers September; fruit ripe September–
October; autumn leaves yellowish.

Chromosomes: Tetraploid (Zeilinga 1964). Apomictic, true from seed.

Hardiness: –21°C (–6°F).

Area: China (Sichuan).

Notes: In their description of *Cotoneaster pseudoambiguus*, Rehder and Wilson (Sargent 1912) stated "Numbers 1270 and 2178 differ from type in their thicker, broader
leaves. Number 2178 has a more numerous flowered corymb, broader sepals, showing
some approach to *C. moupinensis* Franchet." *Wilson 1270* and *2178* were collected in
Sichuan in the vicinity of Kangding, whereas *Wilson 2179* (the holotype for *C. ambiguus*)
was collected west of Kuan-hsien in Pan-lan Shan.

13. *Cotoneaster villosulus* (Rehder & E. H. Wilson) Flinck & B. Hylmö in Bot. Not.
(Lund) 115: 383 (1962). Synonym: *C. acutifolius* Turczaninov var. *villosulus* Rehder
& E. H. Wilson (1912). Type: China, W Hubei, Xingshan Xian, October 1907,
E. H. Wilson 327 [right-hand branch] (holo A, iso E).

Shrub or small tree, multistemmed, 3–5 m. Branches erect, arched and spreading, coarse;
branchlets distichous or spiraled, brown, initially densely villous-strigose. Leaves deciduous, subcoriaceous to chartaceous, on sterile shoots elliptic or ovate, 50–65 × 29–36
mm, apex acuminate or acute, base obtuse or cuneate, upper surface rugose, dark reddish
green, shiny, soon dark green, dullish, pilose-strigose, veins 5–8 lightly impressed, lower
surface mid-green, shiny, sparsely pilose-strigose; petiole 2–5 mm, strigose. Fertile shoots
25–50 mm, including 4 leaves and a 3- to 5(–7)-flowered inflorescence; pedicels 3–7 mm,
densely strigose; flowers (including hypanthium) 6 mm long. Hypanthium cupulate,
tomentose-strigose; sepals acute, obtuse or apiculate, strigose, border broad, brown, gla-

brous, margin tomentose. Corolla with small opening; petals erect-incurved, red with ruby base and white border. Stamens 18–20; filaments pale pink with white apex; anthers white. Fruit cylindrical or obovoid, 9–11 mm, purple-black, villous, calyx lobes flat, margin forming star over navel. Nutlets 2(–3), style remains $^4/5$ from base.

Seasons: Flowers May–June, often reflowers September; fruit ripe September; autumn leaves purple and rich dark red.

Chromosomes: Tetraploid (Klotz 1968b; Bailey, pers. comm.). Apomictic, true from seed.

Hardiness: −21°C (−6°F).

Area: China (Hubei).

Notes: *Cotoneaster villosulus* is a very handsome and vigorous shrub giving excellent autumn color. It withstands semishade very well.

14. *Cotoneaster washanensis* J. Fryer & B. Hylmö, *sp. nov.* Synonym: *C. wenchuanensis* hort. Type: China, W Sichuan, Wa Shan, September 1908, *E. H. Wilson 857B* (holo A). **PLATE 128.**

Shrub or small tree, 4–6 m. Branches narrowly erect and arched; branchlets distichous or spiraled, brown, initially strigose-pilose. Leaves deciduous, subcoriaceous, on sterile shoots elliptic or ovate, 62–105 × 36–54 mm, apex acuminate or acute, base obtuse or cuneate, upper surface rugose, mid to dark green, slightly shiny, initially sparsely strigose, veins 6–8 impressed, lower surface sparsely villous-strigose midrib more dense so; petiole 6–10 mm, strigose-pilose. Fertile shoots 40–70 mm, including 4 leaves and a lax, 5- to 15-flowered inflorescence; pedicels 3–8 mm, strigose; flowers (including hypanthium) 7 mm long. Hypanthium cupulate or infundibulate, sparsely strigose; sepals acute or obtuse, sparsely strigose or subglabrous, margin villous. Petals erect-incurved, yellow-greenish white with ruby base and white border. Stamens 18–20; filaments red with pink; anthers white. Fruit globose, 8–10 mm, black, calyx lobes flat. Nutlets 3–4.

Seasons: Flowers May–June; fruit ripe September–October; autumn leaves intense reddish purple-green.

Chromosomes: Unknown. Apomictic, true from seed.

Hardiness: −21°C (−6°F).

Area: China (Sichuan).

Notes: *Cotoneaster washanensis* can sometimes be found in cultivation as *C. moupinensis*, the name under which the seed of *Wilson 857B* was originally distributed (Rehder and Wilson in Sargent 1912).

15. *Cotoneaster yulingkongensis* J. Fryer & B. Hylmö *sp. nov.* Type: China, Sichuan, Kangding, Yulingkong, 17 October 1934, *Harry Smith 12813* (holo UPS). **PLATE 129.**

Shrub, 2–4 m. Branches narrowly erect; branchlets distichous, light brown, lenticellate, initially pilose-strigose. Leaves deciduous, chartaceous, on sterile shoots elliptic or obovate, 55–75 × 29–35 mm, apex acuminate, base cuneate, upper surface rugose, brownish red and green with a pink and yellow border, soon mid to dark green, slightly shiny, pilose-strigose, veins 5–7 impressed, lower surface becoming red-reticulate, villous-strigose; petiole 3–8 mm, pilose-strigose. Fertile shoots 30–70 mm, including 4–5 leaves and a lax, 3- to 9-flowered inflorescence; pedicels 2–9 mm, sparsely strigose; flowers (including hypanthium) 5–6 mm long. Hypanthium cupulate, sparsely strigose; sepals obtuse or shortly acute, sparsely strigose, margin sparsely villous. Corolla with small opening; petals erect-incurved, red with off-white base and border, margin white. Stamens 10–16; filaments pale pink with off-white; anthers white. Fruit cylindrical or obovoid, 8–10 mm, purple-black, shiny, sparsely hairy, calyx lobes flat. Nutlets 2–3, style remains ³/₄ from base.

  Seasons: Flowers May–June; fruit ripe August–September; autumn leaves purple-red.
  Chromosomes: Unknown. Apomictic, true from seed.
  Hardiness: –21°C (–6°F).
  Area: China (Sichuan).
  Notes: *Cotoneaster yulingkongensis* is beautiful in early spring when the bronzed young leaves emerge, and again in autumn with its contrasting fruit and leaf color. It was rediscovered in Kangding, on Zhedo Shan, in 2005 by Mikinori Ogisu (*MO 5119*).

26. Series *Bullati* Flinck & B. Hylmö in Bot. Not. (Lund) 119: 455 (1966).

Medium shrubs to small trees. Leaves subcoriaceous, 25–210 mm, upper surface strongly bullate, veins 3–12, mostly deeply impressed. Fertile shoots 25–170 mm, including 5- to 50(–70)-flowered inflorescence. Corolla mostly closed; petals greenish white with red. Fruit red, maroon, orange, or black. Nutlets (2–)3–5.

  Mostly mid to late season.
  China (Sichuan, Yunnan, Gansu, Guizhou). Tibet. Taiwan.
  19 species: *C. ataensis, C. atuntzensis, C. boisianus, C. bullatus, C. cornifolius, C. emeiensis, C. hilleri, C. hualiensis, C. ignescens, C. lancasteri, C. moupinensis, C. obscurus, C. ogisui, C. pseudoobscurus, C. rehderi, C. reticulatus, C. sikangensis, C. taiwanensis, C. wanbooyensis.*

Key to Series *Bullati*

1a. Pedicels mostly 2–5 mm; fruit orange, orange-red or red 2
1b. Pedicels mostly 3–10 mm; fruit ruby, maroon, purple-black 10
2a. Leaves 26–60 mm; sepals, acute or acuminate; fruit orange or orange-red 3
2b. Leaves 35–210 mm; sepals short, acute, obtuse or apiculate; fruit red. 5
3a. Leaves broadly elliptic or rhomboid; pedicels 2–8 mm; hypanthium cupulate; nutlets 3–4
     (–5) . . . .*C. ignescens*
3b. Leaves elliptic or ovate; pedicels 1–3 mm; hypanthium infundibulate; nutlets (3–)4–5 4
4a. Leaves chartaceous, elliptic, 46–60 mm, dull; fertile shoots 30–60 mm. . . . .*C. boisianus*
4b. Leaves subcoriaceous, ovate, 26–40 mm, shiny, fertile shoots 25–40 mm. . . . . .*C. sikangensis*

5a. Leaves 35–50 mm, veins 4–6; inflorescence 3- to 9-flowered; fruit obovoid; nutlets (2–)3(–4) **6**

5b. Leaves 55–210 mm, veins 6–12; inflorescence 7- to 40(–150)-flowered; fruit mostly globose; nutlets (3–)4–5 ....**7**

6a. Leaves chartaceous, petiole 4–6 mm; hypanthium sparsely strigose, sepals apiculate or acute...*C. ataensis*

6b. Leaves subcoriaceous, petiole 2–4 mm; hypanthium strigose, base strigose-tomentose, sepals acute or obtuse..*C. hualiensis*

7a. Leaves chartaceous, narrowly elliptic, upper surface pilose; fertile shoots ≤ c. 50 mm.......
....*C. taiwanensis*

7b. Leaves subcoriaceous, elliptic or ovate, upper surface sparsely pilose becoming glabrous; fertile shoots ≤ 100–170 mm..**8**

8a. Leaves 68–210 mm, veins 7–12 deeply impressed; fertile shoots ≤ 120–170 mm; nutlets 3–5 ....**9**

8b. Leaves 55–90 mm, veins 6–7 impressed; fertile shoots ≤ 100 mm; nutlets mostly ....
....*C. bullatus*

9a. Leaves ≤ 210 mm, upper surface strongly bullate, shiny; fertile shoots ≤ 120 mm; inflorescence 12- to 30-flowered; nutlets 4–5....................................*C. rehderi*

9b. Leaves ≤ 160 mm; upper surface bullate, dull; fertile shoots ≤ 170 mm; inflorescence 20- to 40(–70)-flowered; nutlets 3–4(–5) ....*C. emeiensis*

10a. Leaves 25–45 mm, veins 3–6; fertile shoots 25–50 mm.................................**11**

10b. Leaves 53–130 mm, veins 6–11; fertile shoots 30–100 mm..............................**12**

11a. Leaves elliptic or lanceo-elliptic, veins 4–7, petiole 4–6 mm; inflorescence 7- to 25-flowered ....*C. pseudoobscurus*

11b. Leaves elliptic, broadly elliptic or ovate, veins 3–5, petiole 2–4 mm; inflorescence 7- to 12-flowered ....*C. obscurus*

12a. Leaves base mostly obtuse, veins 7–11, strongly reticulate; nutlets (4–)5..................**13**

12b. Leaves base mostly cuneate, veins 6–9, not or weakly reticulate, nutlets (3–)4(–5) **14**

13a. Leaves 53–80 mm; inflorescence 5- to 30-flowered, pedicels 2–8 mm; fruit maroon.........
....*C. cornifolius*

13b. Leaves 65–130 mm; inflorescence 15- to 50-flowered, pedicels 1–4 mm; fruit purple-black..
....*C. moupinensis*

14a. Leaves obovate or elliptic, apex long-acuminate; fertile shoots ≤ 70; fruit ≤ c. 7 mm, purple-black..*C. lancasteri*

14b. Leaves broadly elliptic or elliptic, apex acuminate or acute; fertile shoots ≤ 90–100 mm; fruit ruby or maroon..**15**

15a. Leaves ≤ 120 mm; inflorescence 5- to 25-flowered; hypanthium infundibulate, nutlets mostly 3–4..*C. atuntzensis*

15b. Leaves ≤ 105 mm; inflorescence 10- to 50-flowered; hypanthium cupulate, nutlets mostly 4–5...*C. wanbooyensis*

1. *Cotoneaster ataensis* J. Fryer & B. Hylmö, *sp. nov.* Synonyms: *C. bullatus* T. T. Yu
   in Bois, Bull. Brit. Mus. (Nat. Hist.), Bot. 1 (5): 133 (1954); *C. bullatus* Bois in W. J.
   Bean, Trees and Shrubs p. 736 (1970). Type: SE Tibet, Ata Zayul, 21 October 1933,
   Kingdon Ward 10906 (holo BM, iso UPS). **PLATE 130.**

Shrub, 2–3 m. Branches erect, arched and spreading; branchlets distichous, maroon,
densely lenticellate, initially strigose. Leaves deciduous, chartaceous, on sterile shoots
broadly elliptic, 35–50 × 25–33 mm, apex acuminate or acute, base cuneate, upper surface slightly bullate, dark green, dull or slightly shiny, initially villous, veins 4–6 impressed, lower surface mid-green, shiny, sparsely villous; petiole 4–6 mm, strigose. Fertile shoots 40–60 mm, including 4 leaves and a compact, 3- to 9-flowered inflorescence;
pedicels 2–5 mm, sparsely strigose; flowers (including hypanthium) 6–7 mm long. Hypanthium cupulate, sparsely strigose; sepals apiculate or acute, glabrescent, margin long-
haired villous. Corolla open; petals erect-incurved, red with blackish purple base and
pink border. Stamens 20; filaments red and pink, anthers white. Fruit obovoid, succulent,
10–11 mm, red, shiny, sparsely strigose, calyx lobes flat, navel wide open. Nutlets (2–)3–4,
style remains $^{3}/_{4}$ from base.

Seasons: Flowers June–July; fruit ripe September–October.

Chromosomes: Unknown. Apomictic, true from seed.

Hardiness: −15°C (5°F).

Area: Tibet. China (Yunnan).

Notes: *Cotoneaster ataensis* is fairly widespread in cultivation, where, despite its
bright scarlet fruit, and so forth, it is wrongly assumed to be *C. bullatus*.

2. *Cotoneaster atuntzensis* J. Fryer & B. Hylmö, *sp. nov.* Type: China, Yunnan,
   Atuntze, Mount Kaakeipu, 26 September 1938, *T. T. Yu 10497* (holo E, iso BM).
   PLATE 131.

Shrub, 2–3 m. Branches narrowly erect, somewhat arched in fruit; branchlets distichous,
grayish black, initially pilose-strigose. Leaves deciduous, chartaceous to subcoriaceous,
on sterile shoots broadly elliptic or elliptic, 55–120 × 30–60 mm, apex acuminate, base
cuneate or obtuse, upper surface bullate, initially reddish purple, soon mid-green, shiny,
pilose, veins 6–9 impressed, lower surface light green, initially villous, veins reddish;
petiole 2–4 mm, pilose-strigose. Fertile shoots 40–100 mm, including 4 leaves and a lax,
5- to 25-flowered inflorescence; pedicels 1–10 mm, sparsely strigose; flowers (including
hypanthium) 5–7 mm long. Hypanthium infundibulate, sparsely pilose-strigose; sepals
acute or apiculate, glabrescent, margin villous. Corolla with small opening; petals erect-
incurved, pale pink and greenish with narrow off-white border. Stamens 20; filaments
pale pink and off white; anthers white. Fruit shortly obovoid, 9–10 mm, ruby to maroon,
shiny, sparsely pilose, calyx lobes flat. Nutlets 3–4(–5), style remains $^{2}/_{3}$ from base.

Seasons: Flowers May–June; fruit ripe September–October; autumn leaves reddish
and purple.

Chromosomes: Unknown. Apomictic, true from seed.

Hardiness: −18°C (−1°F).

Area: China (Yunnan, Sichuan).

Notes: *Cotoneaster atuntzensis* is the earliest species in series *Bullati* to flower and fruit. It is extremely handsome and attracts much attention, especially when loaded with shiny fruit which characteristically turn from deep pink-red to ruby-red and finally maroon, contrasting well with the glowing autumn leaf color. Recently reintroduced into cultivation.

3. **Cotoneaster boisianus** G. Klotz in Wiss. Z. Friedrich-Schiller-Univ. Jena, Math.-Naturwiss. 21: 987 (1972). Type: cult. France, Les Barres garden. D. Bois, 25 September 1902, #4483, collector for M. L. de Vilmorin in 1897 in China, Sichuan near Kangding, #2123 (holo P).

Shrub, 2–3 m. Branches erect, arched and spreading; branchlets distichous, maroon, strigose-pilose. Leaves chartaceous, on sterile shoots elliptic, 46–60 × 22–32 mm, apex acuminate or acute, base cuneate or obtuse, upper surface slightly bullate, dark green, dull, pilose-strigose, veins 6–8 impressed, lower surface reticulate, yellowish pilose; petiole 2–3 mm, tomentose-strigose. Fertile shoots 30–60 mm, including 4 leaves and a lax, 9- to 18-flowered inflorescence; pedicels 1–3 mm, densely yellowish strigose-pilose; flowers (including hypanthium) 6–7 mm. Hypanthium infundibulate, yellowish strigose; sepals acute or acuminate, sparsely strigose, border broad, reddish brown, glabrous, margin tomentose. Corolla closed; petals erect-incurved, red, base dark red, border pale pink and off-white. Stamens 18–20; filaments red and pink; anthers white. Fruit obovoid, 9–11 mm, orange-red, shiny, base pilose, calyx lobes flat, densely pilose. Nutlets (3–)4–5, style remains 2/3 from base.

Seasons: Flowers July; fruit ripe September–October; autumn leaves shiny rich red.

Chromosomes: Tetraploid (McAllister, pers. comm.; Klotz and Krügel 1983a). Apomictic, true from seed.

Hardiness: −18°C (−1°F).

Area: China (Sichuan).

Notes: *Cotoneaster boisianus* has long been in cultivation, often misnamed as *C. glomerulatus* or *C. obscurus* and sometimes as *C.* 'Firebird'. It is a lovely shrub for autumn fruit and leaf color. Recently reintroduced into cultivation.

4. **Cotoneaster bullatus** Bois in Bull. Soc. Bot. France 51: 153 (1904); illustr. Curtis's Bot. Mag. 135: t. 8248 (1909) as *C. moupinensis* f. *floribunda*. Type: cult. France, Les Barres garden, 25 September 1902, herb. Maurice L. de Vilmorin (lecto designated P).

Shrub, 3–5 m. Branches erect, arched and spreading, robust; branchlets spiraled or distichous, maroon, initially yellowish pilose-strigose. Leaves deciduous, subcoriaceous, on sterile shoots elliptic or ovate, 55–90 × 26–46 mm, apex acuminate, base cuneate or obtuse, upper surface bullate, initially reddish brown, soon dark green, shiny, initially pilose, veins 6–9 impressed, lower surface villous, midrib densely so; petiole 2–4(–5) mm, pilose-strigose. Fertile shoots 40–100 mm, including 4–5 often obovate leaves and a lax, 12- to 30-flowered inflorescence; pedicels 2–5 mm, strigose-pilose; flowers (including hypanthium) 5–7 mm long. Hypanthium cupulate, sparsely strigose-villous or subglabrous; sepals acute, acuminate or obtuse, initially sparsely villous, margin villous. Corolla closed or with small opening; petals erect-incurved, red and pale pink, border greenish pink and off-white. Stamens 20; filaments pale pink; anthers white. Fruit globose or obovoid, 7–8 mm, rich red to red, slightly shiny, glabrescent, calyx lobes depressed, subglabrous. Nutlets 5, rarely 4, style remains ¹/₂ from base.

Seasons: Flowers July, reflowers September–October; fruit ripe October.

Chromosomes: Tetraploid (Moffett 1931; Zeilinga 1964; Hensen 1966; Kroon 1975; Bailey, pers. comm.). Apomictic, true from seed.

Hardiness: −21°C (−6°F).

Area: China (Sichuan).

Notes: *Cotoneaster bullatus* has for many years been common in gardens and collections throughout Europe and can frequently be found escaped from cultivation, where wild birds feast on its plentiful fruit. It is a robust shrub that withstands windy situations well; hence, it is excellent for coastal areas and also for roadside plantings. Due to the flowers opening in sequence, buds, flowers, and nearly ripe fruit are commonly found in the same inflorescence.

Cultivar: 'Samantha Jane' (PLATE 132), fruit dark red, finally maroon-brown. Has magnificent autumn leaf color. Probably a new species.

5. ***Cotoneaster cornifolius*** (Rehder & E. H. Wilson) Flinck & B. Hylmö in Bot. Not. (Lund) 115: 379 (1962). Synonym: *C. obscurus* Rehder & E. H. Wilson var. *cornifolius* Rehder & E. H. Wilson (Sargent 1912). Type: China, W Sichuan, Tu-fi-liang Shan, Lungan Fu, August 1910, *E. H. Wilson 4543* (holo A, iso K). PLATE 133.

Shrub, multistemmed, 4–5 m. Branches narrowly erect; branchlets spiraled and distichous, maroon, initially yellowish strigose. Leaves deciduous, subcoriaceous, on sterile shoots elliptic or obovate, 53–80 × 28–41 mm, apex acuminate or acute, base obtuse or cuneate, upper surface bullate, mid-green, dull, initially sparsely strigose, veins 7–10 deeply impressed, lower surface light green, sparsely villous-strigose, petiole 3–5 mm, strigose. Fertile shoots 30–100 mm, including 3–4 leaves and a lax, 5- to 30-flowered inflorescence; pedicels 2–8 mm, strigose; flowers (including hypanthium) 5–7 mm long. Hypanthium cupulate, sparsely strigose; sepals acute or obtuse, few strigose hairs or glabrous, margin villous. Corolla with small opening; petals erect-incurved, red with dark red, off-white border. Stamens 20; filaments pale pink; anthers white. Fruit obovoid, 8–10 mm, ruby maroon (drying nearly black), shiny, glabrous, calyx lobes flat. Nutlets (4–)5, style remains ²/₃ from base.

Seasons: Flowers May–June; fruit ripe August–September; autumn leaves red.

Chromosomes: Unknown. Apomictic, true from seed.

Hardiness: −21°C (−6°F).

Area: China (Sichuan).

Notes: Despite being distributed since 1935 by nurseries in Germany (incorrectly as *Cotoneaster bullatus*), *C. cornifolius* is not common in cultivation. It was rediscovered in Sichuan, Shanlinggang, Leibo, in 2007 by Mikinori Ogisu (*MO 447*). A lovely shrub with rich-colored fruit and beautiful autumn leaf color.

6. *Cotoneaster emeiensis* J. Fryer & B. Hylmö, *sp. nov.* Type: China, W Sichuan, N Emei Shan, 2500 m, October 1980, *R. Lancaster 494* [cult. England, Froxfield, J. Fryer 1399, August 2000] (holo BM). PLATE 134.

Shrub, 3–4 m. Branches erect and spreading, branchlets divaricate or distichous, greenish brown with cream lenticels, initially pilose-strigose. Leaves deciduous, subcoriaceous, on sterile shoots elliptic or ovate, 120–160 × 55–60 mm, apex acuminate or acute, base obtuse, cuneate or subauriculate, upper surface bullate, rugose, mid-green, dull, pilose, veins 7–12 deeply impressed, lower surface reticulate, yellowish villous, more dense on veins; petiole very short (leaves subsessile). Fertile shoots 100–170 mm, including 4, lanceolate leaves and a lax, 20- to 40(–70)-flowered inflorescence; pedicels strigose-pilose; flowers (including hypanthium) 7–8 mm long, purple in bud. Hypanthium cupulate, few strigose-villous hairs; sepals acute, glabrous, margin villous. Corolla closed; petals erect-incurved, red with brownish red base, border pale pink. Stamens 20; filaments white to very pale pink; anthers white. Fruit globose or depressed-globose, 8–9 mm, orange-red to bright red, glabrous, calyx lobes slightly depressed. Nutlets (3–)4(–5), style remains $^2/_3$ from base.

Seasons: Flowers June; fruit ripe September–October; autumn leaves reddish.

Chromosomes: Unknown. Apomictic, true from seed.

Hardiness: −18°C (−1°F).

Area: China (Sichuan).

Notes: *Cotoneaster emeiensis* was collected in Sichuan by the horticultural expert, presenter, and personality Roy Lancaster and featured in his book on his travels in China, *A Plantsman's Paradise* (1989), in which there is an illustration on page 99. Recently reintroduced into cultivation.

7. *Cotoneaster hillieri* J. Fryer & B. Hylmö *sp. nov.* Type: China, Sichuan, 1936, K. L. Chu (holo BM). PLATE 135.

Shrub or small tree, 2.5–3 m. Branches stiffly erect; branchlets distichous, maroon-brown, initially strigose-pilose. Leaves deciduous, subcoriaceous, on sterile shoots elliptic or ovate, 40–62 × 20–33 mm, apex acuminate, base obtuse or cuneate, upper surface bullate, dark brownish green, dull, glabrescent, veins 5–6 deeply impressed, lower surface initially densely yellow villous; petiole 3–4 mm, villous. Fertile shoots 40–50(–70) mm long, including 3–4 leaves and a 5- to 8-flowered inflorescence; pedicels 1–4 mm, densely pilose; flowers (including hypanthium) 6–7 mm long. Hypanthium cupulate, sparsely pilose; sepals acute with mucro or acuminate, sparsely pilose, margin sparsely villous. Corolla closed; petals erect-incurved, dark red and pink. Stamens 18–20; filaments dark red with pink or off-white apex; anthers white. Fruit obovoid, 10 × 9 mm, blood red, glabrous, calyx lobes flat. Nutlets (3–)4–5, style remains ²/₃ from base.

Seasons: Flowers May–June, reflowers September; fruit ripe September–October; autumn leaves gold.

Chromosomes: Unknown. Apomictic, true from seed.

Hardiness: –18°C (–1°F).

Area: China (Sichuan).

Notes: *Cotoneaster hillieri* has been in cultivation for many years in various places (especially in Ireland) under various names. It was probably collected by George Forrest on his 7th expedition to Yunnan; both the Marquess of Headfort in County Meath, and the Marchioness of Londonderry in County Down in Ireland subscribed to this his final expedition. This species, with what was probably a seed list number *Forrest 80733* (not 30733), was originally considered possibly to be *C. reticulatus* which was shown to be false when Mikinori Ogisu rediscovered *C. reticulatus* in Sichuan in 1994. *Cotoneaster hillieri* is named in honor of the great plantsman Sir Harold Hillier in whose arboretum in Hampshire (England) this species was first noticed. Not in key.

8. *Cotoneaster hualiensis* J. Fryer & B. Hylmö in New Plantsman 8: 231, 236 (2001).
Synonym: *C. konishii*, non Hayata in T. H. Hseih & T. C. Huang Taiwania 42: 48 (1997); illustr. *C. konishii*, non Hayata, Illustr. of Native and Introduced Ligneous plants of Taiwan (1960) (excluding B with spreading petals). Type: Taiwan, Hua-lien County, below summit of Shimen Shan (an outlying peak of Hohuan Shan), 13 October 1992, *A. Kirkham & M. Flanagan 81* (holo K, iso FRY). **PLATE 136.**
Shrub, 1.5–2.5 m. Branches erect, arched, ascending and spreading; branchlets spiraled or distichous, maroon, initially densely strigose-pilose. Leaves deciduous, subcoriaceous, on sterile shoots broadly ovate or broadly elliptic, 40–50 × 22–31 mm, apex shortly acuminate or acute, base obtuse or cuneate, upper surface bullate, dark green, shiny, initially strigose, veins 4–6 impressed, lower surface pilose-villous; petiole 2–4 mm, strigose-pilose. Fertile shoots 25–60 mm, including 4–5 leaves and a compact, 3- to 8-flowered inflorescence; pedicels 1–4 mm, strigose-tomentose; flowers (including hypanthium) 6–7 mm long. Hypanthium cupulate, strigose-tomentose; sepals acute or obtuse, strigose, border very broad, brown-purple, glabrous, margin villous. Corolla closed or with small opening; petals erect-incurved, pink, base red base and border pale pink or off-white. Stamens (18–)20; filaments red and whitish; anthers white. Fruit obovoid or globose, 9–10 mm, rich red to red, shiny, sparsely pilose, calyx lobes flat with white-villous hairs on margins forming star over slightly open navel. Nutlets (2–)3(–4), apex swollen and slightly recurved, style remains ³/₄ from base.

Seasons: Flowers May–July; fruit ripe September–October; autumn leaves intense red.

Chromosomes: Unknown. Apomictic, true from seed.

Hardiness: −18°C (−1°F).

Area: Taiwan.

Notes: In several floras and publications in Taiwan, *Cotoneaster hualiensis* was mis-named as *C. konishii* (a species closely related to *C. cordifolius*), which differs in being 1–1.5 m high, with leaves 15–25 mm and nutlets 2 per fruit. The reason for this mistaken identification can be traced to the original description of *C. konishii* which wrongly states that the nutlets are 3–5 per fruit. *Cotoneaster hualiensis* is proving to be an extremely desirable and garden-worthy shrub of good habit; the numerous flowers are much loved by bees, and later it is laden with fruit which contrast well with the striking autumn leaf color. The new young leaves in spring are often bronzed. The species was also collected in 1996 in Taiwan by Bleddwyn & Sue Wynn-Jones (*BSWJ 3143*) between Tayuling to Hohaun Shan.

9. *Cotoneaster ignescens* J. Fryer & B. Hylmö in New Plantsman 8: 232, 236 (2001).
Synonyms: *C. bullatus* Bois 'Firebird' (W. J. Hooftman); *C.* 'Firebird' F. J. Grootendorst and Sons, p. 35 (1959/60); W. J. Hooftman ex Boom Ned. Dendr. 5: 262 (1965); *C.* 'Firebrand' W. J. Hooftman p.18 (1959/60). Type: *C.* 'Firebird', cult. W. J. Hooftman Nurseries, #36327, Boom (holo L). **PLATE 137.**

Shrub, 2–3 m. Branches erect, arched and spreading; branchlets distichous, maroon, initially pilose-strigose. Leaves deciduous, subcoriaceous, on sterile shoots broadly elliptic or rhomboid, sides sometimes unequal, 38–50 × 23–28 mm, apex acute or acuminate, base obtuse or cuneate, upper surface bullate, dark green, shiny, strigose, veins 5–7 deeply impressed, lower surface densely whitish pilose-villous; petiole 2–4 mm, strigose. Fertile shoots 25–60 mm, including 2–5 leaves and a compact, 3- to 13-flowered inflorescence; pedicels 2–8 mm, strigose; flowers (including hypanthium) 5–6 mm long. Hypanthium cupulate, strigose; sepals acute or acuminate, strigose, border broad, brown, glabrous, margin villous. Corolla with small opening; petals erect-incurved, reddish brown, border pink or off-white. Stamens 16–20; filaments red and pink; anthers white. Fruit ob-ovoid or depressed globose, 9–10(–12) mm, orange-red, shiny, very sparsely pilose, calyx lobes flat, strigose, navel open. Nutlets 3–4(–5), style remains ²/₃ from base.

Seasons: Flowers June–July; fruit ripe September–November; autumn leaves purple-red.

Chromosomes: Tetraploid (McAllister, pers. comm.). Apomictic, true from seed.

Hardiness: −18°C (−1°F).

Area: China (Yunnan).

Notes: *Cotoneaster ignescens* has been in cultivation since 1938 under the incorrect *Yu number 7941*, erroneously named *C. bullatus* var. *floribundus*. First noticed in 1950 by C. Verboom of W. J. Hooftman Nurseries, Boskoop, Netherlands, when raised from seed obtained from RHS Wisley in England as *C.* Hupeh (without number); it was given the names *C.* 'Firebird' and *C.* 'Firebrand' by two different nurseries. It was collected again in

1996 by J. Fryer (*JFYU 098*) in Yunnan, between Xiao Zhongdian and Qiastou, Thong Giang gorge. *Cotoneaster ignescens* gives an excellent show in the autumn with its bright fruit, which in mild winters can last until January, and vivid autumn leaf color.

10. *Cotoneaster lancasteri* J. Fryer & B. Hylmö in New Plantsman 8: 233, 237 (2001).
Type: China, NW Sichuan, Wolong Valley, 6 August 1986, *R. Lancaster 1527* [cult. Sweden, Bjuv, type collected 5 July 1996, Bertil Hylmö] (holo E). **PLATE 138.**
Shrub, 1.5–2.5 m. Branches erect, arched and spreading; branchlets distichous, reddish brown, initially strigose. Leaves deciduous, chartaceous, on sterile shoots obovate or elliptic, 65–100 × 33–46 mm, apex long-acuminate, base cuneate, obtuse, upper surface slightly bullate, mid-green, slightly shiny, glabrous, veins 6–10 impressed, lower surface sparsely yellowish villous-strigose more dense on veins; petiole 3–5 mm, strigose. Fertile shoots 30–70 mm, including 2–6 leaves, and a very lax, 7- to 20-flowered inflorescence; pedicels 1–8 mm, glabrous; flowers (including hypanthium) 5–6 mm long. Hypanthium cupulate, glabrescent; sepals acute or obtuse, glabrous, margin sparsely villous. Corolla closed or with small opening; petals white with red base. Stamens 20; filaments off-white or pale pink; anthers white. Fruit depressed globose, 6–7 mm, maroon to purple-black, shiny, glabrous, calyx lobes flat. Nutlets (3–)4–5, style remains $^2/_3$ from base.

Seasons: Flowers June–July, reflowers September; fruit ripe September–October; autumn leaves bright orange-red.

Chromosomes: Unknown. Apomictic, true from seed.

Hardiness: −18°C (−1°F).

Area: China (Sichuan).

Notes: *Cotoneaster lancasteri* is a really handsome shrub with numerous clusters of fruit which are initially red, but when fully ripened hang on long red pedicels along the undersides of the branches and resemble little blackcurrants. Recently reintroduced into cultivation.

11. *Cotoneaster moupinensis* Franchet in Nouv. Arch. Mus. Hist. Nat., ser. 2, 8: 224 (1885). Type: China, Sichuan, Moupine, June 1869, A. David (holo P). **PLATE 139.**
Shrub or small tree, 3–4 m. Branches erect, arched and spreading; branchlets distichous, brown, initially pilose-strigose. Leaves deciduous, subcoriaceous, on sterile shoots elliptic, broadly elliptic, obovate or ovate, 65–130 × 30–48 mm, apex acuminate, base obtuse, cuneate or truncate, upper surface bullate, dark green, slightly shiny, glabrescent, veins 8–11 impressed, lower surface light green, villous; petiole 1–4 mm, pilose-strigose. Fertile shoots 40–100 mm, including 3–4 leaves and a lax, 15- to 50-flowered inflorescence; pedicels 1–4 mm, strigose; flowers (including hypanthium) 5–6 mm long. Hypanthium cupulate, glabrescent; sepals acute or obtuse, glabrescent, margin sparsely villous. Corolla closed; petals erect-incurved, pink or red with purple-red, border white. Stamens 20; filaments pale pink; anthers white. Fruit depressed globose, 9–10 mm, purple-black, shiny, glabrous, calyx lobes flat, navel open. Nutlets (4–)5, style remains $^2/_3$ from base.

Seasons: Flowers May–June, reflowers September; fruit ripe September-October; autumn leaves dark red-purple.

Chromosomes: Tetraploid (Kroon 1975). Apomictic, true from seed.

Hardiness: –18°C (–1°F).

Area: China (Sichuan, Gansu).

Notes: With its spreading habit, shiny black fruit hanging on red pedicels, and rich autumn tints, *Cotoneaster moupinensis* is a handsome species. It is excellent for amenity plantings. It is also tolerant of a certain amount of shade. Recently reintroduced into cultivation.

12. *Cotoneaster obscurus* Rehder & E. H. Wilson in Sargent, Pl. Wilson. 1: 161 (1912).
Type: China, W Sichuan, Pan-lan Shan, west of Kuan-hsien, October 1910, *E. H. Wilson 4306* (holo A, iso K).

Shrub, 2–2.5 m. Branches erect and arched; branchlets distichous, maroon, initially yellowish strigose. Leaves deciduous, subcoriaceous, on sterile shoots elliptic, broadly elliptic or ovate, 25–45 × 12–28 mm, apex acuminate, base obtuse or cuneate, upper surface bullate, dark green, slightly shiny, initially strigose, veins 3–5 impressed, lower surface slightly reticulate, yellowish tomentose-villous; petiole 2–4 mm, strigose. Fertile shoots 25–40 mm, including 4–5 leaves and a compact, 7- to 12-flowered inflorescence; pedicels 3–10 mm, strigose; flowers (including hypanthium) 5–6 mm. Hypanthium cupulate, strigose; sepals acute, obtuse or apiculate, strigose, border broad, reddish, glabrous, margin villous. Corolla closed; petals erect-incurved, pink and greenish white with dark red, few hairs on lower surface. Stamens (16–)20; filaments red and pink; anthers white. Fruit shortly obovoid, 7–9, red to maroon, shiny, glabrous, calyx lobes flat, sparsely pilose. Nutlets 3–4(–5), style remains 2/3 from base.

Seasons: Flowers June–July; fruit ripe September–October; autumn leaves purple and red.

Chromosomes: Tetraploid (Zeilinga 1964). Apomictic, true from seed.

Hardiness: –21°C (–6°F).

Area: China (Sichuan, Gansu).

Notes: *Cotoneaster obscurus* is fairly common in cultivation. This bushy shrub has numerous shiny, rich maroon fruit. Sometimes, although looking nothing like this species, it is found in cultivation as *C. apiculatus*.

13. *Cotoneaster ogisui* J. Fryer & B. Hylmö, *sp. nov.* Type: China, Sichuan, Yinqiing,
20 October 1995, *M. Ogisu 95105* (holo TI). **PLATE 140**.

Shrub, 3–5 m. Branches erect, arched, coarse; branchlets distichous; branchlets erect, arched, coarse, maroon, shiny lenticellate, initially densely strigose. Leaves deciduous, subcoriaceous, on sterile shoots ovate or elliptic, 90–170 × 55–70 mm, apex acuminate, base truncate, subauriculate, rarely rotund, upper surface strongly bullate, dark green, dull, pilose-villous, veins 8–10 impressed, lower surface yellow villous veins and midrib dense, petiole 1–2 mm, strigose. Fertile shoots 120–150 mm, including 2–4 leaves and a lax, 10- to 50-flowered inflorescence; pedicels 3–10 mm, strigose; flowers (including hypanthium) 6–8 mm long. Hypanthium cupulate, strigose, sepals acute or obtuse, glabrous, margin villous. Corolla closed or opening small; petals erect-incurved, maroon and off-white with brownish margin. Stamens 20; filaments white or very pale pink; anthers white. Fruit depressed-obovoid, 7–11 mm, orange-red to bright red, shiny, glabrous, calyx lobes depressed. Nutlets 4(–5), style remains ²/₃ from base.

Seasons: Flowers June–July; fruit ripe October–November; autumn leaves shades of gold.

Chromosomes: Tetraploid (Jewsbury, pers. comm.).

Hardiness: −18°C (−1°F).

Area: China (Sichuan).

Notes: *Cotoneaster ogisui* is a magnificent species with branches bowed in autumn due to the weight of the numerous, huge fruit. It is newly introduced into cultivation by the intrepid plant collector Mikinori Ogisu who has discovered some fine new species during his travels. Not common in cultivation. Not in key.

14. *Cotoneaster pseudoobscurus* J. Fryer & B. Hylmö *sp. nov.* Type: China, Sichuan,
Kangding, Yulingkong, 17 October 1934, *Harry Smith 12805* (holo UPS). PLATE 141.
Shrub, 3–4 m. Branches narrowly erect and arched; branchlets distichous, slender, maroon, initially yellowish strigose. Leaves deciduous, subcoriaceous, on sterile shoots elliptic or lanceo-elliptic, 30–44 × 13–22 mm, apex acuminate, base obtuse or cuneate, upper surface bullate, dark green, slightly shiny, initially pilose-strigose, veins 4–7 impressed, lower surface tomentose-villous; petiole 4–6 mm, pilose-strigose. Fertile shoots 25–50 mm, including 4–5 leaves and a lax, 7- to 25-flowered inflorescence; pedicels 3–10 mm, strigose; flowers (including hypanthium) 5–6 mm long. Hypanthium cupulate, strigose; sepals acute, acuminate or obtuse, strigose, border broad, reddish brown, glabrous, margin villous. Corolla closed; petals erect-incurved, off-white, pale pink and greenish white with red or pink base. Stamens 20; filaments pale pink and white; anthers white. Fruit obovoid, 8–10 mm, maroon, pruinose (dropping purple-black), glabrous, calyx lobes flat. Nutlets (3–)4–5, style remains ²/₃ from base.

Seasons: Flowers June–July; fruit ripe September–October.

Chromosomes: Unknown. Apomictic, true from seed.

Hardiness: −21°C (−6°F).

Area: China (Sichuan).

Notes: *Cotoneaster pseudoobscurus* is rare in cultivation, although it can sometimes found in cultivation as *C. reticulatus*. Good autumn color.

15. *Cotoneaster rehderi* Pojarkova in Not. Syst. Inst. Bot. Acad. Sci. USSR 17: 184
(1955). Synonym: *C. bullatus* Bois var. *macrophyllus* Rehder & E. H. Wilson (1912).

Type: China, W Sichuan, Wa Shan, September 1908, *E. H. Wilson 873* (holo A, iso K). **PLATE 142.**

Shrub, 2–5 m. Branches erect and arched; branchlets distichous or spiraled, maroon, lenticellate, initially pilose-strigose. Leaves deciduous, subcoriaceous, on sterile shoots elliptic or obovate, 70–210 × 45–90 mm, apex acuminate or acute, base cuneate, obtuse, truncate or auriculate, upper surface strongly bullate, mid-green, shiny, initially sparsely pilose, veins 8–11 deeply impressed, lower surface light green, initially yellowish strigose; petiole absent to 3 mm, pilose-strigose. Fertile shoots 60–120 mm, including 4 leaves and a 10- to 30-flowered inflorescence; pedicels 2–4 mm, pilose-strigose; flowers (including hypanthium) 5–6 mm long. Hypanthium shallowly cupulate, shiny, sparsely pilose-strigose; sepals acute, shiny, glabrous, margin villous. Corolla closed; petals erect-incurved, red or maroon with pink border. Stamens 20; filaments pink; anthers white. Fruit globose or depressed globose, 8–11 mm, cardinal-red, shiny, calyx lobes flat, glabrous. Nutlets 4–5, style remains ³/₄ from base.

Seasons: Flowers May–June; fruit ripe October; autumn leaves intense butter yellow and reddish purple.

Chromosomes: Unknown. Apomictic, true from seed.

Hardiness: −18°C (−1°F).

Area: China (Sichuan, Yunnan).

Notes: *Cotoneaster rehderi* is a large, extremely handsome shrub with the shiny, rich red fruit contrasting well with an outstanding display of autumn leaf color. The species has been collected Keith Rushforth (*KR 158*) in Sichuan, Emei Shan, below Leidonping, in 1980. Received RHS Award of Merit in 1912.

16. *Cotoneaster reticulatus* Rehder & E. H. Wilson in Sargent, Pl. Wilson. 1: 160 (1912). Type: China, W Sichuan, west and near Wen-chuan Hsien, 15 October 1910, *E. H. Wilson 4191* (holo A, iso K).

Small tree, 2.5–4 m. Branches erect, spreading; branchlets distichous, maroon, initially villous-strigose. Leaves deciduous, subcoriaceous, on sterile shoots elliptic, 25–35 × 10–16 mm, apex acuminate or acute-apiculate, base obtuse, broadly cuneate or truncate, upper surface glabrous, strongly bullate, dark green, slightly shiny, veins 4–8 deeply impressed, lower surface tomentose-villous; petiole 2–5 mm, densely pilose-strigose. Inflorescence 35–50 mm, including 3–5 leaves and a 10- to 40-flowered inflorescence; pedicels 2–5 mm, strigose-pilose; flowers (including hypanthium) 6–7 mm long. Hypanthium cupulate, strigose-pilose; sepals acute, obtuse, apiculate, densely villous. Corolla closed; petals erect-incurved, brownish green, greenish off-white and red. Stamens 20; filaments pale pink; anthers white. Fruit obovoid or depressed-globose, 6–8 mm, rich red to maroon, subglabrous, calyx lobes slightly depressed. Nutlets (3–)5.

Seasons: Flowers May–June; fruit ripe September–October.

Hardiness: −18°C (−1°F).

Area: China (Sichuan).

Notes: *Cotoneaster reticulatus* has been reintroduced into cultivation by Mikinori Ogisu (*MO 94307*). In his original description, Ernest Wilson described the fruit as black, but also referred to *C. reticulatus* as resembling *C. obscurus*, which is maroon-fruited, without mentioning the difference in fruit color. It may have been that when Wilson collected fruit of *C. reticulatus* it was already past its prime. Not in key.

17. *Cotoneaster sikangensis* Flinck & B. Hylmö in Bot. Not. (Lund) 115: 376 (1962).
    Synonym: *C. franchetii* Bois in Rehder & E. H. Wilson (1912). Type: China, Sichuan, Kangding, Cheto valley, 20 October 1934, *Harry Smith 12928* (holo UPS, iso BM).
    PLATE 143.
Shrub, 2–4 m. Branches narrowly erect; branchlets distichous, maroon, initially yellowish pilose-strigose. Leaves deciduous, subcoriaceous, on sterile shoots ovate, 26–40 × 13–24 mm, apex acuminate or acute, base obtuse or cuneate, upper surface bullate, dark green, shiny, pilose-strigose, veins 4–6 impressed, lower surface densely villous-pilose; petiole 2–4 mm, pilose-strigose. Fertile shoots 25–40 mm, including 4 leaves and a 3- to 15-flowered inflorescence; pedicels 2–3 mm, strigose; flowers (including hypanthium) 6–7 mm long. Hypanthium infundibulate, strigose; sepals acuminate or acute, strigose, border broad, reddish brown, glabrous, margin long-haired villous. Corolla closed or small opening; petals erect-incurved, pink with greenish brown or white stripe, border off-white. Stamens 20; filaments pale pink; anthers white. Fruit obovoid, 9–11 mm, orange-red, shiny, subglabrous, calyx lobes flat. Nutlets 3–5, mostly 5, style remains $^2/_3$ from base.
    Seasons: Flowers June–July; fruit ripe October; autumn leaves red.
    Chromosomes: Triploid (Klotz 1968b; Kroon 1975).
    Hardiness: −21°C (−6°F).
    Area: China (Sichuan).
    Notes: In the 1970s at the National Botanic Gardens, Glasnevin, in Ireland, a shrub of *Cotoneaster sikangensis* was found still bearing its original label as *C. franchetii* W. 995 3-09, confirming that the number W. 995 had been carefully preserved at Glasnevin for more than 60 years. *Cotoneaster sikangensis* is of considerable garden merit, very hardy, with fruit produced in numerous quantities and striking autumn leaf color.

18. *Cotoneaster taiwanensis* J. Fryer & B. Hylmö, *sp. nov.*; illustr. Formosan Trees, R. Kanehira 258: 202 (1936), as *C. konishii*, non Hayata, excluding (C) flower. Also in Woody Flora of Taiwan, Hui-Sin Li p. 270 (1963), as *C. konishii*, non Hayata.
    Type: Plants of Formosa (Taiwan), Nokozan, 1919, *Matuda-Eizi 2829* (holo LD).
Shrub or small tree, 3–6 m. Leaves deciduous, chartaceous, on sterile shoots narrowly elliptic, 68–70 × 28–32 mm, apex acuminate, base cuneate, upper surface bullate, dark green, sparsely long-haired pilose, veins 6–9 impressed, lower surface pilose-strigose; petiole 2–5 mm, sparsely strigose. Fertile shoots 30–50 mm, including 4 leaves, and a lax, 7- to 20-flowered inflorescence; pedicels 2–8 mm, strigose; flowers (including hypanthi-

um) 5–6 mm long. Hypanthium infundibulate, strigose; sepals obtuse or acute, glabrescent, margin tomentose. Petals erect, red and pink. Stamens c. 20; filaments red and pink; anthers probably white. Fruit probably maturing red (unripe), calyx lobes flat. Nutlets 3–5, style remains ¹/₂ from base.

Area: Taiwan.

Notes: *Cotoneaster taiwanensis*, a large shrub or small tree, is confused in literature with *C. konishii*, which is a small shrub of 1–1.5 m high, with leaves 15–25 mm long and fruit containing 2 nutlets. *Cotoneaster taiwanensis* is not known in cultivation. The above description is compiled from the type specimen.

19. *Cotoneaster wanbooyensis* J. Fryer & B. Hylmö, *sp. nov.* Type: China, Guizhou, Wan
   Boo Yen, 18 October 1985, *Simmons, Fliegner & Russell 116* (holo K). **PLATE 144.**
Shrub or small tree, 2–3 m. Branches erect, arched and spreading; branchlets distichous, maroon, initially strigose. Leaves deciduous, subcoriaceous, on sterile shoots elliptic, 85–110 × 40–55 mm, apex acuminate or acute, base cuneate or obtuse, upper surface strongly bullate, brownish green, soon dark green and intensely shiny, sparsely strigose-pilose, veins 7–9 deeply impressed, lower surface sparsely villous, more dense on veins; petiole 2–4 mm, strigose. Fertile shoots 30–90 mm, including 2–4 leaves, and a lax, 15- to 50-flowered inflorescence; pedicels 2–8 mm, strigose; flowers (including hypanthium) 5–7 mm long. Hypanthium cupulate, villous-strigose; sepals obtuse or acute, glabrous, margin villous. Corolla closed or small opening; petals erect-incurved, dark red with pale pink border. Stamens 20; filaments red and pink; anthers white. Fruit depressed globose or obovoid, 8–11 mm, red to ruby, shiny, subglabrous, calyx lobes flat. Nutlets 4(–5), rarely 3, style remains ²/₃ from base.

Seasons: Flowers June–July; fruit ripe September–October; autumn leaves rich yellow to gold.

Chromosomes: Unknown. Apomictic, true from seed.

Hardiness: –18°C (–1°F).

Area: China (Guizhou).

Notes: *Cotoneaster wanbooyensis* is one of the few species of *Cotoneaster* found in the Chinese province of Guizhou (formerly Kweichow).

27. Series *Shannanense* J. Fryer & B. Hylmö in New Plantsman 8: 237 (2001).
Shrubs medium to large. Leaves 16–36 mm, upper surface flat, dark green, dull; veins 3–5. Fertile shoots 15–35 mm, including 2- to 9-flowered inflorescence; pedicels 3–9 mm. Corolla open; petals dark red and pink with off-white. Filaments red sometimes with pink apex; anthers often pinkish in bud. Fruit red, ruby, or maroon.

Early to late season.

China (Yunnan). Tibet.

3 species: *C. kingdonii*, *C. shannanensis*, *C. yui*.

Key to Series *Shannanense*

1a. Leaves broadly elliptic or suborbicular, veins not impressed or lightly impressed; inflorescence 3- to 5-flowered; fruit ruby to maroon . . . .*C. yui*
1b. Leaves elliptic or broadly elliptic, veins impressed; inflorescence 3- to 9-flowered; fruit red
. . . .**2**
2a. Leaves elliptic, lower surface densely villous, petiole 3–4 mm; petals glabrous; nutlets (2–)3–4(–5) . . . .*C. kingdonii*
2b. Leaves broadly elliptic, lower surface pilose, petiole 4–6 mm; petals often few hairs at base; nutlets 2(–3) . . . .*C. shannanensis*

1. *Cotoneaster kingdonii* J. Fryer & B. Hylmö in New Plantsman 8: 233, 237 (2001).
Type: SE Tibet, Ata, Zayul, Rong-Tu Chu valley, September 1933, *F. Kingdon Ward 10901* (holo BM). PLATE 145.
Shrub, 3–4 m. Branches erect and arched; branchlets distichous, maroon, initially yellowish pilose-strigose. Leaves deciduous, chartaceous, on sterile shoots elliptic, 16–32 × 10–18 mm, apex acute, or acuminate, mucronulate, base cuneate or obtuse, upper surface dark green, dull, pilose, veins 3–4 impressed, lower surface grayish green, densely villous; petiole 3–4 mm, pilose-strigose. Fertile shoots erect, 20–35 mm, including 3–4 leaves and a 3- to 7-flowered inflorescence; pedicels 3–6 mm, pilose-strigose; flowers (including hypanthium) 4–6 mm long. Hypanthium cupulate, pilose-strigose; sepals cuspidate, acuminate or acute, pilose, border membranous, brownish red, margin villous. Corolla with small opening; petals erect-incurved, pink with blackish red base and off-white border. Stamens (17–)20; filaments dark red with pink apex; anthers white. Fruit obovoid, 8–10 mm, red, shiny, sparsely pilose, calyx lobes flat, pilose, margin villous. Nutlets 3–4(–5), rarely 2, style remains $^2/_3$ from base.
Seasons: Flowers June–July; fruit ripe October; autumn leaves red and purple.
Chromosomes: Triploid (Bailey, pers. comm.; Jewsbury, pers. comm.).
Hardiness: −21°C (−6°F).
Area: Tibet. China (Yunnan).
Notes: *Cotoneaster kingdonii* can be found in cultivation in several botanic gardens and large private collections. A good shrub for its combination of fruit and lovely autumn leaf color. *Cotoneaster kingdonii* has also been collected by Keith Rushforth (*KR 2787*) in Yunnan, Xiao Zhongdian, in 1993.

2. *Cotoneaster shannanensis* J. Fryer & B. Hylmö in New Plantsman 8: 234, 237 (2001). Type: SE Tibet, Kongbo province, Molo, Lilung Chu, 26 June 1938, *F. Ludlow, G. Sherriff & G. Taylor 5671* (holo BM).
Shrub, 2–3 m. Branches erect and arched; branchlets distichous, brown-purple, initially pilose-strigose. Leaves deciduous, chartaceous, on sterile shoots broadly elliptic, 24–30 × 15–20 mm; apex acute, sometimes acuminate, base cuneate or obtuse, upper surface dark

green, dull, sparsely pilose, veins 3–5 impressed, lower surface grayish green, pilose; petiole 4–6 mm, pilose. Fertile shoots erect, 20–35 mm, including 3–4 leaves and a lax, 3- to 9-flowered inflorescence; pedicels 2–5 mm, pilose; flowers (including hypanthium) 5–7 mm long. Hypanthium turbinate, pilose-strigose; sepals cuspidate, apiculate and acute, sparsely pilose, margin villous. Corolla with large opening; petals erect-incurved, pink with dark red base and white and pink border, often few hairs at base. Stamens (17–)20; filaments red, apex pink; anthers white (pinkish in bud). Fruit obovoid, 9–10 mm, red, shiny, glabrescent, calyx lobes flat, glabrescent, margin villous. Nutlets 2(–3), style remains $^2/_3$ from base.

Seasons: Flowers June–July; fruit ripe September; autumn leaves coppery red and purple.

Chromosomes: Tetraploid (Bailey, pers. comm.; Jewsbury, pers. comm.). Apomictic, true from seed.

Hardiness: −21°C (−6°F).

Area: Tibet. China (Yunnan).

Notes: *Cotoneaster shannanensis* has been in cultivation since at least 1934, mostly as *C. desfontanesii* or *C. racemiflorus* var. *desfontanesii*. Neat and fairly dense in habit, abundant pink-red flowers followed by shiny red fruit and a magnificent, long lasting display of autumn leaf color. *Cotoneaster shannanensis* has also been collected Keith Rushforth (*KR 4178*) in the Zhongdian-Yangtze of Yunnan at Chong Jiang He gorge in 1996.

3. *Cotoneaster yui* J. Fryer & B. Hylmö in New Plantsman 8:235, 237 (2001). Type: China, NW Yunnan, Zhongdian plateau, 11 November 1937, *T. T. Yu 13693* (holo E, iso BM).

Shrub, to 3 m. Branches erect and arched; branchlets distichous, brown-purple, initially densely pilose-strigose. Leaves deciduous, chartaceous, on sterile shoots broadly elliptic or suborbicular, 25–36 × 19–24 mm, apex acuminate or apiculate, mucronulate, base obtuse or cuneate, upper surface dark green, dull, pilose-strigose, veins 3–4 sometimes lightly impressed, lower surface grayish green, pilose; petiole 3–5 mm, pilose. Fertile shoots erect, 15–25 mm, including 4 leaves, and a 3- to 5-flowered inflorescence; pedicels 3–6 mm, pilose-strigose; flowers (including hypanthium) 5–6 mm long. Hypanthium cupulate, pilose-strigose; sepals cuspidate or acuminate, sparsely villous, border membranous, mostly purple, glabrous, margin villous. Corolla open; petals erect-incurved, red and pink with dark red, border pale pink or white. Stamens (16–)20; filaments dark red, apex pink; anthers white. Fruit obovoid, 9–12 mm, ruby to maroon, shiny, sparsely pilose, calyx lobes flat, tips erect. Nutlets (2–)3, rarely 4, style remains $^2/_3$ from base.

Seasons: Flowers May–July; fruit ripe September; autumn leaves intense purple.

Chromosomes: Unknown. Apomictic, true from seed.

Hardiness: −18°C (−1°F).

Area: China (Yunnan).

Notes: *Cotoneaster yui* has been in cultivation in numerous botanic gardens and collections since its introduction in 1937. Outstanding in its combination of numerous rich red fruit and spectacular autumn leaf color. Named in honor of Tse Tsun Yu (1908–1986) of the Institute of Botany, Chinese Academy of Sciences, Beijing, who introduced many new and valuable cotoneasters to Western gardens. The species has been collected by Jeanette Fryer (*JFYU 084*) in Yunnan in 1996.

28. Series *Glomerulati* Flinck & B. Hylmö in Bot. Not. (Lund) 119: 455 (1966).

Medium to large shrubs. Leaves deciduous or semievergreen, upper flat or bullate; veins impressed. Inflorescences compact. Corolla with small opening. Fruit mostly small (5–9 mm), globose, orange-red, rich red, ruby, or black, very shiny.

Early to late season.

China (Yunnan, Hubei, Sichuan).

7 species: *C. camilli-schneideri*, *C. cinerascens*, *C. daliensis*, *C. foveolatus*, *C. glomerulatus*, *C. kuanensis*, *C. tengyuehensis*.

Key to Series *Glomerulati*

1a. Upper leaf surface glabrous or nearly so, veins 4–8; nutlets 2–4(–5); fruit dark red or black
. . . .**2**

1b. Upper leaf surface strigose, veins 3–5; nutlets 3–5; fruit orange-red or red. **4**

2a. Leaves mostly obovate; inflorescence 3- to 4(–5)-flowered; fruit black . . . .*C. foveolatus*

2b. Leaves elliptic, ovate or lanceolate; inflorescence 3- to 20-flowered; fruit red **3**

3a. Leaves ≤ 88 mm, upper surface purple-red later blackish green, dull, veins lightly
impressed; nutlets (2–)3(–4); fruit subglobose, 7–9 mm . . . .*C. camilli-schneideri*

3b. Leaves ≤ 65 mm, upper surface light green, intensely shiny, veins deeply impressed;
nutlets (2–)3–4(–5); fruit globose, 5–7 mm. . . . . *C. glomerulatus*

4a. Leaves elliptic or broadly elliptic; inflorescence mostly 3- to 15-flowered; hypanthium
campanulate or cupulate **5**

4b. Leaves ovate or elliptic; inflorescence 3- to 9-flowered; hypanthium cupulate **6**

5a. Leaves chartaceous to subcoriaceous; hypanthium campanulate to cupulate, densely
strigose; sepals acuminate or cuspidate, densely pilose-strigose; fruit strigose . . . .
. . . .*C. daliensis*

5b. Leaves thinly chartaceous; hypanthium cupulate, sparsely strigose; sepals apiculate, acute
or acuminate, sparsely strigose or subglabrous; fruit sparsely pilose . . . . *C. kuanensis*

6a. Leaves dull; fertile shoots 40–60 mm; sepals mostly obtuse or acute; petals greenish white
with pink stripes. . . . .*C. cinerascens*

6b. Leaves shiny; fertile shoots 25–40 mm; sepals acuminate or cuspidate; petals dark red and
white . . . . *C. tengyuehensis*

1. *Cotoneaster camilli-schneideri* Pojarkova in Not. Syst. Inst. Bot. Acad. Sci. USSR 17: 180 (1955). Type: China, Hubei, 1889, *A. Henry 6750* (holo LE). PLATE 147.

Shrub, 1.5–2 m. Branches erect, arched; branchlets distichous, maroon, initially strigose. Leaves deciduous, chartaceous on sterile shoots elliptic or lanceolate, 62–88 × 24–40 mm, apex acuminate or acute, base cuneate, upper surface red-purple, slowly becoming very dark green, dull, glabrous, veins 5–8 lightly impressed, lower surface green, sparse strigose hairs more dense on midrib; petiole 6–9 mm, sparsely strigose. Fertile shoots 25–50 mm, including 3–5 leaves and a compact, 2- to 20-flowered inflorescence; pedicels 2–10 mm, strigose; flowers (including hypanthium) 5–7 mm long. Hypanthium cupulate, strigose; sepals acute or acuminate, strigose, margin villous. Corolla closed or with small opening; petals erect-incurved, red with blackish red, border white. Stamens c. 20; filaments white to pink; anthers white. Fruit subglobose, 7–9 mm, red, shiny, sparsely strigose, calyx lobes flat, navel wide open. Nutlets 2–3, rarely 4, style remains ³/₄ from base.

Seasons: Flowers May–June; fruit ripe September–October; autumn leaves purple-red.

Chromosomes: Unknown. Apomictic, true from seed.

Hardiness: −18°C (−1°F).

Area: China (Hubei).

Notes: Despite the divergence of some details with Antonina Pojarkova's description, and following close scrutiny of the type specimen, it is certain that the Sino-American Botanical Expedition (SABE) collections are *C. camilli-schneideri*. Pojarkova states that the leaf apex is shortly acute or sometimes obtuse, but this does not fit well with her description of the many (6–8 pairs) veins. The type specimen has 2- to 3-flowered inflorescences but in cultivation inflorescence is frequently 10- to 20-flowered. *Cotoneaster camilli-schneideri* has been introduced into cultivation from SABE collections (*#1789* and *#1801*). It is a striking *Cotoneaster* with unusual, rich red-purple leaves which later in the season become blackish green, the dark flowers and leaves together are a beautiful sight, and the rich-colored fruit are very handsome.

2. **Cotoneaster cinerascens** (Rehder) Flinck & B. Hylmö in Bot. Not. (Lund) 115: 383 (1962). Synonym: *C. franchetii* Bois var. *cinerascens* Rehder (1923). Type: cult. United States, Oregon, Beaverton, Weed Landscape Nursery, *Cotoneaster* sp. Schneider 309, June 1922, H. Weed (holo A).

Shrub, 2–3 m. Branches erect and arched; branchlets distichous, light brown, initially densely strigose. Leaves deciduous or semievergreen, chartaceous, on sterile shoots ovate or elliptic, 37–47 × 15–20 mm, apex acuminate or acute, base cuneate, upper surface dark to mid-green, dull, densely strigose, veins 4–5 impressed, lower surface densely villous-strigose; petiole 3–5 mm, strigose. Fertile shoots 40–60 mm, including 4–5 leaves and a compact, 3- to 9-flowered inflorescence; pedicels 2–4 mm, strigose; flowers Including hypanthium) 5–6 mm long. Hypanthium cupulate, densely strigose; sepals obtuse, acute or acuminate, tomentose-strigose, margin villous. Corolla with small opening; petals erect-incurved, greenish white and pink. Stamens 20; filaments pink; anthers white. Fruit globose or obovoid, 7–9 mm, orange-red to red, shiny, sparse strigose hairs more dense at apex, calyx lobes flat, densely strigose, navel slightly open. Nutlets (3–)4(–5), style remains ½ from base.

Seasons: Flowers June–July; fruit ripe September–October; autumn leaves green and orange.

Chromosomes: Triploid (Bailey, pers. comm.; Jewsbury, pers. comm.).

Hardiness: −18°C (−1°F).

Area: China (Yunnan).

Notes: *Cotoneaster cinerascens* was originally described from a cultivated shrub, an offspring from the Schneider collection 309 and was distributed in 1915 by the Arnold Arboretum. This number is not among Schneider's herbarium specimens and hence the origin of the holotype is missing. This species did not prove very hardy in the Arnold Arboretum and died. Recent collections from Yunnan display all the characters of the Oregon raised type, including the long fertile shoots. We know that in September of 1914 Schneider traveled from Dali going southwest to Yongping and Yongchang and nearly to the Salween. This is the area in which *C. cinerascens* has been refound by the Chungtien, Lijiang, and Dali expedition (*CLD 1440*). This is probably the area in which Schneider collected his seed 309. This species is very closely related to *C. tengyuehensis*.

3. **Cotoneaster daliensis** J. Fryer & B. Hylmö, *sp. nov.* Type: China, Yunnan, Dali, Tsang Shan, road to Longquan peak, 15 October 1990, Chungtien Lijiang Dali expedition, *CLD 1299* (holo E). **PLATE 148.**

Shrub, 2–3 m. Branches erect, arched; branchlets distichous, maroon, initially densely strigose. Leaves deciduous, chartaceous to subcoriaceous, on sterile shoots elliptic or broadly elliptic, 30–45 × 15–22 mm, apex acuminate or acute, base cuneate or obtuse, upper surface slightly rugose, mid-green, shiny, pilose-strigose, veins 3–5, deeply impressed, lower surface grayish green, pilose-villous; petiole 3–5 mm, pilose-strigose. Fertile shoots 20–40 mm, including 3–4 leaves and a compact, 3- to 7(–14)-flowered inflorescence; pedicels 2–5 mm, pilose-strigose; flowers (including hypanthium) 5–6 mm long. Hypanthium widely cupulate, densely strigose; sepals acuminate or cuspidate, densely pilose-strigose, margin villous. Corolla with small opening; petals erect-incurved, red with broad off-white or greenish white border. Stamens 20; filaments pink; anthers white. Fruit depressed obovoid, 7–9 mm, orange-red to red, strigose, shiny, calyx lobes flat, pilose-strigose. Nutlets 3–4(–5), style remains ¾ from base.

Seasons: Flowers May–July; fruit ripe October–November.

Chromosomes: Tetraploid (McAllister, pers. comm.). Apomictic, true from seed.

Hardiness: −18°C (−1°F).

Area: China (Yunnan).

Notes: *Cotoneaster daliensis* is known at present only from the type collection. This is very closely related to *C. cinerascens*.

4. *Cotoneaster foveolatus* Rehder & E. H. Wilson in Sargent, Pl. Wilson. 1: 162 (1912).
Type: China, W Hubei, Chang-lo Hsien, September 1907, *E. H. Wilson 147* (holo A,
iso K).

Shrub, 3–4 m. Branches narrowly erect; branchlets distichous or spiraled, maroon, minutely verruculose, initially densely villous-strigose. Leaves deciduous, chartaceous, on sterile shoots obovate or elliptic, 60–90 × 25–41 mm, apex acuminate or acute, base cuneate or obtuse, upper surface reddish, shiny, soon light green to mid-green, dull, glabrescent, veins 6–8 deeply impressed, lower surface grayish green, initially strigose-villous; petiole 2–5 mm, villous-strigose. Fertile shoots 20–50 mm, including 3–4 leaves and a (2–)3- to 4(–8)-flowered inflorescence; pedicels 2–5 mm, villous-strigose; flowers (including hypanthium) 5–7 mm long. Hypanthium shallowly cupulate, strigose; sepals acute or apiculate, strigose, border greenish red, glabrous, margin villous. Corolla with small opening; petals erect-incurved, reddish brown with broad off-white or greenish white border. Stamens 18–20; filaments red and pink; anthers white. Fruit globose or depressed globose, 7–8 mm, black, shiny, sparsely hairy, calyx lobes suberect, navel wide open. Nutlets (3–)4–5, style remains ⁴/₅ from base.

Seasons: Flowers May–June; fruit ripe September; autumn leaves orange and scarlet.

Chromosomes: Unknown. Several tetraploid counts for *C. foveolatus* have been reported but it is doubtful whether they were from the correct species.

Hardiness: −18°C (−1°F).

Area: China (Hubei).

Notes: In the 1950s *C. foveolatus* was growing in the Swedish botanic gardens of Copenhagen and Göteborg, as well in the Hesse nursery in Germany. Comparison with the type specimen showed that these were quite likely to be offspring from the type. Most shrubs found in cultivation as *C. foveolatus* belong to other species, frequently *C. hsingshangensis*.

5. *Cotoneaster glomerulatus* W. W. Smith in Not. Roy. Bot. Gard. Edinburgh 10: 21
(1917). Synonyms: *C. nitidifolius* C. Marquand (1930); *C. mingkwongensis* G. Klotz
(1972). Type: China, Yunnan, Shweli valley, September 1913, *G. Forrest 12046* (holo
E, iso K). **PLATE 149.**

Shrub, 2–3 m. Branches erect and arched; branchlets distichous, slender, greenish brown to maroon, initially tomentose-pilose. Leaves deciduous or semievergreen, chartaceous, on sterile shoots ovate or ovate-lanceolate, 45–65 × 15–37 mm, apex acuminate or acute, base cuneate, upper surface slightly rugose, light green, intensely shiny, glabrescent, veins 4–8 deeply impressed, lower surface initially densely pilose-villous; petiole 3–5 mm, pilose-tomentose. Fertile shoots 20–50 mm, including 4 leaves and a compact, 3- to 15-flowered inflorescence; pedicels 2–6 mm, villous-strigose; flowers (including hypanthium) 5–6 mm long. Hypanthium cupulate, densely villous-strigose; sepals acute or acuminate, villous, border broad, glabrous, margin densely villous. Corolla with small opening; petals erect-incurved, pink, margin off-white. Stamens 16–20; filaments pink;

anthers white. Fruit globose, 5–7 mm, red to ruby, shiny, sparsely villous, calyx lobes suberect, villous. Nutlets (2–)3(–4), rarely 5, style remains ³/₄ from base.

Seasons: Flowers June–July; fruit ripe September–November; autumn leaves lime green, gold, and orange.

Chromosomes: Unknown. A sexual, outbreeding species, variable from seed.

Hardiness: –18°C (–1°F).

Area: China (Yunnan).

Notes: *Cotoneaster glomerulatus* is an attractive shrub with leaves which have a rich range of autumn colors which complement the clusters of shiny currantlike fruit. This species has been in cultivation since at least 1924. In 1930 in England at the RBG Kew, Cecil Marquand designated a new species, *C. nitidifolius*, but in 1958 seed of this shrub produced variable offspring—including some identical to *C. glomerulatus*. Also, Klotz described *C. mingkwongensis* in 1972 without taking into account the sexual and variable nature of *C. glomerulatus*.

6. Cotoneaster kuanensis J. Fryer & B. Hylmö, *sp. nov.* Type: China, N Sichuan, Ata Zang, Wen-chuan Hsien, 80 km from Dujiangyan city following the Pitiao river, 11 September 1988, Erskine, Fliegner, Howick, and McNamara, *SICH 56a* (holo K).
   PLATE 150.

Shrub, 2–3 m. Branches loosely erect, arched, spreading; branchlets distichous, maroon, pilose-strigose, glabrescent. Leaves semievergreen, chartaceous, on sterile shoots elliptic or broadly elliptic, 25–40 × 15–26 mm, apex acuminate or acute, base cuneate or obtuse, upper surface becoming dark-green and shiny, densely pilose-strigose, veins 3–4 impressed, lower surface tomentose-pilose; petiole 3–5 mm, strigose. Fertile shoots 20–35 mm, including 3–4 leaves and a compact, 3- to 15-flowered inflorescence; pedicels 1–4 mm, strigose; flowers (including hypanthium) 5–6 mm long. Hypanthium cupulate, sparsely strigose; sepals apiculate, acute or acuminate, glabrescent, border brown, glabrous, margin tomentose. Corolla with small opening; petals erect-incurved, pink or off-white with dark red base. Stamens 20; filaments pink; anthers white. Fruit depressed-globose, 7–8 mm, red, shiny, sparsely pilose, calyx lobes flat, tips erect. Nutlets 3–4(–5), style remains ¹/₂ from base.

Seasons: Flowers July; fruit ripe October–November; autumn leaves gold.

Chromosomes: Tetraploid (Bailey, pers. comm.; Jewsbury, pers. comm.). Apomictic, true from seed.

Hardiness: –18°C (–1°F).

Area: China (Sichuan).

Notes: *Cotoneaster kuanensis* is an unusual shrub which is closely related to *C. glomerulatus* which is a tetraploid, whereas *C. glomerulatus* is a diploid.

7. Cotoneaster tengyuehensis J. Fryer & B. Hylmö in Watsonia 21: 338 (1997). Type: cult. Sweden, Bjuv, garden of B. Hylmö, raised from seed from National Botanic

Gardens at Glasnevin, Ireland, as plant #9876 *C.* 'Tengyueh', 1 July 1974, B. Hylmö (holo E). **PLATE 151.**

Shrub, 2–2.5 m. Branches narrowly erect, arched; branchlets distichous, grayish maroon, initially densely strigose. Leaves semievergreen, chartaceous, on sterile shoots ovate or elliptic, 35–46 × 17–24 mm, apex acuminate or acute, base cuneate or obtuse, upper surface dark to mid-green, shiny, pilose-strigose, veins 3–5 impressed, lower surface grayish green, villous-strigose; petiole 1–4 mm, strigose. Fertile shoots 25–40 mm, including (3–)4 leaves and a compact, (3–)5- to 7(–9)-flowered inflorescence; pedicels 1–4 mm, densely strigose; flowers (including hypanthium) 5–6 mm long. Hypanthium cupulate, strigose; sepals acuminate or cuspidate, strigose, border reddish brown, glabrous, margin villous. Corolla with small opening; petals erect-incurved, dark red or maroon with white border. Stamens 20; filaments pale pink; anthers white. Fruit depressed globose or obovoid, 7–9 mm, red, sparsely strigose, calyx lobes flat or suberect, strigose. Nutlets 3–4(–5), style remains ⅔ from base.

Seasons: Flowers June–July; fruit ripe October–November.

Chromosomes: Tetraploid (Krügel 1992a) as *Cotoneaster* 'New York'. Apomictic, true from seed.

Hardiness: −18°C (−1°F).

Area: China (Yunnan).

Notes: *Cotoneaster tengyuehensis* is an attractive shrub with fruit noticeably ripening in stages showing green, yellow, orange, red to rich red in the same cluster. It has been grown for 40–50 years in the gardens of Europe and the United States, variably named as *C. franchetii*, *C. wardii*, *C. dielsianus*, *C. elegans*, or *C. cinerascens*. In Ireland, at the National Botanic Gardens in Glasnevin, a shrub existed for many years labeled as *Cotoneaster* 'Tengyueh'. In the United States, at the herbarium of the Arnold Arboretum of Harvard University (AAH), are many *Cotoneaster* specimens cultivated in England at the RBG Kew in 1923; among these is *Forrest 12497*, collected in Tengchong (formerly Tengyueh) in the autumn of 1913 on Forrest's 1912–1914 expedition to China (E, BM, K), this is *C. tengyuehensis*, raised at Kew in 1914. Recently reintroduced into cultivation. This species is very closely related to *C. cinerascens*.

9. Section *Franchetioides*, stat. nov. Basionym: series *Franchetioides* Flinck & B. Hylmö in Bot. Not. (Lund) 115: 383 (1962).

Shrubs often dense and multistemmed. Leaves mostly dark green, lower surface tomentose or densely villous. Pedicels short (0.5–6 mm). Hypanthium tomentose, or pilose-strigose; sepals mostly cuspidate or acute. Anthers white, mauve, or pink.

3 series: *Franchetioides, Sterniani, Dielsiani.*

29. Series *Franchetioides* Flinck & B. Hylmö in Bot. Not. 115: 383 (1962). Including series *Yunnanenses* G. Klotz (1972).

Small to large shrubs. Leaves often wide-spaced, evergreen, coriaceous, upper surface flat or slightly rugose, lower surface mostly whitish silky tomentose. Fertile shoots 10–100 mm including up to 60-flowered inflorescence. Hypanthium mostly long-haired silky tomentose; sepals often recurved. Petals semispreading or erect. Anthers mostly mauve or pink becoming purple. Fruit orange. Nutlets mostly 2–3.

Mid to late or very late season.

China (Yunnan, Sichuan). Tibet.

8 species: *C. amoenus, C. franchetii, C. mairei, C. nohelii, C. tardiflorus, C. teijiashanensis, C. vilmorinianus, C. wardii.*

Key to Series *Franchetioides*

1a. Height 1.5–2.5 m; branchlets mostly spiraled or divaricate; leaves 10–22 mm, veins 2–3 2
1b. Height 2–6 m; branchlets distichous; leaves 20–45 mm, veins 3–6 3
2a. Leaves broadly elliptic to suborbicular, upper surface very shiny, veins deeply impressed; inflorescence 1- to 5(–7)-flowered; fruit depressed globose ....*C. teijiashanensis*
2b. Leaves ovate or elliptic, upper surface slightly shiny soon dull, veins lightly impressed; inflorescence 3- to 9(–15)-flowered; fruit ellipsoid .... *C. amoenus*
3a. Fertile shoots 60–100 mm; inflorescence 20- to 80-flowered; hypanthium infundibulate; petals off-white .... *C. tardiflorus*
3b. Fertile shoots 20–80 mm; inflorescence 3- to 20(–25)-flowered; hypanthium cupulate; petals red, pink and white 4
4a. Leaves chartaceous, narrowly elliptic or narrowly ovate, fertile shoots ≤ 80 mm; inflorescence somewhat lax .... *C. wardii*
4b. Leaves subcoriaceous, elliptic or ovate, often broadly so; fertile shoots ≤ 60 mm; inflorescence mostly compact..5
5a. Leaves broadly elliptic or broadly ovate; fruit mostly depressed globose, orange-red becoming red or crimson..6
5b. Leaves ovate or elliptic not broadly so; fruit obovoid, orange-red remaining so 7
6a. Leaves ≤ 42 mm, petiole 3–4 mm; petals erect-incurved; nutlets mostly 2........*C. nohelii*
6b. Leaves ≤ 25 mm, petiole 4–7 mm; petals erect to semispreading; nutlets 2–3.............. ....*C. vilmorinianus*
7a. Fertile shoots 20–35 mm; inflorescence 3- to 7(–15)-flowered; filaments dark red with pink or white apex; anthers white... *C. mairei*
7b. Fertile shoots 30–60 mm; inflorescence 5- to 15(–25)-flowered; filaments purplish pink; anthers pink becoming purple..*C. franchetii*

1. *Cotoneaster amoenus* E. H. Wilson in Gard. Chron. 51: 2 (1912); Pl. Wilson. 1: 165 (1912). Synonym: *C. mairei* H. Léveillé var. *albiflos* H. Léveillé. Type: cult., raised from seed collected on 10 November 1899 some 10 miles southwest of Mengtze, Yunnan, leg. E. H. Wilson, Hort. Veitch coll. Wilson June 1911 (holo A). PLATE 152. Shrub dense, 1.5–2 m. Branches loosely erect, arched, spreading, slender; branchlets divaricate, distichous or spiraled, frequently ending in fertile shoots, maroon, initially tomentose-pilose. Leaves evergreen, coriaceous, on sterile shoots ovate or elliptic, 10–22 × 6–11 mm, apex acute with long mucro, base broadly cuneate, upper surface drying rugose, dark grayish green, slightly shiny soon dull, pilose, veins 2–3 lightly impressed, lower surface greenish white tomentose; petiole 2–5 mm, tomentose. Fertile shoots 20–30 mm, including 3–4 leaves and a compact, 3- to 9(–15)-flowered inflorescence; pedicels 1–4 mm, densely pilose; flowers (including hypanthium) 5–6 mm long. Hypanthium cupulate, densely pilose; sepals recurved, cuspidate or acuminate, densely pilose, border membranous, purple, glabrous, margin villous. Petals semispreading to erect, off-white with small pink dots. Stamens 20; filaments white or pale pink to red; anthers purple to black. Fruit ellipsoid, 6–7 mm, cardinal-red, pilose, calyx lobes erect, tomentose. Nutlets (2–)3, style remains ³/₄ from base.

Seasons: Flowers June–July; fruit ripe November.

Chromosomes: Tetraploid (Jewsbury, pers. comm.; Bailey, pers. comm.). Apomictic, true from seed.

Hardiness: –15°C (5°F).

Area: China (Yunnan).

Notes: *Cotoneaster amoenus* was introduced by Ernest Wilson to the Coombe Wood nursery in London in 1899. This is a good shrub for the smaller garden. Recently reintroduced into cultivation.

2. *Cotoneaster franchetii* Bois in Rev. Hortic. 2: 380 (1902); illustr. Bull. Soc. Bot. France 51: 152 (1904); cf. Curtis's Bot. Mag. 140: t. 8571 (1914). Type: cult. *Cotoneaster* 4535, from seed 1342, Les Barres garden, June 1900, herb. Maurice L. de Vilmorin, type shrub, 24 September 1900 (lecto designated P). PLATE 153.

Shrub, 2–3 m. Branches erect, arched, lax, slender and graceful; branchlets distichous, often ending in fertile shoots, maroon, initially densely pilose-strigose. Leaves evergreen, wide (often to 30–40) mm apart, coriaceous, on sterile shoots ovate or elliptic, 25–37 × 13–19 mm, apex acute or acuminate, base cuneate or obtuse, upper surface drying slightly rugose, grayish green, slightly shiny, pilose, veins 4–5 impressed, lower surface silvery tomentose; petiole 2–4 mm, tomentose-pilose. Fertile shoots 30–60 mm, including 4 leaves and a compact, 5- to 15(–25)-flowered inflorescence; pedicels 1–4 mm, with dense long silky hairs; flowers (including hypanthium) 5–6 mm long. Hypanthium cupulate, with dense long silky hairs; sepals cuspidate or acuminate, with silky hairs, border purple, glabrous, margin villous. Corolla with small opening; petals erect-incurved, pink with dark red, border off-white. Stamens 20; filaments purplish pink; anthers pink to purple. Fruit obovoid, 8–10 mm, orange-red, shiny, sparsely pilose, calyx lobes erect to semispreading, tomentose. Nutlets (2–)3, rarely 4 in apex fruit, style remains ³/₄ from base.

Seasons: Flowers June–July; fruit ripe October–November.

Chromosomes: Tetraploid (Zeilinga 1964; Hensen 1966; Klotz and Krügel 1983a; Bailey, pers. comm.). Apomictic, true from seed.

Hardiness: –15°C (5°F).

Area: China (Yunnan).

Notes: The type specimen of *Cotoneaster franchetii* was probably collected from a plant raised from a Jean Delavay collection from central Yunnan. The species has been common in cultivation since early 1900 in areas of Europe where the winters are not too cold, and on the west coast of North America. Recently reintroduced into cultivation. The shrub is extremely attractive in autumn when weighed down with orange-red, pear-shaped fruit which contrast well with the silvery-gray foliage. It is wind-tolerant and good for planting in coastal regions. Received RHS Award of Merit in 1984.

3. **Cotoneaster mairei** H. Léveillé in Bull. Geogr. Bot. 25: 45 (1915). Synonyms: *C. dielsianus* E. Pritzel f. *major* Rehder & Wilson (1912); *C. franchetii* Bois in Rehder (1932). Type: China, Yunnan, June 1912, E. E. Maire (excluding second branchlet from left) (holo E, iso S).

Shrub, 2–3 m. Branches erect and spreading; branchlets distichous, maroon, initially tomentose-pilose. Leaves evergreen, frequently wide (30–40 mm) apart, coriaceous, on sterile shoots ovate or elliptic, 27–40 × 14–23 mm, apex acuminate or acute, base obtuse or cuneate, upper surface slightly rugose, dark green, shiny, pilose, veins 3–5 impressed, lower surface grayish tomentose-pilose, petiole 2–4 mm, tomentose-pilose. Fertile shoots 20–35 mm, including 4–5 leaves and a compact, 3- to 7(–15)-flowered inflorescence; pedicels 2–5 mm, silky tomentose; flowers (including hypanthium) 6–7 mm long. Hypanthium cupulate, silky tomentose; sepals cuspidate, silky tomentose, border reddish purple, glabrous, margin villous. Corolla with large opening; petals erect, red and pink with dark red base and off-white border. Stamens 20; filaments dark red, apex pink or white; anthers white. Fruit obovoid, 8–9 mm, orange-red, shiny, pilose, calyx lobes 2 flat with remaining three erect, tomentose. Nutlets 2(–3), style remains $^3/_4$ from base.

Seasons: Flowers June–July; fruit ripe October–November.

Chromosomes: Tetraploid (Zeilinga 1964; Jewsbury, pers. comm.). Apomictic, true from seed.

Hardiness: –15°C (5°F).

Area: China (Yunnan).

Notes: *Cotoneaster mairei* has been in cultivation since at least 1914. It is very tough and will grow well even in the poorest of soils; it also seems to be tolerant to intense traffic pollution and so is useful for urban plantings. *Cotoneaster mairei* can be found in many gardens in Europe, as well as in North America, South Africa, and Australia, frequently misnamed as *C. dielsianus* var. *major*, *C. sternianus* or *C. hypocarpus* hort. This species has been rediscovered after an absence of about 80 years. It was found in Yunnan near Kunming in 1980 by Roy Lancaster (*RL 693*).

4. *Cotoneaster nohelii* J. Fryer & B. Hylmö, *sp. nov.* Type: China, Yunnan, north
end of Hoching valley near Hsi-Ho, May 1910, *G. Forrest 5543* (holo E, iso BM).
PLATE 154.

Shrub or small tree, 2–5 m. Branches loosely erect, arched, coarse; branchlets distichous,
maroon, initially grayish tomentose-pilose. Leaves evergreen, coriaceous, on sterile
shoots broadly elliptic or ovate, 20–42 × 14–25 mm, apex acuminate or acute, base obtuse
or cuneate, upper surface slightly rugose, dark green, shiny, pilose, veins 4–5 impressed,
lower surface grayish silky tomentose; petiole 3–5 mm, tomentose. Fertile shoots 25–50
mm, including 4–5 leaves and a compact, 5- to 20-flowered inflorescence; pedicels 1–4
mm, silky tomentose; flowers (including hypanthium) 5–6 mm long. Hypanthium cupulate, silky tomentose; sepals recurved, cuspidate, silky tomentose, margin villous. Corolla with small opening; petals erect-incurved, pink with dark red base and white border.
Stamens (18–)20; filaments pale pink to red; anthers pink to mauve. Fruit depressed-
globose, 9–12 mm, orange-red to red, shiny, sparsely pilose, calyx lobes suberect, pilose.
Nutlets 2(–3), apex tomentose, style remains ³/₄ from base.

Seasons: Flowers June–July; fruit ripe November.

Chromosomes: Unknown. Apomictic, true from seed.

Hardiness: −15°C (5°F).

Area: China (Yunnan).

Notes: *Cotoneaster nohelii* has long been in cultivation, frequently as *C. glaucophyllus*, although not resembling this species. Named in honor of Antonin Nohel, dendrologist and emeritus director of the botanic garden at Mendel University, Brno, Czech Republic, who grew this *Cotoneaster* and insisted it was like nothing else. A good useful
evergreen shrub, heavily fruiting, makes an excellent hedge. Also collected c. 20 km
north of Lijiang, Yunnan, in 1996 by Jeanette Fryer (*JFYU 123*).

5. *Cotoneaster tardiflorus* J. Fryer & B. Hylmö in New Plantsman 5: 139 (1998). Type:
China, SW Sichuan, mountains southwest of Muli, October 1922, *G. Forrest 22952*
(holo E, iso A, K). PLATE 155.

Shrub or small tree, 4–6 m. Branches erect, gracefully arched, wide-spreading; branchlets distichous, purplish brown, initially tomentose. Leaves evergreen, coriaceous, on
sterile shoots elliptic, 23–38 × 13–19 mm, apex acuminate or acute and mucronulate, base
cuneate, upper surface grayish green, slightly shiny, initially pilose, veins 3–4 lightly impressed, lower surface grayish silky tomentose; petiole 4–7 mm, tomentose. Fertile shoots
60–100 mm, including 4 leaves and a somewhat lax, 20- to 60-flowered inflorescence;
pedicels 0.5–3 mm, tomentose. Flower buds white with pale purple stripes. Hypanthium
infundibulate, silky tomentose; sepals recurved, acute, cuspidate, tomentose, margin villous. Corolla 6–8 mm, petals semispreading, off-white with pale pink blotches. Stamens
20; filament white with base pale pink or mauve; anthers mauve to purple-maroon. Fruit
obovoid, 5–7 mm, orange-red, pilose, base tomentose, calyx lobes erect, tomentose. Nutlets 2(–3), style remains ³/₄ from base.

Seasons: Flowers August; fruit ripe December, remaining throughout winter.
Chromosomes: Tetraploid (Jewsbury, pers. comm.). Apomictic, true from seed.
Hardiness: −12°C (10°F).
Area: China (Sichuan, Yunnan).
Notes: Widely distributed, frequently mistakenly as *Cotoneaster pannosus*, *C. tardiflorus* is an elegant, silvery-leaved evergreen shrub, pretty in flower and, due to the extremely late ripening of fruit, good winter garden value, and hence should be much more widely grown. Recently reintroduced into cultivation.

6. ***Cotoneaster teijiashanensis*** J. Fryer & B. Hylmö, *sp. nov.* Type: China, Yunnan, roadside south of Lijiang on way to Dali, 15 September 1987, *C. D. Brickell & A. C. Leslie 12416* (holo WSY, iso E). **PLATE 156.**

Shrub dense, 1.5–2.5 m. Branches narrowly erect and arched, branchlets mostly spiraled, slender, maroon, initially villous. Leaves evergreen, coriaceous, on sterile shoots broadly elliptic, broadly ovate or suborbicular, 10–22 × 8–15 mm, apex acute and mucronate, base obtuse or cuneate, upper surface rugose, dark green, intensely shiny, villous, veins 2–3 deeply impressed, lower surface whitish tomentose; petiole 1–2 mm, tomentose. Fertile shoots 10–30 mm, including 2–4 leaves and a (1–)3- to 5(–7)-flowered inflorescence; pedicels 1–2 mm, tomentose. Hypanthium densely silky pilose, sepals acuminate or cuspidate, tomentose, margin villous. Flowers (including hypanthium) 5–6 mm long; petals erect, off-white with pink. Stamens 20; filaments white or pale pink; anthers off-white with pink to red. Fruit depressed globose or obovoid, 5–7 mm, orange-red to crimson, shiny, calyx lobes erect, tomentose. Nutlets 2(–3), style remains 4/5 from base.
Seasons: Flowers July; fruit ripe October–November.
Chromosomes: Unknown. Apomictic, true from seed.
Hardiness: −15°C (5°F).
Area: China (Yunnan).
Notes: *Cotoneaster teijiashanensis* is dense and narrowly erect in habit with multitudes of flowers and fruit. This species is excellent for hedges. It was also collected by Jeanette Fryer (*JFYU 126*) in Yunnan in 1996.

7. ***Cotoneaster vilmorinianus*** G. Klotz in Wiss. Z. Friedrich-Schiller-Univ. Jena, Math.-Naturwiss. 21: 992 (1972). Type: cultivated in the botanic garden in Halle, Germany, "Maurice Vilmorin 7258" seed from France, herb. Maurice L. de Vilmorin, G. Klotz, 16 June 1962 (holo JE). **PLATE 157.**

Shrub, 2–3 m. Branches erect, arched, slender and graceful; branchlets distichous, maroon, initially tomentose-pilose. Leaves evergreen, coriaceous, on sterile shoots broadly elliptic or ovate, 20–26 × 11–19 mm, apex acute or acuminate, base cuneate or obtuse, upper surface drying slightly rugose, grayish green, slightly shiny, pilose, veins 3–4 impressed, lower surface white-tomentose; petiole 4–7 mm, tomentose-pilose. Fertile shoots 25–50 mm, including 4 leaves and a compact, 7- to 15(–20)-flowered inflorescence; pedicels 1–4 mm, densely silky pilose; flowers (including hypanthium) 5–7 mm long. Hypanthium cupulate, densely silky pilose; sepals recurved, cuspidate or acuminate, border broad, purple, glabrous, margin villous. Petals semispreading, pale mauve with red base. Stamens 20; filaments red and pink; anthers pink-mauve. Fruit depressed-globose or obovoid, 8–9 mm, cardinal-red, shiny, pilose, calyx lobes erect to semispreading, tomentose. Nutlets 2(–3), style remains 3/4 from base.

Seasons: Flowers July; fruit ripe November–December.

Chromosomes: Tetraploid (Klotz and Krügel 1983a). Apomictic, true from seed.

Hardiness: −15°C (5°F).

Area: China (Yunnan).

Notes: *Cotoneaster vilmorinianus* has been in cultivation since around 1920 under various names. The original introduction was probably made by George Forrest from central Yunnan. A very attractive and garden-worthy shrub, it is sometimes found in cultivation mistakenly as *C. pannosus*. Recently reintroduced into cultivation.

8. *Cotoneaster wardii* W. W. Smith, Not. Roy. Bot. Gard. Edinburgh 10: 25 (1917).

Type: SE Tibet, Ka-Gwr-Pw temple, near the Chinese frontier (north of Doker-La), 27 July 1913, *F. Kingdon Ward 916* (holo E iso K). PLATE 158.

Shrub, 2–3 m. Branches loosely erect, arched, spreading; branchlets distichous, brown, initially tomentose-pilose. Leaves semievergreen, wide (30–40 mm) apart, chartaceous, on sterile shoots narrowly elliptic or narrowly ovate, 25–45 × 15–20 mm, apex acuminate or acute, base cuneate or obtuse, upper surface slightly rugose, dark green, glabrescent, veins 4–6 impressed, lower surface silvery silky tomentose; petiole 3–5 mm, tomentose-strigose. Fertile shoots 30–80 mm, including 4–6 leaves and a 3- to 9(–20)-flowered inflorescence; pedicels 2–5 mm, silky pilose; flowers (including hypanthium) 5–6 mm long. Hypanthium cupulate, silky tomentose; sepals cuspidate or acuminate, silky tomentose, border purple, glabrous, margin villous. Petals erect, dark red with white border. Stamens 20; filaments pink and red; anthers white. Fruit obovoid, 9–10 mm, orange-red, villous, calyx lobes flat, densely villous. Nutlets 2–3, style remains 3/4 from base.

Seasons: Flowers June–July; fruit ripe November.

Chromosomes: Tetraploid (Hensen 1966; Bailey, pers. comm.). Apomictic, true from seed.

Hardiness: −15°C (5°F).

Area: Tibet. China (Yunnan).

Notes: *Cotoneaster wardii* is a very attractive shrub not often encountered in cultivation. However, the name *C. wardii* has been used extensively for other taxa including *C. sternianus*, *C. mairei*, and *C. franchetii*. In the type description *C. wardii* is said to have flowers entirely white, but maybe these were taken from a shaded shrub, as the white-bordered petals have a red base. Recently reintroduced into cultivation.

30. Series *Sterniani* J. Fryer & B. Hylmö, J. Bot. Res. Inst. Texas 2 (1). 2008.
Small to medium shrubs, often densely branched. Leaves deciduous or semievergreen, subcoriaceous or coriaceous, upper surface rugose, lower surface tomentose. Fertile shoots 10–70 mm including up to 20-flowered inflorescence. Hypanthium tomentose-pilose. Anthers mostly white. Fruit orange-red. Nutlets (2–)3–4(–5).

Mid to late season.

China (Yunnan, Sichuan). Tibet. Burma.

12 species: *C. aurantiacus, C. elegans, C. fastigiatus, C. huahongdongensis, C. hypo-carpus, C. induratus, C. insculptus, C. leveillei, C. naoujanensis, C. qungbixiensis, C. ster-nianus, C. taofuensis.*

Key to Series *Sterniani*

1a. Leaves ≤ 17–25 mm; fertile shoots 10–30 mm, inflorescence 1- to 4(–7)-flowered 2

1b. Leaves ≤ 25–60 mm; fertile shoots 20–80 mm, inflorescence 3- to 20-flowered 4

2a. Height 1–2 m; leaves 10–20 mm, chartaceous, veins lightly impressed; fertile shoots 10–20 mm; hypanthium strigose or strigose-pilose 3

2b. Height 2–4 m; leaves 18–25 mm, coriaceous, veins deeply impressed; fertile shoots 15–30 mm; hypanthium tomentose-pilose . . . . *C. insculptus*

3a. Leaves suborbicular or broadly elliptic; sepals acuminate or acute, sparsely strigose; stamens 14–18; nutlets 3(–4) . . . .*C. fastigiatus*

3b. Leaves elliptic; sepals cuspidate or acuminate, pilose; stamens 20; nutlets 3–4 roughly equal . . . . *C. aurantiacus*

4a. Leaves narrowly elliptic, ellipto-lanceolate or narrowly ovate, 27–60 mm. 5

4b. Leaves broadly elliptic, suborbicular or ovate, 11–35(–49) mm 6

5a. Leaf apex truncate, fertile shoots ≤ 50 mm, inflorescence 5- to 15-flowered . . . .
. . . .*C. qungbixiensis*

5b. Leaf apex acuminate, fertile shoots ≤ 80 mm, inflorescence 3- to 9-flowered . . . .
. . . . *C. huahongdongensis*

6a. Leaves evergreen or semievergreen; inflorescence 5- to 20-flowered; anthers white with pink or purple. 7

6b. Leaves mostly deciduous; inflorescence 3- to 9-flowered; anthers white. 8

7a. Leaves 37–49 mm, veins 4–5 deeply impressed; fertile shoots ≤ 70 mm; inflorescence compact; sepals acute or acuminate; fruit suborbicular . . . . *C. sternianus*

7b. Leaves 20–30 mm, veins 3–4 lightly impressed; fertile shoots ≤ 50 mm; inflorescence lax; sepals cuspidate or acuminate; fruit obovoid . . . . *C. naoujanensis*

8a. Fertile shoots ≤ 50–60 mm; hypanthium pilose or sericeous; nutlets mostly 3–4. 9

8b. Fertile shoots ≤ 25–40 mm; hypanthium pilose-strigose; nutlets mostly 2–5 10

9a. Leaves subcoriaceous, broadly elliptic or suborbicular, ≤ 20 mm, veins deeply impressed; hypanthium sericeous-tomentose; inflorescence compact; fruit obovoid. . . . .*C. leveillei*

9b. Leaves chartaceous, ovate or elliptic, ≤ 35 mm, veins lightly impressed; hypanthium pilose; inflorescence somewhat lax; fruit mostly depressed-globose . . . .*C. hypocarpus*

10a. Leaves chartaceous, upper surface sparsely pilose; hypanthium infundibulate; sepals
acuminate; fruit depressed globose . . . . ***C. elegans***

10b. Leaves subcoriaceous, upper surface pilose-strigose; hypanthium cupulate; sepals
cuspidate; fruit obovoid **11**

11a. Branchlets, petioles and pedicels tomentose; inflorescence 3- to 5-flowered; nutlets mostly
3–4 . . . . ***C. induratus***

11b. Branchlets, petioles and pedicels strigose-pilose; inflorescence mostly 5- to 9-flowered;
nutlets 3(–5) . . . . ***C. taofuensis***

1. ***Cotoneaster aurantiacus*** J. Fryer & B. Hylmö, *sp. nov.* Type: China, Sichuan,
Kangding, 24 October 1934, *Harry Smith 13000* (holo UPS, iso LD, S). **PLATE 159**.
Shrub dense, 1–2 m. Branches erect, arched and spreading; branchlets distichous, maroon, initially pilose-strigose. Leaves deciduous, chartaceous, on sterile shoots elliptic,
10–20 × 6–13 mm, apex acute or acuminate, base cuneate or obtuse, upper surface slightly
rugose, dark green, shiny, pilose-strigose, veins 3–4 impressed, lower surface whitish
tomentose; petiole 1–3 mm, pilose-strigose. Fertile shoots 10–20 mm, including 2–4
leaves and a 1- to 3(–4)-flowered inflorescence; pedicels 1–3 mm, pilose-strigose; flowers
(including hypanthium) 5–6 mm long. Hypanthium cupulate, pilose-strigose, sepals
cuspidate or acuminate, pilose, margin villous. Corolla closed, petals erect-incurved,
dark red with black base and pink border. Stamens 20; filaments dark red, anthers white.
Fruit depressed-globose or obovoid, 6–8 mm, light orange, shiny, glabrous, calyx lobes
flat, pilose. Nutlets (2–)3–4(–5), style remains $^2/_3$ from base.
Seasons: Flowers June; fruit ripe October–November; autumn leaves orange-red to
bronze.
Chromosomes: Triploid (Bailey, pers. comm.; Jewsbury, pers. comm.).
Hardiness: –18°C (–1°F).
Area: China (Sichuan).
Notes: *Cotoneaster aurantiacus* is a very pretty little shrub, especially in autumn
when a profusion of small, bright pale orange fruit smother the branches among the
dainty little pointed leaves.

2. ***Cotoneaster elegans*** (Rehder & E. H. Wilson) Flinck & B. Hylmö in Bot. Not.
(Lund) 115: 383 (1962). Synonym: *C. dielsianus* E. Pritzel var. *elegans* Rehder &
Wilson (1912). Type: China, W Sichuan, Kangding, October 1908, *E. H. Wilson
1287* (holo A, iso E, K).
Shrub, 1–2 m. Branches erect and arched, slender; branchlets distichous, maroon, initially tomentose-pilose. Leaves deciduous, chartaceous, on sterile shoots elliptic or ovate,
11–28 × 8–14 mm, apex acute, base cuneate or obtuse, upper surface slightly rugose, dark
green, slightly shiny, sparsely pilose, veins 3–4 impressed, lower surface tomentose; petiole 2–3 mm, tomentose-pilose. Fertile shoots 20–30 mm, including 4–5 leaves and a compact, 5- to 9-flowered inflorescence; pedicels 1–3 mm, strigose-pilose; flowers (including

hypanthium) 5–6 mm long. Hypanthium infundibulate, base strigose-pilose; sepals acuminate, tomentose-pilose, margin villous. Corolla closed; petals erect-incurved, red with white border. Stamens (16–)20; filaments red; anthers white. Fruit depressed-globose or obovoid, 6–8 mm, orange-red, shiny, sparsely pilose, calyx lobes flat, tomentose. Nutlets 4(–5), style remains ³⁄₄ from base.

Seasons: Flowers June; fruit ripe October.

Chromosomes: Tetraploid (Klotz 1968b; McAllister, pers. comm.; Bailey, pers. comm.). Despite tetraploid counts, there is strong evidence that this species is not always breeding true.

Hardiness: –18°C (–1°F).

Area: China (Sichuan).

Notes: *Cotoneaster elegans* is a good shrub for autumn color, both fruit and leaves. This species needs further investigation.

3. **Cotoneaster fastigiatus** J. Fryer & B. Hylmö, *sp. nov.* Type: China, Sichuan, Kangding, on sunny slopes, 29 October 1934, *Harry Smith 13023* (holo UPS, iso LD, S). PLATE 160.

Shrub dense, 1.5–2 m. Branches erect and arched, spreading; branchlets distichous, brown, initially pilose-strigose. Leaves deciduous, chartaceous, on sterile shoots suborbicular or elliptic, 12–17 × 8–14 mm, apex acute, base obtuse, upper surface slightly rugose, dark green, shiny, pilose-strigose, veins 3–4 impressed, lower surface whitish tomentose; petiole 2–3 mm, pilose-strigose. Fertile shoots 10–20 mm, including 3–5 leaves and a 1- to 3(–4)-flowered inflorescence; pedicels 1–4 mm, sparsely pilose-strigose; flowers (including hypanthium) 4–6 mm long. Hypanthium cupulate, sparsely strigose; sepals acuminate or acute, sparsely strigose, border broad, purple, glabrous, margin tomentose. Corolla with small opening; petals erect-incurved, red with dark red base. Stamens 14–18; filaments dark red; anthers white. Fruit shortly obovoid, 8–9 mm, orange to orange-red, shiny, glabrous, calyx lobes flat, pilose. Nutlets 3(–4), style remains ²⁄₃ from base.

Seasons: Flowers June–July; fruit ripe September–October.

Chromosomes: Unknown. Apomictic, true from seed.

Hardiness: –18°C (–1°F).

Area: China (Sichuan).

Notes: *Cotoneaster fastigiatus* has a neat, erect (somewhat fastigiate) habit and hence is good for the smaller garden. Fruits well.

4. **Cotoneaster huahongdongensis** J. Fryer & B. Hylmö, *sp. nov.* Type: China, Yunnan, western hills of Kunming, Hua Hong Dong, October 1980, *H. van de Laar 80654* [cult. Netherlands, Wageningen BG, 86BG N1003, September 1998] (holo WAG). PLATE 161.

Shrub, 2–3 m. Branches erect, arched; branchlets distichous, maroon, initially tomentose-pilose. Leaves evergreen or semi, subcoriaceous, on sterile shoots narrowly elliptic or ellipto-lanceolate, 27–62 × 10–32 mm, apex acuminate, base obtuse or cuneate, upper surface rugose, dark green, shiny, pilose, veins 3–5 deeply impressed, lower surface whitish tomentose; petiole 2–4 mm, tomentose. Fertile shoots 30–80 mm, including 4–6 leaves and a compact, 3- to 10-flowered inflorescence; pedicels 1–4 mm, tomentose-pilose; flowers (including hypanthium) 7–8 mm long. Hypanthium cupulate, silky tomentose; sepals cuspidate, silky tomentose, margin tomentose. Petals erect, pink and dark red with white border. Stamens c. 20; filaments pale pink and off-white; anthers white. Fruit obovoid, 10–12 mm, orange to orange-red, villous, calyx lobes depressed, silky tomentose. Nutlets 3(–5), style remains ²/₃ from base.

Seasons: Flowers June–July; fruit ripe October–November.
Chromosomes: Unknown. Apomictic, true from seed.
Hardiness: –15°C (5°F).
Area: China (Yunnan).
Notes: Showing some similarity to *Cotoneaster franchetii*, *C. huahongdongensis* is more closely related to *C. sternianus*. This is another lovely species introduced by Harry van de Laar.

5. *Cotoneaster hypocarpus* J. Fryer & B. Hylmö, *sp. nov.* Type: China, Yunnan, north of Lijiang, at base of Gang Ho Ba, Yulong Shan, 15 September 1987, *C. D. Brickell & A. C. Leslie 12236* (holo WSY, iso E, KUN). **PLATE 162.**

Shrub, 2–3 m. Branches erect, arched and pendulous; branchlets distichous, reddish brown, initially strigose-pilose. Leaves deciduous or semievergreen, chartaceous, on sterile shoots ovate or elliptic, 25–35 × 15–22 mm, apex acute-obtuse or acute, base obtuse or cuneate, upper surface slightly rugose, mid-green, pilose, veins 2–5 impressed, lower surface grayish tomentose; petiole 2–3 mm, strigose-pilose. Fertile shoots 30–60 mm, including 4–6 leaves and a 3- to 9-flowered inflorescence; pedicels 2–6 mm, strigose-pilose; flowers (including hypanthium) 6–7 mm long. Hypanthium cupulate, pilose; sepals cuspidate, pilose, border purple, glabrous, margin long-haired villous. Corolla open; petals erect-incurved, pink with dark red base and off-white border. Stamens 20; filaments pink; anthers white. Fruit depressed-globose or obovoid, 8–9 mm, orange to orange-red, sparsely pilose, calyx lobes suberect, sparsely pilose. Nutlets 3(–4), rarely 2, style remains ³/₄ from base.

Seasons: Flowers June–July; fruit ripe October–November.
Chromosomes: Tetraploid (Bailey, pers. comm.; McAllister, pers. comm.). Apomictic, true from seed.
Hardiness: –18°C (–1°F).
Area: China (Yunnan, Sichuan).
Notes: The name *Cotoneaster hypocarpus* has been used for this species in cultivation since at least 1940. The Hesse Nursery in Germany probably obtained *C. hypocarpus* from a collection by George Forrest (*Forrest 11190*), which was grown in the nursery

of Vilmorin of France. Also distributed by German nurseries as *C. hybridus* 'Gloire de Versailles'.

6. **Cotoneaster induratus** J. Fryer & B. Hylmö in Watsonia 21: 339 (1997). Type: China, NW Yunnan, on the northwestern flank of the Lijiang range, September 1922, *G. Forrest 22352* (holo E). PLATE 163.

Shrub, 2–3 m. Branches narrowly erect, arched in fruit; branchlets distichous or spiraled, purplish brown, initially tomentose-strigose. Leaves deciduous or semievergreen, coriaceous, on sterile shoots elliptic to ovate, 19–27 × 10–14 mm, apex acute, acuminate, mucronulate, base cuneate, upper surface rugose, dark green, shiny, pilose-strigose, veins 3–4 impressed, lower surface grayish tomentose-pilose; petiole 2–3 mm, tomentose-strigose. Fertile shoots 20–30 mm, including 4 leaves and a compact 3- to 5-flowered inflorescence; pedicels 2–4 mm, silky tomentose; flowers (including hypanthium) 5–7 mm long. Hypanthium cupulate, pilose-strigose; sepals cuspidate, acute or obtuse, silky, margin tomentose. Corolla with small opening; petals erect-incurved, reddish maroon and pink with off-white border. Stamens 20; filaments red or pink; anthers white. Fruit obovoid or globose, 9–10 mm, orange-red, shiny, pilose, calyx lobes suberect, margin tomentose. Nutlets 3(–4), rarely 2, style remains ³/₄ from base.

Seasons: Flowers June–July; fruit ripe November.

Chromosomes: Tetraploid (Zeilinga 1964; McAllister, pers. comm.). Apomictic, true from seed.

Hardiness: −25°C (−13°F). Very hardy.

Area: China (Yunnan).

Notes: Along with other George Forrest introductions, *Cotoneaster induratus* was trialed before 1939 in the Danish nursery Brandekjaerhoej, where, as it was found to withstand extremely severe winter temperatures, the nursery owner Axel Olsen gave it the epithet "Hardy." It can still be found in some gardens bearing this nickname. This species is of great horticultural value. It is frequently cultivated in the cold climes of Scandinavia. Abundantly fruiting, it is spectacular in autumn when the weight of the fruit often bows the branches to the ground. It is sometimes found cultivated as *C. wardii*. Recently reintroduced into cultivation.

7. **Cotoneaster insculptus** Diels in Not. Roy. Bot. Gard. Edinburgh 5: 273 (1912). Type: China, Yunnan, Salween valley, Salween-Irrawaddy divide, Lu-Chang, November 1903 (1904), *G. Forrest 800* (holo E). PLATE 164.

Shrub, 2–4 m. Branches erect, arched and spreading; branchlets distichous, maroon, minutely verruculose, initially tomentose-pilose to tomentose-strigose. Leaves deciduous or semievergreen, coriaceous, on sterile shoots broadly elliptic or suborbicular, 18–25 × 11–22 mm, apex acuminate or acute, base obtuse or cuneate, upper surface rugose, dark green, intensely shiny, initially densely pilose, veins 3–4 deeply impressed, lower surface whitish tomentose; petiole 2–4 mm, tomentose-pilose. Fertile shoots 15–30 mm, including 4 leaves and a 1- to 5(–7)-flowered inflorescence; pedicels 2–3 mm, tomentose-pilose; flowers (including hypanthium) 4–5 mm long. Hypanthium cupulate, tomentose-pilose to pilose; sepals cuspidate or acuminate, tomentose-pilose, border broad, reddish, glabrous, margin tomentose. Corolla closed; petals erect-incurved, brownish red and pink with pale pink border. Stamens 20; filaments red to pink; anthers white. Fruit obovoid, 7–9 mm, orange-red, shiny, sparsely pilose, calyx lobes flat, navel wide open. Nutlets 3–4, rarely 2, style remains $2/3$ from base.

  Seasons: Flowers June–July; fruit ripe October–November.
  Chromosomes: Unknown. Apomictic, true from seed.
  Hardiness: –18°C (–1°F).
  Area: China (Yunnan).
  Notes: *Cotoneaster insculptus* is not common, although it can be found in cultivation as *C. amoenus* or *C. reticulatus*. This attractive shrub has branches fanning horizontally, super shiny, crinkly leaves, and bright, shiny fruit. The Forrest holotype, collected in November, was incorrectly said by Forrest to have white flowers. The species was also collected in 1996 by Jeanette Fryer (*JFYU 023*) in Yunnan, Cangshan, beside track to Lonquan peak.

8. *Cotoneaster leveillei* J. Fryer & B. Hylmö, *sp. nov.* Type: China, Yunnan, western hills of Kunming, 20 September 1994, Alpine Garden Society China Expedition, *ACE 1034* (holo E). **PLATE 165.**

Shrub, 2–3 m. Branches erect and arched; branchlets distichous, maroon, initially tomentose-pilose. Leaves deciduous or semievergreen, subcoriaceous, on sterile shoots broadly elliptic to suborbicular, 15–20 × 12–13 mm, apex acute or acuminate, base obtuse or cuneate, upper surface rugose, dark green, slightly shiny, villous, veins 2–4 deeply impressed, lower surface whitish tomentose; petiole 3–5 mm, tomentose. Fertile shoots 25–50 mm, including 4–5 leaves, and a compact, 3- to 9-flowered inflorescence; pedicels 2–5 mm, silky tomentose; flowers (including hypanthium) 5–6 mm long. Hypanthium cupulate, base tomentose-silky; sepals cuspidate, silky tomentose, border narrow, purple, margin tomentose. Petals erect, red with white border. Stamens 20; filaments red and pink; anthers white. Fruit obovoid, 8 mm, orange-red, calyx lobes flat, tomentose. Nutlets (2–)3(–4), style remains $3/4$ from base.

  Seasons: Flowers June–July; fruit ripe October.
  Chromosomes: Tetraploid (Bailey, pers. comm.; Jewsbury, pers. comm.). Apomictic, true from seed.
  Hardiness: –15°C (5°F).
  Area: China (Yunnan).
  Notes: *Cotoneaster leveillei*, named in honor of Hector Léveillé for his work with *Cotoneaster*, has often been mistaken for *C. mairei* or *C. amoenus*, both of which come from the Kunming area of Yunnan. Harry van de Laar also collected *C. leveillei* (*80675*) in Hua Hong Dong in Yunnan in 1980.

9. **Cotoneaster naoujanensis** J. Fryer & B. Hylmö, *sp. nov.* Type: China, Yunnan, roadside between Dali and Lijiang, 15 September 1987, *C. D. Brickell & A. C. Leslie 12022* (holo WSY, iso E, KUN). **PLATE 166.**

Shrub, 1.5–2.5 m. Branches erect and arched; branchlets distichous or spiraled, maroon, initially pilose-strigose. Leaves evergreen, chartaceous or subcoriaceous, on sterile shoots broadly elliptic, 22–29 × 13–18 mm, apex acuminate or acute, base cuneate or obtuse, upper surface slightly rugose, mid-green, shiny, pilose, veins 3–4 impressed, lower surface tomentose; petiole 3–6 mm, tomentose-strigose. Fertile shoots 30–50 mm, including 4–6 leaves and a lax 5- to 15-flowered inflorescence; pedicels 2–5 mm, pilose-strigose; flowers (including hypanthium) 5–6 mm long. Hypanthium infundibulate, silky tomentose, sepals cuspidate, pilose-strigose, border broad, purple, glabrous, margin tomentose. Corolla open; petals erect-incurved, red with darker base and a narrow pink or white border. Stamens 20; filaments red, apex pink; anthers white mostly pink-tinged becoming purple. Fruit obovoid, 8–9 mm, orange to orange-red, shiny, sparsely pilose, calyx lobes flat, pilose. Nutlets (2–)3–4(–5), style remains ³/₄ from base.

Seasons: Flowers June–July; fruit ripe October–November.

Chromosomes: Unknown. Apomictic, true from seed.

Hardiness: −18°C (−1°F).

Area: China (Yunnan).

Notes: *Cotoneaster naoujanensis* is an outstanding shrub of good habit. It is attractive in leaf and flower (although flowers are small there are multitudes of them), and when in fruit the branches are absolutely laden with numerous loose clusters of striking orange-red fruit. Recently reintroduced into cultivation.

10. **Cotoneaster qungbixiensis** J. Fryer & B. Hylmö, J. Bot. Res. Inst. Texas 2 (1). 2008. Type: China, Yunnan, near Dali, eastern slope of Cangshan, Qung Bi Xi, 15 September 1987, *C. D. Brickell & A. C. Leslie 12455* (holo WSY, iso E, KUN). **PLATE 167.**

Shrub, 2–3 m. Branches erect and arched, spreading; branchlets distichous or spiraled, reddish brown, initially strigose-pilose. Leaves deciduous or semievergreen, chartaceous, on sterile shoots narrowly ovate or narrowly elliptic, 28–42 × 13–21 mm, apex acute-truncate (very typical) or acute, base cuneate or obtuse, upper surface slightly rugose, dark green, shiny, initially pilose, veins 2–4 impressed, lower surface grayish tomentose; petiole 3–4 mm, often red, strigose-pilose. Fertile shoots 30–50 mm, including 4–6 leaves and a compact, 3- to 9(–15)-flowered inflorescence; pedicels 1–3 mm, strigose-pilose; flowers (including hypanthium) 7–8 mm long. Hypanthium infundibulate, silky tomentose; sepals cuspidate or acuminate, tomentose. Corolla open; petals erect-incurved, pink with dark red base and yellowish and off-white border. Stamens 20; filaments dark red; anthers white. Fruit globose or obovoid, 8–10 mm, orange-red, slightly shiny, pilose, calyx lobes flat, tomentose. Nutlets (2–)3(–4), very rarely 5, style remains ²/₃ from base.

Seasons: Flowers June–July; fruit ripe October–November.

Chromosomes: Tetraploid (Bailey, pers. comm.; McAllister, pers. comm.). Apomictic, true from seed.

Hardiness: −18°C (−1°F).

Area: China (Yunnan).

Notes: *Cotoneaster qungbixiensis* is a good shrub for autumn fruit color. It was also collected by Charles Wingfield (*772*) in Yunnan above a small temple on Cangshan in 1985.

11. *Cotoneaster sternianus* (Turrill) Boom in Jaarboek Nederland Dendrology Ver. 20: 81 (1957). Synonym: *C. franchetii* Bois var. *sternianus* Turrill (1950). Type: N Burma, Hpimaw, 23 September 1919, *R. Farrer 1325* (lecto designated E). **PLATE 168.**

Shrub, multistemmed and dense, 3–4 m. Branches erect and arched, stiff; branchlets distichous, maroon, whitish tomentose-pilose. Leaves evergreen, coriaceous, on sterile shoots elliptic to broadly ovate, 37–49 × 20–28 mm, apex acute or acuminate, base obtuse or cuneate, margin recurved, upper surface very rugose, dark green, slightly shiny, pilose, veins 4–5 deeply impressed, lower surface whitish tomentose; petiole 4–6 mm, tomentose-pilose. Fertile shoots 25–70 mm, including 3–5 leaves and a compact 7- to 20-flowered inflorescence; pedicels 1–4 mm, tomentose-pilose; flowers (including hypanthium) 5–6 mm long. Hypanthium cupulate, silky tomentose; sepals acute or acuminate, silky tomentose, border purple, glabrous, margin villous. Corolla with small opening; petals erect-incurved, dark red with minute black dots with pink or white border. Stamens 20; filaments red with pink and white apex; anthers white with pink-tinged border. Fruit globose or depressed globose, 9–10 mm, orange-red, pilose, calyx lobes flat, tomentose, margins creating perfect five pointed star over navel. Nutlets (2–)3–4(–5), style remains $^3/_4$ from base.

Seasons: Flowers June–July; fruit ripe October–November.

Chromosomes: Tetraploid (Hensen 1966). Apomictic, true from seed.

Hardiness: −15°C (5°F).

Area: Burma. China (NW Yunnan).

Notes: *Cotoneaster sternianus* was named in honor of Sir Frederick Stern, who raised the type collection in his Highdown garden, in Goring-by-Sea, Sussex, England. The species is common in cultivation, though frequently found as *C. franchetii* or *C. wardii*. The fruit are produced in great abundance, often the older leaves falling in bright shades of orange at the same time. Recently reintroduced into cultivation. Received RHS Award of Merit in 1939 (as *C. wardii*), and Award of Garden Merit in 1953 (as *C. franchetii* var. *sternianus*).

12. *Cotoneaster taofuensis* J. Fryer & B. Hylmö, *sp. nov.* Type: China, Sichuan, Taofu, Kuku-la, December 1934, *Harry Smith 13912* (holo UPS). **PLATE 169.**

Shrub dense, 2–3 m. Branches erect and arched; branchlets distichous, maroon, initially pilose-strigose. Leaves deciduous, subcoriaceous or chartaceous, on sterile shoots elliptic or ovate, 18–25 × 9–14 mm, apex acute or rarely acuminate, base cuneate or obtuse, upper surface slightly rugose, mid to dark green, initially pilose-strigose, veins 3–4 lightly impressed, lower surface grayish tomentose; petiole 2–3 mm, pilose-strigose. Fertile shoots 20–25 mm, including 4–5 leaves and a compact, (3–)5- to 9(–11)-flowered inflorescence; pedicels 1–3 mm, pilose-strigose; flowers (including hypanthium) 5–6 mm long. Hypanthium cupulate, pilose-strigose; sepals cuspidate or acuminate, densely villous, border gray or purple, glabrous, margin villous. Corolla closed; petals erect-incurved, red and pink with dark red base and pink border. Stamens (18–)20; filaments dark red; anthers white. Fruit shortly obovoid, 8–9, orange-red, shiny, sparsely pilose, calyx lobes flat, tomentose. Nutlets (3–)4(–5), rarely 2, style remains $2/3$ from base.

Seasons: Flowers June–July; fruit ripe October–November.

Chromosomes: Triploid (Bailey, pers. comm.; Jewsbury, pers. comm.).

Hardiness: −18°C (−1°F).

Area: China (Yunnan).

Notes: *Cotoneaster taofuensis* is in cultivation in a few gardens originating from the Harry Smith collection. This shrub is frequently abundantly fruiting, the fruit smothering the branches.

31. Series *Dielsiani* G. Klotz in Wiss. Z. Friedrich-Schiller-Univ. Jena, Math.-Naturwiss. 21: 991 (1972).

Small to large shrubs. Leaves mostly deciduous, chartaceous or subcoriaceous, upper surface flat or slightly rugose, veins mostly 2–3, lower surface initially with grayish tomentose or densely pilose hairs. Fertile shoots 10–40 mm including up to 7(–10)-flowered inflorescence. Hypanthium mostly pilose-strigose. Anthers white. Fruit rich red, rarely orange. Nutlets 2–5.

Early to mid season.

China (Sichuan, Yunnan, Hubei).

8 species: *C. bradyi*, *C. declinatus*, *C. dielsianus*, *C. floridus*, *C. froebelii*, *C. fruticosus*, *C. soulieanus*, *C. splendens*.

Key to Series *Dielsiani*

1a. Leaves mid-green, lower surface densely pilose; fruit orange-red . . . . **C. splendens**

1b. Leaves dark green, lower surface tomentose; fruit red or ruby 2

2a. Branches slender; leaves narrowly elliptic; flowers 4–5 mm, fruit 6–7 mm . . . . . **C. declinatus**

2b. Branches coarse; leaves ovate or elliptic, often broadly so; flowers 5–7 mm; fruit
(6–)8–11 mm 3

3a. Leaves 11–20 mm; fertile shoots 10–25 mm; sepals mostly acute . . . . **C. bradyi**

3b. Leaves 15–26 mm; fertile shoots 20–40 mm; sepals mostly cuspidate 4

4a. Leaves mostly chartaceous, elliptic, upper surface dull, strigose; pedicels 2–6 mm; stamens 14–17; fruit obovoid, 10–11 mm, nutlets (2–)3(–4) . . . .**C. *floridus***

4b. Leaves mostly coriaceous, ovate, upper surface shiny, pilose; pedicels 1–3 mm; stamens 20; fruit mostly globose, 6–8 mm; nutlets (3–)4(–5). . . . . **C. *dielsianus***

1. *Cotoneaster bradyi* E. C. Nelson & J. Fryer in Glasra 2:127 (1995); illustr. Curtis's Bot. Mag. 198: 201 (1995). Type: cult. Ireland, National Botanic Gardens, Glasnevin (accession #1962.008603), E. C. Nelson, 16 June 1994 (holo DBN, iso E, K).   .
    PLATE 170.

Shrub dense, 1.5–2 m. Branches narrowly erect and arched; branchlets distichous or divaricate, brown, initially tomentose-strigose. Leaves deciduous, chartaceous, ovate, on sterile shoots 11–20 × 8–16 mm, apex acute, mucronate, base obtuse, upper surface slightly rugose, dark green, shiny, sparsely pilose-strigose, veins 2–3 lightly impressed, lower surface tomentose-villous; petiole 2–5 mm, strigose. Fertile shoots 10–25 mm, including 4 leaves and a 1- to 4(–5)-flowered inflorescence; pedicels 2–3 mm, sparsely pilose; flowers (including hypanthium) 5–6 mm long. Hypanthium cupulate, greenish red, pilose-strigose; sepals acute, mucronate, pilose-strigose, margin villous. Corolla small opening; petals erect-incurved, pink with red base and white border. Stamens 12–16; filaments red, anthers white. Fruit globose or obovoid, 9–10 mm, rich red to ruby, shiny, sparsely pilose, calyx lobes flat, villous. Nutlets (2–)3–4(–5), style remains $^3/_4$ from base.

    Seasons: Flowers June; fruit ripe October.

    Chromosomes: Triploid (Bailey, pers. comm.; McAllister, pers. comm.).

    Hardiness: –18°C (–1°F).

    Area: China (Sichuan).

    Notes: *Cotoneaster bradyi* is named in honor of Aiden Brady, director of the National Botanic Gardens, Glasnevin, Ireland, from 1968 to 1993. The shrub is spectacular in autumn when its branches are studded with masses of shiny red fruit. It is sometimes found in cultivation as *C.* 'Glasnevin'.

2. *Cotoneaster declinatus* J. Fryer & B. Hylmö, *sp. nov.* Type: China, Sichuan, between Nitou and Hualinping, Fei-Ye-Ling, 16 November 1934, *Harry Smith 13444* (holo UPS). PLATE 171.

Shrub, 1.5–2 m. Branches erect, slender and weak; branchlets distichous or spiraled in habit, maroon, lenticellate, initially densely pilose-strigose. Leaves deciduous, chartaceous, on sterile shoots narrowly elliptic, on sterile shoots 16–19 × 8–12 mm, apex acute or acuminate, base obtuse or cuneate, upper surface dark green, shiny, initially pilose, veins 3 impressed, lower surface grayish tomentose; petiole 2–3 mm, pilose. Fertile shoots 15–25 mm, including 3–4 leaves and a 3- to 5(–7)-flowered inflorescence; pedicels 2–3 mm, pilose-strigose; flowers (including hypanthium) 4–6 mm long. Hypanthium infundibulate, pilose; sepals acuminate or acute, pilose, border broad, purple, glabrous, margin villous. Corolla closed or with small opening; petals erect-incurved, greenish white with red base and off-white border. Stamens 20; filaments red and pink, apex off-white; anthers white. Fruit globose, 6–7 mm, rich red, shiny, sparsely pilose, calyx lobes flat, pilose. Nutlets (3–)4(–5), style remains ⅔ from base.

Seasons: Flowers May–June; fruit ripe September–October.

Chromosomes: Unknown. Apomixis to be checked.

Hardiness: –21°C (–6°F).

Area: China (Sichuan, Yunnan).

Notes: Although a very garden-worthy shrub with a wealth of attractive shiny bead-like fruit, *Cotoneaster declinatus* is not common in cultivation. A hedge of this species which was growing at the National Botanic Gardens in Glasnevin, in the 1960s was labeled *C. declinatus*, but the origin of both name and shrub was unknown. It is known that a number of Harry Smith collections were received at Glasnevin, although this species has never been detected growing among the many Smith numbers in Sweden. It is more likely that it originated from a collection made by Augustine Henry in the mountains near Mengtze in Yunnan. Recently reintroduced into cultivation.

3. *Cotoneaster dielsianus* E. Pritzel in Bot. Jahrb. Syst. 29: 385 (1900). Synonym:

C. applanatus Duthie ex Veitch (1906). Type: China, E Sichuan, Nanchuan,

Paomuwan, August 1891, *C. Boch & A. v. Rosthorn 492* (holo O). **PLATE 172.**

Shrub, 2–4 m. Branches narrowly erect and spreading; branchlets distichous, grayish brown, initially tomentose-pilose. Leaves deciduous, coriaceous or subcoriaceous, on sterile shoots ovate or broadly ovate, 21–26 × 11–26 mm, apex acute or acuminate, base obtuse or cuneate, upper surface slightly rugose, grayish green, shiny, pilose, veins 2–3 lightly impressed, lower surface grayish tomentose; petiole 2–4 mm, tomentose-pilose. Fertile shoots 20–35 mm, including 4 leaves and a compact, 3- to 7(–10)-flowered inflorescence; pedicels 1–3 mm, tomentose-strigose; flowers (including hypanthium) 6–7 mm long. Hypanthium infundibulate, base tomentose-strigose, apex tomentose-pilose; sepals cuspidate or apiculate, pilose, border broad, reddish purple, glabrous, margin tomentose. Corolla closed; petals erect-incurved, red with dark red, border off-white. Stamens 20; filaments dark red or pink; anthers white. Fruit globose, depressed-globose or obovate, 6–9 mm, rich red, slightly shiny, pilose, calyx lobes flat, navel open, tomentose. Nutlets (3–)4(–5), style remains ⅔ from base.

Seasons: Flowers June; fruit ripe October.

Chromosomes: Tetraploid (Zeilinga 1964; Hensen 1966; Kroon 1975). Apomictic, true from seed.

Hardiness: –21°C (–6°F).

Area: China (Sichuan, Hubei).

Notes: *Cotoneaster dielsianus*, introduced from a German expedition, is very common in central Europe and Scandinavia. It has branches often ending in fan-shaped clusters of branchlets. In autumn, when crowded with fruit, the branches are sometimes arched to the ground. Received an RHS Award of Merit in 1907 and First Class Certificate in 1912.

4. ***Cotoneaster floridus*** J. Fryer & B. Hylmö, J. Bot. Res. Inst. Texas 2 (1). 2008. Type: China, Yunnan, Muli, Washin area, near the lamasery, 5 October 1937, *T. T. Yu 14430* (holo E, iso A, BM). PLATE 173.

Shrub, 1.5–2 m. Branches erect and arched; branchlets distichous, maroon and minutely verruculose, initially pilose-strigose. Leaves deciduous, chartaceous or subcoriaceous, on sterile shoots elliptic often broadly so, on sterile shoots 15–25 × 11–25 mm, apex acuminate or acute, base cuneate or obtuse, upper surface dark green, dull, strigose, veins 3(–4) lightly impressed, lower surface whitish tomentose-pilose; petiole 3–4 mm, strigose. Fertile shoots 20–40 mm, including mostly 4 leaves and a 2- to 5-flowered inflorescence; pedicels 2–6 mm, strigose; flowers (including hypanthium) 5–6 mm long. Hypanthium turbinate, densely strigose; sepals cuspidate or acuminate, densely strigose, border membranous, reddish brown, glabrous, margin villous. Corolla closed; petals erect-incurved, pink with dark red base and white and pink border. Stamens 14–17; filaments dark red or red and pink; anthers white. Fruit narrowly obovoid, 10–11 mm, rich red, intensely shiny, sparsely pilose, calyx lobes flat, densely pilose. Nutlets (2–)3(–4), style remains $^2/_3$ from base.

> Seasons: Flowers June; fruit ripe September–October.
> Chromosomes: Unknown. Apomictic, true from seed.
> Hardiness: –21°C (–6°F).
> Area: China (Yunnan, Sichuan, probably Jiangsu).
> Notes: *Cotoneaster floridus* is frequently found in cultivation as *C. rubens* hort., non W. W. Smith, a misnomer under which it was distributed as seed from RHS Wisley in England. It can also be found grown as *C. dielsianus* var. *rubens* hort. Unfortunately, T. T. Yu's collection numbers have become confused in cultivation; hence, various species of *Cotoneaster* can sometimes be found under a single collection number.

5. ***Cotoneaster froebelii*** Sax ex Vilmorin in Journ. Arn. Arb. 35: 340 (1954). Type: China, NE Yunnan, between Yiliang and Xiaocuba, 5 October 1995, *Cox & Hutchinson 7104* (lecto designated E). PLATE 174.

Shrub, 1.5–2 m. Branches erect, spreading. Leaves deciduous, sometimes semievergreen, chartaceous or subcoriaceous, on sterile shoots broadly ovate, 18–28 × 10–18 mm, apex acute, base obtuse, upper surface slightly rugose, dark green, sparsely strigose, veins deeply impressed, lower surface gray tomentose. Fertile shoots 22–28 mm, including 1- to 3(–6)-flowered inflorescence. Hypanthium with sepals acute or acuminate, pilose-strigose, margin tomentose. Petals erect, incurved, red and pink. Stamens 13–20; filaments red with off-white base; anthers white. Fruit subglobose or broadly-obovate, 9–10 mm, bright red, sparsely pilose, calyx lobes flat, densely pilose, navel closed or small opening. Nutlets (3–)4(–5), style remains $^1/_2$–$^2/_3$ from base.

Seasons: Flowers June–July; fruit ripe October.

Chromosomes: Tetraploid (Zeilinga 1964).

Hardiness: −21°C (−6°F).

Area: China (Yunnan).

Notes: *Cotoneaster froebelii* has long been a somewhat lost species, although it has possibly been in cultivation in the United States. The collection by Peter Cox and Peter Hutchinson from the corner of Yunnan bordering with Sichuan and Guizhou has provided the material needed for the further investigation of this species. Not in key.

6. *Cotoneaster fruticosus* J. Fryer & B. Hylmö, *sp. nov.* Type: China, Yunnan, Chungtien, Huachiapouh, 27 November 1937, *T. T. Yu 14994* (holo E, iso BM).

    PLATE 175.

Shrub, 2–3 m. Branches coarse, erect, arched, spreading; branchlets distichous, brown, pilose-strigose, glabrescent. Leaves deciduous, subcoriaceous, on sterile shoots widely spaced, broadly ovate or suborbicular, 23–30 × 18–21 mm, apex acute, base obtuse or cuneate, upper surface slightly rugose, dark green, shiny, pilose-strigose, veins 3–4 impressed, lower surface grayish tomentose; petiole 2–4 mm, pilose-strigose. Fertile shoots 20–40 mm, including 4 leaves and a 3- to 7-flowered inflorescence; pedicels 2–6 mm, pilose-strigose; flowers (including hypanthium) 6–8 mm long. Hypanthium cupulate, pilose-strigose; sepals acuminate or acute, pilose, border broad, purple, glabrous, margin tomentose. Corolla with small opening; petals erect-incurved, pink with dark reddish brown base and off-white border. Stamens (18–)20; filaments dark brownish red; anthers white. Fruit obovoid, succulent, 9–11 mm, orange-red to bright-red, intensely shiny, subglabrous, calyx lobes flat, pilose, navel wide open. Nutlets 3–4(–5), style remains ²/₃ from base.

Seasons: Flowers June–July; fruit ripe September–October.

Chromosomes: Tetraploid (Bailey, pers. comm.). Apomictic, true from seed.

Hardiness: −21°C (−6°F).

Area: China (Yunnan).

Notes: *Cotoneaster fruticosus* is known only from the type collection, but, due to the recent upsurge of seed collecting in this area of China, the species is likely to be rediscovered. Not in key.

7. *Cotoneaster soulieanus* G. Klotz in Wiss. Z. Friedrich-Schiller-Univ. Jena, Math.-Naturwiss. 21: 1014 (1972). Synonym: *C. rotundifolius* Wallich ex Lindley var. *tongolensis* Rehder (1906). Type: China, W Sichuan, Tongolo, near border with E Tibet, *J. A. Soulie 684* (holo P).

The type herbarium specimen of *Cotoneaster soulieanus* is without flowers. The leaves are broadly elliptic, around 20–25 mm, with the apex obtuse and mucronate or cuspidate, and the base rotund or obtuse, the upper surface hairs are pilose-villous, with the lower surface yellowish gray tomentose, veins c. 3 pairs; the only fruit with the specimen are misshapen.

Notes: This species is probably related to *Cotoneaster splendens*. Possibly not in cultivation. Not in key.

8. *Cotoneaster splendens* Flinck & B. Hylmö in Bot. Not. (Lund) 117: 124 (1964). Synonym: *C.* ×*sabrina* Hadden ex Krüssmann (1951). Type: China, Sichuan, Kangding, Cheto valley, 22 October 1934, *Harry Smith 12925* (holo UPS, iso BM, E). **PLATE 176**.
Shrub somewhat dense, 1–2 m. Branches ascending, arched; branchlets distichous, maroon, initially pilose-strigose. Leaves deciduous, chartaceous, on sterile shoots suborbicular or broadly elliptic-ovate, 17–24 × 13–18 mm, apex acute, base obtuse, upper surface mid-green, slightly shiny, pilose-strigose, veins 2–3 lightly impressed, lower surface densely pilose; petiole 2–3 mm, strigose. Fertile shoots 20–30 mm, including 4–5 leaves and a 3- to 7-flowered inflorescence; pedicels 1–2 mm, pilose-strigose; flowers (including hypanthium) 5–6 mm long. Hypanthium infundibulate, base strigose, apex pilose; sepals acuminate or acute, pilose, border broad, purple, glabrous. Corolla small opening; petals erect-incurved, dark red with pink or off-white border. Stamens (16–)20; filaments dark red; anthers white. Fruit obovoid or depressed globose, 9–11, orange-red, shiny, subglabrous, calyx lobes flat, tomentose. Nutlets (3–)4, rarely 5, style remains $^2/_3$ from base.

Seasons: Flowers June–July; fruit ripe September–October.

Chromosomes: Tetraploid (Zeilinga 1964; Hensen 1966; Kroon 1975; Klotz and Krügel 1983a). Apomictic, true from seed.

Hardiness: −21°C (−6°F).

Area: China (Sichuan).

Notes: Harry Smith, coming upon this shrub for the first time in the wild, noted that it was indeed a splendid shrub covered with many shiny orange fruit and suggested it be given the name *Cotoneaster splendens*. In cultivation the charm of this species was soon realized. In Somerset, England, it grew in the garden of Norman Hadden, who, believing it to be a hybrid arisen there, named it *C.* ×*sabrina*. Under this name it received an RHS Award of Merit in 1950. Seed from Harry Smith collections were widely distributed and shrubs with his numbers can be found in several English gardens. In Sweden, *C. splendens* and *C.* ×*sabrina* were studied in cultivation for over 40 years and found to be identical. *Cotoneaster splendens* can be found in some botanic gardens as *C. distichus* var. *tongolensis*.

10. Section *Cotoneaster*

Branchlets spiraled or distichous, often initially tomentose. Leaves with lower surface tomentose or densely pilose-villous. Pedicels 1–20 mm. Petals off-white or very pale pink, sometimes with green. Fruit often dull or pruinose, calyx lobes somewhat succulent.

4 series: *Zabelioides, Tomentosi, Cotoneaster, Ignavi*.

32. Series *Zabelioides* Flinck & B. Hylmö in Bot. Not. (Lund) 119: 456 (1966).

Small to medium shrubs. Branchlets mostly slender, distichous or irregular. Leaves on sterile shoots mostly ovate. Inflorescences lax. Hypanthium often villous. Petals erect or semispreading. Anthers pale pink or white. Fruit pendent on long pedicels, obovate. Nutlets 2–3, large (to 7 × 6 mm).

Early to late season.

China (Hubei, Shaanxi, Henan, Ningxia, Gansu, Shanxi, Hebei, Shandong, Sichuan). Mongolia. Korea.

13 species: *C. alashanensis, C. difficilis, C. fangianus, C. genitianus, C. giraldii, C. globosus, C. gracilis, C. kitaibelii, C. miniatus, C. schantungensis, C. shansiensis, C. svenhedinii, C. zabelii.*

Key to Series *Zabelioides*

1a. Leaves mostly elliptic, upper surface of leaves, hypanthium, sepals and fruit glabrous or subglabrous. **2**

1b. Leaves mostly ovate or suborbicular, upper surface of leaves, hypanthium, sepals and fruit pilose, villous or tomentose. **3**

2a. Branches slender; leaves ≤ 24 mm, apex mostly obtuse; fertile shoots 30–40 mm; inflorescence lax, pedicels thin, 3–10 mm; fruit orange . . . . **C. gracilis**

2b. Branches coarse; leaves ≤ 40 mm, apex mostly acute; fertile shoots 20–30 mm; inflorescence compact, pedicels coarse, 2–5 mm; fruit red . . . . **C. giraldii**

3a. Petals mostly pink; petioles pilose or villous; pedicels 5–10 mm; nutlets 2; fruit orange **4**

3b. Petals mostly off-white; petioles tomentose; pedicels 2–8 mm; nutlets mostly 1–3; fruit red **5**

4a. Leaves yellowish green, veins impressed, lower surface pilose; fertile shoots ≤ 45 mm; inflorescence ≤ 18-flowered; fruit 4–8 mm . . . .**C. miniatus**

4b. Leaves grayish green, veins not impressed, lower surface tomentose; fertile shoots ≤ 60 mm; inflorescence ≤ 30-flowered; fruit 10–11 mm . . . . **C. shansiensis**

5a. Branches mostly ascending; leaves ovate or elliptic; pedicels 3–8 mm; petals and filaments mostly white or off-white. **6**

5b. Branches mostly erect; leaves broadly ovate or suborbicular; pedicels 2–5 mm; petals and filaments mostly pink or green. **7**

6a. Branches slender; leaves thinly chartaceous, ≤ 34 mm, mid-green, veins lightly impressed; stamens 16–20; fruit ripening currant red, dull. . . . . **C. svenhedinii**

6b. Branches thicker; leaves subcoriaceous, ≤ 40 mm, dark green, veins deeply impressed; stamens 20; fruit ripening ruby, shiny . . . .**C. zabelii**

7a. Leaves ≤ 35 mm, apex obtuse or acute, upper surface dull; sepals acute; petals pink; fruit ruby; nutlets (1–)2 . . . . **C. fangianus**

7b. Leaves ≤ 43 mm, apex acute or acuminate, upper surface shiny; sepals mostly obtuse; petals greenish; fruit orange-red with crimson; nutlets 2–3 . . . . **C. kitaibelii**

1. ***Cotoneaster alashanensis*** J. Fryer & B. Hylmö, *sp. nov.* Type: China, Ningxia, Ala Shan, in valley, 27 August 1933, *W. Y. Hsia H3903* (holo A, iso PE).

Shrub, 1.5–2 m. Branches narrowly erect, robust; branchlets divaricate, maroon, initially tomentose-pilose. Leaves deciduous, chartaceous to subcoriaceous, on sterile shoots suborbicular, 19–28 × 16–19 mm; apex obtuse, base obtuse or cuneate, upper surface green, dull, pilose, veins 3–4 impressed, lower surface reticulate, gray tomentose-villous; petiole 3–5 mm, tomentose-villous. Fertile shoots 10–20 mm, including 2–3 leaves and a 2- to 5-flowered inflorescence; pedicels 3–5 mm, sparsely villous. Sepals acute or obtuse, villous. Flowers non visa. Stamens 20. Fruit pendent, obovoid, red, sparsely villous; calyx lobes villous. Nutlets 2–3.

Area: China: (Ningxia, Qinghai).

Notes: *Cotoneaster alashanensis*, originating from northern provinces of China where records of cotoneasters are very few, is invaluable for investigation into the connection between the cotoneasters of China and those of Mongolia and E Siberia. Rare in cultivation. Not in key.

2. ***Cotoneaster difficilis*** G. Klotz in Wiss. Z. Friedrich-Schiller-Univ. Jena, Math.-Naturwiss. 21: 1017 (1972). Type: China, W Sichuan, valley of Hsao-ho near Monkong Ting, June 1908, *E. H. Wilson 2169* (holo A, iso K, LE).

Shrub, 1.5–2.5 m. Branches erect, spreading and gracefully arched, divaricate; branchlets distichous, initially tomentose. Leaves deciduous or semievergreen, chartaceous or subcoriaceous, on sterile shoots ovate, ovate-elliptic, or broadly-elliptic, 7–22 × 6–10 mm, apex obtuse or acute, base rotund or obtuse, upper surface slightly rugose, mid-green, dull, sparsely initially pilose, lower surface initially tomentose-pilose; petiole 1–2 mm, tomentose-strigose. Fertile shoots 20–30 mm, including 2–3 leaves and a 1- to 3(–6)-flowered inflorescence; pedicels 10–12 mm, pilose-strigose to subglabrous. Hypanthium cupulate, sparsely pilose-strigose, sepals sparsely pilose-strigose. Corolla open; petals erect or semispreading, exceeding sepals by 1.7 mm, pale pink. Stamens 17–20. Fruit pendent, obovoid, 7–8 mm, orange to orange-red, pilose, calyx lobes flat to slightly depressed, pilose-villous. Nutlets (2–)3, style remains $^1/_2$–$^1/_3$ from base.

Seasons: Fruit ripe October.

Chromosomes: Unknown.

Area: China (Sichuan, Gansu).

Notes: *Cotoneaster difficilis*, rediscovered by Mikinori Ogisu (*MO 93303*) in 1993 in Nanchuan, in the Sichuan province of China, needs further investigation. Not in key.

3. ***Cotoneaster fangianus*** T. T. Yu in Acta Phytotax. Sin. 8: 219 (1963). Type: China, Hubei, Enh-Shih, 18 June 1958, *M. Y. Fang 24314* (holo PE).

Shrub, 2–2.5 m. Branches erect, arched and spreading; branchlets distichous, maroon, initially tomentose-pilose. Leaves deciduous, subcoriaceous, on sterile shoots broadly ovate or suborbicular, 21–35 × 15–28 mm, apex obtuse or acute, base obtuse or truncate, upper surface slightly rugose, dark green, dull, pilose, veins 4–6 deeply impressed, lower surface grayish densely villous; petiole 2–4 mm, tomentose. Fertile shoots 20–30 mm, including mostly 3 leaves and a compact, 5- to 15-flowered inflorescence; pedicels 2–5 mm, tomentose-pilose; flowers (including hypanthium) 4–5 mm. Hypanthium cupulate, densely villous; sepals acute, villous, border whitish, glabrous, margin villous. Corolla with large opening; petals erect, exceeding sepals by 1 mm, pink. Stamens 16–20; filaments pale pink; anthers white. Fruit pendent, obovoid, 8–9 mm, succulent, crimson to ruby, villous, calyx lobes flat, navel slightly open. Nutlets (1–)2, style remains ⅔ from base.

Seasons: Flowers June–July; fruit ripe October.

Chromosomes: Unknown. Apomictic, true from seed.

Hardiness: −21°C (−6°F).

Area: China (Hubei).

Notes: *Cotoneaster fangianus* is common in central Europe and Scandinavia, mostly as *C. zabelii* and often found in mixed plantings with the latter species. *Cotoneaster fangianus* can easily be distinguished by its leaves which fall nearly one month earlier than those of *C. zabelii*. *Cotoneaster fangianus* was grown in several botanic gardens originating from *Wilson 331*, which was collected in the same area as the type. In Yu's description of *C. fangianus*, the upper surface of the leaves is said to be glabrous and the nutlets 3, but the type specimen in the Chinese National Herbarium, Beijing, has pilose leaves and 2 nutlets.

4. *Cotoneaster genitianus* Hurus in Acta Phytotax. Geobot. 13: 233 (1943). Type: Korea, Kankyo-Hokudo province, Mozan, 19 August 1933, G. Koidzumi (holo TI, iso TI).

Shrub, 1.5–2 m. Branches erect, arched, slender; branchlets divaricate, maroon, initially tomentose-pilose. Leaves deciduous, chartaceous, on sterile shoots elliptic or ovate, 26–40 × 15–20 mm, apex obtuse, base obtuse, upper surface slightly rugose, dull green, villous, veins 3–4 impressed, lower surface villous-pilose; petiole 3–5 mm, villous. Fertile shoots 20–30 mm, including a 3- to 5-flowered inflorescence. Hypanthium sparsely villous; sepals obtuse or acute, villous, margin villous. Stamens 20. Fruit pendent, obovoid, 7–9 mm, light red. Nutlets 2–3, style remains ⅔ from base.

Notes: *Cotoneaster genitianus* is not known in cultivation. The above is compiled from the original diagnosis plus photographs of the type and isotype herbarium specimens. Not in key.

5. *Cotoneaster giraldii* Flinck & B. Hylmö ex G. Klotz in Wiss. Z. Friedrich-Schiller-Univ. Jena, Math.-Naturwiss. 21: 1018 (1972). Synonym: *C. zabelii* C. K. Schneider f. *glabriusculus* (1906/07). Type: China, N Shaanxi (*C. zabelii* C. K. Schneider var. *glabrescens*), 1897, leg. *G. Giraldi 7163* (lecto K).

Shrub, 1.5–2 m. Branches erect, arched and spreading; branchlets distichous or divaricate, yellowish brown, initially densely villous-pilose. Leaves deciduous, chartaceous, on sterile shoots elliptic or ovate, 21–40 × 13–21 mm, apex acute or acuminate, base obtuse or cuneate, upper surface reddish green, shiny, soon dark-green, dull, glabrescent, veins 5–7 lightly impressed, lower surface greenish gray tomentose-villous; petiole 2–3 mm, tomentose-villous. Fertile shoots 20–30 mm, including 3–4 leaves and a compact, 5- to 13-flowered inflorescence; pedicels 2–5 mm, glabrous or sparsely pilose; flowers (including hypanthium) 5–6 mm long. Hypanthium cupulate, glabrescent; sepals obtuse, acute or apiculate, glabrous, margin villous. Corolla with large opening; petals erect to semi-spreading, pink with red base. Stamens 18–20; filaments pink, apex off-white; anthers white. Fruit pendent, obovoid, 8–9 mm, red to crimson, glabrous, calyx lobes suberect, glabrous, navel open. Nutlets 2, style remains $2/3$ from base.

Seasons: Flowers June; fruit ripe September; autumn leaves red.

Chromosomes: Unknown. Apomictic, true from seed.

Hardiness: –21°C (–6°F).

Area: China (Shaanxi).

Notes: *Cotoneaster giraldii* is not common in cultivation. At the Arnold Arboretum of Harvard University, a specimen collected in England at the RBG Kew in 1923 claims it was seeded there as early as 1895. Seed at the Arnold Arboretum, originating from the Hesse nursery in Germany and planted in 1931, was sent in 1958 to Bjuv, Sweden, and raised there as *C. giraldii*. Gerhard Klotz, when visiting the cotoneasters in Bjuv in 1967, gathered this information for his description of *C. giraldii*.

6. *Cotoneaster globosus* (Hurusawa) G. Klotz in Wiss. Z. Friedrich-Schiller-Univ. Jena, Math.-Naturwiss. 21: 1017 (1972). Synonym: *C. dielsianus* E. Pritzel var. *globosus* Hurusawa (1943). Type: China, Nei Monggol, Chahar province, Kalgan, August 1938, Auro Otuka (holo TI).

Shrub, 1.5–2 m. Branchlets distichous, maroon, initially tomentose-pilose. Leaves deciduous, chartaceous, on sterile shoots ovate or elliptic, 17–40 × 10–20; apex acute or obtuse, base obtuse or cuneate, upper surface slightly rugose, mid-green, dull, sparsely pilose, veins 4–5 lightly impressed, lower surface villous; petiole 3–5 mm, tomentose-villous. Fertile shoots 15–30 mm, including 2–4 leaves and a 3- to 5-flowered inflorescence; pedicels 3–8 mm, sparsely villous. Hypanthium villous; sepals acute or obtuse, villous. Stamens 20. Fruit pendent, globose or obovoid, red, sparsely villous, calyx lobes villous. Nutlets 2, style remains $4/5$ from base.

Area: China (Hebei, Nei Mongolia).

Notes: *Cotoneaster globosus* is not known in cultivation. Isao Hurusawa classified this species to series *Dielsiani*, species of which are southern in origin. It is obvious though that *C. globosus* is related to species in series *Zabelioides*, from more northern areas. This classification was later accepted by Klotz when raising *C. globosus* from a variety to a species. Not in key.

7. **Cotoneaster gracilis** Rehder & Wilson in Sargent, Pl. Wilson. 1: 167 (1912). Type: China, W Hubei, Xingshan Xian, June 1907, *E. H. Wilson 2176* (holo A, iso BM, E, K). Shrub, 1.5(–2) m. Branches erect, arched and spreading, slender; branchlets distichous, maroon, initially tomentose-pilose. Leaves deciduous, chartaceous, on sterile shoots elliptic, 15–24 × 11–18 mm, apex obtuse or acute, base obtuse or truncate, upper surface light to dark green, dull, glabrous, veins 5–6 lightly impressed, lower surface greenish white tomentose-pilose; petiole 2–3 mm, tomentose-pilose. Fertile shoots 30–40 mm, including 2–3 leaves and a lax, 5- to 11-flowered inflorescence; pedicels 3–10 mm, glabrous or base pilose; flowers 5 (including hypanthium) mm long. Hypanthium cupulate, glabrous; sepals obtuse, rarely acute, glabrous, border membranous, margin villous or subglabrous. Corolla with large opening; petals erect, exceeding sepals by 1 mm, pink. Stamens 20; filaments white or very pale pink; anthers white. Fruit pendent, obovoid, 6–9 mm, orange, glabrous, calyx lobes flat. Nutlets 2(–3), style remains ²/₃ from base.

Seasons: Flowers May–June; fruit ripe October.

Chromosomes: Triploid (Bailey, pers. comm.; Jewsbury, pers. comm.).

Hardiness: –21°C (–6°F).

Area: China (Sichuan, Hubei).

Notes: *Cotoneaster gracilis* is a pretty little shrub with delicate, soft pink flowers and pale tangerine fruit. It can easily be grown in a container and is very effective when grown on a single stem as a standard. Recently reintroduced into cultivation.

8. **Cotoneaster kitaibelii** J. Fryer & B. Hylmö, *sp. nov.* Synonym: *C. kitaibelii* hort. Type: China, Sichuan, Nanjiang, southwest of Wei Jian Ba, 23 September 1996, Kirkham, Flanagan, Howick, & McNamara, *SICH 1809* (holo K). **PLATE 177.** Shrub, 2–3 m. Branches erect and ascending; branchlets distichous, maroon, initially tomentose-pilose. Leaves deciduous, chartaceous, on sterile shoots broadly ovate, 23–43 × 18–30 mm, apex acute or acuminate, base obtuse, upper surface slightly rugose, dark green, shiny, villous, veins 3–5 deeply impressed, lower surface grayish tomentose-villous; petiole 2–3 mm, tomentose-villous. Fertile shoots 30–40 mm, including 4 leaves and a compact, 3- to 13-flowered inflorescence; pedicels 2–4 mm, tomentose-pilose; flowers (including hypanthium) 5–6 mm long, pink in bud. Hypanthium cupulate, tomentose-pilose; sepals obtuse or apiculate, tomentose-villous, border broad, brown, glabrous, margin whitish tomentose. Corolla with small opening; petals erect-incurved, pale green tinged red. Stamens 18–20; filaments pink, soon red; anthers white. Fruit pendent, obovoid, 9–10 mm, orange-red with crimson tint, shiny, pilose, calyx lobes flat, tomentose, navel open. Nutlets 2(–3), style remains ²/₃–³/₄ from base.

Seasons: Flowers June; fruit ripe October–November.

Chromosomes: Tetraploid (Klotz and Krügel 1983a). Apomictic, true from seed.

Hardiness: –25°C (–13°F). Very hardy.

Area: China (Sichuan, probably also some surrounding provinces).

Notes: This species has long been in cultivation as *Cotoneaster kitaibelii* hort. It was reintroduced by the 1996 expedition to Sichuan as *SICH 1809*—but seeds were collected from six different shrubs. Possibly originally introduced into cultivation from the Wilson collection 1167 from Hubei.

9. *Cotoneaster miniatus* (Rehder & E. H. Wilson) Flinck & B. Hylmö in Bot. Not. (Lund) 119: 456 (1966). Synonym: *C. zabelii* C. K. Schneider var. *miniatus* Rehder & Wilson (1917). Type: cult. United States, Arnold Arboretum, *Cotoneaster* 153 Wilson, *C. zabelii miniata* collected 3 July 1914, raised from seed collected in China, W Hubei, Chang-lo Hsien, autumn 1907, *E. H. Wilson 153* (holo A).

Shrub, 1.5 (–2) m. Branches erect, spreading, slender and weak; branchlets distichous, divaricate, light brown, initially tomentose-pilose. Leaves deciduous, chartaceous, on sterile shoots ovate or elliptic, 30–40 × 19–25 mm, apex acute or obtuse, base cuneate or obtuse, upper surface yellowish green, dull, pilose, veins 3–5 impressed, lower surface reticulate, pilose; petiole 3–5 mm, densely pilose. Fertile shoots 35–45 mm, including 4 leaves and a lax, 8- to 18-flowered inflorescence; pedicels 5–10 mm, slender, pilose; flowers (including hypanthium) 4–5 mm long. Hypanthium cupulate, villous-pilose; sepals obtuse, villous, margin villous. Corolla with large opening; petals erect, exceeding sepals by 1 mm, pink tinged red. Stamens 20, white or pale pink; anthers white. Fruit pendent, depressed-globose or obovoid, 4–9 mm, orange-red, sparsely villous, calyx lobes flat, villous, navel slightly open. Nutlets 2(–3), style remains ³/₄ from base.

Seasons: Flowers July; fruit ripe October; autumn leaves intense yellow.

Chromosomes: Tetraploid (Zeilinga 1964). Apomictic, true from seed.

Hardiness: –21°C (–6°F).

Area: China (Hubei, Henan, Shaanxi).

Notes: *Cotoneaster miniatus*, although a pretty little shrub, is uncommon in cultivation, except in the United States where it grows very well in the climate of the Seattle (Washington) area. It is very effective grown on a single stem as a standard. Recently reintroduced into cultivation.

10. *Cotoneaster schantungensis* G. Klotz in Wiss. Z. Friedrich-Schiller-Univ. Jena, Math.-Naturwiss. 21: 1018 (1972). Type: China, Shandong, Lung tung near Tsi-nan fu, 7 September 1930, *C. Y. Chiao 3074* (holo BM, iso B, C, PE).

Shrub, 1.5–2.5 m. Branches erect, arched and spreading; branchlets distichous, maroon, initially tomentose-pilose. Leaves deciduous, chartaceous or subcoriaceous, on sterile shoots elliptic or ovate, 21–35 × 15–20 mm, apex acute or obtuse, base obtuse, upper surface slightly rugose, dark green, villous, dull, veins 3–5 impressed, lower surface tomentose-villous; petiole 2–5 mm, villous. Fertile shoots 35–40 mm, including 3 leaves and a spreading, lax, 3- to 6-flowered inflorescence; pedicels 2–8 mm, villous; flowers (including hypanthium) 8 mm long. Hypanthium widely cupulate, villous; sepals obtuse or acute, villous, border membranous, margin villous. Corolla open; petals erect, exceeding sepals by 1.5 mm. Stamens 20, filaments pale pink or white; anthers white. Fruit pendent, obovoid, 6–8 mm, red. Nutlets 2.

Seasons: Flowers June–July; fruit ripe October–November; autumn color good.

Hardiness: −21°C (−6°F).

Area: China (Shandong).

Notes: *Cotoneaster schantungensis* is not common in cultivation and is mainly found in botanic gardens and large private collections. It holds its fruit well into late autumn and hence is loved by the birds. Not in key.

11. *Cotoneaster shansiensis* J. Fryer & B. Hylmö in New Plantsman 5: 135 (1998).

Synonym: *Cotoneaster schansiensis* Flinck & Hylmö nom. nud. in Klotz, Wiss. Z. Friedrich-Schiller-Univ. Jena, Math.-Naturwiss. 21: 1016 (1972) name only. Type: cult. Sweden, Bjuv, garden of B. Hylmö, as plant #9495 raised from seed collected in the botanic garden at Göteborg University in 1958 from *Harry Smith 11 286* (seed), China, Shanxi, Mei Shan, 3 October 1924. 4 July 1964, B. Hylmö (holo E). **PLATE 146.**

Shrub, 1.5 (–2) m. Branches erect, gracefully arched, spreading; branchlets slender, yellowish brown, initially pilose-tomentose. Leaves deciduous, chartaceous, on sterile shoots suborbicular, elliptic or ovate, 21–35 × 17–24 mm, apex obtuse or acute, base obtuse, upper surface grayish green, pilose-villous, veins 2–4, lower surface grayish green pilose-tomentose; petiole 4–6 mm, villous. Fertile shoots 30–60 mm, including 2–4 leaves and a lax, 15- to 30-flowered inflorescence; pedicels 5–8 mm, villous; flowers (including hypanthium) 5 mm long. Hypanthium cupulate, villous-tomentose; sepals obtuse or acute, villous-tomentose. Corolla open, 8–9 mm, petals semispreading, exceeding sepals by 1.5–2 mm, pink with darker pink centre. Stamens 20; filaments white, base pink; anthers white. Fruit pendent, obovoid, 10–11 mm, orange, sparsely pilose-villous, calyx lobes flat, pilose-villous. Nutlets 2, style remains ²/₃ from base.

Seasons: Flowers May–June, sometimes reflowers September; fruit ripe September–October; autumn leaves yellow.

Chromosomes: Tetraploid (Krügel 1992; McAllister, pers. comm.). Apomictic, true from seed.

Hardiness: −21°C (−6°F).

Area: China (Shanxi, Shaanxi, Henan, Hubei).

Notes: *Cotoneaster shansiensis* is one of the loveliest cotoneasters. This graceful, elegant shrub has many pretty soft pink flowers and droplet-shaped pale orange fruit which hang attractively in numerous quantities on long, slender pedicels along the undersides of the branches. It can be trained on a single stem as a standard. *Cotoneaster shansiensis* seems to be the most common species of series *Zabelioides* in the wild.

12. *Cotoneaster svenhedinii* J. Fryer & B. Hylmö, *sp. nov.* Type: China, SW Gansu, Lower Tebbu country, Wantsang valley, September 1926, *J. F. Rock 14829* (holo A). **PLATE 178.**

Shrub, 1–2 m. Branches 2–3 m, ascending, slender; branchlets distichous, maroon, initially tomentose-pilose. Leaves deciduous, thinly chartaceous, on sterile shoots ovate or elliptic, 26–34 × 16–18 mm, apex acute, base obtuse, upper surface mid-green, dull, pilose, veins 4–5 lightly impressed, lower surface tomentose-pilose; petiole 3–4 mm, tomentose-villous. Fertile shoots 20–40 mm, including 3–4 leaves and a 7- to 17-flowered inflorescence; pedicels 3–7 mm, slender, pilose; flowers (including hypanthium) 4–5 mm long. Hypanthium cupulate, brick-red, long-haired villous; sepals obtuse or acute, villous, border broad and white, margin villous. Corolla wide open; petals erect to semi-spreading, off-white with pale pink blotch at base. Stamens 16–20; filaments white or pale pink; anthers white. Fruit pendent, obovoid, 9–11 mm, light red, dull, sparsely villous, calyx lobes flat. Nutlets 2(–3), style remains 2/3 from base.

Seasons: Flowers June; fruit ripe September.
Chromosomes: Unknown. Apomictic, true from seed.
Hardiness: –21°C (–6°F).
Area: China (Gansu).
Notes: *Cotoneaster svenhedinii* is named in honor of the Swedish explorer Sven Hedin, leader of the 1931 expedition to Gansu. A very garden-worthy shrub.

13. *Cotoneaster zabelii* C. K. Schneider in Illustr. Handb. Laubholzk. 1: 749 (1906); cf. Feddes Repert. 3: 220 (1906). Type: China, Mount Kan-Y-San, Shaanxi, 12 June 1897, G. Giraldi is (lecto designated A). PLATE 179.

Shrub, 1.5–2 m. Branches ascending, spreading; branchlets distichous, maroon, initially tomentose-pilose. Leaves deciduous, chartaceous to subcoriaceous, on sterile shoots ovate or elliptic, 32–40 × 20–23 mm, apex acute or obtuse, base obtuse, upper surface rugose, dark green, dull, sparsely pilose, veins 3–5 somewhat deeply impressed, lower surface tomentose-villous; petiole 3–5 mm, tomentose-villous. Fertile shoots 15–45 mm, including 4 leaves and a 3- to 13-flowered inflorescence; pedicels 3–8 mm, pilose; flowers (including hypanthium) 7 mm long, pale pink in bud. Hypanthium cupulate, tomentose-villous; sepals obtuse or acute, villous, margin villous. Corolla open. Petals erect to semi-spreading, exceeding sepals by 1.5, white with few pink dots. Stamens 20; filaments white; anthers white. Fruit pendent, obovoid, 10–11 mm, red to ruby, shiny, succulent, sparsely villous, calyx lobes flat, densely villous, navel slightly open. Nutlets 2(–3), style remains 4/5 from base.

Seasons: Flowers June; fruit ripe October; autumn leaves bright yellow to russet.
Chromosomes: Tetraploid (Hensen 1966; Krügel 1992a). Apomictic, true from seed.
Hardiness: –21°C (–6°F).
Area: China (Shaanxi).
Notes: We reject the lectotype for *Cotoneaster zabelii* designated by Klotz (1972a, 1016), which was said not to be the same as *C. zabelii* commonly in cultivation. The Schneider description is complete and obviously based on living material which probably originated from the nurseries of central Europe and is identical *C. zabelii* at present in cultiva-

tion. The species was introduced to the United Kingdom in 1907. Received an RHS Award of Merit in 1912.

33. Series *Tomentosi* J. Fryer & B. Hylmö, *ser. nov.*

Medium shrubs. Branches narrowly erect, arched. Fertile shoots 25–70 mm, including a mostly erect inflorescence. Hypanthium tomentose. Petals erect-incurved, greenish white with pink. Nutlets 3–5.

Early to mid season (but later flowering and fruiting than series *Cotoneaster*).

Europe (Alps, Pyrenees, Tatras, Balkans). Caucasus (area between Black and Caspian Seas).

3 species: *C. intermedius, C. soczavianus, C. tomentosus.*

Key to Series *Tomentosi*

1a. Leaves ≤ c. 40 mm; inflorescence 3- to 7-flowered; pedicels pilose-villous; sepals mostly low obtuse, sparsely villous . . . .*C. intermedius*

1b. Leaves ≤ 65 mm; inflorescence 5- to 12-flowered; pedicels tomentose; sepals mostly acute, tomentose 2

2a. Branches ascending; leaves elliptic or suborbicular, apex mostly obtuse, upper surface dark green; fertile shoots ≤ 50 mm; inflorescence compact . . . .*C. tomentosus*

2b. Branches erect and arched; leaves obovate or elliptic, apex mostly acute, upper surface light green; fertile shoots ≤ 70 mm; inflorescence lax . . . . *C. soczavianus*

1. *Cotoneaster intermedius* H. J. Coste (*pro. hybr.*) in Bull. Soc. Bot. France 40: 1 22 (1893). Type: France, Aveyron, Le Larzac, Viala-du-pas-de-Jaux, 8 May 1893, leg. H. J. Coste 274 (lecto selected Flinck, Fryer et al. 1997 P).

Shrub, 1.5–2 m. Branches erect and ascending; branchlets spiraled, grayish maroon, shiny, lenticellate, initially tomentose-pilose. Leaves deciduous, chartaceous, on sterile shoots broadly elliptic or broadly ovate, 30–65 × 17–30 mm, apex or obtuse, base rotund or truncate, upper surface slightly rugose, mid-green, dull to slightly shiny, initially pilose, veins 5–10 impressed, lower surface tomentose-pilose; petiole 4–9 mm, tomentose-villous. Fertile shoots 25–55 mm, including 3–4 leaves and a semispreading, lax 2- to 7-flowered inflorescence; pedicels 3–10 mm, densely pilose-villous; flowers (including hypanthium) 4–6 mm long. Hypanthium cupulate, densely pilose-villous, apex often sparsely so; sepals low, acute or obtuse, sparsely villous, border narrow, membranous and glabrous, margin tomentose. Corolla open; petals erect, slightly incurved, exceeding sepals by 1.5–2 mm, greenish off-white with pink. Stamens 16–20; filaments off-white with pink; anthers white. Fruit depressed-globose, rich red, slightly shiny, sparsely pilose, calyx lobes flat, succulent, navel open. Nutlets (2–)3–4(–5), style remains $^{1}/_{2}$–$^{2}/_{3}$ from base.

Seasons: Flowers May; fruit ripe October–November; autumn leaves gold and red.

Hardiness: −21°C (−6°F).

Area: France. Italy.

Notes: *Cotoneaster intermedius*, from the Central Massif and the W Alps, has recently been brought into cultivation from collections made in the borders of France and Italy by Luc Garraud, curator of the National Alpine Botanical Conservatory in Gap, France. Reports of *C. intermedius* from Greece are *C. parnassicus*.

2. *Cotoneaster soczavianus* Pojarkova in Not. Syst. Inst. Bot. Acad. Sci. USSR 17: 179 (1955). Type: Caucasus, at river Malaja Laba, 14 September 1945, V. Soczava, A. Gavrilevicz & M. Schik (holo LE). **PLATE 180**.

Shrub, 1.5–2 m. Branches erect and arched; branchlets spiraled, greenish brown to maroon, lenticellate, initially tomentose-pilose. Leaves deciduous, chartaceous, on sterile shoots obovate or elliptic, 45–63 × 28–37 mm, apex obtuse or acute, base obtuse or cuneate, upper surface light green, dull or slightly shiny, initially pilose, veins 5–7 impressed, lower surface tomentose; petiole 5–8 mm. Fertile shoots 50–70 mm, including 4 leaves and an erect, lax, 5- to 12-flowered inflorescence; pedicels 2–8 mm, tomentose, flowers (including hypanthium) 5–6 mm. Hypanthium cupulate, often deep yellow, tomentose; sepals acute or obtuse, tomentose, border membranous, glabrous, margin red-brown and tomentose. Corolla with small opening; petals erect, incurved, exceeding sepals by 1–2 mm, off-white and pinkish. Stamens 20; filaments white; anthers white. Fruit depressed-globose or obovoid, 9–10 mm, red, shiny, sparsely villous, calyx lobes depressed, villous, navel open. Nutlets (4–)5, rarely 3, style remains $^2/_3$ from base.

Seasons: Flowers May–June, often reflowers August; fruit ripe September–October; autumn leaves pure yellow.

Chromosomes: Tetraploid (Gladkova 1968; Klotz and Krügel 1983a).

Hardiness: −25°C (−13°F).

Area: Armenia. Azerbaijan. Georgia.

Notes: In 1959 seed from the type collection of *Cotoneaster soczavianus* was personally given to Bertil Hylmö by Antonina Pojarkova and shrubs raised from this seed exist in cultivation in Bjuv, Sweden (hort. 9330). A garden-worthy shrub.

3. *Cotoneaster tomentosus* (Aiton) Lindley in Trans. Linn. Soc. London 13: 101 (1822). Synonyms: *Mespilus tomentosa* Aiton in Hort. Kew. Cat. 2: 174 (1789); *Cotoneaster nebrodensis* in Flora Europaea (Tutin et al. 1968). Type: Baenitz, Herbarium europaeum, Dalen, Austria, August 1875 (lecto designated K).

Shrub, 1–2 m. Branches to 2 m, erect, ascending, or spreading prostrate with constant weight of winter snows; branchlets greenish brown to maroon, lenticellate, initially tomentose-pilose. Leaves deciduous, chartaceous, on sterile shoots elliptic or suborbicular, 34–65 × 23–48 mm, apex obtuse seldom acute, base obtuse, upper surface dark green, dull, pilose, veins 4–5 impressed, lower surface tomentose; petiole 4–6 mm, tomentose. Fertile shoots 25–50 mm, including 3–4 leaves and an erect, compact 5- to 12-flowered inflorescence; pedicels 3–6 mm, tomentose; flowers (including hypanthium) 5–7 mm

long. Hypanthium cupulate, tomentose; sepals acute or obtuse, tomentose, border narrow, membranous, glabrous, margin tomentose. Corolla with small opening; petals erect,
incurved, exceeding sepals by 2 mm), off-white tinged green and pink ageing brownish
red. Stamens (18–)20; filaments white with pinkish base; anthers white. Fruit depressed-
globose or obovoid, 9–12 mm, red, pilose, calyx lobes depressed, tomentose. Nutlets (4–)5,
rarely 3, style remains $1/2$ from base.

Seasons: Flowers May–June, reflowers August–September; fruit ripe October–
November; autumn leaves red.

Chromosomes: Tetraploid (Zeilinga 1964; Hensen 1966; Gladkova 1968; Klotz 1968b;
Kroon 1975; Jewsbury, pers. comm.). Pentaploid (Favarger 1975 as quoted in Löve 1975;
Klotz and Krügel 1983a; Krügel 1992a; Jewsbury, pers. comm.).

Hardiness: –25°C (–13°F). Very hardy.

Area: Europe: Alps, Tatras, Balkans. Turkey. Records from the Pyrenees not confirmed.

Notes: In 1789 W. Aiton described *Cotoneaster tomentosus* (as *Mespilus tomentosa*)
as having 5 nutlets per fruit. Over the years this species has been raised from seed obtained
from 7 different botanic gardens, and indeed 80 percent of the time the fruit contained 5
nutlets. The type shrub, originating from the Tyrol and propagated at the RBG Kew, was
quite likely the original source of *C. tomentosus* in all 7 gardens. In the western Alps
the fruit of *C. tomentosus* contains mostly 3–4 nutlets, rarely 5. In the area of the Balkans
this species needs further investigation. It is quite likely that there are several taxa shar-
ing the name *C. tomentosus*. Collected by Jeanette Fryer (*JFIT 01*) in 1991 in Italy above
Lake Como.

34. Series *Cotoneaster*

Dwarf to medium shrubs. Branches erect, ascending, decumbent or prostrate. Fertile
shoots mostly 10–25 mm including a pendent, 1- to 7-flowered inflorescence. Hypanthium glabrous; sepals often ligulate. Petals erect-incurved, equal to or exceeding sepals,
1–2 mm. Fruit mostly subsessile or on short pedicels. Nutlets 2–4(–5).

Very early to early season.

Europe. Western and Central Asia.

17 species: *C. alatavicus*, *C. alaunicus*, *C. antoninae*, *C. cambricus*, *C. canescens*, *C.
cinnabarinus*, *C. estiensis*, *C. favargeri*, *C. integerrimus*, *C. juranus*, *C. kullensis*, *C. obtusisepalus*, *C. raboutensis*, *C. scandinavicus*, *C. tjuliniae*, *C. uniflorus*, *C. uralensis*.

Notes: Species of series *Cotoneaster* are the most widespread of any series in geographical range, from Wales in the west, throughout Europe, western and central Asia to
Kashmir, and northwest to the area surrounding lake Baikal. Also it is probably the most
problematic series of *Cotoneaster* in Europe. As early as 1875 Michel Gandoger had separated *C. juranus* and *C. obtusisepalus* from *C. integerrimus*. However, these two species
were disregarded in *Flora Europaea* (Tutin et al. 1968). Subsequent to the understanding

of apomixis in *Cotoneaster*, Hrabětová-Uhrová's (1962) *Cotoneaster* varieties from the Czech Republic and Slovakia need further investigation.

Key to Series *Cotoneaster*

1a. Fertile shoots 15–50 mm; inflorescence 3- to 8(–10)-flowered; nutlet with style remains $^2/_3$ from base **2**

1b. Fertile shoots 5–25 mm; inflorescence 1- to 3(–4)-flowered; nutlet with style remains $^1/_2$ from base **4**

2a. Branchlets divaricate; upper leaf surface glabrous; pedicels 2–8 mm; sepals mostly acute; filaments off-white . . . .***C. raboutensis***

2b. Branchlets spiraled; upper leaf surface initially pilose; pedicels 3–15 mm; sepals mostly obtuse; filaments pale pink **3**

3a. Leaves ≤ 44 mm, broadly elliptic or suborbicular, apex mostly obtuse, veins lightly impressed; fertile shoots ≤ 50 mm . . . . ***C. canescens***

3b. Leaves ≤ 55 mm, broadly ovate, apex mostly acute, veins deeply impressed; fertile shoots ≤ 25(–35) mm . . . .***C. integerrimus***

4a. New growth mostly pilose or villous; leaves ≤ 30–40(–45) × 19–24(–31) mm; inflorescence 1- to 2(–4)-flowered **5**

4b. Branchlets mostly tomentose; leaves ≤ 40–70 × 27–50 mm; inflorescence (1- to) 2- to 4(–5)-flowered **9**

5a. Upper leaf surface glabrous, dull, veins not impressed; fertile shoots 5–10 mm; pedicels ≤ 3 mm, glabrous. **6**

5b. Upper leaf surface initially pilose, shiny, veins impressed; fertile shoots 8–20 mm; pedicels 1–18 mm, pilose or tomentose **7**

6a. Branchlets pilose-villous, soon glabrous; leaves narrowly elliptic or narrowly ovate, apex mostly acute . . . .***C. uniflorus***

6b. Branchlets tomentose-pilose; leaves broadly elliptic, broadly ovate or suborbicular, apex mostly obtuse . . . . ***C. cinnabarinus***

7a. Leaves mostly broadly elliptic, ≤ 30 mm, apex mostly obtuse; flowers (including hypanthium) 4–5 mm; petals equal sepals or exceeding by 1 mm; sepals ligulate; fruit 5–8 mm. . . . . ***C. cambricus***

7b. Leaves mostly ovate, ≤ 40–45 mm, apex mostly acute; flowers (including hypanthium) 6–7 mm; petals to twice length sepals; sepals mostly obtuse; fruit 8–10 mm. **8**

8a. Branches ascending or prostrate; flowers (including hypanthium) 1–3(–4); pedicels 1–5 mm; fruit ruby over-ripe maroon. . . . . ***C. alatavicus***

8b. Branches mostly erect; flowers 1(–3); pedicels 8–18 mm; fruit orange-red, densely pruinose . . . . ***C. tjuliniae***

9a. Leaves 28–47 mm, mostly glaucous; pedicels 3–10 mm **10**

9b. Leaves 31–70 mm, shiny becoming dull; pedicels 1–8 mm **12**

10a. Leaves ovate; sepals ligulate; nutlets 2–3(–4) . . . . *C. juranus*

10b. Leaves mostly broadly elliptic or broadly ovate; nutlets (2–)3–4 . . . .**11**

11a. Upper leaf surface light to mid-green, apex obtuse, veins not impressed, petiole 2–4 mm; fertile shoots 8–13 mm; flowers (1–)2–3. . . . . *C. scandinavicus*

11b. Upper leaf surface dark to bluish green, apex acute, veins becoming lightly impressed, petiole 4–8 mm; fertile shoots 10–20 mm; flowers 1(–3). . . . . *C. obtusisepalus*

12a. Branchlets brown-maroon; leaves ovate or elliptic, apex acute, margin undulate; flowers (1–)2–3(–5); filaments pale pink to nearly off-white. . . . . *C. kullensis*

12b. Branchlets purple-black; leaves broadly ovate, broadly elliptic or suborbicular, apex mostly obtuse, margin flat; flowers 1–4; filaments white **13**

13a. Branches stiffly erect; leaves to 40 mm, petiole tomentose; sepals ligulate, erose; fruit blood-red to pale ruby . . . . *C. alaunicus*

13b. Branches ascending or erect; leaves ≤ 45 65 mm, petiole pilose; sepals mostly obtuse, entire, fruit orange-red, ripening currant-red. **14**

14a. Branches mostly erect; leaves mostly suborbicular, ≤ 45 mm, base mostly truncate; pedicels 2–8 mm, pilose; fruit globose; 8–10 mm . . . . *C. uralensis*

14b. Branches ascending; leaves mostly broadly elliptic or broadly ovate, ≤ 65 mm, base rotund; pedicels 1–5 mm, subglabrous; fruit obovoid, 7–8 mm. . . . . *C. antoninae*

1. *Cotoneaster alatavicus* Popov in Bull. Soc. Imp. Nat. Mosc. 47: 86 (1938). Synonym: *C. pojarkovae* Zakirov (1955). Type: China, Xinjiang, Trans-Ili Alata mountains, Turgen river, Tesken-Su springs, 28 August 1936, M. G. Popov (holo LE).

Shrub, 0.5–1 m. Branches narrowly ascending or prostrate; branchlets spiraled, reddish brown to purple-black, initially pilose-strigose. Leaves deciduous, chartaceous, on sterile shoots ovate or elliptic, 22–45 × 15–31 mm, apex acute or obtuse, base rotund or cuneate, upper surface slightly rugose, dark green, shiny, initially sparsely long-haired pilose, veins 4–5 lightly impressed, lower surface densely pilose-villous; petiole 3–5 mm, often red, pilose-villous. Fertile shoots 10–20 mm, including 2–3 leaves and a pendent, 1- to 3(–4)-flowered inflorescence; pedicels 1–5 mm, pilose or glabrous; flowers (including hypanthium) 6 mm long. Hypanthium cupulate, glabrous; sepals rotund or obtuse, glabrous, border membranous, reddish purple, margin sparsely villous. Corolla with small opening; petals erect or suberect, exceeding sepals by 1–2 mm, pink and red with off-white stripe. Stamens 20; filaments off-white or pale pink; anthers white. Fruit globose or obovoid, succulent, 8–9 mm, ruby to maroon, glabrous, calyx lobes flat. Nutlets 2–4, style remains $^1/_2$–$^3/_4$ from base.

Seasons: Flowers May; fruit ripe August; autumn leaves purple-red with yellow patches.

Chromosomes: Unknown. Apomictic, true from seed.

Hardiness: −21°C (−6°F).

Area: China (Xinjiang) to Kyrgyzstan.

Notes: *Cotoneaster alatavicus* is uncommon in cultivation but is well worth growing for its autumn leaf color alone. It was collected in August 2005 by Géza Kósa of Vácrátót, Hungary, between Bishkek and Issyk Kul lake in the Tian Shan range, Kyrgyzstan.

2. *Cotoneaster alaunicus* Golitsin in Nov. Syst. Pl. Vasc. (Leningrad) p.145 (1964).

Type: Russia, province Orlovskaja, Galitshia Gora reserve, at Botki, by the river Jasenek, 30 August 1949, S. Golitsin (holo LE).

Shrub, 1.5–2 m. Branches narrowly erect, slender; branchlets spiraled, divaricate, purple-black, initially tomentose-pilose. Leaves deciduous, chartaceous, on sterile shoots broadly ovate, broadly elliptic or suborbicular, 34–40 × 22–29 mm, apex rotund or acute, base rotund or truncate, upper surface sometimes slightly rugose, mid-green, dull, initially sparsely pilose, veins 4–5, lower surface reticulate, densely-pilose; petiole 4–7 mm, tomentose. Fertile shoots 10–25 mm, including 2–4 leaves and a pendent, 1- to 4-flowered inflorescence; pedicels 2–8 mm, sparsely pilose; flowers (including hypanthium) 5–6 mm long. Hypanthium cupulate, glabrous; sepals ligulate, glabrous, border membranous, red, margin erose and villous. Corolla open; petals suberect, exceeding sepals by 1–2 mm, off-white with pink stripe. Stamens 20; filaments white; anthers white. Fruit globose or obovoid, 7–8 mm, red to pale ruby, glabrous, calyx lobes suberect, navel open. Nutlets (2–)3(–4), style remains ¹/₂ from base.

Seasons: Flowers April–May; fruit ripe July; autumn leaves purple-red.
Chromosomes: Tetraploid (Klotz 1968b; Krügel 1992a). Apomictic, true from seed.
Hardiness: –25°C (–13°F).
Area: S Russia. NW Caucasus.

Notes: Sergei Golitsin described *Cotoneaster alaunicus*, a species well known in the southeastern part of European Russia, as having fruit dark brown to black (perfecta fusco-nigri nec nigris), but as the type was collected late in its season of fruiting (30 August), they were probably over ripe. Klotz (pers. comm.) said offspring of the type in the botanic garden of Moscow produced fruit which were a darker red than those of *C. integerrimus*. *Cotoneaster alaunicus* is closely related to both *C. uralensis* and *C. antoninae*, differing in, among other details, its narrowly erect habit and darker fruit color.

3. *Cotoneaster antoninae* Juzepczuk in Not. Syst. Inst. Bot. Acad. Sci. 13: 33 (1950).

Type: Russia, Murmansk, Velikij island in Kandalaksha bay on the White Sea, 3 August 1951, Kuzeneva & Ponomareva (lecto LE, iso KIROUSK).

Shrub, 0.5–1 m. Branches ascending; branchlets spiraled, purple-black, lenticellate and minutely verruculose, initially densely pilose. Leaves deciduous, chartaceous, on sterile shoots broadly elliptic, 31–65 × 24–50 mm, apex rotund or acute, base rotund, upper surface green, dull, initially sparsely pilose, veins 4–5, lower surface reticulate, pilose-villous; petiole 4–6 mm, pilose. Fertile shoots 10–15 mm including 1–3 leaves and a pendent, 1- to 4-flowered inflorescence; pedicels 1–5 mm, subglabrous; flowers (including hypanthium) 4–5 mm long. Hypanthium cupulate, glabrous; sepals obtuse or acute, border broad, membranous, reddish purple, margin short haired villous. Corolla with large opening; petals suberect, exceeding sepals by 1 mm, off-white with pink. Stamens 20; filaments off-white; anthers white. Fruit obovoid, 7–8 mm, orange-red ripening red, glabrous, calyx lobes flat. Nutlets (2–)3(–4), style remains $^1/_2$ from base.

Seasons: Flowers April; fruit ripe July; autumn leaves red.

Chromosomes: Tetraploid (Gladkova 1968). Apomictic, true from seed.

Hardiness: −25°C (−13°F). Very hardy.

Area: NW Russia (Kola Peninsula, Karelia).

Notes: Orlova (1959) treated *Cotoneaster antoninae* as a hybrid, but repeated propagation by seed has proved it to be an apomictic species. Originating from the Russian provinces north of Lake Ladoga, this species is rarely found in cultivation. It is lovely when grown with heathers (*Erica* sp.), spreading its sparse branches with silvery-haired young leaves just above their heads.

4. *Cotoneaster cambricus* J. Fryer & B. Hylmö in Watsonia 20: 62 (1994); illustr. Ross-Craig. Drawings of British Plants 9: 37 (1956). Synonym: *C. integerrimus* Medikus var. *anglicus* Hrabětová (1962). Type: British Isles, Wales, Caernarvonshire, Llandudno, c. 1936, *L. Price H 899* (60) 4 (holo K).

Shrub, 1–1.5 m. Branches erect; branchlets spiraled, greenish brown to purple-black, initially densely villous. Leaves deciduous, chartaceous, on sterile shoots broadly elliptic or suborbicular, 17–30 × 14–20 mm, apex obtuse or acute, base obtuse, upper surface ageing slightly rugose, gray-green, slightly shiny, initially pilose, veins 4–5 lightly impressed, lower surface tomentose; petiole 3–7 mm, tomentose. Fertile shoots 8–20 mm, with up to 2 leaves and a pendent, 1- to 2(–4)-flowered inflorescence; pedicels 2–5 mm, tomentose; flowers (including hypanthium) 4–5 mm long. Hypanthium cupulate, base pilose; sepals ligulate, border broad, membranous, margin villous. Corolla open; petals erect-incurved, equal to or exceeding sepals by 1 mm, off-white sometimes pink tinged. Stamens 20; filaments off-white; anthers white. Fruit globose, 5–8 mm, red with orange tones, glabrous, calyx lobes depressed. Nutlets (2–)3–4, style remains $^1/_2$–$^2/_3$ from base.

Seasons: Flowers May; fruit ripe August–September.

Chromosomes: Tetraploid (McAllister, pers. comm.; Jewsbury, pers. comm.). Apomictic, true from seed.

Hardiness: −21°C (−6°F).

Area: British Isles (Wales).

Notes: *Cotoneaster cambricus* is endemic to the cliffs of the Great Orme peninsula in N Wales. Its closest relative is probably *C. kullensis* of S Sweden. *Cotoneaster cambricus* is also related to *C. integerrimus* but differs in its later-dehiscing leaves, which are smaller and more suborbicular with an obtuse apex, much fewer-flowered inflorescence, and fruit red with orange tones. There are many collections of *C. cambricus* in herbaria throughout the British Isles—mostly labeled *C. integerrimus*.

5. *Cotoneaster canescens* Vestergren ex B. Hylmö in Svensk. Bot. Tidskr. 87: 319
  (1993). Type: Sweden, Öland, Borgholm, 20 July 1917, *Gustaf Neander 281*
  (holo S).

Shrub, 1.5–2.5 m. Branches erect, spreading; branchlets spiraled, reddish brown, initially
tomentose-pilose. Leaves deciduous, chartaceous, on sterile shoots broadly elliptic or
suborbicular, 30–44 × 23–30 mm, apex obtuse, seldom acute, base obtuse or truncate,
margin undulate, upper surface mid-green, shiny soon dull, initially pilose, midrib remaining pilose, veins 5–6 lightly impressed, lower surface grayish tomentose-villous;
petiole 4–8 mm, tomentose. Fertile shoots 15–50 mm, including mostly 2–3 leaves and a
pendent, (1–)3- to 5(–10)-flowered inflorescence; pedicels 3–15 mm, pilose; flowers
(including hypanthium) 4–6 mm long. Hypanthium cupulate, glabrous; sepals obtuse,
rarely acute, glabrous, border broad, membranous, margin villous. Corolla with small
opening; petals erect-incurved, exceeding sepals by 1–2 mm, off-white with pink stripe
and border. Stamens (18–)20; filaments pale pink or white tinged pink; anthers white.
Fruit globose or obovoid, 8–10 mm, succulent, red to pale ruby, glabrous, calyx lobes
depressed. Nutlets (2–)3(–4), style remains $^2/_3$ from base.

  Seasons: Flowers April–May; fruit ripe July–August.

  Chromosomes: Tetraploid (Bailey, pers. comm.; Jewsbury, pers. comm.). Apomictic,
true from seed.

  Hardiness: −25°C (−13°F).

  Area: Sweden (Öland, Gotland).

  Notes: *Cotoneaster canescens* is the largest of the species in series *Cotoneaster*. It is
rare in cultivation but can be found in some specialist collections. Recently reintroduced
into cultivation.

6. *Cotoneaster cinnabarinus* Juzepczuk in Not. Syst. Inst. Bot. Acad. Sci. USSR 13:
  32 (1950); illustr. Oulova, Flora Murmanskoj Oblasti 14: 54 (1959). Type: Plantae
  Finlandiae exiccatae 752 *C. integerrimus* Medikus var. *uniflorus* (Bunge), Russia,
  Lapland, Schelesna, near Kandalaksha city, 25 July 1913, *Harald Lindberg 752* (holo
  LE, iso LD).

Shrub, sparsely branched, 0.2–0.5 m. Branches 1–1.5 m, decumbent, slender; branchlets
spiraled, purple-black, initially tomentose-pilose. Leaves deciduous, chartaceous, on
sterile shoots broadly elliptic, broadly ovate or suborbicular, 22–31 × 17–21 mm, apex
obtuse or acute, base obtuse or cuneate, upper surface mid-green, shiny soon dull, glabrous, veins 4–5, lower surface reticulate, sparsely yellowish pilose hairs more dense on
midrib and veins; petiole 3–7 mm, pilose. Fertile shoots 5–10 mm, including 1–2 leaves
and a pendent, 1(–3)-flowered inflorescence; pedicel absent to 2 mm; flower (including
hypanthium) 4 mm long. Hypanthium cupulate, glabrous; sepals ligulate, obtuse or
acute, border broad, membranous, margin glabrous or short haired villous. Corolla with
small opening; petals erect-incurved, not reaching above sepals, greenish white sometimes
pink-tinged. Stamens 20; filaments off-white; anthers white. Fruit globose or depressed-

globose, succulent, 7–8 mm, orange-red, glabrous, calyx lobes depressed. Nutlets 3–4, style remains ¹/₂ from base.

Seasons: Flowers April; fruit ripe July.

Chromosomes: Tetraploid (Gladkova 1968; Klotz and Krügel 1983a). Apomictic, true from seed.

Hardiness: –25°C (–13°F). Very hardy.

Area: NW Russia (Kola Peninsula, Archangelsk).

Notes: *Cotoneaster cinnabarinus*, due to its very early flowering when the pollen beetles are scarcely active, has a poor fruit set. It is the earliest into leaf of the species in series *Cotoneaster*.

7. *Cotoneaster estiensis* J. Fryer & B. Hylmö, *sp. nov.* Type: Estonia, Rapla, Lipstunömme, 1982, R. Cinovskis et al. (holo RIG). **PLATE 181.**

Shrub, 1–1.5 m. Branches mostly erect; branchlets spiraled, light brown or red-brown, initially tomentose-pilose. Leaves deciduous, chartaceous, on sterile shoots broadly elliptic or obovate elliptic, 35–55 × 23–38 mm, apex acute, obtuse, mucronulate, sometimes apiculate, base rotund, obtuse or truncate, margin slightly undulated, upper surface becoming rugose, mid-green, dull or very slightly shiny, initially very sparsely pilose, veins 4–5 impressed, lower surface villous-pilose, petiole 4–8 mm, villous-strigose. Fertile shoots 10–25 mm, including 2–3 leaves and a somewhat pendent 2- to 3(–4)-flowered inflorescence, pedicels 8–10 mm, pilose-villous; flower (including hypanthium) 6–7 mm long. Hypanthium cupulate, pale green flushed brownish, glabrous; sepals acute or apiculate, glabrous, margin villous. Corolla open, petals erect-incurved, exceeding the sepals by 1 mm, white with pink center and border. Stamens c. 20; filaments white; anthers white. Fruit globose or subglobose 7–10 mm, deep ruby, glabrous; calyx lobes flat, navel open. Nutlets (2–)3–4, style remains ²/₃ from base.

Seasons: Flowers April–May; fruit ripe September; autumn leaves red.

Chromosomes: Unknown. Apomictic, true from seed.

Hardiness: –25°C (–13°F).

Area: Estonia. Latvia.

Notes: *Cotoneaster estiensis*, rarely found in cultivation, is an attractive shrub with good autumn color. Closely related to *C. kullensis*. Not in key.

8. *Cotoneaster favargeri* J. Fryer & B. Hylmö, *sp. nov.* Type: France, Pyrenees, Circque de Gavarnie, 7 August 1975, *Halliwell, Mason & Smallcombe 1184* (holo K). **PLATE 182.**

Shrub, 0.3–1 m. Branches decumbent or suberect, spreading; branchlets divaricate, spiraled, greenish brown to soft purple, initially tomentose-pilose. Leaves deciduous, chartaceous, on sterile shoots broadly ovate, ovate, lanceolate or suborbicular, 25–45 × 10–30 mm, apex acute or obtuse, base obtuse, upper surface mid-green, dull and slightly waxy, initially pilose, veins 4–5, lower surface tomentose-pilose, petiole 2–4 mm, pilose. Fertile shoots 10–15 mm, including 2–3 leaves and a pendent, 1- to 3(–5)-flowered inflorescence, pedicels 4 mm, sparsely pilose; flower (including hypanthium) 5–7 mm long. Hypanthium cupulate, yellowish green and pink with gold; sepals ligulate or high obtuse, gold and orange with red border. Corolla open; petals erect-incurved, just exceeding sepals, off-white. Stamens 15–21; filaments very pale pink; anthers white. Fruit globose, 8–10 mm, orange-red, glabrous. Nutlets (3–)4–5, rarely 2, style remains $^2/_3$ from base.

Seasons: Flowers April–May; fruit ripe July–August.

Chromosomes: Diploid (Favarger 1969, 1975 as quoted in Löve 1975; Jewsbury, pers. comm.). Sexual, outbreeding, variable from seed.

Hardiness: –21°C (–6°F).

Area: Spain. France. Italy. Switzerland.

Notes: *Cotoneaster favargeri* was named in honor of the geneticist Claude Favarger in recognition of his work with *Cotoneaster*. Due to its variable nature, this species has caused much confusion in identification. A lovely specimen of this species is growing at the RBG Kew (#180-74-07179); it originated in the French Pyrenees, from Saillagouse, a small town in the southeastern department of Pyrenees-Orientales. Recently reintroduced into cultivation.

9. **Cotoneaster integerrimus** Medikus, Gesch. Bot. p. 85 (1793); based on *Mespilus cotoneaster* Lindley, Species plantarum p. 479 (1753). Type: *Mespilus folio subrotundo fructu rubro* in Clifford herbarium (lecto BM). **PLATE 183.**

Shrub, 1.5–2 m (3–4 m supported). Branches erect, arched and spreading, coarse (to 25 mm in diameter); branchlets spiraled, maroon with large lenticels, initially tomentose-pilose. Leaves deciduous, chartaceous, on sterile shoots broadly ovate, 32–55 × 21–38 mm, apex acute or acuminate, base obtuse or truncate, margin undulate, upper surface rugose, grayish green, initially pilose, veins 4–6 deeply impressed, lower surface tomentose; petiole 3–8 mm, tomentose. Fertile shoots 15–25(–35) mm, including 2–4 leaves and a pendent, (1–)3- to 4(–6)-flowered inflorescence; pedicels 5–15 mm, sparsely pilose; flowers (including hypanthium) 6–7 mm long. Hypanthium cupulate, glabrous; sepals obtuse, glabrous, margin sparsely villous. Corolla open; petals erect-incurved, exceeding sepals by 1 mm, pale pink and off-white. Stamens 20; filaments white with pale pink base; anthers white. Fruit globose or depressed-globose, succulent, 8–11 mm, red, glabrous, calyx lobes depressed. Nutlets (2–)3(–4), style remains $^2/_3$ from base.

Seasons: Flowers April–May, reflowers August; fruit ripe July–August.

Chromosomes: Tetraploid (Klotz 1968b; Favarger 1969, 1975 as quoted in Löve 1975; Krügel 1992a); other records exist but being uncertain of the quality of identification and as few geneticists keep herbarium records, it is better to omit counts which have not been confirmed. Apomictic, true from seed.

Hardiness: –25°C (–13°F).

Area: Central Europe.

Notes: According to Charles Jarvis (pers. comm.), original elements of Linnaeus's

Mespilus cotoneaster described in *Species plantarum* (1753, 479) are the specimen *Mespilus folio subrotundo fructu rubro* in the Clifford herbarium, *LINN 646.22, 646.23*, and *646.24*, and Herb. *Burser 23:75* and *23:76*. The identities of these collections are discussed here. The specimen *Clifford 33* is very well preserved and complete. The larger leaves are partly acuminate and have an obtuse to truncate base, the inflorescences are long and contain 3–5 flowers. This clearly represents the taxon occurring in the mountains of central and eastern Europe. The specimen *LINN 646.22* was collected in early spring. The branch is straight and coarse with one secondary branch diverging at a very acute angle; the upper surface of the immature leaves are rugose and subglabrous. This seems to represent the same taxon as the Clifford specimen. But the specimen *LINN 646.23* is *Cotoneaster niger*. And the specimen *LINN 646.24* has branchlet leaves with single hairs on the upper surface and possibly represents *C. juranus*. The large leaves (on sheet) probably belong to *C. niger*. The sheet *Burser 23.75* contains two specimens: the upper specimen, probably from "Stygia," is *C. tomentosus*; the lower specimen, probably from "Misnia" (Meissen in Germany), has young leaves pilose above, and represents the same taxon as the Clifford specimen. The sheet *Burser 23:76* also contains two specimens: the left-hand one, probably from the Pyrenees, is similar to *C. juranus*; the right-hand one, probably from Gletscher Valle Augusta, is *C. juranus*. The Clifford specimen is obviously the best choice for the lectotype. This specimen is the most complete, and it is quite clear which taxon it represents. It has been marked with "6. *Mespilus Cotoneaster*" by Linnaeus. Among the references given in *Species plantarum*, the one to *Hortus Cliffortianus* was placed first. Also, the taxon it represents is probably the most widespread in series *Cotoneaster*. This specimen is therefore selected as the lectotype of *Mespilus cotoneaster* Lindley. The name *C. integerrimus* is to be reserved for the shrub with a wide distribution in Europe. The fruit of *C. integerrimus* have in the past been used in the treatment of diarrhea. Collected by Jeanette Fryer (*JFSL 01*) in the Tatranska Lomnice area of Slovakia at Liptovsky Hradek in 1990.

10. *Cotoneaster juranus* Gandoger in Flore Lyonnaise, Gallia p. 87 (1875). Synonym:
   C. mathonneti Gandoger (1875 invalid). Type: cult. Spain, Hort. Lugo, 8 October
   1872, from the Jura mountains, M. Gandoger (lecto designated LY).
Shrub, 0.5–1 m. Branches ascending, wide-spreading, slender; branchlets spiraled, purple-black, initially tomentose. Leaves deciduous, chartaceous, on sterile shoots ovate, 28–40 × 22–27 mm, apex acute, base obtuse, upper surface ageing slightly rugose, dark green, slightly waxy, glabrous, veins 4–6 lightly impressed, lower surface whitish tomentose-villous; petiole 4–8 mm, tomentose. Fertile shoots 10–25 mm, including mostly 2–3 leaves and a pendent, (1–)2- to 3(–4)-flowered inflorescence; pedicels 4–10 mm, pilose; flowers (including hypanthium) 5–6 mm long. Hypanthium cupulate, glabrous; sepals occasionally 6, high ligulate sometimes obtuse, glabrous, margin villous. Corolla open; petals erect-incurved, just exceeding sepals, off-white tinged reddish. Stamens 20; filaments off-

white; anthers white. Fruit globose or depressed-globose, 8–10 mm, orange-red to red, glabrous, calyx lobes depressed. Nutlets 2–3(–4), style remains ¹/₂ from base.

Seasons: Flowers April–May; fruit ripe July–August; autumn leaves yellow.

Chromosomes: Tetraploid (Favarger 1969, 1975 as quoted in Löve 1975; Jewsbury, pers. comm.). Apomictic, true from seed.

Hardiness: −25°C (−13°F).

Area: France. Switzerland. Italy.

Notes: *Cotoneaster juranus*, from the Jura and the Alps, has in the past been confused with *C. integerrimus* which grows in the same area. Alberto Giussani (pers. comm.) demonstrated that in the Italian and Swiss Alps *Cotoneaster* species are zoned according to altitude: *C. tomentosus* grows at the lowest, between 400 and 1500 m; *C. juranus* at the highest, between 1450 and 2250 m; and *C. integerrimus* in between and overlapping the previous two ranges. *Cotoneaster juranus* was found in Switzerland, near Maloja in 1992 by Jeanette Fryer (*JFSW 01*).

11. *Cotoneaster kullensis* B. Hylmö in Svensk Bot. Tidskr. 87: 322 (1993). Type: Sweden, Skåne, Brunnby, Arild (just west of) Stensnäs, 14 July 1971, Thomas Karlsson (holo LD, iso S). **PLATE 184.**

Shrub, 1–1.5 m. Branches to 3 m, ascending; branchlets spiraled, brown-maroon, initially tomentose-pilose. Leaves deciduous, chartaceous, on sterile shoots ovate or elliptic, 50–70 × 27–42 mm, apex acute, base obtuse or cuneate, margin with protracted undulations, upper surface soon slightly rugose, mid-green, shiny soon dull, initially pilose, veins 4–5 lightly impressed, lower surface grayish green, reticulate, tomentose-pilose; petiole 4–8 mm, tomentose. Fertile shoots 10–25 mm, including 2–3 leaves and a pendent, (1–)2- to 4(–5)-flowered inflorescence; pedicels 3–8 mm, pilose; flowers (including hypanthium) 4–5 mm long. Hypanthium cupulate, glabrous or few hairs at base; sepals ligulate, acute or obtuse, glabrous, margin broad and membranous, margin villous. Corolla with small opening; petals erect-incurved, exceeding sepals by 1 mm, off-white with pink border and stripe. Stamens (18–)20; filaments very pale pink; anthers white. Fruit globose, 6–10 mm, succulent, orange-red to red, glabrous, calyx lobes depressed. Nutlets 2–3(–4).

Seasons: Flowers April–May; fruit ripe July; autumn leaves intense yellow.

Chromosomes: Tetraploid (Bailey, pers. comm.). Apomictic, true from seed.

Hardiness: −25°C (−13°F).

Area: Sweden (Skåne).

Notes: *Cotoneaster kullensis* is endemic to the province of Skåne in southernmost Sweden, where it grows in three separate areas along the NW coastal cliffs. Karl Flinck, Jeanette Fryer, Bertil Hylmö, and Antonin Nohel collected *JFSU 01* on a rocky outcrop of the Kullen Peninsula in 1993. The closest relative to *C. kullensis* is *C. cambricus*.

12. *Cotoneaster obtusisepalus* Gandoger in Flore Lyonnaise, Gallia p. 87 (1875).
Type: France, West-Alps, Mont Rachet, 20 April 1890, ex herb. Chararis, det.
M. Gandoger (holo LY).
Shrub, 0.5–1 m. Branches to 1.5 m, decumbent, ascending or erect, slender; branchlets spiraled, purple-black, initially tomentose. Leaves deciduous, chartaceous, on sterile shoots 30–47 × 20–38 mm, elliptic or ovate (mostly broadly so) or suborbicular, apex acute, base mostly obtuse or truncate, upper surface becoming slightly rugose, dark green to blue-green, glabrous or sparse long pilose hairs mostly on midrib, veins 4–5 lightly impressed, lower surface tomentose-villous; petiole 4–8 mm, tomentose. Fertile shoots 10–20 mm, including mostly 2–3 leaves and a pendent, 1- to 3-flowered inflorescence; pedicels 3–10 mm, sparsely pilose; flowers (including hypanthium) 4–5 mm long, pinkish in bud. Hypanthium cupulate, glabrous or few hairs at base; sepals broadly obtuse or ligulate, glabrous, border membranous, often reddish, margin long-haired villous. Corolla open; petals erect-incurved, scarcely exceeding sepals, off-white with pale pink. Stamens 20; filaments white; anthers white. Fruit globose, 8–10 mm, orange-red to red, glabrous, calyx lobes suberect. Nutlets 3–4, rarely 5, style remains 1/2 from base.
Seasons: Flowers April–May; fruit ripe July–August; autumn leaves yellow to reddish.
Chromosomes: Diploid (Favarger 1969, 1975 as quoted in Löve 1975; Kroon 1975). Tetraploid (Favarger 1969, 1975 as quoted in Löve 1975; Bailey, pers. comm.; Jewsbury, pers. comm.). Sexual, outbreeding; slightly variable from seed.
Hardiness: –25°C (–13°F).
Area: France. Switzerland.
Notes: Claude Favarger demonstrated that *Cotoneaster integerrimus* in its broadest sense in Jura in the W Alps and in the Pyrenees to be both diploid and tetraploid. Despite the type specimen of *C. obtusisepalus* being somewhat inadequate, it seems most likely that (having studied both Favarger's herbarium specimens and also his living shrubs) both the diploid and also some of the tetraploids are *C. obtusisepalus*. More research is needed into this species. Recently reintroduced into cultivation.

13. *Cotoneaster raboutensis* Flinck, Fryer, Garraud, Hylmö & Zeller in Bull. Soc.
Linné. de Lyon 67: 272 (1998). Type: cult. from seed collected in France, Dauphiné,
Bois de Rabou, near the town of Gap, 18 September 1964. Cult. Sweden, Bjuv, 9 June
1969, *B. Hylmö 1245*.
Shrub, sometimes suckering, to 2 m. Branches ascending, spreading, coarse; branchlets divaricate, purple-black, initially densely pilose. Leaves chartaceous or subcoriaceous, on sterile shoots broadly ovate or broadly elliptic, 36–42 × 23–30 mm, apex obtuse or acute, base obtuse or truncate, upper surface slightly rugose, dark green, dull, glabrous, veins 4 impressed, lower surface tomentose-pilose; petiole 5–7 mm, tomentose. Fertile shoots 30–40 mm, including 4 leaves and a pendent, 3- to 8-flowered inflorescence; pedicels 2–8 mm, pilose. Hypanthium cupulate, glabrous or pilose hairs at base; sepals acute or obtuse, glabrous, margin villous or glabrous. Corolla with large opening; petals erect-

incurved, much longer than sepals, off-white with pink dots at base. Stamens (15–)18–20; filaments off-white; anthers white. Fruit depressed-globose, 8–10 mm, crimson to red, glabrous or base sparsely pilose, calyx lobes depressed. Nutlets (2–)3(–4).

Seasons: Flowers April–May, reflowers August; fruit ripe September.

Chromosomes: Tetraploid (Jewsbury, pers. comm.). Apomictic, true from seed.

Hardiness: −25°C (−13°F).

Area: France (Alps).

Notes: *Cotoneaster raboutensis* flowers and fruits a full 2–3 weeks later than *C. integerrimus* and is the last species in series *Cotoneaster* to shed (in November) its leaves.

14. *Cotoneaster scandinavicus* B. Hylmö in Svensk Bot. Tidskr. 87: 317 (1993). Type: Sweden, Halland, Apelviken, 21 May 1925, Sten Svensson (holo LD). **PLATE 185.**

Shrub, 1–1.5 m. Branches to 1.5 m (2.5 m when supported), ascending or decumbent, coarse (28–30 mm in diameter); branchlets spiraled, yellowish to reddish brown, initially tomentose-pilose. Leaves chartaceous, on sterile shoots elliptic or ovate (mostly broadly so), 29–41 × 18–27 mm, apex obtuse, seldom acute, base obtuse, upper surface light to mid-green, glaucous, glabrous, veins 4–5, lower surface pale grayish green, reticulate, tomentose-pilose; petiole 2–4 mm, tomentose. Fertile shoots 8–13 mm, including mostly 2 leaves and a pendent, (1–)2- to 3-flowered inflorescence; pedicels 3–8 mm, sparsely pilose or subglabrous; flowers (including hypanthium) 5–6 mm long. Hypanthium cupulate, glabrous; sepals obtuse or acute, glabrous, margin villous. Corolla with small opening; petals erect-incurved, exceeding sepals by 1 mm, off-white to pale pink, tinged red and green. Stamens (16–)20; filaments off-white or pale pink; anthers white. Fruit globose or depressed-globose, 8–10 mm, orange-red to red tinged yellow, glabrous, calyx lobes depressed, navel slightly open. Nutlets (2–)3(–4), style remains $^1/_2$ from base.

Seasons: Flowers April–May; fruit ripe July.

Chromosomes: Tetraploid (Klotz 1968a). Hexaploid (Favarger 1969) as *C. integerrimus* from Sweden, Halland, Olmevalla (an area from which only *C. scandinavicus* has been discovered). Hexaploids are extremely rare in *Cotoneaster*, the only other known hexaploid is a stunted freak seeded from *C. ignescens* (McAllister, pers. comm.). This could be the case with Favarger's hexaploid. Apomictic, true from seed.

Hardiness: −25°C (−13°F).

Area: Sweden. Norway. Denmark (Bornholm). Finland.

Notes: *Cotoneaster scandinavicus* is native to all Swedish provinces except Blekinge, and in all Norwegian provinces up to 63N, growing from sea level to 950 m in Sweden, and to 1250 m in Norway. It is also found on the island of Bornholm in Denmark and in SW Finland. Recently reintroduced into cultivation.

15. *Cotoneaster tjuliniae* Pojarkova ex G. A. Peschkova in Nov. Syst. Pl. Vasc. (Leningrad) 15: 232 (1979). Type: Central Siberia, Lake Baikal, islands of Bolischoj Uschkanij, 29 July 1959, M. Ivanova (holo LE, iso IRK).

Shrub, to 2 m. Branches erect or ascending. Leaves deciduous, on sterile shoots ovate, 28–40 × 17–24 mm, apex acute or obtuse, sometimes acuminate, base obtuse or truncate, upper surface initially sparsely pilose, veins 4–6 impressed, lower surface yellowish white tomentose. Fertile shoots 10–20 mm, including a pendent, 1(–3)-flowered inflorescence; pedicels 8–18 mm, sparsely pilose; flowers (including hypanthium) 6–7 mm long. Hypanthium cupulate, sparsely pilose or glabrous; sepals obtuse. Petals erect-incurved, twice as long as sepals, off-white and red. Fruit 8–10 mm, orange-red, pruinose, glabrous. Nutlets (2–)3(–4).

Area: Russia (Siberia).

Notes: *Cotoneaster tjuliniae* is the easternmost species in series *Cotoneaster*. It is extremely rare in cultivation. The above description is mostly compiled from the original description plus the type herbarium specimen. More research needs to be undertaken on the only known living specimen in the University of Kiev botanical garden in Ukraine, which was collected in Siberia, Hozo-za, in 1983 by Anna Terentiyevna Grevtsova.

16. *Cotoneaster uniflorus* Bunge in Ledebour, Fl. Altaica 2: 220 (1830); illustr. Ic.
   Plant. Fl. Rossicae t. 269 (1831). Type: *C. uniflora* Bunge, fr. alt. leg. Bunge (lecto designated C).

Shrub, to 0.5 m. Branches ascending or decumbent, short; branchlets spiraled, purple-black, initially pilose-villous. Leaves deciduous, chartaceous, on sterile shoots narrowly elliptic or narrowly ovate, 25–30 × 12–19 mm, apex acute or obtuse, base cuneate or obtuse, upper surface mid-green, dull, glabrous, veins 4–5 impressed, lower surface reticulate, initially sparsely villous; petiole 4–6 mm, villous. Fertile shoots 5–10 mm, including 1–2 leaves and a pendent, 1(–2)-flowered inflorescence; pedicels 1–3 mm, glabrous. Hypanthium cupulate, glabrous; sepals acute or ligulate, glabrous, margin villous. Petals erect-incurved, shorter than sepals, greenish white tinged pink. Stamens 20; filaments white; anthers white. Fruit globose, 6–7 mm, probably orange-red to red. Nutlets 3–4, style remains 1/2 from base.

Chromosomes: Diploid (Gladkova 1968; Krasnoborov et al. 1980). Sexual, outbreeding, variable from seed.

Area: Russia (Siberia). Probably also Kazakhstan.

Notes: *Cotoneaster uniflorus* is rare in cultivation but can be found in Latvia at the National Botanic Garden in Salaspils. Herbarium material of this species from the Altai area shows the variation in this diploid species.

17. *Cotoneaster uralensis* B. Hylmö & J. Fryer in Acta Bot. Fennica 162: 181 (1999).
   Type: Russia, Polar Ural, basin of river Lyapina, branch of river Sev. Sosna, upper part of river Hulga, 27 August 1926, *B. N. Gorodkov* 297 (holo LE, iso C).

Shrub, 0.5–1 m. Branches erect or ascending, slender; branchlets spiraled, purple-black, initially tomentose-pilose. Leaves deciduous, chartaceous, on sterile shoots suborbicular or broadly ovate, 32–45 × 23–28 mm, apex obtuse or acute, base truncate or obtuse, upper surface becoming slightly rugose, light to mid-green, dull to slightly shiny, waxy, very sparsely pilose, veins 4–5, lower surface green, reticulate, pilose; petiole 3–5 mm, initially pilose. Fertile shoots 10–20 mm, including 2–4 leaves and a pendent, 1- to 3-flowered inflorescence; pedicels 2–8 mm, pilose hairs decreasing; flowers (including hypanthium) 4–6 mm long. Hypanthium cupulate, glabrous; sepals short, obtuse or ligulate, glabrous, membranous border often reddish, margin villous or glabrous. Corolla with large opening; petals erect-incurved, exceeding sepals by 1–2 mm, off-white with very pale-pink flush and green stripe. Stamens 20; filaments white; anthers white. Fruit globose, 8–10 mm, orange-red to red, glabrous, calyx lobes depressed. Nutlets (2–)3(–4), style remains ½ from base.

 Chromosomes: Unknown. Apomictic, true from seed.

 Hardiness: –25°C (–13°F). Very hardy.

 Area: Russia (Urals).

 Notes: A native of the northeastern part of European Russia, *Cotoneaster uralensis* has often previously been included in *C. uniflorus*. Recently reintroduced into cultivation.

35. Series *Melanocarpi* (Pojarkova) Hurusawa in Inf. Ann. Hort. Bot. Sci. Univ.

 Tokyo. p. 6 (1967). Synonym: series *Melanocarpae* Pojarkova (1939).

Small to large shrubs, multistemmed. Branches mostly narrowly erect, often coarse. Fertile shoots 15–100 mm, including a mostly pendent, lax 2- to 60-flowered inflorescence. Hypanthium glabrous or with sparse hairs. Petals erect or semispreading. Fruit mostly purple-black, frequently bluish pruinose. Nutlets 2–4(–5).

 Very early to mid season.

 Europe (mostly Central and Eastern).

 13 species: *C. altaicus*, *C. commixtus*, *C. hylanderi*, *C. laxiflorus*, *C. melanocarpus*, *C. narynensis*, *C. niger*, *C. orientalis*, *C. polyanthemus*, *C. popovii*, *C. rannensis*, *C. talgaricus*, *C. yakuticus*.

 Notes: Series *Melanocarpi* in Poland, Czech Republic, Hungary, and Romania, where maybe the lost species *C. matrensis* Domokos awaits rediscovery, needs more research.

Key to Series *Melanocarpi*

1a. Fertile shoots 30–100 mm; inflorescence 10- to 50-flowered 2

1b. Fertile shoots 15–50 mm; inflorescence 2- to 15-flowered. 3

 2a. Leaves 34–62 mm, mid-green, dull; fertile shoots 30–80 mm; flowers 5–6 mm, pedicels sparsely villous or subglabrous; hypanthium infundibulate . . . . **C. *laxiflorus***

 2b. Leaves 40–73 mm, dark green, shiny; fertile shoots 40–100 mm; flowers 6–8 mm, pedicels densely pilose, hypanthium cupulate . . . . **C. *polyanthemus***

3a. Leaf veins impressed; fertile shoots ≤ 30–50 mm, inflorescence 3- to 15-flowered 4

3b. Leaf veins not impressed or lightly impressed; fertile shoots ≤ 25–40 mm, inflorescence
mostly 2- to 9-flowered 8

4a. Branches slender; pedicels 5–20 mm; hypanthium infundibulate; petals off-white, sometimes with pale pink blotches; nutlets (2–)3(–4) . . . . *C. commixtus*

4b. Branches coarse; pedicels 2–14 mm; hypanthium cupulate; petals red or pink; nutlets
2–3(–5) 5

5a. Leaves light green, upper surface intensely shiny, petiole 2–4 mm; sepals mostly ligulate
. . . .*C. narynensis*

5b. Leaves mostly dark green, upper surface dull or only slightly shiny, petiole 4–8 mm; sepals
acute or obtuse 6

6a. Branches loosely erect; leaf apex, and sepals mostly acute; fertile shoots ≤ 30 mm;
inflorescence with 3 4 leaves; pedicels 3 8 mm . . . . *C. melanocarpus*

6b. Branches stiffly erect; leaf apex, and sepals mostly obtuse; fertile shoots to 40–50 mm;
inflorescence with 2–3 leaves; pedicels 5–14 mm 7

7a. Height 1–1.5 m; leaves subcoriaceous; hypanthium and fruit base villous; nutlets
(2–)3(–5); petals erect . . . .*C. rannensis*

7b. Height 2–3 m; leaves chartaceous; hypanthium glabrous; nutlets 2–3; petals semispreading
. . . .*C. yakuticus*

8a. Leaves mostly elliptic, upper surface dull; inflorescences lax; nutlets 2(–3) 9

8b. Leaves mostly ovate, upper surface shiny or initially shiny; inflorescences ± compact;
nutlets 2–4 11

9a. Inflorescence with 2 large leaves overtopping the 2- to 5-flowered inflorescence; fruit
mostly obovoid . . . . *C. orientalis*

9b. Inflorescence with 2–4 leaves not overtopping the 3- to 9(–14)-flowered inflorescence; fruit
globose or depressed-globose. 10

10a. Branches coarse, narrowly erect; inflorescence 3- to 9(–14)-flowered; fruit 8–9 mm, purple-
black, pruinose . . . .*C. altaicus*

10b. Branchlets slender, erect; inflorescence 3- to 5-flowered; fruit 6–8 mm black, not pruinose
. . . .*C. talgaricus*

11a. Leaves ≤ 50 mm, upper surface intensely shiny; pedicels ≤15 mm; sepals obtuse; nutlets
2–3(–4) . . . . *C. popovii*

11b. Leaves ≤ 77 mm, upper surface dull or only initially slightly shiny; pedicels ≤ 10 mm; sepals
mostly acute; carpels 2(–4). . . . . *C. niger*

1. ***Cotoneaster altaicus*** J. Fryer & B. Hylmö, *sp. nov.* Synonym: *C. melanocarpus*
G. Loddiges var. *altaicus* G. Klotz nom. nud. Wiss. Z. Martin-Luther-Univ. Halle-
Wittenberg, Math.-Naturwiss. 6: 963 (1957). Type: cult. Sweden, Bjuv, 4 May 1993,
B. Hylmö 2026, from Asia Media, Tian Shan, Trans-Ili Altau range at the mouth of
the Almatinka Minor river, 1971, R. Cinovskis et al. (holo GB). PLATE 186.

Shrub, 2–2.5 m. Branches narrowly erect, coarse; branchlets spiraled, grayish brown, initially tomentose-pilose. Leaves deciduous, chartaceous, on sterile shoots elliptic, 33–75 × 20–43 mm; apex obtuse or acute, base obtuse or truncate, upper surface light green to dark green, dull, initially pilose, veins 4–6 lightly impressed, lower surface sometimes slightly rugose, paler green, tomentose soon pilose-villous; petiole 6–8 mm, pilose-villous. Fertile shoots 20–30 mm, including 2–4 leaves and a pendent, lax 3- to 9(–14)-flowered inflorescence; pedicels 4–15 mm, villous; flowers (including hypanthium) 5–6 mm long. Hypanthium cupulate, glabrous; sepals obtuse or ligulate, glabrous, margin glabrous. Petals erect to semispreading, exceeding sepals by 1–2 mm, off-white with red stripe and pink base. Stamens 20; filaments white or pale pink; anthers white. Fruit depressed-globose, 8–9 mm, succulent, purple-black, pruinose, glabrous, calyx lobes flat. Nutlets 2(–3), style remains ⅔ from base.

> Seasons: Flowers April–May; fruit ripe July; autumn leaves purple-red.
> Chromosomes: Tetraploid (Bailey, pers. comm.). Apomictic, true from seed.
> Hardiness: –21°C (–6°F).
> Area: Kazakhstan.
> Notes: *Cotoneaster altaicus* originates from the Tian Shan range. This is a good shrub

with a neat habit and lovely autumn color. The dull black fruit are an added bonus.

2. *Cotoneaster commixtus* (C. K. Schneider) Flinck & B. Hylmö in Bot. Not. (Lund) 119: 454 (1966). Synonym: *C. melanocarpus* G. Loddiges var. *commixtus* C. K. Schneider (1906). Illustr. of *C. laxiflorus* Lindley in Bot. Mag. 63: 3519 (1836). Type: 122 *C. laxiflorus* J. F. Jacquin, Herb. Dendrol. Hort. Berol., flowered 13 May 1896 (lecto designated H).

Shrub, 1.5–2 m. Branches erect, slender; branchlets spiraled, greenish gray, lenticellate, initially pilose-villous. Leaves deciduous, chartaceous, on sterile shoots elliptic, narrowly elliptic or narrowly ovate, 45–65 × 24–46 mm, apex acute or obtuse, base obtuse or cuneate, upper surface slightly rugose, mid-green, dull, initially pilose-villous, veins 4–6 lightly impressed, lower surface light green, pilose-villous; petiole 5–8 mm, villous. Fertile shoots 30–40 mm, including 1–4 leaves and a pendent, lax 7- to 15-flowered inflorescence; pedicels 5–20 mm, subglabrous; flowers (including hypanthium) 5–6 mm long. Hypanthium infundibulate, pale green, glabrous; sepals obtuse or acute, glabrous, margin villous. Petals erect, exceeding sepals by 1.5 mm, off-white, sometimes with pink blotch at base. Stamens 20; filaments white, base sometimes pale pink; anthers white. Fruit depressed-globose, 6 mm, purple-black, bluish pruinose, glabrous, calyx lobes suberect, glabrous. Nutlets 2–3(–4).

> Seasons: Flowers May–June; fruit ripe August.
> Chromosomes: Unknown. Apomictic, true from seed.
> Hardiness: –25°C (–13°F).
> Area: Russia (Siberia).

Notes: The silvery white hair covering of *Cotoneaster commixtus* gives the shrub a very attractive ethereal appearance, especially noticeable in early spring.

3. *Cotoneaster hylanderi* J. Fryer & B. Hylmö, *sp. nov.* Type: Sweden, Öland,
Vickleby, 10 June 2001, K. E. Flinck (holo E). **PLATE 187.**

Shrub, 1–2 m. Branches stiffly erect; branchlets spiraled, red-brown, shiny, pilose-villous, glabrescent. Leaves deciduous, chartaceous, on sterile shoots broadly-elliptic or sub-orbicular, 30–55 × 20–40 mm, apex obtuse or acute, base truncate or obtuse, upper surface convex, slightly rugose, light to mid-green, dull, long-haired pilose-villous, veins 4–5 impressed, lower surface tomentose-villous, petiole 4–5 mm, villous. Fertile shoots 15–25 mm, including 3 leaves and a pendent, 2- to 7-flowered inflorescence, pedicels 4–14 mm, tomentose; flowers (including hypanthium) 5–6 mm long; flower buds red. Hypanthium cupulate, glabrous; sepals ligulate or obtuse, green-red, sometimes pilose, margin villous. Corolla with small opening; petals exceeding sepals by 1.5 mm, white and pink with red stripe and border. Stamens 20, white; anthers white. Fruit depressed-globose or globose, 7–9 mm, ruby to black, glabrous, calyx lobes flat, navel open. Nutlets 2(–3), style remains ³/₅ from base.

Seasons: Flowers April–May; fruit ripe August.

Chromosomes: Unknown. Apomictic, true from seed.

Hardiness: –25°C (–13°F).

Area: Sweden (Öland).

Notes: *Cotoneaster hylanderi* is endemic to the island of Öland off the southern coast of Sweden. It is a pretty shrub, compact in habit, with little red-striped flowers and sooty fruit. The species was named in honor of Nils Hylander, a botany professor at the University of Uppsala who was after Carl Linnaeus probably Sweden's most important botanist. *Cotoneaster hylanderi* is rare in cultivation. Not in key.

4. *Cotoneaster laxiflorus* (J. F. Jacquin) Lindley in Edward's Bot. Reg. 15: t. 1229
(1829); illustr. 1305. Type: cult. England, Hort. Soc. London, 25 April 1828 (lecto
designated K). **PLATE 188.**

Shrub, 2–2.5 m. Branches erect and spreading; branchlets spiraled, maroon, lenticellate, initially pilose. Leaves deciduous, chartaceous to subcoriaceous, on sterile shoots broadly elliptic, 34–62 × 25–40 mm, apex acute or obtuse, base obtuse, margin sometimes undulate, upper surface slightly rugose, mid-green, dull, initially sparsely pilose, veins 5–6 lightly impressed, lower surface grayish green, densely pilose-villous; petiole 5–7 mm, villous. Fertile shoots 30–80 mm, including 3–4 leaves and a pendent, lax, 10- to 50-flowered inflorescence; pedicels 5–20 mm, sparsely villous or subglabrous; flowers (including hypanthium) 5–6 mm long. Hypanthium infundibulate, glabrous; sepals obtuse or acute, glabrous, margin villous. Petals erect to semispreading, exceeding sepals by 2 mm, pink. Stamens (18–)20; filaments off-white; anthers white. Fruit globose or obovoid, 7–10 mm, purple-black, pruinose, glabrous, calyx lobes flat. Nutlets 2(–3), rarely 4, style remains $^2/_3$ from base.

Seasons: Flowers May–June; fruit ripe August; autumn leaves colorful.

Chromosomes: Tetraploid (Bailey, pers. comm.). Apomictic, true from seed.

Hardiness: –25°C (–13°F).

Area: Russia (Siberia, Mongolia). N China (Xinjiang).

Notes: *Cotoneaster laxiflorus* was introduced to England from Vienna in 1826. This really lovely shrub has large hanging clusters of pale pink flowers on long pedicels which contrast well with the silvery, softly hairy young growth. It is equally attractive in early autumn with hanging, sooty, blackcurrant-like clusters of fruit and lovely autumn leaf color.

5. *Cotoneaster melanocarpus* (G. Loddiges) Hurusawa in Inf. Ann. Hort. Bot. Fac. Sci. Univ. Tokyo. p. 5 (1967); illustr. *C. melanocarpus* nom. nud. in Loddiges' Bot. Cab. 16: 1531 (1829). Type: cult. Sweden, Bjuv (hort.) 1762, B. Hylmö, 20 May 1996, from Ukraine, Tjeremsjini, Lvov (lecto designated GB). **PLATE 189.**

Shrub, 2–2.5 m. Branches loosely erect; branchlets spiraled, yellow-brown and shiny, lenticellate, initially densely pilose. Leaves deciduous, chartaceous, on sterile shoots elliptic or ovate, 33–45 × 20–32 mm, apex acute or rotund, base obtuse, upper surface rugose, mid to dark green, dull to slightly shiny, sparsely pilose, veins 5–7 impressed, lower surface densely silvery pilose-villous; petiole 4–7 mm, tomentose-villous. Fertile shoots 25–30 mm, including 3–4 leaves and a pendent, lax, 5- to 13-flowered inflorescence; pedicels 3–8 mm, sometimes sparsely villous; flowers (including hypanthium) 6–7 mm long. Hypanthium cupulate, dark reddish brown, glabrous; sepals acute or obtuse, glabrous, margin erose, apex often villous. Petals erect, greenish white with pink, red and white. Stamens 20(–22); filaments white; anthers white. Fruit obovoid or globose, 7–9 mm, purple-black, pruinose, glabrous, calyx lobes suberect, navel open. Nutlets 2(–3), rarely 4, style remains $^2/_3$ from base.

Seasons: Flowers April–May; fruit ripe July–August.

Chromosomes: Tetraploid (Bailey, pers. comm.). Apomictic, true from seed.

Hardiness: –25°C (–13°F). Very hardy.

Area: Ukraine.

Notes: The beautiful color illustration of *Cotoneaster melanocarpus* in Loddiges' *Botanical Cabinet* was drawn from a shrub grown at the RGB Kew, which was raised from seed distributed by the botanical garden of Dnipropetrovsk (formerly Ekaterinoslav) National University in central Ukraine. *Cotoneaster melanocarpus* has been reintroduced from collections made by Jeanette Fryer (*JFUK 1–12*) in Ukraine in the Dietropietrowska district, Sofijewskij region, near Demurieno-Warwariewka, beside the river Demurino, in 2003.

6. *Cotoneaster narynensis* Tkatschenko ex J. Fryer & B. Hylmö, *sp. nov.* Type: cult. Sweden, Bjuv, 9 June 1979, B. Hylmö 1627, seed from Kyrgyzstan, W Tian Shan, Sussamyr plateau, junction of W Karakol and Sussamyr rivers, Dzhumgoltau mountains, 13 August 1968, R. Cinovskis et al. (holo GB). **PLATE 190**.

Shrub, 2–2.5 m. Branches narrowly erect; branchlets spiraled, reddish brown to gray, initially pilose. Leaves deciduous, chartaceous, on sterile shoots broadly elliptic, elliptic or ovate, 45–63 × 27–41 mm, apex acute or rotund, base obtuse or rotund, upper surface rugose, light green, intensely shiny, initially sparsely pilose, veins 4–6 impressed, lower surface grayish green, densely villous-pilose; petiole 2–4 mm, pilose. Fertile shoots 30–40 mm, including up to 4 leaves and a pendent, lax 5- to 12-flowered inflorescence; pedicels 3–13 mm, sparsely villous; flowers (including hypanthium) 5–6 mm long. Hypanthium cupulate, glabrous; sepals ligulate or obtuse, glabrous, margin villous. Petals semispreading, red and pink. Stamens 20; filaments white, anthers white. Fruit globose, 8–9 mm, black, pruinose, glabrous, calyx lobes erect, navel open. Nutlets 2(–3), style remains ³⁄₄ from base.

Seasons: Flowers May; fruit ripe July–August.

Chromosomes: Tetraploid (Krügel 1992a). Apomictic, true from seed.

Hardiness: –25°C (–13°F).

Area: Kyrgyzstan. Kazakhstan.

Notes: Vasily Tkatschenko of the botanical garden at the National Academy of Science (formerly Frunze) in Bishkek, Kyrgyzstan, who frequently led expeditions in Central Asia (this species was collected by Raymonds Cinovskis who was present on Tkatschenko's 18th expedition), suggested this *Cotoneaster* be named *C. narynensis* after the river Naryn that flows through the area in which it was first discovered.

7. *Cotoneaster niger* (Wahlberg) Fries in Summa veg. Scand. 1: 175 (1845). As *Mespilus cotoneaster* f. *nigra* Wahlberg in Fl. Gothob. 1: 53 (1820). Type: Sweden, På, Varberg 1819, herb. Wahlberg (lecto UPS).

Shrub, 1.5–2.5 m. Branches narrowly erect, often becoming arched; branchlets spiraled, yellowish to reddish brown, initially densely pilose. Leaves deciduous, chartaceous, on sterile shoots ovate or elliptic, 23–77 × 15–40 mm, apex acute, obtuse or rotund, base rotund, margin undulate, upper surface red-brown and slightly shiny, soon dark green and dull, initially pilose, veins 4–6, lower surface densely grayish pilose-strigose; petiole 4–7 mm, pilose-villous. Fertile shoots 15–40 mm, including 2–3 leaves (1 of which is small) and a pendent, 3- to 5(–9)-flowered inflorescence; pedicels 3–10 mm, initially pilose-villous; flowers (including hypanthium) 6 mm long. Hypanthium cupulate, subglabrous; sepals broad, acute or obtuse, brownish red, glabrous, margin villous. Petals erect, exceeding sepals by 2 mm, off-white with pink. Stamens (15–)20; filaments pink, anthers white. Fruit globose or depressed-globose, 6–10 mm, maroon to black, pruinose, glabrous, calyx lobes flat. Nutlets 2(–3), rarely 4, style remains ²⁄₃ from base.

Seasons: Flowers May–June, reflowers late summer mostly on terminal shoots; fruit ripe July–August.

Chromosomes: Unknown. Apomictic, true from seed.

Hardiness: –25°C (–13°F). Very hardy.

Area: Scandinavia (excluding Finland).

Notes: In the cold climate of the areas to which *Cotoneaster niger* is native, the branches of this species gradually become more arched with age due to succeeding winters' weight of snow. In flower the pale petals contrast well with the dark calyx, and the fruit are quite unusual in being almost brown before turning black. No longer in the Baltic states. Recently reintroduced into cultivation.

8. *Cotoneaster orientalis* A. Kerner in Osterreichische Bot. Zeitschr. 19: 270 (1869). Non *Mespilus orientalis* Miller (1768). Synonym: *C. matrensis* Domokos (1941). Type: Romania, Biharia, Batnima plateau at Stana Oncesa, c. 1865, A. J. von M. Kerner (holo W).

Shrub, to 2 m. Branches erect; branchlets spiraled, brown, initially pilose-villous. Leaves deciduous, chartaceous, on sterile shoots elliptic or ovate, 20–40 × 10–30 mm, apex obtuse, rotund or acute, mucronate, base rotund, upper surface slightly rugose, dark green, dull, sparsely pilose or subglabrous, veins 4–6 lightly impressed, lower surface white-tomentose; petiole 4–7 mm, tomentose. Fertile shoots 15–25 mm, including 2 leaves and a pendent, lax 2- to 5-flowered inflorescence; pedicels 3–12 mm, villous; flowers (including hypanthium) 5–7 mm long. Hypanthium cupulate, glabrous or few hairs at base; sepals obtuse or acute, glabrous, margin villous. Petals suberect to erect, incurved, red and pink. Stamens 20; filaments white; anthers white. Fruit obovoid or subglobose, 8 mm, bluish black, glabrous. Nutlets 2(–3).

Area: Hungary. Romania. Possibly also in Poland and Czech Republic.

Notes: Not having yet seen the type herbarium sheet for *Cotoneaster orientalis*, we wrote the above description mostly based on Kerner's original diagnosis. Kerner did not use *Mespilus orientalis* (syn. *C. tomentosus*) as the base for his description of *C. orientalis*. He knew *C. tomentosus* well and separated *C. orientalis* from this species. Janós Domokos, when describing *C. matrensis*, compared his new species with *C. integerrimus* and *C. niger*, but totally overlooked *C. orientalis*, which is native to the same area. *Cotoneaster hrabetovae sp. nov.* J. Fryer & B. Hylmö (unpublished) from the Czech Republic is similar to *C. orientalis*, but is in fact closer to the description Domokos gives for *C. matrensis*. These three cotoneasters—*C. orientalis*, *C. matrensis*, and *C. hrabetovae*—need further research. Recently reintroduced into cultivation.

9. *Cotoneaster polyanthemus* E. L. Wolf in Mitt. Deutsch. Dendrol. Ges. 34: 325 (1924). Type: cult. Russia, St. Petersburg, garden of V. L. Komarov Botanical Institute, raised from seed collected in Turkistan, near Almaty, c. 1906 (holo LE).

PLATE 191.

Shrub, 2–4 m. Branches erect, coarse; branchlets spiraled, light brown, lenticellate, initially pilose-villous. Leaves deciduous, chartaceous to subcoriaceous, on sterile shoots elliptic or broadly elliptic, 41–73 × 26–44 mm, apex acute, acuminate or obtuse, base rotund, upper surface slightly rugose, dark green, shiny, initially sparsely villous on veins, veins 4–7 impressed, lower surface tomentose, soon pilose-villous; petiole 4–7 mm, pilose-villous. Fertile shoots 40–100 mm, including 2–5 leaves and a pendent, lax 15- to 50-flowered inflorescence; pedicels 5–10 mm, densely pilose; flowers (including hypanthium) 6–8 mm long. Hypanthium cupulate, sparsely pilose; sepals acute, obtuse or acuminate, glabrous, margin villous. Petals erect to semispreading, exceeding sepals by 2–3 mm, off-white with pink base. Stamens (16–)20; filaments off-white with pale pink; anthers white. Fruit globose or obovoid, 7–11 mm, black, pruinose, glabrous, calyx lobes flat, navel open. Nutlets (2–)3(–4), style remains $^2/_3$ from base.

Seasons: Flowers May–June; fruit ripe September–October; autumn leaves yellow.

Chromosomes: Unknown. Apomictic, true from seed.

Hardiness: –25°C (–13°F). Very hardy.

Area: Kazakhstan. Mongolia.

Notes: *Cotoneaster polyanthemus* is described in an excellent paper by Egbert Ludwigowitsch Wolf (1924), in which he begins the separation of the many taxa of Central Asia and Siberia which were until then included in *C. melanocarpus*. *Cotoneaster polyanthemus* is the largest, and one of the most striking and easily identified species in series *Melanocarpi*. It is extremely winter hardy. Reintroduced from the Khentey Mountains in Mongolia in 1997 by Géza Kósa, curator of the Institute of Ecology and Botany of the Hungarian Academy of Sciences at Vácrátót.

10. *Cotoneaster popovii* Peschkova in Nov. Syst. Pl. Vasc. (Leningrad) 15: 231 (1979).

Synonyms: *C. melanocarpus* G. Loddiges var. *chailaricus* G. Klotz nom. nud. (1957); *C. chailaricus* Flinck & B. Hylmö nom. nud. (1966). Type: Siberia, Lake Baikal, Vydrino, 4 August 1952, L. Bardunov (holo LE).

Shrub, 1.5–2.5 m. Branches narrowly erect, arched, slender; branchlets reddish brown with large lenticels, initially pilose. Leaves deciduous, chartaceous, on sterile shoots ovate-lanceolate or oblong-ovate, 15–60 × 10–45 mm, apex obtuse or acute, base obtuse or truncate, upper surface slightly rugose, reddish green soon dark green, intensely shiny, sparsely pilose, veins 4–6 lightly impressed, lower surface tomentose-villous; petiole 4–7 mm, villous. Fertile shoots 20–30 mm, including 1–2 leaves and a pendent, lax, 2- to 6(–9)-flowered inflorescence; pedicels 2–15 mm, subglabrous; flowers (including hypanthium) 6–7 mm long. Hypanthium cupulate, often maroon, subglabrous; sepals obtuse, triangular, broad and low, margin sparsely villous. Petals erect or semispreading, exceeding sepals by 1 mm, red and pink or entirely pale pink. Stamens 20; filaments white or pale pink; anthers white. Fruit globose, 6–9 mm, maroon to purple-black, pruinose, glabrous, calyx lobes flat. Nutlets (2–)3(–4), style remains $^2/_3$ from base.

Seasons: Flowers May; fruit ripe July; autumn leaves yellow.

Chromosomes: Unknown. Apomictic, true from seed.

Hardiness: −25°C (−13°F). Very hardy.

Area: Russia (Siberia, Mongolia).

Notes: *Cotoneaster popovii* is an extremely hardy species and, along with other species here in series *Melanocarpi*, is a very useful addition to the early spring garden. Recently reintroduced into cultivation.

11. *Cotoneaster rannensis* B. Hylmö & J. Fryer in Acta Bot. Fennica 162: 183 (1999).
Type: Estonia, Kose, 11 August 1923, Rickard Sterner (holo LD). **PLATE 192.**
Shrub, 1–1.5 m. Branches erect; branchlets spiraled, reddish purple to gray, initially tomentose. Leaves deciduous, subcoriaceous, on sterile shoots suborbicular, broadly elliptic or broadly ovate, 22–40 × 16–36 mm; apex obtuse, rotund or acute, base obtuse or rotund, upper surface rugose, dark green, shiny becoming dull, initially pilose-villous, veins 4–5 impressed, lower surface tomentose-villous; petiole 4–6 mm, villous-pilose. Fertile shoots 15–40 mm, including 2–3 leaves and a pendent, 2- to 15-flowered inflorescence; pedicels 5–14 mm, pilose-villous; flowers (including hypanthium) 5–6 mm long. Hypanthium cupulate, base villous; sepals obtuse or acute, glabrous, margin long-haired villous. Petals erect, exceeding sepals by 2 mm, pinkish red. Stamens 18–20; filaments off-white; anthers white. Fruit depressed-globose, 8–9 mm, maroon-purple maturing black, few hairs at base, calyx lobes depressed. Nutlets (2–)3(–4), rarely 5, style remains ½ from base.

Seasons: Flowers April–May; fruit ripe August; autumn leaves golden yellow.

Chromosomes: Unknown. Apomictic, true from seed.

Hardiness: −25°C (−13°F). Very hardy.

Area: Estonia. Latvia. Russia (Karelia).

Notes: *Cotoneaster rannensis* is similar to *C. hylanderi*, both differing from the closely related *C. niger* in their reddish flowers. *Cotoneaster rannensis* is an attractive, well-shaped shrub of close-branching habit, very early flowering, with beautiful autumn leaf color. Reintroduced into cultivation in 1981 by Raymonds Cirovskis and Maija Bice from Estonia.

12. *Cotoneaster talgaricus* Popov in Bull. Soc. Imp. Nat. Mosc. 44: 126 (1935). Type:
Kazakhstan, left side river W Talgar, below Kok-Assik gorge and creek from Bogda glacier, 13 September 1933, M. J. Popov & N. I. Rubtzov (holo A).
Shrub, 1.5–2 m. Branches erect, slender; branchlets spiraled, reddish brown to light gray, initially pilose. Leaves deciduous, chartaceous, on sterile shoots elliptic or elliptic-lanceolate, 40–65 × 21–36 mm, apex acute, obtuse or acuminate, base rotund, obtuse or cuneate, upper surface mid-green, dull, initially pilose, veins 4–6, lower surface light green, pilose-villous; petiole 5–8 mm, pilose-villous. Fertile shoots 25–35 mm, including 2–4 leaves and a pendent, lax 3- to 5-flowered inflorescence; pedicels 4–10 mm, pilose-villous or subglabrous; flowers (including hypanthium) 6 mm long. Hypanthium cupulate,

glabrous; sepals obtuse, acute or ligulate, glabrous, margin villous. Petals semispreading, white with pink. Stamens 20; filaments white; anthers white. Fruit globose or subglobose, 6–8 mm, black, glabrous, calyx lobes flat. Nutlets 2(–3), style remains $^2/_3$ from base.

Seasons: Flowers May–June; fruit ripe August.

Chromosomes: Unknown. Apomictic, true from seed.

Hardiness: −21°C (−6°F).

Area: Kazakhstan. Kyrgyzstan.

Notes: In *Flora URSS* (1932), *Cotoneaster talgaricus* was mistakenly treated as *C. melanocarpus* and *C. uniflorus*. This species, from the Tian Shan range, is not common in cultivation.

13. *Cotoneaster yakuticus* J. Fryer & B. Hylmö, *sp. nov.* Type: Siberia, Dahurien, Nertchinsu, in bushes by the Nertz river, 1892, *F. Karo 89* (holo GB, iso E).

   PLATE 193.

Shrub, 2–3 m. Branches narrowly erect; branchlets spiraled, reddish brown, initially densely pilose. Leaves deciduous, chartaceous, on sterile shoots elliptic or ovate, 38–58 × 21–33 mm, apex obtuse or acute, base obtuse or truncate, upper surface dark grayish green, dull or slightly shiny, sparsely pilose, veins 5–6 impressed, lower surface gray tomentose-pilose; petiole 4–7 mm, densely pilose. Fertile shoots 30–50 mm, including 2–3 leaves and a pendent, lax 3- to 10-flowered inflorescence; pedicels 3–12 mm, slender, glabrescent; flowers (including hypanthium) 7 mm long. Hypanthium cupulate, glabrous; sepals obtuse, glabrous, margin sparsely villous. Petals semispreading, exceeding sepals by 1.5 mm, pale pink and off-white. Stamens 20; filaments white; anthers white. Fruit suborbicular, purple-black, glabrous. Nutlets 2–3, style remains $^4/_5$ from base.

Seasons: Flowers April–May; fruit ripe July.

Chromosomes: Triploid (Bailey, pers. comm.; Jewsbury, pers. comm.).

Hardiness: −25°C (−13°F). Very hardy.

Area: Russia (Siberia).

Notes: As one would expect from a species native to such a northerly region, *Cotoneaster yakuticus* is extremely hardy. Recently reintroduced into cultivation.

36. Series *Ignavi* Hurusawa in Inf. Ann. Hort. Bot. Fac. Sci. Univ. Tokyo. 11 (5–7): 208 (1973). Synonym: series *Oliganthae* Pojarkova nom. nud. (1939).

Shrubs dwarf to medium. Branches mostly stiffly erect. Leaves with lower surface densely pilose or villous. Inflorescences mostly erect; flowers small (including hypanthium) 3–6 mm long. Hypanthium pilose or villous. Petals mostly semispreading and pink. Stamens 10–20. Fruit red, ruby, or maroon. Nutlets 1–3.

Early to mid season.

Kazakhstan. Turkey. Armenia. Iran. Tajikistan. Uzbekistan. Kyrgyzstan.

9 species: *C. armenus*, *C. browiczii*, *C. erratus*, *C. goloskokovii*, *C. ignavus*, *C. neoantoninae*, *C. oliganthus*, *C. peduncularis*, *C. zeravschanicus*.

Key to Series *Ignavi*

1a. Height ≤ 0.5, fertile shoots 10–15 mm, inflorescence 1- to 3(–4)-flowered. . . . . *C. erratus*

1b. Height > 0.5 m, fertile shoots 15–55 mm, inflorescence 2- to 20-flowered 2

2a. Lower leaf surface villous-pilose; fertile shoots 35–55 mm, inflorescence lax, 7- to 20-flowered . . . .*C. ignavus*

2b. Lower leaf surface densely pilose; fertile shoots 15–30 mm, inflorescence mostly compact, 2- to 15-flowered 3

3a. Leaves broadly elliptic, broadly ovate or suborbicular, petiole 3–5 mm; nutlets 2(–3) 4

3b. Leaves elliptic or ovate, petiole 4–9 mm; nutlets 1–3. 5

4a. Branches stiffly erect; leaves ≤42 mm; inflorescence 7- to 12-flowered; pedicels 1–10 mm; hypanthium glabrous; stamens (10–)14; fruit ruby to maroon . . . . *C. zeravschanicus*

4b. Branches ascending; leaves ≤ 30 mm; inflorescence 2- to 5-flowered, pedicels 3–5; stamens 18–20; hypanthium sparsely pilose; pedicels 3–5 mm; fruit red. . . . . *C. browiczii*

5a. Branches ascending; leaves ≤ 40 mm, veins not impressed; petals mostly white; stamens 18–20 . . . .*C. oliganthus*

5b. Branches stiffly erect; leaves ≤ 53–55 mm, veins impressed; petals pink; stamens (10–)14 . .6

6a. Inflorescence compact; hypanthium base densely pilose; fruit obovate, ruby to maroon; nutlets 1–3 . . . .*C. armenus*

6b. Inflorescence lax; hypanthium base glabrous or sparsely pilose; fruit globose, pure or cherry red; nutlets 2(–3). . . . . *C. peduncularis*

1. *Cotoneaster armenus* Pojarkova in Not. Syst. Inst. Bot. Acad. Sci. USSR 17: 202 (1955). Type: Armenia, vicinity of Erevan, near the Gehart monastery, 17 October 1937, *A. Pojarkova 385* (holo LE, iso A, LE).

Shrub, 1.5–2 m. Branches narrowly erect; branchlets spiraled, maroon with large lenticels, initially tomentose-pilose. Leaves deciduous, chartaceous, on sterile shoots elliptic or ovate, 30–55 × 20–32 mm, apex acute or obtuse, base obtuse or cuneate, upper surface mid-green, dull, pilose, veins 5–6 impressed, lower surface densely pilose; petiole 5–8 mm, pilose. Fertile shoots 15–30 mm, including 2–3 leaves and a compact, 7- to 15-flowered inflorescence; pedicels 2–4 mm, pilose; flowers (including hypanthium), 4–5 mm long, pink in bud. Hypanthium cupulate, base densely pilose, apex glabrous; sepals obtuse, sometimes pilose, margin villous. Corolla 6–8 mm, petals spreading to semispreading, pale pink. Stamens 10–14 rarely to 20; filaments white or pale pink; anthers white. Fruit obovoid, 8 × 7 mm, ruby to maroon, sparsely villous, calyx lobes suberect, navel open. Nutlets (1–)2, rarely 3, exserted through apex, style remains $^3/_4$ from base.

Seasons: Flowers May–June; fruit ripe September–October.

Chromosomes: Tetraploid (Hensen 1966; Gladkova 1968; Krügel 1992a; Bailey, pers. comm.). Apomictic, true from seed.

Hardiness: –21°C (–6°F).

Area: Turkey. Armenia. Iran.

Notes: *Cotoneaster armenus* can be found, often overlooked or identified as other species, in several botanic gardens and collections. It was reintroduced in 1987 from a collection made in Armenia by Géza Kósa of Vácrátót, Hungary.

2. *Cotoneaster browiczii* J. Fryer & B. Hylmö, *sp. nov.* Type: cult. Sweden, Sweden, Bjuv, 3 June 1995, B. Hylmö 2157, raised from seed collected in E Armenia, Zangezur Mountains, near Tandzatap village, 1987, Géza Kósa (holo GB). **PLATE 194.**

Shrub, to 0.7 m. Branches to 1.5 m, ascending, spreading; branchlets spiraled or distichous, maroon with large lenticels, initially densely pilose. Leaves deciduous, chartaceous, on sterile shoots broadly elliptic or suborbicular, 19–30 × 18–19 mm, apex obtuse or acute, base obtuse, cuneate or truncate, upper surface dark green, dull, glabrous, veins 4–6, lower surface densely pilose; petiole 3–5 mm, pilose. Fertile shoots 15–25 mm, including 2–4 orbicular leaves and a compact, 2- to 5-flowered inflorescence, pedicels 3–5 mm, pilose; flowers (including hypanthium) 5–6 mm long, red in bud. Hypanthium cupulate, base sparsely pilose; sepals obtuse or acute, pilose or glabrous, margin villous. Corolla 8–9 mm, petals semispreading to spreading, white with purple stripe. Stamens 18–20; filaments white; anthers white. Fruit depressed-globose or obovoid, 8–9 mm, red or slightly orange-red, glabrous, calyx lobes suberect, navel open. Nutlets 2(–3), style remains ¾ from base.

Seasons: Flowers May–June; fruit ripe September.

Chromosomes: Unknown. Apomictic, true from seed.

Hardiness: −18°C (−1°F).

Area: Turkey. Armenia. Iran.

Notes: *Cotoneaster browiczii* is named in honor of Kasimiriez Browicz, professor of botany at the Polish Academy of Science, Kornik, Poland. It is a useful little open shrub that will spread itself over the heads of heathers. It is as yet uncommon in cultivation.

3. *Cotoneaster erratus* J. Fryer & B. Hylmö, *sp. nov.* Synonym: *C. oliganthus* Pojarkova in Not. Syst. Inst. Bot. Acad. Sci. USSR 17: 200 (1955); non Addendum et emendandum ad descriptionem (1940). Type: cult. Sweden, Bjuv, 11 June 1957, B. Hylmö 9558, from seed collected in Tajikistan, Hissar Mountains, on the way to Ziddy, 1955, A. Pojarkova 6513 (holo GB). **PLATE 195.**

Shrub, to 0.5 m. Branches to 1 m, ascending, spreading, slender; branchlets spiraled, maroon, initially densely pilose. Leaves deciduous, chartaceous, on sterile shoots elliptic, 17–27 × 10–17 mm, apex acuminate or acute, base cuneate or obtuse, upper surface light green, dull, initially sparsely pilose, veins 5–6, lower surface pale grayish green, pilose; petiole 3–7 mm, pilose. Fertile shoots 10–15 mm, including 3 leaves and a compact, 1- to 3(–4)-flowered inflorescence; pedicels 2–5 mm, pilose; flowers (including hypanthium) 4 mm long, pale pink and red in bud. Hypanthium cupulate, glabrous, base sparsely pilose; sepals obtuse, acute, apiculate or ligulate, glabrous, margin erose, villous. Corolla 6–8 mm, petals spreading, pale pink. Stamens 16–20; filaments white; anthers white. Fruit depressed-globose, 7–9 mm, red to crimson, sometimes single hairs, calyx lobes suberect, navel open. Nutlets 2(–3), style remains $^2/_3$ from base.

Seasons: Flowers May; fruit ripe August–September.

Chromosomes: Tetraploid (Bailey, pers. comm.). Apomictic, true from seed.

Hardiness: –18°C (–1°F).

Area: Tajikistan. Uzbekistan.

Notes: In the botanic garden of Moscow, seed of the white-flowered *Cotoneaster oliganthus* from Kazakhstan and the pink-flowered *C. erratus* from Tajikistan became mixed (see notes for *C. oliganthus*). Bertil Hylmö received seed of *C. erratus* from Antonina Pojarkova in Leningrad 1959 in error as *C. oliganthus*.

4. *Cotoneaster goloskokovii* Pojarkova in Opred. Rast. Sred. Azii 5: 245 (1976). Type: Kazakhstan, Turaigyr mountains (a branch of the Trans-Ili Alatau), 29 September 1962, *A. Pojarkova 458* (holo LE).

Shrub, 1.5–2 m. Branches erect, arched. Leaves deciduous, subcoriaceous, on sterile shoots oblong or rhomboid-elliptic, 15–45 × 7–23 mm, apex acute or acuminate, upper surface sparsely pilose-strigose, lower surface sparsely pilose; petiole densely pilose. Fertile shoots with a compact, 3- to 12-flowered inflorescence; pedicels densely pilose, Hypanthium densely long-haired pilose; sepals truncate, obtuse or acute, pilose or sparsely so, margin densely pilose. Petals spreading to recurved, white. Stamens 20. Fruit subglobose or depressed-globose, 6–8 mm, purple-red, pilose, apex open. Nutlets 1(–2), apex tomentose, style remains $^2/_3$ from base.

Seasons: Flowers June; fruit ripe September.

Area: Kazakhstan. Kyrgyzstan.

Notes: *Cotoneaster goloskokovii*, which comes from the Tian Shan and Alatau ranges bordering China, is rare in cultivation. Not in key.

5. *Cotoneaster ignavus* E. L. Wolf in Bull. Imp. For. Inst. St. Petersburg 15: 240 (1907). Type: cult. Sweden, Bjuv, 5 June 1971, B. Hylmö 9381, RBG Edinburgh received from Arnold Arboretum (lecto designated GB). **PLATE 196**.

Shrub, 1.5–2 m. Branches narrowly erect; branchlets spiraled or distichous, slender, maroon to brownish with large lenticels, initially densely pilose. Leaves deciduous, chartaceous, on sterile shoots broadly elliptic, 35–55 × 23–40 mm, apex acute or obtuse, base truncate or obtuse, upper surface mid-green, dull, initially pilose, veins 4–5 impressed, lower surface villous-pilose; petiole 7–9 mm, pilose. Fertile shoots 35–55 mm, including 3 leaves and a lax, dichotomous 7- to 20-flowered inflorescence; pedicels 3–13 mm, sparely pilose; flowers (including hypanthium) 4–5 mm long, red in bud. Hypanthium cupulate, glabrous or extreme base pilose; sepals obtuse or acute, glabrous, margin villous. Corolla 7–8 mm, petals semispreading, pale pink. Stamens (16–)20; filaments white; anthers white. Fruit pendent, globose or obovoid, 6–7 mm, maroon to purple-black, pruinose, glabrous, calyx lobes flat, navel open. Nutlets 2(–3), style remains $^4/_5$ from base.

Seasons: Flowers May–June; fruit ripe August–September.

Chromosomes: Tetraploid (McAllister, pers. comm.). Apomictic, true from seed.

Hardiness: –21°C (–6°F).

Area: Kazakhstan. Kyrgyzstan.

Notes: *Cotoneaster ignavus* has been in cultivation since around 1890, but there has been some confusion surrounding its origin and classification. Egbert Wolf believed that cultivated shrubs descended from a collection made by Albert von Regel in eastern Turkestan. However, Popov (1935) identified *C. ignavus* from the Alatau mountains near Almaty, Kazakhstan, in the knowledge that Regel had also collected in this area, although he (Popov) believed this to be a hybrid between *C. melanocarpus* and *C. multiflorus*. In 1971 Raymond Cinovskis of the National Botanic Garden, Salaspils in Latvia found *C. ignavus* growing near Issyk Kul lake in Kyrgyzstan.

6. Cotoneaster neoantoninae A. Vassiliev in Flora Kazakhstana 6: 444 (1963). Synonym: *C. antoninae* A. Vassiliev (1961), non Juzepczuk. Type: SW Alatau (Kazakhstan), Dschungari, Mt. Matai Tuzasu, 16 June 1956, V. Goloskokov (holo LE, iso E).

Shrub, 1.5–2 m. Branches erect; branchlets reddish brown and shiny, initially tomentose-pilose. Leaves deciduous, on sterile shoots ovate or elliptic, 20–35 × 15–20 mm, apex obtuse, rarely apiculate, margin undulate, upper surface dark green, glabrous, lower surface white tomentose; petiole 4–6 mm long, pilose. Fertile shoots with a 3- to 5-flowered inflorescence; pedicels tomentose. Hypanthium tomentose-pilose. Carpels 2.

Area: Kazakhstan.

Notes: The opportunity to study the type herbarium specimen of *Cotoneaster neoantoninae* has not arisen. The above description is based on Vassiliev's type diagnosis, from which it seems this species is near *C. oliganthus* but with the upper surface of the leaves glabrous. Not known in cultivation. Not in key.

7. Cotoneaster oliganthus Pojarkova in Not. Syst. Inst. Bot. Acad. Sci. USSR 8: 141 (1940). Type: Kazakhstan (former region of Semipalatinsk), on the western slope of the Arkat mountain range, 19 May 1914, N. Schipczinsky (holo LE).

Shrub, to 0.7 m. Branches to 1.5 m, ascending, spreading; branchlets spiraled or distichous, maroon to purple-black with large lenticels, initially densely pilose. Leaves deciduous, chartaceous, on sterile shoots elliptic, 24–40 × 15–23 mm, apex acute or obtuse, base obtuse or cuneate, upper brownish soon dark green, dull, sparsely pilose, veins 4–6, lower surface densely pilose; petiole 4–7 mm, pilose. Fertile shoots 15–25 mm, including a compact, 3- to 11-flowered inflorescence; pedicels 1–4 mm, villous; flowers (including hypanthium) 4–5 mm long, pinkish in bud. Hypanthium cupulate, sparsely villous; sepals obtuse, subglabrous, margin villous. Corolla 8–10 mm, petals erect to spreading, white with few pink blotches. Stamens 18–20; filaments white or pale pink; anthers white. Fruit depressed-globose or obovoid, 8–9 mm, red to ruby, pruinose, sparsely pilose, calyx lobes suberect, navel open. Nutlets (1–)2, rarely 3, style remains ⅔ from base.

Seasons: Flowers May–June; fruit ripe August–September.

Chromosomes: Tetraploid (Klotz 1968b; Jewsbury, pers. comm.). Apomictic, true from seed.

Hardiness: −18°C (−1°F).

Area: Kazakhstan. Kyrgyzstan. Turkmenistan

Notes: In Pojarkova's (1940) original description for *Cotoneaster oliganthus*, the inflorescence is described as 3- to 11-flowered, petals erect to spreading, white. Later (1955), without realizing she was looking at two different species, Pojarkova altered this description to inflorescence 1- to 3-flowered, petals spreading, pink. The latter description is of *C. erratus*, raised from seed given to Bertil Hylmö by Pojarkova.

8. *Cotoneaster peduncularis* Boissier in Diagn. Plant. Orient. 3: 8 (1943). Type: Herb. Boissier, Turkey, Bursa Ula Dag, Mount Olympus in summit, July 1842 (lecto designated BORD).

Shrub, 1.5–2 m. Branches narrowly erect; branchlets spiraled, greenish to maroon, minutely verruculose, initially densely pilose. Leaves deciduous, chartaceous, on sterile shoots elliptic or ovate, 33–53 × 19–34 mm, apex acute, obtuse sometimes acuminate, base obtuse, upper surface slightly rugose, mid-green, initially sparsely pilose, veins 4–5 lightly impressed, lower surface densely pilose; petiole 7–9 mm, densely pilose. Fertile shoots 20–30 mm, including 2–3 leaves which exceed the flowers, and a lax, 5- to 13-flowered inflorescence; pedicels 2–4 mm, slender, sparsely pilose; flowers (including hypanthium) 4–5 mm long. Hypanthium cupulate, subglabrous; sepals obtuse, acute or ligulate, border membranous, whitish, margin villous. Corolla 8–9 mm, petals spreading to semispreading, pink. Stamens 10–14; filaments white; anthers white. Fruit pendent, globose or depressed-globose, 7–8 mm, red to crimson, glabrous, calyx lobes suberect, navel open. Nutlets 2(–3), style remains ³/₄ from base.

Seasons: Flowers May–June; fruit ripe October.

Chromosomes: Unknown. Apomictic, true from seed.

Hardiness: −18°C (−1°F).

Area: Turkey. Armenia. Iran.

Notes: *Cotoneaster peduncularis* has long been a forgotten species. In Turkish floras it has been treated as *C. integerrimus*, *C. melanocarpus*, or even *C. multiflorus*. *Cotoneaster peduncularis* seems to be fairly common in some areas of Turkey. Recently reintroduced into cultivation.

9. *Cotoneaster zeravschanicus* Pojarkova in Not. Syst. Inst. Bot. Acad. Sci. USSR 17: 208 (1955). Type: Tajikistan, Lake Iskander-kul, on the northern slope of the Hissar Mountains, May 1892, V. Komarov (holo LE).

Shrub dense, 2–2.5 m. Branches narrowly erect; branchlets spiraled, maroon, initially densely pilose. Leaves deciduous, chartaceous, on sterile shoots broadly ovate, suborbicular or broadly elliptic, 23–42 × 20–37 mm; apex obtuse, base obtuse or truncate, upper surface mid-green, slightly shiny soon dull, initially sparsely pilose, veins 4–6, lower surface densely pilose; petiole 3–5 mm, pilose. Fertile shoots 20–30 mm, including 2–3 leaves and a compact, 7- to 12-flowered inflorescence; pedicels 1–10 mm, pilose; flowers (including hypanthium) 3–5 mm long, pink in bud. Hypanthium infundibulate, subglabrous; sepals obtuse or low acute, glabrous, margin villous. Corolla 8–9 mm, petals semispreading, off-white with small pink blotches. Stamens (10–)14; filaments white; anthers white. Fruit obovoid, 8–10 mm, ruby to maroon, pruinose, calyx lobes suberect. Nutlets 2, style remains ³/₄ from base.

> Seasons: Flowers May–June; fruit ripe August–September.
> Chromosomes: Unknown. Apomictic, true from seed.
> Hardiness: –21°C (–6°F).
> Area: Tajikistan. Kazakhstan.
> Notes: *Cotoneaster zeravschanicus* is an unusual species which can be found in some botanic gardens and large private collections. It is especially easy to identify in spring when the fertile shoots are covered with dense, white hairs which give the shrub an attractive, ethereal appearance.

11. Section *Megalocarpi*, stat. nov. Basionym: series *Megalocarpi* (Pojarkova)

> G. Klotz in Wiss. Z. Martin-Luther-Univ. Halle-Wittenberg, Math.-Naturwiss. 15: 847 (1966).

Branches narrowly erect, slender; branchlets spiraled, divaricate or distichous. Leaves on sterile shoots distichous or spiraled, veins mostly not impressed. Inflorescences erect. Petals erect or semispreading, white or pink, often with hairs at base of inner surface and sometimes on margins. Fruit mostly globose, dull. Nutlets with style remains near or at apex.

> 1 series: *Megalocarpi*.

37. Series *Megalocarpi*

Small to large shrubs. Leaves deciduous, upper surface initially with sparse pilose hairs mostly on midrib. Inflorescences mostly erect. Fruit crimson, red, ruby, maroon, rarely purple-black. Nutlets (1–)2–3.

> Very early to mid season.
> Kazakhstan. Kyrgyzstan. Afghanistan. Mongolia. Korea (Ullŭng island). India.
> 11 species: *C. cinovskisii, C. karatavicus, C. krasnovii, C. megalocarpus, C. mongolicus, C. nedoluzhkoi, C. osmastonii, C. roborowskii, C. roseus, C. songoricus, C. wilsonii.*

Key to Series *Megalocarpi*

1a. Petals rose-pink; filaments pink; nutlets 1–2, c. 50–50%. . . . . ***C. roseus***
1b. Petals white, rarely pink-tinged; filaments white; nutlets (1–)2(–3) **2**

2a. Leaves broadly elliptic or suborbicular; fruit crimson or cherry; nutlet with style remains ± at apex **3**

2b. Leaves elliptic or ovate; fruit mostly ruby, maroon or plum-purple; nutlet with style remains 2/3–4/5 from base **5**

3a. Fertile shoots 35–60 mm; inflorescence 9- to 25-flowered; hypanthium glabrous; sepals obtuse ....*C. songoricus*

3b. Fertile shoots 15–30 mm; inflorescence 3- to 10-flowered; hypanthium pilose or villous; sepals acute or acuminate **4**

4a. Branches narrowly erect; hypanthium pilose-villous often densely so; stamens mostly 18–20 ....*C. karatavicus*

4b. Branches erect; hypanthium sparsely villous; stamens mostly 12–16 .... *C. krasnovii*

5a. Leaves narrowly elliptic or oblong-elliptic; inflorescence 3- to 6(–7)-flowered ....
....*C. mongolicus*

5b. Leaves ovate or elliptic; inflorescence mostly 5- to 15-flowered **6**

6a. Leaf apex mostly acuminate, sometimes acute; fertile shoots 40–60 mm; petals white tinged red and pink ....*C. wilsonii*

6b. Leaf apex mostly acute, sometimes obtuse or acuminate; fertile shoots 20–50 mm, petals white or off white **7**

7a. Leaves 38–70 mm; hypanthium glabrous; sepals mostly acute or obtuse; corolla 7–8 mm
....*C. cinovskisii*

7b. Leaves 32–48 mm; hypanthium pilose; sepals cuspidate; corolla 10–12 mm ....
....*C. megalocarpus*

1. *Cotoneaster cinovskisii* J. Fryer & B. Hylmö, *sp. nov.* Type: cult. Sweden, Bjuv, 10 June 1973, B. Hylmö 1629, from National Botanic Garden of Latvia, Salaspils, as seed from Kyrgyzstan, Tian Shan, Sussamyr plateau, Tschitschkan, It-Agar, 1969, R. Cinovskis et al. (holo GB). **PLATE 197.**

Shrub, 2–3 m. Branches narrowly erect, arched; branchlets spiraled, slender, brown, lenticellate, initially pilose-strigose. Leaves deciduous, chartaceous, on sterile shoots ovate or elliptic, 38–70 × 23–37 mm, apex acute, acuminate or obtuse, base obtuse or cuneate, upper surface mid to dark green, dull, initially sparsely pilose, veins 4–7, lower surface light green, pilose; petiole 6–9 mm, pilose. Fertile shoots 20–50 mm, including 2–4 leaves, and a lax 3- to 15-flowered inflorescence; pedicels 3–10 mm, glabrous. Flower buds white. Hypanthium cupulate, glabrous; sepals obtuse, acute or ligulate, glabrous, border membranous, whitish green, margin glabrous or single hairs. Corolla 7–8 mm, petals spreading to semispreading, white, sometimes with hair-tuft. Stamens (16–)20; filaments white; anthers white. Fruit globose, 9–10 mm, red with crimson, glabrous, calyx lobes flat to suberect. Nutlets 2(–3), style remains 4/5 from base.

Seasons: Flowers April–May, frequently reflowers July–August at ends of long shoots; fruit ripe August.

Chromosomes: Tetraploid (Bailey, pers. comm.). Apomictic, true from seed.

Hardiness: −18°C (−1°F).

Area: Kazakhstan. Kyrgyzstan.

Notes: *Cotoneaster cinovskisii*, named in honor of the late Raymonds Cinovskis, dendrologist of the National Botanic Garden in Latvia, Salaspils, is narrowly erect in habit, early flowering and fruiting, and is very pretty when displaying both its second-season flowers and beadlike fruit at the same time.

2. *Cotoneaster karatavicus* Pojarkova in Not. Syst. Inst. Bot. Acad. Sci. USSR 21: 184 (1961). Type: S Kazakhstan, Karatau, Kurgan-Sai, Atabaevka, 12 September 1956, *E. Korotkova, O. Knorring & T. Adylov 5514* (holo LE).

Shrub, 1.5–2 m. Branches narrowly erect, thin; branchlets spiraled, reddish brown to purple, lenticellate, initially strigose-pilose. Leaves deciduous. subcoriaceous, on sterile shoots broadly elliptic or suborbicular, 20–32 × 16–29 mm, apex acute, apiculate or obtuse, base cuneate, upper surface dark green, dull, sparsely pilose, veins 3–5, lower surface light green, pilose-villous; petiole 4–6 mm, pilose. Fertile shoots 15–25 mm, including mostly 2–3 leaves and a compact, 4- to 10-flowered inflorescence; pedicels 3–8 mm. Flower buds white. Hypanthium cupulate, pilose-villous, often densely so; sepals acute or acuminate, sparsely villous, border membranous often reddish purple, margin villous. Corolla 7–10 mm, petals spreading, white, sometimes with very small hair-tuft. Stamens (16–)18–20; filaments white; anthers white. Fruit depressed-globose or obovoid, 7–8 mm, crimson to red, sparsely pilose, calyx lobes flat. Nutlets (1–)2, frequently joined but separating easily, style remains at apex.

Seasons: Flowers May–June; fruit ripe August–September.

Chromosomes: Tetraploid (Gladkova 1968; Kroon 1978; Jewsbury, pers. comm.). Apomictic, true from seed.

Hardiness: −21°C (−6°F).

Area: Kazakhstan. Kyrgyzstan.

Notes: *Cotoneaster karatavicus*, from the Karatau and Alatau mountains, is a sparsely branched shrub which is closely related to *C. krasnovii*.

3. *Cotoneaster krasnovii* Pojarkova in Not. Syst. Inst. Bot. Acad. Sci. USSR 21: 187 (1961). Type: SE Kazakhstan, Alatau mountains, Songoria, Mt. Tshulak in Mont sha-Sai, 29 May 1955, V. Goloskokov (holo LE, iso E).

Shrub, 1.5–2 m. Branches narrowly erect; branchlets reddish brown to purple, lenticellate, initially strigose-pilose. Leaves deciduous, subcoriaceous, on sterile shoots broadly elliptic or suborbicular, 19–32 × 14–29 mm, apex acute, apiculate or obtuse, base cuneate, upper surface dark green, dull, sparsely pilose, veins 5–7, lower surface light green, pilose-villous; petiole 5–7 mm, pilose. Fertile shoots 15–30 mm, including 2–3 leaves and a compact, 3- to 8-flowered inflorescence. Hypanthium cupulate, sparsely villous; sepals acute, few obtuse, glabrous or few villous hairs, border membranous, often reddish purple, margin villous. Flower buds white with pink dots. Corolla 9–11 mm, petals spreading, white, sometimes very small hair-tuft. Stamens 12–16 (20); filaments white; anthers white. Fruit depressed-globose or globose, 7–8 mm, crimson to red, sparsely pilose, calyx lobes flat. Nutlets (1–)2, frequently joined but separating easily, style remains at apex.

Seasons: Flowers June; fruit ripe September–October.

Hardiness: –21°C (–6°F).

Area: Kazakhstan.

Notes: Pojarkova presented *Cotoneaster krasnovii* in the same paper as *C. karatavicus*, without making any comparisons between the two species. The diagnoses are similar, showing only minor differences. Both originate from the Alatau mountain range, *C. karatavicus* from the west (Karatau) and *C. krasnovii* from the east (Songoria).

4. *Cotoneaster megalocarpus* Popov in Bull. Soc. Imp. Nat. Mosc. 44: 128 (1935). Type: Kazakhstan, in the vicinity of Almaty, 19 September 1933, M. G. Popov (holo LE).

Shrub, 2–2.5 m. Branches loosely erect and irregularly spreading; branchlets spiraled, maroon, initially pilose-strigose. Leaves deciduous, chartaceous, on sterile shoots ovate or elliptic, 32–48 × 20–28 mm, apex acute or acuminate, base obtuse, upper surface dark green, shiny, initially sparsely pilose-strigose, veins 5–6 lightly impressed, lower surface pilose; petiole 3–6 mm, pilose-strigose. Fertile shoots 25–40 mm, including 2–4 leaves and a lax, 5- to 15-flowered inflorescence; pedicels 3–8 mm, pilose. Flower buds pink-tinged. Hypanthium cupulate, pilose hairs dense at base; sepals long cuspidate, light green with red tip, glabrous, few hairs at margin. Corolla 10–12 mm, petals spreading to semispreading, white, glabrous. Stamens 16–20; filaments white; anthers white. Fruit globose or obovoid, 11–13 mm, red to ruby, dull, glabrous, succulent, skin splitting at maturity, calyx lobes flat, glabrous. Nutlets (1–)2, rarely 3, style remains $^4/_5$ from base.

Seasons: Flowers April–May, often reflowers late summer; fruit ripe August.

Chromosomes: Tetraploid (Gladkova 1968; Klotz and Krügel 1983a). Apomictic, true from seed.

Hardiness: –21°C (–6°F).

Area: Kazakhstan.

Notes: *Cotoneaster megalocarpus*, from the Tian Shan range, has inflorescences in which the period of flowering is extended to such a degree that flowers and fruit appear in the same inflorescence simultaneously. Recently reintroduced into cultivation.

5. *Cotoneaster mongolicus* Pojarkova in Not. Syst. Inst. Bot. Acad. Sci. USSR 17: 196 (1955). Type: E Mongolia, Mount Kheseg, river Urtu, 22 August 1945, *D. Tsevegmid 8348* (holo LE).

Shrub, 2–2.5 m. Branches erect; branchlets spiraled or divaricate, purplish brown, initially pilose-villous. Leaves deciduous, subcoriaceous, on sterile shoots narrowly elliptic or oblong-elliptic, 35 × 18 mm, apex obtuse, acute or apiculate, base cuneate or obtuse, upper surface green, glabrous or few pilose hairs, veins lightly impressed, lower surface initially glaucous, densely pilose to pilose; petiole pilose. Fertile shoots with 2–3 leaves and a 3- to 6(–7)-flowered inflorescence; pedicels 2–3 mm. Hypanthium cupulate, glabrous; sepals acute, border membranous, purple, glabrous, margin villous. Corolla 9–10 mm, petals spreading becoming slightly recurved, white, glabrous. Stamens 20. Fruit obovoid to globose, succulent, 8–9 mm, dark red to purple-black, glabrous, calyx lobes flat, navel open. Nutlets 2, style remains near or at apex.

Hardiness: −21°C (–6°F).

Area: Mongolia.

Notes: *Cotoneaster mongolicus* was reintroduced into cultivation in 1997 from a collection made in the Khentey Mountains of Mongolia by Géza Kósa of Vácrátót, Hungary. It has not been possible as yet to undertake an in-depth study of this species. The above description is based mostly on the original diagnosis.

6. *Cotoneaster nedoluzhkoi* Tzvelev in Bot. Zhurn. (Moscow & Leningrad) 87 (7): 115 (2002). Type: Russia, province Primorskje, near the town of Nachodka, in Sestra at the mouth of the river Partizanskaja (formerly Suczan), 30 September 1989, *N. Tzvelev 224* (holo LE).

Shrub, 0.3–1 m. Branchlets strongly divaricate, dark brown and gray. Leaves deciduous, elliptic, 8–15 × 6–9 mm, apex rotund often minutely apiculate, base rotund or broadly cuneate, upper surface green, dull, sparsely pilose-villous on veins, veins impressed, lower surface lax tomentose; petiole 1–4 mm, lax tomentose. Inflorescence c. 2- or 3-flowered; pedicels 5–7 mm, lax tomentose. Fruit subglobose (ovate-globose), 5–7 mm, becoming red, dull.

Notes: At fruiting time *Cotoneaster nedoluzhkoi* is said to have pendent, solitary fruits hanging on arched pedicels. Neither herbarium nor living specimen were seen. The above description is compiled from Nikolai Tzvelev's original description. Not in key.

7. *Cotoneaster osmastonii* G. Klotz in Wiss. Z. Martin-Luther-Univ. Halle-Wittenberg, Math.-Naturwiss. 15: 850 (1966). Type: N India, Kumaon, Niti valley opposite Laung, 4 June 1915, *A. E. Osmaston 641* (holo DD). **PLATE 198.**

Shrub, 2–3 m. Branches erect, slender; branchlets divaricate, maroon to purple-black, initially yellowish pilose-strigose. Leaves deciduous, chartaceous, on sterile shoots elliptic or ovate, 15–55 × 12–32 mm, apex obtuse or acute, base mostly obtuse or rotund, upper surface mid-green, sparsely pilose, veins 6–8 slightly impressed, lower surface paler with pilose hairs initially dense; petiole 2–7 mm, strigose-villous. Fertile shoots 25–35 mm, including 1–2 leaves and somewhat lax, 3- to 7-flowered inflorescence; pedicels 1–3 mm, initially pilose-villous, flowers (including hypanthium) 4–6 mm long, pinkish red in bud. Hypanthium cupulate, pilose-villous; sepals acuminate, acute or lingulate, initially sparsely villous. Corolla 8–9 mm, petals semispreading, pink with red, with hairtuft. Stamens 15–20; filaments pink; anthers white. Fruit depressed-globose, 7–10 mm, orange-red with pale lenticels, shiny, glabrous; calyx lobes suberect, navel open, nutlets exeorted. Nutlets 2.

Seasons: Flowers May–June; fruit ripe August–September.

Hardiness: –18°C (1°F).

Area: India (Uttaranchal Pradesh, Himachal Pradesh). Pakistan.

Notes: Although it is uncommon in cultivation, this species but can be seen under *Helmut Ern 7557*, a collection made in Pakistan in 1983. *Cotoneaster osmastonii* is similar to *C. roseus* but with more hairs in most parts, fewer flowers in the inflorescence, and orange-red fruit. Not in key.

8. *Cotoneaster roborowskii* Pojarkova in Not. Syst. Inst. Bot. Acad. Sci. USSR 21: 190 (1961). Type: SE Kazakhstan, Turaigyr, Tsharyn river, Kartagoi, 20 May 1953, V. Goloskokov (holo LE, iso E).

Shrub, 2–4 m. Branches erect, long and slender; branchlets divaricate, purplish, initially densely pilose. Leaves deciduous, chartaceous, on sterile shoots elliptic or ovate, 25 × 16 mm, apex shortly acute, petiole 2–6 mm, grayish pilose. Fertile shoots 15–40 mm, including a 3- to 10-flowered inflorescence; pedicels 2–7 mm, densely pilose. Hypanthium cupulate, sparsely pilose; sepals broadly acute, densely pilose, border purple. Corolla 10–12 mm, petals spreading to reflexed, white, with hair-tuft. Stamens 18–20. Fruit obovoid, 6–7 mm, red-purple. Nutlets 2.

Chromosomes: Unknown.

Hardiness: –18°C (–1°F).

Area: Kazakhstan. Kyrgyzstan.

Notes: *Cotoneaster roborowskii*, from the Tian Shan and Alatau ranges, is very rarely found in cultivation. The above description is based on the original diagnosis. Not in key.

9. *Cotoneaster roseus* Edgeworth in Trans. Linn. Soc. London 20: 46 (1846). Type: Afghanistan, Kuram valley, high forest up Shedloi gorge, 3000 m, July 1879, *M. P. Edgeworth 782* (lecto designated BM). **PLATE 199.**

Shrub or small tree, 2–4 m. Branches erect, arched; branchlets distichous, maroon, initially pilose-strigose. Leaves deciduous, chartaceous, on sterile shoots ovate or elliptic, 33–55 × 16–35 mm, apex acute or acuminate, base cuneate or truncate, upper surface mid-green, initially pilose, veins 6–8, lower surface initially sparsely pilose; petiole 4–8 mm, pilose or glabrous. Fertile shoots 25–40 mm, including 3–4 leaves and a lax, 7- to 15-flowered inflorescence; pedicels 2–5 mm, sparsely pilose. Flower buds reddish. Hypanthium cupulate, glabrous or single long hairs; sepals acute or lingulate, glabrous, margin tomentose. Corolla 8 mm, petals spreading, rose-pink, hair-tuft at base of upper surface. Stamens 18–20; filaments pink; anthers white. Fruit globose or obovoid, 9 mm, crimson to ruby, dull, glabrous, calyx lobes flat or suberect, navel open. Nutlets 1–2, style remains $^9/_{10}$ from base.

Seasons: Flowers May–June; fruit ripe August–September.

Chromosomes: Tetraploid (Zeilinga 1964) as *C. multiflorus* (Klotz 1968b; Kroon 1975; Klotz and Krügel 1983a). Apomictic, true from seed.

Hardiness: −21°C (−6°F).

Area: Afghanistan. Kashmir. Pakistan.

Notes: According to Charles Nelson (Walsh and Nelson 1990), *Cotoneaster roseus* was named by Michael Pakenham Edgeworth of Edgeworthstown, County Longford, Ireland. The species is a somewhat sparsely branched but very pretty and unusual rose-pink-flowered *Cotoneaster*. There are many collections of this species in herbaria.

10. *Cotoneaster songoricus* (Regel) Popov in Bull. Soc. Imp. Nat. Mosc. 44: 128 (1935).
Synonyms: *C. fontanesii* Spach var. *songoricus* Regel (1873); *C. allochrous* Pojarkova (1961). Type: Kazakhstan, Songaria, 15 June 1857, *Semenov 381* (holo LE).

Shrub, 1.5–2 m. Branches erect, arched, slender; branchlets spiraled, slender, reddish brown, initially pilose-strigose. Leaves deciduous, chartaceous, on sterile shoots broadly elliptic to suborbicular, 29–35 × 17–32 mm, apex obtuse or acute, base cuneate or obtuse, upper surface light to mid-green, initially few pilose hairs, veins 4–6, lower surface light green, pilose-villous; petiole 5–10 mm, initially pilose-strigose. Fertile shoots 35–60 mm, including 2–4 mostly leaves and a lax, 9- to 25-flowered inflorescence; pedicels 3–7 mm, slender, glabrous or few pilose hairs. Flower buds white. Hypanthium cupulate, glabrous; sepals obtuse, glabrous, margin sparsely villous. Corolla 6–8 mm, petals semispreading, white, sometimes with hair-tuft. Stamens (18–)20; filaments white; anthers white. Fruit globose, 9 mm, pale crimson, glabrous, calyx lobes suberect, villous, navel open. Nutlets (1–)2, style remains at apex.

Seasons: Flowers May–June; fruit ripe August–September.

Chromosomes: Tetraploid (Gladkova 1968; Krügel 1992a). Apomictic, true from seed.

Hardiness: −18°C (−1°F).

Area: Kazakhstan. China (Xinjiang).

Notes: *Cotoneaster songoricus*, from the Tian Shan range, is a very pretty shrub which has quite a long flowering period. It is uncommon in cultivation.

11. *Cotoneaster wilsonii* Nakai in Bot. Mag. (Tokyo) 32: 104 (1918). Type: Korea,
Ullüng island, Dö-dong, 20 July 1917, *T. Nakai 6142-3* (holo TI). **PLATE 200.**

Shrub 1.5–2 m. Branches erect, arched; branchlets distichous or spiraled, slender, brown, lenticellate, initially strigose-pilose. Leaves deciduous, chartaceous, on sterile shoots ovate or elliptic, 45–78 × 22–32 mm, apex acuminate or acute, base cuneate, upper dark green, shiny, initially long-haired pilose, veins 5–7 lightly impressed, lower surface slightly reticulate, villous-pilose; petiole 5–10 mm, pilose-villous. Fertile shoots 40–60 mm, including 3–4 leaves and a lax, 5- to 15-flowered inflorescence; pedicels 3–12 mm, pilose. Flower buds white or reddish. Hypanthium cupulate, initially sparsely long-haired pilose; sepals acute or acuminate, glabrous or single hairs, margin long-haired villous.

Corolla 8–10 mm, petals semispreading, white tinged red and pink, glabrous. Stamens 16–20; filaments white, anthers white. Fruit obovoid to subglobose, 10–12 mm, ruby, maroon to purple-black, glabrous, calyx lobes flat. Nutlets 2(3), rarely 1, apex tomentose, style remains $^9/_{10}$ from base.

Seasons: Flowers May; fruit ripe September; autumn leaves yellow to red.

Chromosomes: Unknown. Apomictic, true from seed.

Hardiness: –18°C (–1°F).

Area: Korea (Ullüng Island).

Notes: *Cotoneaster wilsonii* is a beautiful shrub of good habit. The branches are pendulous when laden with fruit, and the butter-yellow autumn leaves contrast well with the multitudes of rich purple bloomy fruit. Recently reintroduced into cultivation. Also worth mentioning is *C. wilsonii* var. *pilocalyx* Hurusawa, Act. Phy. Geobot. 13: 229 (1943), from Korea, 1 June 1917, T. Nakai (TI)—possibly a new species.

Latin Descriptions of New Taxa

New Species

Cotoneaster alashanensis J. Fryer & B. Hylmö, *sp. nov.*
Affinis *C. zabelii* C. K. Schneider sed ramis rigidus erectus, foliis surculorum sterilum suborbicularis, serculo fertilis 10–20 mm longis, inflorescentiis 2–5-floris differt.

    Cotoneaster alashanensis is closely related to *C. zabelii*, which differs in its ascending branches, leaves ovate or elliptic, sterile shoots 15–45 mm, and inflorescence 3- to 13-flowered.

Cotoneaster altaicus J. Fryer & B. Hylmö, *sp. nov.*
Affinis *C. laxiflorus* (Jacquin) Lindley sed serculo florenti 20–30 mm longis, inflorescentiis 3–9-floris, nuculis 2–3 differt.

    Cotoneaster altaicus is closely related to *C. laxiflorus*, which differs in its longer (30–80 mm) fertile shoots, 10- to 50-flowered inflorescence, and nutlets 2–4 per fruit.

Cotoneaster ataensis J. Fryer & B. Hylmö, *sp. nov.*
Affinis *C. boisianus* G. Klotz sed foliis subtus purus viridis nitidus albidus villosis petiolis 4–6 mm, inflorescentiis compactis 3–9-floris hypanthiis cupuliformis differt.

    Cotoneaster ataensis is closely related to *C. boisianus*, which differs in its leaves with lower surface paler with yellowish pilose hairs, petiole 2–3 mm, inflorescences lax, 9- to 18-flowered, and hypanthium infundibulate.

Cotoneaster atrovinaceus J. Fryer & B. Hylmö, *sp. nov.*
Affinis *C. nitens* Rehder & Wilson sed frutex 0.5–1 m altus, foliis supra villoso-strigosis, pedicellis 2–4 mm longis, poma atrovinaceus obscuris differt.

    Cotoneaster atrovinaceus is closely related to *C. nitens* which differs in its taller (2–3 m) habit, leaves with upper surface glabrous, pedicels 2–4 mm long, and black shiny fruits.

Cotoneaster atrovirens J. Fryer & B. Hylmö, *sp. nov.*
Affinis *C. atropurpureus* Flinck & B. Hylmö sed foliis subcoriaceus atroviridis, pedicellis 0.5–3 mm longis strigosis, poma globosus 10 mm sanguineus ad rubris orientalis differt.

    Cotoneaster atrovirens is closely related to *C. atropurpureus* which differs in its thinner (chartaceous), paler green leaves, pedicles 1–2 mm, villous, and its obovoid, 7–8 mm, orange-red fruits.

Cotoneaster atuntzensis J. Fryer & B. Hylmö, *sp. nov.*

Affinis *C. bullatus* Bois sed hypanthiis infundibuliformis, poma 8–10 mm longis rubineus ad marroninus cum 3–4(–5) nuculis differt.

Cotoneaster atuntzensis is closely related to *C. bullatus*, which differs in its cupulate hypanthium, fruits 7–8 mm, rich red to red, with (4–)5 nutlets per fruit.

Cotoneaster aurantiacus J. Fryer & B. Hylmö, *sp. nov.*

Affinis *C. induratus* Flinck & B. Hylmö sed rami hornotini piloso-strigosis, foliis chartaceis, serculo fertilis 10–20 mm longis, poma 8–10 mm longis, pallide aurantiacus.

Cotoneaster aurantiacus is closely related to *C. induratus*, which differs in its new growth being tomentose, leaves coriaceous, fertile shoots 20–30 mm, and fruits orange and 9–10 mm.

Cotoneaster beimashanensis J. Fryer & B. Hylmö, *sp. nov.*

Affinis *C. nanshan* Vilmorin ex Mottet sed foliis surculorum sterilum ad 20 mm longis supra nitidus, inflorescentiis 1(–2)-floris, flores 6–7 mm (cum hypanthiis) longis, petalis apice pallidus roseus differt.

Cotoneaster beimashanensis is closely related to *C. nanshan* which differs in its larger (to 25 mm) leaves with upper surface dull, inflorescences 2- to 4-flowered, flowers (including hypanthium) 7–10 mm long, and petals with an off-white border.

Cotoneaster browiczii J. Fryer & B. Hylmö, *sp. nov.*

Affinis *C. oliganthus* Pojarkova sed foliis surculorum sterilum late ellipticis vel suborbicularis supra glabris, inflorescentiis 2–5-floris, gemmis rubris differt.

Cotoneaster browiczii is closely related to *C. oliganthus*, which differs in its elliptic leaves that are sparsely pilose on the upper surface, 3- to 11-flowered inflorescences, and flowers that are white or only slightly pinkish in bud.

Cotoneaster bumthangensis J. Fryer & B. Hylmö, *sp. nov.*

Affinis *C. simonsii* Baker sed foliis surculorum sterilum 12–24 mm longis supra concavis, venis 2–3 bini, sepalis obtusis vel apiculatis, nuculis (2–)3 differt.

Cotoneaster bumthangensis is closely related to *C. simonsii*, which differs in its leaves which are longer (19–33 mm) with upper surface flat, veins in 4–5 pairs level with surface, sepals long acuminate or cuspidate, and fruits with nutlets (2–)3(–4) per fruit.

Cotoneaster campanulatus J. Fryer & B. Hylmö, sp. nov.

Affinis *C. paradoxus* G. Klotz sed foliis surculorum sterilum 48–83 × 19–46 mm subtus villoso-tomentosis, poma atropurpureus differt.

Cotoneaster campanulatus is closely related to *C. paradoxus*, which differs in its smaller (22–44 × 10–19 mm) leaves, with lower surface sparsely pilose-strigose, and red to ruby fruits.

Cotoneaster capsicinus J. Fryer & B. Hylmö, *sp. nov.*
Affinis *C. forrestii* G. Klotz sed frutex 0.5–1 m altus, ramis horizontaliter arcuatis, foliis venis 3–4 bini petiolis 3–5 mm, flores 5 mm longis differt.
    Cotoneaster capsicinus is closely related to *C. forrestii* which differs in being 2–3 m tall with a stiffly erect habit, leaves with 2–3 pairs of veins, and the petiole 2–3 mm long.

Cotoneaster cardinalis J. Fryer & B. Hylmö, *sp. nov.*
Affinis *C. apiculatus* Rehder & Wilson sed frutex ad 1 m altus, foliis surculorum sterilum apice obtusis supra laetus viridis, petalis cardinalis, nuculis interdum 1 plerumque 2 raro 3 differt.
    Cotoneaster cardinalis is closely related to *C. apiculatus* which differs in its shorter (to 0.7 m) habit, leaves on sterile shoots with an apex apiculate or acute, upper surface dark green, petals dark red, and (2–)3 nutlets per fruit.

Cotoneaster chadwellii J. Fryer & B. Hylmö, *sp. nov.*
Affinis *C. royleanus* (Dippel) J. Fryer & B. Hylmö sed serculo fertilis 25–50 mm longis, inflorescentiis 10–50-floris, antheris purpureus, 2 nuculis differt.
    Cotoneaster chadwellii is closely related to *C. royleanus*, which differs in its shorter (15–25 mm) fertile shoots, 5- to 9(–12)-flowered inflorescence, anthers white or only very pale pink, and nutlets 1(–2) per fruit.

Cotoneaster chuanus J. Fryer & B. Hylmö, *sp. nov.*
Affinis *C. rokujodaisanensis* Hayata sed frutex 1.5 m alto, ramis ascendentibus horizontaliter arcuatis, foliis surculorum sterilum orbicularis vel suborbicularis, staminibus 10(–14), nuculis 2–3 differt.
    Cotoneaster chuanus is closely related to *C. rokujodaisanensis*, which differs in its shorter (0.5 m) habit, branches procumbent or decumbent, leaves broadly elliptic or broadly ovate, stamens 16–20, and nutlets 3–4.

Cotoneaster chulingensis J. Fryer & B. Hylmö, *sp. nov.*
Affinis *C. langei* G. Klotz sed ramis ascendens vel procumbens, foliis supra glabris, petalis erecto-patentis, atrosanguineus caudacus differt.
    Cotoneaster chulingensis is closely related to *C. langei*, which differs in its more erect habit, leaves with upper surface strigose, petals erect with apex incurved, red and pink with a white border, persistent.

Cotoneaster cinovskisii J. Fryer & B. Hylmö, *sp. nov.*

Affinis *C. megalocarpus* Popov sed foliis in surculorum sterilum 40–70 mm longis, hypanthiis glabris, sepalis obtusis vel acutis, corolla 7–8 mm diametro differt.

Cotoneaster cinovskisii is closely related to *C. megalocarpus*, which differs in its shorter (32–48 mm) leaves, hypanthium pilose, sepals long cuspidate, and the corolla 12 mm in diameter.

Cotoneaster coadunatus J. Fryer & B. Hylmö, *sp. nov.*

Affinis *C. ambiguus* Rehder & Wilson sed arbuscula vel frutex ad 5 m altus, foliis chartaceis, poma 10–15 mm longis, styli et nuculis 2 ex parte coadunatis differt.

Cotoneaster coadunatus is closely related to *C. ambiguus*, which differs in its lower stature (2–3 m), thinner leaves, and smaller (c. 8 mm) fruits with 2–3 free nutlets.

Cotoneaster convexus J. Fryer & B. Hylmö, *sp. nov.*

Affinis *C. kongboensis* G. Klotz sed foliis in surculorum sterilis 50–70 mm longis supra convexus, petiolis 3–5 mm longis, serculorum fertilis 25–45 mm longis, pedicellis 6–8 mm longis, hypanthiis cupuliformis differt.

Cotoneaster convexus is closely related to *C. kongboensis*, which differs in its shorter (40–53 mm) leaves that are not convex, longer (4–6 mm) petiole, fertile shoots 15–30 mm, pedicels 3–5 mm, and a cupulate hypanthium.

Cotoneaster creticus J. Fryer & B. Hylmö, *sp. nov.*

Affinis *C. parnassicus* Boissier & Heldreich sed foliis suborbicularis supra glabrescentibus subtus glabris, hypanthiis parc piloso-strigosis differt, poma rubineus ad marroninus.

Cotoneaster creticus is closely related to *C. parnassicus*, which differs in its ovate or elliptic leaves with upper surface persistently sparsely strigose and lower surface tomentose, hypanthium with a tomentose base, and fruits red.

Cotoneaster daliensis J. Fryer & B. Hylmö, *sp. nov.*

Affinis *C. tengyuehensis* J. Fryer & B. Hylmö sed foliis deciduo in surculorum sterilum late ellipticis, hypanthiis campanuliformis vel cupuliformis.

Cotoneaster daliensis is very closely related to *C. tengyuehensis*, which differs in its evergreen or semievergreen leaves that are mostly ovate, and cupulate hypanthium.

Cotoneaster decandrus J. Fryer & B. Hylmö, *sp. nov.*

Affinis *C. notabilis* G. Klotz sed frutex 1.5–2 m altus, serculo fertilis 20–60 mm longis, inflorescentiis 2–10-floris, staminibus 10(–12), poma 12–13 mm longis differt.

Cotoneaster decandrus is closely related to *C. notabilis*, which differs in its taller (3–4 m) habit, leaves 13–44 mm, inflorescence 1- to 4-flowered, stamens mostly 10, and smaller (c. 9 mm) fruits.

Cotoneaster declinatus J. Fryer & B. Hylmö, *sp. nov.*
Affinis *C. dielsianus* E. Pritzel sed frutex 1.5–2 m altus, ramis tenuis et debilis, foliis chartaceis in surculorum sterilum anguste ellipticus minus quam 20 mm longis differt.

Cotoneaster declinatus is closely related to *C. dielsianus*, which differs in its taller (2–4 m), more robust habit and in its leaves that are thicker (coriaceous or subcoriaceous), 21–26 mm, and ovate or broadly ovate.

Cotoneaster drogochius J. Fryer & B. Hylmö, *sp. nov.*
Affinis *C. harrysmithii* Flinck & B. Hylmö sed frutex 3–4 m altus, foliis surculorum sterilum 25–40 mm longis, petalis basis atropurpureus in centro rubris albomarginatus differt.

Cotoneaster drogochius is closely related to *C. harrysmithii*, which differs in its shorter (1–2 m) habit, leaves 13–17 mm, and petals pink with a maroon base and a white border.

Cotoneaster emeiensis J. Fryer & B. Hylmö, *sp. nov.*
Affinis *C. moupinensis* Franchet sed foliis surculorum sterilum 120–160 mm longis venis 7–8 bini, serculo fertilis 100–170 mm longis, poma rubris ribis differt.

Cotoneaster emeiensis is closely related to *C. moupinensis*, which differs in its longer (65–130 mm) leaves with 8–11 pairs of veins, fertile shoots 40–100 mm, and fruits purple-black.

Cotoneaster encavei J. Fryer & B. Hylmö, *sp. nov.*
Affinis *C. verruculosus* Diels sed foliis supra strigosis nervis 4 binatum paginis planus, pedicellis 2–4 mm longis differt.

Cotoneaster encavei is closely related to *C. verruculosus*, which differs in its slightly rugose leaves with upper surface only very sparsely strigose, veins 2–3 impressed, and pedicels 1–2 mm.

Cotoneaster erratus J. Fryer & B. Hylmö, *sp. nov.*
Affinis *C. oliganthus* Pojarkova sed foliis in surculorum sterilum angusto-ellipticis supra laetus viridis, inflorescentiis 1–3-floris, nuculis 2–3 plerumque 3 differt.

Cotoneaster erratus is closely related to *C. oliganthus*, which differs in its darker green and more widely elliptic leaves, 3- to 11-flowered inflorescences, and nutlets (1–)2 per fruit.

Cotoneaster estiensis J. Fryer & B. Hylmö, *sp. nov.*
Affinis *C. scandinavicus* B. Hylmö sed ramis erectus, petiolis 4–8 mm longis, sed serculo fertilis 10–25 mm longis, poma rubris differt.

Cotoneaster estiensis is closely related to *C. scandinavicus*, which differs in its branches ascending or decumbent, leaves with petiole 2–4 mm, fertile shoots 8–13 mm long, and fruits orange-red to red.

Cotoneaster fastigiatus J. Fryer & B. Hylmö, *sp. nov.*
Affinis *C. induratus* Flinck & B. Hylmö sed ramis fastigiatus, foliis chartaceous in surculorum sterilum 12–17 mm longis, staminibus 14–18, poma capsicinus differt.

Cotoneaster fastigiatus is closely related to *C. induratus*, which differs in its more spreading habit, leaves thicker (coriaceous) and larger (19–27 mm), stamens 20, and fruits orange-red.

Cotoneaster favargeri J. Fryer & B. Hylmö, *sp. nov.*
Affinis *C. juranus* J. Fryer & B. Hylmö sed foliis medius viridis, stamenibus 15–21 filamentis pallidus roseus, poma capsicinus cum (2–)3–5 nuculis, chromosomatibus 2*n* = 34 differt.

Cotoneaster favargeri is closely related to *C. juranus*, which differs in its darker green leaves, stamens 20, filaments off-white, fruits red with nutlets 2–4, and also in being tetraploid (2*n* = 68).

Cotoneaster fruticosus J. Fryer & B. Hylmö, *sp. nov.*
Affinis *C. induratus* J. Fryer & B. Hylmö sed frutex crassus ramosus, ramis erectus et effusis arcutis, foliis surculorum sterilum late ovatis vel suborbicularis, sepalis apice acutis, styli et nuculis 3–5 differt.

Cotoneaster fruticosus is closely related to *C. induratus*, which differs in its thinner branches which are stiffly erect (becoming arched in fruit), elliptic or ovate leaves, cuspidate sepals, and nutlets (2–)3–4.

Cotoneaster gonggashanensis J. Fryer & B. Hylmö, *sp. nov.*
Affinis *C. albokermesinus* J. Fryer & B. Hylmö sed foliis surculorum sterilum apice acutis vel obtusis venis 5–7 bini, hypanthiis campanuliformis verruculosis, poma carmesinus et rubris differt.

Cotoneaster gonggashanensis is closely related to *C. albokermesinus*, which differs in its leaves with apex mostly obtuse and veins 3–5, hypanthium cupulate without verrucules, and fruits creamy white with crimson blush.

Cotoneaster hedegaardii J. Fryer & B. Hylmö, *sp. nov.*
Affinis *C. gamblei* G. Klotz sed foliis supra primus sordidus, inflorescentiis compactis, corolla 10–12 mm diametro glabris, poma 12 mm diametro, nitens differt.

Cotoneaster hedegaardii is closely related to *C. gamblei*, which differs in its leaves with upper surface shiny, inflorescences lax, smaller flowers (corolla 8–10 mm wide), petals often with tuft of hairs at base of upper surface, and smaller (10 mm), dull fruits.

Cotoneaster hersianus J. Fryer & B. Hylmö, *sp. nov.*
Affinis *C. potaninii* Pojarkova sed foliis surculorum sterilum 53–60 mm longis, petiolis

5–9 mm longis, serculo fertilis 25–60 mm longis, antheris albis, poma 14–17 mm longis differt.

Cotoneaster hersianus is closely related to *C. potaninii*, which differs in its larger (10–26 mm) leaves with petiole 3–5 mm, fertile shoots 15–35 mm, anthers purple, and fruits c. 7 mm.

Cotoneaster hicksii J. Fryer & B. Hylmö, *sp. nov.*
Affinis *C. taylorii* G. Klotz sed foliis surculorum sterilum ad 30 mm longis supra densis strigosis, flores solitarius differt.

Cotoneaster hicksii is closely related to *C. taylorii* which differs in its longer (to 38 mm) leaves with upper surface sparsely strigose and a 2- or 3(–4)-flowered inflorescence.

Cotoneaster hillieri J. Fryer & B. Hylmö, *sp. nov.*
Affinis *C. reticulatus* Rehder & Wilson sed ramis rigidus erectus, venis 5–6 bini, inflorescentiis 5–8-floris differt.

Cotoneaster hillieri is closely related to *C. reticulatus*, which differs in its more spreading branching habit, leaves with 4–8 pairs of veins, and a 10- to 40-flowered inflorescence.

Cotoneaster huahongdongensis J. Fryer & B. Hylmö, *sp. nov.*
Affinis *C. sternianus* (Turrill) Boom sed foliis subcoriaceis in surculorum sterilum angusto-ellipticis vel elliptico-lanceolatis, apice acuminatis, inflorescentiis 3–10-floris, poma obovoideus differt.

Cotoneaster huahongdongensis is closely related to *C. sternianus*, which differs in its leaves being broadly elliptic or broadly ovate with apex mostly acute, the inflorescences 7- to 20-flowered, and the fruits obovoid.

Cotoneaster hylanderi J. Fryer & B. Hylmö, *sp. nov.*
Affinis *C. niger* (Wahlberg) Fries sed foliis surculorum sterilum late ellipticis vel orbicularis laetus viridis, petalis alabastro rubris, filamentis albis, poma initio rubris differt.

Cotoneaster hylanderi is closely related to *C. niger*, which differs in its darker green, ovate or elliptic leaves, off-white to pale pink flower buds, pink filaments, and fruits initially brownish.

Cotoneaster hypocarpus J. Fryer & B. Hylmö, *sp. nov.*
Affinis *C. elegans* (Rehder & E. H. Wilson) Flinck & B. Hylmö sed foliis in surculorum sterilum 26–35 mm, serculo fertilis 30–60 mm longis, hypanthiis cupuliformis, nuculis 3–4 differt.

Cotoneaster hypocarpus is closely related to *C. elegans*, which differs in its smaller (11–28 mm) leaves, fertile shoots 20–30 mm, hypanthium infundibulate, and nutlets 4–5 per fruit.

Cotoneaster kangdingensis J. Fryer & B. Hylmö, *sp. nov.*

Affinis *C. harrysmithii* Flinck & B. Hylmö sed rami hornotini verruculosus, foliis, petiolis, pedicellis, hypanthio et calycis dentibus strigosis, corolla praeclusus.

    Cotoneaster kangdingensis is closely related to *C. harrysmithii*, which differs in its new growth not being verruculose, the hairs on the leaves, petioles, pedicels, hypanthium, and sepals pilose, and an open corolla.

Cotoneaster kitaibelii J. Fryer & B. Hylmö, *sp. nov.*

Affinis *C. zabelii* C. K. Schneider sed foliis supra nitidis, pedicellis 2–3 longis, gemmis rubris, petalis reclusus viridi-albus suffusus rubris, filamentis roseus differt.

    Cotoneaster kitaibelii is closely related to *C. zabelii*, which differs in its dull leaves, pedicels 3–8 mm, flowers pale pink in bud, petals erect to semispreading, white with pink dots, and the filaments white.

Cotoneaster kuanensis J. Fryer & B. Hylmö, *sp. nov.*

Affinis *C. glomerulatus* W. W. Smith sed foliis surculorum sterilum ellipticis vel late ellipticis supra strigosis venis 3–4 bini, hypanthiis et sepalis sparsus strigosis, tetraploid ($2n = 68$) differt.

    Cotoneaster kuanensis is closely related to *C. glomerulatus*, which differs in its ovate to ovate-lanceolate leaves with upper surface glabrous or single pilose hairs, veins 4–8, hypanthium densely villous, and in being a diploid ($2n = 34$).

Cotoneaster leveillei J. Fryer & B. Hylmö, *sp. nov.*

Affinis *C. sternianus* (Turrill) Boom sed foliis surculorum sterilum suborbicularis ad 20 mm longis venis 2–4 bini, inflorescentiis 3–9-floris, sepalis cuspidatis differt.

    Cotoneaster leveillei is closely related to *C. sternianus*, which differs in its longer (to 50 mm), broadly elliptic or broadly ovate leaves, with 4–5 pairs of veins, inflorescences 7- to 20-flowered, and sepals acute or acuminate.

Cotoneaster marroninus J. Fryer & B. Hylmö, *sp. nov.*

Affinis *C. harrysmithii* Flinck & B. Hylmö sed sepalis plerumque longiacuminatis interdum acutis, poma marroninus nitensissimus calycis dentibus depressus differt.

    Cotoneaster marroninus is closely related to *C. harrysmithii*, which differs in its sepals being mostly acute or sometimes acuminate, fruits black, dull to shiny with calyx erect.

Cotoneaster milkedandaensis J. Fryer & B. Hylmö, *sp. nov.*

Affinis *C. encavei* J. Fryer & B. Hylmö sed foliis chartaceis valde undulatus, nuculis 1–2 differt.

    Cotoneaster milkedandaensis is closely related to *C. encavei*, which differs in its subcoriaceous, much less heavily undulate leaves, and nutlets 2–3 per fruit.

Cotoneaster naninitens J. Fryer & B. Hylmö, *sp. nov.*
Affinis *C. nitens* Rehder & Wilson sed frutex 1–1.5 m altus, ramis ascendentibus effusis, foliis surculorum sterilum 10–13 mm longis, poma 5–6 mm longis differt.

    Cotoneaster naninitens is closely related to *C. nitens*, which differs in its taller habit (to 3 m), branches erect becoming pendulous, branchlets divaricate, leaves longer (to 27 mm), and fruits 7–10 mm.

Cotoneaster nantouensis J. Fryer & B. Hylmö, *sp. nov.*
Affinis *C. verruculosus* Diels sed foliis surculorum sterilum suborbicularis versus fere quadratus, staminibus 10, nuculis 2 differt.

    Cotoneaster nantouensis is closely related to *C. verruculosus*, which differs in its orbicular, suborbicular, or broadly obovate leaves, stamens 12–16, and nutlets 2–4 per fruit.

Cotoneaster naoujanensis J. Fryer & B. Hylmö, *sp. nov.*
Affinis *C. sternianus* (Turrill) Boom sed foliis surculorum sterilum 20–30 mm longis apice acuminatis, sepalis cuspidatis, poma obovoideus differt.

    Cotoneaster naoujanensis is closely related to *C. sternianus*, which differs in its thicker, longer (37–50 mm) leaves with apex mostly acute, sepals acute or acuminate, and globose fruits.

Cotoneaster narynensis Tkatschenko ex J. Fryer & B. Hylmö, *sp. nov.*
Affinis *C. niger* (Wahlberg) Fries sed foliis surculorum sterilum late ellipticis supra laetus viridis valde nitidis petiolis 2–4 mm longis, inflorescentiis 5–12-floris differt.

    Cotoneaster narynensis is closely related to *C. niger*, which differs in its darker green and dull, ovate or sometimes elliptic leaves, longer (4–7 mm) petioles, and mostly 3- to 5-flowered inflorescences.

Cotoneaster natmataungensis J. Fryer, B. Hylmö & E. C. Nelson, *sp. nov.*
Affinis *C. forrestii* G. Klotz sed serculo fertilis 5–10 mm longis, flores solitari subsessiles differt.

    Cotoneaster natmataungensis is closely related to *C. forrestii* which differs in its longer (10–20 mm) fertile shoots with 1- or 2(–3)-flowered inflorescence with pedicels mostly 3–4 mm.

Cotoneaster nohelii J. Fryer & B. Hylmö, *sp. nov.*
Affinis *C. vilmorinianus* G. Klotz sed arbusculus vel frutex ad 5 m altus, foliis surculorum sterilum ad 42 × 25 mm supra rugulosis, petalis basis atrorubens centralis roseus candidomarginatus, nuculis 2 differt.

    Cotoneaster nohelii is closely related to *C. vilmorinianus*, which differs in its shorter (2–3 m) habit, smaller (20–26 mm) leaves with smooth upper surface, petals pale mauve with red base, and nutlets 2–3 per fruit.

Cotoneaster ogisui J. Fryer & B. Hylmö, *sp. nov.*
Affinis *C. sikangensis* Flinck & B. Hylmö sed foliis surculorum sterilum 90–170 mm longis, serculo fertilis 120–150 mm longis, venis 8–10 bini, inflorescentiis 10–50-floris, nuculis 4–5 plerumque 4 differt.

Cotoneaster ogisui is closely related to *C. sikangensis*, which differs in its smaller (26–39 × 13–24 mm) leaves, veins in 4–6, fertile shoots 25–40 mm, inflorescence 3- to 15-flowered, and nutlets mostly 5 per fruit, sometimes 3–4.

Cotoneaster omissus J. Fryer & B. Hylmö, *sp. nov.*
Affinis *C. monopyrenus* (W. W. Smith) Flinck & B. Hylmö sed foliis sempervirens coriaceis venis 6–8 bini, poma rubris cum 1–2 plurumque 2 nuculis differt.

Cotoneaster omissus is closely related to *C. monopyrenus*, which differs in its deciduous and thinner (subcoriaceous) leaves with 4–5 veins, fruits ruby to purple-black, containing mostly a solitary nutlet.

Cotoneaster pseudoobscurus J. Fryer & B. Hylmö, *sp. nov.*
Affinis *C. obscurus* Rehder & Wilson sed foliis surculorum sterilum ellipticis ad ellipticolanceolatis venis 4–7 bini, sepalis acuminatis vel acutis, poma marroninus ad pruninus differt.

Cotoneaster pseudoobscurus is closely related to *C. obscurus* which differs in its broader, elliptic or ovate leaves with 3–5 veins, sepals obtuse, acute or apiculate, and shiny maroon fruits.

Cotoneaster spongbergii J. Fryer & B. Hylmö, sp. nov.
Affinis *C. horizontalis* Decaisne sed foliis chartaceis in surculorum sterilum obovatus vel ellipticus, sepalis cuspidatis vel caudatus differt.

Cotoneaster spongbergii is closely related to *C. horizontalis*, which differs in its thicker (subcoriaceous) leaves that are mostly suborbicular or orbicular, and in the sepals that are acute or acuminate.

Cotoneaster svenhedinii J. Fryer & B. Hylmö, *sp. nov.*
Affinis *C. zabelii* C. K. Schneider sed ramis tenuis, foliis tenuis chartaceis supra planities medius viridis, hypanthiis villosis differt.

Cotoneaster svenhedinii is closely related to *C. zabelii*, which differs in its coarser branches, leaves thicker (chartaceous to subcoriaceous), rugose, and dark green, and the hypanthium tomentose-villous.

Cotoneaster taiwanensis J. Fryer & B. Hylmö, *sp. nov.*
Affinis *C. bullatus* Bois sed foliis chartaceis in surculorum sterilum angusto-ellipticis persistenter pilosis, sepalis obtusis vel acutis glabris, styli et nuculis 3–5 differt.

Cotoneaster taiwanensis is closely related to *C. bullatus*, which differs in its thicker (subcoriaceous), elliptic or ovate, glabrescent leaves, sepals mostly acute or acuminate, and 4–5 nutlets per fruit.

Cotoneaster tanpaensis J. Fryer & B. Hylmö, *sp. nov.*
Affinis *C. calocarpus* (Rehder & E. H. Wilson) Flinck & B. Hylmö sed inflorescentiis 5–10-floris, hypanthiis late campanuliformis glabris, petalis erecto-patentis differt.
Cotoneaster tanpaensis is closely related to *C. calocarpus*, which differs in its up to 15-flowered inflorescence, hypanthium cupulate with base sparsely pilose, and petals spreading.

Cotoneaster taofuensis J. Fryer & B. Hylmö, *sp. nov.*
Affinis *C. induratus* J. Fryer & B. Hylmö sed ramis arcutis, foliis subcoriaceis vel chartaceis, inflorescentiis 5–9-floris, nuculis 3–5 plerumque 3 differt.
Cotoneaster taofuensis is closely related to *C. induratus*, which differs in its more erect branches, thicker (coriaceous) leaves, 3- to 5-flowered inflorescences, and nutlets 3–4 per fruit.

Cotoneaster teijiashanensis J. Fryer & B. Hylmö, *sp. nov.*
Affinis *C. amoenus* Wilson sed ramis rigidus erectus, petiolis 1–2 mm longis, antheris albokermesinus, poma plus minusve globosus cum nuculis 2–3 plerumque 2 differt.
Cotoneaster teijiashanensis is closely related to *C. amoenus*, which differs in its branches loosely erect and spreading, leaves with petiole 2–5 mm, anthers purple becoming black, fruits ellipsoid with (2–)3 nutlets each.

Cotoneaster tripyrenus J. Fryer & B. Hylmö, *sp. nov.*
Affinis *C. nitens* Rehder & Wilson sed foliis surculorum sterilum 12–16 mm longis, serculo fertilis 10–15 mm longis, inflorescentiis 3–5-floris, nuculis 3 raro 2 differt.
Cotoneaster tripyrenus is closely related to *C. nitens*, which differs in its longer (to 27 mm) leaves, fertile shoots 15–30 mm including 1–3 flowers, and nutlets mostly 3 per fruit.

Cotoneaster tsarongensis J. Fryer & B. Hylmö, *sp. nov.*
Affinis *C. vernae* C. K. Schneider sed foliis surculorum sterilum ad 92 mm longis, inflorescentiis ad 70-floris, hypanthiis cupuliformis, petalis glabris differt.
Cotoneaster tsarongensis is closely related to *C. vernae*, which differs in its shorter (to 52 mm) leaves, inflorescence with up to 150 flowers or fruits, hypanthium infundibulate, and petals with hair-tuft at the base of upper surface.

Cotoneaster undulatus J. Fryer & B. Hylmö, *sp. nov.*
Affinis *C. nitens* Rehder & Wilson sed foliis surculorum sterilum usque ad 40 mm longis apice acuminatis vel acutis margine valde undulatus, inflorescentiis 3–4(–5)-floris differt.

Cotoneaster undulatus is closely related to *C. nitens*, which differs in its smaller (to 27 mm) leaves with apex obtuse or acute and mucronate, margin not flat, and 1- to 3-flowered inflorescences.

Cotoneaster verokotschyi J. Fryer & B. Hylmö, *sp. nov.*

Affinis *C. royleanus* (Dippel) J. Fryer & B. Hylmö sed foliis nervis 3–4 binatum paginus planus, petiolis 3–5 mm longis piloso-strigosis, inflorescentiis 3–5-floris, sepalis obtusis vel acutis, corolla 7–8 mm diametro, poma rubris differt.

Cotoneaster verokotschyi is closely related to *C. royleanus*, which differs in its leaves with 4–5 slightly impressed pairs of veins, petiole 5–7 mm, pilose-villous, inflorescence 5- to 9(–12)-flowered, sepals acuminate or acute, corolla 9–11 mm wide, and fruits crimson red.

Cotoneaster wanbooyensis J. Fryer & B. Hylmö, *sp. nov.*

Affinis *C. rehderi* Pojarkova sed foliis surculorum sterilum 85–110 mm longis, inflorescentiis 15–50-floris, nuculis (3–)4(–5) differt.

Cotoneaster wanbooyensis is closely related to *C. rehderi*, which differs in its larger (70–210 mm) leaves, 10- to 30-flowered inflorescences, and 4–5 nutlets per fruit.

Cotoneaster washanensis J. Fryer & B. Hylmö, *sp. nov.*

Affinis *C. hummelii* J. Fryer & B. Hylmö sed foliis subcoriaceis venis 6–8 bini, nuculis 3–4 differt.

Cotoneaster washanensis is closely related to *C. hummelii*, which differs in its thinner (chartaceous) leaves with 5–6 veins, and with 2–3 nutlets per fruit.

Cotoneaster yakuticus J. Fryer & B. Hylmö, *sp. nov.*

Affinis *C. popovii* Peschkova sed foliis supra nitidulus, persistenter longipilosis, serculo florenti 30–50 mm longis differt.

Cotoneaster yakuticus is closely related to *C. popovii*, which differs in its intensely shiny leaves that are pilose only upon emergence from bud, very soon glabrous, and in the shorter (20–30 mm) fertile shoots.

Cotoneaster yalungensis J. Fryer & B. Hylmö, *sp. nov.*

Affinis *C. verruculosus* Diels sed ramis ascendentibus effuses, staminibus 20, poma cinnabarino cum 2–3 nuculis differt.

Cotoneaster yalungensis is closely related to *C. verruculosus*, which differs in its more erect habit, 12–16 stamens, fruits rich red with 2(–4) nutlets per fruit.

Cotoneaster yinchangensis J. Fryer & B. Hylmö, *sp. nov.*

Affinis *C. horizontalis* Decaisne sed foliis chartaceus in surculorum sterilum late ellipticis apice acutis vel acuminatis, nuculis 2(–3) differt.

Cotoneaster yinchangensis is closely related to *C. horizontalis*, which differs in its thicker (subcoriaceous) leaves that are mostly suborbicular or orbicular with apex apiculate or obtuse, and nutlets (2–)3.

Cotoneaster yulingkongensis J. Fryer & B. Hylmö, *sp. nov.*
Affinis *C. hummelii* J. Fryer & B. Hylmö sed frutex 2–3 m altus, inflorescentiis 3–9-floris, poma 8–9 mm longis cum nuculis 2–3 differt.

    Cotoneaster yulingkongensis is closely related to *C. hummelii*, which differs in its taller (3–4 m) habit, 7- to 15-flowered inflorescence, and larger (11–13 mm) fruits with (2–)3 nutlets per fruit.

New Series

Series *Aitchisonioides* J. Fryer & B. Hylmö, *ser. nov.*
Affinis ser. *Racemiflori* (Pojarkova) G. Klotz sed foliis surculorum sterilum distichus vel spiralis ad 70 × 50 mm, alabastris albis, poma depresso-globosus sepalis depressus differt.
    Type: *C. aitchisonii* C. K. Schneider
    Series *Aitchisonioides* is closely related to ser. *Racemiflori*, which differs in its species having leaves on sterile shoots spiraled, very rarely distichous, smaller leaves (to 40 × 30 mm), flower buds pink, and fruits mostly obovoid with calyx suberect or erect over navel.

Series *Mucronati* J. Fryer & B. Hylmö, *ser. nov.*
Affinis ser. *Kongboense* J. Fryer & B. Hylmö sed foliis sempervirens vel semisempervirens, sepalis acuminatis vel cuspidatis, poma rubellus differt.
    Type: *C. mucronatus* Franchet
    Series *Mucronati* is closely related to ser. *Kongboense*, which differs in its species having deciduous leaves, with sepals mostly acute or obtuse, and the fruits maroon to purple-black.

Series *Tomentosi* J. Fryer & B. Hylmö, *ser. nov.*
Affinis ser. *Cotoneaster* sed serculo fertilis ad 70 mm longis, inflorescentiis erectis, hypanthiis tomentosis, sepalis plerumque acutis tomentosis, poma parc pilosis cum nuculis 3–5 differt.
    Type: *C. tomentosus* (Aiton) Lindley
    Series *Tomentosi* is closely related to series *Cotoneaster*, which differs in its species having fertile shoots to 50 mm, inflorescences pendent, pedicels pilose, hypanthium glabrous with sepals obtuse or lingulate, glabrous, and fruits glabrous with nutlets mostly 2–4.

Glossary

acuminate tapering, terminating gradually to a point

acute terminating in a point, without tapering in any degree

adpressed lying flat against

apiculate terminating abruptly in a little point

ascending having a direction upward from an oblique base

attenuate becoming thin or fine

auriculate with ear-shaped appendage

bullate blistered or puckered

caducous falling early

campanulate bell-shaped

camptodromous of a vein running outwards but curving before the margin and uniting with the vein above

caudate tailed, excessively acuminated with a long, weak point

chartaceous papery, having the consistency of writing paper, opaque

ciliate having fine hairs resembling an eyelash at the margin

conduplicate folded together lengthwise

conjoined joined together

coadunate united, fused together

connate fused so as not to be separated without injury

coriaceous leathery, consistency of leather

cordate heart-shaped, having two round lobes at the base

cupulate cup-shaped

cuneate wedge-shaped, inversely triangular with rounded angles

cuspidate tapering gradually into a rigid point, also used for abruptly acuminate

cylindrical solid with two parallel planes bounded by identical curves

decumbent reclining upon the earth and rising again from it at the apex

depressed flattened vertically

diffuse wide-spreading (loosely, irregularly)

distichous arranged in two rows one opposite to the other

divaricate straggling, irregular

ellipsoid a solid, flattened sphere, acute at each end

elliptic oval, in outline like an ellipsoid

emarginate having a notch at the end

epigynous situated on the upper part of the ovary

erect pointing towards the sky

erecto-patent semispreading

erose ragged, having a margin irregularly toothed as if bitten

facultative apomicts plants that reproduce with or without fertilization and thus produce both genetically identical offspring and genetically variable offspring.

fastigiate all parts nearly parallel with each other pointing to the sky

floccose covered with dense hairs which fall away in little tufts

glabrescent becoming glabrous or nearly so

glabrous without hair

glaucous covered with a fine "bloom" of the color of a cabbage leaf

globose forming nearly true sphere

hypanthium a receptacle joined to the ovary from the base of the petals and stamens

infundibulate funnel-shaped

irregular having symmetry destroyed by some inequality of parts (disordered, haphazard)

lanceolate narrowly elliptical, tapering equally to each end

lingulate tongue-shaped

linear narrow, short, two opposite margins parallel

mucronate abruptly terminated by a hard point, formed wholly of the midrib

nitidus shiny, having a smooth, even, polished surface

obligate apomicts plants that reproduce without fertilization and thus produce genetically identical offspring

oblong elliptical, obtuse at each end

obovate oblong or elliptical—broadest at upper end

obovoid a solid oblong—broadest at upper end

obtuse terminating gradually in a rounded end

orbicular having the outline of a perfect circle

ovate oblong or elliptical—broadest at lowest end

papillose pimpled, covered with soft minute tubercles of uneven size

pendent hanging downwards

pendulous hanging downwards in consequence of the weakness of its support

plane flat, a perfectly level or flat surface

planoconvex being flat on one side and convex on the other in cross section

pilose hairy, covered with short, weak, thin hairs (can become villous with age)

procumbent spread flat over the surface of the ground

prostrate lying upon the ground or any other object

pruinose having a waxy, whitish, powdery "bloom" on a surface

pubescent hairy, as opposed to glabrous

radicans rooting, putting forth aerial roots

regular having all parts symmetrical (uniform)

repens, reptans creeping, prostrate and rooting

reticulate netted, covered with netlike lines which project a little

revolute with edges rolled back on each side

rotund rounded

rugose wrinkled, covered with reticulated lines, spaces between which are convex

semi half

sericeous covered with very fine close-pressed hairs, silky to the touch

sessile without a stalk, sitting closely on the body that supports it

spathulate having a broad, rounded upper part, tapering gradually downwards into a stalk, spoon-shaped

spiral revolving around a common axis

strigose covered with sharp, adpressed, rigid hairs

sub situated under or beneath

subulate linear, very narrow, tapering to a very fine point from a broad base

tomentose thickly and evenly covered (cannot see surface) with matted hairs

triangular shaped like a triangle

trigonous triangular in cross section

truncate terminating very abruptly, cut off

tubate trumpet-shaped, dilated at one extremity, like the end of a trumpet

undulate wavy, having an uneven, alternately convex and concave margin

ungulate clawed

verruculose covered with small, wartlike outgrowths (glandular-based hairs)

villous covered with long, weak (shaggy) hairs

Bibliography

Apgar, A. C. 1910. *Ornamental Shrubs of the United States.*

Aitchison, J. E. T. 1880–1881. *On the Flora of the Kuram Valley, etc., Afghanistan.*

Aiton, W. 1789. *Mespilus tomentosus. Hortus Kewensis.* 2: 174.

Alanko, P., L. Hämet-Ahti, A. Palmén, and P. M. A. Tigerstedt. 1992. *Suomen puu–ja pensaskasvio.*

André, E. 1875. *Cotoncaster nepalensis. L'illustr. Hort.* 22: 95.

André, E. 1889. *Cotoneaster nepalensis. Revue Horticole* 61: 348.

Arnold-Forster, W. 1948. *Shrubs for Milder Counties.* 69.

Bailey, L. H. 1949. *Manual of Cultivated Plants.*

Bailey, L. H., and E. Z. Bailey. 1976. *Hortus Third.*

Bartish, I. V., B. Hylmö, and H. Nybom. 2001. RAPD analysis of interspecific relationships in presumably apomictic *Cotoneaster* species. *Euphytica* 120: 273.

Bartish, I. V., and H. Nybom. 2005. Genetic relatedness among Asian *Cotoneaster* species investigated with DNA marker analysis. *International. Journ. Hort. Science* 11 (4): 43.

Bartish, I. V., and H. Nybom. 2007. Taxonomy of apomictic *Cotoneaster. Taxon* 56 (1): 119.

Bean, W. J. 1970. *Trees and Shrubs Hardy in the British Isles.* 8th ed. 1–4: 729.

Bean, W. J. 1988. *Trees and Shrubs Hardy in the British Isles.* 8th ed. Supplement.

Blackburn, B. 1952. *Trees and Shrubs in Eastern North America.* 125.

Bois, D. 1893–1899. *Dictionaire of Horticulture.* 377.

Bois, D., and P. Berthault. 1918. *Cotoneaster adpressus* var. *praecox. Revue Horticole.* 90.

Boissier, E. 1838. *Elenchus Plantarum Hisp. Austr.* Geneva. 71.

Boissier, E. 1843. *Diagnosae Plantarum Orientalium novarum*, ser. 3, 8.

Boissier, E. 1856. *Diagnosae Plantarum Orientalium novarum*, ser. 2.

Boissier, E. 1872. *Flora Orientalis.* 2nd vol.

Bosse, J. F. W. 1849. *Vollständiges Handbuch der Blumengartneri.* 4: 177.

Brandis, D. 1874. *Forest Flora of North-West and Central India.* 208.

Broertjes, K. 1956. Reactie op vraagstukken ronon het *Cotoneaster* sortiment. De *Boomkwekerij* 11.

Browicz, K. 1958. *Cotoneaster tomentosa* in the Polish Tatra Mountains. *Florist. Geobot.* 1–2: 153.

Browicz, K. 1959. Species of the genus *Cotoneaster* in Poland. *Arb. Kornickie* 4: 5.

Browicz, K. 1968. Genus *Cotoneaster* Medikus. In *Flora Europaea.* Eds. T. Tutin, V. Heywood, A. Burges, and D. Valentine. 2: 72–73.

Buia, A. 1956. *Flora Republich Populare Romine.* 4: 191.

Campbell, C. S., M. J. Donoghue, B. G. Baldwin, and M. F. Wojciechowski. 1995. Phylo-genetic relationships in *Maloideae* (*Rosaceae*): Evidence from sequences of the internal transcribed spacers of nuclear ribosomal DNA and its congruence with morphology. *American Journal of Botany* 82: 903–918.

Carrière, E.-A. 1871. *Cotoneaster reflexus. Revue Horticole* 342: 520.

Carrière, E.-A. 1873. *Revue Horticole.* 464.

Carrière, E.-A. 1875. *Revue Horticole.* 160.

Chatenier, C. 1922–1923. Plantes rares et critiques du Bassin moyen du Rhone. *Bulletin de la Société Botanique de France* 69 (9–10): 710.

Collett, H. 1902. *Flora Simlensis.* 171.

Coombes, A. J. 1991. *The Hillier Manual of Trees and Shrubs.* 6: 127.

Corbet, S. A., and A. Westgarth-Smith. 1993. *Cotoneaster* for bumble bees and honey bees. *BBC Wildlife Magazine.* 10.

Coste, H. 1893. *Cotoneaster intermedius. Bulletin de la Société Botanique de France* 40: 122.

Craib, W. G. 1914. *Cotoneaster turbinatus. Curtis's Botanical Magazine* 140: t. 8546.

Czerepanov, S. K. 1995. *Vascular Plants of Russia and Adjacent States.*

Davis, P. H. 1972. *Flora of Turkey and the East Aegean Islands.* 4: 128.

de Candolle, A. P. 1825. *Rosaceae. Prodromus Systematis Naturalis.* 2: 525.

Diels, L. 1900. *Cotoneaster rugosus. Botanische Jahrbücher für Systematik.* 29: 385.

Domokos, J. 1941. *Megegyszer: terem-e Cotoneaster integerrima az Osmatraban.* Bull. Royal Hungarian Hort. Col. 7:4 7.

Dostál, J. 1989. *New Flora of Czechoslovakia.* 490.

Emberger, L., and R. Maire. 1941. *Catalogue des Plantes du Maroc.* 5: 1021.

Favarger, C. 1969. Notes de carylogie alpine V. *Bulletin de la Société Neuchâteloise des Sciences Naturelles* 92: 13.

Favarger, C. 1971. Relations between the Mediterranean flora of detached areas in Central Europe with submediterranean vegetation. *Boissiera* 19: 149.

Favorka, S., and V. Csapody. 1939. *Iconographia Florae Hungaricae.* 231.

Fennane, M., M. Ibn Tattou, J. Mathez, A. Ouyahya, and J. Oualidi, eds. 1999. *Flore Pratique du Maroc.* 1: 483.

Fischer, F. E. L., and C. A. Meyer. 1835. *Cotoneaster nummularius. Index Seminum* (St. Petersburg) 2: 34.

Flinck, K. E., and J. Fryer. 1993. *Cotoneaster hylmoei,* an overlooked *Cotoneaster. The Plants-man* 15: 1.

Flinck, K. E., J. Fryer, L. Garraud, B. Hylmö, and J. Zeller. 1998. *Cotoneaster raboutensis. Bulletin Mensual de la Société Linnéene de Lyon* 67 (10): 272.

Flinck, K. E., and B. Hylmö. 1958. Cotoneaster som tradgardsrymling (Cotoneasters as gar-den escapes). *Botaniska Notiser* 3: 650.

Flinck, K. E., and B. Hylmö. 1962a. *Cotoneaster harrysmithii,* a new species from western China. *Botaniska Notiser* 115: 29.

Flinck, K. E., and B. Hylmö. 1962b. Two recently described species of *Cotoneaster* of north-western Europe. *Botaniska Notiser* 115: 343.

Flinck, K. E., and B. Hylmö. 1962c. *Cotoneaster sikangensis*, a new species from western China. *Botaniska Notiser* 115: 376.

Flinck, K. E., and B. Hylmö. 1964. *Cotoneaster splendens*, a new species from western China. *Botaniska Notiser* 117: 124.

Flinck, K. E., and B. Hylmö. 1966: A list of series and species in the genus *Cotoneaster*. *Botaniska Notiser* 119: 445.

Flinck, K. E., and B. Hylmö. 1967. Cotoneaster i Svensk odling. *Lustgarden* 5.

Flinck, K. E., and B. Hylmö. 1991. Two new species of *Cotoneaster*. *Watsonia* 18: 311.

Flinck, K. E., and B. Hylmö. 1992. Slaktet cotoneaster—oxbar. *Lustgarden* 35.

Flinck, K. E., and B. Hylmö. 1998. Slaktet cotoneaster—oxbar. *Tradgardsamatoren* 60, 80.

Franchet, A. 1886. *Cotoneaster salicifolius*. *Nouvelles Archives du Muséum d'Histoire Naturelle (Paris)*, ser. 2, 8: 224, 225.

Franchet, A. 1889–1890. *Plantae Delavayanae* 3.

Fries, E. 1845. *Cotoneaster niger. Summa Vegetabilium Scandinaviae*. 1: 175.

Fryer, J. 1990. A key to the 20 *Cotoneaster* species most likely to be found naturalized in the British Isles. *BSBI News* (Botanical Society of the British Isles) 54: 9.

Fryer, J. 1993. Determination of *Cotoneaster* collections in three European botanic gardens. Combined Proceedings of the International Plant Propagators' Society 43: 185.

Fryer, J. 1994. The genus *Cotoneaster* in the British Isles. In *The Common Ground of Wild and Cultivated Plants*. Eds. A. R. Perry and R. G. Ellis. 151–157.

Fryer, J. 1995. New *Cotoneaster* taxa in the flora of Britain and Ireland. *BSBI News* (Botanical Society of the British Isles) 69: 53.

Fryer, J. 1996. Undervalued versatility. *The Garden* 121: 11.

Fryer, J., and B. Hylmö. 1994. The native British cotoneaster—great orme berry—renamed. *Watsonia* 20: 61.

Fryer, J., and B. Hylmö. 1995. Cotoneasters. *European Garden Flora* 4: 426.

Fryer, J., and B. Hylmö. 1997. Five new species of *Cotoneaster* Medik. (*Rosaceae*) naturalized in Britain. *Watsonia* 21: 335.

Fryer, J., and B. Hylmö. 1998. Seven new species of *Cotoneaster* in cultivation. *The New Plantsman* 5 (3): 132.

Fryer, J., and B. Hylmö. 2001. Captivating cotoneasters. *The New Plantsman* 8 (4): 227.

Fryer, J., and B. Hylmö. 2008. Two new cotoneasters (*Cotoneaster, Rosaceae*) from Yunnan Province, China. *J. Bot. Res. Inst. Texas* 2 (1).

Fryer, J., B. Hylmö, and P. Zika. (in prep.) Cotoneasters. *Flora of North America*.

Fryer, J., and E. C. Nelson. 1995a. Two new species of *Cotoneaster* (*Rosaceae*) at the National Botanic Gardens, Glasnevin, Dublin. *Glasra* 2: 127.

Fryer, J., and E. C. Nelson. 1995b. *Cotoneaster bradyi*. *Curtis's Botanical Magazine* 2 (4): 198.

Gandoger, M. 1875. *Cotoneaster juranus*. *Flore Lyonnaise*. 87.

Gandoger, M. 1916. *Flora Cretica*. 35.

Garraud, L. 1994. *Cotoneaster delphinensis* Chatenier, endemic plant of the Baronnies (Drôme and Hautes-Alpes), France. *Le Monde des Plantes.* 450: 13.

Garraud, L. 1998. *Cotoneaster atlanticus* Klotz, un nouvel arbuste pour la flore française. *Le Monde des Plantes.* 463: 11.

Garraud, L. 2006. *Flore de la Drôme.* 743.

Gladkova, V. N. 1967. Chromosome numbers of some species of *Cotoneaster* Med. and *Crataegus* L. *Botanicheskii Zhurnal* 52: 3.

Gladkova, V. N. 1968. Karyological studies on the genera *Crataegus* L. and *Cotoneaster* Medik. (Maloideae) as related to their taxonomy. *Botanicheskii Zhurnal* 53 (9): 1263–1273.

Godwin, H. 1960. Studies of the post-glacial history of British vegetation; XIV. Late- glacial deposits at Moss Lake, Liverpool. *Philosophical Transactions of the Royal Society of London*, ser. B: vol. 1.

Goldblatt, P. , ed. 1981. *Index to Plant Chromosome Numbers 1975–1978.* Monographs in Systematic Botany from the Missouri Botanical Garden, vol. 5.

Golitsin, S. 1964. *Cotoneaster alaunicus. Nov. Syst. Pl. Vasc.* (Leningrad). 145

Grevtsova, A. T. 1997. *Cotoneasters in Ukraine* (in Russian).

Grevtsova, A. T. 1999. *Atlas of cotoneasters.*

Grierson, A. J. C., and D. G. Long. 1987. *Flora of Bhutan.* 1 (3): 588.

Grootendorst, H. J. 1966. Low-growing cotoneasters. *Dendroflora* 3: 20.

Hara, H., W. T. Stearn, and L. J. H. Williams. 1978. *An Enumeration of the Flowering Plants of Nepal.* Vol. 1.

Hara, H., and L. H. J. Williams. 1979. *An Enumeration of the Flowering Plants of Nepal.* Vol. 2.

Hayata, B. 1911–1921. *Icones plantarum Formosanarum.* 10 vols.

Hegi, G. 1935. *Illustrierte Flora von Mitteleuropa* 4 (2): 682.

Hensen, K. J. W. 1966. Het geslacht Cotoneaster. *Dendroflora* 3: 17.

Herner, G. 1988. Harry Smith in China—notes of his botanical travels. *Taxon* 37 (2): 299.

Hjelmqvist, H. 1962. The embryo sac development of some *Cotoneaster* species. *Botaniska Notiser* 115: 208.

Hooker, J. D. 1878–1879. *The Flora of British India.* 2: 384.

Hrabětová-Uhrová, A. 1962. Beitrag zur Taxonomie und Verbeitung der Gattung *Cotoneaster* in der Tschechoslowakei. *Acta Acad. Sci. Čechoslovenicae Basis Brunensis.* 34: 197.

Hsieh, T.-H., and T.-C. Huang. 1997. Notes on the flora of Taiwan (28)—The genus *Cotoneaster* Medic. (*Rosaceae*). *Taiwania* 42 (1): 43.

Hurusawa, I. 1943. *Cotoneaster* Asiae Orientalis. *Acta Phytotaxonomica et Geobotanica* (Kyoto) 13: 225.

Hurusawa, I. 1973. Taxonomische Untersuchungen der Gattang *Cotoneaster* (*Rosaceae*) auf karpologischer Grundlage. *Inform. Annuales Hort. Bot. Fac. Sci. Univ. Tokyo* 3 (2): 195.

Hurusawa, I. 1996. *Horticultural Use of Cotoneaster.* 30–33: 99.

Hurusawa, I., S. Kawakami, and Y. Ito. 1967. Revisio Generis *Cotoneaster* quoad Species in Horto Botanico Koishikawaensi Cultas (1). *Inform. Annuales Hort. Bot. Fac. Sci. Univ. Tokyo.* 1.

Hutchinson, J. 1920. *Cotoneaster serotinus. Curtis's Botanical Magazine* 146: t. 8854.

Hylmö, B. 1993. Oxbär, *Cotoneaster,* i Sverige (The genus *Cotoneaster* in Sweden). *Svensk Botanisk Tidskrift* 87: 305.

Hylmö, B., and J. Fryer. 1999. Cotoneasters in Europe. *Acta Botanica Fennica* 162: 179–184.

Jahandiez, E., and R. Maire. 1932. *Catalogue des Plantes du Maroc.* 332.

Jerzak, E. 2000. Gatunki rodzaju *Cotoneaster* Medik. (*Rosaceae*) uprawiane w Polsce Część I. Irgi serii *Adpressi. Rocznik Dendrologiczny* 48:53.

Jerzak, E. 2001. Gatunki rodzaju *Cotoneaster* Medik. (*Rosaceae*) uprawiane w Polsce Część II. Irgi serii *Multiflori* Pojark. *Rocznik Dendrologiczny* 49: 159.

Jerzak, E. 2001. Gatunki rodzaju *Cotoneaster* Mcdik. (*Rosaceae*) uprawianc w Polscc Część III. Irgi serii *Lucidi* Pojark. *Rocznik Dendrologiczny* 49: 167.

Jerzak, E. 2002. Gatunki rodzaju *Cotoneaster* Medik. (*Rosaceae*) uprawiane w Polsce Część IV. Irgi seria *Bullati* Flinck et B. Hylmö. *Rocznik Dendrologiczny* 50:153.

Juzepczuk, S. V. 1950. Species novae endemicae peninsulae Kolaensis. *Not. Syst. Herb. Inst. Bot. Komarov. Acad. Sci. URSS* 13: 32.

Kanehira, R. 1936. *Formosan Trees.* 258.

Kanijal, U. N. 1938. *Flora of Assam.* 2: 225.

Kerner, A. 1869. Die Vegetations—Verhaltnisse. *Österreische Bot. Ztschr.* 19: 268.

Khatamsaz, M. 1988. New *Rosaceae* from Iran. *Iranian Journal of Botany* 4 (1): 113.

Khatamsaz, M. 1991. New *Rosaceae. Iranian Journal of Botany* 5 (1): 3.

Kitamura, S. 1960. *Flora of Afghanistan.* 94.

Klotz, G. 1957. Uebersichtueber die in Kulture befindlichen *Cotoneaster,* Arten und Formen. *Wissenschaftliche Zeitschrift der Martin-Luther-Universität Halle-Wittenburg, Math.-Naturwiss.* 6: 945.

Klotz, G. 1963a. The cotoneasters of the *C. nitidus* Jacques Group. *Bulletin of the Botanical Survey of India* 5 (³/₄): 207.

Klotz, G. 1963b. Neue oder kritische *Cotoneaster*—Arten I. *Wissenschaftliche Zeitschrift der Martin-Luther-Universität Halle-Wittenbrug, Math.-Naturwiss.* 12: 753.

Klotz, G. **1963**c. Neue oder kritische *Cotoneaster*—Arten II. *Wissenschaftliche Zeitschrift der Martin-Luther-Universität Halle-Wittenburg, Math.-Naturwiss.* 12: 769.

Klotz, G. 1966a. Neue oder kritische *Cotoneaster*—Arten III. et Beitrage zur Flora und Vegetation Indiens. *Wissenschaftliche Zeitschrift der Martin-Luther-Universität Halle-Wittenburg, Math.-Naturwiss.* 15: 529.

Klotz, G. 1966b. Neue oder kritische *Cotoneaster*—Arten IV. *Wissenschaftliche Zeitschrift der Martin-Luther-Universität Halle-Wittenburg, Math.-Naturwiss.* 15: 84.

Klotz, G. 1967a. *Zwei neue Cotoneaster—Arten aus dem Bereich der Flora Iranica.* Feddes Repert. 76: 201.

Klotz, G. 1967b. *Numerische Taxonomie und moderne Verwandtschaftsforschung.* Feddes Repert. 75 (1–2): 115.

Klotz, G. 1968a. Neue oder kritische *Cotoneaster*—Arten V. *Wissenschaftliche Zeitschrift der Friedrich-Schiller-Universität Jena, Math.-Naturwiss.* 17: 333.

Klotz, G. 1968b. Zur zytologischen Struktur der Gattung *Cotoneaster* Medik. *Wissenschaftliche Zeitschrift der Friedrich-Schiller-Universität Jena, Math.-Naturwiss.* 17: 349.

Klotz, G. 1970: Die Hybridization, ein wichtiger Evolutionsfaktor in der Gattung *Cotoneaster* Medik. *Wissenschaftliche Zeitschrift der Friedrich-Schiller-Universität Jena, Math.-Naturwiss.* 19: 329.

Klotz, G. 1972a. Neue oder kritische *Cotoneaster*—Arten VI. *Wissenschaftliche Zeitschrift der Friedrich-Schiller-Universität Jena, Math.-Naturwiss.* 21.

Klotz, G. 1972b. Neue oder kritische *Cotoneaster*—Arten VII. *Wissenschaftliche Zeitschrift der Friedrich-Schiller-Universität Jena, Math.-Naturwiss.* 21.

Klotz, G. 1975. *Cotoneaster otto-schwarzii*—eine neue Acutifolii—Siooe aus Yunnan. *Wissenschaftliche Zeitschrift der Friedrich-Schiller-Universität Jena, Math.-Naturwiss.* 24.

Klotz, G. 1978. Neue oder kritische *Cotoneaster*—Arten VIII. *Wissenschaftliche Zeitschrift der Friedrich-Schiller-Universität Jena, Math.-Naturwiss.* 27.

Klotz, G. 1982. Synopsis der Gattung *Cotoneaster* Medik. 1. *Beiträge zur Phytotaxonomie* 10: 47.

Klotz, G. 1996a. *Cotoneaster melanotrichus* (Franch.) Klotz eine bisher verkannte *Cotoneaster*—Sippe aus Yunnan. *Mitteilungen der Deutschen Dendrologischen Gesellschaft* (Berlin) 82: 66.

Klotz, G. 1996b. Neue oder kritische *Cotoneaster*—Arten 1X. Die weidenblattrigen Felsmispeln (*Cotoneaster* sect.*Densiflos* Yu ser. *Salicifolii* Yu) in der Natur und Kultur. *Mitteilungen der Deutschen Dendrologischen Gesellschaft* (Berlin) 82: 67.

Klotz, G., and T. Krügel. 1983a. Zur zytologischen Struktur der Gattung *Cotoneaster* Medik. 11. *Wissenschaftliche Zeitschrift der Friedrich-Schiller-Universität Jena, Math.-Naturwiss.* 32: 901.

Klotz, G., and T. Krügel. 1983b. *Cotoneaster* ×*mirabilis* Klotz & Krügel, eine bemerkenswerte hybridogene Merkmalskombiation in der Gattung *Cotoneaster*. *Wissenschaftliche Zeitschrift der Friedrich-Schiller-Universität Jena, Math.-Naturwiss.* 32: 909.

Koehne, E. 1893. *Deutsch. Dendrol.* 224.

Krasnoborov, I. M., T. S. Rostovtseva, and S. A. Ligus. 1980. Chromosome numbers of some plant species of South Siberia and the Far East. *Botanicheskii Zhurnal* 65: 659–668. (In Russian)

Kroon, G. H. 1975. Polyploidy in *Cotoneaster* 11. *Acta Bot. Neerl.* 24: 5, 417

Krügel, T. 1992a. Zur zytologischen Structur der Gattung *Cotoneaster* (*Rosaceae, Maloideae*) 111. *Beiträge zur Phytotaxonomie* 15: 69.

Krügel, T. 1992b. Zur zytologischen Structur von ×*Sorbocotoneaster pozdnjakovii* Pojarkova (*Rosaceae, Maloideae*). *Beiträge zur Phytotaxonomie* 15: 87.

Krüssmann, G. 1984. *Handbuch der laubgehölze*. 381.

Lancaster, R. 1983. *Plant Hunting in Nepal*.

Lancaster, R. 1989. *Travels in China: A Plantsman's Paradise*.

Ledebour, C. F. 1830. *Flora Altaica*. 2: 218.

Ledebour, C. F. 1844–1846. *Flora Rossica*. 2: 91.

Léveillé, H. 1915. *Cotoneaster mairei*. Bull. Géogr. Bot. 25: 45.

Li, H.-L. 1963. *Woody Flora of Taiwan*. 270.

Lindley, J. 1822. Observ. nat. gr. pl. *Pomaceae. Transactions of the Linnean Society of London* 13: 88.

Linnaeus, Carl. 1753. *Species Plantarum*. 1st ed.

Liu, T.-S. 1960. *Illustrations of Native and Introduced Ligneous Plants of Taiwan*. 1: 430.

Liu, T.-S., and H.-J. Su. 1977. In *Flora of Taiwan*. 3: 57.

Loiacono Pojero, M. 1891. *Flora Sicula*. 7: 208.

Loudon, J. C. 1838. *Arboretum et Fruticetum Britannicum*. 2:869.

Loudon, J. C. 1842. *An Encyclopaedia of Trees and Shrubs*. 405.

Löve, A. 1975. IOPD chromosome number report XLIX. *Taxon* 24 (4): 510.

Maire, R. 1923. *Cotoneaster fontanesii* var. *tomentella. Bulletin de la Société d'Histoire Naturelle de l'Afrique du Nord* 14: 143.

Marquand, C. V. B. 1930. *Cotoneaster cooperi. Hooker's Icones Plantarum*. t. 3146.

Marquand, C. V. B. 1935. *Cotoneaster hebephylla* var. *monopyrena. Curtis's Bot. Mag.* 48: 9389.

Meikle, R. D. 1977. *Flora of Cyprus*. 1: 637.

Meyer, C. A. 1831. *Verzeichniss der Pflanzen*. 171.

Miller, Philip. 1759. *The Gardener's Dictionary*. 7th ed. 22.

Moffett, A. A. 1931. A preliminary account of chromosome behaviour in Pomoideae. *Journal of Pomology and Horticultural Science*. 9.

Molero Mesa, J., and F. P. Raya. 1991. *La Flora de Sierra Nevada*. 130.

Mottet, S. 1925. *Les Arbres et les Arbustres d'ornement de pleine terre*. 107.

Nakai, T. 1918. *Cotoneaster wilsonii. Botanical Magazine* (Tokyo) 32: 104.

Nyman, C. F. 1854–1855. *Sylloge Florae Europaeae*. 267.

Oborny, A. 1851. *Flora von Mahren und Ostrr. Schlesien*. 2: 868.

Orlova, N. I. 1959. *Cotoneaster* Medik. *Flora Murmanskoi oblasti*. 4: 54.

Osmaston, A. E. 1927. *A Forest Flora of Kumoan*. 222.

Pampanini, R. 1910. Piante Vascolari Dell'Hupeh. *Nuovo Giornale Botanica Italiano*. 17: 288.

Panigrahi, G., and A. Kumar. 1986. *Cotoneaster glacialis. Bulletin of the Botanical Survey of India*.

Panigrahi, G., and A. Kumar. 1988. A conspectus of the 74 taxa of *Cotoneaster* in India. *Bulletin of the Botanical Survey of India* 28 (1): 63.

Parker, R. N. 1924. *A Forest Flora for the Punjab*. 231.

Peschkova, G. A. 1979. Notulae ad florum Sibericae 3. *Flora URSS*. 15: 231.

Phipps, J. B., K. R. Robertson, P. G. Smith, and J. R. Rohrer. 1990. A checklist of the subfamily *Maloideae* (*Rosaceae*). *Canadian Journal of Botany*. 68: 2209–2269.

Phitos, D., A. Strid, S. Snogerup, and W. Greuter. 1995. *The Red Data Book of Rare and Threatened Plants of Greece*.

Pignatti, S. 1982. *Flora d'Italia*. 1: 610.

Pohl, J. E. 1815. *Tentamen Florae Bohemiae*. 164.

Pojarkova, A. I. 1938–1939. *Cotoneaster* Med. *Flora URSS*. 9: 319.

Pojarkova, A. I. 1940. De speciebus novis generis *Cotoneaster* Med. *Flora URSS*. 8: 136.

Pojarkova, A. I. 1950. *Flora Turkmenii*. 5.

Pojarkova, A. I. 1954a. Addend. gen. *Cotoneaster* Med. *Flora URSS*. 16: 109.

Pojarkova, A. I. 1954b. ×*Sorbocotoneaster* Pojark. hybrida intergenerica nova naturalis. *Bot. Mater. Gerb. Inst. Bot. Acad. Nauk Kazakhsk. SSR* 14: 90.

Pojarkova, A. I. 1955. Addend. gen. *Cotoneaster*. *Flora URSS*. 17: 179.

Pojarkova, A. I. 1961. Florae USRR et Chinae genersis *Cotoneaster* Med. spec. nov. *Not. Syst.* 21: 161.

Pojarkova, A. I. 1976. *Cotoneaster goloskokovii*. *Opred. Rast. Sred. Azii* 5: 245.

Popov, M. G. 1935. Plantae novae vel criticae in montibus Altau transiliensis Tienschan orientalis), prope opp. Alma-Ata collectae. *Bulletin de la Sociétè Imperiale des Naturalistes de Moscou*, Sekt. Biol., n.s., 44: 125.

Prior, C. 2005. Plant Pathology Leaflet. Royal Horticultural Society Wisley.

Rechinger, K. H. 1943. *Flore Aegaea*. 309.

Redakcijā, P. G. 1957. *Latvijas PSR Flora*. 43.

Rehder, A. 1927. *Manual of Cultivated Trees and Shrubs*. 1st ed.

Rehder, A. 1932. *Cotoneaster franchetii* Bois. *Journal of the Arnold Arboretum* 13: 302.

Rehder, A. 1940. *Manual of Cultivated Trees and Shrubs*. 2nd ed. 347.

Rehder, A. 1949. *Bibliography of Cultivated Trees and Shrubs Hardy in the Cooler Temperature Regions of the Northern Hemisphere*. 234.

Riedl, H. 1969. *Flora Iranica*. 13.

Robertson, K. R., J. R. Rohrer, J. B. Phipps, and P. G. Smith. 1991. A synopsis of genera in subfamily *Maloideae* (*Rosaceae*). *Systematic Botany* 16: 376–394.

Rohrer, J. R., K. R. Robertson, and J. B. Phipps. 1992. Variation in structure among fruits of *Maloideae* (*Rosaceae*). *American Journal of Botany* 78: 1617–1635.

Ross-Craig, S. 1956. *Drawings of British Plants* 9: 37.

Roxburgh, W. 1832. *Flora Indica*. 2: 509.

Ruprecht, F. J. 1860. *Flora Ingrica*. 1: 350.

Rutkowski, L. 2003. *Klucz do oznaczania roslin naczyiowzch Polski nizowej*. 182.

Saunders, W. W. 1869. *Refugium Botanicum*. 1: 48.

Sax, A. 1954. Polyploidy and apomixis in *Cotoneaster*. *Journal of the Arnold Arboretum* 35: 334.

Schlechtendal, D. F. L. 1854. Corollar. observat. pl. Hort. Hal. Saxon. *Linnaea* 27: 534.

Schneider, C. K. 1906. *Illustriertes Handbuch der Laubholzkunde*. 1: 744.

Schneider, Ir. F. 1964. *Cotoneaster* 'Gracia' and *C.* 'Valkenburg'. *Dendroflora* 1: 35.

Silva Tarouca, E., and C. K. Schneider. 1922. *Unsere Freiland-Laubgehölze.* 2nd ed. 163.

Silva Tarouca, E., and C. K. Schneider. 1931. *Unsere Freiland-Laubgehölze.* 3rd ed. 140.

Simon, T. 1992. *Determination of Hungarian Vascular Flora.* 149.

Soo, R. 1966. *Synopsis Systematico-Geobotanica Florae Vegetationisque Hungariae.* 2: 98.

Spach, M. E. 1834. *Histoire Naturelle des Vegetaux. Phanerogames* 2: 73.

Stace, C. A. 1997. *New Flora of the British Isles.* 2nd ed. 378.

Stapf, O. 1929. *Cotoneaster glaucophylla. Botanical Magazine* (London) 153: 9171.

Steudel, E. T. 1840. *Nomenclator Botanicus.* 2: 426.

Strid, A. 1986. *Mountain Flora of Greece.* 1: 437.

Timm, J., and Company. 1959–1960. *Baustein fur den Modernen Garten.* 85.

Townsend, C. C., E. Guest, and A. Al-Rawi. 1966. *Flora of Iraq.* Vol. 2.

Turczanivow, Nicolai. 1832. *Cotoneaster acutifolius. Bulletin de la Société Imperiale des Naturalistes de Moscou* 4: 190.

Tutin, T., V. Heywood, A. Burges, and D. Valentine, eds. 1968. *Flora Europeae.* Vol. 2, *Rosaceae to Umbelliferae.*

van de Laar, H. 1994. *Darthuizer Vademecum.* 160.

Vassiliev, A. N. 1961. *Flora Kazakhstana.* 4: 395.

Vvedensky, A. I. 1976. *Conspectus Florae Asiae Media.* 2: 131.

Walsh, W. F., and E. C. Nelson. 1990. *A Prospect of Irish Flowers.* 8.

Wenzig, T. 1875. *Die Famille Pomaiae (Pomaceae) Lindley.* Berlin Monatsschrift Gartenbau-Vereins. 227.

Wenzig, T. 1883. Pomaceen. *Jahrbuch des Königlichen Botanischen Gartens und des Botanischen Museums zu Berlin.* 2: 304.

Wight, R. 1845. *Icones Plantarum India Orientalis.* Figures 3: 2, t. 992.

Wilson, E. H. 1907, 1908, 1910. *Plantae Wilsonianae.* 3 vols.

Wilson, E. H. 1927. *Cotoneaster. Bulletin of the Arnold Arboretum* 3 (1): 17.

Wilson, E. H. 1928. *More Aristocrats of the Garden.* 144.

Wolf, E. L. 1907. *Cotoneaster ignavus.* Izvestiya Imperatorskago Lesnogo Instituta (St. Petersburg) 15: 240.

Wolf, E. L. 1924. *Cotoneaster polyanthemus. Mitteilungen der Deutschen Dendrologischen Gesellschaft* (Berlin) 34: 325.

Yu, T. T. 1954. Cotoneasters from the Eastern Himalaya. *Bulletin of the British Museum (Natural History), Botany* 1 (5): 125.

Yu, T. T. 1963. Taxa nova Rosacearum sinicarum. *Acta Phytotaxonomica Sinica* 8: 14.

Zabel, H. 1897. Die Gattung der Zwergmispelm, *Cotoneaster. Mitteilungen der Deutschen Dendrologischen Gesellschaft* (Berlin) 6: 14.

Zabel, H. 1898. *Cotoneaster pekinensis. Mitteilungen der Deutschen Dendrologischen Gesellschaft* (Berlin) 7: 348.

Zakirov, K. 1955. Duae species novae ex Asia media. *Not. Syst. Herb. Inst. Bot. Komarov. Acad. Sci. URSS* 17: 26.

Zeilinga, A. E. 1964. Polyploidy in *Cotoneaster. Botaniska Notiser* 117: 262.

Zhou, L.-H., and Z.-Y. Wu. 1999. The taxonomic revision of *Cotoneaster conspicuus* Messel. (*Rosaceae*). *Acta Botanica Yunnanica* 21 (2): 160–160.

Zhou, L.-H., and Z.-Y. Wu. 2000. Taxonomic studies on *Cotoneaster dammeri* Schneid. (*Rosaceae*). *Acta Botanica Yunnanica* 22 (4): 379–382.

Zhou, L.-H., and Z.-Y. Wu. 2001. Taxonomic revision on series *Buxifolii* in genus *Cotoneaster* (*Rosaceae*). *Acta Botanica Yunnanica* 23 (1): 29–36.

Zielinski, J. 1991. *Cotoneaster tomentosus* (*Rosaceae*): a new species for the flora of Turkey. *Polish Acad. Sci. Inst. Dendr. Kornik.*

Index

In this index, accepted names are given in **boldface**; synonyms and common names appear in regular font. **Boldface** numbers indicate main entry pages.

acuminate-leaved cotoneaster. See *C. acuminatus*.
Acuminati (series), 36, 203–208
acute-leaved cotoneaster. See *C. acutifolius* Turczaninov.
Acutifolii (section), 34, 208–240
Acutifolii (series), 29, 36, 208–219
Adpressi (section), 33, 148–189, 202
Adpressi (series), 23, 35, 167–174
'Afterglow'. See *C. salicifolius* 'Repens'.
Aitchisonioides (series), 15, 35, 60–67, 319
'Aldenhamensis'. See *C. salicifolius* 'Aldenhamensis'.
Alpigeni (section), 25, 33, 115–143
Altai cotoneaster. See *C. lucidus*.
ambiguous cotoneaster. See *C. ambiguus*.
Ampfield cotoneaster. See *C. laetevirens*.
'Anne Cornwallis'. See *C. henryanus* 'Anne Cornwallis'.
'Antonin Nohel'. See *C. marginatus* 'Antonin Nohel'.
Antonin's cotoneaster. See *C. nohelii*.
apiculate-leaved cotoneaster. See *C. apiculatus*.
'Arnold-Forster'. See *C. prostratus* 'Arnold-Forster'.
ascending cotoneaster. See *C. ascendens*.
Assam cotoneaster. See *C. assamensis*.
autumn fire. See *C. salicifolius* 'Herbstfeuer'.
'Avondrood'. See *C. salicifolius* 'Repens'.

Bacillares (series), 34, 79–84
bearberry cotoneaster. See *C. dammeri*.
bearberry Nepal cotoneaster. See *C. uva-ursi*.
beautiful cotoneaster. See *C. amoenus*.
bellflower cotoneaster. See *C. campanulatus*.
black cotoneaster. See *C. niger*.
black-drop cotoneaster. See *C. otto-schwarzii*.

black-grape cotoneaster. See *C. ignotus*.
'Blazovice'. See *C. marginatus* 'Blazovice'.
Bois's cotoneaster. See *C. boisianus*.
box-leaved cotoneaster. See *C. buxifolius*.
Brady's cotoneaster. See *C. bradyi*.
'Brandekjaerhoej'. See *C. ×watereri* 'Brandekjaerhoej'.
Brandis's cotoneaster. See *C. brandisii*.
brickberry cotoneaster. **See** *C. tomentosus*.
Brickell's cotoneaster. See *C. brickellii*.
'Brno'. See *C. marginatus* 'Brno'.
'Brno Orangeade'. See *C. salicifolius* 'Brno Orangeade'.
broad-leaved cotoneaster. See *C. latifolius*.
Browicz's cotoneaster. See *C. browiczii*.
bullate cotoneaster. See *C. rehderi*.
Bullati (series), 15, 25, 29, 36, 152, 208, 219–232
Buxifolii (series), 14, 34, 119–125

'Canu'. See *C. adpressus* 'Canu'.
'Cardinal'. See *C. dammeri* 'Cardinal'.
carpet cotoneaster. See *C. procumbens*.
Chaenopetalum (subgenus), 14–15, 30, 33, 37–143, 165
Chaenopetalum (section), 33, 56–91
cherry-red cotoneaster. See *C. zabelii*.
Chinan cotoneaster. See *C. foveolatus*.
circular-leaved cotoneaster. See *C. hissaricus*.
common cotoneaster. See *C. integerrimus*.
congested cotoneaster. See *C. congestus*.
'Conglomeratus'. See *C. adpressus* 'Conglomeratus'.
Conspicui (series), 34, 115–119
Cooper's cotoneaster. See *C. cooperi*.
'Copra'. See *C. apiculatus*.
'Coral Beauty'. See *C. ×suecicus* 'Coral Beauty'.
'Coral Bunch'. See *C. salicifolius* 'Coral Bunch'.
'Corina'. See *C. henryanus* 'Corina'.
cornseed cotoneaster. **See** *C. hebephyllus*.
'Cornubia'. See *C. frigidus* 'Cornubia'.
Cotonea. See *Cotoneaster* (genus).
Cotoneaster (genus), 14, 17, 19–25, **32–37**

C. zabelii, 22, 263, **268–269**, 307, 314, 316, Plate 179

    f. *glabriusculus*. **See** *C. giraldii*.

    var. *miniatus*. See *C. miniatus*.

C. zaprjagaevae. See *C. hissaricus*.

C. zayulensis, **114–115**

C. zeravschanicus, 24, **298–299**

cranberry cotoneaster. See *C. apiculatus*.

Crataegus integrifolius. See *Cotoneaster integri-folius*.

creeping cotoneaster. See *C. adpressus*.

Crimea cotoneaster. See *C. tauricus*.

crimson-flowered cotoneaster. See *C. cardinalis*.

crisp's cotoneaster. See *C. crispii*.

dark-green cotoneaster. See *C. atrovirens*.

'Decor'. See *C. salicifolius* 'Decor'.

'Decorus'. See *C. conspicuus* 'Decorus'.

Densiflori (section), 33, **37–56**

Densiflos (section). See *Densiflori* (section).

Diels cotoneaster. See *C. dielsianus*.

Dielsiani (series), 37, **255–260**, 264

Distichi (series), 15, 35, **157–167**, 208

distichous cotoneaster. See *C. rotundifolius* Wallich ex Lindley.

dwarf cotoneaster. See *C. nanshan*.

ear-leaved cotoneaster. See *C. cochleatus*.

earthquake cotoneaster. See *C. hodjingensis*.

'Eastleigh'. See *C. marginatus* 'Eastleigh'.

elegant cotoneaster. See *C. elegans*.

'Emerald Carpet'. See *C. salicifolius* 'Emerald Carpet'.

'Emerald Spray'. See *C. microphyllus* 'Emerald Spray'.

engraved cotoneaster. See *C. insculptus*.

entire-leaved cotoneaster. See *C. integrifolius*.

Eriobotria elliptica. See *Cotoneaster ellipticus*.

European cotoneaster. See *C. integerrimus*.

'Exburyensis'. See *C. salicifolius* 'Exburyensis'.

'Exbury Variety'. See *C. frigidus* 'Exbury Variety'.

Fang's cotoneaster. See *C. fangianus*.

'FCC Variety'. See *C. frigidus* 'FCC Variety'.

few-flowered cotoneaster. See *C. nitens*.

fireberry cotoneaster. See *C. ignescens*.

'Flameburst'. See *C. conspicuus* 'Flameburst'.

Flinck's cotoneaster. See *C. flinckii*.

floccose cotoneaster. See *C. floccosus*.

Forrest's cotoneaster. See *C. forrestii*.

Franchetioides (section), 25, 34, **240–260**

Franchetioides (series), 37, **240–246**

Franchet's cotoneaster. See *C. franchetii* Bois (1902).

Frigidi (series), 34, **56–60**

fringed cotoneaster. See *C. marginatus*.

'Fructuluteo'. See *C. frigidus* 'Fructuluteo', *C. salicifolius* 'Fructuluteo'.

Gamble's cotoneaster. See *C. gamblei*.

glabrate cotoneaster. See *C. glabratus*.

glandular cotoneaster. See *C. verruculosus*.

glaucous cotoneaster. See *C. glaucophyllus*.

Glomerulati (series), 36, **235–240**

Godalming cotoneaster. See *C. transens*.

graceful cotoneaster. See *C. gracilis*.

Granada cotoneaster. See *C. granatensis*.

Gymnopyrenium. See *Cotoneaster* (genus).

handsome cotoneaster. See *C. suavis*.

hardy cotoneaster. See *C. induratus*.

Harry Smith's cotoneaster. See *C. harrysmithii*.

'Heaseland's Coral'. See *C. ×watereri* 'Heaseland's Coral'.

Hebephylli (series), 15, 35, 49, **107–115**

hedge cotoneaster. See *C. lucidus*.

Henry's cotoneaster. See *C. henryanus*.

'Herbstfeuer'. See *C. salicifolius* 'Herbstfeuer'.

herringbone cotoneaster. See *C. horizontalis*.

Himalayan cotoneaster. See *C. frigidus*.

Hissarici (series), 15, 30, 35, **84–91**

Hjelmqvist's cotoneaster. See *C. hjelmqvistii*.

hollyberry cotoneaster. See *C. bullatus*.

'Holstein Resi'. See *C. dammeri* 'Holstein Resi'.

Horizontales (series), 15, 35, **174–182**, 199

Hsing-Shan cotoneaster. See *C. hsingshangensis*.

Hummel's cotoneaster. See *C. hummelii*.

Hupeh cotoneaster. See *C. hupehensis*.

Hupehenses (series). See *Multiflori* (series).

'Hybridus Pendulus'. See *C. dammeri* 'Hybridus Pendulus'.

Hylmö's cotoneaster. See *C. hylmoei*.

'Ifor'. See *C. ×suecicus* 'Ifor'.

Ignavi (series), 36, **293–299**

'Inchmery'. See *C. frigidus* 'Inchmery'.

Insignes (series). See *Hissarici* (series).

intermediate cotoneaster. See *C. intermedius*.